W9-AGL-697

THE FAMILY IN SOCIAL CONTEXT

THE
FAMILY
IN
SOCIAL
CONTEXT

SIXTH EDITION

GERALD R. LESLIE
SHEILA K. KORMAN

NEW YORK   OXFORD
OXFORD UNIVERSITY PRESS
1985

OXFORD UNIVERSITY PRESS
Oxford London New York Toronto
Delhi Bombay Calcutta Madras Karachi
Kuala Lampur Singapore Hong Kong Tokyo
Nairobi Dar es Salaam Cape Town
Melbourne Auckland
and associated companies in
Beirut Berlin Ibadan Mexico City Nicosia

Copyright © 1967, 1973, 1976, 1979, 1982, 1985 by Oxford University Press, Inc.
Published by Oxford University Press, 200 Madison Avenue, New York, New York 10016
All rights reserved. No part of this publication may be reproduced, stored in a retrieval
system, or transmitted, in any form or by any means, electronic, mechanical, photocopy-
ing, recording, or otherwise, without the prior permission of Oxford University Press.
Library of Congress Cataloging in Publication Data
Leslie, Gerald R.
    The family in social context.
    Bibliography: p.
    Includes indexes.
    1. Family—United States. 2. Family. I. Korman,
Sheila K. II. Title.
HQ536.L47 1985 306.8′1′0973 84-876
ISBN 0-19-503478-3

PRINTING (LAST DIGIT): 9 8 7 6 5
Printed in the United States of America

Preface

The sixth edition of this book retains the basic features that caused earlier editions to be so widely praised and so widely used. It is scholarly, comprehensive, and readable.

It is a big book, including most of the material usually covered in courses offered under such titles as the Modern Family, the Sociology of the Family, Marriage and the Family, and the American Family. Not all instructors will be able to cover all of it in one term. They should, however, find ample material to get into their courses the specific emphases they want. Moreover, by assigning the whole book to be read, they can give their students what often requires a textbook and a book of readings combined.

One feature of the book is unusually extensive coverage of cross-cultural and historical material. With the trend toward inclusion of more such material in family courses, many instructors will want to spend considerable time on Parts I and II. Those instructors who do not want to emphasize the family systems of other societies will want to move more quickly to Part III, Contemporary American Families.

Several features are new to this edition. The chapter on Conceptual Approaches in Family Study replaces the earlier chapter on Theories of Family Structure and Family Change. Those instructors who desire more conceptual sophistication will approve of the change. Those who prefer a more descriptive approach will find ample material available.

The restructuring of the chapters on Contemporary American Families provides better integration of those materials. A new chapter on the Influence of Religion has been added. The proliferation of research in all areas of family study is indicated by the fact that 438 new names appear in the Name Index. All of this has been accomplished without lengthening the book.

The last nine chapters of the book continue to be organized in a life-cycle framework, providing a wealth of detail on the functioning of contemporary families from adolescence through old age. Some instructors will interpret these materials in strictly institutional terms; some will use a more functional approach. The needs of both groups should be met fully.

Finally, the book continues to avoid confusing profundity with obscurantism. It assumes that the conceptual apparatus essential to an understanding of the field can be employed in a clear and simple writing style to make learning a pleasure.

Gainesville, Fla.   G.R.L.
September 1984   S.K.K.

Contents

I
Cross-Cultural Perspectives

Paul S. Conklin, Monkmeyer Press Photo Service

I
The Nature of the Family

The family is, as far as we know, the toughest institution we have. It is, in fact, the institution to which we owe our humanity. We know no other way of making human beings except by bringing them up in a family. Of course this does not mean that widows cannot bring up children; but the widowed mother brings up her children to know that their father is dead, that they had a father, and that the children next door have a father. The model is still there. And of course this holds for the widower as well. But we know no other way to bring children up to be human beings, able to act like men and women, and able to marry other men and women and bring up children, except through the family.[1]

The paragraph above was written over a generation ago by one of America's most respected social scientists. Many people today ask whether it is still true, whether the family is the toughest institution we have, and whether the only way to raise children successfully is in families. Although this book will do far more than simply answer these questions, it will attempt to answer them in the context of both several thousand years of human experience and in the context of the rapid changes of recent years.

It is a large task. Even if we exclude analyses of the family in genetic, embryological, anatomical, and physiological terms, to say nothing of legal, economic, and political ones, and confine our analysis to the family as a social institution, we still must consider humankind's experience over several thousand years and over the entire world. We must analyze the family in its total social context.

1. Margaret Mead, "The Impact of Cultural Changes on the Family," *The Family in the Urban Community*, Detroit: The Merrill-Palmer School, 1953, p. 4.

SOCIETY AND THE SOCIAL CONTEXT

Conventionally, the term *society* has been used to refer to substantial collections of people living in near isolation from other such collections, having definite geographic boundaries, and enacting distinctive cultures. The term is easy to apply to preliterate peoples, but more difficult to apply to modern industrial nations where there is less isolation and where cultural boundaries and national boundaries do not always coincide.

Anthropologists estimate that there have been 4000 separable societies in the world since the dawn of human experience.[2] These range from preliterate societies of fewer than 400 people to modern societies of over 900 million. Not even a majority of these societies has been systematically studied. The most adequate analysis has been done by Murdock who compiled the *Ethnographic Atlas* of 1170 carefully selected societies.[3] Among those 1170 societies, some are known through history and some exist now, some are preliterate and some are civilized societies.

Few people, except social scientists, know that there have been so many societies. Moreover, when they become aware of this tremendous range of human groups, many people wonder how relevant the experience of small preliterate societies in the mid-Pacific, the Andes, or Africa is to the problem of complex societies such as the United States. They wonder whether the experience of 178 people isolated and virtually without material possessions should be compared with the customs of a society of 230 million people who have created an automated, computerized economy and one in which the arts and humanities flourish.

The problems of comparing societies are complex, but we need not get into them here. Suffice it to say that anthropologists believe that it is legitimate and useful to compare large and small societies when the purpose is to try to understand the full range of solutions to universal human problems. Regardless of the size or technological advancement, each society's customs and institutions constitute an independent solution to the problem of ensuring survival. The family system of a society of 178 people might not be practical in the United States, but it does represent another means of coping with the same general human problems that we face. Moreover, if we see that the majority, or even a significant minority, of societies have family systems that differ significantly from our own, it becomes more difficult for us to believe that our own system is divinely ordained or even inherently superior.[4]

2. George P. Murdock, "World Ethnographic Sample," *American Anthropologist* 59 (Aug. 1957), pp. 664–87.
3. George P. Murdock, *Ethnographic Atlas*, Pittsburgh: University of Pittsburgh Press, 1967.
4. The tendency of people to regard their own ways of doing things as the best is, of course, the concept of ethnocentrism. Ethnocentrism serves the valuable function of

Social Institutions

The concept of social institutions will appear throughout this book, for social scientists are much concerned with the institutional aspects of the family. At this point, our task is to discuss briefly the major social institutions and to place the family institution within the context of the society's larger institutional structure.

Sociologists use the term *institution* in a different and more technical way than does the average person. Sociologists view institutions as systems of social norms. Norms are society's rules of conduct for its members. Norms range from the formal—each person may have only one spouse—to the informal—letting father have the largest piece of pie. The number of such rules, or customary behaviors, is exceedingly large and covers almost every aspect of life. Growing up in a society means learning its norms so that as an adult one will be able to function successfully with other similarly socialized people.

Although most people may not be aware of it, norms are organized into patterns. In the family, for example, there are norms that specify which persons are eligible to marry, how many spouses they may have, who is eligible to marry whom, when they should marry, who should be the boss in the family, where they should live, what the division of labor should be, the proper attitudes toward children and oldsters, and so on. Detailed examination of the normative system controlling family behavior will appear in subsequent chapters.

In all societies, complex normative patterns appear in certain basic areas. There is always a normative system governing the legitimate use of power in the society. We call this system of norms government. Similarly, another normative system defines the production, distribution, and consumption of goods and services: the economic institution. A third normative system regulates our relation to the supernatural: the religious institution. The educational institution is concerned with the transmission of values, attitudes, knowledge, and skills from one generation to the next. And there are always rules regulating adult sexual relationships and procreation: the family institution.

All societies have these major institutions: family, government, economic system, education, and religion. The content of a society's institutions determines in large measure its character. Understanding these basic institutions leads to understanding of the society.[5]

---

promoting loyalty to one's own society and its institutions, but it makes it difficult for us to see the relativity of cultural practices. The principle of cultural relativity holds that the functions and meaning of practices can be understood only in the context of the larger culture in which they are found—not in the context of our values and practices.

5. Unfortunately, sociologists occasionally use the term *institution* not only in its tech-

In every known society, at least some persons consider themselves kin of at least some other persons, living and dead. The way in which kinship is expressed and the kinds of behavior which follow from the recognition of this relationship vary from culture to culture.

PHILIP K. BOCK, *Modern Cultural Anthropology: An Introduction*, New York: Alfred A. Knopf, 1969, pp. 87–88

The institutions of a society are related to one another. Government, for example, impinges on the family in many ways. The authority wielded within the family may well stand in some inverse relation to the power vested in the government: when the government is weak, the family may exercise considerable control of individual behavior and vice versa. Government may provide a host of services to families and their members or it may require that families be largely self-sufficient.

Moreover, the interrelations among a society's institutions may vary over time. There was a time in our history when there was relatively little differentiation among the major institutions: when the family performed many of what today are the functions of government, religion, and the schools. Later on, Western religious institutions became powerful and restricted and controlled family life. Still other changes saw government come to exercise great regulatory power, and current interrelations between the family and the economy have much to do with the nature of present-day family problems. One social institution can be understood only in the context of its relations with other institutions.

Functional Requisites for Societal Survival

The fact that certain institutions are found in all known societies suggests that societies may not be able to exist without them. Or, to put it differently, the major social institutions play a very large role in accomplishing those basic functions that are essential to a society's survival.

Apparently, there are certain minimum tasks that must be performed in all societies. Unless they are performed adequately, the society will cease to exist. An analogy may help to make the point. We might hypothesize that a quality-control department is essential to the survival of a manufacturing company. A company might survive if it occasionally put out defective merchandise, but if much of its product were defective, customers would take their business elsewhere and the company would go bankrupt. Perhaps the only way to prevent this from happen-

---

nical sense but also in its lay usage. Thus, people refer to prisons and hospitals as institutions. Actually institutionalization is a process that is going on in many areas of life simultaneously.

ing is to have a quality-control department to make sure that the company's product uniformly meets predetermined standards.

Notice that we are not saying that the conscious purpose of a quality-control department is to keep a company in business. Nor are we saying that a company could not be established and operate without a quality-control department. We are saying that, in the long run, a company that does not develop effective means of quality control is likely not to be able to meet the competition and, hence, is likely not to survive.

So it is with societies. To speak of there being functional requisites to a society's survival does not mean that each society is aware that certain tasks must be performed and that it consciously creates arrangements to provide for them. Nor is it to say that there have never been societies in which these tasks were not properly provided for. It is to say that if such societies existed, they have long since ceased to exist.

Social scientists, from their studies of societies, have concluded that there are certain minimum conditions that must be met. These functional requisites that are met principally through a society's major institutions include: (1) provision for the continued adequate biological functioning of the members of the society, (2) provision for the reproduction of new members of the society, (3) provision for the adequate socialization of new members of the society, (4) arrangements for the production and distribution of goods and services, (5) provision for the maintenance of order within the group and with outsiders, and (6) the meaning of life must be defined and the motivation for group and individual survival must be maintained.

Continued Biological Functioning. In our analysis of human social life, we should never forget that we are biological organisms who share problems of survival with all other animal species. Our survival depends on provision of the basic necessities of food, clothing, and shelter. Without these, we could not remain healthy—and the maintenance of health is a part of this requisite to societal survival. People must also be relatively healthy to reproduce successfully, and reproduction is a part of the maintenance of biological functioning. The provision of food, clothing, and shelter, of course, implies that there must be an organized pattern of work. Food, clothing, and shelter must be produced and distributed, according to some notion of equity, among the society's members. Except in the simplest societies, the provision for continued biological functioning does not stop at this rudimentary level. In societies above the subsistence level, the basic necessities are elaborated into standards of nutrition, comfort, style, medical care, family planning, and so on. But whatever the level at which the society operates, certain minimum provisions in this area are essential to survival.

Two institutions are deeply involved in meeting this functional requisite for societal survival. The production and distribution of goods and services occur through the economic system. The usual consumption unit for goods and services is the family. Moreover, the family is the unit of reproduction and the primary source of care for ailing persons. It is no accident that the meeting of functional requisites is accomplished significantly through social institutions. Institutions develop originally in response to societies' needs to survive.

Adequate Reproduction. That the various functional requisites are interrelated has been shown by our reference to reproduction when talking primarily about continued biological functioning. The problem of replacement of members of the society is so fundamental, however, that it deserves separate discussion.

Unless a society provides for an adequate number of children to be born and cared for, the population will dwindle and eventually disappear. All societies have normative systems that regulate childbearing and childrearing. These societal rules define who is qualified to bear children, when reproduction may begin, how many children should be born, how the children should be cared for, and so on. These norms make up part of the institution of the family.

Even in this area, which seems to fall squarely within the institutional sphere of the family, other institutions are involved. The educational system shares with the family the care and training of the young. The replacement of societal members may occur also through recruitment from other societies. This process sometimes assumes large proportions through immigration. Immigrants require resocialization into the normative system of the new society, again involving the educational institution. No society for long, however, depends on immigration to provide new members. New adults are not so dependable a source of replacement as are infants born into the society, and infants are not faced with conflicts between two normative systems. In all societies, the replacement of members occurs primarily through reproduction.

Socialization of New Members. The term *socialization* encompasses learning the values, attitudes, knowledge, skills, and techniques that a society possesses—in short, it involves learning the culture. A very important part of the culture is the normative system, including the major institutions. Socialization molds the child's biological potential into the pattern of functioning that we call human personality.

Socialization covers all learning, including the indirect and unanticipated learning that occurs whenever the child observes parents or others in interaction. Thus, the child learns socially disapproved as well as approved behaviors and masters the nuances that are not taught in school, in college, or in apprenticeship.

No society allows socialization to proceed according to chance. The family institution includes norms defining proper parental behavior. It defines what parents properly may teach children and what they may not. Beyond the familial contribution, and intertwined with it, there always lies a body of knowledge and practice that is shared by the society at large and that the society transmits to all new members. For unless the members of a society share a common core of values, beliefs, and practices, the organization of the society cannot be maintained.

The organization of the socialization process outside the family is, of course, what we call the educational institution. It may be rudimentary and nonspecialized, involving only a few wise elders passing on the ancient lore to youngsters working in informal apprenticeship with adults, or it may be highly organized and complex, including nursery schools, schools, colleges, and graduate schools.

Socialization does not cease when adulthood is reached. The socialization of the young is so dramatic that most of our attention has focused on it. We are realizing more and more, however, that learning occurs throughout life. College seniors have only begun to prepare for their occupational roles, and it takes considerable learning to transform them into the mature, poised, knowledgeable, self-confident leaders they may be as middle-aged adults. Similarly, becoming a husband or wife and a parent involves learning attitudes, sentiments, and skills that are not learned in school. Even becoming old involves complicated learning that the young and middle-aged cannot appreciate. The need for society to socialize its members may be most dramatic in the early years of life, but the continued functioning of a society is equally dependent on the continued socialization of its adult members.

Production and Distribution of Goods and Services. All known societies have norms defining what goods will be produced, how, and by whom. At bottom is the problem of ensuring the survival of individuals. But the regulation of economic activity does not stop here. All societies elaborate their regulations to provide for a division of labor among the members of the society. The economic and family institutions become intertwined, for there is always a division of labor among family members, influenced by sex and age. Work roles considered appropriate to sex and age groups derive from the family and are also influenced by it. Further, the production of goods results in the accumulation of property and necessitates rules for transmitting property from one generation to the next. Such rules again are involved in both the family and the economic system.

The adequate functioning of these various sets of norms ensures that the necessary goods will be produced, that they will be distributed in predictable fashion, and that competition among the members of the society will be limited and controlled.

Maintenance of Order. The rules that maintain order within societies range from informal customs to legally enforced codes. All societies have such customs and codes to govern relationships among members of the society and between members of the society and outsiders.

This is the general area involving the legitimate use of power and force; what we call government. Through organizations ranging from a few tribal elders to large nation-states, societies regulate behavior in the interests of the group. Police forces, regulatory commissions, courts, prisons, and the like are representative of the enforcement apparatus. Such apparatus usually is conspicuous in the society, and people remain quite aware of the potential threats thus presented.

Yet it is inherent in social organization that the threat of force is a far more effective deterrent to deviation from approved behavior than is the actual use of force. In fact, the need to use force on any great scale is symptomatic of ineffective social organization. Even in the most complex society with the most elaborate regulatory and enforcement agencies, there cannot be enough police and other officers to force people to conform. Imagine, for example, what would happen if most citizens did not habitually obey traffic laws or voluntarily abstain from stealing. The vast majority of violators would go unapprehended, and those who were caught would overflow the jails and swamp the courts. The threat of force is effective only if it does not often have to be used, and all societies depend primarily on other means for securing conformity.

The primary technique for gaining conformity in all societies is the thorough socialization of individuals. Socialization normally produces persons who have so thoroughly learned the official and unofficial norms that not only do they not want to violate them but it does not often occur to them that they might do so. It is common knowledge, for example, that small children take things that don't belong to them. Five-year-olds pick up attractive items in a store with little guilt because they have not yet learned how much other people disapprove. A few years later, they may still steal small items they want, but now with furtiveness and guilt. By the time they reach adulthood, they ordinarily do not have to be watched, and they now help teach other younger persons that stealing is reprehensible. The word *conscience* is used to refer to this internalization of norms within the personality.

Here, again, the family institution and the political institution interpenetrate. Parents and siblings, aided by the formal educational system, teach conformity to the norms, which the political system has the official responsibility for enforcing. Without effective cooperation among the institutions, order would soon break down and the society would disintegrate.

Maintaining Motivation for Survival. To some degree the adequate performance of all of the preceding functional requisites depends on this last one. There is a universal human problem of ascribing meaning to life itself and providing people with motivation for survival.

The rationale for valuing existence varies among societies, but some rationale always is provided. In one society, the purpose of life may be to provide for worship of the Almighty. In a second, the goal may be continuation of the family line. Alternative and overlapping goals in life might include the appreciation of nature, the destruction of enemies, and hedonistic enjoyment. Some combination of goals is often found.

The religious institution is deeply involved in this area. One of the functions of religion is to define and strengthen ultimate values and to define relationships with the supernatural. The interpenetration of the religious and the family institution in this connection is obvious. In relatively undifferentiated societies, it may be the father, himself, who serves as priest. In more complex societies, it is still likely to be the family that guides the young into the formal religious organizations and that complements the instruction of the church with family devotions and home worship. This complementariness is well illustrated by holidays such as Christmas and Easter, Chanukah and Yom Kippur, in which family, church, and synagogue are deeply involved.

The functional requisites for societal survival are the minimum conditions for its continued existence. We have emphasized the family's involvement in these tasks and the overlapping of the roles of the family with those of other institutions.

THE NATURE OF FAMILY ORGANIZATION

The family is sometimes called the basic social institution. For, although the major institutions are found in all societies, their relative importance and the clarity with which they are defined varies from one society to another. The family is always a conspicuous feature of social organization. The family is always easy to locate, is in the constant awareness of people, and is deeply involved in the performance of the functional requisites. These are sweeping generalizations. They are true enough— but not without qualification. There follow several hundred pages of qualifications!

The Nuclear Family

Not only is the family universal, but a specific form of it—the nuclear family—comes close to being a cultural universal.[6] Americans easily un-

6. George P. Murdock, *Social Structure*, New York: Macmillan, 1949, ch. 1.

derstand the nuclear family because, in our society, the nuclear family is virtually synonymous with the family in general. The United States has the nuclear family as the basic residential family unit.

The term *nuclear family* refers simply to two adults of opposite sex living in a socially approved sexual relationship and living with their own or adopted children. It is the familiar unit of mother, father, and children. Data from societies all over the world point overwhelmingly to the central role the nuclear family plays in human experience.

One indication of the significance and utility of a scientific generalization is the amount of research and writing stimulated by it, which activity seeks to test, expand, and qualify the generalization. By this test, Murdock's generalization that the nuclear family is a distinct functional unit in all societies must be one of the most seminal contributions to twentieth-century social science. Virtually all work in this area for the past 35 years has used Murdock's analysis as a starting point.

Some scholars argue that there are exceptions to the universality of the nuclear family, but their evidence for exceptions is less impressive than Murdock's evidence for universality. The challengers generally use data from groups that do not constitute independent societies and in which partial exceptions typically fail to endure for as long as two full generations even where they do occur.[7] One of their favorite illustra-

---

. . . Whatever the degree of intensity with which kinship ties are utilized to forge social bonds, no society so far has managed to dispense with an irreducible minimum of kinship-based social relationships. And until Huxley's *Brave New World* is realized and bottles are substituted for mothers, they are unlikely ever to be dispensed with. . . .

ROBIN FOX, *Kinship and Marriage*, Baltimore: Penguin Books, 1967, p. 16

---

tions is the Nayar of Malabar. The Nayar, for a while, had an arrangement in which the husband lived with his sister's family and visited his wife only at night for sexual purposes. The Nayar are not a separate society however. They are a caste in the south of India. Moreover, this custom has not survived even among the Nayar who are tending toward

7. See Ira L. Reiss, *Family Systems in America*, New York: Holt, Rinehart & Winston, 1976. See also Lewellyn Hendrix, "Nuclear Family Universals: Fact and Faith in the Acceptance of an Idea," *Journal of Comparative Family Studies* 6 (Autumn 1975), pp. 125–38; Gary R. Lee, *Family Structure and Interaction: A Comparative Analysis*, Philadelphia: J. B. Lippincott, 1977; and Betty Yorburg, "The Nuclear and the Extended Family: An Area of Conceptual Confusion," *Journal of Comparative Family Studies* 6 (Spring 1975), pp. 5–14.

the nuclear family as a prominent residential unit.[8] A second alleged exception, the Kibbutzim of modern Israel are not a separate society either, and they, too, give increasing prominence to the nuclear family.

More significant than these cases for understanding family structure are the facts that nuclear families often are incomplete and often are incorporated into larger families. In any society, some nuclear families contain only one adult and some contain more than two adults. Similarly, there may or may not be children present. If the husband has died or been divorced, the wife may continue the family alone and vice versa. Or there may be a grandparent or unmarried brother or sister living with the family. Either the married couple may have had no children or they may have children who have grown and gone. The important thing about these exceptions is that they are exceptions. People who live temporarily in expanded or contracted nuclear families prepare the children to form intact nuclear families when they grow into adulthood.

Despite its heavy load of evolutionary and traditional social functions, the family is a popular concept. Families are personally important to individuals and, generally, have proved adaptive to modern requirements. The idea of the family is a reference point for people. A family represents love, security, and certain values even if, in reality, one's own family is mean-minded and distant. Families also have wider meaning as a cohesive force. They connote responsibility, especially toward the very young and very old. People believe that families are the group of first and last resort. . . .

ROBERT W. FOGEL, et al., eds., *Aging: Stability and Change in the Family,* New York: Academic Press, 1981, p. xix.

In many societies, nuclear families exist as parts of larger kinship units. Even where the nuclear family is embedded in a network of grandparents, grandchildren, cousins, uncles, and so on, however, it tends to be a distinct unit and to have its own private quarters. Moreover, the nuclear family ordinarily is the smallest kinship unit that is treated as a separate unit by the rest of the society.

Before proceeding further, it may be helpful to distinguish the family from marriage. We reserve *marriage* not for the married couple itself but for the complex of customs that regulates the relationship between husband and wife and provides for the creation of a family. Marriage specifies the appropriate way of establishing a relationship, the normative structure for ordering it, and often includes provision for terminating it.

8. See Joan P. Mencher, "The Nayars of South Malabar," in Meyer F. Nimkoff, *ed.,* *Comparative Family Systems,* Boston: Houghton Mifflin, 1965, pp. 163–91.

The Family of Orientation and the Family of Procreation. To view the nuclear family as a set of parents and their children is to view it in static, cross-sectional fashion. It describes the nuclear family at any given point in time, but it fails to describe the experience in the nuclear family of any given person.

Normally, during his or her lifetime, each person is a member of two different, overlapping nuclear families. He or she is born into a nuclear family composed of self, siblings (brothers and sisters), and parents. This family is called the *family of orientation.* At marriage, the individual leaves the family of orientation to create a new family composed of self and spouse and their children. This new nuclear family in which the individual lives as an adult is called the *family of procreation.* The families of orientation and procreation are diagrammed in Figure 1.1. The word *ego*, the Latin word for self, is used to stand for any individual.

The term *nuclear family* refers either to the family of orientation or to the family of procreation. Note that ego is the only person who is a member of both of these nuclear families. If we were to diagram the nuclear families of each other member of ego's nuclear families (mother, spouse, or sibling), the same thing would be true. Each pair of nuclear families would have only one member in common. This has much to do with the complexity of kinship structure.

Nuclear Family Functions. If we look at the common characteristics of nuclear families in various societies, we see that they parallel closely the functional requisites for societal survival. We find that (1) the marriage relationship always provides for meeting the sexual needs of adults, (2) the nuclear family is the unit of reproduction, (3) the nuclear family is a unit of common residence, (4) the nuclear family is the primary unit of economic cooperation, and (5) the nuclear family has important responsibility for the socialization of children.

1. The nuclear family, through the marital relationship, always provides for meeting the sexual needs of its adult members. Sex is a power-

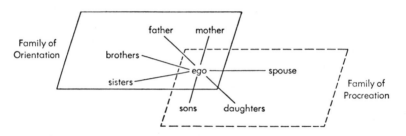

Figure 1.1. Diagram of the families of orientation and procreation

ful impulse that is nowhere permitted expression without regulation; unregulated sexual expression would threaten the cooperative relationships necessary within the family and society. Neither do societies deny regular sexual gratification to any sizable proportion of their adult members. Some adults, or even defined groups of adults, may remain celibate, but what evidence is available suggests that whenever sexual access is denied to a sizable segment of men or women, the society is likely to become unstable and major social change will occur.

It would be a mistake, however, to assume that the availability of sex within marriage accounts for the existence of marriage. In our own society, before the recent liberalization of sexual attitudes, this might have seemed true. Even today, a large proportion of American youth have difficulty establishing satisfactory sexual relationships before marriage. Many other societies, however, grant considerable sexual freedom to unmarried adolescents and young adults, imposing more restrictions on the availability of sexual partners after a person is married than before. If sex were the only, or even the chief, reason for marriage, we would expect persons in these societies to resist marriage. Such is not the case. People marry just as predictably in these societies as in our own. Most societies assign full adult status only to married people, and adult functioning, because of the sexual division of labor, is more difficult for the single person. We need to look to the full patterns of relationships between men and women to account for the universality of marriage.

2. The relationship between husband and wife is expected to produce children. Even today, when societies are becoming conscious of overpopulation, the expectation is that most marriages will produce at least one child. The fact that all societies place high value on having children testifies to the necessity of children to the society's survival. In all societies, the reproductive function of the nuclear family is emphasized.

It even appears that some societies make the sexual relationship between husband and wife contingent on reproduction rather than the other way around. The Banaro of New Guinea, for example, forbid the husband to have intercourse with his wife until after she has borne a child by another man chosen for the purpose. The husband is granted sexual access to the wife only after her ability to produce children has been established.

3. In most societies, the residential kin group is not limited to the nuclear family. It may include grandparents and grandchildren. There may be brothers and their wives, sisters and their husbands. There may also be siblings, aunts, nephews, and so on. A residential kin group may be larger than the nuclear family. Always included with a residential kin group, however, and identifiable within it, is the nuclear family.

Where larger residential kin units are found, there may be common facilities such as cooking space, dining space, and space for relaxation, but there are usually separate dwellings or apartments also. Each nuclear family ordinarily has some private quarters.

4. Economic cooperation within the nuclear family along with the sexual relationship between the father and mother binds it together. This cooperation is rooted in biological differences between the sexes and is reinforced by the culturally defined division of labor. Men everywhere are generally physically more powerful; women with children may have their freedom of movement hampered by pregnancy and nursing. All societies have developed a sex-based division of labor so that the work roles of men and women complement each other. Neither the man nor the woman can function at full efficiency without the services of the other.[9]

All societies also have a division of labor by age, assigning certain lighter tasks to children. Our own urban industrial society has restricted such childhood tasks severely, but even here there exist tasks ranging from mowing the lawn to walking the dog, from going to the grocery to baby-sitting with younger siblings. In most agriculture-oriented societies, the economic contribution of children is more obvious and greater. This division of labor continues into subsequent stages of the family life cycle when the dependency patterns may become reversed. One day the parents will need support, and their adult children will be in a position to provide it. Both across sexual lines and generational levels, economic cooperation helps to account for the importance of the nuclear family.

Despite the profound changes in the nature of the family that have come with the industrialization and urbanization of the past century, today's family remains the basic unit for the protection and rearing of young children, and the center of emotional life. Indeed, its role as the major source of psychological support for its members has, if anything, greatly increased. The family is a "haven in a heartless world," an oasis of stable, diffuse, and largely unquestioned love and support.

LENORE J. WEITZMAN, "Changing Families, Changing Laws," *Family Advocate* 5 (Summer 1982), pp. 2–3.

---

9. The women's movement argues that conditions of modern life have removed most of the necessity for a sex-based division of labor. For critiques of this topic, see Jack Balswick and Christine Proctor Avertt, "Differences in Expressiveness: Gender, Interpersonal Orientation, and Perceived Parental Expressiveness as Contributing Factors," *Journal of Marriage and the Family* 39 (Feb. 1977), pp. 121–27; William D. Crano and Joel Aronoff, "A Crosscultural Study of Expressive and Instrumental Role Complementarity in the Family," *American Sociological Review* 43 (Aug. 1978), pp. 463–71; Anne Statham Macke and William R. Morgan, "Maternal Employment, Race, and Work Ori-

5. Even in highly specialized societies, the nuclear family has responsibility for the care and socialization of children during their early years. The facts of parturition and nursing determine that there will be early and intense contact with the mother. Ordinarily, she assumes most of the responsibility for physical care of the infant and only gradually does the father become involved in training the child. The training ultimately is much more complex than mere physical care and requires the combined efforts of both parents. Only the father can transmit to his sons the skills required of adult men in the society, and only the mother can provide comparable training for her daughters. Boys and girls learn from both of their parents how to interact with members of the opposite sex. The more elaborate the society, the more agencies are likely to share in this socialization, but in all societies, the nuclear family plays an important role.

The nuclear family almost everywhere is characterized by sexual, reproductive, residential, economic, and socialization functions. Groups and agencies outside the family often share in the fulfillment of these tasks but never to the exclusion of the nuclear family. No society has yet found a satisfactory substitute for the nuclear family.

Kinship Organization

The nature of Western family organization makes it easy for American students to grasp the concept of the nuclear family. To a large extent the nuclear family is exemplified by the family in the United States. This same family structure is a handicap, however, when it comes to understanding kinship organization throughout most of the rest of the world. For in most societies, nuclear families do not exist in relative isolation from other kin units. Most societies have additional forms of family or kinship organization. Nuclear families may be combined through plural marriage or through extension of the parent-child relationship into composite families. In addition, the means of tracing descent often produce larger kinship units, known variously as lineages, moieties, clans, and so on. None of these other forms of kinship organization is universal. It is important, however, to emphasize, along with the primacy of the nuclear family, that most societies have a kinship organization more elaborate and complex than ours.

The Family as a Social Group

So far we have emphasized the family as a social institution, as a normative system. It consists of more or less formal rules and regulations con-

entation of High School Girls," *Social Forces* 57 (Sept. 1978), pp. 187–204; and Lynn K. White and David B. Brinkerhoff, "The Sexual Division of Labor: Evidence from Childhood," *Social Forces* 60 (Sept. 1981), pp. 170–81.

cerning the conduct of a major aspect of life. The family institution is not limited to the particular form given to it by a particular group of people, by the Jones family, say, or the Kowalskis. The family institution does not come into existence with the Joneses or the Kowalskis, and it does not die with them. The family as an institution is an abstraction or, rather, a series of abstractions from behavior. By observing the behavior of a sufficiently large and representative group of people in a society and by studying its official codes, we can state that the family institution of that society has certain features. This form of analysis provides a powerful tool for understanding human behavior.

There is yet another way of viewing families and their behavior. It focuses on the specific groups of people through whom the family institution is enacted and transmitted to subsequent generations. The distinction is not completely clear-cut: it is a matter of emphasis. The nuclear family, for example, is an institutional form—a series of prescriptions and proscriptions—about the relationships among its members and also refers to a specific group of people—mother, father, sons, and daughters.

In addition to the nuclear family, there are a number of fairly common family groups in the United States. People who think that it is desirable to live in independent nuclear families sometimes live in different circumstances. To understand the operation of our nuclear family system fully, it is necessary to have an awareness of some of these variations.[10]

Family Household. A family household consists of at least one adult member who maintains a household and shares a common dwelling with a spouse, children, or relatives. This group may be united by ties of marriage, blood, or adoption. There are many nuclear families that have unmarried relatives or aged parents living with them. Family households need not include children.

Married-Couple Family. A married-couple family is one in which both spouses maintain the household with or without children. Couples joined through remarriage may also constitute married-couple families. Children from one or both partners may share the common household.

Other Family, Male Householder. A male householder is a single parent who maintains a dwelling without his wife present. Children may or may not reside with the father, but some family member is usually present. This may be a sibling, aged parent, or grown child.

10. Lynda Henley Walters, "Are Families Different from Other Groups?" *Journal of Marriage and the Family* 44 (Nov. 1982), pp. 841–50.

Other Family, Female Householder. A female householder is a single parent who maintains a household without her husband present. In this case, children usually reside with the mother. Other relatives may share the household.

Nonfamily Household. A nonfamily household is one in which an individual maintains a household without other family members present. Young adults who are not yet married, the permanently single, divorced persons, and widows and widowers may fall into this category. One or more unrelated persons may share the household.

Male Householder. Male householders either live alone or share a residence with unrelated people. They may also live in institutional settings.

Female Householder. Female householders may be single, divorced, or widowed women living apart from relatives. They may live alone, have boarders living with them, or may share a dwelling with other, nonrelated people.

Trends in U.S. Family Groups

Recent years have witnessed substantial changes in the household and family arrangements of the U.S. population. As Table 1.1 clearly shows, the majority of households still consists of married couples, almost 60 percent. Over 9 million households, however, are now headed by women.

Table 1.1. Households in the United States, 1981 (in thousands)

Type of unit		1981
Family households		
Married-couple family	49,294	
Other family, male householder	1,933	
Other family, female householder	9,082	
Total		60,309
Nonfamily households		
Male householder	9,279	
Female householder	12,780	
Total		22,059
Total households		82,368

Source: After U.S. Bureau of the Census, *Household and Family Characteristics: March 1981*, Current Population Reports, Series P-20, No. 371, U.S. Government Printing Office (Washington, D.C., 1982), pp. 2–3.

Most of these are divorced women who have minor children living with them. Slightly less than 2 million households are headed by men without their wives present. Thus, approximately 2 percent of all households are mostly divorced and widowed men living without their children. The growth in the number of female-headed families was one of the major changes in the 1970s. This growth is expected to continue through the 1980s.

There has also been a marked increase in nonfamily living arrangements in recent years. In 1981, over 22 million people in the United States maintained their own households, living alone or with people unrelated to them. About 8 out of 10 of these people live alone, with most of the remainder living with an unrelated person of the opposite sex. Most of the latter are young adults who are living together, delaying the time of marriage.

The living arrangements of children also have changed appreciably. Slightly over three fourths of noninstitutionalized, unmarried children under the age of 18 lived in two-parent families in 1980. This figure takes into account the rising occurrence of children living with one natural parent and a stepparent. Another 20 percent lived with one parent, usually the mother. Approximately 4 percent of all children lived with neither parent but with relatives, usually grandparents. Almost three times as many children were living apart from their parents as were living in father-only households.[11] Although more than two thirds of all children still live with both natural parents, the number of children living with just one parent and with stepparents has been increasing rapidly. More details on these changes will be provided in later chapters.

SUMMARY

No one knows just how many human societies there are and have been, for societal boundaries often are difficult to define. There are, however, at least 4000 identifiable societies, ranging from preliterate to modern. The culture of each of these societies constitutes an independent solution to the common human problem of group living. Study of these societies will help us to understand our own society and our own family system.

The term *institution* is used by social scientists to refer to complex systems of social norms organized about the preservation of basic societal values. All societies have certain basic institutions—government, an economic system, an educational system, a religious institution, and the family. The institutions in a society are interrelated. Each impinges on the others, and the relationships among them change over time.

Institutions play major roles in performing the tasks essential for the

11. Raymond Montemayor and Geoffrey K. Leigh, "Parent-Absent Children: A Demographic Analysis of Children and Adolescents Living Apart from Their Parents," *Family Relations* 31 (Oct. 1982), pp. 567–73.

society's survival. Such tasks are called functional requisites. Functional requisites include provision for (1) continued adequate biological functioning, (2) reproduction, (3) the socialization of new members of the society, (4) the production and distribution of goods and services, (5) the maintenance of order within the group, and (6) maintenance of the motivation for individual and group survival. The family plays an important role in the performance of each of these essential tasks, sharing the responsibility differentially with the other major institutions.

The nuclear family, composed of a married pair and their offspring, is a family unit of special importance. Normally, people are members of two such units during their lifetimes, the family of orientation and the family of procreation. The nuclear family (1) provides regular sexual outlet for adults, (2) is the unit of procreation, (3) is the basic unit of economic cooperation, (4) maintains a common residence, and (5) has basic responsibility for the indoctrination of the young.

In most societies, nuclear families are organized into larger kinship units. This may be accomplished either through the practice of plural marriage or through the extension of the parent-child relationship. The means of tracing descent, through lineages, clans, and the like, often encourage larger family units also. Adequate understanding of social structure requires analysis of the whole of kinship organizations, not just of the nuclear family.

When the family is viewed as a social institution, the norms governing family forms and functions are emphasized. There is yet another important way of analyzing family patterns however. Families are also social groups. Institutions consist of social norms, whereas groups consist of people in interaction. When one focuses on the family as a social group, attention is directed more toward its internal functioning than toward its relationships with other aspects of the society. There are many ways to classify family groups, but one of the most useful ways is to follow the usages of the Bureau of the Census. The census classifies households into family households and nonfamily households. Family households are further subdivided into married-couple families, other family-male householders, and other family-female householders. Most households are organized around married couples, but the number of single-parent families, particularly those headed by women, have been increasing rapidly. The number of individuals living alone has also been rising steadily. The census classifies these nonfamily households as male householders and female householders.

SUGGESTED READINGS

Bernard, Jessie, *The Future of Motherhood*, New York: Penguin Books, 1974. A leading scholar examines the past, present, and future of motherhood in the United States and the world. Fascinating reading.

Burr, Wesley R., *Theory Construction and the Sociology of the Family*, New York: John Wiley & Sons, 1973. A sophisticated and technical volume that analyzes the process by which sociologists construct theories of family behavior. Good preparation for advanced study in the field.

Carter, Hugh, and Glick, Paul C., *Marriage and Divorce: A Social and Economic Study*, Cambridge, Mass.: Harvard University Press, 1976. A monograph of the American Public Health Association, this book contains a wealth of information about the structure and functioning of American families.

Clayton, Richard R., *The Family, Marriage, and Social Change*, Lexington, Mass.: D. C. Heath, 1978. A comprehensive sociological analysis of the family. Written as a textbook for college courses on the family.

Nye, F. Ivan, and Berardo, Felix M., *eds., Emerging Conceptual Frameworks in Family Analysis* (2nd ed.), New York: Macmillan, 1981. Systematic analysis of 11 different theoretical approaches to the analysis of family data. Includes anthropological, psychoanalytic, economic, legal, and religious approaches.

Rosenfeld, Jeffrey P., *ed., Relationships: The Marriage and Family Reader*, Glencoe, Ill.: Scott, Foresman, 1982. Contains contributions from more than 40 authors covering a myriad of marriage and family topics.

Scanzoni, John, *Shaping Tomorrow's Family: Theory and Policy for the 21st Century*, New York: Russell Sage Foundation, 1983. Proposes a progressive model that intertwines the family as an institution with public policy.

FILMS

Beginnings of Conscience (McGraw-Hill, Text-Film Division, 1221 Avenue of the Americas, New York, N.Y. 10020), 16 minutes. The social conscience that James Bruce, the adult, manifests is traced back to his socialization as a child. The conscience that he gradually develops in childhood, through experiencing such social sanctions as force, exclusion, and ridicule, later functions almost automatically in adulthood to make him a social being.

A Cross-Cultural Approach to the Acquisition of Sex Roles and Social Standards (Harper & Row Media, 10 East 53rd Street, New York, N.Y. 10022), 25 minutes. Children in Guatemala, Kenya, and Japan learn sex-role standards through observation, imitation, praise, and punishment.

Excited Turkeys (Grove Press Film Division, 53 East 11th Street, New York, N.Y. 10003), 10 minutes. Focuses on the traditional Thanksgiving dinner to examine the "apple pie" family. Studies the myths that Americans have created about their cultural and rational identity.

The Family: Lifestyles of the Future (Document Associates, 211 East 43rd
Street, New York, N.Y. 10017), 20 minutes, color. Margaret Mead nar-
rates an examination of traditional values and current unconventional
forms of family life. Concludes that there will be diversity in family
forms in the future.

A House, a Wife, and a Singing Bird (available through Oklahoma State
University Audio-Visual Center, Stillwater, Okla. 74074), 30 minutes,
color. A wise man tells a youth that old men dream dreams, but it is
the young men who make them come true; and to be happy, a man
must have a wife, a house, and a singing bird. Set in Indonesia, it shows
a young Indonesian searching for a place to live, ways that people make
a living, customs, and finally the marriage ceremony.

Windy Day (Grove Press Film Division, 53 East 11th Street, New York,
N.Y. 10003), 12 minutes. An animated film, featuring the voices of two
young girls, that deals with the responses of children to romance, marriage, and adulthood. The children muse about their parents getting
married, growing old, and dying.

QUESTIONS AND PROJECTS

1. Explain how we can learn about the American family system from
   knowledge of the family systems of preliterate societies.
2. Define the concept *social institution.* How are institutional patterns inferred from behavior?
3. Name the basic social institutions and give a brief definition of each. In
   what ways are the various institutions of a society interrelated? Illustrate.
4. Define the term *functional requisites.* Have there ever been societies that
   did not provide for meeting the functional requisites? If so, what happened to them?
5. Show, through illustration, how the family is involved in meeting each
   of the functional requisites.
6. Why is the family sometimes called the *basic social institution?*
7. Define the term *nuclear family.* Does the fact that some members of a
   society do not live in nuclear units detract from the importance of the
   nuclear family? Why or why not?
8. Distinguish between the family and marriage. What is the relationship
   between the two?
9. What is the family of orientation? The family of procreation? Draw a
   diagram indicating the relationship between them.
10. What are the principal functions of the nuclear family? Illustrate each.
11. What is meant by the family "as a social group"? How is the family as
    a social group different from the family as an institution?
12. Define each of the following terms: *family household, married-couple
    family, other family-male householder, other family-female householder,
    nonfamily household, male householder, female householder.*

Monkmeyer Press Photo Service

2

The Family in World Perspective

The most powerful man in the village had the most wives (nine) and twelve mistresses. The husbands and lovers of these women were a source of friendship and of agricultural labor, as well as support in situations of conflict. . . . Men who belonged to relatively large kin groups with considerable strength in garden farms were the ones able to attract women as mistresses, and to afford bride-wealth for more wives. In turn, the supporters acquired through these women bolstered the size and productivity of his farms and enhanced the prestige and well-being of his kin group. Some evidence suggests that men who could not aspire to leadership or ritual positions occasionally sought out Big Men to become lovers of their wives.[1]

Marriage and family forms vary widely over the world and even within the United States. Polygamy, or more precisely polygyny, occurs on a small scale in several western states. Other variations in U.S. family patterns shall be described in detail later on in this book. For now, we shall concentrate on variations in family patterns over the world.

COMPOSITE FAMILY FORMS

The nuclear family is the basic building block in family structure. In most societies, nuclear families are combined into larger units in one of two ways. They are combined through plural marriage or through extension of the parent-child relationship. Nuclear families combined through plural marriage are called *polygamous families* and those combined through the parent-child relationship are called *extended families*.

1. Audrey Smedley, "The Implications of Birom Cicisbeism," *Journal of Comparative Family Studies* 11 (Summer 1980), p. 349.

Polygamous Families

Polygamy is the general term used to refer to all marriage forms that involve the taking of plural spouses. Under polygamy, the spouses may be either husbands or wives. Although this might seem to be a foreign notion to Americans used to a monogamous system of marriage, in many parts of the world, it is actually the preferred marital form.

Many Americans hear the word *polygamy* and think of the sexual aspects of marriage. We are likely to imagine polygamy as one long sexual orgy. Nothing could be further from the truth.

In the first place, polygamous marriage is based on more than extension of the sexual privilege. Most societies grant sexual privileges with persons to whom the individual is not, and probably will never be, married. Also, in marriages in which plural spouses are present, sex may become more of a chore than a pleasure. Polygamy often requires that spouses be treated equally so that sexual intercourse must be accomplished on a regular, routine basis. Meeting the intimacy and sexual needs of multiple mates then becomes an obligation, and, as such, may lose much of its erotic appeal. Jealousies may arise if one wife thinks a co-wife is getting more than her fair share of attention or time. Men with plural spouses may worry about their ability consistently to oblige seemingly overwhelming sexual demands. Under situations such as these, sex may even become a burden.

In any case, marriage involves more than just an approved sexual relationship. In marriage, there is also the expectation of reproduction, common residence, and economic cooperation. Polygamy, as a marital system, is intimately tied up with economic functioning and status considerations. Also, as a normative system, it places a series of obligations on men and women. People in polygamous societies may react to these obligations much as we react to the obligations in our own monogamous system.

As we said earlier, under polygamy, marriage mates may be either husbands or wives. The marital system that allows the taking of multiple wives is called *polygyny*. *Polyandry* involves one wife with plural husbands. Polygyny is more common, whereas polyandry tends to be a rare occurrence.[2]

Polygyny. Again, because of our own cultural biases, it is not too difficult for most Americans to imagine polygynous societies. We may

2. Gerald D. Berreman, "Polyandry: Exotic Custom Vs. Analytic Concept," *Journal of Comparative Family Studies* 11 (Winter 1980), pp. 377–83; and Charles E. Welch, III, and Paul C. Glick, "The Incidence of Polygamy in Contemporary Africa: A Research Note," *Journal of Marriage and the Family* 43 (Feb. 1981), pp. 191–93.

misunderstand polygyny, but at least we can imagine it. Having several wives can be quite profitable in tribal economies. In areas where land is widely available, polygyny encourages its cultivation. Men with plural wives gain additional workers for their land and producers of children, two factors that contribute to economic wealth and social status and prestige.

Wives in polygamous marriages are not unhappy with the system or at least no more unhappy than monogamous wives are in Western cultures.[3] They may welcome additional wives to help with household duties and child care, to share with work in the fields, or for the friendship and closeness that could develop. Conflict and jealousy within the household is usually minimized by a set of rules that specify such things as how often the husband sleeps with each wife and how often each wife cooks for the husband.

Polygyny further subdivides into two basic types, *sororal* and *nonsororal*. The Latin word *soror* means sister. Under sororal polygyny the wives are sisters. Under nonsororal polygyny, the wives may be unrelated.

To most Americans, the best known sororal polygynous society may be that of the Hebrews. Students will remember the story of Jacob, Rachel, and Leah. Jacob wished to marry Rachel, the younger daughter of Laban. Jacob worked for seven years to earn the "bride price" for Rachel, only to be told that the younger daughter could not be married until the elder daughter was married. So Jacob took Leah and worked another seven years for Rachel.

Sororal polygyny is widespread over the world. Polygyny does produce problems of adjustment for the people who practice it (as does any form of marriage), and sororal polygyny seems to minimize some problems. Co-wives who are sisters are more likely to get along with one another than are co-wives who are not sisters. Having grown up together, they are likely to have similar values, attitudes, and ways of doing things. Jealousy is also less likely than between unrelated women. This situation is often reflected in housing arrangements. The separation of the dwellings of the co-wives is likely to be more marked if they are not sisters.

A special form of sororal polygyny is the *sororate*. This form results

3. See Louise Lamphere, "Strategies, Cooperation, and Conflict Among Women in Domestic Groups," in Michelle Zimbalist Rosaldo and Louise Lamphere, eds., *Woman, Culture, and Society*, Stanford, Calif.: Stanford University Press, 1974. See also Helen Ware, "Polygyny: Women's Views in a Transitional Society, Nigeria 1975," *Journal of Marriage and the Family* 41 (Feb. 1979), pp. 185–95. Interviews with 250 wives in a society where almost half of all marriages are polygynous showed that most of the women would be pleased if their husbands took another wife, particularly if they had a voice in selecting the new wife.

Figure 2.1. Diagram of independent, polygynous family

when there is a cultural rule that specifies the preferred mate for a widower is the sister of his deceased wife. Under the sororate, the marriages are successive rather than concurrent.

Many societies practice both sororal and nonsororal polygyny. The Mormons and the Crow Indians in the early days of the United States are examples. The breakdown of Mormon polygyny often is attributed to the fact that the Mormons permitted unrelated wives to live in close contact and to the fact that Mormon husbands often showed preference for the most recent wife.

The men of Kenya were worried: a new government bill threatened to restrict their right to marry as many wives as they could afford. Though polygamy would remain legal, . . . a man would be required to get permission from his first wife before marrying a second one.

Attorney General Charles Njonjo, who drafted the bill, is personally opposed to polygamy on the ground that it is "a luxury and too expensive." His compromise marriage law was designed to be more acceptable to Kenya's parliamentarians, the majority of whom are polygamists. Even so, many of them had serious reservations. Kimunai Arap Soi, an M.P. representing one of the Kalenjin tribal areas, charged that the bill would make it impossible to teach wives "manners" by beating them. "Even slapping your wife would be out," he fumed. . . .

Arguing that the proposed legislation was "very un-African," Arap Soi warned that "we are moving too far too fast in Kenya." He need not have worried: Parliament, by an overwhelming majority, shelved the bill for six months. For the time being, therefore, Kenyans may continue to slap as many wives as they can afford.

Time, The Weekly Newsmagazine, August 6, 1979, p. 56; Copyright © 1979 Time Inc. Reprinted by permission from Time.

Murdock has prepared estimates of the incidence of polygyny for one sample of 250 societies and for an expanded sample of 565 societies. Polygyny was found in 75 percent of the first sample of societies and in 81 percent of the second.[4]

Where it exists, polygyny usually is accorded higher status than is monogamy. Yet, even where polygyny is preferred, it tends to be practiced only by a small segment of the population. In some instances, the right to take multiple wives is limited to ruling families or to high-status persons. But even where such restrictions do not exist, most persons in polygynous societies remain monogamous. There are at least two reasons for this: (1) the economic factor, and (2) the sex ratio.

1. The existence of polygyny implies relatively high living standards. It means that one man must be capable of supporting at least two women and their children. Even where the highest living standards prevail, not many men can afford this. Most men in the United States, for example, could not afford two wives even if it were permitted. Thus, as an economic necessity, most men in polygynous societies have only one wife. Only the very wealthy are likely to afford more than one.

2. The second factor that exerts a push in the direction of monogamy is biological. In all societies, the sex ratio hovers about 100. The sex ratio is the number of men per 100 women in the society. The denominator of the fraction usually is not stated. If, for example, there are 110 men for every 100 women, the sex ratio is 110. If there are 97 men for every 100 women, the sex ratio is 97, and so on.

There are *primary*, *secondary*, and *tertiary* sex ratios. The primary sex ratio is the ratio at conception and is variously estimated to range from 120 to 150. Mortality rates are higher among male fetuses than among female fetuses and, by birth, the ratio is down to 105 or 106. The sex ratio at birth is the secondary sex ratio. Males continue to have higher mortality rates during childhood, and by adulthood, the sex ratio in most societies (the tertiary sex ratio) is around 100.

As indicated in Chapter 1, all societies afford marriage and regular sexual intercourse to most adults. Because there are approximately equal numbers of men and women, monogamy for most people is the only circumstance possible. For every man who has three wives, there may be two men who will have none. The number of males might be held in check through male infanticide, but children, particularly male infants, tend to be highly valued. The result is that polygyny is found in many places over the world, but it is not common even where preferred. Polygyny is more widely valued, but monogamy is more widely practiced.

Polyandry. For most people in our society, polyandry is difficult to imagine. As a matter of fact, polyandry is difficult to imagine outside of

---

4. George P. Murdock, *Social Structure*, New York: Macmillan, 1949, p. 28; and Murdock, "World Ethnographic Sample," *American Anthropologist* 59 (Aug. 1957), p. 686.

our society too, and it is very rare. Murdock found only 4 societies out of 565 to practice it—less than 1 percent.[5]

Polyandry also is divided into two types: fraternal, where the husbands are brothers; and nonfraternal, where the husbands may be unrelated. When nonfraternal polyandry is practiced, the husbands are likely to have separate dwellings. The Todas, in Southern India, practice fraternal polyandry,[6] and the Marquesan Islanders practice nonfraternal polyandry.[7]

A special variant of taking brothers as husbands is the custom of *levirate*. The levirate is a cultural norm specifying that the preferred mate for a widow is the brother of her deceased husband, as among the ancient Hebrews. In a polygynous society where the brother is married, the widow often becomes a secondary spouse to him. The caution should be added that the terms *levirate* and *sororate* are appropriate only when there is a societal preference and resulting social pressure for the arrangement to be followed. The terms do not apply to societies like our own, where such marriages occur occasionally but are not the general practice.

Polyandry creates one problem that polygyny does not: that of determining paternity. Obviously, the biological father generally remains unknown. The customs of the Todas are instructive in this respect. First, there is no great emotional investment on the part of the husbands in establishing paternity. For legal and ceremonial purposes, paternity is established through a ceremony in which one of the husbands presents a toy bow and arrow to the pregnant wife. That husband becomes the father of the child. During subsequent pregnancies, the rite may be repeated by other husbands if they wish to become fathers. Thus, the social status of father has no necessary connection with the biological fact of having sired a child.

There are so few cases of polyandry that only tentative explanations for it have been developed. It appears that polyandry is associated with extreme societal poverty, that it is found in societies existing very close

---

5. Murdock, "World Ethnographic Sample," *loc. cit.* See also Nancy E. Levine and Walter H. Sangree, "Asian and African Systems of Polyandry," *Journal of Comparative Family Studies* 11 (Summer 1980), pp. 385–410; John F. Peters and Chester L. Hunt, "Polyandry Among the Yanomama Shirishana," *Journal of Comparative Family Studies* 6 (Autumn 1975), pp. 197–207; and John F. Peters, "Polyandry Among the Yanomama Shirishana Revisited," *Journal of Comparative Family Studies* 13 (Spring 1982), pp. 89–95. When monogamy became a possibility in this culture, polyandry ceased, pointing to the fragility of this marital form.
6. His Royal Highness, Prince Peter of Greece and Denmark, "The Tibetan Family System," in Meyer F. Nimkoff, *ed.*, *Comparative Family Systems*, Boston: Houghton Mifflin, 1965, pp. 192–208.
7. Murdock, "Sample," pp. 675–86.

to the minimum subsistence level. We can't say that poverty causes polyandry because there are many poverty-ridden societies that are not polyandrous. A true cause-and-effect relationship exists only where the alleged cause invariably is followed by the supposed effect.

As an adjustment to poverty, polyandry has certain advantages. If the level of living were so low that a man could not produce sufficient food for a wife and children, he might be able to have a wife and children by sharing their support with other men. Polyandry also keeps the birthrate low and, thus, keeps the population in check. The reproductive potential for any society is set by the number of women who have the opportunity for sexual outlet. Because each woman can produce only one child every nine months, it does not matter how many husbands are involved. The polyandrous society, thus, can provide sexual outlet for a large number of men and still keep the birthrate low. There is some evidence of a tendency in polyandrous societies to keep the sex ratio in proper balance through ritual female infanticide. His Royal Highness Prince Peter of Greece and Denmark, a foremost student of the Tibetan family system, believes that fraternal polyandry among the Tibetans is a device for keeping the family property intact. Polyandry permits all the brothers to continue living on the land and permits them to transfer it intact to the next generation. Such an explanation, of course, is consistent with the idea of an association between poverty and polyandry.

Group Marriage. Continuing debate over whether or not group marriage exists illustrates a startling fact about our own society and its kinship system. We are accustomed to thinking of our society as complex and of other societies as being much less so. In fact, we often use value-laden adjectives such as simple and primitive to describe preliterate societies. In some respects, our society *is* complex. Its technology and its economic and political institutions are intricate and involved. But when we come to family and kinship, the institutions of many so-called simple societies are more complex than our own. It appears, literally, that persons reared in our relatively simple system and handicapped by a language associated with such simplicity of kinship are unable to conceptualize adequately the marital, family, and kinship customs of many other societies.

Western anthropologists use the term *group marriage* to refer to a situation in which a group of men and a group of women are married in common to one another. And they cannot agree whether or not such practices exist. Murdock says that group marriage "appears never to exist as a cultural norm."[8] He acknowledges, however, that among the

8. Murdock, *Social Structure*, p. 24.

Kaingang of Brazil,[9] 8 percent of all recorded marriages over a period of 100 years were group marriages. Linton describes the Marquesan Islanders as practicing group marriage.[10] The Dieri of Australia and the Chukchee of Siberia also have been reported to practice group marriage.

In fact, it appears that the categories of polygyny, polyandry, and group marriage are inadequate to describe the marriage forms in some preliterate societies. Both polygyny and polyandry and combinations of them exist in some societies. In addition, there may be the sharing of sexual privileges without the common residence and economic cooperation that we regard as essential to true marriage. Whether or not group marriage exists seems almost a question of semantics. It may be that the answer is less significant than the fact that we are ill equipped to understand fully the complex kinship institutions of many societies.

Polygamy and the Economy. Monogamy, polygyny, and polyandry are widely scattered over the world. Moreover, what associations have been discovered between them and other aspects of social structure are far from perfect. There are certain very rough relationships between the type of marriage and the economic situation in the society. The following tentative generalizations may be hazarded. First, when small family units are as efficient as large ones, monogamy may be favored. Second, where women have relatively little economic contribution to make, polyandry may be preferred. Finally, where large family units are advantageous and one man can support several women, polygyny may be favored.[11] In pastoral societies—keeping herds and flocks—one man and his sons may be able to shepherd enough animals to keep several women busy processing meat, hides, and milk and operating the household.

Extended Families

The second mode of combining nuclear families into larger units is through the parent-child relationship. Such combination produces residential units of three or more generations—at least grandparents, parents, and children. Extended families may be compounded of either monogamous or polygamous families. Families need not be either polygamous or extended; they can be both. A simple diagram of a three-generation extended family is given in Figure 2.2. For simplicity, a monogamous

9. Jules Henry, *Jungle People*, New York: Random House (Vintage Books), 1964, p. 45. Henry uses the term *joint marriage* instead of the term *group marriage*.
10. Ralph Linton, *The Study of Man*, New York: D. Appleton-Century, 1936, pp. 181–82.
11. For an analysis of how demographic conditions limit opportunities to maintain extended family households, see Karen K. Petersen, "Demographic Conditions and Extended Family Households: Egyptian Data," *Social Forces* 46 (June 1968), pp. 531–37.

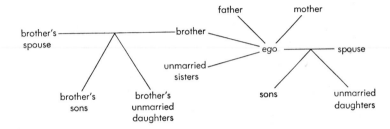

Figure 2.2. Diagram of three-generation extended, patrilocal, monogamous family

family is shown. Note that there are three separate nuclear families—the families of procreation of ego's father, of ego, and of ego's brother. These are dependent nuclear families in contrast with the independent polygynous family diagrammed in Figure 2.1. Nuclear families or polygamous two-generation families are called independent. The nuclear families included in an extended family unit are referred to as dependent families.

Consanguine and Conjugal Family Types. In structuring kinship, priority tends to be assigned either to marital ties or to blood ties. When priority is given to marital ties, the system is called *conjugal.* Our own family system is a conjugal one. Independent nuclear or polygamous family systems ordinarily are conjugal systems.

In contrast, extended family systems emphasize blood ties—those between parents and children or between brothers and sisters—over marital ties. These are *consanguine* systems. In a conjugal system, a man may leave his parents and "cleave unto his wife." In a consanguine system, the wife (or husband) is an outsider whose wishes and needs must be subordinated to the continuity and welfare of the extended kin group.

Conjugal families, including only two generations, are transitory in character. They disintegrate with the death of the parents. The family of orientation of the offspring ceases to exist and the family of procreation comes into being. The family of procreation creates a new family of orientation for its offspring and in turn will disappear with the death of the new parents. Thus, conjugal families are short lived. With their short duration and the drastic break from one generation to the next, they are not good vehicles for the maintenance of family traditions or for keeping family property intact over the generations. On the other hand, because conjugal families involve relatively few people, there may be little need for roles to be prescribed in great detail. There may be more improvisation permitted on the role of husband, daughter, and so on. We pride ourselves in the United States on the opportunities for personal development and personal freedom that our system provides. At the same time, many of us know little about our great-grandparents, and few of us hold substantial family property.

In contrast, consanguine families are immortal. The continued existence of the family does not depend on any one person or any couple. At marriage, one of the spouses remains with the family of orientation and is joined by husband or wife. The couple raise their children in a large family setting, and even if the mother or father should die prematurely, there are other kin present to absorb the several facets of the parental role. Eventually, when the grandparents retire or die, control and property pass without great fanfare to the next generation.

The advantages and limitations of the consanguine family are the reverse of those of the conjugal family. Whereas the conjugal family tends to produce the splitting of family property at each generation, the consanguine family permits it to be transmitted intact. Because consanguine families ideally involve a sizable number of persons spread over at least three generations, the role behaviors for each family member at each stage in life are laid down in considerable detail. One is under pressure to enact the roles of son, elder brother, husband, father, and eventually grandfather as they have been traditionally enacted. Whether one is well suited temperamentally to play these roles has little to do with it. Instead of the personal freedom emphasized in a conjugal family system, emphasis is placed on the faithful performance of prescribed roles.

A widely discussed variant of the extended family deserves brief mention. This is the so-called *joint family* of India.[12] The joint family is the traditional Indian family in which adult brothers live together with their respective families of procreation. In addition to maintaining a common residence, they hold property in common and assume joint responsibility for the education of younger siblings.

This Indian joint family actually is characteristic of just one stage in the life cycle, with persons typically passing through several stages during their lifetime. The process begins when the sons remain in the parental home following their marriage. While the father is alive, the In-

12. M. S. Gore, "The Traditional Indian Family," in Meyer F. Nimkoff, *ed., Comparative Family Systems*, Boston: Houghton Mifflin, 1965, pp. 209–31. See also George H. Conklin, "Emerging Conjugal Role Patterns in a Joint Family System: Correlates of Social Change in Dharwar, India," *Journal of Marriage and the Family* 35 (Nov. 1973), pp. 742–48; Ann Baker Cottrell, "Outsiders' Inside View: Western Wives' Experiences in Indian Joint Families," *Journal of Marriage and the Family* 37 (May 1975), pp. 400–407; A. A. Khatri, "The Adaptive Extended Family in India Today," *Journal of Marriage and the Family* 37 (Aug. 1975), pp. 633–42; and S. B. Singh Parmar, "Jointness and Nuclearity of the Hindu Family in Rural Settings," *The Eastern Anthropologist* 32 (July–Sept. 1979), pp. 193–99.

dian family does not differ significantly from other extended families. Following the father's death, the true joint family comes into existence when the brothers keep the extended household intact. This joint family is preserved until all the younger siblings are educated and married, at which time, the brothers split off their families of procreation and divide the family property among them. Thus, for a time, nuclear units exist separately. Soon, however, the sons of the brothers are ready for marriage and the process begins again.

Composite Families and the Economy

In Murdock's analysis of 250 societies, he found that approximately one fourth of them had the nuclear family only, another one fourth had polygamous but not extended families, and about one half had extended family systems, which could be either monogamous or polygamous. Nimkoff and Middleton subsequently analyzed data from 549 of the cultures included in Murdock's "World Ethnographic Sample."[13] They correlated the type of family system with certain economic factors, particularly the subsistence pattern and the amount of family property. More recently, Osmond,[14] as well as Blumberg and Winch[15] analyzed data from Murdock's *Ethnographic Atlas* and related familial complexity to societal complexity.

The results of these studies lead to the following tentative generalizations. First, the independent nuclear family is found at both ends of the economic scale. It predominates in societies with primitive hunting and gathering economies, where the food supply is uncertain, and also in modern industrial societies. Second, the extended family predominates in agricultural economies and reaches its fullest development in farming economies that combine agriculture with animal husbandry. Finally, independent nuclear families and extended families occur with about equal frequency in societies that depend on hunting and fishing and in societies that depend primarily on animal husbandry or where animal husbandry exists along with fishing. Thus, the independent nuclear family

13. Meyer F. Nimkoff and Russell Middleton, "Types of Family and Types of Economy," *American Journal of Sociology* 66 (Nov. 1960), pp. 215–25. See also Hsien-Jen Chu and J. Selwyn Hollingsworth, "A Cross-Cultural Study of the Relationship Between Family Types and Social Stratification," *Journal of Marriage and the Family* 31 (May 1969), pp. 322–27.
14. Marie W. Osmond, "A Cross-Cultural Analysis of Family Organization," *Journal of Marriage and the Family* 31 (May 1969), pp. 302–10.
15. Rae L. Blumberg and Robert F. Winch, "Societal Complexity and Familial Complexity: Evidence for the Curvilinear Hypothesis," *American Journal of Sociology* 77 (March 1972), pp. 898–920.

is found both at the top and at the bottom of the scale, with extended family systems being more prevalent in the middle.[16]

FAMILY STRUCTURE AND THE REGULATION OF SEX

All societies regulate sexual behavior. They all provide regular sexual outlet for most adults, but nowhere is the selection of partners simply a personal choice. Instead there are obligations, alternatives, possibilities, discouragements, and prohibitions. Moreover, these prescriptions and proscriptions are intricately bound up with family and kinship.

As with the more complicated combinations of plural marriage, intercultural variation in the regulation of sexual behavior is difficult for many Americans to put in proper perspective. Our own society is one of a very few that traditionally have completely prohibited sexual intercourse outside marriage. Murdock estimates the proportion of such societies in the world to be less than 5 percent.[17] People who have grown up in such a society are prone to make moralistic judgments about patterns that provide for a range of sexual partners both before and after marriage. It is well to keep in mind that patterns different from our own can be understood only in the larger social context in which they are found.

In the United States and much of the rest of the Western world, sex itself has been the focus of regulation. Sex is still frequently seen as a necessary evil. It is not so in most other societies. Most commonly, sexual regulation is part of the broader regulation of marriage, reproduction, kinship, and social status. What we encounter in most of the world is a series of permissions and restrictions in relation to these other phenomena.

Premarital Sexual Relationships

The marriage relationship is one of the major foci of sexual regulation. Most societies see nothing inconsistent between the regulation of sex in marriage and considerable sex freedom before marriage; consequently, complete premarital chastity is a minority pattern over the world. In some societies, there is almost complete freedom of premarital sexual relationships, with boys and girls allowed to take and to change partners

16. For an analysis of the relation between plural marriage and the economy, see Gary R. Lee, "Marital Structure and Economic Systems," *Journal of Marriage and the Family* 41 (Nov. 1979), pp. 701–13.
17. Murdock, *Social Structure*, p. 264.

at will. Surprisingly, the incidence of pregnancies appears to be quite low. Some writers attribute this to the relative youthfulness and undeveloped fecundity of the persons involved. In some cases, birth control techniques may be employed, but it is difficult to gather data on this. Generally, when pregnancy does occur, it is not the tragedy that a premarital pregnancy in our society might be. It may even be that the girl's marriageability will be enhanced by her own proven ability to have children.

Murdock found premarital sex relationships to be fully approved in 65 societies, to be conditionally approved in 43, to be mildly disapproved in 6, and to be forbidden in 44. In some societies where complete premarital freedom is not sanctioned, intercourse with selected persons—such as cross cousins,[18] who are potential marriage partners—is permitted. In sum, about 70 percent of the societies for whom data are available permit premarital intercourse. In most of the others, the taboo falls particularly on females and seems to be based on the necessity to prevent pregnancies. In most societies, it is less of a moral issue than with us.

Social Status and Sexual Relationships

The rules of *endogamy* and *exogamy* are two conspicuous examples of the relation between sexual regulation and social status. Technically, endogamy and exogamy define potential marriage partners and, indirectly, sexual partners. Endogamy requires a person to select a marriage partner from within the tribe, community, social class, nationality, race, or other grouping. Such requirements exist in virtually all societies and often have strong sanctions attached to them. Conversely, exogamy requires a person to select a marriage partner from outside certain groups. Exogamous requirements appear to result from extensions of the incest taboos that prohibit sexual relationships with close kin.

Exceptions to existing sexual regulations sometimes are made for high-status persons. The custom of *jus primae noctis* in medieval times and in some preliterate societies has received considerable public attention. Under *jus primae noctis*, the feudal lord, a priest, chief, or other high-status man selected for the purpose is entitled and obligated to have the first sexual intercourse with each bride. This custom has been interpreted to reinforce the headman's proprietary interest in the persons and property of his subjects and as a means of offering proof to the society that a

---

18. Cross cousins are the children of a father's sister or of a mother's brother. In many societies, cross cousins are preferred marriage partners. Parallel cousins are the children of a father's brother or of a mother's sister.

bride is virginal.[19] Exceptions to prevailing incest taboos are also known to have existed for members of royal families in some societies.

Kinship and Sexual Regulation

Sexual freedom before marriage does not necessarily mean sexual freedom in marriage, for most societies regulate closely the sexual behavior of married people. Most societies forbid intercourse between a married man and an unrelated woman. At the same time, however, few societies are as restrictive as ourselves in allowing intercourse only between spouses.

Most societies recognize some "privileged relationships" both before marriage and for married persons that give the person legitimate sexual outlet with certain classes of kin. Before marriage, the most common privileged relationship is with cross cousins where they are preferred marriage partners. In Murdock's 250 societies, 11 allow intercourse with a father's sister's daughter and 14 with a mother's brother's daughter.[20]

Within marriage, a comparable situation exists, particularly where the levirate and sororate are found. The privileged relationships are with the siblings-in-law who are potential spouses. Nearly two thirds of the sample societies permit intercourse with brothers-in-law or sisters-in-law.

In many societies, there is an assumption that men, particularly, suffer if denied sex for very long. The assumption for women is less explicit, the argument sometimes being that women do not experience sexual frustrations comparable to those of men. In some societies, also, there are taboos on intercourse during menstruation, pregnancy, and during a lactation period, which may last for three or four years. Granting sexual access to other female relatives often is rationalized as a means of relieving the sexual frustration that would be experienced during these periods.

This logic has been institutionalized in a few societies in the custom of *sexual hospitality*. The custom is found in societies in which men travel and are away from their wives during their travel. When they stop with a family for the night, it is obligatory on the host to provide a sleeping partner, just as he provides food and shelter. It is generally equally obligatory on the guest to accept the sexual partner, just as he accepts

19. This is another practice regularly misinterpreted by many Westerners. Many of us think of *jus primae noctis* as a highly erotic situation and as an uncomplicated privilege of rank. It is sobering to realize that privilege tends to shade off into duty and that the lord or chief may not be free to take only the brides attractive to him. As for the brides themselves, it is impossible to know if they consider this practice a high honor or an onerous obligation. Societal expectations in such matters usually take precedence over personal feelings.
20. Murdock, *Social Structure*, p. 268.

food. Failure to accept an offered bed partner, even one the guest considers to be totally undesirable, would be seen by the host to be a gross and intolerable insult.[21]

The regulation of sexual behavior in and out of marriage is part of the regulation of family behavior. Sexual regulation cannot be understood apart from the larger normative system of which it is a part. Moreover, understanding of the larger system requires understanding of its constituent parts. One set of sexual regulations that have great significance for family structure has yet to be discussed.

THE STRUCTURAL IMPLICATIONS OF INCEST TABOOS

An important factor in the analysis of family structure is the understanding of the nature and effects of incest taboos. The term *incest* refers to the prohibition of sexual intercourse with close blood relatives. Such taboos exist in all known societies.

Sexual intercourse between members of the nuclear family always is taboo, except between husband and wife. No society regularly permits intercourse between father and daughter, mother and son, or brother and sister. Virtually all societies also proscribe sexual relationships with adoptive parents, adoptive children, stepchildren, godparents, and godchildren—persons who occasionally stand in lieu of regular members of the nuclear family. Not only are such relationships prohibited, but most people react to incestuous relationships with aversion and disgust.[22]

As with most rules, there are a few exceptions. It is known, for example, that intermarriage of brothers and sisters has been permitted or required in certain royal families. Among the ancient Egyptians of the Ptolemaic period, among the Inca Indians, and within the old Hawaiian aristocracy, brother-sister marriage occurred within royal families. The practice generally is interpreted as a device for keeping property and power within the family. Murdock also reports that the Dobus, a Melanesian people, regard intercourse with one's mother after the father's death as a private sin, not as a public offense.[23] The Balinese permit twins to marry on the assumption that they have already been too inti-

21. Appreciation of the customs of one composite people practicing sexual hospitality may be gained from a pair of novels by Hans Ruesch—*Top of the World*, New York: Pocket Books, 1959; and *Back to the Top of the World*, New York: Charles Scribner's Sons, 1973. These fascinating novels are anthropologically sound.

22. For an argument that proposes the disappearance of the incest taboo owing to advancing technology and an emphasis on personal freedom, see Yehudi Cohen, "The Disappearance of the Incest Taboo," in Jeffrey P. Rosenfeld, *ed., Relationships: The Marriage and Family Reader*, Glencoe, Ill.: Scott, Foresman, 1982.

23. Murdock, *Social Structure*, p. 13.

mate in the womb. And an African people, the Thonga, are reputed to permit father-daughter incest in extraordinary preparation for a great hunt. These exceptions, of course, do not apply to whole societies, and their very nature emphasizes the universality of incest taboos.

There are two instances reported of societies where incestuous relationships within the nuclear family may have been more widespread. Slotkin claims that father-daughter, mother-son, and brother-sister incest were all generally permitted in ancient Persia.[24] Middleton also believes that brother-sister marriage in Roman Egypt occurred among commoners as well as within the royal family.[25] He interprets these marriages as a device for keeping property within the family. Unfortunately, it is not possible to gather additional data concerning these possible exceptions. Comparable situations apparently do not exist in any contemporary society. Suffice it to say that even should these two interpretations prove valid, the prohibition of sexual intercourse within the nuclear family is the most nearly universal social custom.

Discontinuity in the Nuclear Family

A primary effect of incest taboos is to make the nuclear family discontinuous. Sons and daughters are forced to go outside the nuclear family to find mates, resulting in a break between the family of orientation and the family of procreation. Were this not true, the nuclear family would be immortal. Brothers would marry their sisters and, thus, property, traditions, and folkways would be transmitted undisturbed from generation to generation. Kinship structure would be simple. Except for distinctions by age and sex, no other differentiation would be necessary.

The selection of mates from outside the nuclear family produces a continuous overlapping of nuclear families. The nuclear family experience of any two persons over their lifetimes is different. Each person becomes related biologically to an ever-expanding number of people. This is illustrated in Figure 2.3.

The terms *primary, secondary,* and *tertiary relatives* describe the degree of relationship between a person and the ever-expanding circle of relatives.[26] Primary relatives are the members of ego's nuclear families—mother, father, brothers, sisters, spouse, sons, and daughters—7 categories in all. Secondary relatives are composed of the primary relatives of ego's primary relatives—33 categories in all. Tertiary relatives are the

24. J. S. Slotkin, "On a Possible Lack of Incest Regulations in Old Iran," *American Anthropologist* 49 (Oct.–Dec. 1947), pp. 612–15.
25. Russell Middleton, "Brother-Sister and Father-Daughter Marriage in Ancient Egypt," *American Sociological Review* 27 (Oct. 1962), pp. 603–11.
26. A. R. Radcliffe-Brown, "The Study of Kinship Systems," *Journal of the Royal Anthropological Institute* 71 (1941), p. 2.

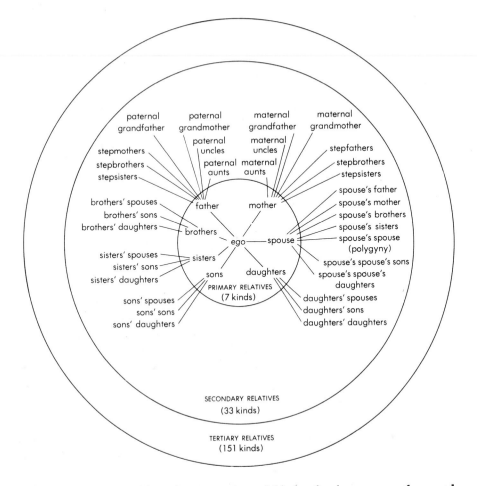

Figure 2.3. Diagram of maximum number of kinds of primary, secondary, and tertiary relatives in a polygamous marriage

primary relatives of ego's secondary relatives—151 different categories. Note that these are categories of relatives and that most categories may include several people. Some perspectives on these degrees of relationship may be gained by realizing that first cousins, generally recognized relatives in our own society, are tertiary relatives.

Where we stop tracing relationship, biologically, is purely arbitrary. It is obvious that even by the time we trace relationships out three degrees we have included so many categories, to say nothing of the larger number of people, that we cannot possibly have close social relationships with all of them. How many of us can name even one person who belongs to each of the 151 different categories of tertiary relatives?

Because of the ever-expanding number of biological kin, all societies select certain categories of kin for recognition and ignore others.[27] All societies have *social* definitions that establish priorities with certain biological kin. Family relationships are social relationships that include norms that govern the sharing of affection, economic cooperation, and the provision of mutual aid in time of need. There isn't enough affection to scatter indiscriminately over several hundred people, and to be entitled to aid from several hundred people is tantamount to receiving aid from no one. The satisfactory performance of family duties requires a group of kin of manageable size with whom orderly relationships may be maintained. To reduce the number of biologically related kin to a manageable social group, all societies have *rules of descent*.

Rules of Descent

Rules of descent are social definitions that determine for individuals who, among the myriad of biological kin, they consider themselves related to. Rules of descent define the family as a social group in contrast to the family as a biological group.

There are four general rules of descent. We shall take them in order of the frequency of their appearance.

Patrilineal descent is the most common form. Under patrilineal descent, the person is assigned at birth to a group of kin who are related through males only. To put it technically, descent is traced through the male lineage. The most important ties are those from father to son to grandson. A wife typically marries into her husband's family and their children become members of the husband's family but not of the family into which the wife was born.

Such unilineal systems of descent obviously are not in accord with the facts of biological relationship. Relationship to biological kin on the father's side is affirmed, whereas relationship to the mother's biological kin is ignored. Some early anthropologists believed that patrilineal descent meant that the people were ignorant of the ties to the maternal kin. This is not true however. Neither is patrilineal descent confined to preliterate peoples. Patrilineal descent has a long history in Eastern and Western civilizations. Unilineal systems of descent do not mean that people deny their biological relationship to the opposite lineage. They do mean that systems of descent are means of defining social relationships and that family structure, although rooted in the facts of biologi-

27. See, for example, Anthony Good, "Elder Sister's Daughter Marriage in South Asia," *Journal of Anthropological Research* 36 (Winter 1980), pp. 475–500; and Jared Tao Keil, "Prescription and Improper Marriage: Kin Category, Social Group, and Relationship Terminology Usage in Buin," *Journal of Anthropological Research* 36 (Winter 1980), pp. 501–16.

cal relationship, is not limited by them. Family structure is social structure.

The second most common system of descent is called *bilateral*. It
involves tracing relationships through two sides of the family—through
the mother's biological kin and the father's biological kin equally. The
size of the kin group is regulated by limiting it to close relatives on each
side. Such a system of tracing social relationships is in accord with the
facts of biological relationship. Because it is the system of descent used
in our own society, it makes sense to most Americans.

Matrilineal descent is the obverse of patrilineal descent. It traces relationship through females and the female line, discarding the father's relatives. Matrilineal descent is less common. As we shall see, descent, residence, inheritance—indeed virtually all family phenomena—are more
frequently determined through males than through females.

The fourth system, *double descent*, is useful simply to provide insight
into how complicated kinship systems can and do get. It is not common.
Where double descent exists, each person at birth is assigned to two kin
groups, one traced through paternal relatives and one through maternal
relatives. He or she becomes a member of the father's patrilineal kin
group and a member of the mother's matrilineal kin group. There are, in
the world, even more complex systems in which relationships are traced
differently for sons and daughters and that zigzag between the sexes,
from generation to generation.[28]

The rules of descent select from the ever-expanding group of biological kin those with whom social relationships are to be maintained. Associated with rules of descent are rules of inheritance.

Rules of Inheritance

Inheritance patterns are more complex than systems of descent and have
been studied less thoroughly. They are complicated by the facts that
some possessions such as clothing, ornaments, and tools are used only by
members of one sex, whereas other possessions such as money are transmitted to either sex. Through most of human history and over much of
the world, inheritance rights have centered on land, dwellings, animals,
and (generally) the means of production. If such property passes to the
heir or heirs through males, the rule is said to be *patrilineal;* if the route
is through females (from a man to his sister's son) then it is *matrilineal.*

Inheritance patterns are further complicated because men and women
may or may not inherit equally and even same-sex siblings may or may

28. Students who wish to read more on this system of descent are referred to Margaret
Mead, *Sex and Temperament in Three Primitive Societies*, New York: New American
Library (Mentor Books), 1950, pp. 119–63.

not inherit equally. More often than not, the inheritance of major property is through males to other males. The inheritance rights of women often are circumscribed and sometimes nonexistent.

The inheritance rights of males may vary with birth order. If all sons do not inherit equally, the most likely situation is for the eldest son to inherit all or a disproportionate part of the property. This arrangement is known as *primogeniture*. Less commonly found is *ultimogeniture*, where the youngest son is favored.

Rules of Residence

The nuclear family is virtually everywhere a residential unit. At marriage, the husband and wife take up residence together. Because they come from different families of orientation, one or the other or both must move at marriage. The alternatives available, in relation to their respective families, are few: they can locate with the husband's family of orientation, with the wife's family, away from both families, or in some combination of these. All societies have developed norms to determine which alternative will be followed. These norms are called rules of residence.

The most common rule is *patrilocal*. Under patrilocal residence, the bride leaves her family of orientation and sets up housekeeping with her husband in the same dwelling with, or adjacent to, his family of orientation. Note that patrilocal residence does not refer to the wife's going to live with the husband but to her going to live with the husband's family. Patrilocal residence is common over the world. A special variant of patrilocal residence is *matri-patrilocal*, where residence is with the bride's family of orientation for a prescribed period after which the couple take up permanent residence with the groom's family. The couple may live with the bride's family for one year or until the first child is born.

Matrilocal residence involves the husband leaving his family of orientation to take up residence with his bride in the locale of her family of orientation. Closely related to matrilineal descent and inheritance is another rule of residence known as *avunculocal*. Under avunculocal residence, the couple take up residence with the maternal uncle of the groom. Thus, the residence rule is built around males of the female line. Few societies have avunculocal residence.

Under *bilocal residence*, the couple is permitted to choose whether they will locate with the husband's or the wife's kin. The strength of the personal ties between the couple and their parents, the relative wealth of the parents and their power in the community, and the need for assistance from the young couple may be determining factors.

Note that the rules of residence discussed so far all favor the development of extended families. All create units of at least three generations. They also put one of the spouses into a favored position. The spouse who stays with his or her family is surrounded by kin sympathetic to his or her cause in disputes with the other spouse. The spouse who has to move, in contrast, is relocated among relative strangers and somewhat isolated from the support of kin. Thus, the rule of residence may influence the distribution of power between the spouses in marriage.

The final rule of residence is *neolocal*. As the term implies, this rule involves the establishment of a new residence apart from both families of orientation. This is the only rule that militates against the development of extended family units and encourages isolation of the nuclear family. This is the rule followed in our society.

It is probably apparent that there are certain logical associations (1) among patrilineal descent, patrilineal inheritance, and patrilocal residence and (2) among matrilineal descent, matrilineal inheritance, and matrilocal residence. Murdock concluded that patrilocal residence is associated with polygyny, warfare, slavery, and an economy that depends on the chase rather than on collecting. Matrilocal residence is favored by the development of agriculture in what previously was a hunting and gathering economy and by the ownership of land by women. Bilocal residence is accompanied by a migratory life in unstable bands and, at a higher economic level, by approximate equality of the sexes in the ownership of property. Finally, neolocal residence is associated with approximately equal economic contributions by men and women, monogamy, extensive poverty, and individualism.

Murdock assigns priority to rules of residence in determining systems of descent and inheritance. He concludes that rules of residence are likely to be affected first by changes in the economic base and by technological development. As the residential kin group alters, changes gradually come about in the means of tracing relationships.[29]

One final set of associations with rules of residence deserves mention. The phenomenon known as *bride price* exists in approximately two thirds of the societies for whom data are available. Bride price refers to a payment of money or goods to the bride's family at marriage, to the exchange of one of the husband's female relatives for the bride, or to a

29. See M. S. Grieco, "Family Structure and Industrial Employment: The Role of Information and Migration," *Journal of Marriage and the Family* 44 (Aug. 1982), pp. 701–7; Robert E. Mitchell, "Residential Patterns and Family Networks (I)," *International Journal of Sociology of the Family* 2 (Sept. 1972), pp. 212–24; Mary Ellen Oliveri and David Reiss, "The Structure of Families' Ties to Their Kin: The Shaping Role of Social Constructions," *Journal of Marriage and the Family* 43 (May 1981), pp. 391–407; and Ellen Fitzgerald Richards, "Network Ties, Kin Ties, and Marital Role Organization," *Journal of Comparative Family Studies* 11 (Spring 1980), pp. 139–51.

period of work-service for the bride. The payment of bride price is associated with rules of residence that remove the bride most drastically from her family of orientation.

Her daughter, Raj Yadav says, was 18 years old and married less than a year when she was held by the arms, doused with gasoline and set afire by her husband or an in-law or both. The daughter died.

She was killed, Mrs. Yadav charged, because neither she nor her parents could produce the $1,200 and a television set that had been demanded as an after-the-marriage "dowry."

Such incidents have become known as "dowry deaths," and one surfaces in India every few days.

WILLIAM K. STEVENS, "The Rise in 'Dowry Deaths' Alarms Many Indian Women," *New York Times*, September 12, 1982.

Some early students of kinship interpreted bride price as outright purchase of the wife, as one would purchase cattle or other property. Such interpretation appears erroneous and misses the true functions of bride price. There appear to be essentially two functions. First, the bride price offers recompense to the bride's family for loss of her services. Particularly when the bride's and groom's families live in different communities and patrilocal residence is followed, the bride's family's economic loss may be very real. Second, the bride price is insurance against maltreatment of the bride by the husband or his family. The sum involved usually is substantial and if the bride is unjustly divorced or forced to return to her parental home because of mistreatment, her family generally retains possession of the bride price. True wife-purchase appears to be rare.

Authority Patterns in the Family

Strictly speaking, the distribution of authority between husband and wife does not derive directly from the incest taboos. The relationships between family authority patterns and rules of descent and residence, however, make brief discussion of them relevant here. We may describe three principal types: patriarchal, matriarchal, and equalitarian.

A *patriarchal* system is one in which power and authority are vested in males, with the eldest male usually wielding arbitrary power. Patriarchal systems have been common through history and over the world. The ancient Hebrews, Greeks, and Romans; the Hindus and Mohammedans; and the Chinese and Japanese provide a few examples.

Patrilineal descent, patrilineal inheritance, patrilocal residence, and primogeniture all are associated with male dominance. In addition, polygyny, a double standard of sexual morality, masculine privilege in divorce, the arrangement of children's marriages by adults, and a low status for women are frequent accompaniments of patriarchy. We do not have quantitative data to indicate what proportion of the world's societies are and have been strong patriarchies, but abundant descriptive data exist. Few would question that male dominance is the rule rather than the exception.[30]

Logically, a *matriarchal* family type is very simple; matriarchy should involve the complete vesting of power in females. There is in fact no true matriarchal society in existence and chances are there never has been. Even in societies organized about women, in societies that follow matrilineal descent, inheritance, and residence, power tends to be held by males in the female lineage. Power usually is held by the women's brothers—from the viewpoint of ego, by the maternal uncle. Male dominance, or a tendency toward it, appears to be nearly universal. A minority of societies are organized around the female lineage, but even then, power, status, and property tend to be held by males.[31]

One common feature of human existence that has put women into positions of power is the tendency for women to outlive men. Men are physically stronger, but women live longer and are less susceptible to genetically transmitted diseases. Patriarchal societies often accord high status to older people, and sons usually are trained to respect their mothers. When the father dies first, the son who assumes power may continue to defer to his mother, thus creating by default a degree of female dominance in the society.

The third logical type, the equalitarian family, implies equal distribution of power and authority between husband and wife.[32] This arrangement is in accord with some of the basic facts of human existence. Few fair-minded people would question that, except perhaps for brute strength, there are many women in any society who are as strong, intel-

30. See Leslie B. Curtin, *Status of Women: A Comparative Analysis of Twenty Developing Countries*, Washington, D.C.: Population Reference Bureau, 1982.

31. See Alice Schlegel, *Male Dominance and Female Autonomy: Domestic Authority in Matrilineal Societies*, New Haven, Conn.: HRAF Press, 1972.

32. Most of the concepts employed in this chapter—patriarchal, matrilineal, neolocal, polygymous, authoritarian, and so on—are *ideal types*. See Max Weber, *The Methodology of the Social Sciences*, translated and edited by Edward A. Shils and Henry A. Finch, Chicago: The Free Press, 1949. Ideal types are concepts created by taking one or more characteristics typical of a phenomenon and accentuating those characteristics to their logical maximum or reducing them to their logical minimum. They are not accurate descriptions of reality but represent logical exaggerations of reality. There is no such thing, for example, as a patriarchal society, if we mean by that a society in which all power is vested in males. There are only societies in which considerable power is held by males. Ideal types are logically extreme standards against which reality is measured. As long as we are careful to avoid the fallacy of *reification*, of confusing the concept with reality, ideal types are useful analytic devices.

ligent, clever, and ambitious as their husbands, if not more so. Even in the most patriarchal societies, strong wives probably have dominated weak husbands. One of the traditional ways of writing *wife* in Chinese characters was to show a woman's hand holding onto a man's ear. The equalitarian family simply represents institutionalization of this situation. The Western family, particularly the family in the United States, has been tending for many decades toward an equalitarian form.

Extension of Incest Taboos Outside the Nuclear Family

All societies taboo all cross-sex relationships within the nuclear family, but no society stops there. Some additional kin are always tabooed. Interestingly, however, there is no one class of kin outside the nuclear family from which it is not acceptable to choose a sex partner in some society. First cousins, aunts, nephews, and so on, are taboo in some societies but not in others. At first glance, there does not appear to be much rhyme or reason to these extensions.

Obviously, the taboos are not extended strictly in accord with biological relationship. In most societies, intercourse is permitted with some fairly close blood relatives and prohibited with more distant ones. The key to these extensions is the family as a social group rather than the family as a biological group. Those groups who are prohibited tend to be those the system of descent defines as closely related. Thus, the *extension* of incest taboos tends to be rooted more in sociology than in biology.

A peculiar feature of incest taboos is their strength and the attitudes that surround them. A peculiar horror attaches to their violation; scarcely can a more heinous offense be imagined. The repugnance is greatest at incest within the nuclear family and becomes less strong as one moves outward from the nuclear family along the socially defined lines of kinship.

The Enforcement of Incest Taboos

The basic technique on which most societies depend for the enforcement of incest taboos is to instill them so thoroughly in the society's members that violations become virtually inconceivable. The learning of the incest taboos is a basic part of socialization. It is commonplace in American society that many small children are relatively free in acting on their sexual impulses and indiscriminate in their choice of partners. It is not unusual, for example, for young brothers and sisters to join in sexual play. By adulthood, however, the taboos have been so thoroughly learned that aversion, bordering on physical illness, may be the response to any prospect of sexual intercourse within the nuclear family. Adult brothers and sisters may sleep in adjoining bedrooms and appear before one another in states of partial undress without arousing any sexual response in either person. This internalization of the taboos within personality is far more effective than any external restraints might be and is the primary mechanism on which most societies depend.

Not all societies, however, depend on internalization alone. In some societies, there are, in addition, patterns of avoidance behavior between persons who are tabooed but between whom intercourse might occur. At puberty, for example, the norms may prescribe that brother and sister shall no longer be alone together. If the sister enters a room and only her brother is present, he may be required to leave. Similarly, the norms may provide that a man may not look directly on his mother-in-law. Whenever they are together, he may be required to keep his face turned away. Murdock found the relationship between a man and his mother-in-law and between a father and his son's wife to be classic avoidance relationships.

Avoidance relationships appear not to be depended on by any society to the exclusion of internalization of incest taboos but rather as supplements thereto, in situations where the internalization process is not wholly effective. A man's relationships with his mother-in-law or his son's wife, for example, are not likely to be so strongly tabooed as are those with his sister or daughter. Avoidance relationships also are quite effective, up to a point. People who cannot be alone together or who cannot look at one another ordinarily are not in great danger of sexual involvement. The superiority of internalization of the taboos as a means of control is that it continues to be effective even when the situational restraints are removed.

Indoctrination of people with social norms is never perfect, and violations of the incest taboos occur in all societies. The few violations appear to be exceptions that validate the rule. Kinsey reports that violations in our society are so rare that it would be misleading to mention specific figures.[33] Weinberg studied 203 cases of incest known to the authorities in Illinois[34] and reports that the detected incidence of incest in the United States in 1920 was 1.9 offenders per 1 million population, in 1930 it was 1.1 per 1 million.

These detected figures probably underestimate the actual incest rates. True rates are probably considerably higher; certainly the experience of social workers and clinicians would indicate so. It is significant, however, that great effort is made to suppress knowledge of specific cases of

33. Alfred C. Kinsey, Wardell B. Pomeroy, and Clyde E. Martin, *Sexual Behavior in the Human Male*, Philadelphia: W. B. Saunders, 1948, p. 558.
34. S. Kirson Weinberg, *Incest Behavior*, New York: Citadel Press, 1955, p. 39.

incest. The maintenance of the taboo is too crucial to the larger society to permit open discussion of violations that do occur.

Explanation of Incest Taboos

People have long sought an adequate explanation of the universality of incest taboos. Dozens of explanations have been proposed, most of them so bizarre that no discussion of them need be given. Of the many proposed explanations, only a few have more than superficial plausibility. On detailed examination, most of those also prove inadequate. We shall examine four of the commonly accepted explanations before arriving at the one that appears most plausible.

Alleged Harmful Effects of Inbreeding. One explanation attributes the taboo between blood relatives to the adverse effects of inbreeding on the quality of the population. It is claimed that inbreeding leads to deterioration of the stock (perpetuation of hemophilia within inbred European families is used as an illustration), and recognition of this fact has led people everywhere to prohibit such relationships.

This explanation has appeal, for inbreeding does tend to bring genetic deficiencies into expression. Most human genetic deficiencies are carried as recessive genes and do not produce harmful effects when the carrier is mated with a person who does not carry the same recessive gene. The odds are much greater that a closely related person also carries the harmful recessive gene and that if these closely related persons are mated, the defect will appear in their offspring.

There are several problems with this logic however. For one thing, this logic might be reversed to promote biological improvement of the species. Inbreeding is precisely what is used in animal science to produce steers that yield more and higher quality beef, chickens that contain more white meat, faster race horses, and so on. If people were completely rational, they might promote inbreeding within certain lines along with prohibiting it in others. It can be argued that until recently, if even now, we did not have sufficient knowledge of human genetics to make such selective regulation possible. Granting this argument, it appears unlikely that vastly improved knowledge of genetics would have much influence on incest taboos.

A more serious difficulty with this explanation is that it assumes a rationality that in some cases is literally impossible. Until recently at least some preliterate peoples lacked adequate knowledge of the reproductive process, occasionally being unaware of the role of the father in procreation. The Arunta and the Trobriand Islanders are illustrations.

Incest taboos are no less complex and are just as strong in these societies that could not possibly connect genetic problems to inbreeding.

Still another problem is that incest taboos in most societies do not coincide with the closeness of biological relationship. Distant biological relatives may be prohibited, whereas procreation with closer relatives is permitted. Thus, we must conclude that although the prohibition of inbreeding has some salutary effects in some instances, the total weight of evidence is against this explanation for most of the incest taboos.

Alleged Instinct Against Inbreeding. The internalization of norms against inbreeding among most people is so effective that revulsion against incestuous relationships seems almost to be a part of the biological structure of the organism. This fact led some writers to posit the existence of an instinct against incest.

Early in the twentieth century, the concept of instinct was seized on to explain a tremendous variety of human behaviors, ranging from simple autonomic reflexes to complex and variable patterns of behavior such as parenthood and war. Gradually, however, the absurdity of postulating hundreds of human instincts became apparent.[35] It was concluded that the term *instinct* has utility only to refer to complex patterns of behavior that are biologically fixed for the species and that cannot be explained as a product of learning.

The concept of instinct cannot explain incest taboos. In the first place, violations of the taboos occur. If there were an instinct operating, violations could not take place unless some people were born without the instinct, an implausible assumption. Second, incest taboos are highly variable. It makes no sense biologically to claim that instincts prohibit intercourse with first cousins in one group and not in another. Third, if there were an instinct against it, there would be no need for the widespread horror of incest. A biological mechanism operates automatically without need for buttressing emotional reactions. The instinct explanation has been generally discarded by biological and social scientists.

Familiarity Breeds Disinterest. Edward Westermarck explained incest taboos by the fact that continued close association between persons of opposite sex lessens their sexual attraction for one another.[36] That some lessening of interest does occur with continued close association seems to be a fact. Virtually all husbands and wives recognize this even in a context where sexual participation is expected. Recently in the kibbutzim of Israel, it has been found that among children reared together

35. Luther L. Bernard, *Instinct: A Study in Social Psychology*, New York: Holt, 1924.
36. Edward Westermarck, *The History of Human Marriage*, New York: Allerton, 1922, Vol. 2, p. 192.

where there are few taboos on nudity and where sexual interest might be expected to develop, it does not. In ancient Egypt, where royal brother and sister were expected to marry, it was usual to separate them in childhood and to keep them apart until adulthood so that they would be sexually attracted to one another.

The problem is not with the facts themselves as with the facts as an explanation of incest taboos. The effects of growing up together cannot explain the frequent extension of incest taboos to kin who are not members of the household and with whom one might not have continuing close association. In the reverse situation, preferential mate selection (the levirate, sororate, and cross-cousin marriage) often calls for marriage with persons with whom one has been associated long and intimately.

There is also reason for questioning the facts. We know that there are many exceptions to the rule and that some persons are attracted sexually to other members of their own nuclear families. The logic of lessened sexual attraction would not explain why sexual relationships should be prohibited in those cases where attraction does exist.

Frustrations in the Oedipal Involvement. Another explanation has come out of psychoanalytic theory. Freud developed the notion of universal sexual attraction of a boy to his mother from Sophocles' *Oedipus Rex*, in which the son, Oedipus, unknowingly slays his father and marries his mother. When he learns what he has done, he is overwhelmed with guilt and blinds himself. In psychoanalytic theory, this became the universal situation where the child's sexual attraction to the parent of opposite sex must be repressed because of the harm that would be done to the child should the parent of the same sex become aware of the incestuous desires. The repression is only partly successful, and the horror that is attached to violations of the incest taboos is interpreted as reaction formation against the partly repressed impulses.

This psychoanalytic interpretation makes sense in the context of Western family organization but not in societies with radically different family organization. Malinowski tested the notion of a universal Oedipal complex through study of the Trobrian Islanders, a matrilineal society in which the role of paternity was not understood and in which the maternal uncle performed most of the functions associated with the father role in Western society. He found that the child's hostility was directed toward the uncle rather than toward the father and that the basis for hostility was not sexual jealousy but resentment against authority. Thus, the Oedipus complex is not universal but is a product of middle-class family structure in Western society.[37]

37. Bronislaw Malinowski, *Sex and Repression in Savage Society*, New York: Harcourt and Brace, 1927.

The Oedipus hypothesis is inadequate in other respects. It does not account for the universal extension of taboos beyond the nuclear family. Nor does it account for variability in the definitions of which relatives are taboo. Psychoanalysis usefully focused attention on the dangers of sexual conflict within the nuclear family, but by itself, it did not provide an adequate explanation of incest taboos.

An Eclectic Explanation. The term *eclecticism* refers to the combination of elements of existing theories into a new, more comprehensive theory. Murdock has proposed an eclectic theory of incest taboos that provides the most satisfactory explanation of them to date. In so doing, he draws on contributions from sociology, cultural anthropology, psychoanalysis, and behavioristic psychology.[38]

The explanation begins by assuming, with the psychoanalysts, that immature sexual responses, or at least responses that adults interpret as sexual, are made by the infant toward its parents as part of responses to feeding, protection, and general care. These incipient responses meet with rebuffs and frustration both because of lack of interest by parents and because of the threats that are inherent in such behavior.

The parents, as sexually experienced adults, feel some sexual attraction toward their children. Having been indoctrinated with restraints on sexual behavior with children and within the nuclear family, the parents react with guilt and anxiety. Their anxiety is heightened because each parent would be threatened by the other's sexual attraction to one of the children. As a consequence, both parents strongly discourage their children from making any sexual overtures.

The explanation of the cultural sanctioning of these tendencies within families comes from sociology. The family is the basic unit of reproduction, economic cooperation, and socialization. Sexual rivalry within the group would jeopardize its efficient functioning and its existence. Fathers competing with sons for the mother and the daughters, and mothers competing with daughters for the father and brothers would tear the group apart. Thus, the self-interest of individuals and the societal interest are consistent with one another. Sexual restraints within the family receive normative support from the society at large.

Kingsley Davis points out, further, that should inbreeding occur, the resulting confusion of statuses would be unbelievable. As he says, "The incestuous child of a father-daughter union . . . would be a brother of his own mother, i.e. the son of his own sister; a stepson of his own grand-

---

38. Murdock, *Social Structure,* pp. 292–300. For other analyses of the incest taboos, see Christopher Bagley, "Incest Behavior and Incest Taboo," *Social Problems* 16 (Spring 1969), pp. 505–19; and Richard L. Means, "Sociology, Biology, and the Analysis of Social Problems," *Social Problems* 15 (Fall 1967), pp. 200–212.

mother; possibly a brother of his own uncle; and certainly a grandson of his own father."[39] All family systems provide definitions of proper behavior between various family members; these definitions would break down in the face of widespread inbreeding.

The extension of incest taboos beyond the nuclear family is explained through the psychological concept of "stimulus generalization." According to this principle, any response elicited by a stimulus will be elicited by other stimuli in direct proportion to their similarity to the original stimulus. Thus, if the mother is tabooed, other women will be tabooed in proportion to their perceived similarity to her. Where maternal aunts are called by the same kinship terms as the mother (as they sometimes are), where they live in the same household, and where the sororate exists, the maternal aunts are likely to be tabooed also.

There still remains the problem of why the taboos are extended further in some cases than in others, both within and among societies. Suffice it to say that anthropologists have determined that kinship systems have both a history and a structure that is somewhat self-limiting. To explain why a particular society has an irregular extension of incest taboos, it is necessary to know both its historical connections with other societies and the particular directions of change that are facilitated and restricted by its existing kinship structure.

SUMMARY

Nuclear families are combined into composite families through plural marriage or through extension of the parent-child relationship. Polygamous marriage, which involves common residence, economic cooperation, and the sexual relationship, is divided into polygyny and polyandry. Polygyny is widespread; polyandry is rare; and group marriage is nowhere the societal norm. Polygamous marriages may involve the taking of siblings as spouses or the multiple spouses may be unrelated. The terms *levirate* and *sororate* refer to preferential marriage with the sibling of a deceased spouse. Although polygyny usually is accorded higher status than monogamy, most persons in any society are monogamous. The sex ratio and the cost of polygynous marriages are influential here.

Extended families may be compounded either of monogamous or polygamous families. Nuclear families become dependent units in extended family systems. Extended families emphasize blood ties over marital ties and are labeled consanguine. Nuclear families that emphasize marital ties are called conjugal. Consanguine families provide for continuity over

39. Kingsley Davis, "Legitimacy and the Incest Taboo," in Norman W. Bell and Ezra F. Vogel, eds., *A Modern Introduction to the Family*, Glencoe, Ill.: The Free Press, 1960, p. 401.

the generations, hold property intact, and prescribe the roles of family members in detail. Conjugal families are short lived, split up the family property, and emphasize flexibility in role performance.

About one fourth of all societies have the nuclear family only, another fourth have polygamous but not extended families, and about half have some form of extended family. The independent nuclear family is found at both the bottom and the top of the economic scale. The extended family predominates in agricultural and pastoral economies.

Because one spouse must move at marriage, rules of residence are necessary. Patrilocal residence is most common, followed by matrilocal residence. Neolocal residence is less common. Some form of bride price is associated with removal of the bride from the community of her parents and is a guarantee of her good treatment. Women seldom are purchased outright.

Authority patterns in the family may be patriarchal, matriarchal, or equalitarian. Even in alleged matriarchies, power is wielded by males of the female lineage.

All societies regulate sexual behavior. Only about 5 percent of societies prohibit all sex behavior outside of marriage however. About 70 percent of societies permit premarital intercourse, sometimes with preferred marriage partners. Intercourse between a married man and an unrelated woman generally is forbidden, but men, in most societies, are granted sexual access to one or more female relatives. The rules of endogamy and exogamy require marriage either within or outside the group.

Universal incest taboos within the nuclear family have striking effects on family structure. The constant overlapping of nuclear families requires social definitions of kinship. This is accomplished through rules of descent. The significant rules are patrilineal, matrilineal, and bilateral. Rules of inheritance may also be patrilineal or matrilineal, with primogeniture—preference given to the eldest son—often being found.

Incest taboos are always extended beyond the nuclear family but not universally to any specified relative. The key to these extensions is the family as a social group rather than a biological group. Societies enforce incest taboos primarily through internalization of the taboos during socialization and secondarily through avoidance relationships.

Among explanations proposed for universal incest taboos are the alleged ill effects of inbreeding, alleged instincts against inbreeding, the sexual disinterest that allegedly accompanies intimate familiarity, and the frustrations encountered in the Oedipal situation. All of these explanations are found wanting. An eclectic explanation finds the roots of the taboos in the suppression of sexual rivalries within the nuclear family and the necessity to preserve the family as a cooperative unit.

SUGGESTED READINGS

Becker, Gary S., *A Treatise on the Family*, Cambridge, Mass.: Harvard University Press, 1981. A mathematically formulated theoretical analysis of the family by a well-known economist. This is an important interdisciplinary contribution to our understanding of family life.

Bullough, Vern L., *Sexual Variance in Society and History*, New York: John Wiley & Sons, 1976. A set of essays demonstrating the potential importance of historical investigation into attitudes toward sexual behavior. Includes the legal and political issues in polygyny.

Duncan, Beverly, and Duncan, Otis Dudley, *Sex Typing and Social Roles: A Research Report*, New York: Academic Press, 1978. A recent research detailing changes in sex roles in the United States in recent years.

Farber, Bernard, *Conceptions of Kinship*, New York: Elsevier, 1981. Provides theoretical models detailing the pluralistic nature of kinship structure and family systems.

Lee, Gray R., *Family Structure and Interaction: A Comparative Analysis*, Philadelphia: J. B. Lippincott, 1977. Designed as a textbook, this well-written volume explores the theory, methodology, and findings of a comparative sociology of the family.

O'Kelly, Charlotte, *Women and Men in Society*, New York: D. Van Nostrand, 1980. Examines the relations of the sexes in various societal settings.

Winch, Robert F., Blumberg, Rae Lesser, Garcia, Maria-Pilar, Gordon, Margaret, and Kitson, Gay C., *Familial Organization: A Quest for Determinants*, New York: The Free Press, 1977. A collection of papers specifying and clarifying the relationship between the family system and other societal systems.

FILMS

Four Families (National Film Board of Canada, 1251 Avenue of the Americas, 16th Floor, New York, N.Y. 10020), 61 minutes. Comparison of family life in India, France, Japan, and Canada. Margaret Mead discusses how the upbringing of a child contributes to a distinctive national character.

Incest: The Victim Nobody Believes (MTI Teleprograms, 4825 N. Scott Street, Suite 23, Schiller Park, Ill. 60176), 23 minutes. Three young women discuss their experiences as victims of incest.

Married Life (Time-Life Films, 43 West 16th Street, New York, N.Y. 10011), 45 minutes. Married life in five different settings: a wife with three husbands in the Himalayas, a couple in a prosperous English community, a man with three wives in New Guinea, another with two wives in Botswana, and a young couple in Lancashire.

QUESTIONS AND PROJECTS

1. Describe two ways in which nuclear families may be combined into composite forms. What terms refer to the two types of composite families?
2. Differentiate among polygamy, polygyny, and polyandry. Why are most people monogamous even in societies that value polygyny highly?
3. What economic conditions in a society favor monogamy? Polygyny? Polyandry? How widespread is each over the world?
4. What are the levirate and the sororate? Does either custom exist in our own society? Why or why not?
5. Distinguish between dependent and independent nuclear families.
6. What is meant by a consanguine family? A conjugal family? Detail the advantages and problems of consanguine and conjugal systems.
7. What are incest taboos? Differentiate between incest taboos and endogamy and exogamy. Illustrate rules of endogamy and exogamy in the United States.
8. How does the existence of universal incest taboos necessitate the development of complex kinship systems? Evaluate the proposition that kinship systems are social systems.
9. Define and describe the major rules of descent; the rules of inheritance; the rules of residence. Which are more common over the world? What associations exist among rules of descent, inheritance, and residence?
10. What is a patriarchal family system? Are there any true matriarchies? In what persons is power usually vested in so-called matriarchal societies?
11. What explanations have been proposed for the universality of incest taboos? Evaluate the strengths and weaknesses of these explanations. What is the most adequate explanation of incest taboos?

David Strickler, Monkmeyer

Mimi Forsyth, Monkmeyer

3
Worldwide Trends in Family Patterns

There are more women working now that ever before, more women in politics, more teaching, more learning. And yet.

Most of the women hold down-scale jobs and draw salaries smaller than a man's for the same work; many live below the poverty line. The majority of American college students now are women, and yet the faculties instructing them are still mostly male. There are, all together, more women in the state legislatures, more in the House and Senate than at any other time in history. And yet. Neither these increasing numbers of women politicians nor their male colleagues could manage to get women something that once looked so elementary, something that should have been so simple: a constitutional guarantee of equal rights under the law. . . . Equality does not eradicate differences in gender, it exalts them, which should be some comfort to cowering sexists still clinging to every advantage they have ever wrangled or wrung out of women. Equality is only a threat if reality is. In the rubble of busted pedestals and shredded stereotypes are the pieces of a new perception: of the real, working, workable way of equality, of self-awareness, of mutual respect.[1]

The continuing subordination of women was a recurrent theme in Chapter 2. The quotation that opened this chapter indicates at least two things. First, there is a women's movement that is attempting to eliminate all vestiges of discrimination against women and second, male domination is resistant to change. The women's movement is not confined to the United States, it is international in scope. In this chapter, we shall examine, briefly, scholarly efforts to find universal evolutionary changes through which family systems have progressed. In light of the failure of those efforts, we shall then analyze current world trends in

1. *Time*, The Weekly Newsmagazine, July 12, 1982, pp. 20, 29; Copyright © 1982 Time Inc. Reprinted by permission from Time.

family patterns, concluding with a description of the contemporary U.S. women's movement.

EVOLUTIONARY THEORY

The publication of two books in 1861 might be taken to establish an arbitrary beginning of sociological interest in the family. One, *Das Mutterrecht*, was written by a Swiss jurist, J. J. Bachofen; the other, *Ancient Law*, was written by the anthropologist Sir Henry Sumner Maine. The two books proposed quite different theories of the development of family organization, but both attempted to trace the evolution of family structure from its beginnings in primitive promiscuity to the final form of permanent monogamy.

Most early writers did not state directly that people lived originally in a promiscuous horde but believed that such a condition could be inferred from the widespread "promiscuous" mating discovered among preliterate peoples. What appeared to be promiscuity to anthropologists, ship captains, and missionaries was not that at all, but only forms of sexual regulation different from Western ones. Nevertheless, this ethnocentric interpretation of preliterate sexual behavior prevailed, and the assumption of original human promiscuity was widespread.

From this beginning, many writers reasoned that family systems everywhere passed through a series of stages eventuating in Western-style monogamy. From an hypothesized original promiscuity Sumner believed that the next stage might have been a more or less durable informal monopoly of one or more women by a man. This stage he called *monandry*. From monandry, the next stage probably was group marriage. Group marriage developed into polyandry, and polyandry into polygyny. The stage of monogyny, one wife plus additional consorts, preceded the final development of monogamy.[2]

There were many variants of the evolutionary scheme. Bachofen assumed an original promiscuity and, along with it, an actual supremacy of women that resulted in the development of a matriarchal, matrilineal society.[3] Gradually, he says, women lost their power and the final stage of the patriarchate emerged. A contrary view was proposed by Maine, who secured his data from ancient legal codes.[4] Not surprisingly, because the societies he studied were strongly patriarchal, he concluded that the human family has been basically patriarchal.

These theories have only historical interest today. Sophisticated an-

2. William Graham Sumner and Albert G. Keller, *The Science of Society*, Vol. 3, New Haven, Conn.: Yale University Press, 1927.
3. J. J. Bachofen, *Das Mutterrecht*, Stuttgart, Germany, 1861.
4. Sir Henry Sumner Maine, *Ancient Law*, London: John Murray, 1861.

thropological study has rendered implausible the proposition that families everywhere have passed through similar stages or that there is any unilinear trend toward the monogamous family. The question of family origins is lost in prehistory, and social scientists have ceased to pursue a problem on which data can never be brought to bear.

CURRENT WORLD TRENDS

Most sociologists trace major changes in the American family to the Industrial Revolution and the consequent urbanization of society. They believe that industrialization was instrumental in transforming the authoritarian, large, stable, rural family system into a more equalitarian, relatively isolated, unstable, nuclear family. They ask whether there may not be a causal connection between industrialization and the nuclear family.

The logic of this position is simple. In an agricultural society, family members work together as an economic unit. Sons become apprenticed to fathers and eventually inherit the land. There is a clear division of labor between men and women, but the division of labor among men is minimal. A person's status in the community is clearly fixed by the family into which the person is born. Large families are advantageous. With industrialization, all of this changes. Work is removed from home to factories. The division of labor becomes complex and schools, not fathers, teach many occupational skills. The use of specialized occupational skills requires that young people move away to the cities. Occupational success produces mobility upward in the social-class structure and further isolates parents and children from grandparents. Property becomes intangible and ties to the land are lost. Thus, the argument runs, industrialization changes extended family systems into nuclear systems.

The argument is persuasive. It accords with the American experience; it is consistent with current happenings in other areas of the world. To provide some test of the argument, Goode assembled family data covering roughly the past 50 years in the West, in Arabic Islam, in sub-Saharan Africa, in India, China, and Japan.

Goode concluded that "the alteration appears to be in the direction of some type of conjugal family pattern—that is toward fewer kinship ties with distant relatives and a greater emphasis on the nuclear family unit of couple and children."[5] Note that Goode does not say that all family systems are becoming more like ours. He says that the trend is toward *some type* of conjugal system. In fact, Goode's study indicates

5. William J. Goode, *World Revolution and Family Patterns*, New York: The Free Press, 1963.

that the problem is more complicated than whether other family systems are becoming more like ours. He adds these cautions:

1. Even if the family systems in diverse areas of the world are moving *to-ward* similar patterns, they *begin* from very different points, so that the trend in one family trait may differ from one society to another—for example, the divorce or illegitimacy rate might be dropping in one society but rising in another.
2. The elements within a family system may each be altering at different rates of speed. . . .
3. Just *how* industrialization or urbanization affects the family system or how the family system facilitates or hinders these processes is not clear.
4. It is doubtful that the amount of change in family patterns is a simple function of industrialization; more likely, ideological and value changes, partially independent of industrialization, also have some effect on family action.
5. Some beliefs about how the traditional family system worked may be wrong.
6. Correlatively, it is important to distinguish *ideal* family patterns from real family behavior and values. . . .[6]

Zelditch, in an independent analysis of the relation between industrialization and family change, reaches similar conclusions. He states that any kind of nonsubsistence expanding economy or even political changes can destroy the authority structure on which the extended family depends.[7] He summarizes the conditions for change as:

1. any change by which kinship and occupational structures become differentiated.
2. where income and status come to depend upon factors not controlled by the extended family.
3. where sons begin to contribute more status and income to the family than do their fathers.
4. where the self interests of family members are not identified with continuity of the family.

These conditions, he says, produce a trend toward the conjugal family whether or not industrialization is involved. In a few generations, all that is left may be a sense of personal obligation and affection toward kin. Gradually, these sentiments are restricted to fewer and fewer kin, and more and more the relatives included are bilateral.

6. *Ibid.*, pp. 1–2.
7. Morris Zelditch, Jr., "Cross-Cultural Analyses of Family Structure," in Harold T. Christensen, *ed., Handbook of Marriage and the Family*, Chicago: Rand McNally, 1964, p. 496.

That there is no simple cause-and-effect relationship between industrialization and the nuclear family is clear. Nuclear family systems are found in primitive, nonindustrialized societies as well as in modern ones. Nor is it clear that it is simply industrialization that is producing the changes that are evident in much of the world.[8] Goode points out that we cannot assume that non-Western family systems were similar to Western family systems at some undefined historical period just before industrialization.

Goode also emphasizes the role of ideological changes—changes in values—that are helping to transform non-Western family systems. He sees all family systems as containing points of strain—features that make them vulnerable to change. Consanguine extended family systems have subjugated women and subordinated the young to their elders. Among women and the young and among intellectuals, radical ideologies have been emerging concurrent with, and even prior to, industrialization.

One such new ideology is that of economic progress, the notion that technological development and the production of wealth is more important than the preservation of traditional customs. A second ideology is that of individualism, the notion that personal welfare is more important than family continuity. A third emerging ideology is that of equalitarianism, the notion that women should have equal rights with men. Taken together, these emerging values may be as instrumental in producing family change as are the effects of industrialization.

It remains now only to summarize the general changes involved in the widespread trend toward some variant of the conjugal, nuclear family. The changes include trends toward: (1) free choice of spouse, (2) more

8. Carolyn Balkwell and Jack Balswick, "Subsistence Economy, Family Structure, and the Status of the Elderly," *Journal of Marriage and the Family* 43 (May 1981), pp. 423–29; George H. Conklin, "The Extended Family as an Independent Factor in Social Change: A Case from India," *Journal of Marriage and the Family* 36 (Nov. 1974), pp. 798–804; Glen H. Elder, Jr., "History and the Family: The Discovery of Complexity," *Journal of Marriage and the Family* 43 (Aug. 1981), pp. 489–519; Greer Litton Fox, "Love Match and Arranged Marriage in a Modernizing Nation: Mate Selection in Ankara, Turkey," *Journal of Marriage and the Family* 37 (Feb. 1975), pp. 180–93; G. David Johnson and Lewellyn Hendrix, "A Cross-Cultural Test of Collins's Theory of Sexual Stratification," *Journal of Marriage and the Family* 44 (Aug. 1982), pp. 675–84; Gary R. Lee and Lorene Hemphill Stone, "Mate Selection Systems and Criteria: Variation According to Family Structure," *Journal of Marriage and the Family* 42 (May 1980), pp. 319–26; V. V. Prakasa Rao and V. Nandini Rao, "Arranged Marriages: An Assessment of the Attitudes of the College Students in India," *Journal of Comparative Family Studies* 7 (Autumn 1976), pp. 433–53; P. K. Roy, "Industrialization and 'Fitness' of Nuclear Family: A Case Study in India," *Journal of Comparative Family Studies* 5 (Spring 1974), pp. 74–86; Rudy R. Seward, "The Colonial Family in America: Toward a Socio-Historical Restoration of its Structure," *Journal of Marriage and the Family* 35 (Feb. 1973), pp. 58–70; and Carol Vlassoff, "Unmarried Adolescent Females in Rural India: A Study of the Social Impact of Education," *Journal of Marriage and the Family* 42 (May 1980), pp. 427–36.

equal status for women, (3) equal rights of divorce, (4) neolocal residence, (5) bilateral kin, and (6) the equality of individuals against class or caste barriers.

Free Choice of Spouse

Extended family systems and the arrangement of marriages by parents have long been associated. Love as a basis for marriage is discouraged because affection between a young couple cannot be permitted to conflict with its obligations to the family group. The spouse who moves at marriage often is subordinated to members of the new family until he or she has been so completely socialized into the new family that opposition to its customs has been completely eliminated. Most often, of course, it is the woman who moves at marriage and who is at greatest disadvantage.

The conditions of urban living often include separation from both families of orientation so that the ability of the new spouse to get along with in-laws is no longer so important. Instead, the relationship between husband and wife assumes greatest importance. Probably in all times and places, certain men and women have been attracted to one another. But whereas extended family systems exclude such attraction as bases for marriage, conjugal family systems often make romantic love the primary basis for marriage. Until recently, the encouragement of romantic love and the right to choose one's own marital partner were not widespread in non-Western countries. Now they are spreading rapidly.

Toward Equal Status for Women

Patrilineal descent and patrilocal residence have been associated with patriarchy and the subordination of women. Polygyny has been widespread, with some women assigned the status of secondary wives. The custom of concubinage, in which women have approved status as additional sexual partners but not the full legal and other rights of wives, also has been widespread. Then there are the more informal, socially disapproved situations where wealthy and influential men have had mistresses who had no rights at all.

The emerging right of women to choose their husbands is doing much to change this. When men must compete for women, inevitably women gain a certain power. Coupled with this is the fact that education for women is spreading rapidly. Women take jobs in the expanding economy and often their salary approaches that of men. The cities, moreover, offer independent living opportunities for women who cannot marry men on terms that are satisfactory to them.

Goode points out that although the philosophy of equal rights for women receives more verbal acceptance in upper social-class levels, the equal rights are more effective at lower-class levels.[9] Upper-class men may believe that they should grant equal rights to women, but their own wealth and power lead them to expect deference from their wives. Lower-class men, on the other hand, have less power over their wives because of the greater economic contribution lower-class wives make to the family. Goode also warns that no family system now grants full equality to women and none is likely to do so as long as the daily work involving house and children is regarded as woman's responsibility.[10]

Equal Rights of Divorce

The modern term *divorce* is somewhat misleading when applied to many non-Western and ancient societies. What has often been found among them might be more usefully referred to as the husband's right of repudiation of the wife. The distinction is important. Divorce may be secured only on specified grounds and with some official body such as the courts determining the equity of the matter. In many non-Western and ancient societies, however, the husband or his family has been the sole judge. With no more ceremony than telling the wife before witnesses or handing her a slip of paper, a so-called bill of divorcement, the husband could end the marriage. The wife often had no recourse and no corresponding rights.

Women in many countries now are demanding protection against unjust repudiation by the husband or his family—that husbands be permitted divorce only for cause. Similarly, they demand equal rights: that the same or comparable grounds for the divorce of a wife should also be grounds for the divorce of a husband. Again, the caution should be added that divorce rights in many societies still favor the husband. There is a *trend only* toward equal divorce rights for women.

9. Goode, *op. cit.*, pp. 21-22, 372.
10. For vigorous protest against this state of affairs, see Shulasmith Firestone, *The Dialectic of Sex: The Case for Feminist Revolution*, New York: Bantam Books, 1971; Charlotte Perkins Gilman, *The Living of Charlotte Perkins Gilman: An Autobiography*, New York: D. Appleton-Century, 1935; Roberta Hamilton, *The Liberation of Women: A Study of Patriarchy and Capitalism*, London: Allen & Unwin, 1978; Annette Kuhn and Ann Marie Wolpe, *eds., Feminism and Materialism: Women and Modes of Production*, London: Routledge & Kegan Paul, 1978; Kate Millett, *Sexual Politics*, New York: Doubleday, 1970; Robin Morgan, *ed., Sisterhood Is Powerful*, New York: Random House, 1970; Sheila Rowbotham, *Hidden from History*, London: Pluto Press, 1973; and Gayle Graham Yates, *What Women Want: The Ideas of the Movement*, Cambridge, Mass.: Harvard University Press, 1975.

Neolocal Residence

Patrilocal residence has been common over the world. Even matrilocal residence, also reflecting extended family organization, has been more common than neolocal residence. As urbanization and industrialization proceed, more and more families of procreation find their residences being determined by the location of their jobs. By default, if not by design, neolocal residence is becoming more common. In some cases, nuclear families plan for decades eventually to return to their extended families. Sometimes they do; often they do not.

Bilateral Kindred

Technically, *kindred* refers to a bilateral kin group. Even where formal unilineages exist, social and geographic mobility and neolocal residence lead to weakening of ties with extended kin. Tasks formerly performed by the lineage either are assumed by the conjugal family or by public and private agencies—police, courts, welfare agencies, and so on. Gradually, ties with kin are reduced to a smaller and smaller group, typically drawn from both the husband's and the wife's lineages. Whether ties are maintained with any kin at all comes to depend on affection for those kin rather than on obligation to them.

Equality of Individuals Against Caste or Class Barriers

The trends toward free mate choice, equality for women, and equal divorce rights are part of a larger ideological change. A pervasive philosophy of individualism appears to be spreading over much of the world—a philosophy that militantly asserts the importance of the person over the continuity of the group. This is a radical philosophy. The worth of the individual comes to be more important than inherited wealth or ethnic group. The individual's status comes to be evaluated not so much by the lineage into which he or she was born as by their own accomplishments. The status of the family, then, must be determined for each generation anew.

   In closing this section, a few cautions are in order. First, the trends described are just that—trends. It would be a mistake to conclude that extended family systems the world over have broken down. Most societies in the world today have unilineal descent, extended families, and male domination. The trends toward conjugal family systems, widespread as they are, generally are confined to urbanized, industrialized regions. The great masses of population in the hinterlands of countries like China and India, to say nothing of preliterate societies, are relatively unaffected. Moreover, these changes, where they appear, often are viewed as social problems, as symptoms of the breakdown of time-honored ways. Men and women, young and old are pitted against one another. One should not construct a stereotype of societies emerging from the darkness of autocratic extended families into the light of conjugal systems held together by ties of affection.

Finally, we should remember how little we know of the cause-and-effect relations underlying these trends. That urbanization and industrialization are involved is obvious; that urbanization and industrialization alone cannot account for the trends is equally obvious. Ideological factors—individualism, democracy, economic progress—are involved and appear to be both cause and effect. To some degree, the ideals, the technology, and the family system are being exported to the rest of the world from the West. But other societies cannot be seen properly as following the West. Other societies, exposed to technological and ideological change, will incorporate the effects of those changes in ways unique to themselves. Each society has a history and a present structure into which change must be incorporated. Other societies, even if they are profoundly altered by it, will adapt the conjugal family system to their own needs.

THE WOMEN'S MOVEMENT

Although trends such as free choice of spouse, equal rights for women, and equal rights of divorce are revolutionary in much of the world, they appear strangely archaic in contemporary American society. The United States has an organized women's movement that began more than a century ago. It has drastically altered relationships between men and women and has assumed new vitality over the past 20 years. The final section of this chapter will summarize the history of the women's movement in the United States, assess its present status, and lay the groundwork for analysis of issues pertaining to the status of women in subsequent chapters.

History of the Movement

Although many people believe that the women's movement had its origins in the turbulent decade of the 1960s, efforts toward changing women's subordinate status actually began in the early 1800s. Enormous changes were taking place in the United States, many of which led to the realization by some people that there existed many inequalities between the sexes. The rise in industrialization found many women employed as factory workers, earning the money to buy what they had once produced in the home. For the first time, women experienced the income inequality of the labor market. Colleges were beginning to open their doors to women, beginning with Oberlin College in 1833. Although women's education was geared toward producing good wives and mothers, women in higher education had the opportunity to hear lectures given by liberal speakers of the time and to interact as intellectual equals.

It was the Abolitionist Movement of the 1830s, however, that provided the strongest impetus to the movement for women's rights in the nineteenth century.[11] Women learned the politics of articulate debate while denouncing slavery as an inhumane institution. They also found that they were barred from abolitionist meetings and, in many places, from actually speaking in public because of their sex. They soon realized that there were many similarities between the position of slaves and the position of women in society. Women began speaking out on women's rights but continued to concentrate on abolishing slavery.

Eight years after Elizabeth Cady Stanton and Lucretia Coffin Mott were barred from participation in the London World Anti-Slavery Convention of 1840, they held the first Women's Rights Convention at Seneca Falls, New York. Although only a small response to the newspaper advertisement announcing the meeting was expected, over 300 people, men and women, met that day to discuss the "social, civil, and religious condition" of women.[12] The two days of speeches and discussions produced the Declaration of Sentiments, based on the American Declaration of Independence, which asserted that "all men and women are created equal." The document also contained resolutions, among which were the right of women to vote, equal educational and occupational opportunities, and the elimination of legal discrimination against women. The issue of the vote for women was considered the most radical of the resolutions and much heated debate ensued before this resolution was accepted by the convention members.

Efforts toward the recognition of women's social, political, and economic equality were frustrated by legislative inattention, and when the Civil War began in 1861, women's rights advocates were urged to abandon their cause and take up the war effort. Following the war, the reins were once again taken up, but this time virtually all feminist activity concentrated on a single issue, that of gaining suffrage for women.

Although nearly all the activists agreed on the necessity of securing

11. Judith Hole and Ellen Levine, *Rebirth of Feminism*, New York: Times Books (Quadrangle Books), 1971, pp. 1–14.
12. Judith Papachristou, *Women Together: A History in Documents of the Women's Movement in the United States*, New York: Alfred A. Knopf, 1976, pp. 23–26.

the vote for women, ideological and tactical differences split the women's movement into two major factions in 1869.[13] The National Woman Suffrage Association, headed by Susan B. Anthony and Elizabeth Cady Stanton, limited its activities strictly to gaining the vote and steered clear of more controversial issues to appear "respectable" to the populace. The American Woman Suffrage Association, led by Lucy Stone, pursued suffrage as a means through which to gain a broad spectrum of women's rights. Gradually though, suffrage became a single-issue campaign, and, in 1890, the National and American associations merged into the National American Woman Suffrage Association. The NAWSA and a variety of organizations—the Women's Trade Union League, the General Federation of Women's Clubs, and the Women's Christian Temperance Union—joined forces to press for women's suffrage.[14] In 1920, 70 years after it first became an issue, the Nineteenth Amendment to the Constitution became effective, and women finally gained the vote.

Popular writing often claims that the women's movement went into eclipse following 1920, but that is oversimplification. The movement became fragmented, and, once again, two factions formed. The radical faction, represented by the National Women's Party founded in 1916, espoused a philosophy of "identical rights" and proposed, in 1923, an equal rights amendment to the U.S. Constitution. The proposed amendment read, "Men and women shall have equal rights throughout the United States, and every place subject to its jurisdiction. Congress shall have power to enforce this article by appropriate legislation." The amendment received little support, and in part because of its identification with the amendment, the National Women's Party also failed to gain widespread support.

In 1920, the NAWSA changed its name to the League of Women Voters and was representative of the more conservative faction of the women's movement until the early 1960s. This conservative wing of the movement promoted a concept of "equivalent rights" for women, which held that women are equal to, but different from, men. That difference, it was held, should be recognized through protective legislation for women establishing minimum wage levels, providing meal and rest periods, limiting the number of hours worked, limiting the loads to be lifted, and so on. The Women's Bureau in the U.S. Department of Labor was created in 1920 and, for the next 40 years, promoted such policies.

13. Olive Banks, *Faces of Feminism: A Study of Feminism as a Social Movement*, New York: St. Martin's Press, 1981, p. 56.
14. Jo Freeman, "The Origin of the Women's Liberation Movement," *American Journal of Sociology* 78 (Jan. 1973), pp. 792–811.

The Revolution of the 1960s

Reaction against the conservatism of the women's rights movement following World War I was symbolized by the publication of Betty Friedan's *The Feminine Mystique* in 1963.[15] Friedan argued that women have been trapped into believing that housewifery and childrearing bring deep and lasting satisfaction when actually they consist of the most menial and humdrum tasks. Women, she said, should use their talents in creative endeavor in the occupational world just as men do.

In the early 1960s, many women who shared Friedan's views allied themselves with the civil rights movement and with the emerging radical left, thinking that those who sought equality for blacks and other minorities would also support equality for women. They were disillusioned on finding that sexism pervaded these movements. One woman activist stated that, "Civil rights has always been a very male-dominated movement. Most radical organizations saw to it that the 'chicks' operated the mimeograph machines and scampered out for coffee while the men ran the show."[16] The most devastating put down of women has been attributed to Stokely Carmichael of SNCC (Student Nonviolent Coordinating Committee) who is reputed to have stated that "the only position for women in the movement is prone."

In the long run, the support of the federal government for the movement may prove more significant than the efforts of any private groups. In 1964, while Congress was debating the banning of racial discrimination in employment as part of the Civil Rights Act of 1964, an amendment was also introduced forbidding discrimination by sex. Although it was apparently intended as a joke and as a delaying tactic, the act as finally passed did forbid such discrimination. For several years, federal administrators did not take the sex discrimination ban seriously, but by the early 1970s, firms receiving federal contracts and universities receiving federal funds came under heavy pressure to develop affirmative action programs to employ women in appropriate numbers in responsible and high-paid positions. Additional pressure was applied through the Equal Employment Opportunity Act of 1972. The need for such remedial action had been documented in 1965 in the report of the President's Commission on the Status of Women. The report showed that working women earned roughly half as much as men and that the ratio of women in professional and executive positions had been dropping.

The year 1966 saw the formation of NOW (National Organization for Women), with Betty Friedan as its first president. The goals of NOW include, ". . . a sex-role revolution for men and women which

15. New York: Dell.
16. *Time,* August 31, 1970, p. 17.

will restructure all our institutions: childrearing, education, marriage, the family, medicine, work, politics, the economy, religion, psychological theory, human sexuality, morality and the very evolution of the race."[17] Friedan insists that the name National Organization *for* Women rather than National Organization *of* Women reflects her realization that men should be included as equal members. She states, further, that she never visualized women as an oppressed class fighting to wrest power away from men.

Nevertheless, meetings of local chapters of NOW often were consciousness-raising quasi-therapy sessions in which participants were encouraged to ventilate their feelings about the frustrations that women face in a male-dominated society and, specifically, their mistreatment at the hands of men. That NOW was not wholly receptive to such man-hating is suggested by the early appearance of radical splinter groups such as WITCH (Women's International Terrorist Conspiracy from Hell) and SCUM (Society for Cutting Up Men). By 1970, lesbianism had become a major issue, and Friedan believes that a small group of radical lesbians set out to take control of NOW. Soon after, though, lesbianism was acknowledged by NOW as a legitimate concern of feminism.[18]

There have been a number of potentially very strong leaders in this second wave of the feminist movement, each sincere in her own conception of how the movement might become more influential. In addition to Friedan, Ti-Grace Atkinson, Gloria Steinem, Robin Morgan, and Kate Millett have been some of the more prominent ones. The movement has not been without its problems however. Media exploitation of feminist demonstrators as frivolous bra burners undoubtedly discouraged many potential advocates from seriously examining the issues involved in feminism. Many potential supporters of women's rights were also turned off by the radical faction of the movement that advocated the rhetoric of sex-class warfare based on the hatred of men. In 1968, when NOW first advocated repeal of all abortion laws, a substantial proportion of its members resigned. As the movement evolved into the 1970s, though, many of the differences dividing various women's groups disappeared or at least blurred. The slogan "Sisterhood Is Powerful" soon became an umbrella under which women worked together on various projects, including celebrating the anniversary of women's suffrage, abortion repeal, and peace moratoriums.

NOW has had a curious history. During its first 10 years or so, it

17. Betty Friedan, "Up from the Kitchen Floor," *New York Times Magazine*, March 4, 1973, p. 30.
18. Barbara Sinclair Deckard, *The Women's Movement* (2nd ed.), New York: Harper & Row, 1979, pp. 374–78.

had a very limited membership base. Estimates indicate that in 1970 it had only 3000 to 5000 members. By 1973, membership was somewhere between 8000 and 15,000.[19] Most of the members were white, middle-class women. Efforts to recruit sizable numbers of minority women have been largely unsuccessful. Some minority women believed that NOW had been unsympathetic to issues concerning them. Others believed that the issues of race and ethnicity must take precedence over the rights of women. Still others believed that the solidarity of their own groups could do more to further their concerns than could NOW. In this regard, a number of organizations composed of minority group members arose during the 1970s, among them were the National Conference of Puerto Rican Women, Black Women Organized for Action, The National Black Feminist Organization, and the Chicana Caucus.[20]

By the mid-1970s, many women who were attracted to the movement were unimpressed with NOW's accomplishments and rejected the leaderships of the movement's pioneers. The movement factionalized into what were called the older and the younger branches.[21] The women of the younger branch emphasized local action programs rather than formal or national organization. They set up and operated women's health centers, information centers, spouse abuse and rape centers, and so on. They maintained a loose network of communication among themselves, but they did not become directly involved in political action. Although these younger women argued that the absence of large-scale organization was a source of strength, many outsiders viewed it as reflecting a serious malaise in the movement.

In 1970, another development gave added strength to the women's movement: a woman's political caucus was founded. The caucus's influence was evident at the 1972 national political conventions where there were large increases in the women delegates. There was also a 20 percent increase in the women elected to public office that year. In 1973, the first National Women's Political Caucus met with 1200 participants representing 30,000 members in all 50 states. The Caucus, learning from NOW's struggles, downplayed the issue of lesbianism and rededicated itself to broad social objectives, not to narrowly feminist ones. The Caucus approved of two basic goals: the election and appointment of more women to public office and improvement of the situation of minorities and the poor through legislation.

The late 1970s and early 1980s were years of spectacular membership growth in NOW. A letter circulated by NOW's national office in

---

19. *Time, loc. cit.;* Jo Freeman, *op. cit.,* p. 799; and Friedan, *op. cit.,* p. 34.
20. Papachristou, *op. cit.,* pp. 240–44.
21. Jo Freeman, *The Politics of Women's Liberation,* New York: David McKay, 1975, pp. 50, 59–63.

September 1977 referred to NOW's 60,000 active members, and a news report in 1979 indicated that the membership had reached 100,000.[22] Three years later, in 1982, the membership roll had risen dramatically to 250,000 and President Judy Goldsmith vowed to bring that number to 1 million during her three-year term.[23] Despite the enormous increases in the numbers of people involved in the women's movement and in political action groups, there is the growing belief that women's rights are being abandoned in favor of a new conservative effort, particularly among younger women to whom feminist struggles are seen as past history.[24] Whether conservative efforts toward turning around feminist issues will be successful or whether young women will have "their consciousness raised" and become politicized when they enter the labor market remains to be seen.

The Equal Rights Amendment (ERA)

Congress, in 1972, showed special interest in an equal rights amendment to the Constitution, almost 50 years after one was first proposed. On May 22, 1972, five months after the House had acted, the Senate authorized an amendment that had three basic provisions: (1) equality of rights under the law could not be denied or abridged by the United States or by any state on account of sex; (2) Congress would have the power to enforce, by appropriate legislation, the provisions of the article; and (3) the amendment would take effect two years after ratification.

Before the amendment could take effect, it had to receive the approval of three fourths (38) of the legislatures of the 50 states. The original requirement was that those approvals had to be secured within seven years, or by May 22, 1979. As that date approached, however, and only 35 states had ratified the amendment, Congress was persuaded to extend the time for ratification until June 30, 1982.

Twenty-two states ratified it in 1972; 13 more by January 1977. Not a single state ratified it after that time. Moreover, seven of the states that ratified—Idaho, Indiana, Kentucky, Montana, Nebraska, South Dakota, and Tennessee—later voted to rescind their ratification. The proponents of ERA argued that the states could not rescind ratification, whereas the opponents argued that the amendment had had much more time for

22. Time, The Weekly Newsmagazine, August 6, 1979, p. 47.
23. Associated Press, November 29, 1982.
24. See David M. Heer and Amyra Grossbard-Schechtman, "The Impact of the Female Marriage Squeeze and the Contraceptive Revolution on Sex Roles and the Women's Liberation Movement in the United States, 1960 to 1978," Journal of Marriage and the Family 43 (Feb. 1981), pp. 49–65; and Time, July 12, 1982, pp. 20–29.

approval than any other amendment and that ratification had to reflect the "contemporaneous consensus" of the states.

One of the reasons why the fate of ERA was so uncertain was because even well-informed people did not know for sure what all of the implications of enactment would be. Proponents argued that the effects on the family would be minimal, whereas some opponents argued that the family would be destroyed. The most informed analyses available were published in the *Yale Law Journal* and the *Harvard Civil Rights-Civil Liberties Law Review*.[25]

Family Relationships. As opponents of the amendment fear, husbands no longer will automatically be liable for their wives' financial support; the obligation to support will fall on whichever spouse is able to provide. Each spouse will become equally vulnerable to requests for alimony in the event of divorce. Women will not be required to take their husband's names at marriage, nor will they be required to accept the husband's domicile. Failure to move with a spouse who takes a new job could be grounds for divorce for husbands as well as wives.

Special laws protecting females from seduction, statutory rape, and obscene language would become unconstitutional. Forcible rape by men undoubtedly will remain a crime because it is based on the unique physical characteristics of men, but women will become vulnerable to charges of assault should they engage in sexual intercourse with underage boys.

Employment. All forms of discrimination in favor of, or against, women will be eliminated. Only jobs where sex clearly is a requirement for successful performance such as wet nurses, sperm donors, and locker-room attendants will be the prerogative of one sex. Women will be eligible to engage in hazardous occupations such as mining, police work, and fire protection. Limitations on the weight that can be lifted and on the number of hours that can be worked will be eliminated or made uniform for the two sexes. Equal pay will be required for equal work.

Military Service. There is little question that women will be eligible for miliatry service on the same basis as men, and that they will be eligible for the draft should conscription be resumed. Height-weight correlations, and IQ scores required for induction will have to be made uniform for the sexes. Women with dependent children will be eligible for enlistment, just as men are. If men are granted deferment because of dependent children, women will have the same right. If the sole surviving son in a family where one child has already died in the service is

25. *New York Times*, June 25, 1973.

eligible for deferment, then the sole surviving daughter will receive deferment as well. The Women's Army Corps and similar female units will have to be abolished. Women will be eligible for combat duties unless it can be shown that they have specific physical disqualifications for them.

In June 1982, the Equal Rights Amendment to the Constitution failed, three states shy of the 38 needed for ratification. Although opponents of the ERA consider this a major victory, efforts are being directed, at the time of this writing, toward reintroducing the amendment as the first bill of the 98th Congress.[26] At present, the measure has 221 cosponsors in the House, the majority of them Democrats. Whatever the outcome of this renewed effort, the struggle for women's rights has been long; and it is not over yet. Women have learned the power of political action: more are voting and seeking public office than ever before.[27] And more are winning.

SUMMARY

Although there has been no universal evolution of family systems, there is, today, an almost worldwide trend toward some variant of the conjugal family. Urbanization and industrialization are involved in this trend, but it is too simple to say that they are the cause. For one thing, conjugal families are found in preindustrial societies. Moreover, ideological changes, including individualism and equalitarianism, play partly independent causal roles.

There are six general components of the change toward some form of conjugal family. They are trends toward: free choice of spouse for both sexes, equal status for women, equal rights of divorce, neolocal residence, bilateral kin, and the equality of individuals against caste or class barriers.

The women's rights movement in the United States is over a century old. After universal suffrage was achieved in 1920, the movement split into conservative and radical factions, with the conservative faction being dominant until the 1960s. A revolutionary phase was entered in the 1960s as women's groups and government efforts combined to give women more political and economic power. An equal rights amendment to the Constitution was approved by Congress in 1972, but it failed to be ratified by the 1982 deadline. Either through constitutional amendment or through legislation, further changes in the status of women and in the nature of family relationships may be expected.

26. Associated Press, January 4, 1983.
27. *Newsweek*, November 1, 1982, pp. 26–30.

SUGGESTED READINGS

Bardwick, Judith M., *In Transition: How Feminism, Sexual Liberation, and the Search for Self-Fulfillment Have Altered America*, New York: Holt, Rinehart & Winston, 1979. A psychologist's analysis and evaluation of the social changes of the last decade. Focuses on changed sex roles and the persistence of sexism.

Chafe, William H., *Women and Equality: Changing Patterns in American Culture*, New York: Oxford University Press, 1977. A historian's analysis of women's struggle for equality in the United States. The author is for equality, but concludes that barriers to full equality still exist.

Freeman, Jo, ed., *Women: A Feminist Perspective* (2nd ed.), Palo Alto, Calif.: Mayfield, 1979. A comprehensive collection of readings that cover virtually all aspects of the contemporary and historical women's movements in America.

Hill, Mary A., *Charlotte Perkins Gilman: The Making of a Radical Feminist, 1860–1896*, Philadelphia: Temple University Press, 1980. Fascinating biography of the woman who was to become the leading intellectual force behind the women's suffrage movement.

Lovenduski, Joni, and Hills, Jill, eds., *The Politics of the Second Electorate: Women and Public Participation*, Boston: Routledge & Kegan Paul of America, 1981. A cross-cultural analysis of women's political participation and contributions.

Rosenberg, Rosalind, *Beyond Separate Spheres: Intellectual Roots of Modern Feminism*, New Haven, Conn.: Yale University Press, 1982. A historical account of the women who were influential in the women's movement of the early 1900s.

FILMS

Growing Up Female (New Day Films, P.O. Box 315, Franklin Lakes, N.J. 07417), 60 minutes. A documentary about the experience of becoming a woman in America, through encounters with six females. Good for introducing the issues involved in women's liberation.

How to Make a Woman (Polymorph Films, 331 Newbury Street, Boston, Mass. 02115), 58 minutes. Illuminates the relationship between men and women. Presents the sexual and personal conflicts motivating women today.

QUESTIONS AND PROJECTS

1. What was the general argument of evolutionary theories of the family? What flaws were evident in such reasoning? What is the status of evolutionary theories today?
2. Toward what general form are family systems over the world changing?

Evaluate critically the proposition that family systems in other parts of the world are coming to be modeled after the American system.

3. What factors, technological and ideological, appear to play causal roles in the trend toward conjugal family systems? Try to specify the role of each type of factor.

4. List five components of the general trend toward conjugal families. Why are these changes described as "trends toward" rather than as accomplished facts?

5. Describe the women's movement in the United States from the mid-nineteenth century to the early twentieth century. What were its major accomplishments? Its major frustrations?

6. Describe the current women's movement in the United States. What have been its major accomplishments? Its major frustrations?

7. What is NOW? Analyze its role in the women's movement.

8. What was the ERA? What changes would have attended its ratification? Of what significance is it to the women's movement? Why did it fail to be ratified?

9. Arrange a classroom panel discussion on the ERA, focusing on the panelists' views of the desirability of enactment and what they perceive the consequences of such an amendment to the Constitution to be. Include among the panelists a black woman, a black man, a white woman, and a white man. Do they seem to speak for their racial and sex groups?

Hiroji Kubota, Magnum Photos Inc.

4
The Family System of China

Yu Luojin, a Peking writer, was mortified by her second husband Cai Zhongpei. In fact, she was sure she had married a bumpkin. He never seemed to talk about aesthetics and the finer things of life, only stupid topics like the price of yellowfish. He flailed and hooted like a child while watching soccer games, and when she hauled him to the theater for some cultural uplift, he laughed when he should have cried. One day Yu tried to coax him into reading a book. He snapped: "I've been selected a model worker every year without reading books and newspapers!" That did it. She rushed to the nearest court and filed for divorce. After much publicity and a judge's stern lecture on socialist morality, Yu won her case, in effect on grounds of incompatibility. Said Yu, piously: "To continue a marriage without love is utterly immoral."[1]

The quotation refers to China in 1982, and it describes an emerging family system radically different from the traditional one to be described in the first part of this chapter. The traditional family was a strong, stable one, which persisted for 2000 years. The traditional family still exists, but increasingly, it is being replaced by the family patterns described in the latter part of this chapter.

ADVANTAGES IN THE STUDY OF THE CHINESE FAMILY

A Major Family Tradition Different from Our Own

Most of this book will be devoted to the analysis of Western family organization and to the family in the United States. Chapters 2 and 3 al-

1. Hunter R. Clark, "Untying the Knot in China," *Time*, February 15, 1982, p. 52.

ready have provided some world perspective but, necessarily, that cross-cultural analysis could not provide a comprehensive, integrated portrayal of any one family system very different from our own. Family practices take on meaning only in the total context in which they appear. Lest strange family customs remain merely as curiosities, we need to present some of them in a context in which they will be wholly intelligible and at the same time to present another major type of family system with which our own can be systematically compared.

The traditional Chinese family is very different from our own. Just as ours may represent Western family systems, the Chinese can represent Eastern systems. Instead of a preliterate society of a few hundred people with tenuous ties to any major civilization, we have selected a society of over 1 billion people, the largest population of any nation in the world, whose practices are somewhat applicable to additional hundreds of millions of people. The cultural stream from which Chinese family practices derive has as long and distinguished a history as our own.

A Model of Stability and Change

The Western family, and the American family in particular, has been characterized by rapid change. In contrast, the Chinese family remained relatively unchanged for approximately 2000 years. No society is ever completely static, of course, and some of the apparent lack of change in Chinese society is a function of the inability of Western scholars to see the change that has occurred. Nevertheless, by Western standards, Chinese social change has been slow.

Even as it serves as a model of stability, however, the Chinese family also presents a model of change. About 150 years ago, urbanization and industrialization began to make their influence felt, and China embarked on rapid change that is still in process. The family system, which had seemed impervious to change, underwent drastic alteration.

Unusually Comprehensive Data Available

There is more reliable literature on the Chinese family than on any other non-Western family system. Both Oriental and Western scholars have been studying China's history and social patterns for decades and, in some cases, centuries. This concerted attention has resulted not only in a massive literature but also in a literature of unusual trustworthiness. The descriptions that follow are not based on the work of one or two people with two or three years of fieldwork experience; they represent the combined efforts of a veritable army of scholars.

Significance in the Modern World

Along with the Soviet Union and the United States, China is one of the world's great powers. It has the largest population of any nation, a huge land area, and virtually untapped natural resources. For three decades, China has presented a formidable ideological, military, and economic challenge to the rest of the world. Whatever the future, it will be profoundly affected by what happens in China.

THE TRADITIONAL CHINESE FAMILY

The phrase *traditional Chinese family* requires qualification. In the broadest sense, it refers to family patterns up to about 75 to 100 years ago. The extensive social change that produced the *transitional family* first became evident about then. More narrowly, the traditional family was most characteristic of the Ch'ing dynasty, which lasted from A.D. 1644 to 1911.[2] Earlier variations of the traditional family did not differ greatly from that of the Ch'ing dynasty. Moreover, it was the Ch'ing dynasty that gave way to the modern Republic of China on January 1, 1912.[3]

During most of its traditional period, China was a land of over 3.5 million square miles (larger than the United States), where dozens of dialects were spoken, and one in which there was great variation from one section to another and from rural to urban areas. Far from there being one family pattern in such a vast land, there were innumerable variations. Some of these variations we shall touch on. For the most part, however, we shall concentrate on the dominant patterns reflected in Confucian teachings, in literature, and in the law.

The Gentry and the Peasantry

A basic distinction for understanding of the traditional family separates the so-called gentry from the vast majority of Chinese peasants. The gentry were defined by several criteria. First, they received income from land they did not cultivate. Abstinence from manual labor was a source of pride and essential for acceptance into the class. By and large, the gentry were intellectuals for whom mastery of knowledge was the

2. The discussion of the traditional Chinese family will depend heavily on that of Marion J. Levy, Jr., *The Family Revolution in Modern China*, Cambridge, Mass.: Harvard University Press, 1949, pp. 41–269.
3. The Republic of China today is represented by the government of Taiwan; the People's Republic of China is represented by the government of mainland China.

route to social advancement. China developed a massive examination
system very early—somewhat analogous to our civil service system—
which theoretically was open to all Chinese and through which positions in government were awarded. Actually, the system was controlled
by the gentry whose opportunities for leisure gave them great advantage
in acquiring the knowledge necessary for success. In addition to their
income as landlords, the gentry received income from governmental
and academic positions they held. As China began to modernize, the
gentry also became involved in industry, commerce, and banking. The
gentry probably accounted for less than one fifth of the population.

China was basically agricultural, and the term *peasantry* accurately
described most of the population. The peasantry, who worked the land,
were very poor by modern standards; physical survival was their primary goal. There was little room in their existence for the elaboration
of social customs, and their family patterns were similar to those of
poverty-ridden people everywhere. Men and women worked together
in the fields and children were pressed into work. There was, however,
widespread aspiration for the attainment of gentry status and just enough
upward mobility to keep the dream alive. Consequently, even among
the peasantry, the family ideals were frequently those of the gentry.[4]

The influence of the gentry cannot be overemphasized. Their ways
were highly regarded and set standards for the entire country. This preoccupation with gentry patterns was so great that little is actually
known about the variety of peasantry patterns. The gentry patterns
were the ideal patterns,[5] and it is with these ideal patterns that we shall
mainly deal.

The Gentry Family

The traditional gentry family was patriarchal, patrilineal, patrilocal, and
monogamous. It included the patriarch and his wife, their sons and the
sons' wives, unmarried daughters, grandsons and their wives, unmarried
granddaughters, great-grandsons and their wives, unmarried great-
granddaughters, and so on. The ideal was to have six generations living
under one roof and to go nine generations without a division of prop-

4. In addition to the gentry and peasantry, there were small merchants, artisans, soldiers,
servants, and the like. These groups were relatively unimportant and generally followed
the social patterns of the peasantry. If their economic status was high enough, they
tended to follow the gentry patterns.
5. Care should be taken not to confuse ideal culture patterns with ideal types. Ideal culture patterns are the models of exemplary conduct toward which a society strives. Real
cultural patterns, in contrast, refer to the actual behavior patterns prevailing in the society. See Ralph Linton, *The Cultural Background of Personality*, New York: D. Appleton-Century, 1945, pp. 52–54.

erty. The gentry family ideally was a very large family all living together and maintaining themselves intact for as many generations as possible.

Family Size. The real gentry patterns, however, deviated from this ideal. In practice, China appears not to have been a nation of exceptionally large families. Comprehensive data are difficult to come by, but several studies have shown an average household size of around 5 persons. Ping-ti Ho reports that a respectable census in A.D. 2 yielded an average household of 4.87 persons and that Chinese family size has not changed appreciably over the past 2000 years.[6] He states further, "the size of the Chinese peasant family was determined primarily by its basic economic needs and by the fiscal burden it bore."[7]

Census figures, of course, would yield averages much closer to the typical size of the peasant family than to that of the gentry family. Yet there is reason to think that the typical gentry family probably fell far short of the large, six-generation ideal.

If nothing else, longevity patterns would prevent six generations of the same family living together. Even in modern America where longevity is greater, we do not often find living families extending from great-grandparents through great-grandchildren. Three or four generations must have been the usual maximum in traditional China.

Even this three- or four-generation group probably was not the most common gentry family. Although the gentry were relatively wealthy, it appears that such large family units were not economically feasible for most of them. It appears that when a man achieved additional wealth, he was likely to use that wealth to increase the size of his household in accord with the concept of the ideal family. But it also appears that economic necessity forced most of the gentry to live in smaller units.[8]

The typical Chinese family probably was the stem family.[9] Under this arrangement, one of the sons brings his bride to live with his parental family, whereas other sons go out of the family to earn their living. Even though large families could not generally be maintained, there were sev-

6. Ping-ti Ho, "An Historian's View of the Chinese Family System," in Seymour Farber, Piero Mustacchi, and Roger H. L. Wilson, eds., *Man and Civilization: The Family's Search for Survival*, New York: McGraw-Hill, 1965, p. 18.

7. *Ibid.* For arguments that actual variations in family size from one society to another are less than differences of family ideals would indicate, see Ansley J. Coale, Lloyd A. Fallers, Marion J. Levy, Jr., David M. Schneider, and Sylvan S. Tomkins, *Aspects of the Analysis of Family Structure*, Princeton, N.J.: Princeton University Press, 1965.

8. Irene Taeuber, "The Families of Chinese Farmers," in Maurice Freedman, *ed.*, *Family and Kinship in Chinese Society*, Stanford, Calif.: Stanford University Press, 1970, pp. 81-85.

9. Pierre Guillaume Frédéric Le Play used the term *famille souche*. See his *Les Ouvriers européens*, Tours, France: 1879, Vol. 1, p. 457.

eral factors operating to prevent the Chinese family from breaking down into a simple conjugal unit. One factor was ancestor worship which virtually all Chinese practiced. The worship of ancestors was both a major responsibility and a major goal in life. If one worshipped one's ancestors dutifully and raised sons properly, one would eventually be worshipped as an ancestor himself. One son remained with the parental family to maintain the family burial ground and continue the ancestor worship.

Supporting factors were the doctrine of filial piety, which emphasized the subordination of the child to the parents, and the practice of holding family property in common. These forces were strong enough to perpetuate the large family ideal in circumstances where economic factors did not favor it. Many married sons were forced to live in conjugal units for much of their lives. Apparently many sons lived as meagerly as possible, sending much of their earnings back to the family home and paving the way for the day when they would be able to return and take their places in the family as distinguished elders.

Division of Property. Ideally, the family was to go nine generations without a division of property. The inheritance rules provided that all sons should inherit equally, although the eldest son often received a larger share. This informal inequality reflected a ceremonial primogeniture, in which the eldest son assumed major responsibility for the ancestor worship. The eldest brother also was destined, if a division of property did not occur, to succeed his father as patriarch. The greater prestige of the eldest brother and the expenses he incurred in maintaining the ancestors' graves often were enough to militate against strictly equal inheritance. In peasant families, younger sons often turned their inheritances over to the eldest son, and then he assumed full responsibility for the ancestor worship.

Although the family remained intact, property was held in common under the patriarch. Given the norms of filial piety, sons were unlikely to ask for a division during the father's lifetime. The same allegiance was not owed to the elder brother however, and there were forces operating to encourage younger brothers to ask for a division at the father's death or retirement. Particularly if the family wealth was not increasing, expansion of the family would reduce each brother's potential wealth accordingly. Thus, the brothers were encouraged to request their inheritances while there still was something to inherit.

When a division of property occurred, each brother separated his straight-line descendants and established a new branch of the family with himself as patriarch. Such a move permitted younger brothers to attain the status of family head, which otherwise would be denied them. But the division of property also was regarded as undesirable, and it appears that this kind of motivation was not prominent. Few families were wealthy enough and sufficiently well integrated to avoid a division of property for nine generations. In fact, division often occurred at the death of the patriarch. The strength of the family ideals is illustrated by their continuance, despite widespread deviation from them.

The Tsu. The traditional family was more important in the institutional structure of China than almost any family system is in any contemporary nation. This was before the development of modern nation-states in Europe, and there was no strong central government in China. The family performed most of the enforcement, judicial, and welfare functions that we associate with government.

Beyond the family, the chief group in traditional China was the clan, or *tsu*. The *tsu* included all persons with a common surname tracing descent from a common ancestor. With the care given to tracing ancestry, the *tsu* might number thousands of persons, and gentry, peasants, servants, and soldiers might be members of a single *tsu*. The importance of the *tsu* varied from one section of the country to another, but in some areas, there were whole villages where everyone belonged to the same *tsu*.

The *tsu* operated through a council of elders and intervened in matters that could not be handled by individual families. Its will was implemented through the patriarch and, in rare instances, against the patriarch himself. A major function of the *tsu* was to aid in the maintenance of the ancestral graves. Its resources were, thus, used to ensure the continuation of the group when that continuance might be in jeopardy.

The *tsu* also exercised broad welfare functions, paid for by the income from property held for this purpose. It paid for the education of an occasional bright son from a poorer branch of the *tsu* and, thus, supported some upward mobility. It loaned money to *tsu* members. It also helped families to organize and to pay for lavish weddings and funerals.

Certain enforcement and judicial functions were handled by the *tsu*. It arbitrated disputes between branches of the *tsu* and enforced its rulings. It served as a tax collection agency for the government. It mediated between family members and government authority, protecting *tsu* members from outside aggression and serving as a parole body for *tsu* members who had committed offenses.

The *tsu* was one of a few sources of power in China outside the individual family. It played a role in helping to maintain the integrity of the family. The *tsu* also came under attack as a competing source of power when the present Communist government came into being.

Age and Sex Roles

The traditional Chinese family is an excellent example of a consanguine system. Consistent with the large family ideal, prescribed roles for members were laid down in detail. Position in the family was all-important; little opportunity was provided for personal idiosyncrasies. What mattered was whether one was an eldest son in a well-to-do family or the newest daughter-in-law—not personality characteristic such as whether one was intelligent, nurturant, or what have you. Little ad-libbing on the prescribed roles was permitted. Everyone knew how the eldest son or the newest daughter-in-law was supposed to think, feel, and act in most situations, and most people conformed to expectations.

Traditional China was highly structured by age and sex. The roles for family members can be described according to the age groups to which they belonged. Moreover, not only was absolute age important—not only were 40-year-olds treated differently from 20-year-olds—but relative age was also important. By relative age we mean the age of one person in relation to that of another person. The Chinese emphasized not only whether people were 20 years or 40 years old but also whether they were younger or older than the people with whom they interacted. Prescribed behavior was also defined by sex. There was marked segregation of sex roles, with quite different behavior expected of males and females.

Infancy. The Chinese were kind and affectionate toward small children. Children were highly valued, particularly sons. Sons were the means to continuation of the family and provided for continued worship of the ancestors. A marriage that did not produce sons was unfortunate indeed.

Girls, too, were valued and welcomed into the family when their birth did not present grave financial problems and when daughters were not born to the exclusion of sons. In poor peasant families, the situation was different. Female infanticide occasionally was resorted to by poverty-stricken parents, and girl babies occasionally were sold. If resources were scarce, the sons, as the most important children, had first priority.

The length of the infancy period was not hard and fast. On the average, it lasted about four years, depending on the wealth of the parents and whether children were born subsequently. Wealthy parents could afford to indulge their children more and if no other siblings were born, infancy could be prolonged.

The child's first years were easy, pleasant ones. Both boys and girls received affection from both parents; discipline was held to a minimum. Weaning and toilet training were accomplished gradually, and during the latter part of the period, training in filial piety was begun. This training took the form of stories, read or told to the children, in which the implicit message was that the children were the property of their parents and ancestors. Children learned to be obedient to their parents and to older brothers and sisters.

Childhood. The term *childhood* is American, not Chinese. The Chinese term for this second age period, *yu-nien*, stresses the immaturity and inexperience of the persons involved.

Early in this period, sex differentiation became marked. Gentry boys moved to the father's section of the house and came under his direct supervision. Schooling began also, and the schoolmaster or tutor wielded authority over boys, which closely paralleled that of the father. The mother remained as a refuge for the boy against unduly harsh treatment, but her position was essentially without power, enabling her only to comfort him. Girls remained under their mother's care and began preparation for their future roles as wives and mothers. Educational training was denied to girls.

The severe discipline of Chinese life began during this period. Boys received arduous intellectual and physical training, being expected to study—essentially learning by rote—for long hours under austere conditions. Disobedience, willfulness, and failure to perform were dealt with by beatings by father and schoolmaster. The relationship between father and son ceased to be one of warmth and acceptance and became based, instead, on awe—a mixture of fear and respect. Complete subservience to the father was instilled along with the notion that one day the son would assume the same role with his own sons.

Rebellion against this severe discipline appears to have been uncommon. Acceptance of the discipline and progress in his studies made life easier for the boy, and even as he was punished, he was made aware of his importance and of the high status that was his to inherit. Too, gentry boys were granted increasing freedom to make contacts outside the household, where their sense of personal importance was increased.

The lives of gentry girls were very different from those of boys. Girls were increasingly segregated from the outside world and even from the males of their own household. They became aware of their roles as temporary members of the family. In some instances, girls were listed in the family genealogical tables only by *nu*, the symbol for female, for at marriage they would cease to be members of their fathers' families and become members of their husbands' families.

This blow to a girl's self-esteem was compensated for by the indulgent relationship with her parents. Her mother, knowing of the difficult times ahead, made the girl's life as easy as possible. The father, too, could lavish on his daughters the affection that was not appropriate with his sons. As a result, in spite of her increasing sense of worthlessness, childhood was often the happiest period of the girl's life.

The peasantry patterns for both boys and girls differed markedly from those of the gentry. The extensive schooling and segregation simply were not possible, and both boys and girls were inducted early into the labors of adult life. Boys accompanied their fathers to the fields. The girls did not work in the fields as a rule, but at periods of peak load they did. Peasant women could not be isolated from outsiders as gentry women were, and peasant girls retained much more contact with male members of their households and with outsiders.

Entrance to Adulthood. The second age period lasted from 4 years of age to 16 or 17. For peasant boys and girls and for gentry girls, this age period was followed by entrance into full adulthood. Not so for gentry males. For them, there was a relatively long and structurally significant period referred to by the term *ch'ing-nien*. This third age period for gentry males lasted until roughly age 30 or until the young man was married.

By contrast with the preceding period, the stage of *ch'ing-nien* was a relatively easy one for gentry males. Discipline was relaxed and was replaced by an almost comradely, consultative relationship in which the father trained his son in the exercise of judgment. The son's academic training had prepared him to take the first examinations, and passing those examinations brought higher status and personal freedom. His continued schooling was likely to take place in the towns and cities away from direct parental supervision and he was given money to spend.

During this period, the gentry male was introduced to the common vices of adult life—drinking, gambling, and extramarital intercourse. His first sex experience was likely to be either with a servant or a prostitute. Most gentry families had servants who were subject to the will of the household's males. The strict separation of female family members and the strong incest taboos reinforced the availability of servant girls. Sexual experimentation also was likely with prostitutes in situations that involved drinking and gambling. Sooner or later, the parents became aware of these activities and viewed them as threats to the stability of the family.

Parental reaction to the son's incipient dissolution was to seek a wife for him. The responsibility for so doing fell on his mother, who acted for her husband. The son was not consulted, for custom provided that he should not meet his bride until the engagement. According to Chinese law, marriage was concluded by the heads of the families, not by the young couple themselves.

Theoretically, there was no emotional involvement between gentry males and young women but such involvements did occur. Gentry girls were carefully chaperoned because sexual intercourse would damage their chances of marrying satisfactorily. In some areas, cross-cousin marriages were preferred and more contact was permitted with these future wives than with unrelated girls. Emotional involvement even with an eligible marriage partner was a threat to the family and an indication that another suitable marriage should be arranged immediately. Rebellion against the wishes of parents appears to have been rare.

Full Adulthood. The next two age periods covered full maturity from marriage to some time between 30 and 40 years of age, then from 30 to 40 years of age and on to old age. Entrance into adulthood was determined more by marriage than by the reaching of a particular age, for marriage was of extreme importance. Except for a small minority of religious celibates, virtually everyone married. Marriage provided for children, and children were essential to obligations to ancestors and to oneself.

Gentry families usually tried to marry their daughters to provide useful family connections. At the minimum, this meant that the man's family should have considerable property. Where possible, the gentry also tried to assure themselves that their daughter would be well received and well treated in her new family.

Peasants faced more extreme problems. The marriage of a son required a gift to the girl's parents, which gift the girl ideally brought back to the marriage as part of her trousseau. Thus, the parents of both families were supposed to make an economic contribution to the marriage, and there was negotiation over these contributions. If the man's parents were very poor, they might be forced to keep the gift made to them by the parents of their daughter's groom to arrange for the marriages of their own younger sons. Such a practice was considered undesirable, but it appears to have been widely followed.

The situation was further complicated by a chronic shortage of marriageable girls, resulting from female infanticide, prostitution, and concubinage. There are no reliable data on the extent of female infanticide, but it is known to have existed. In times of famine, drought, high taxes, and the like, it probably reached large proportions. Goode emphasizes that outright infanticide may have been accompanied by more widespread neglect of daughters during times of great privation so that their death rate may have been considerably higher.[10]

Prostitution flourished, and many peasant girls were sold into prostitu-

10. William J. Goode, *World Revolution and Family Patterns,* New York: The Free Press, 1963, pp. 307-9.

tion by parents who, thus, escaped the costs of the girl's rearing and marriage. Concubinage was uncommon among the peasants, who could not afford it, but was common among the gentry, who usually secured their concubines from peasant families. The factors of infanticide, prostitution, and concubinage combined to produce a shortage of peasant girls, forcing many peasant men to delay marriage.

Chinese girls, including gentry girls, were married early—as soon as possible after puberty. No accurate figures on age at marriage are available, but the present Chinese government is harshly critical of the old "feudalistic pattern of early marriage." Gentry men married at considerably older ages. Goode reports data from one clan in Canton that show the average age of the father at the time of the birth of his first living son to have been 33 years from A.D. 1150 to 1500, 31 years from 1630 to 1800, and 23 years from 1800 to 1880.[11] The average age at marriage would be slightly younger, of course, but given the emphasis on bearing sons, the different probably would not be great.

Marriage normally was arranged by go-betweens, for families seldom dealt directly with outsiders. Generally, these were male relatives who were trusted members of the family and yet could negotiate with the families of prospective spouses without committing the family. The procedure called for investigation of each family and several ritual exchanges of gifts and information. The information exchanged included the names and birth dates of the couple, which were presented to the ancestors and were subjected to astrological interpretation. If the interpretation was favorable, the negotiations continued. If unfavorable, the negotiations were dropped. There is some evidence that astrologers took into account more than the stars and that if a marriage did not seem mutually advantageous, an unfavorable interpretation provided a mutually face-saving way of calling it off. Eventually, if all went well, the marriage contract was signed and the wedding ceremony held.

The essence of the marriage ceremony, however elaborately embellished, was the transport of the bride to the home of the groom's parents where she was introduced to the worship of their ancestors. The wife, thus, became a member of her husband's family and her name was eligible for listing in their genealogical tables. After the ceremony, the couple were permitted to spend the night together, but early the next morning, the bride arose and served tea to her mother-in-law in bed. This began a period of service to the husband's family and particularly to the mother-in-law, the function of which was to take the bride, as an outsider, and to make her a docile member of her new family.

Marriage almost amounted more to the parents taking a daughter-in-

11. *Ibid.*, p. 286.

law than to the son taking a wife. The priority of the parents' relationship with the bride was emphasized by the fact that the lack of affection between the bride and groom was considered irrelevant. Indeed, should affection develop, display of it before other family members was taboo. Hsu reports that newlyweds were expected to occupy the same bed for only seven days, after which they were supposed to occupy separate beds. When a man's parents died, he was expected to show grief that was barely short of suicide. If his wife died, he was "expected to show some grief, but never enough to make him forget his filial duties."[12]

Marriage usually brought about the last major change in the man's status. Not so for the woman. For her, there remained the birth of her first son and the retirement of her mother-in-law. The period from marriage to the birth of her first son often was the hardest period in the woman's life. She was removed from her parents to people who had no reason to consider her feelings. As an outsider, she had no right to consideration and was dominated not only by the mother-in-law but by all other family members. The parents, her husband, and the husband's siblings all sided against her in the case of disagreement.

About the only relief the young wife had were occasional visits to her parental family. These may have been used consciously to lessen the pressure. If she became pregnant, the pressure might ease somewhat in anticipation of the birth of a son. The bearing of sons would improve the wife's position; the bearing of daughters might worsen it. In cases of exceptional mistreatment, the wife's parental family might threaten the use of force, with resulting shame to the husband's family.

Occasionally, wives were pushed into suicide. Reliable data on suicide rates are not available, but it is believed that, unlike the situation in the West, suicide in traditional China occurred primarily among women between 17 and 35. Actual suicide by harassed wives appears to have been less common than were unsuccessful attempts at it. If the wife were to commit suicide, the husband's family would be shamed for its harsh treatment of her and would have difficulty in securing another wife for their son. If she attempted suicide but was not successful, the husband's family might be intimidated into according her better treatment.

The wife's status improved as she bore sons, as she became a smoothly functioning member of the family, and as other younger daughters-in-law were added. Each woman prepared for the day when the mother-in-law should die or retire and she would assume the responsibility for inducting other younger women into the family.

Life for men was less complicated. Marriage and the birth of sons were important, but they were not accompanied by such drastic changes

12. Francis L. K. Hsu, *Under the Ancestor's Shadow*, Garden City, N.Y.: Doubleday, 1967, p. 59.

as were true for women. The man gradually moved into adult work under the increasingly gentle supervision of his father. The fear and respect for the father lessened, and their relationship often developed considerable warmth. Not uncommonly, the father retired or died fairly early in his sons' adulthood, and the eldest son became the patriarch.

Old Age. The last period began at about age 55, considerably before what we usually regard as old age. Longevity was not so great in traditional China, however, and people of 55 probably were at least as "old" as most Americans of 65 today. This was the most secure and comfortable period for both men and women. By this time, the man usually was the head of the family and his wife rather than being an outsider was now partner to her husband in maintaining the family intact. Furthermore, age was venerated. Oldsters, as the closest living contacts with ancestors, received deference from younger family members and had first claim on the family's resources.

The couple made provision for their old age by having sons and now, as grandchildren came along, the grandparents were free to enjoy them as they had never been to enjoy their own children. Gradually, the father turned over responsibility to his sons, who shouldered the burden but maintained deference to the father. By now, father and son usually saw things alike, and there was a minimum of friction.

With widowhood, the mother might come out from under male domination for the only time in her life. The official Confucian prescriptions required that she be subordinate to her sons, but actually, she often commanded obedience from them, born of long years of affection and respect and because she was a member of an older generation.

Relative Age Roles. Not only absolute age but also relative age was important. Unlike our society, where the relationship between brothers is influenced little, if at all, by their relative ages, the Chinese had separate terms for older and younger siblings. Moreover, it was common to use the terms for older brother and younger brother rather than their given names. The term *older brother* was one of great respect, and about the highest honor bestowed on a friend was to refer to him as "my older brother."

Younger siblings were expected to defer to older siblings, and the allegiance of brothers to the eldest son was counted on to keep the family intact and prevent a division of property at the father's death. Normally, older sons and daughters were married before younger siblings, and the wives' status was dependent on the relative ages of their husbands. Occasionally, when an older sibling married a much younger woman, this resulted in the older women married to his brothers being subordinated to the younger woman, and this created confusion and conflict.

Concubinage and Prostitution

The traditional family was monogamous,[13] but it was a different monogamy from that in the United States. Concubinage was fully sanctioned and among the gentry was widely practiced. Yang reports that the Chinese family was like a balloon, ready to expand whenever there was wealth to inflate it. As soon as there was opportunity to employ the married sons, they would remain in the father's household. Should wealth increase further, concubines and their children would be added.[14]

Part of the rationale for concubinage lay in the importance attached to sons. Sons were necessary to meet one's obligations to ancestors and to ensure one's own future worship as an ancestor. A man without sons might adopt them, but the practice was disapproved of. Men did not like to give up their sons, sons did not like to change surnames, and adopted sons were looked down on. Occasionally, peasant families permitted their sons to be adopted into gentry families, but the more common solution was for gentry men to take concubines.

If a marriage did not produce sons, the patriarch might demand that his son take a concubine, and even the unfortunate wife might cooperate. Sometimes the wife urged that her own sister be taken so that her position in the family would not be so threatened and to ease the adjustment to having another woman in the household. Gentry families might wish to aid such an unfortunate daughter, but they did not relish having their other daughters becoming concubines. The concubines generally were secured from peasant families, often being purchased outright.

Concubinage played another role. It offered males relief from their otherwise carefully ordered lives. From boyhood, the male's structurally important relationship with his father was nearly devoid of affection; spontaneity and emotional freedom were sacrificed on the altar of filial piety. When it was time for him to marry, he took the wife selected by his parents and with whom emotional intimacy was not encouraged. His

13. Variation from the basic monogamy has been reported. Goode cites the ancient custom of *chien t'iao*, according to which a man might make his nephew his heir while the boy remained his own father's heir also. In 10 provinces, custom permitted such boys to take two wives, each of whom took charge of the worship of one of the groups of ancestors. Van der Valk also reports that forms of polyandry were found in 3 different provinces. M. H. Van der Valk, *Conservatism in Modern Chinese Family Law*, Leiden, The Netherlands: E. J. Brill, 1956, pp. 45–47, cited in Goode, *op. cit.*, pp. 279–83.

14. C. K. Yang, *The Chinese Family in the Communist Revolution*, Cambridge, Mass.: MIT Press, 1959, p. 9.

relationships with his own sons—indeed with almost everyone—were structured in terms of responsibility and the subordination of personal needs to family goals. Concubines were likely to be women of his own choosing with whom the relationship was romantic and erotic. Hsu found that in more than half of his cases concubines were taken where the wife had already borne sons.[15]

Large-scale prostitution in traditional China is explained in similar terms. The tea house, to which men repaired to conduct business and to gain relief from their unending obligations, offered drinking, gambling, opium smoking, feminine companionship, and sexual intercourse. Young men who were introduced to these pastimes before marriage often continued them afterward. Yang reports that "merchants as well as government officials transacted much of their business, and traditional scholars wrote some of their best lines of poetry, in whorehouses." He goes on to say that, "a recent well-known Chinese writer who used to entertain his father in houses of prostitution was praised by friends as a filial son who catered to his father's desires."[16]

Thus, concubinage and prostitution provided safety valves that drained off emotions that otherwise might have threatened the stability of the family. Neither concubinage nor prostitution was disapproved on moral grounds. Only when they threatened the stability of the family were they regarded as harmful. A man might be censured for neglecting his wife and children in favor of his concubine, but his right to take concubines was unassailable. Similarly, visits to prostitutes were matters of concern only if family duties were neglected or if the accompanying drinking and gambling threatened to get out of hand.

The incorporation of concubinage into the family system stressed the dominant position of the wife and the priority of her children's rights. There was no ceremony involved in taking a concubine. A concubine had no recognized share in the family income and was assigned menial tasks under the wife's supervision. She was not included among the man's relatives, she was excluded from mourning the man's deceased family members, and she could never, herself, be worshipped as an ancestor. The concubine's children were legitimate but had limited rights of inheritance unless the wife bore no sons.

Divorce and Remarriage

There were three kinds of divorce possible in traditional China: divorce by mutual consent; divorce on the husband's initiative; and divorce under compulsion by the authorities.

15. Hsu, *op. cit.,* pp. 105–6.
16. Yang, *op. cit.,* p. 57.

Divorce by mutual consent required the consent of the heads of the families, not of the couple themselves, and the very existence of this form of divorce emphasizes the strength of the family. Divorce was regarded as tragic, and if the patriarchs agreed to a divorce, there could be no question that continuation of the marriage would be harmful to the families involved. In this form of divorce, it was the welfare of the family that was involved, not that of the couple.

Wives could be divorced by husbands on any one of seven grounds: (1) disobeying the husband's parents, (2) failing to have children, (3) acquiring a loathsome disease, (4) committing adultery, (5) displaying jealousy, (6) being overly talkative, and (7) stealing. In spite of these liberal grounds, however, women were not often repudiated and the divorce rate was low. The poor could not afford divorce and remarriage, and the wealthy did not welcome it. Besides, more acceptable alternatives were available to men. Most of their recreation was outside the home, and feminine companionship and sexual intercourse were readily available. Men also were expected to meet their needs through concubines rather than by disrupting the marriage relationship.

Divorce was tragic for women. A divorced woman could only be returned to her family; there was no other place for her to go. And her repudiation—early in marriage essentially by her mother-in-law or her later divorce by her husband for cause—brought shame on her and her family. Other families would not consider her a suitable marriage prospect, she was not entitled to inherit property, and she was denied the opportunity to achieve honor and respect as wife and mother-in-law.

This double standard of morality also applied to the remarriage of widows. Widowed men could remarry without restraint, and gentry men sometimes elevated a concubine to the status of wife on the death of the first wife. The remarriage of widows was frowned on, however, and their husbands' families could actually block a remarriage of which they did not approve. Nor could the widow take property with her into a remarriage. The only way a widow could retain a position of honor was to stay as the elderly mother in the home of her sons. The remarriage of gentry widows apparently was rare. Among the peasantry, however, economic conditions forced many remarriages.

THE TRANSITIONAL FAMILY

It is not possible to specify precisely when the Chinese family began to undergo major change. The system never was completely static, of course, and change proceeded slowly throughout the 2000-odd years of apparent stability. Until 1830, however, there was no political, military, or industrial power that could successfully break China's self-imposed isolation from the rest of the world. Marked change followed on England's successful opening of trade with the Chinese mainland.

With the development of international trade, the Chinese coastal areas began to industrialize and to develop large-scale commercial enterprises. The impact of these developments on the society and the family was tremendous. The requirements of an industrial economy and the traditional family system were incompatible at many points.

The Influence of Western Ideals

Trade not only encouraged industrialization but also brought extensive contact with Western ideals that subverted the traditional order. The Western concept of treating women as near-equals with men and as full companions was revolutionary. The concept of individualism, which elevates the well-being of individuals to superiority over the welfare of the family, was equally striking. Although Western religion did not make great impact, its emphasis on the sacredness of the individual had far-reaching repercussions. Finally, the idea of political freedom—of individuals exercising collective control over the conditions of their existence—formed part of the base for a new social order.

An Alternative Way of Life

The combination of industrialization and ideals of political freedom, individualism, and social equality provided what no influences on Chinese life had done for 2000 years—the prospect of an alternative way of living. With the growth of cities and factory employment, single persons, married couples, and nuclear families could live apart from their extended families permanently. The separation of the kinship and occupational structures led to a weakening of parental authority; income and status came to depend more on one's place in the occupational system than upon family ties; industrialization provided new sources of wealth greater than those of the old agricultural system; and people began to think of their individual interests as taking priority over extended family obligations.

No one set of influences brought about these changes. Nor it is possible to assign priority to one of them. It was a combination of industrialization, ideals of individualism, equality, freedom, and the possibility of an alternative way of life that produced the transitional family.

Emerging Patterns

The family structure of traditional China was an integrated, stable entity. Not so with the transitional family because it is not clear that a new, stable form has yet emerged.[17] Change has been under way for over a century and has been complicated recently by the family policies of the Communist government. How much effect and what kind of effect such policies will have is a matter of debate. What can be done

---

Two men hurled a large sack into a river in northeast China and a curious peasant fished it out. Inside was a drowned baby girl, a few months old. A heavy stone was tied to her feet.

In the northeast city of Chenyang, a woman committed suicide by drinking seven bottles of DDT because her husband beat and cursed her for having a girl. "Go and die," he ordered her. "I will go and find a woman to bear a son."

. . . In sophisticated Shanghai, many women weep on learning they have borne a girl. . . . One woman murdered her girl baby by throwing her out the hospital window. . . .

Chinese women have made great advances since the days of footbinding, but feudal thinking dies slowly and Chinese Communist society is dominated by men.

A torrent of recent press reports reveal widespread abuse of women and girls because of the powerful desire to have sons for posterity, inheritance, labor in the fields and insurance in old age.

Recent articles also complain about job discrimination against women who say that employers don't even want women college graduates.

Associated Press, October 31, 1982.

---

here is to indicate the direction in which the family has been moving and to indicate possible future developments.

Changing Status of Women. For the first time, women and children have become potential sources of additional income. Legally, today, Chinese women have full inheritance rights with men. That Chinese women often do not yet get their full legal rights only underscores the radical nature of the transformation.[18]

17. The changes in Chinese family patterns are most typical of, and may (in many cases) be confined to, urban and coastal areas that have undergone industrialization. The vastness of China, the numerous dialects, and the limited ability of the government to impose policies in the hinterland probably leave hundreds of millions still living according to traditional ways.

18. Lawrence K. Hong, "The Role of Women in the People's Republic of China: Legacy and Change," *Social Problems* 23 (June 1976), pp. 545–57; Kay Ann Johnson, "Women in China: Problems of Sex Inequality and Socioeconomic Change," in Joan I. Roberts, ed., *Beyond Intellectual Sexism: A New Woman, a New Reality*, New York: David McKay, 1976, pp. 286–319; William T. Liu and Elena S. H. Yu, "Variations in Women's Roles and Family Life Under the Socialist Regime in China," *Journal of Comparative*

In childhood, less segregation of the sexes now occurs and both boys and girls come more under the influence of their mothers. Formal education has been extended to almost the entire society and tends to be co-educational. There is less need to marry girls young, and their average age at marriage has been rising. The mother-in-law/daughter-in-law relationship remains difficult. But with the increasing separation of the nuclear family from the extended family, it is becoming less so. Chinese women have not yet gained the near-equality of Western women, but the official ideologies are pushing them in that direction.

Development of a Youth Culture. For 2000 years, Chinese culture venerated age and assigned inferior status to youth. That situation has been changing rapidly and may now be reversed.

Chinese youth and young adults have been cut loose in a drastic sense. As they became involved in industry, they were forced, for the first time, to make decisions on their own. This produced an individualism by default, if not by design. The Communist movement in China is largely a youth movement that, because it is articulate, assumes importance beyond the number of people involved.

The freeing of youth from notions of family responsibility has produced a problem in relation to the aged. The old norms called for support of one's own parents, but it carried no responsibility for the aged in general. Now the number of aged persons is increasing and many are in danger of being left without financial support. The government is, thus, faced with a dilemma. It wishes to substitute allegiance to the government for allegiance to the family, but its success in destroying the sense of family obligation increases the problem of support for the aged.

Development of Romantic Love. With urban living, freer association between the sexes emerged and romantic love is threatening to replace parental arrangement as the basis for marriage. High school and college students mingle freely, and the attractions of specific boys and girls to one another demand consideration.[19] There are three forms of deviation from the old pattern of arranged marriage: (1) parents arrange the marriage but ask their children's consent, (2) young people select their own

---

Family Studies 8 (Summer 1977), pp. 201-15; *U.S. News & World Report,* "Chinese Men and Women are Equal—But Men Are More Equal," June 28, 1982, p. 54; and Joyce Jennings Walstedt, "Reform of Women's Roles and Family Structures in the Recent History of China," *Journal of Marriage and the Family* 40 (May 1978), pp. 379-92.
19. Lucy J. Huang, "Mate Selection and Marital Happiness in the Mainland Chinese Family," *International Journal of Sociology of the Family* 2 (Sept. 1972), pp. 121-38.

More and more, boys and girls are going out to dinner together and to the movies, and on hand-in-hand strolls through the parks. Last fall, the authorities in Peking started closing the city's parks at dusk in an effort to stop an outbreak of kissing on benches and in the shrubbery. The onset of cold weather has since put a natural end to the epidemic.

FOX BUTTERWORTH, "Love and Sex in China," *New York Times Magazine,* January 13, 1980, p. 44.

---

mates but ask their parents' approval, and (3) the young people marry without asking parental consent.[20]

A drastic change that is an accompaniment of romantic love is the appearance of groups of unmarried men and women in the cities. Under traditional norms, the unmarried state for adults was regarded almost as perverted and there were no satisfactory social arrangements for single persons. Now, however, with the emergence of apartment living, hotels, restaurants, laundries, and the like, the old definitions of the single state are breaking down.

Increased Rates of Divorce, Suicide, and Illegitimacy. Although trustworthy figures are not available, divorce rates have been increasing. Under the traditional system, divorce rates were low and divorce often involved repudiation of the wife by the husband's family. Revisions of the marriage laws have sought to equalize divorce rights of husbands and wives, and most divorces now result from mutual consent or from insistence by either party. One clue to the increase in divorce is found in recent educational campaigns by the government aimed at lowering divorce rates.

Levy reports that suicide rates apparently have been increasing also.[21] Moreover, the pattern has been changing. Whereas suicide was predominantly an alternative for young women under the traditional system, it is more often found now among middle-aged and older persons. Levy

20. For an analysis of kinship structure on contemporary Taiwan, see Solomon S. Chu, "Some Aspects of Extended Kinship in a Chinese Community," *Journal of Marriage and the Family* 36 (Aug. 1974), pp. 628–33. See also Hugh J. R. Baker, *Chinese Family and Kinship,* New York: Columbia University Press, 1980; Elizabeth Croll, *The Politics of Marriage in Contemporary China,* New York: Cambridge University Press, 1981; Lau Siu-Kai, "Chinese Familism in an Urban-Industrial Setting: The Case of Hong Kong," *Journal of Marriage and the Family* 43 (Nov. 1981), pp. 977–92; and Fai-Ming Wong, "Industrialization and Family Structure in Hong Kong," *Journal of Marriage and the Family* (Nov. 1975), pp. 985–1000.

21. Levy, *op. cit.,* p. 337.

attributes the change to the responsibilities placed on middle-aged people by urban living and to the difficult position of aged parents.

Illegitimacy, in the Western sense, is almost a new problem in China. Lack of free association between the sexes and marriage at early ages, especially for girls, kept illegitimacy rates low during the traditional period. Too, the extramarital wanderings of men were institutionalized in the custom of concubinage. Now it is increasingly difficult for a man to maintain a concubine either within his household or outside it. China never had puritanical attitudes toward sex; when young people are free to associate intimately, sexual intercourse often occurs. The government is now urging a puritanical morality in an effort to reduced illegitimacy rates.

THE INFLUENCE OF THE CHINESE COMMUNIST GOVERNMENT

The policies and programs of the government of the People's Republic of China are of importance to the entire world. The government's policy is formulated in reaction to the traditional family system as well as in accordance with political, economic, and military goals.

The basic stance of the government is exemplified by the Marriage Law that became effective in May 1950, less than eight months after the establishment of the new government. A more extensive version of the law was released on January 1, 1982.[22] The new law, which actually is a code for the regulation of many aspects of family life, establishes the following principles: (1) monogamy without concubinage, (2) free choice of spouse, (3) equal inheritance rights for both sexes, (4) protection of children's rights, and (5) divorce by mutual consent or on insistence by either spouse. It is a complete departure from the traditional system. Noteworthy in the law are provisions for protection of the rights of women and children. Women are given full legal rights; and it has become high fashion for a married woman to retain her own family name. Children born out of wedlock have equal rights with legitimate offspring.

To achieve the goal of modernization and to raise the standard of living for its people, the Chinese government has embarked on an ambitious program of population control.[23] A vigorous campaign has been

22. Lucy Jen Huang, "The New Marriage Law of the People's Republic of China: An Analysis of the Articles on the Use of Names, Family Membership and Residence, Age of Marriage, and Family Planning." Paper presented at the National Council of Family Relations, Washington, D.C., October 1982.
23. See C. C. Ching, "The One-Child Family in China," *Studies in Family Planning* 13 (June/July 1982), pp. 208–12; Henry P. David, "Incentives, Reproductive Behavior, and Integrated Community Development in Asia," *Studies in Family Planning* 13 (May

launched to limit families to one child per couple and to deter couples from producing "excess children." Free birth control counseling, clinics, and devices are widely available and their use encouraged. Abortion is also freely available and encouraged in the case of an unscheduled second pregnancy.[24] The goal of the government is to get a substantial proportion of young couples to sign a pledge promising to have no more than one child. To accomplish this goal, educational programs, peer pressure, and a number of strong economic incentives have been initiated. The incentives include small supplementary monthly payments and food rations; free health care and schooling; preferences for housing and jobs; preferences for the child's higher education; and, higher pensions for those who work for the state. Couples who sign the pledge and subsequently deliver a second child must repay all the benefits they received for signing the pledge.[25] The age of legal marriage has also been raised in China to aid in population control. In urban areas, men may marry when they reach the age of 27, and women when they reach the age of 25.[26]

Despite such efforts, questions remain whether China will be able to achieve its goal of population control. Eighty percent of the people of mainland China live in the countryside where large families are the custom.[27] The rate of illiteracy is quite high, which hinders effective use of birth control. Despite efforts to change long-standing custom, male children are still preferred. Couples may continue procreating until they have borne the son tradition calls for. Female children may be subject to infanticide in increasing numbers so that the one child allowed per couple is male. As with any radical change that usurps traditional practices, the national birth control movement of China is meeting with resistance, but efforts will undoubtedly continue.[28] Whether or not they are successful remains to be seen.

Much public attention has been given to the reported efforts of the Communist government to eliminate the family as a threat to its own hold over the populace. The Marriage Law of 1950 and the revised edition of 1982 are not consistent with such a position but seem instead to embody the highest ideals of Western societies. Where the govern-

---

1982), pp. 159–73; and Lucy Jen Huang, "Planned Fertility of One-couple/One-child Policy in the People's Republic of China," *Journal of Marriage and the Family* 44 (Aug. 1982), pp. 775–84.

24. Henry P. David, "China's Population Policy: Glimpses and a 'Mini-Survey,'" *Intercom* 10 (Sept./Oct. 1982), pp. 3–4.

25. *Intercom*, 9 (Aug. 1981), pp. 1, 12–14.

26. Huang, "Planned Fertility . . . ," p. 778.

27. *U.S. News & World Report*, November 8, 1982, p. 38.

28. Christopher S. Wren, "Chinese Region Showing Resistence to National Goals for Birth Control," *New York Times*, May 16, 1982.

ment has attacked the family system is in all of those areas formerly controlled by the *tsu*.[29] The government's substitute for the *tsu* is the commune.

The new government required years to consolidate its hold over major areas of China, and it broke up *tsu* land holdings wherever possible and redistributed them among the peasants. It then followed land reform by organizing agricultural cooperatives designed to nationalize farm production. The government regulated production of major crops, leaving each farmer free to raise his own garden crops. By the middle of 1955, there were more than 600,000 cooperatives involving 14 percent of the farm population; by the end of 1956, almost all peasant families were members of collectives. These cooperatives were not too satisfactory. Their management was not too competent, and farm production failed to meet expectations.

The cooperatives were replaced by communes. The first showplace commune was established in April 1958; by November of that year, 99 percent of the rural population had been grouped into communes of about 5000 households each. In August 1958, 173 urban communes were formed in Honan; by 1960 urban communes were being organized on a grand scale. Up to 20 million people are said to have been involved.

The new communes were bigger than the old collectives and involved the collectivization of much more of daily living. In addition to agricultural production, they were to have charge of such tasks as banking and the building of dams and steel mills. Common dining rooms were provided, nurseries were established for the care of children, and women were expected to play a full role in the occupational system. Universal primary education was offered to children, inexpensive weddings and funerals were provided, and homes for the aged were established.

Western attitudes toward these communes were quite negative. The communes were widely interpreted as an attack on the family—as an attempt to eliminate the family as we know it from Chinese society. Actually, it appears that nothing so drastic was intended. Many Westerners also predicted that the communes were bound to fail; an oversimplified prediction to say the least.

In sober retrospect, the communes appear to have been designed to replace the network of authority and loyalty that was part of the extended family system and the clan organization, not to replace the family itself. The Communists complain that the old system was corrupt and that it led to the degradation of all but the gentry families who held power. They point to the fact that the allegedly universalistic examination system was actually under the control of the gentry; they point to

29. See Janet W. Salaff, "The Emerging Conjugal Relationship in the People's Republic of China," *Journal of Marriage and the Family* 35 (Nov. 1973), pp. 705–17.

the rampant nepotism that kept positions of wealth, power, and prestige within the gentry; they point to infanticide, prostitution, and the sale of women as degrading. And they present themselves as representing the interests of all the people against the tyranny of the traditional family system. They have sought to free women and children from that tyranny and to redistribute wealth in the society.

China underwent political and economic upheaval during the latter 1960s, the Cultural Revolution, and confirmed anti-Communists in the West were quick to conclude that the collective system was on the point of collapse. By the early 1970s, however, the Cultural Revolution was over, the government was in firm control of the country, and the system showed considerable strength.

The communes still are conspicuous features, but there are indications that they may be dying out.[30] China's leaders believe that for economic modernization to occur, the country must dramatically increase the production of food and raw materials. Many of the communes have been found to be economically inefficient and almost 3000 of them have been abolished. Capitalist-style free enterprise has been introduced and individual initiative in profit making seems to be replacing communal work and living arrangements. Individuals may sign production contracts and sell to cooperatives or corporations whatever they have agreed to produce. The worker then has free control over the surplus production. Private enterprise does not equate with democracy however. The Communist party still sets and oversees procedures and policies.

Farming and farm values dominate the village of Xitang, a name meaning "west of the pond." Early to bed, early to rise is a way of life today, just as it has been since the village was first established nearly four centuries ago.

By 6 a.m., people are selling produce from private plots in the free market. And by 8 a.m., they are at work in communal fields, laboring until the hour-long break at lunch—a Communist tradition that has become as firmly ingrained as the Latin siesta. Communal work ends at 5 p.m., except during planting and harvest season.

"I get up at 5 o'clock to do my housework before we open the store at 8," says Cheng Fengzhu, 38, a shop clerk and housewife. "Sometimes we watch television in the evening, but we are always in bed before 10."

U.S. News & World Report, February 2, 1981, p. 63.

---

30. *U.S. News & World Report,* January 17, 1983, pp. 30-32.

It is too early to say that the transformation of the Chinese family system is complete. The Communist government has now been in power for more than 30 years however, and it continues to urge the family in the same general direction as it is moving in the West.[31]

SUMMARY

Study of the Chinese family has both theoretical and practical implications. First, it serves as a model of an extended, patriarchal, patrilineal system. Second, after 2000 years of relative stability, it is now undergoing rapid change. Finally, China is the most populous nation in the world and may pose a grave political, economic, and military threat to the West.

To understand the Chinese family, one must distinguish between the gentry, whose customs and ideals were universally admired and widely imitated, and the vast peasantry, who lived close to the minimum subsistence level and for whom little elaboration of social patterns was possible.

The traditional family was patriarchal, patrilineal, patrilocal, and monogamous. Ideally, it involved six generations and went nine generations without a division of property. Actually, few families contained more than three or four generations and the modal family may have been the stem family. Ancestor worship and the doctrine of filial piety probably kept the family from changing to a simple conjugal system.

The *tsu*, or clan, was composed of all persons of a given surname tracing descent from a common ancestor. The *tsu* served as a buffer between the extended family and the larger society and performed educational, welfare, religious, and judicial functions.

Traditional Chinese society was rigidly structured according to age and sex. Old age was highly esteemed and men dominated women. Role prescriptions for each family member were laid down in detail.

Gentry boys and girls were segregated early in childhood. Boys were remanded to the strict discipline of fathers and tutors, whereas girls were affectionately indulged by both parents. As they grew in responsibility, boys' lots improved, whereas girls could look forward only to harsh treatment at the hands of their husbands' families.

Marriages were arranged by parents. The man's status changed little

---

31. Jane Cassels Record and Wilson Record, "Totalist and Pluralist Views of Women's Liberation: Some Reflections on the Chinese and American Settings," *Social Problems* 23 (April 1976), pp. 402–14; and Judith Stacey, "Toward a Theory of Family and Revolution: Reflections on the Chinese Case," *Social Problems* 26 (June 1979), pp. 499–508.

at marriage, but the bride began a period of servitude to the husband's family, the function of which was to properly socialize her into her new family. The mother-in-law treated the girl harshly, and the resulting antagonisms between them were a source of strain in the family.

The husband continued to grow in responsibility and personal freedom; the wife's status improved as she bore sons. As they moved into old age the relationship between them became quite strong and they received complete deference from their children.

Escape from the order and responsibility of everyday life was provided for men through concubinage and through widespread commercial prostitution. Concubines sometimes were elevated to the status of wife, and the children of concubines were legitimate.

Divorce was uncommon during the traditional period and was regarded as undesirable. Divorce might occur with the mutual consent of the families involved or the husband might divorce his wife on any one of seven specified grounds. Remarriage was common among men but very difficult for women. Similarly, widowers generally remarried but the remarriage of widows was strongly disapproved of.

Extensive changes began early in the 1880s. As China began to industrialize, the family system came into conflict with the occupational system. Western ideals of individualism, equality, and political freedom helped to subvert the traditional system. The transition finally was made possible by the development of urban institutions that made an alternative way of life possible.

The character of the transitional family is not fully established. There is an unmistakable trend toward the conjugal form based on romantic love and with more equality between the sexes. Divorce and illegitimacy rates have risen. With the rebellion of youth against the traditional system, care of the aged has become a problem.

The Communist government, which came into power in 1949, has supported these changes and has attacked the traditional system as feudalistic. It demands full equality for women and protection of the rights of children. A massive population-control program has been instituted to limit family size to one child per couple.

The most controversial of the Communist innovations are the communes, which were established on a large scale. Westerners often interpret the communes as an attempt to destroy the family. In reality, the communes are intended as a substitute for the *tsu* and for the extended family, not for the conjugal unit, on which the government already depends. Although firmly entrenched in the Chinese social order, communal living may give way to free enterprise as the government steps up efforts to increase food and raw materials production.

SUGGESTED READINGS

Adams, Carolyn Teich, and Winston, Kathryn Teich, *Mothers at Work: Public Policies in the United States, Sweden and China*, New York: Longman, 1980. A cross-cultural examination of public policies for working women.

Cohen, Myron L., *House United, House Divided: The Chinese Family in Taiwan*, New York: Columbia University Press, 1976. A carefully drawn portrait of the modernizing of the traditional family. Based on extensive fieldwork in a farming village.

Curtin, Katie, *Women in China*, New York: Pathfinder Press, 1975. A brief analysis, by a socialist and feminist, of the changes that have taken place in the status of women since the Chinese Cultural Revolution.

Davin, Delia, *Woman-Work: Women and the Party in Revolutionary China*, New York: Oxford University Press, 1979. Traces the impact of party policy on the status of women in the countryside and in the cities.

Eberhard, Wolfram, *The Upperclass Family in Traditional China*, in Charles E. Rosenberg, *ed., The Family in History*, Philadelphia: University of Pennsylvania Press, 1975, pp. 59–94. A comprehensive analysis covering the whole 2000 years of traditional family patterns.

Kessen, William, *ed., Childhood in China*, New Haven, Conn.: Yale University Press, 1975. A report based on the visit to China of a number of U.S. specialists in child development. Among other things, focuses on the emergence of traditional sex-role differences in a system supposedly committed to egalitarianism.

Parish, William L., and Whyte, Martin King, *Village and Family in Contemporary China*, Chicago: University of Chicago Press, 1978. Examines the impact of new political and economic policies on peasant life. Focuses on how much of the traditional way of life survives in Communist China.

FILMS

Born Chinese: A Study of the Chinese Character (Time-Life Films, 43 West 16th Street, New York, N.Y. 10011), 57 minutes. Shows the daily life of the Lung family, Hong Kong refugees from Red China. The camera studies their daily routine and analyzes the motives behind their behavior. No Westerners are seen.

China: A Hole in the Bamboo Curtain (Association Films, 866 Third Avenue, New York, N.Y. 10022), 28 minutes, color. A documentary odyssey, ranging from Shenyang to Peking, Shanghai, and Canton, that shows lifestyles, children in school, and people's thoughts of the present and future.

China: Land of My Father (New Day Films, P.O. Box 315, Franklin Lakes, N.J. 07417), 28 minutes. First-person perspective of China as a journalist searches for the roots of her father's family.

QUESTIONS AND PROJECTS

1. Distinguish between the gentry and the peasantry. Why were the gentry patterns so important in traditional China?
2. Describe the "ideal" gentry family, using the concepts of family structure presented in Chapter 2. How did the "real" gentry patterns differ from the ideal? How did the peasantry patterns differ from the gentry patterns?
3. Explain the inheritance patterns in the traditional family. How was ceremonial primogeniture important? How was the division of property provided for? How often did it occur?
4. What was the *tsu* and what was its relationship to the extended family? What specific functions did the *tsu* perform?
5. Describe the infancy and childhood periods in the lives of gentry boys and girls. In what way did the relationship between boys and their father become a source of strain in the family?
6. Who were the interested parties in arranging a marriage? What was the essence of the marriage ceremony?
7. What was the significance of relative age in the traditional family?
8. What functions were served by concubinage? How was the stability of the family linked to extramarital sexual activity on the part of men?
9. What regulations governed divorce in the traditional family? Explain how the practice of divorce by mutual consent actually reflected the strength of the family. How common was divorce in traditional China?
10. What forces finally led to disruption of the traditional family system? Assess the roles of industrialization, ideals of individualism and equality, and the possibility of an alternative way of life.
11. How and why is China attempting to limit its population growth? How likely are they to succeed?
12. What has been the influence of the People's Republic of China on the family? Describe how communes are consistent with the government's family policy. Are communes likely to survive in China? Describe the changes likely to occur with the introduction of free enterprise.

Copyright © Jean Shapiro

5
Utopian Experiments and Alternative Life Styles

Like most of Israel's 370 other communal settlements, Ein Hahoresh has been unable to survive on the income from its orange, avocado, and cotton crops and from raising chickens. Seventy percent of its income is now derived from industry. For 1981 the container factory will have an estimated volume of $9 million and a $500,000 profit.

. . . Except for outside workers, salaries are not paid to individuals but are deposited in a village account from which the kibbutz expenses are paid. Committees allocate expenditures for housing, clothing, communal dining, training, and vacation trips. The communal account also pays for cultural events such as concerts, lectures, and films—and for TV sets for individual families.[1]

By law, the women of Russia are guaranteed rights that would be the envy of any American committed to the equal-rights amendment. . . . But the stark realities bear little resemblance to the legal guarantees. Few women are emancipated. . . . A great deal of women's discontent springs from the fact that economic necessity and Soviet custom require everyone to hold a job. . . . Wives and divorced mothers, as a result, spend 8 hours a day earning a livelihood and then more weary hours devoted to shopping and housework. . . . Working women spend more than 30 hours a week on those two activities. And while husbands in their 20s and 30s are more willing to help at home than their own fathers were, a recent survey of the Russian Republic disclosed that on the average men spend only 15 hours a week on household chores.[2]

Attempts, large and small, to find better ways of living have been going on for a long time. They have ranged from small communities to whole

1. Manfred F. Schroeder, "The Kibbutzim Go Industrial," *World Press Review*, July 1981, p. 54.
2. *U.S. News & World Report*, June 28, 1982, p. 53.

nations. Recently, in the United States, they have emphasized fairly individualistic searches for alternatives to nuclear family living. Most such attempts to create utopian ways of living have been fairly short-lived.

Analysis of a representative sample of efforts to do away with the family would require more space than we have available. What we shall do is consider the Oneida experiment in nineteenth-century America, the Russian experiment after World War I, and the kibbutzim in Israel as background for assessment of proposals for alternative life styles on the contemporary scene.

THE ONEIDA COMMUNITY

The story of the Oneida Community is inextricably linked with the personality and religious beliefs of John Humphrey Noyes.[3] Noyes graduated from Dartmouth and began the practice of law. He underwent religious conversion at a revival meeting, gave up law, and entered the seminary, where the zealousness that was to characterize his later years became evident. He decided that the doctrine of repentance for sinning was wrong and that people should strive instead to live a perfect life here on earth. Noyes narrowly escaped being expelled from the seminary, and soon after he began to preach, his license was revoked.

Noyes continued to preach his doctrine of *perfectionism*. Gradually, he gathered a group of believers at his home in Putney, Vermont; this group became, in 1846, the Putney Community—a group who lived together in the first stages of what came to be called *complex marriage*.

The detailed origins of complex marriage may never be known. It was part of a larger "Bible communism" that involved a sharing of wealth, the elimination of private property, and the principle that every adult man should have sexual privileges with every adult woman and vice versa. The Putney Community started when Noyes arranged for his two sisters to marry two men in the group. The actual sexual communism began later, when Noyes became attracted to one of the other women who had joined the group. He began to have sexual relations with her after he first consulted with his wife and with the woman's husband.

Noyes was a complicated man. His charismatic leadership made men loyal to him and attracted women, sexually and otherwise. He fathered at least 11 children by various women. At the same time, Noyes was a deeply religious man who genuinely eschewed lust and personal selfish-

3. Constance Noyes Robertson, *ed.*, *Oneida Community: An Autobiography, 1851–1876,* Syracuse, N.Y.: Syracuse University Press, 1970.

ness. Such men usually are not easily tolerated by those around them, and, in 1848, Noyes and his little band were driven out of Putney.

The group reestablished itself in central New York State on the Oneida Creek, where it existed for approximately 30 years. The group grew to about 300 people and, after a difficult start, prospered financially. Unlike most utopian American communities that emphasized farming, Oneida developed a sizable industrial base. One of the members invented a steel trap, which was widely used; shortly before the community broke up, it embarked on the manufacture of silverware. The silverware business was profitable and continued after the breakup of the community as the well-known Oneida, Limited.

Complex Marriage

According to the principle of complex marriage, all men should love all women and all women should love all men. Romantic love and monogamy were seen as both cause and effect of selfishness and jealousy, selfishness and jealousy being barriers to leading the perfect life.

Consistent with these beliefs, the Oneidans practiced group marriage, in which a man had the right to seek sexual relations with any woman. Women were free either to accept or reject a specific proposal. If a man wished to initiate a relationship, he was supposed to convey his request to the woman through a Central Committee. An older woman member of the Committee relayed the proposal to the woman, making it easy for her to respond either way without embarrassment. Women seldom refused. The man then appeared at the woman's room at bedtime and retired to his own room again before going to sleep. Such an elaborate procedure may have been used only when a new relationship was begun and probably, after the first visit, matters were more informally handled by the couples involved.

The absence of any right to demand sex is said to have resulted in Oneida men and women remaining more attentive to one another than is usually true in conventional situations. For couples to develop romantic attachments, however, was regarded as unseemly and sanctions occasionally were applied; the couple might be chided and one member of the couple might be sent out of the community for a time.

The Oneidans distinguished between the right to sex and the right to reproduction. The community agreed that during its first 20 years there should be no childbearing. After the community was firmly established and child-care facilities provided, a committee was appointed to determine which men and women should reproduce. Although modern eugenics did not yet exist, Noyes had been influenced by Galton and Darwin and called his planned parenthood program *stirpiculture*.

Eventually some 53 women and 38 men were selected to become parents and 58 children were born. For the most part, the parents were the authorized ones, but a few unauthorized women were highly desirous of having children and managed to become pregnant.

The birth control technique used by the Oneidans casts light on their concept of appropriate sexual relationships. They practiced *coitus reservatus*, in which intercourse is continued without the man reaching ejaculation. It calls for a high degree of control on the part of the man however—enough so that there is doubt of its feasibility for whole populations. Moreover, it alters the character of the sexual relationship; replacing the explosive sexual climax with a suffused lower key pleasure. The combination of free sexual access with intentional toning down of the erotic seems consistent with the deeply religious nature of the Oneida Community.

Associated with this concept of sex was the "principle of ascendance," according to which men learned the techniques of control by having their early sex experiences only with older, experienced women—often those beyond menopause who could not become pregnant. Similarly, young women were taught the intricacies of sex by older men who were "properly spiritual" and would not be carried away.

Apparently, the birth control technique was effective. There was, however, grumbling on the part of younger men, and this may have been one of the factors leading to the breakup. It may have been responsible, also, for John Humphrey Noyes's leaving and going to Canada, where he died. There are unsubstantiated rumors that some of the younger women were under "the age of consent" and that Noyes believed that he might be prosecuted for statutory rape.

Complex marriage also removed the childrearing function rather completely from the parents. When children attained the age of 15 months, they were removed from the care of their mothers and housed in the children's wing of the great mansion house, which by that time, had been built. The children had a visiting period with their mothers once each day. All adults were supposed to love all children and all children to love all adults; so the relationship to children was not impersonal or distant.

Students of the Oneida Community have placed emphasis on the structure of the mansion house in determining the social patterns within the group. Although each adult had his or her room and although there was a separate wing for the children, there were common dining, recreation, and living areas. The seeking of privacy was discouraged and communal living was expected. Life in the mansion was pleasant, and there was a high degree of sharing interests and activities.

The Oneidans' communistic practices extended through the economic sphere, were buttressed by an ascetic morality, and were accompanied by a lively interest in the arts. Private property was done away with. Property was jointly held, and even clothing and personal effects were furnished from a central supply. Sexual attractiveness was not emphasized. The women wore their hair short and wore knee-length dresses over loose-fitting trousers that extended to the feet. Even the children held their toys in common. There was one brief period when small children were provided with their own dolls, but this encouraged personal selfishness and the privately owned dolls were ritually destroyed.

Effort was made to reinforce the inherent dignity of all work, and status distinctions among different tasks were played down. Whenever possible, people were rotated from one job to another so that permanent status distinctions would not appear. Yet the Oneidans managed their enterprises well, and the community prospered.

Another paradox appeared in that dancing and card playing, which were defined as healthy social activities, were encouraged, whereas alleged personal vices such as smoking, drinking coffee, and the use of alcohol were prohibited. The community also sponsored musical and other cultural programs, which outsiders from the surrounding areas were permitted to attend. Except for these occasions, contact between members of the community and outsiders were kept to a minimum.

The Breakup of the Community

Even as the community prospered, its radical ways led to pressures, from within and without, that proved to be its undoing. What priority should be assigned to the various factors cannot be said for sure. But by 1880, barely 30 years after its beginning, the community had broken up.

As nearly as can be determined, most individual members of the community were well thought of by outsiders. They had the reputation of being sober, hard-working, religious people who bothered no one. But complex marriage was too radical for surrounding communities. Rumors grew of sexual orgies, "free love," and the breeding of human beings "like cattle." Older men having sexual relationships with young girls not only outraged public morality but also appeared to be in violation of the laws against statutory rape. The pressure grew greater until, by 1879, the community was forced to give up complex marriage and return to official monogamy.

Some of the pressure came from within the community, which was not entirely successful in indoctrinating its young people with their parents' values. Some of the children were sensitive to the taunts of outsiders, who referred to them as "bastards" and "Christ boys." To their parents' dismay, some of the younger people also assumed the romantic and monogamous attitudes of outsiders.

The fate of the community also was linked to the leadership of John Humphrey Noyes. Like many charismatic leaders, he gave unstintingly of himself for the community's welfare, but he failed to provide adequately for his own succession. Power in the community was vested in its elders, with the balance of power often being held by Noyes. The younger generation was not trained to leadership and became a divisive force within the community. In 1877, John Humphrey Noyes resigned as leader and was replaced by one of his sons. In 1879, Noyes left for Canada and soon afterward the community dissolved.

Of the many utopian experiments within the United States, Oneida was the most successful. For 30 years and among some 300 people, the family virtually ceased to exist. It is significant, however, that the experiment did not last through the raising of even one generation.

THE SOVIET FAMILY EXPERIMENT

In turning to the great family experiment in the Soviet Union, we jump from an isolated experiment among 300 people to analysis of a system with some 200 million people composed of several ethnic groups and as many as 175 separate nationalities.

The major cultural division in prerevolutionary Russia was between the Slavs who were concentrated in European Russia and the non-Slavic peoples located in the Caucasus, Central Asia, the Steppes, and Siberia. The Slavs composed four fifths of the population and had a family pattern that loosely associated the conjugal family with a larger bilateral kindred. This stood in contrast to the Kayakh family, which was a patrilineal, extended family attached to a larger clan group and governed by Moslem law. The situation was further complicated by differences between the urban minority (about 30 percent of the population) and the vast peasant masses in the hinterlands.

The dominant, bilateral, conjugal family was large by modern standards, tending toward an extended family system. Particularly among the wealthier segments, there was strict patriarchal control associated with the ownership of large tracts of land. The power of these elite families traced directly from the Czar and was supported by the powerful Eastern Orthodox Church. It was against the concentration of power in these three places that the Bolshevik Revolution of 1917 was directed.

Early Soviet Policy

The new Soviet regime, in its second month, issued decrees regulating marriage and divorce. One decree replaced religious marriage with civil marriage; another made divorce available at the request of one or both parties. In 1918, a comprehensive code supplemented these decrees with the stipulation that, "birth itself shall be the basis of the family. No differentiation whatsoever shall be made between relationships by birth, whether in or out of wedlock."[4] The code provided, further, that neither parents nor children should have rights to one another's property and that their obligations to support one another should be conditioned on "destitution and the inability to work." Thus, the Soviet regime adopted policies that attacked the foundations of the family: the church was forbidden to solemnize marriages; divorce was made easy; penalties attached to illegitimacy were removed; the legal obligations of parents and children to one another were minimized; and the family inheritance of property was attacked.

The most radical policies, however, were still to come. In 1926, the Code on Domestic Relations was enacted by the largest Soviet state and was soon adopted by the other Soviet republics. The new code did not require registration of marriages and declared only that registration offered the best proof that a marriage existed. The courts also recognized marriages where there was "the fact of cohabitation, combined with a common household, evidence of marital relations before third parties or in personal correspondence and other documents, mutual financial support, the raising of children in common if supported by circumstantial evidence, and the like."[5] In brief, none of the rights and obligations of spouses, parents, or children were to depend on whether a marriage had been registered.

The code of 1926 was equally drastic in its provision for divorce. The couple jointly, or either spouse, could request divorce without giving any reasons. There was no trial or other judicial procedure. Divorces simply were registered, as marriages were registered. If the divorce was registered by one party only, the other party was notified to appear at the Registry, not to contest the dissolution but to acknowledge it. Failure to appear brought notice of the divorce through the mail.

Laws relating to sex were conspicuous early in the regime by their absence. One of the few laws legalized abortion in 1920. Other laws dropped adultery, bigamy, and incest as punishable offenses. The pre-

4. Vladimir Gsovski, "Family and Inheritance in Soviet Law," in Alex Inkeles and H. Kent Geiger, *eds., Soviet Society: A Book of Readings*, Boston: Houghton Mifflin, 1961, p. 531.
5. *Ibid.*, p. 532.

vailing attitude was that there should be no barriers to free sexual relationships. Contraceptive devices were made readily available, and all stigma was removed from illegitimacy.

The conclusion is inescapable that the Soviets sought to eliminate the family. Perhaps the most explicit Bolshevik spokesman on marriage and the family was Friedrich Engels, who wrote that "the modern monogamous family is founded on the open or disguised domestic slavery of women."[6] Engels equated marriage with prostitution and foresaw the demise of the family in the socialist state.

The Effects of the Soviet Policies

It did not take long for the effects of the new policies to appear. The traditional family system was greatly altered and the family itself was weakened. Some of the changes were consistent with socialist ideology and were approved by the government; some unanticipated consequences, however, eventually forced reversal of the earlier policies.

The Emancipation of Women. The Soviet leaders sought complete equality between men and women. "Bourgeois marriage" involved the subjugation of women and was forbidden by socialist morality. Moreover, if women could be induced to rebel against marriage, the threat to the new regime posed by the family would be removed. Too, the Soviet Union needed workers. If women worked outside the home, industrialization would proceed faster.

The marriage laws removed the legal disabilities attached to woman's status. At marriage, she was permitted to adopt the husband's surname, or he could take her surname, or they were permitted to retain their own surnames. Their place of residence had to be fixed by mutual consent. If the husband moved to another location, the wife was under no obligation to follow him. Neither the husband nor the wife was liable for the other's support unless one of them was incapacitated; then the other partner was liable, irrespective of sex. The husband and wife were equally liable for their children and they had equal rights of divorce.

Discrimination in employment was prohibited, and women streamed into factories. They performed manual labor, worked at clerical tasks and, as their educational levels increased, moved into the professions. By 1935, two thirds of all able-bodied women of working age were employed, compared with about two fifths in the United States. By 1940, the percentage of all workers who were women was 38 percent in the Soviet Union, compared with 31 percent in Germany and only 24 per-

6. Friedrich Engels, *The Origin of the Family, Private Property, and the State,* Chicago: Charles H. Kerr and Co., 1902, p. 89.

cent in the United States. By that time, 75 percent of the medical students, 50 percent of the education students, and 23 percent of the engineering students in Russia were women. The peak was reached during World War II when 53 percent of all workers were women. Since then, the proportion has stabilized at just under 50 percent.[7]

The new regime was successful in raising the status of women. The status of women, relative to men, may be higher in the Soviet Union today than anywhere else in the Western world. Some writers point out that this literal equality may mean a heavier burden on women because they must carry most of the reproductive burden along with the work function.[8]

Rise in the Divorce Rate. The unavailability of systematic data makes it impossible to specify the rise in the divorce rate precisely, but the increase was enough to alarm the Soviet leadership. Accounts were published of marriages contracted only for convenience—for example, to qualify for rooms and apartments in the crowded cities—and immediately followed by divorce. A widely circulated story concerned a maiden schoolteacher who, unable to find a husband, offered a sizable sum to a woman friend if she would locate a husband for her. The scheming friend, already married, arranged for her own husband to divorce her and marry the schoolteacher. As soon as she received the money, the husband was then supposed to divorce the schoolteacher. In attacking such practices, the Soviet press gleefully pointed out that the husband decided that he preferred the schoolteacher and remained married to her.

It was reported in *Izvestia* that the divorce rate in Moscow in 1934 was 37 divorces per 100 marriages and in 1935 the rate climbed to 38.3. These figures are believed to be about 50 percent higher than those during the latter part of the czarist period. The regime became concerned about the divorce rate, both as a symptom of the decay of socialist morality and as a contributor to the falling birthrate.

Fall in the Birthrate. The precipitous fall in the birthrate was caused by increases in legalized abortion and divorce. Some 154,000 abortions were performed in Moscow in 1934, whereas only 57,000 children were actually born in the city. In 1935, there were 155,000 abortions to

7. H. Kent Geiger, *The Family in Soviet Russia*, Cambridge, Mass.: Harvard University Press, 1968, p. 178.
8. See Michael P. Sacks, "Unchanging Times: A Comparison of the Everyday Life of Soviet Working Men and Women Between 1923 and 1966," *Journal of Marriage and the Family* 39 (Nov. 1977), pp. 793–805; and Janet S. Schwartz, "Women Under Socialism: Role Definitions of Soviet Women," *Social Forces* 58 (Sept. 1979), pp. 67–88. See also Vladimir Shlapentokh, "The Study of Values as a Social Phenomenon: The Soviet Case," *Social Forces* 61 (Dec. 1982), pp. 403–17.

70,000 live births. About 60 percent of the abortions were done for "social" rather than medical reasons. The alarmed government restricted abortion again in 1936, and the Moscow birthrate for the first half of 1937 doubled over that for the preceding year.

Rise of Hooliganism. In its efforts to destroy the family, the government sought to make wives independent of their husbands and to take much of the socialization of children from parents. Universal primary education was instituted, and the educational level of the population was raised markedly. Part of the schooling consisted of indoctrination in socialist ideology, and this indoctrination was carried out even more vigorously in the youth organizations such as Komsomol and the Pioneers.

Education during the revolutionary years emphasized complete loyalty to the state and attacked religion and the family as sources of corrupt capitalist beliefs. The authority of parents was undermined and, for a time, children actually were encouraged to report counterrevolutionary sentiments on the part of their parents to the authorities. How much open spying developed within families is difficult to say, but we do know that one effect was a rapid increase in what we call juvenile delinquency, and what the Russians call hooliganism.

By 1929, hooliganism was a major problem. Adolescent gangs roamed the cities, making vicious unprovoked attacks on helpless citizens. Vandalism, stealing, robbery, rape, and even murder occurred with increasing frequency.[9]

During the early 1930s, the government began to rethink its family policies. Universal primary education and the raising of the status of women had brought some beneficial results. But they had been accompanied by widespread increases in almost every form of pathology associated with family life. To cope with these unanticipated problems, the regime reversed itself drastically.

Revised Family Policy

The second stage in the Russian family revolution began in the middle 1930s and extended into the 1950s. This was a period of reaction against the radicalism of the postrevolutionary phase. A law outlawing homosexuality, for example, was passed in 1934 and, in 1935, another law made parents responsible for the delinquent acts of their children. Major recodifications occurred in 1936 and again in 1944.[10]

9. Walter D. Connor, "Juvenile Delinquency in the U.S.S.R.: Some Quantitative and Qualitative Indicators," *American Sociological Review* 35 (April 1970), pp. 283–97.
10. Rudolph Schlesinger, *ed., Changing Attitudes in Soviet Russia: The Family in the U.S.S.R.,* London: Routledge & Kegan Paul, 1949.

After 1944, only officially registered marriages were recognized as legal. Common law marriage was outlawed and illegitimacy was reestablished. The fathers of illegitimate children were not liable for their support, and such children had no right to inherit from their fathers.

Requirements for divorce became increasingly strict, until divorce in the Soviet Union became more difficult to get than in the United States. The divorce might be petitioned for by either partner, but both had to be summoned to court and the specific grounds for divorce proved to the court's satisfaction. Even then, the People's Court could not grant the divorce but sought reconciliation of the couple. If that failed, the suit had to be filed again in a higher court. That court might or might not grant the divorce, depending on whether it judged the divorce to be in the interest of the state. The whole process was also quite expensive.

Such measures were characteristic of the period through World War II and until after the death of Joseph Stalin. Then, in the 1950s, the pendulum began to swing the other way. Abortion was made legal again in 1955, apparently largely to stamp out the flourishing illegal abortion practices that existed.

The extreme difficulty of securing divorces came under attack because it was believed that such difficulty encouraged people to enter informal liaisons without having been divorced from their former partners. Recodification came in 1965 when the People's courts were authorized to grant divorces. Subsequently, even court hearings were done away with where neither partner objected and where there were no minor children. In recent years, 85 percent of Russian divorces have been granted by filling out a form at the Registry, with the divorce becoming final after three months.

The Russians also are trying to make marriage more attractive. Although only civil marriage is recognized, great effort is made to make the registration a solemn affair. The Registry offices are large, attractive, and well furnished. The date for the registration of a marriage must be set in advance, and parents and friends are invited to witness the ceremony. Attractive certificates of the registration are issued, and even wedding rings may be used.

In addition to revising its regulations concerning marriage and divorce, the Soviet Union has continued to support the practice of mothers working and has sought to encourage large families. Although the bulk of Soviet women still are engaged in heavy, unskilled work, women now comprise 63 percent of specialists with secondary education and 53 percent of professionals with higher education.[11] Women receive

11. Norton D. Dodge, *Women in the Soviet Economy: Their Role in Economic, Scientific, and Technical Development*, Baltimore: Johns Hopkins University Press, 1966.

two months' paid leave before and after their babies are born. Both factories and collective farms maintain nurseries, and mothers receive time off every three hours to nurse their infants. The state also operates kindergartens for children between the ages of three and eight, where the children receive three full meals and medical care. This may work better in theory than in practice, for Bronfenbrenner reports that only 10 percent of children under two are enrolled in preschool institutions, with the comparable percentage for three- to six-year-olds being 18 percent.[12]

Large families are encouraged through monetary subsidies, beginning with the birth of the fourth child and increasing through the eleventh child. Initial grants are paid as well as monthly payments from the time the child is a year old until he or she reaches the age of five. Obviously, because the payments end at age five, couples cannot expect to produce children for a profit, but the payments do provide some incentive.[13]

The modal family in the Soviet Union today appears to be a two-generation conjugal family. The birthrate continues to decline under the impact of urbanization and industrialization. A three-generation unit also appears to be relatively common. It involves one or more grandparents living with the parents and children, with the grandparents assuming many household and child-care duties. This arrangement nicely relieves the state of much responsibility for the care of both children and oldsters. Such extended units also are advantageous in the cities, where housing is allotted on the basis of family size.

Many a Soviet male has never seen his wife naked, and creative lovemaking is not high on the husband's list of living priorities. Ignorance is partly to blame, and some of that is being overcome by Western influences. One Moscow woman says her "naive, inexperienced husband" has been performing heroically since she showed him a smuggled copy of *The Joy of Sex*. A slowly improving standard of living has had an impact too. Many couples who once made love under the covers in an apartment crowded with relatives now have their own apartments and are more relaxed about sex. Says one such wife: "Now I feel freer to tell my husband what gives me pleasure and what doesn't."

Time, The Weekly Newsmagazine, June 23, 1980, p. 65.

12. Urie Bronfenbrenner, "The Changing Soviet Family," in Michael Gordon, *ed.*, *The Nuclear Family in Crisis: The Search for an Alternative*, New York: Harper & Row, 1972, p. 133.
13. David M. Heer and Judith G. Bryden, "Family Allowances and Population Policy in the U.S.S.R.," *Journal of Marriage and the Family* 28 (Nov. 1966), pp. 514–19.

Final Evaluation of the Soviet Experiment

The Russian attempt to do away with the family is the largest such effort ever made. Unlike the Communist Chinese, who sought to destroy only the extended family, the Russians tried to do away with the family altogether. Significantly, again, this radical effort did not last for more than a generation. The revolution occurred in 1917, and by the early 1930s, the ground was being laid for strengthening the family again. The Soviet family today appears to be remarkably similar to the family in the United States, having many of the same strengths and problems. The great Soviet effort to eliminate the family has ended and few direct results of the effort remain.

THE KIBBUTZ

The American utopian communities were very small, the Russian experiment was on a grand scale, and the kibbutzim fall in between. There are over 240 kibbutzim in Israel, involving some 100,000 members.[14] These kibbutzim are organized into five major federations, one of which—Marxist in ideology and Soviet in inclination—has been most carefully studied. The kibbutz patterns described in this section represent the most completely collectivized and the most antireligious of the kibbutzim.[15]

The kibbutz is an agricultural collective in which virtually all property is collectively owned, work and consumption are collectively organized, there are communal living arrangements, and the rearing of children is assumed by the group. The original kibbutz settlers were middle-class European intellectuals who migrated to Israel and made physical labor the highest vocational goal. Rather than aspiring to upward mobility, these pioneers deliberately created a socialist enterprise in which all persons would experience satisfaction from working the soil.

The kibbutzim date back to the 1880s when Russian Jews established the first collectives in what, at that time, was Palestine. Between 1882 and 1903, some 25,000 Jews migrated to Palestine. Forty thousand more went between 1904 and the start of World War I. After World War I, the migration continued. By 1931, 116,000 more immigrants arrived. Persecution of the Jews under Hitler brought 225,000 more between

14. Rosanna Hertz, "Family in the Kibbutz: A Review of Authority Relations and Women's Status," *Marriage and Family Review* 5 (Summer 1982), pp. 29–50.
15. See Melford E. Spiro, "Is the Family Universal?—The Israeli Case," in Norman W. Bell and Ezra F. Vogel, eds., *A Modern Introduction to the Family* (Rev. ed.), New York: The Free Press, 1968, pp. 68–79.

1932 and 1939. And in 1948, the State of Israel came into being.[16] By 1936, there were 47 kibbutzim in Palestine, by 1948 there were 149, in 1954 the number reached 227.

The kibbutzim range in size from 40 to 50 members to more than 2000 members. The pattern was for a nucleus of original settlers to be joined by other groups who had received some training in kibbutz life and organization. The settlers tended to be young, with men substantially outnumbering women. Each collective was operated as though it were a single large household. A general assembly was the governing body, aided by a secretariat and a series of committees.

Living conditions in the early kibbutzim were austere. One of their goals was the reclamation of arid and barren land on the frontier, necessitating a joint economic effort and a low living standard on the part of members. All income, from whatever source, was paid into the common treasury, which in turn provided a small personal allowance to each member. Clothing was provided from the central supply. The members lived in small rooms—sometimes several persons to a room—in which there was a minimum of furniture and no conveniences. Bathrooms and showers were centrally located and jointly used.

There was a playing down of differences between persons and between the sexes. All work was regarded as noble and rewarding, with physical labor in the fields being the most noble of all. To the extent to which status differences existed, administrative and clerical personnel had lower, not higher, status. In the early stages, women wore masculine clothes and used no makeup or other personal adornment. Women worked in the fields equally with men, and women did military service. Actually, some division of labor by sex emerged quite early. Certain of the heavier agricultural tasks simply could not be handled by women, and women disproportionately became involved in the collective's service enterprises—the nurseries, schools, kitchens, dining rooms, and laundries.

The most distinguishing feature of the kibbutz has been its attitude toward the family and the practices it evolved to implement that attitude. Talmon hypothesizes that "there is a certain fundamental incompatibility between commitment to a radical revolutionary ideology and intense collective identification on the one hand and family solidarity on the other."[17] The kibbutz considered itself to be an effort to revolution-

16. Raphael Patai, *Israel Between East and West: A Study in Human Relations*, Westport, Conn.: Greenwood Press, 1970, pp. 59–72.
17. Yonina Talmon, "The Family in a Revolutionary Movement—the Case of the Kibbutz in Israel," in Meyer F. Nimkoff, *ed., Comparative Family Systems*, Boston: Houghton Mifflin, 1965, pp. 259–86. See also Eliezer Ben-Rafael, "Dynamics of Social Stratification in Kibbutzim," *International Journal of Comparative Sociology* 21 (March–June 1980), pp. 88–100; Orit Ichilov and Schmuel Bar, "Extended Family Ties and the

ize society, and it considered family ties to be incompatible with that goal. Family and kinship are based on ties between the generations and on the passing of tradition from one generation to the next. Revolutionary movements seek to break the ties with the past. Thus, from the beginning, the kibbutz was antifamilistic. It sought to eliminate the family as an institution and as a social group.

Kibbutz Morality

The kibbutz rejected the morality of middle-class European society. That society's values of chastity, lifelong sexual fidelity, a double standard for men and women, and widespread premarital and extramarital intercourse were seen as hypocritical. The kibbutz taught that sexual relationships should reflect physical needs and the emotional relationship between the persons involved. There were to be no barriers to premarital sexual intercourse, and both sexual relationships and marriage should continue only so long as there was a deep emotional relationship. Kibbutz members were seen as free men and women entitled to form and to dissolve relationships at will.

Some people may view such liberal norms as an invitation to license. On the contrary, kibbutz morality was restrained and almost ascetic. In most kibbutzim, there was a disavowal of the erotic and little promiscuity. Nudity was accepted, men and women often slept in the same room without erotic complications, showers were shared, and there was little overt preoccupation with sex. Part of the explanation appears to lie in the conservative family backgrounds of most kibbutz members; ideologically liberal, they remained behaviorally tied to the standards of their upbringing. Important, too, was the commitment to renunciation of physical comfort and pleasure that characterized the kibbutz.

Sexual relationships among youth of high school age generally were frowned on. After that, however, young people were free to become involved without censure. No special notice was taken of these relationships, and no sanction was given to them. After some experimentation, most youth settled down to one partner and became monogamous. At some point in their relationships, they were likely to request that they become a "couple" and have a separate room assigned to them.

Marriage

Marriage, because it implied the development of an ominous solidarity within the kibbutz, was given little support. The couple simply applied

Allocation of Social Rewards in Veteran Kibbutzim in Israel," *Journal of Marriage and the Family* 42 (May 1980), pp. 421–26; and Hyman Tarlo, "Some Socio-Legal Aspects of the Kibbutz," *Jewish Journal of Sociology* 22 (Dec. 1980), pp. 103–23.

for a room and moved into it with no fanfare. In many kibbutzim, there was a shortage of sleeping rooms and the couple might have to wait months for a room. If the shortage was severe, they might also have to accept sharing the room occasionally with another person. There were no restrictions on the right of separation and divorce.

Marriage was accompanied by no discernible shift in status, either for the man or the woman. Wives could keep their maiden names and usually did. Husbands and wives were not allowed to work at the same jobs and often did not even have the same day off. For some time, radios and electrical utensils were not permitted in the rooms, to discourage couples from spending time there. Virtually all free time was supposed to be spent in the public areas, with other members of the collective.

There was avoidance of public acknowledgment of the relationship. The husband and wife often did not eat together but ate with other members, as if to reinforce their primary loyalty to the kibbutz. The word *marriage* was not used. Instead the two people "became a couple." The man referred to his wife as "my young woman" or called her by her given name and vice versa. Public display of affection was considered to be in bad taste and aroused feelings of shame in the participants. Ordinarily, a wedding ceremony was held at the birth of the first child, but only because the state required it for the legitimization of the offspring.

Family and Parental Roles

There was no basis for one spouse to dominate the other. Each remained on the kibbutz rolls as a separate person and continued to receive a personal allowance. They shared equally in the little housework required to keep their room in order, and both parents assumed responsibility for children. Anniversaries and birthdays, which might place unseemly emphasis on family relationships, were not celebrated.

Childrearing was separated as completely as possible from marriage. New-born infants went directly from the hospital to the nursery. From birth, they lived in special children's houses. This arrangement had at least two advantages. First, it permitted children to have a higher standard of living than their parents. In spite of the antifamilistic ideology, children were the means to perpetuation of the collectivist ideology and were highly valued; regardless of what privations parents might undergo, children received the best of food, clothing, and medical care. Separate child-care arrangements also left parents free to work in the community and reduced the number of persons required to care for children.

Children spent some time each day with their parents, usually the afternoon and early evening hours. Parents also went to the nursery to put young children to sleep each night. Saturdays and holidays also brought families together. Emotional relationships between parents and their young children were surprisingly close. The relationship was non-authoritarian, discipline being the function of the persons who supervised the children's upbringing rather than that of the parents. The parents provided security and love and played a crucial role in the psychological development of the child. The relationship between all adults and children was a warm, rewarding one. Children were likely to refer to their parents by their given names instead of by kinship terms, whereas adults referred to all children as "son" and "daughter."

In the children's houses, each age group had its own section. Nurses and teachers were primary sources of indoctrination with the history, norms, and values of the kibbutz. Several writers have pointed out that the relationship among members of each age group became much like that among brothers and sisters in a family. The psychological character of this bond is reflected in the fact that, as they grow to adulthood, these age groups are voluntarily and almost completely exogamous. There are no barriers to marriage within the group, but the young men and women react to one another as though they truly were brothers and sisters.

Thus, in its unique way, the kibbutz went as far as either Oneida or the Soviet Union in attempting to do away with the family. The experiment is still going on today. Moreover, some of the kibbutzim already have lasted longer than either of the other experiments did. Some kibbutz-born children already are adults and, themselves, full-fledged kibbutz members. But the kibbutzim are changing rapidly. The revolutionary fervor of the 1930s and 1940s is fading. As it fades, the kibbutzim are having to accord a more prominent place to the conjugal family.

Emerging Kibbutz Patterns

The kibbutzim began as agricultural collectives, and they still are heavily involved in agriculture. There are now, however, some 350 kibbutz factories, generating about $500 million in 1981.[18] This industrial production has become the chief source of income and is responsible for vastly improved living standards. Private living quarters have become the norm, radios and kitchen facilities are common—private TV sets are becoming so. Many families have some "good" clothes, which are cared

18. Manfred F. Schroeder, "The Kibbutzim Go Industrial," *World Press Review*, July 1981, p. 54.

for at home and treated as private possessions. Afternoon tea in the family quarters is common, and some families eat part or all their meals "at home." Children spend more time with their parents, even going so far as to sleep in the parents' quarters.

Part of what is happening here is the result of a generalized process of differentiation occurring within the kibbutz. The kibbutzim are no longer peopled just by the original pioneers; groups of varying backgrounds and ages have been added. Relationships among the subgroups become complicated by intellectual, religious, political, and economic differences. Hostility develops and social distance widens. With the appearance of differences within the group, the family comes to be assigned a place among the subgroups.

Differentiation within the family itself plays a major role. As long as the kibbutz was peopled predominantly by young persons and gained its recruits primarily through immigration, it did not have to cope with the whole range of family ties. As the kibbutz birthrate rose, generational ties emerged. As parents grow old and children grow to adulthood, these ties become more numerous and more complex. Such ties are reflected in changes in the living quarters. The typical private living quarters may now be a semidetached flat instead of a room. Grandparents may be housed in separate buildings or they may have quarters adjoining those of their children. The ties also are reflected in terminological changes. Parents are more likely to address offspring as "my son" and "my daughter," and the terms "my man" and "my woman" are taking on connotations usually associated with the terms "husband" and "wife."

The relationships among the sabras,[19] as they grow into adulthood also are different from those that prevailed among their parents. There is less deeroticization than formerly. People are dressing more attractively and there is more public display of affection by couples. The sexual norms have become more conservative. Although there still is no taboo on premarital intercourse, promiscuity is strongly discouraged, liaisons tend to be short and to precede marriage immediately, and increasingly couples are not engaging in sex until marriage. Marriage ceremonies, before beginning life together, are becoming common, and wives increasingly take their husbands' names. Divorce is becoming rare.[20]

In short, the antifamilism of the kibbutz movement seems largely to

19. Persons born in Israel.
20. Harvey Peskin, Zvi Giora, and Mordecai Kaffman, "Birth Order in Child-Psychiatric Referrals and Kibbutz Family Structure," *Journal of Marriage and the Family* 36 (Aug. 1974), pp. 615–18; and Yaffa Schlesinger, "Sex Roles and Social Change in the Kibbutz," *Journal of Marriage and the Family* 39 (Nov. 1977), pp. 771–79.

have ended. For a while, the kibbutz appeared to have functioned without the family because the community itself functioned as a family.

ALTERNATIVE LIFE STYLES

The late 1960s and the early 1970s in the United States produced an effort quite different from the utopian experiments in Oneida, Russia, and the kibbutzim to promote alternatives to conventional family living. The movement was diffuse, unorganized, and extremely varied; collectively, it promoted the development of alternative life styles.

The Social Context

The 1960s was a decade of great social turbulence. Black people, joined later by white people, embarked on an aggressive struggle for equality. Originally an offshoot of the civil rights movement, the feminist movement became a major effort in its own right. Then the Vietnam War divided the country as it had seldom been divided before. College students rioted. Drug use spread into the middle classes and young people not only dropped out of college, they dropped out of the "straight" life. Hippie crash pads sprang up all over the country and bizarre communal settlements clustered both in the cities and in isolated rural areas from California to the Appalachians.

Obviously, many factors contributed to the widespread need to reject traditional ways of living and to find new and better ways. Two such factors were an unprecedented demographic phenomenon and the hesitant movement of the nation toward the postindustrial era.

The Demographic Factor. For approximately a decade after World War II, birth rates were very high. Then in 1957, they began to drop, and they are still dropping.

The effects of these changes began to be noticed in 1964 when the babies who had been born in 1947 reached the age of 17, and 17-year olds became the largest single age group in the nation. Each year from 1964 through 1971 saw more people reaching age 17 than had the year before. After 1971, the number of people reaching 17 each year began to drop. It will continue to drop for another decade or so. According to one analyst, this bulge in the teenage segment of the population was far greater than had ever occurred before or is likely to ever happen again.[21]

The impact of this huge number of teenagers and young adults was

21. Daniel P. Moynihan, " 'Peace'—Some Thoughts on the 1960's and 1970's," *Public Interest* 32 (Summer 1973), pp. 3–12.

great. The teen years are years of rebellion against parental authority in particular and societal authority in general. It is the time when teenagers leave the parental home to seek separate identities for themselves. It is also the period of greatest vigor in life. Given these facts, the large-scale emphasis during the late 1960s on creating alternative life styles probably was not an accident. It was a predictable outcome of a situation in which young people were so numerous that their values, their standards, and their way of life had major influence on the whole society.

Toward the Postindustrial Society. The 1960s not only saw unprecedented numbers of teenagers and young adults, they also brought living conditions that alienated young people from the values of the larger society. Casual analysts blamed marriage, arguing that marriage had become irrelevant to the needs of modern society. This analysis was too facile and ignored major social-structural changes that had been proceeding from about the end of World War II.

What happened was that there was a change in the family life cycle that involved the prolongation of adolescence. We refer to adolescence as a stage in social life rather than a stage in physical maturation, although viewed within a longer time frame, even biological adolescence has been lengthening through a lowering of the age of menarche. Socially, the introduction of prepubescent and barely pubescent youth to experiences formerly reserved for older persons was startling. Both vicariously through the mass media and directly through experience, many youngsters of the 1960s, were more knowledgeable about sex and drugs than were adults of a generation earlier.

If adolescence began earlier, however, its prolongation into adulthood was even more dramatic. This came about as the result of the movement of the nation toward a postindustrial stage in which it does not need and cannot use all of its potentially productive adult labor. That the nation was somewhat aware of the problem was revealed by debates concerning whether the work week should be shortened below 40 hours and whether the age for retirement should be lowered from 65.

Universities during the 1950s and 1960s ceased to be just educational institutions and became, figuratively, storehouses for vast numbers of young people for whom there was no place in the adult labor market. Whereas, in earlier times, people generally entered the labor market at about age 18—or if they went to college, at around 22—the situation now changed drastically. Going to college became almost a way of life rather than a brief interlude between childhood and adulthood. Most people began college on schedule, but often they dropped out for a year or two on the way to the B.A. degree. After five or six years at that stage, they entered graduate schools in greatly increased numbers, where, again, they prolonged their stays by dropping out for extended periods and through general procrastination.[22]

The connection between this and the demographic and economic conditions described in the preceding section should be obvious. An affluent society, accommodating itself to tremendous numbers of young people, could afford, as never before, to keep a sizable portion of its young adults in a stage of financial dependence. If we can broaden the concept of adolescence to include those who remained in this limbo between the child world of being educated and the adult world of gainful employment, then there were large groups of 20-, 25-, and 30-year-old adolescents, and some even older than that.

These conditions were ideal for promoting the youth counterculture that emerged during the early 1960s. The leaders of this movement—generally the articulate, idealistic progeny of prosperous parents—had an ambiguous relationship to the adult world that made them especially sensitive to hypocrisy; thus, they joined forces with blacks, other ethnic groups, and the opponents of the Vietnam War. Being essentially free of the necessity of earning a living, they had time to devote to moral causes. Being basically antiacademic and anti-intellectual, they were unfettered by the lessons of history in their enthusiasm for the development of new social forms. For approximately a decade, they experimented conspicuously with alternative life styles, which included group marriage and communal living.

Group Marriage

Group marriages, by definition, involved three or more people in any distribution by sex that functioned as a family, sharing both interpersonal and sexual intimacy. The most common pattern was four adults, usually the members of two former couples. Occasionally, as many as six adults were involved.[23] The average age of the participants was about 30, and they varied widely in income level. Because of public disapproval, most group marriages were at least semisecret, and it is difficult to know how many people actually tried them. There may have been a

---

22. This section closely follows Bennett M. Berger, "The New Stage of American Man—Almost Endless Adolescence," *New York Times Magazine*, Nov. 2, 1969, pp. 32–33, 131–36.
23. Larry L. Constantine and Joan M. Constantine, "Where Is Marriage Going?" *Futurist* (April 1970), p. 44; and James W. Ramey, "Emerging Patterns of Behavior in Marriage: Deviations or Innovations?" *Journal of Sex Research* 8 (Feb. 1972), pp. 6–30.

few thousand of them, but the proportion of the total population was exceedingly small.[24]

Many group marriages combined flexibility in the performance of "masculine" and "feminine" roles within the marriage, with a fairly conventional adaptation to the outside world. The men typically went to their jobs each morning as other husbands did. One or more of the women often held outside employment, too, and sometimes one of them remained at home in the primary housewife and mother role. Whatever the occupational arrangements, the members of group marriages often were committed to equality between the sexes and to the sharing of roles in the home. Men and women often shared meal preparation, cleaning, and child care. One of the explicit goals was to provide extra attention to children—who were believed to thrive on the security provided to them by multiple, more relaxed, less harried parents and who were encouraged to avoid the sexual stereotyping believed inherent in more conventional marriages.

Sharing was intended to characterize all aspects of group marriages. Self-disclosure to other members of the group was emphasized, with intimacy with others and personal growth being the goals. Sex was shared also, with the couples typically pairing off informally or on a regular rotation basis. Group sex appears to have been the exception rather than the rule and, where it existed, to have occurred in marriages that had existed for some time.[25]

The reported advantages of group marriages were several. Men and women could share roles flexibly. There were multiple opportunities for intimacy and personal growth. There was sexual variety. Children could grow up in a nonsexist environment. And it was cheaper to maintain one household than two or three. Nevertheless, after a few years of experimentation, even sympathetic analysts concluded that group marriages had many serious disadvantages.[26]

Secrecy was difficult to maintain and many group marriages were subjected to pressure from neighbors and the community. As children of the couples approached adolescence, they often were shamed by, or morbidly preoccupied with, their parents' sleeping arrangements. Although jealousy among the adults was disapproved, it developed anyway. Some of the jealousy was sexual; some of it was over leadership in the group. As a consequence of all of these things, many group mar-

24. Albert Ellis, "Group Marriage: A Possible Alternative?" in Gorden F. Streib, *ed.*, *The Changing Family: Adaptation and Diversity*, Reading, Mass.: Addison-Wesley, 1973, p. 86.
25. Larry L. Constantine and Joan M. Constantine, "Sexual Aspects of Multilateral Relations," *Journal of Sex Research* 7 (Aug. 1971), p. 214.
26. Larry L. Constantine, and Joan M. Constantine, "Where Is Marriage Going?" *op. cit.*; and Albert Ellis, *op. cit.*, p. 82.

riages broke up after a while, their members sometimes returning to conventional married living, sometimes divorcing their legal spouses, and sometimes going on to try other alternative life styles.

Group marriages, or something approximating them, probably have been tried by occasional sets of couples in many times and places. The late 1960s and early 1970s in the United States undoubtedly saw them tried on a larger scale and publicized more than ever before. By the mid-1970s, however, one expert reported, "The majority of them don't work, or they work only for a limited time—a year, two years, four years. They fall apart because of the tremendous complexities . . . the sexual interaction is the least important confusion; they can handle that. It's the other interpersonal relationships—dominance, money, child care, for example—that aren't so simple to contend with."[27]

Group marriages still exist and, undoubtedly, they will continue to do so.[28] Their numbers were never large, however, and are much smaller today than they were a few years ago. They may continue to provide an alternative life style for a small minority, but the challenge they provided to more conventional family living has passed.

Communal Living

Experiments with communal living have a longer and much more explicit history than does group marriage, as evidenced by the discussions of the Chinese family, Oneida, the Russian family experiment, and the kibbutzim. Currently in the United States, there are also a variety of religious communes, many of which are intensely familistic and fiercely monogamous.[29] Our discussion will be limited to the groups that emerged during the 1960s and that sought to eliminate conventional family living.

Communal-living groups differ from group marriages in several important respects. First, they are larger, ranging from half a dozen to 200 people or even more. Second, communes often seek to provide a total way of life, minimizing contacts with the surrounding community. Third, the distinctions between men's and women's work may almost be obliterated. Fourth, many communes strive for economic self-sufficiency. And, fifth, private property, including possessiveness of people, usually is disavowed.

As with group marriages, no one knows precisely how many com-

27. Wardell B. Pomeroy, "Playboy Panel: New Sexual Life Styles," *Playboy*, Sept. 1973, p. 86.
28. Shelley Ann Peabody, "Alternative Life Styles to Monogamous Marriage: Variants of Normal Behavior in Psychotherapy Clients," *Family Relations* 31 (July 1982), pp. 425–34.
29. Benjamin Zablocki, *The Joyful Community*, Baltimore: Penguin Books, 1971.

munes sprang up in the United States during the late 1960s and early 1970s. A *New York Times* survey in 1971 turned up some 2000 communes in 34 different states. At about the same time, an estimate from the National Institute of Mental Health put the number at approximately 3000. Whichever the correct figure, a moment's computation will demonstrate that not more than a few hundredths of 1 percent of the U.S. population was involved.

The advantages claimed for commune living were essentially those claimed by group marriages, only more so: the complete sharing of relationships and possessions, personal growth and development, and freedom from the hang-ups of conventional society. For a while, at least, some members of some communes appeared to achieve these goals.[30] By the mid-1970s, however, the number of such communes had shrunk drastically, and many of the remaining ones, particularly around college campuses, had come to emphasize their cost-sharing arrangements more than their ideologies.

Many communes were unstable. People moved into them and moved out again, without staying long. Many members came from broken marriages; other marriages broke under the pressures of commune living. Where stable, monogamous marriages persisted, there were often tensions between them and other commune members. Many of the communes, themselves, survived for only a few months or a few years.

The communal ideal of economic self-sufficiency was not often achieved. Leather goods shops, farms, health food stores and restaurants, candle-making operations, and other such enterprises were established, but a sustained work ethic was not part of the communal value system. The work often did not get done, and most communes depended heavily on outside support. Members applied for unemployment compensation, surplus commodities, and food stamps. They went on welfare. And they welcomed divorcees with alimony checks and child-support payments. For a while, such precarious circumstances lent excitement to the venture but eventually threatened the stability of the group.

The highly valued sexual freedom and sharing also created problems.[31] Sometimes, sex became an unofficial arena of competition, with

30. Betty E. Cogswell, "Variant Family Forms and Life Styles: Rejection of the Traditional Nuclear Family," *Family Coordinator* 24 (Oct. 1975), pp. 391–406; Teresa Donati Marciano, "Variant Family Forms in a World Perspective," *Family Coordinator* 24 (Oct. 1975), pp. 407–20; and Rosabeth Moss Kanter, Dennis Jaffe, and D. Kelly Weisberg, "Coupling, Parenting, and the Presence of Others: Intimate Relationships in Communal Households," *Family Coordinator* 24 (Oct. 1975), pp. 433–52.
31. Patrick W. Conover, "An Analysis of Communes and Intentional Communities with Particular Attention to Sexual and Genderal Relations," *Family Coordinator* 24 (Oct. 1975), pp. 453–64.

some members of each sex becoming defined as more desirable than others. Some had their self-concepts enhanced by being sought after, whereas others suffered the pain of not being wanted and the deprivation that results from not being entitled to claim the sexual favors of some other person.

Most communes also had difficulty with, or did not confront, the generational problem. Childbirth was an important ceremonial event in which the whole commune participated, but after the first few months, the care of babies and small children was usually left to their often-disillusioned mothers. Few communes lasted long enough to have to face the problem of educating older children. Finally, there were few older people in these communes. The emphasis was on youth, and there was no place for grandparents and other elders.[32]

The unprecedented social upheaval that began in the 1960s was all but over by the mid-1970s.[33] The Vietnam War was ended, and the population center of gravity had moved up from the teen years. It is clear that although, undoubtedly, a limited number of communes and group marriages still exist in the United States, the social movement toward these types of family forms has ended at least for the present. What they have pointed out to us, however, is that the term *family* is not limited to a single definition. It is broad enough to encompass a wide spectrum of variant forms, each capable of handling the needs of the people involved. Some of these such as cohabitation, single-parent families, and stepfamilies, we shall be discussing in subsequent chapters. For the present, there is an alternative life style that merits discussion as a growing movement in the United States—that of homosexual couples.

Homosexual Couples

Although controversial, the fact remains that there is an outspoken and visible movement toward the acknowledgement and acceptance of homosexual rights. This is particularly true on college campuses today[34] and in sections of the country where this nontraditional life style is openly accepted. In San Francisco, considered the mecca for homosexuals, single adults now outnumber the married, and homosexuals make

32. Robert C. Hauhart, "Children in Communes: Some Legal Implications of a Modern Life Style," *Family Coordinator* 26 (Oct. 1977), pp. 367–71; and Thomas H. Shey, "Why Communes Fail: A Comparative Analysis of the Viability of Danish and American Communes," *Journal of Marriage and the Family* 39 (Aug. 1977), pp. 605–13.
33. James L. Spates, "Counterculture and Dominant Culture Values: A Cross-National Analysis of the Underground Press and Dominant Culture Magazines," *American Sociological Review* 41 (Oct. 1976), pp. 868–83.
34. Gerald Lubenow, "Gays and Lesbians on Campus," *Newsweek*, April 5, 1982, pp. 75–77.

up 15 to 20 percent of the population.[35] Because homosexuality is an un-conventional life style, it is impossible to know with any certainty what proportion of the population is actively involved in it. Also, the grow-ing body of research on gay couples is based on self-selected samples, that is, those willing to acknowledge their sexual preferences and openly discuss their life styles. For these reasons, it is difficult to generalize the information gathered as to the general homosexual population. There is, however, a growing body of research on homosexual couples, and it is that research we want to discuss.

Contrary to popular belief, gay (male) and lesbian (female) relation-ships are not based on the belief that one partner should be dominant and the other passive. Peplau reports that homosexual dyads tend to re-semble a best friend relationship.[36] Roles, duties, and responsibilities are shared on a more or less equal basis, constantly shifting between the partners as needs arise. The respondents in Peplau's sample report that one great advantage to homosexual relationships is that they reject the restrictive role playing that traditional marriage is based on and feel free to share everything that living together entails.

Another myth surrounding homosexuals is the notion that they en-gage in widespread promiscuity. Movies often portray gay men cruising bars night after night seeking seemingly endless one-night stands. Al-though this may be true of a minority of homosexuals, as it is true of some heterosexuals, a large number of lesbians and gays enjoys durable, long-lasting relationships based on affection, love, and companionship.[37]

Although love does not always ensure that same-sex relationships will continue, neither can heterosexual couples predict the course of their future together. Relationships can and do break apart, regardless of sex-ual preferences. If some same-sex dyads are of a shorter duration, a rea-son for this might be that there exist fewer barriers to ending relation-ships. Rarely is one partner financially dependent on the other; there are seldom legal formalities to go through; and same-sex partners do not produce children for whom they could claim custody rights.

Apart from public disapproval, the issue of children is a factor that appears to present some homosexuals great disappointment in their lives.

35. *Time*, December 13, 1982, p. 74.
36. Letitia Anne Peplau, "What Homosexuals Want in Relationships," *Psychology Today*, March 1981, pp. 28–34, 37–38. See also Letitia Anne Peplau, Susan Cochran, Karen Rook, and Christine Padesky, "Loving Women: Attachment and Autonomy in Lesbian Relationships," *Journal of Social Issues* 34 (Summer 1978), pp. 7–27.
37. Alan P. Bell and Martin S. Weinberg, *Homosexualities*, New York: Simon & Schus-ter, 1978; Joseph Harry, "The 'Marital' Liaisons of Gay Men," *Family Coordinator* 28 (Oct. 1979), pp. 622–29; Serena Nanda and J. Scott Francher, "Culture and Homosex-uality, *Eastern Anthropologist* 33 (April–June 1980), pp. 139–52; and Siegrid Schaefer, "Sociosexual Behavior in Male and Female Homosexuals," *Archives of Sexual Behavior* 6 (Dec. 1977), pp. 355–67.

The desire to have and raise children leads many lesbians and gays into heterosexual marriages. Although studies of lesbian mothers are few, evidence indicates that at least 25 percent of self-identified gay men father children.[38] This number, undoubtedly, underestimates the actual occurrence in the general population. Although there is great apprehension about the deleterious effects of gay parents on their young children, the facts do not support these fears.[39] Homosexual fathers do not molest their children nor do they have a disproportionate number of gay children. Relationships between children and gay fathers even appear to improve as the parents move from an unhappy heterosexual marriage into an openly gay one. The most important factor in a good parent-child relationship appears to be the parent's openness and honesty with the child about coming out.

There is a growing realization that sexual preference does not affect the ability to be a good parent. For a long time, homosexuals virtually had no chance of being awarded custody of their children at the time of divorce. Today, about 15 percent of lesbian mothers are awarded custody of their children.[40] Gay fathers are now actively seeking custody of their children, and the incidence of homosexual couples seeking to adopt is growing. In New York City and San Francisco, homosexuals are fighting hard to gain the same legal rights that are granted to married couples, including health and other spousal benefits, for their partners.[41] What precedents these efforts will set or what the future outcomes will be is impossible to say at this point. What is clear is that individuals are beginning to confront the question of sexual options and those who choose homosexuality are finding a growing subculture that is supportive, or at least tolerant, of this alternative life style.

SUMMARY

The Oneida Community was founded in 1848 by John Humphrey Noyes, with whose life and teachings the community is inseparably linked. Noyes preached perfectionism and saw monogamous marriage and private property as barriers to the unselfishness required by the perfectionist doctrine. Complex marriage was based on the assumption that all men should love all women and vice versa. Young men were initiated

38. M. Saghir and E. Robins, *Male and Female Homosexuals*, Baltimore: Williams & Wilkins, 1973; and Martin S. Weinberg and C. J. Williams, *Male Homosexuals*, New York: Oxford University Press, 1974.
39. Brian Miller, "Gay Fathers and Their Children," *Family Coordinator* 28 (Oct. 1979), pp. 544–52.
40. Brenda Maddox, "Homosexual Parents," *Psychology Today*, February 1982, pp. 62, 66–69.
41. *Time*, December 13, 1982, p. 74.

into sex by older women, young women by older men, according to the principle of ascendance. Only persons approved by a committee were entitled to become parents. Children were reared apart from their parents. The community prospered financially but encountered resistance from the surrounding society. Children of the community were ridiculed by outsiders, and there were rumors of legal prosecution of adults. Some of the children failed to accept the teachings of the community. In 1877, Noyes resigned as leader, and by 1880 the community had broken up.

The Soviet family experiment followed the Bolshevik Revolution, and lasted into the 1930s. The Soviets sought to do away with the family as a corrupt bourgeois institution. Marriage and divorce became simple matters of registration. Abortion was made legal, birth control was encouraged, and children were urged to break ties with parents who evidenced counterrevolutionary tendencies. By the middle 1930s, a reverse trend had set in. Rising divorce rates, falling birthrates, and rampant juvenile delinquency were by-products the Soviets had not counted on. Laws from 1936 to 1944 reemphasized the solemnity and permanence of marriage and made divorce very difficult. The equality of women was upheld, and allowances were provided to parents of large families. The Soviet Union now sees a stable family as a bulwark of socialism.

The kibbutzim are agricultural collectives in Israel. Communistic in ideology, they sought to eliminate the family as a competing source of identification. All production and consumption were collectivized and all kinship ties were discouraged. Marriage virtually was done away with, couples simply applying for a room when they wished to make their relationships permanent. Relationships also could be dissolved at will. Children were reared in groups apart, visiting their parents at prescribed times. Time has seen changes in the kibbutzim. Marriage has become somewhat regularized, more adequate quarters have been provided for families, and more functions are being transferred to the home. Extended family relationships are being formed, and contact with kin outside of the kibbutz is increasing.

The 1960s saw a major effort to promote alternatives to family living in the United States. Changing birthrates had produced, relatively, the largest group of teenagers the nation had ever seen, and the teen years are years of rebellion and physical and intellectual vigor. The nation was also moving toward a postindustrial stage in which the labor of many young people was not needed. Social adolescence was prolonged, with resulting chaos.

Group marriages constituted one alternative life style. They were intended to promote unselfishness and sharing, variety in sexual experience, and interpersonal intimacy. They also had financial advantages. Such marriages encountered major problems however. There was harassment from neighbors and the community. Young children often thrived on the attention they received from multiple parents, but teenage children often were upset by their parents' arrangements. Sexual and interpersonal jealousy also developed. The complexity of group marriage proved almost overwhelming, and few of them lasted for more than a year or two.

Communal living attracted other people. These communes generally abolished private property and sought financial self-sufficiency. They also believed in the open sharing of persons and relationships. In addition to serious financial problems, many of them were also plagued by high membership turnover. As in group marriages, sexual and personal rivalries developed. Children posed special problems, and there were few older people in communes.

Compared with heterosexual marriages, homosexual relationships may be based on egalitarian principles, with both partners sharing duties and responsibilities. Promiscuity is characteristic of some gays, but most engage in steady relationships with one partner. The desire for children leads many gays and lesbians into heterosexual marriages. Children appear to be quite accepting of gay parents, and there is a growing movement among gays to gain custody of their children, adopt children, and to gain the same benefits for their partners that spouses would be entitled to.

SUGGESTED READINGS

Bell, Alan P., Weinberg, Martin S., and Hammersmith, Sue Kiefer, *Sexual Preference: Its Development in Men and Women*, Bloomington: Indiana University Press, 1981. This report from the Kinsey Institute suggests that homosexuality may be determined before birth and is not influenced by factors in the home.

Gerson, Menachem, *Family, Women, and Socialization in the Kibbutz*, Boston: Lexington Books, 1978. Examines the psychological factors determining the role of the family and the status of women in second-generation kibbutzim.

Kephart, William M., *Extraordinary Groups: The Sociology of Unconventional Life-Styles*, New York: St. Martin's Press, 1976. A fascinating account of several experimental communities and life styles: Oneida, the Old Order Amish, the Father Divine Movement, the Shakers, the Mormons, the Hutterites, and contemporary communes.

Lapidus, Gail Warshovsky, *Women in Soviet Society: Equality, Development, and Social Change*, Berkeley: University of California Press,

1978. Bolshevik ideology has had less to do with the status of women in Russia than has the dual burden of work at lower status occupations combined with childbearing and childrearing.

Macklin, Eleanor D., and Rubin, Roger H., eds., *Contemporary Families and Alternative Lifestyles: Handbook on Research & Theory*, Beverly Hills, Calif.: Sage Publications, 1983. A synthesis of theory and research concerning the wide variety of family forms.

Robertson, Constance Noyes, *Oneida Community: The Breakup, 1876–1881*, Syracuse, N.Y.: Syracuse University Press, 1972. A sequel to the volume cited in the chapter, covering the final years of the experiment.

Spiro, Melford E., *Gender and Culture: Kibbutz Women Revisited*, Durham, N.C.: Duke University Press, 1979. One of the original investigators of kibbutz life finds that the effort to transform traditional sex roles has failed.

FILMS

Blackjack's Family (G. V. Hood Films, P.O. Box 22213, Milwaukee, Ore. 97222), 53 minutes. A documentary about a former communal couple's efforts to find their own solutions to universal family problems.

A Great Family on a Collective Farm (National Council of American-Soviet Friendship, 156 Fifth Avenue, New York, N.Y. 10010), 20 minutes. The daily life of a family with 6 children and 30 grandchildren on a prosperous collective farm. Methods of payment to farmers and collective social services are discussed.

Serafima Kotova (National Council of American-Soviet Friendship, 156 Fifth Avenue, New York, N.Y. 10010), 20 minutes. Pictorial story of a Soviet woman made an orphan in World War II. Mrs. Kotova works in a textile mill where she is now a forelady. She is also a Deputy of the Supreme Soviet of the Soviet Federation. Film shows her relationships with her husband and her young son.

The Year of the Communes (Association-Sterling Films, 866 Third Avenue, New York, N.Y. 10022), 52 minutes. A survey of communes, ranging from the ascetic to the hedonistic. Honest, beautifully filmed, and informative.

QUESTIONS AND PROJECTS

1. Describe the role of John Humphrey Noyes in the development of the Oneida Community. What is meant by, "Noyes was a charismatic leader"?

2. What factors led to the breakup of the Oneida Community? What are the implications of the Oneida experience for family sociology?

3. Why was the Soviet regime opposed to the family? What steps did it take to eliminate the family?

4. What were the effects of the Soviet family legislation of the 1920s on

divorce rates and birthrates? On the status of women? On juvenile delinquency?

5. Sketch briefly the history of the kibbutzim. Describe the economic organization, the level of living, and the ideology of the traditional kibbutz.

6. What has been the long-term kibbutz experience in attempting to do away with the family? What trends appear likely in the kibbutz in the future?

7. How was the decade of the 1960s in the United States demographically unique? What impact did that uniqueness have on the nation?

8. Trace the ways in which social adolescence was prolonged over the past two or three decades. How is this a function of movement toward a postindustrial society?

9. Differentiate between group marriages and communes in terms of: (a) size, (b) clarity of boundaries, (c) sex roles, (d) attitude toward property, and (e) stability.

10. What special problems did communes encounter in the areas of: (a) finances, (b) operationalizing the communal value system, (c) sex and jealousy, and (d) children?

11. Why is it difficult to gather information on homosexual couples? How are homosexual relationships different from heterosexual ones? How are they similar? What rights are homosexuals seeking to obtain?

II

Historical and Theoretical Perspectives

David Strickler, Monkmeyer

6
History of the Western Family

It is likely that some form of marriage *must* form the basis of a large social structure. For civilization to continue, new generations must be born and nurtured, educated and civilized. . . . The forms that family patterns take are multivariate, and are only partially constructed by the individual members. Society and culture place powerful constraints on certain features of any design; for instance, on the roles of men and women within the family, on the presence or absence of children, on sexual conduct, etc. Some of the means by which these constraints operate are laws about marriage, divorce, inheritance, and sex, family pressures to conform, one's own previous enculturation, and a multitude of other overt and covert measures. . . . The family will probably endure, in one form or another, as long as humanity exists.[1]

Change in the Western family has been rapid and continuous. We can trace our family system back 3000 years or so and learn a great deal about how the American family functions today. During that 3000 years, the focus shifts many times and the family changes from a strongly patriarchal, patrilineal, patrilocal, polygynous one to a nearly equalitarian, monogamous, bilateral, conjugal one.

THE ANCIENT HEBREW FAMILY SYSTEM

The family system of the ancient Hebrews is the earliest direct antecedent of our own system about which there is comprehensive knowledge. The earliest Hebrew records go back approximately 4000 years. Not surprisingly, the earliest records are fragmentary and difficult to interpret. By the dawn of history, the Hebrews were a nomadic desert

1. James L. McCary, *Freedom and Growth in Marriage* (2nd ed.), New York: John Wiley & Sons, 1980, pp. 4–5.

people with a pastoral economy. They roamed the countryside seeking pasture for their herds and maintaining an elaborate kinship organization. Beyond the family, there was a *sib*, a group of kinsmen related through males (a patrilineal descent group), and a *clan*, which included the wives as well. Several related clans made up a *tribe*, and 12 tribes constituted the nation of Israel.[2]

By about the twelfth century before Christ, the Hebrews began to develop agriculture and to settle in towns. The old tribal organization was gradually replaced by a more centralized organization around a king.

During the nomadic period, the Hebrew family was patriarchal, patrilineal, patrilocal, polygynous, and extended. There is evidence of a quite different form of organization before recorded history,[3] and the patriarchy was considerably modified as settled agriculture developed.

Patriarchy

The Hebrew family was a strong patriarchy, the authority of the father being nearly absolute. All women were under the control of one or more men, the only exception being a widowed mother. Sons were trained in obedience to their mother; other women were considered to be a man's property.[4] The husband could put his wife to death for adultery but not for any other reason. All of this implies a low status for women, and their status *was* low. Yet there is little evidence that women were abused. On the contrary, wives were highly regarded and often wielded great power. Marriages often were made to cement ties between two extended families, and the wife's family retained an interest in her welfare.

The father had even greater power over his children. The familiar story of Abraham's near sacrifice of Isaac indicates that he held the power of life and death. Hebrew children were expected to be obedient

2. Stuart O. Queen and Robert W. Habenstein, *The Family in Various Cultures*, Philadelphia: J. B. Lippincott, 1974, pp. 153–59.
3. Some scholars believe that the Hebrew family once was both matrilineal and matrilocal. The generations of Esau are traced, in Genesis, through his wives rather than through himself, and Leah and Rachel are referred to as the women who did "build the house of Israel." The incest taboos permitted the marriage of half brothers and sisters where the common parent was the father but not where the common parent was the mother. Certain of the patriarchs and their wives are also known to have lived with their wives' fathers over long periods of time. See Queen and Habenstein, *ibid.*, p. 157; and Panos D. Bardis, "Family Forms and Variations Historically Considered," in Harold T. Christensen, *ed., Handbook of Marriage and the Family*, Chicago: Rand McNally, 1964, p. 416.
4. Willystine Goodsell, *A History of Marriage and the Family*, New York: Macmillan, 1939, p. 54.

and respectful, and the Mosaic law provided that persistently disobedient children should be put to death. That there was some limitation on the father's power is indicated by the fact that a stubborn or gluttonous son was to be stoned by his fellow Israelites after the father had testified against him; but he was not to be killed by the father himself.[5]

The father could marry off his children and could sell their labor. Theoretically, the young persons' consent to marriage was required, but they seldom refused. The father's power again was restricted, in that he was forbidden to make his daughter a prostitute,[6] and could not sell his children to foreigners (non-Hebrews).

Polygyny

The Hebrews practiced polygyny and concubinage. Several wives were common among patriarchs and kings, additional concubines being taken from among servant and slave girls. One rationalization for concubinage was the high value placed on sons. Barren wives might give their female servants to their husbands as concubines, claiming the children as their own. Concubines were treated well and sometimes were raised to the status of wife after a wife died. Children of concubines could inherit, although not so much as children of wives.

Polygyny was not without problems, although it did not yield completely to monogamy until the Middle Ages. Some jealousy developed among wives and concubines, and it was common for each wife and her children to have a separate dwelling.[7] Sororal polygyny helped to keep antagonisms in check. The vast majority of Hebrews must have been monogamous of course. Beyond the biological facts of the sex ratio, the custom of bride price restricted polygyny to the well-to-do.

Betrothal and Marriage

According to Talmudic law, the minimum ages for marriage was 13 for boys and 12 for girls. Fathers could betroth children at younger ages, but the nuptials could not take place until they became of age. In earliest times, betrothal was regarded as the beginning of marriage even though the marriage was not consummated until later;[8] sometimes nuptials were not even held.

5. Deuteronomy 21:18–21.
6. Leviticus 19:29.
7. Genesis 31:33.
8. Sexual intercourse with a person other than the betrothed was regarded as adultery and was punished as such.

Gradually, betrothal became distinct from marriage and, when the parties were of age, one year commonly elapsed between betrothal and marriage. Betrothal took two forms: the transfer of money or the preparation of a written instrument. *Kaseph* involved the man giving a coin to the woman and saying, "Be thou consecrated to me." Kaseph is believed to be a symbol of the earlier explicit wife purchase. The other ceremony, *kiddushin,* involved the man's giving the woman a document that probably read, "I do hereby betroth thee according to the law of Moses and Israel." Two witnesses were required in both cases, and a benediction was given by the bride's father or by a rabbi.

The marriage ceremony was a private family affair in which the bride was transported to the groom's house to receive the benediction. A rabbi was not required, but 10 witnesses were necessary. By the first century B.C., the *ketubah,* or marriage contract, came to be separate from the betrothal agreement. In addition to the vows, the *ketubah* stated the bride price, or *mohar,* it enumerated the property the bride brought to the marriage (the dowry); it defined the mode of inheritance in case no children were born; and it specified the wife's right to support from her husband and his obligation to have sexual intercourse regularly with her.[9]

Marriage was highly valued; to remain celibate was a religious crime. There are many reasons for the high value put on marriage. First, it was designed to produce sons so that a man's house "should not die out of Israel." Second, marriage was a more acceptable alternative than illicit sexual activity.[10] Third, the Hebrews were keepers of herds and flocks, and children, especially sons, were economic assets.

The importance of sons was institutionalized in the levirate. If a man died without sons, the widow was expected to marry the deceased husband's brother. The first son born was then regarded as the offspring of the deceased brother. Because the Hebrews were polygynous, the levirate was possible even if the brother were already married. The only way that the brother could escape the duty of the levirate was to humiliate himself through the custom of *chalitza,* according to which the widow loosened the brother's shoe, spat in his face, and accused him of

9. The husband's obligation to have regular sexual intercourse with each of his wives placed a practical limitation on the number of wives a man could take. Both husband and wife could be fined if they failed in their marital duties. More important than the right to sexual satisfaction was the importance attached to having children. If sexual intercourse were not had regularly, the production of children would be threatened.

10. Sexual attitudes among the Hebrews were characterized by prudery and by preoccupation with avoiding prostitution and perversion. Nudity was regarded as shameful; only foreign women were acceptable as prostitutes; sodomy was considered repulsive yet may have been widely practiced. Students will recall the story of Lot and the destruction of the cities of Sodom and Gomorrah.

failing to do his duty to his brother—all in a public ceremony. The levirate prevailed among the Hebrews well into the Middle Ages.[11]

Descent and Inheritance

By the time of the patriarchs, patrilineal descent and inheritance were well established. During the earliest period, there was something very close to complete primogeniture. The eldest son received the father's blessing and inherited almost all of the property. During this period, daughters did not inherit.

Later, as agriculture developed, the eldest son received a double portion, with the other sons inheriting equally.[12] If there was no son, property passed to the daughters; if there were no children, it passed to brothers or uncles.[13] Sometimes, if there were no sons, the patriarch would marry his daughter to a male slave and make the slave his heir.[14] Property, thus, passed from patriarch to grandson, with the slave as intermediary.

Divorce

Until nearly the time of Christ, the Hebrew husband had almost unlimited power to divorce his wife. The Mosaic law provided, simply, that the husband should hand his wife a bill of divorcement stating, "Be thou divorced from me," and send her out of the house.[15]

Over the centuries, resistance developed to the husband's power to repudiate his wife and, by the time of Christ, the authorities would accept divorce only on certain grounds: adultery, indecency, refusal to cohabit, barrenness, change of religion, refusal to observe ritual laws, and insulting the husband. Gradually, the wife also gained rights of divorce. By the Roman period, the wife could divorce her husband for: impotence, change of religion, refusal to support her, commission of a serious crime, extreme dissoluteness, and affliction with a loathsome dis-

11. The crime of Onan (onanism), which is widely regarded today as masturbation, was actually Onan's refusal to impregnate his brother's widow. In his relations with the widow, Onan practised coitus interruptus.

12. Deuteronomy 21:15–18.

13. Numbers 27:1–11.

14. The extended family often was quite large. In addition to the patriarch, his wives and concubines, their unmarried children, married sons and their wives and children, there often were servants and slaves. And sometimes, even nonrelatives who had placed themselves under the authority of the patriarch. Servants and slaves were well treated—almost as family members. Consequently, taking a slave as a son-in-law and heir did not seem too unusual.

15. Deuteronomy 24:1–2.

ease (leprosy). At first, the wife could not divorce a husband for adultery. Later, the rabbis secured power to separate couples either for adultery or barrenness.

Women who were unjustly divorced did not suffer greatly. They became free agents. They were no longer under the power of their fathers or their husbands. They were also entitled to the return of their dowries, which provided them with an income. If they were divorced for cause however—and the causes were by modern standards trivial—then they lost their dowries and suffered loss of status as well.

The Gradual Development of Public Control

The traditional Hebrew family was an organization of great strength and unity. It existed in a social context where there were no other elaborately developed institutions. Political power was held largely by patriarchs; the economy was rudimentary; even religion was primarily a family matter. The patriarch served as priest at worship and presided over ceremonial activities.[16] There was not yet a separate class of rabbis. Under these conditions, the family performed many functions and was a strong and stable unit.

Gradually, with the development of agriculture, other sources of power developed. In the eighth century B.C., Israel was conquered by the Assyrians. Then, in the sixth century B.C., came the Babylonian conquest, and eventually Israel fell under the power of Rome. The public authorities, as they expanded control over the society, undertook increasing regulation of marriage and family matters.

Gradually, too, a class of religious functionaries—the rabbis—emerged. At first, the rabbis did not challenge the power of the patriarchs. But gradually, they interpreted the Scriptures to limit the power of husbands over wives and of fathers over children. A body of rabbinical law became the foundation for marriage and family life.

The changes brought about by public authorities and rabbis are illustrated by the transformation of the custom of wife purchase and the accompanying changes in the status of women. In earliest times, husbands apparently purchased wives outright—almost as they would cattle. Gradually, bride price became compensation to the girl's father for loss of her services and a guarantee of her good treatment. The bride price was paid either in service or in money. During this period, women were regarded as chattels.

The rabbis sought to protect women through the marriage contract.

16. There is a possibility that in prehistory the Hebrews were ancestor worshippers. The graven images of the Old Testament are thought to be symbols of ancestors. Moreover, the family burial ground was a sacred place.

The *ketubah* spelled out the economic interests and rights of both families. As the rabbis took control of marriages, the parties became less the two families and more the particular man and woman. The *ketubah* listed the bride price, which was gradually transformed into a dower right—money or property to be held for the wife in the event of the husband's death or her unjust divorce. The dowry, too—essentially the wife's family's economic contribution to the marriage—was listed. The husband was given life use (usufruct) of the dowry but, again, the wife retained interest in it and might have it returned if she were divorced by her husband.

THE ANCIENT GREEK FAMILY SYSTEM

Description of the family system of ancient Greece is complicated both by continuous social change and by differences between Athens and Sparta. During the earliest (Homeric) period, Greece's economy was mainly agricultural, and its family system reflected that economic base. The family was a strong patriarchy in which divorce was uncommon. Beyond the extended family there was the *gens*, a clan consisting of all the extended families that traced descent from a common ancestor. The *gens* established the legitimacy of children, prevented the alienation of land, and saw to it that legitimate heirs were provided. The dominant family patterns became those of the cities of Athens and Sparta. During the Golden Age of Greece, its family system was an urban one, which evolved from its patriarchal land-oriented precursor.

Athens was an aristocratic state in which the cultivation of knowledge was highly regarded. Most of the Greek contributions to philosophy, literature, architecture, and engineering originated here. The Athenians also emphasized athletic skills, but Sparta made virtually a fetish of these. The Spartans were militaristic, emphasizing the production of warriors. Spartan boys at the age of seven generally left their parental homes to live in military-style barracks, where they underwent arduous physical training and where they continued to live during most of their adult lives. The separation of husbands and wives entailed by this existence produced different relationships between the sexes than in Athens. Spartan women were freer, more aggressive, and more nearly equal with their husbands.

Patriarchy

The Greek father, like his Hebrew counterpart, was exceedingly powerful. Unlike the Hebrew, however, the Greek father did not hold power in his own right. His power derived from his position as trustee of the family estates and from his role as priest in the worship of ancestors. Membership in the family was based on being eligible to worship the ancestors and coming under control of the family head.

Athenian men dominated women almost completely. Women were defined as biologically, intellectually, and emotionally inferior. They were minors who had no legal status, were poorly educated, and were inadequate companions to their learned husbands. Mature men of about 30 often were married to adolescent girls. Once married, a woman was confined to the women's apartments and unable to leave the house without permission. On the streets, she had to be veiled and accompanied by a slave chaperone. When her husband had guests, she was not permitted to eat with them. The husband held power of life and death over his wife only for adultery. If he discovered his wife and her lover in the act, the husband could kill them. If he did not kill his wife immediately, he could only beat her and confine her to the house.

Spartan wives also occupied a very inferior position and were treated without sentiment. There was almost no wedding ceremonial. The bride was taken forcibly to the groom's house,[17] where a servant cut her hair in ragged boyish style, dressed her in men's clothing and shoes, and left her in the dark to await her husband. The husband visited her for sexual purposes and little else. Even in their sexual relationship, the emphasis was on the production of heirs and not on physical and emotional satisfaction. For companionship and pleasure, the husband turned to a special class of women who were available for the purpose.

The father's power over children was even more extreme. In the early period, he could expose (desert) infants, sell their labor, and bestow them in marriage. The father may have had authority to determine whether any child lived or died. Probably, the right to expose an infant was linked to the emphasis on healthy children who could inherit property and carry on the family line. Exposure seems to have been limited mainly to illegitimate and deformed or sickly children. Girls were more likely to be exposed than boys. Girls could not serve in the military, and their marriage carried heavy dowry obligations.

During the early period, the father could sell both sons and daughters. He probably could not sell them into genuine slavery but rather into indentured servitude while they were growing up. Even this power was eventually restricted.

In the early period, too, sons remained under the father's control as

17. There are references in Greek literature to wife capture, and there has been speculation whether this was the prevailing means of mate selection in the prehistoric era. The Spartan ceremonial and the Athenian custom of carrying a bride—who feigned resistance—over the threshold are sometimes interpreted as symbolic of earlier wife capture. There is no way to tell whether a general practice of wife capture ever existed.

long as the father lived. The father could emancipate the son through a ceremony that excluded the son from worship of the family ancestors and released him from paternal authority. Sons were highly valued however, and emancipation was rare. Later on, it became common to emancipate the son at maturity.

Inheritance and Descent

Patrilineal descent was tied to ancestor worship.[18] Only men could carry on worship of the ancestors, so descent was traced through males only. This extreme form of patrilineal descent, in which relationship is traced only through males, is known as *agnation*. Primogeniture existed with landed property, all of the family estates being inherited by the eldest son. The younger sons left home with the movable property; daughters did not inherit.

Great emphasis was placed on the provision of legitimate heirs. If a man produced daughters but no sons, his daughter was required to marry the father's brother. Because the Greeks were monogamous, this sometimes meant that the brother had to divorce his wife to marry his niece. Or the father might give the daughter in marriage to some other man on condition that the first son be given to him as his own.[19]

Spartan inheritance laws were more liberal. Women could inherit land as well as movable property, and one of the effects of Greece's wars was to concentrate property in the hands of women.

Marriage

Marriage was a sacred obligation. It was the means to continued worship of the ancestors, and it provided for inheritance of the family property. Celibacy was a legal offense; both Athens and Sparta passed laws punishing those who remained single.

Legislation intended to give married women an equal voice with their husbands in all matters of family life was unanimously adopted this week by the Greek Parliament. . . . Henceforth, under the new law, husband and wife must decide together all matters pertaining to their common family life. . . . No longer would a married woman have to get her husband's permission to set up a business, take their children abroad or even choose a school for them. . . .

---

18. The Greeks may have practiced matrilineal descent in prehistoric times.
19. In the more liberal Sparta, older men who were childless sometimes encouraged their younger wives to have intercourse with younger men so that they might become pregnant.

For the first time in Greece, divorce would be possible based on mutual consent. . . . Other provisions . . . would allow a wife to keep her own name for legal questions and to choose whichever family name she wished.

One amendment abolishes the institution of dowry, which has become a system of tax evasion. Under a law enacted by the colonels who ruled Greece from 1967 to 1974, dowries were taxed by only half as much as gifts or inheritance. . . . In the future . . . the transfer of property can be made to son or daughter, with or without marriage, and will be taxed at the normal rate.

MARVINE HOWE, "New Law in Greece Gives Women an Equal Voice in Family Matters," *New York Times*, January 30, 1983. Copyright © 1983 by The New Times Company. Reprinted by permission.

During the Homeric period marriage was simple. The groom made "gifts" to the bride's father—a not very subtle form of bride price—and the girl was handed over to her husband. At this stage, the wife ordinarily brought no property to the marriage. As Greece developed, the arrangements became elaborate. Betrothal and marriage were separated. Betrothal was a business contract between the parents, setting forth the bride price and the dowry. The husband was permitted to administer the dowry, but it was returned to the wife at the husband's death or in the event of her unjust divorce.

The Athenian wedding ceremony was an extravagant religious affair. The principal ceremonies occurred either in the bride's home or in a temple. There was a ritual eating of sesame-seed cakes to ensure fertility; the bride's father offered sacrifices to the gods and handed his daughter over to her husband by releasing her from his own power and from the worship of his ancestors. Then there was an elaborate parade to the groom's home, more ritual eating, and the commending of the bride to the husband's ancestors. No special religious functionaries participated. The fathers acted as priests; marriage was a private family affair.

Concubinage and Prostitution

The Greeks were monogamous,[20] but supplemented monogamy with concubinage and prostitution. Concubines were taken by wealthy men generally from among slaves or women who had been captured in war. Concubines had lower status even than wives and were not permitted to

20. Bardis reports that both polygyny and polyandry may have existed in prehistoric times, *op. cit.*, pp. 423–24.

worship family ancestors. Their children were not true family members and could not inherit property.

The best known women of ancient Greece are the *hetaerae*. The *hetaerae*—trained from childhood in knowledge, the arts, and social graces—were captured women of noble birth or were Greek girls who had survived exposure and who were reared to be the social and sexual companions of wealthy men. These women were remarkably free in their daily activities, were highly regarded, and often wielded power and influence. For poorer Greeks, there were ordinary prostitutes. Again, they were either exposed girls from poor families or captured women. The city-states licensed houses of prostitution and heavily taxed prostitutes' income. The taxing was less a matter of morality than of financing the state.

Divorce

If divorce existed during the earliest period, it was rare. Even during Homeric times, the indissolubility of marriage was emphasized. Gradually, however, the husband's right to repudiate his wife emerged. He had only to state his displeasure with her in the presence of witnesses. On either of two grounds—adultery or barrenness—the husband was regarded as justified in divorcing his wife. Gradually, the law came to demand annulment for flagrant adultery on the part of the wife.

At least during the period of urbanization, the wife also had limited rights of divorce. She could not, however, divorce her husband for adultery no matter how flagrant. Only if he were physically cruel or neglected his family was she entitled to divorce. Even then she had to seek permission from the public authorities, which she could not do unless her husband permitted her to leave the house.

THE ROMAN FAMILY SYSTEM

According to legend, Rome was founded in 753 B.C. Little is known of this period, except that Rome was a village occupied by Latin-speaking tribes. Gradually, these tribes increased in military power and conquered the whole of what today is Italy. The development of the Roman family system is even more progressive than that of the Hebrews and Greeks. For convenience, we divide Roman history into two main periods from 753 B.C. until the close of the Punic Wars in 202 B.C. and from 202 B.C. until the fall of the Empire in the third century A.D.

Before the Punic Wars

The early Roman family was the strongest patriarchy of which we have knowledge. Descent was patrilineal. Marriage was monogamous, and a three-generation extended family was common.

Patriarchy. The family was a large, strong, stable unit. It performed many functions, and those functions were concentrated in the patriarch, the *pater familias.* The father was priest of the ancestor worship, he was the only "legal" person in the family, and he held ownership of all property. His power over his children was called *potestas* and extended throughout his lifetime; some famous Roman generals were still under *potestas* and were unable to control their own property or earnings. Newborn infants were brought to their fathers to determine whether they should live or die. If the father decided to expose them, they were left in the countryside to die or to be taken as slaves to some other family. The father also could sell children into slavery, banish them from the country, or kill them. Before he could kill them, he had to consult with the adult men of his *gens,* but, after doing so, no matter what their recommendations, he was free to do as he wished. The father could both marry off and divorce his children even against their will. Even married sons and their sons remained under the patriarch's power. Before the father's death, the only escape from *potestas* was emancipation, a mock sale that freed the son to become a *pater familias* himself. Sons were highly valued however, and emancipation was rare.

Daughters also fell under *potestas* and at marriage were transferred to the *manus* (hand) of their husbands. Theoretically, no Roman woman was ever a free agent. The husband could name a guardian for his wife after his own death. Because women were not legal persons, the husband was responsible for crimes his wife committed, and he could punish her accordingly. If she caused him financial loss, he could sell her labor to pay it. After consulting with the adult men of both his *gens* and his wife's, he could kill her. If she committed adultery, he could kill her immediately. Paradoxically, Roman women had generally high status. They were respected mistresses of their households, were free to come and go, and were social and intellectual companions of their husbands. Their status is symbolized by the phrase they uttered on being carried over the threshold by their new husbands: "Where thou art lord, I am lady." In the home, the Roman woman was located not in women's apartments but in the atrium, the central room of the house.

Descent and Inheritance. The *familia* was a unit of the *gens,* a patrilineal descent group. Like the Greeks, the Romans practiced *agnation,* tracing descent through males only. The *gens* was composed of all *familia* who traced descent from a common ancestor. In earliest times, the *gens* held property, provided guardians for dependent or defective members, conducted religious services, maintained burial grounds, and passed resolutions that were binding on its members.

There was no place for unattached persons. Everyone belonged to a household and came under the control of the family head. At the death of the *pater familias*, each adult son inherited an equal share of the estate and set up his own *familia*. Later on, the widow and daughters who lived at home and were under *potestas* came to receive equal shares. Such daughters had to have the consent of the *gens* to marry, and they were not permitted to dispose of their shares of the estate.

Marriage. The emphasis on ancestor worship and continuing the family line made marriage both a patriotic and a religious duty. Single persons were heavily taxed, and widowed and divorced persons were urged to remarry. Girls were married young. Often men of 25 were married to girls of 15. Marriage forms and ceremonies varied according to the social status of the participants. The highest status group were the patricians, or Roman citizens. Then came the plebeians and, finally, the slaves.

Betrothal was common among the patricians. Breaking of an engagement, although disapproved, could be done by either family without penalty. It was not unusual to betroth girls of 10 or 12, and if a betrothed girl were subsequently to engage in sexual intercourse with another man, she was guilty of adultery. The major function of betrothal was the setting of a girl's dowry, which tended to become increasingly large. The dowry was controlled by the husband, who received income from it but was not permitted actually to own or dispose of it. At his death, or on divorce, the dowry was returned to the girl's family.

There were two basic forms of marriage: *matrimonium justum* and *matrimonium nonjustum*. Until 445 B.C., *matrimonium justum* could be entered into only by Roman citizens; after that, it could be arranged between a citizen and a noncitizen. *Matrimonium justum* established both *potestas* and *manus*, and the children were Roman citizens. *Matrimonium nonjustum* carried neither *potestas* nor *manus*, and the children could not become citizens.

There were three ways of celebrating marriage with *manus*. The first, *confarreatio*, was an elaborate religious ceremony presided over by priests and 10 witnesses. The bride was carried in elaborate procession to the groom's house, where a sheep was slain, and there was a ritual eating of sacred cake. This ceremony was most common among the patricians or citizens. A second type of ceremony, *coemptio*, rested solely on the consent of the parties (the parents of the bride and groom), and it consisted of a mock sale of the bride. The passing of a coin symbolized the woman's being brought under *manus*. The least highly regarded custom was that of *usus* (use), where the marriage grew out of cohabitation. If the man and woman lived together for a year without the woman being absent from the man's home for three consecutive days, she was automatically brought under *manus*. This form was most common among the plebeians.

Although the Romans were monogamous, *matrimonium nonjustum* was a form of concubinage. It was a socially sanctioned relationship between two people who could not legally marry according to *matrimonium justum* and in which the woman had low status and the offspring were not recognized as members of the man's family.

Divorce. The Roman husband always could divorce his wife for adultery, preparation of poisons, or wine drinking.[21] Divorce was discouraged during the early centuries however, and it was uncommon. Before a man could repudiate his wife, even when she had committed the specified acts, he had to consult with the adult men of both *gentes*. The breaking of a marriage entered into by *confarreatio* was even more difficult. The couple had to endure a *diffarreatio* ceremony, to which all of those who had attended the wedding were invited.

Divorce was not interfered with by public authorities. As the centuries progressed, divorce became more common, and a distinction between just and unjust divorce emerged. The case of Spurius Carvilius Ruga about 230 B.C. is cited as the first instance of a man divorcing his wife for other than the three specified causes. He was compelled to forfeit half of his property and to turn over the other half to his divorced wife. A man who divorced his wife without cause was required to return her dowry.

After the Punic Wars

There was not, of course, a sharp change in Roman family patterns in 202 B.C. Change had been occurring for centuries and was aggravated by Rome's long wars with Carthage. The immediate effect was to take men off to war and to leave their wives, by default, with increasing power. The wives were not under *potestas* while their husbands were away. Women took over the management of family estates and ap-

---

21. This is the first instance of a man being *unable* to divorce his wife for barrenness. Although childbearing was highly regarded, a man suffered economic penalties for divorcing his wife because she was childless.

parently managed them well. Inevitably, a shift in the power relations between the sexes occurred. Men, when and if they returned, found many wives unwilling to submit to *manus*.

These changes were associated with vastly increased family wealth. Rome emerged victorious over Carthage and went on to subjugate the entire Mediterranean region. The wealth of the provinces was siphoned away to Rome, and a vast number of servants and slaves were accumulated. As wealth increased, the size of dowries increased proportionately, and daughters came to inherit property from their fathers. Fathers became more reluctant to see this property going to their daughter's husbands, and after the second Punic War, marriage without *manus* became common. Theoretically, this left the wife under *potestas*, but practically, it worked to free women from direct male control. Many women became quite wealthy. Moreover, some women became learned and active in public affairs. As they did, changes in marriage and family practices took place.

Potestas declined. Civil authorities gradually freed the property of adult sons from the control of their fathers. Caesar gave sons the right to dispose of property acquired in their military careers. The power of the father over children was restricted also. Infant exposure, never common, still was permitted, but the power of life and death over children was taken away. Only very poor parents were permitted to sell their children's labor, and public officials assumed jurisdiction over children who committed legal offenses. Daughters indirectly escaped from *potestas* through marriage without *manus*.

Change in the marriage ideals was not striking. Marriage still was highly regarded, and marriages on the whole remained stable. The wedding had always been a private family matter, resting on the consent of the two families involved. It remained so, but the consent of the husband and wife became more prominent. The customs of *confarreatio*, *coemptio*, and *usus* all but disappeared. The formal trappings of the wedding, in the form of an elaborate torchlight parade and banquet, remained, but much of the substance withered away.

Erosion of marriage ideals took place most conspicuously at the top of the socioeconomic order. Within the leisure class, marriage ceased to be a sacred obligation and became primarily a matter of personal satisfaction and convenience. Both men and women married for financial gain or they married not at all. *Matrimonium nonjustum* degenerated into men simply taking mistresses. Prostitution increased markedly. The drop in the marriage rate became a matter of concern, and by the time of Christ, legislation was passed penalizing the unmarried. Single adults were disqualified from receiving inheritances unless they married.

The birthrate also fell. Abortion was widely practiced, and the exposure of infants reached scandalous proportions. To correct this situation, laws were passed taxing inheritances of childless couples at 50 percent. The laws exempted children by adoption however, and it became fashionable to adopt adult children for the purpose of receiving inheritances. Both the couples doing the adopting and the adopted entered such relationships according to calculated advantage. The state grew more concerned, and the birthrate continued to fall.

Divorce, too, became common. Divorce, like marriage, was a private matter, and divorce by mutual consent became possibly simply by transferring a bill of divorcement in the presence of seven witnesses. There are no rates of divorce available, of course, so we can judge their increase only by the public concern. This concern is reflected in the following statements by famous men:

Tertullian: "The fruit of marriage is divorce."
Juvenal: "Some women divorce their husbands before the marriage garlands have faded."
Seneca: "Women no longer measure time in terms of the administrations of Roman consuls, but by the number of their husbands."

The famous Julian Law, in 17 B.C., provided that a woman guilty of adultery should be deprived of half her dowry, one third of her property, and be banished to a desert island. Ironically, one of the women punished was Julia, daughter of Emperor Augustus who had had the law passed. The same law deprived an adulterous husband of half his property, all his wife's dowry, and banished him from Rome.

THE INFLUENCE OF CHRISTIANITY

The Christians did not have a family system as such. They were not a nation, nor even an ethnic group. They began as a small sect within Judaism and gradually made converts from among Romans, Greeks, traditional Hebrews, and others. Rome remained as the center of political power, and the Christians, as they gained in strength and numbers, contested with the Roman government for control of marriage and family matters.

The new religion spread slowly, for it challenged, both directly and indirectly, the power of the state. The Christians taught that the power of the church was superior to that of the state. They refused to celebrate the emperor's birthday, they would not offer sacrifices to the spirits of departed emperors, and they discouraged their members from serving in the Roman armies. Whereas the emperors were passing laws to penalize celibacy, the Christians taught that the virgin state was an exalted one. As a result of such teachings, the Christians were persecuted by the authorities and by much of the general populace.

The teachings of the Christian church must be seen both in the context of religious history and in terms of the prevailing morality in Rome. In some ways, the Christians sought to resurrect the stern morality of earlier Hebrew, Greek, and Roman periods. For their concept of the relationship between the mind and the body, the spirit and the flesh, they went back to the Persian philosophy of dualism, which was some 2000 years old. They saw the demands of the spirit and the flesh as being mutually opposed and believed in suppressing the demands of the flesh. Rome appeared to be catering to the flesh. Divorce, celibacy, infanticide, prostitution, childlessness, and worldliness were common. Christian policies were formed both from tradition and in reaction against the prevailing conditions in Rome.

The church did not immediately take positions on marriage and divorce. It did not develop its own wedding ceremonies. It continued to accept the Roman ideas of marriage and divorce as private matters and sought to express its ideals within the framework of Roman law and customs. Until the fourth century A.D., the state was clearly dominant. By A.D. 311, the Christians had grown too numerous and too powerful to be suppressed. Finally in 313, Christianity became an officially tolerated religion of Rome.

Attitudes and Policies Concerning Marriage

It is ironic that the Christians should have drastically lowered the status of marriage. Yet under Christian influence, marriage and the family were more lowly regarded than ever before or since. The Christians began by attacking adultery, abortion, infanticide, and child exposure. But in so doing, they became victims of a conception of marriage as a purely sexual union—as a slightly more desirable alternative than fornication. The development and the implications of this concept have ever since been a matter of debate among theologians. Some early church fathers held lofty views of marriage. But over the centuries, the dominant view became that represented by some of the writings of St. Paul. Paul's statement that "it is better to marry than to burn" is widely quoted.[22] The Christians did not actually condemn marriage for Christ

22. This statement is widely misinterpreted. Some have concluded that Paul offered marriage as an alternative to the fires of hell. Actually, the phrase "to burn" referred to the fires of passion, and Paul's statement should be interpreted to say that those who cannot abstain from illicit sexual intercourse should marry.

had given approval to it. What they did was to regard the highest state as that of virginity, next came celibacy after marriage, then marriage, and finally, fornication.

Sexual intercourse in marriage was considered a necessary evil rather than a source of pleasure. It was necessary for producing children and the virgins idealized by the church. At the fourth Council of Carthage in A.D. 398, it was declared that bride and groom should abstain from intercourse on their wedding night out of respect for the benediction. Later, the period was extended to three nights. The couple could avoid the obligation by paying a moderate fee to the church.

Marriage gradually was denied to priests and nuns. For a while, the church also encouraged married couples who had borne children to reassume the celibate state in marriage. The resulting friction was so great, however, that the policy was modified to include only marriages where the husband and wife agreed on celibacy. Second marriages also were condemned. An early Christian manual stated that "a second marriage is wicked, a third one indicative of unbridled lust, and one after the third, synonymous with fornication."[23]

The church disapproved of the Roman practice of permitting first cousins to marry, and it gradually created prohibited relationships within which people might not marry. Relatives by blood (consanguinity) were taboo within seven degrees of kinship. Relatives by affinity (marriage) likewise were prohibited within seven degrees. Even persons who presided as godfathers and godmothers at baptisms and confirmations were considered to be related (spiritual affinity) and were forbidden to marry. Within a few generations, almost everyone in the villages and towns of the day was related within prohibited degrees. For 1000 years, however, efforts were made to check on such relationships; in the thirteenth century, the obligatory publishing of banns in the churches was designed to give those who knew of impediments a chance to speak. By their nature, these prohibitions were not enforceable, and they gave rise to problems.

Christianity had no marriage ceremonies of its own for centuries. It accepted the Roman customs; later on, it accepted the customs of the Teutonic invaders from the north. What the church did was to urge the couple to seek the blessing of a priest after the nuptials. Not until the ninth century was marriage within the church firmly established. The reaction against marriage was harshest in the early centuries of the Christian era and gradually softened over the years. The sacred nature of marriage was emphasized increasingly as the church gained control;

23. Quoted in Bardis, *op. cit.*, p. 442.

by the twelfth century, marriage was defined as one of the seven sacraments.

The Status of Women

The early Christian attitude toward women was paradoxical. On the one hand, men and women were equal in the sight of God, both being possessed of divine souls. Virgins were highly regarded. As "brides of Christ," they were assigned duties of caring for the sick and for needy widows and orphans, of visiting prisoners and administering relief programs. Widows, too, who forsook remarriage had high status and were employed in charitable activities.

On the other hand, the idea of the inferiority of women was pronounced. Women were assumed to represent the evils of sex and to be the unwholesome tempters of men.

You are the devil's gateway: You are the unsealer of that forbidden tree: You are the first deserter of the divine law: You are she who persuaded him whom the devil was not valiant enough to attack. You destroyed so easily God's image, man. On account of your desert—that is, death—even the Son of God had to die.[24]

Women were considered to be tainted with the sin of Eve. They were admonished to confine themselves to housework and prayer. Women were not permitted to teach religion or to perform baptisms.

Divorce

The Christian attitude toward divorce required many centuries to crystallize. As in other areas, there was a split within the church. Christ had seemed to sanction divorce where adultery had been committed. In general, however, the sentiment was against divorce: "What therefore God hath joined together, let not man put asunder."[25]

By A.D. 140, the church permitted divorce only on grounds of idolatry, apostasy, covetousness, and fornication. Over the next century or two, the policy wavered but tended toward increasingly strict regulation of divorce. In A.D. 314, the Council of Arles affirmed the principle of the indissolubility of marriage but did not make it mandatory. Finally, at the Council of Carthage in A.D. 407, the church took an irreversible stand against divorce. Then in the twelfth century, civil law

24. Tertullian, *On the Apparel of Women*, Book I, Chapter I, Vol. 4, p. 14, quoted in Queen and Habenstein, *op. cit.*, p. 203.
25. Matthew 19:6.

was brought into complete conformity with canon law and absolute divorce almost disappeared from Europe.

THE GERMAN-ENGLISH FAMILY SYSTEM OF THE MIDDLE AGES

The Roman Empire finally succumbed to conquest at the end of the fourth century. For about 200 years, various portions of the empire were overrun by loosely federated tribes, ranging from the Vandals, Visigoths, Lombards, East Goths, Alemanni, and Burgundians in the south to the Angles, Saxons, Frisians, and Jutes in the north. Eventually, Britain was invaded by the Angles, Saxons, and Jutes, carrying the cultural stream that was to be transported to America. Our knowledge of this period is not complete or reliable. The word *barbarian*, which is customarily attached to the Teutonic tribes, connotes among other things a disrespect for learning that produced few written records.

Inheritance and Descent

The kinship system of the Germanic and English peoples was a considerable departure from the earlier patrilineages of the Hebrews, Greeks, and Romans. Both peoples (the Anglo-Saxons in England and the Saxons and Frisians on the Continent) practiced double descent. Relationship was traced both through the father's line and the mother's line, with each person being a member of two separate kin groups. These extended kin groups were called the *maegth* in Britain and the *sippe* on the Continent. In each case, membership in the kin group was traced from the grandchildren of a common set of ancestors.

The *sippe* occupied a position between the household and the state, comparable to the position of the *tsu* in China. The state depended on the *sippe* to enforce the law among its members, and the *sippe* wielded power over the households and individuals. Membership in the *sippe* was by blood or adoption. Illegitimate children had no rights of inheritance; wives remained members of their own *sippes* after marriage. The father admitted each child to the *sippe*. The child was brought to him before it had tasted food, to be accepted or to be condemned to exposure. Although the father could not kill children who had tasted food, infanticide and exposure were permissible at least until the eleventh century.

Among these warlike peoples, membership in a kin group was the primary individual protection. If an individual was killed, his kin avenged the death or extracted payment (*wergild*) from the slayer's kin. If he killed someone else, then the paternal kin paid two thirds of the *wergild* and the maternal kin paid one third. A major function of the *sippe* was to restrain its landless male members from aggressive behavior.

In spite of the system of double descent, property passed from father to son in the male line. Wives and daughters were not prohibited from inheriting however, and sometimes did so. In later centuries, the wife's inheritance rights became increasingly fixed through the dower.

Patriarchy

The father's power over children was not so great as among the ancients. Fathers could punish children vigorously, but the laws of the Jutes, for example, provided that he should not break their bones. Anglo-Saxon children could be sold into slavery until they became seven years old; among the Germanic peoples, both wives and children could be sold in time of famine. The power of the *sippe* always was available to protect wives and children from abuse beyond permissible limits.

Anglo-Saxon fathers could give their daughters in marriage without the girls' consent until the eleventh century. They could also commit children to monasteries and nunneries. Girls, whose entrance into a convent often was accompanied by a substantial gift to the church, were not entitled to seek release from the convent even at adulthood.

The rights of sons exceeded those of daughters. Although fathers generally had the usufruct of their children's property, the Anglo-Saxon father could not claim his son's earnings. Moreover, the father's power over his sons was drastically restricted when the sons reached majority, most commonly at 12 years of age.

The husband's power over his wife was limited by her membership in her own *sippe*. Her *sippe* remained responsible for crimes she committed, and the *sippe* collected *wergild* in the event that harm was done to her. Short of doing severe bodily injury however, the husband was expected to chastise her for misdeeds. A man who failed to punish an unruly wife might himself be punished by neighbors.

Betrothal and Marriage

By the late Middle Ages, betrothal and the nuptials had become quite distinct among the Germanic peoples. The betrothal, called *beweddung*, originated in an agreement betwen the groom and the bride's father for a bride price of cattle, money, or arms. Gradually, however, the interval between *beweddung* and *gifta* (marriage) lengthened until it became common to betroth children and even infants.[26] With child be-

26. George E. Howard, *A History of Matrimonial Institutions*, Chicago: University of Chicago Press, 1904, Vol. 1, pp. 258–72.

trothal, only a token sum was paid to the father as a kind of deposit on the full bride price. Eventually, it became common to pay the money to the bride herself and still later, the payment took the form of a ring—the precursor of the modern engagement ring. The bride price also was transformed from an actual payment to the bride's father into a dower right in the husband's property in the event that the husband should die before she did. This dower right often amounted to half of the husband's property. *Beweddung* was the first step in marriage, and subsequent sexual intercourse on the part of the girl was severely punished.

Gifta, the marriage ceremony, was a private family matter, involving the bride's being turned over to her husband by her father. In some cases, the father also handed over a hat, sword, and mantle, which were the husband's symbols of authority over the wife. In some tribes, the groom then stepped on the bride's foot as a means of reinforcing the symbols. No religious officials were involved. After the tenth century, the girl sometimes selected another male relative to give her away or she gave herself in marriage. This giving of oneself in marriage, *self-gifta*, later evolved into common-law marriage.

These customs were little influenced by the spreading Christian church. As it had among the Romans, the church accepted the native customs for centuries. The church emphasized the sacred character of marriage and urged the couple to seek the blessing of a priest following *gifta*. Attending mass on the day following *gifta* became common, and by the tenth century *gifta* was often performed just outside the church entrance and in the presence of the priest. The presence of a priest was not necessary however; marriage remained a private matter, based on the consent of the parties.

Divorce

The Germanic peoples like the ancients had permitted the repudiation of wives. As this power became restricted, the influence of Rome was felt in the appearance of divorce by mutual consent—mutual consent, with the advantages lying with the husband. Adultery by the woman not only was cause for divorce but produced such moral outrage that she might be driven through the village and beaten to death. Men ordinarily could not be divorced for adultery. A man caught in adultery might be killed, not on moral grounds, but for violating the property rights of another man!

The church, it will be recalled, had established the indissolubility of marriage by the fifth century. For another 500 years, however, it continued to compromise with secular customs. Divorce by mutual consent was recognized, and even remarriage was permitted. Often, the bishops demanded that their consent be secured before remarriage. The church even gave slight encouragement to divorce in cases where one of the partners had converted to Christianity but the other had not.

During these 500 years, the church consolidated its power and steadily assumed control over divorce until by the tenth century, it had wrested control from the civil authorities. The bishops' courts came to hear all divorce cases and canon law replaced civil law. Canon law permitted two remedies to discontented couples: *divortium a vinculo matrimonii* and *divortium a mensa et thoro.*

Divortium a vinculo matrimonii, meaning divorce from the bonds of matrimony, was not divorce as we know it, but annulment—an ecclesiastical declaration that a valid marriage never existed in the first place. There were ample grounds on which annulment might be sought, for the church prohibited marriage within seven degrees for both consanguinity and affinity and between those who had been religious sponsors for a child. Annulment also was permitted where either the husband or wife had entered into a previous verbal contract of marriage in words of the present tense. By the nature of such a contract, no records were available and the procedure was subject to abuse.

Divortium a mensa et thoro, literally divorce from bed and board, was not absolute divorce either. It was separation, permitted and enforced by the church. The parties remained legally married and escaped none of the obligations of marriage other than cohabitation. *Divortium a mensa et thoro* was permitted on three grounds: adultery, cruelty, and apostasy (heresy).

With *divortium a vinculo matrimonii*, the church opened Pandora's box. Most couples, if they were determined, could find grounds for annulment. Moreover, the church often was a not too reluctant partner in fraud. Annulments were granted to wealthy persons on the payment of sums of money, and dispensations permitting marriage within the prohibited degrees were available for the proper consideration.

To understand this situation, one must be aware that the church was not only a religious institution but also an increasingly powerful political one. In contest with civil authorities over morals, the church wielded economic power with good effect. It missed few opportunities to increase its wealth or its holdings in land. Be that as it may, the church established definitions that were to create problems for centuries.

THE IMPACT OF FEUDALISM

Feudalism developed on the Continent, where the countryside was divided into estates accumulated and held through military power. Kings bestowed vast portions of land on nobles, who constituted a landed aristocracy paying tribute to the king and contributing armies to his service. In turn the nobles farmed their holdings with the labor of serfs who were bound to the soil and who served in the nobles' armies. In addition, there were freemen, or yeomen, who owned their farms and who occasionally became prosperous. Finally, there was a growing class of artisans and tradesmen who lived in the towns. It was a more rigidly stratified society than had existed since the Roman Empire. This feudal economy was transferred to England with the Norman invasion, where it was dominant until the time of the Reformation.

Feudalism had major impact on inheritance, marriage, and the status of women. These changes all stemmed from the necessity to hold estates intact and to keep them under the control of male heirs who could protect them against plunder.

Unogeniture and *entail* became firmly established. Unogeniture means that the estate is transmitted intact to one of the sons. Primogeniture was most common, but ultimogeniture also was found. Entail involved lands being inalienably settled on a man and his straight-line descendants. Thus, great emphasis was placed on "heirs of the body," and if a man had sons, no other relatives could inherit his land. Occasionally, younger sons inherited recently acquired lands that were not considered part of the traditional estate, but by the fourteenth century, even that practice had given way to providing younger sons with life interests in the income from rents and trusts. Wives had only their dower interests, and this was defined as not to include the man's house, which must go instead to his heir.

Feudalism deprived women again of much of the status they had begun to recoup during the early Middle Ages. The husband owned the wife's dowry as long as the marriage survived, and he had a life interest in it after her death. If he died first, she might have difficulty in acquiring control of her dower. For a woman to hold land outright, if just for her lifetime, threatened the lord's interest in it: she might marry a man who would alienate the land or the land might be wrested from her by force. Consequently, when a man died, the lord acquired control of the widow almost as he did of the land. She had to secure his consent to a proposed remarriage or the lord might actually marry the widow off to a knight of his choice to protect his interest in the land.

The plight of children under feudalism was more difficult than that of women. Discipline was harsh, with beatings the approved way of securing obedience and respect. Children often were sent away from home to be trained by other families who would instill discipline and virtue without sentiment. If the father died, his children came under the power of the lord, who could arrange their marriages or sell that right to someone if he did not wish to avail himself of it.

Arranging marriages became a matter of calculated bargaining in which children were used as pawns in building estates. Although marriages could not be consummated until the boy reached 14 and the girl 12, much younger children were involved in marriage agreements. Queen and Habenstein quote Coke as writing that a 9-year-old widow should have her dower, "of what age soever her husband be, albeit he were but four years old."[27] Children of 7 could legally contract marriage.

The Influence of Chivalry

As feudalism matured, standards of living of the upper classes improved. The castle served as home, fortress, and social center. Boys and men were trained in warfare, whereas girls learned spinning, sewing, and weaving. There was even some cultivation of knowledge—sometimes directly, sometimes through the stories and songs of wandering troubadours.

All of this was accompanied by changes in the relations between men and women. Medieval women acquired power when their husbands went to war, just as Roman women before them had done. Left in charge of the castles and servants, many women developed competence and assurance in the management of their affairs. Too, women could inherit property. If a man died without heirs of the body, his widow might become wealthy and powerful. Women, isolated in their castles, gradually became preoccupied with manners and etiquette. How much sheer boredom had to do with it, we cannot say. Then there was the fact that women could not act directly in their own behalf; a woman wronged could only seek recourse through some man who might champion her cause. A man might champion his own wife's cause, but not out of sentiment. Marriage had been arranged on economic grounds, and its purpose was to provide heirs to keep the estates intact. Because emotional needs were not met in marriage, both sexes sought to satisfy those needs outside of marriage in extramarital intrigue, which has since come to be called *chivalry*.

Chivalry appears to have been two-sided. On the one hand, it was lusty and sensual. There was much overt sex seeking, with little regard for the feelings or reputations of the persons involved or their families. On the other hand, chivalry fostered an idealization of love and the partner; this had no counterpart in the ancient world. In short, chivalry produced the concept of romantic love. Romantic love and marriage were widely regarded as incompatible with one another, but the ideal of seeking continued, intense satisfaction in a member of the opposite sex was created as a legacy to be passed on to future generations.

27. Queen and Habenstein, *op. cit.,* p. 255.

How widespread chivalry became in the later Middle Ages is unknown. Probably, it was confined to the upper classes, serving only as an ideal for the great mass of men and women who worked their modest holdings or at trades in the towns. Much less is known of the actual family behavior of people in the Middle Ages than of the ideal standards the age set for them.

CHURCH POLICY THROUGH THE REFORMATION

After the tenth century, the church vigorously contested the concept of marriage as a private matter not requiring the participation of clergy. As long as the father gave the bride in marriage, the clergy did not complain openly; but when it became common for other laymen to do it, the clergy demanded that only a priest should give a woman in marriage. Laymen who bestowed a bride in marriage were threatened with excommunication. Much of the Continent, however, and most of England was not prepared to surrender the concept of marriage as a private affair. One result of the church's stand was the spread of clandestine marriage.

The old custom of *self-gifta* had evolved into the right of a man and woman to marry simply by stating their vows "in words of the present tense." As the church opposed this custom, it became common for the vows to be said in secret and often without witnesses.

The church was caught in a dilemma. If it refused to recognize such marriages, it would drive the participants from the church and condemn their children to illegitimacy. If it recognized the marriages, it would abdicate its power to regulate family life. During the twelfth century, Peter the Lombard attempted to find a way out by declaring that vows in words of the present tense (I take thee) produced a marriage, but that vows spoken in words of the future tense (I will take thee) did not. The result was chaos. Clandestine marriages were held to be binding. Moreover, in neither English nor German is there any clear distinction between the present and future tenses. If a man says "I will" to a woman, does it mean that he will right now or at some time in the future?[28]

The church's logic was supported by a distinction it created between *legal* and *valid* marriages. Legal marriages were those that met the formal requirements of the church. Marriages that occurred without church sanction, although illegal, were still recognized as valid. The church discouraged marriage in words of the present tense by requiring penance of those who were so married, but to no avail. Clandestine marriages in-

---

28. A common form of marriage ceremony in use at the present time uses the phrase "I will" rather than the phrase "I do."

creased rapidly, and there were abuses. Some children were held to be validly married, whereas other couples who had lived together for years were declared not to be married. Unscrupulous men escaped from marriages where there were no witnesses.

In 1215, Pope Innocent III decreed that banns must be read in the church three times before a marriage ceremony could be performed, but the decree was not rigidly enforced. Finally, at the Council of Trent in 1563, it was declared that in the future valid marriages must be celebrated in the presence of a priest and two or three witnesses. The Council also decreed that publishing of the banns should be enforced. Even then, however, the church failed to make publication of the banns a condition of valid marriage; high-status persons continued to secure their licenses without the banns being read.

In at least two other areas, the church was plagued by scandal. First, there were continuing abuses centering on *divortium a vinculo matrimonii*. It had proved impossible to enforce kinship restrictions within seven degrees, and Innocent III, in 1215, specified that the prohibited relationships extend only to the fourth degree. Still, the prohibitions were erratically applied. In some instances, spiritual affinity was held to impose restrictions within four or seven degrees, whereas in other cases, persons consanguineally related within three degrees were given dispensation to marry. Even more irksome, persons of wealth and influence continued to secure annulments when less fortunate persons could not.

Another scandal revolved around the requirement for a celibate priesthood. Enforcement was lax, and there were continuous rumors of licentious behavior by priests. On the Continent, some priests took women, had children by them, and then married them just before they died so that the children might inherit their property.[29] The church even taxed clergy for the privilege of keeping concubines.

The Reformation

A crisis was reached at the end of the fifteenth century, in a revolt against the abuses with which the church was plagued. Martin Luther was a symbol of the revolt, and he was influential in reintroducing the concept of civil marriage. Luther held marriage in high regard and objected to clandestine marriage, to the abuses associated with clerical celibacy, to fraud in the granting of special dispensation to marry, and to annulments. Consequently, he held that marriage was not a sacrament but a civil contract blessed by God. It followed from this that marriage and divorce should be regulated by the state, not by the

29. O. E. Feucht, *ed., Sex and the Church*, St. Louis: Concordia Publishing House, 1961, p. 63, quoted in Panos D. Bardis, *op. cit.,* p. 451.

church. Luther himself, in 1525, married a nun who had fled from a convent.

The church fragmented into Catholic and Protestant factions, and civil authorities gradually assumed control of family matters. Performance of the marriage ceremony was left to the church for another generation. Nor was there immediate change in the prohibition of divorce; with the restriction on fraudulent annulments, marriage actually became more binding than before.

One early effect of the Reformation was the removal of most of the impediments to marriage. Prohibitions for spiritual affinity were done away with and barriers owing to consanguinity were removed beyond the third degree. Interestingly for modern-day America, the Protestant churches continued to forbid marriages between Christians and non-Christians—so-called mixed marriages.

Ironically, the Reformation helped preserve one of the evils against which it was directed. The Church of England continued to recognize marriage in words of the present tense until the eighteenth century. Canon law and civil law were in conflict, for although canon law declared the children of such marriages to be legitimate, civil law held that they could not be legitimated even by the subsequent religious marriage of their parents. The church gained power to force a subsequent religious marriage and could jail persons who refused to do so. Be that as it may, the stage was set for the transport of common-law marriage to America.

THE ENGLISH FAMILY: THE SIXTEENTH CENTURY TO THE EIGHTEENTH CENTURY

After the feudal era, the class structure changed because of the diversification of occupations, thus increasing settlement in cities and towns and the development of trade. Ties to the land were not so universal as before: the top three classes—nobles, freeholders, and yeomen—constituted only about one fifth of the population. Four fifths of the population was composed of professionals, tradesmen, craftsmen, and laborers—people who sold their labor for a living.

Then English family remained patriarchal, although not so rigidly as before. As late as 1663, a man was legally entitled to beat his wife. Wealthy men remained as the heads of large households, holding authority over kin and non-kin alike who resided within them. On a smaller scale, the same thing applied to craftsmen, tradesmen, and farmers. Marriages still were arranged by parents, but there were the beginnings of free choice based on romantic love. Children began to go to school in greater numbers, but the majority were still placed in apprenticeship or loaned out to other families to learn discipline and the social graces.

Marriage

Probably the majority practice was that of child betrothal and marriage. Queen and Habenstein report the marriage of a boy 3 years old,[30] and Goodsell refers to a widow of 9.[31] These child brides and grooms continued to live with their own parents until they reached 12 and 14 years old. Their marriages were arranged frankly on the basis of financial consideration, to ensure the welfare of parents and to provide for the inheritance of property.

Clandestine marriages increased during the seventeenth and eighteenth centuries. Certain rectors of the Church of England discovered that marrying people without licenses could be profitable and did it on a large scale. Even more notorious were the fleet marriages, performed by clergymen who had been imprisoned for debt. These enterprising gentlemen sometimes even arranged to have offices outside the prison where they performed illegal marriages. After several unsuccessful attempts to do away with such marriages, the Hardwicke Act in 1573 required that all marriages should be performed before two witnesses by an Anglican clergyman after the publication of banns or the securing of a license. Registers of marriages were kept, and destroying or falsifying a register was punishable by death.

Descent and Inheritance

Inheritance laws changed little from medieval times. Primogeniture and entail were followed with landed property, younger brothers leaving the family home to make their own way. Daughters inherited only in the absence of sons. Wives had a dower right in their husband's property, which amounted to life use of one third of his property if there were children and one half of his property if there were not.

One sign of the times was the increased number of men and women who lived apart from kin. During the Middle Ages, the church had maintained monasteries, nunneries, hospitals, and the like, to which unattached persons repaired as the *sippe* or *maegth* declined. Now with the role of the church restricted, laws were passed making families financially responsible for their indigent members. Where families were not able to provide support, the obligation was now defined as a public

30. Queen and Habenstein, *op. cit.*, p. 278.
31. Goodsell, *op. cit.*, p. 329.

responsibility. The Poor Laws of 1597 saw government entrance into a field that formerly had been exclusively the prerogative of the family.[32]

Divorce

There was little change in regard to separation and divorce. Divorce became legally possible, although the Roman church still insisted on the indissolubility of marriage. Divorce cases were heard in the bishops' courts on grounds of adultery, impotence, refusal to cohabit, and cruelty. Apparently, few divorces were granted. Somewhat later, powerful and wealthy people sometimes were granted divorces by special act of Parliament. Stigma, however, was attached to divorce, and few persons endured the ordeal. The groundwork was being laid, however, for more liberal divorce practice in the future.

Transition to the Nuclear Family

Some time after the year 1500, the decline of the *sippe* and the *maegth*, which supported the ideal of extended family living, began to give way to positive sentiments toward nuclear family living. How much of this occurred by default and how much by design is impossible to say. On the one hand, legal changes came to hold individuals rather than clan groups responsible for misdeeds. On the other hand, increased geographic mobility both reduced ties to the land and resulted in more people working for wages. Positively, the church began to promote the ideal of family living based on conjugal affection.

Whatever the precise combination of causes, nuclear families had become the bases for most households by the mid-1600s. Recent research has shown the average household size to have been about five persons. This is smaller than was previously believed and has led some scholars to conclude that extended families and stem families were not only uncommon in the seventeenth century but also may not have been common earlier. Because data are not available for earlier periods, the latter point can neither be substantiated nor refuted. The former point requires very careful evaluation.

First, we must again distinguish between ideal and real cultural patterns. That the ancient Hebrews, Greeks, and Romans valued extended families is indisputable. It is also possible, even probable, that economic and other circumstances forced many of them to live in nuclear family circumstances for extended periods of time. We saw in Chapter 4 that

32. Kenneth W. Eckhardt, "Family Responsibility and Legal Norms," *Journal of Marriage and the Family* 32 (Feb. 1970), pp. 105–9.

the Chinese ideal of extended family living was not achieved by most of
the populace.

This leads to the second point: regardless of the ideal family norms
and even if extended family living is systematically achieved, cross-
sectional studies will always show most families to be nuclear and
household size to be relatively small. Take the stem family as an example. Even if every eldest son brings his bride to live in the parental
home, surveys will show them to be living as extended families only for
the relatively brief period between the son's marriage and the parents'
deaths. Moreover, all of the other sons will leave the parental home at
marriage and set up nuclear families. Thus, even in societies where the
stem family ideal is carefully adhered to, the majority of households at
any one time will be organized around nuclear families.

THE FAMILY IN THE AMERICAN COLONIES

No clan organization was transported to America. The immigrants
came, not in extended families but in nuclear families and as single persons. Particularly in the southern colonies, there were large numbers of
unattached men. Consequently, the basic social units of the New World
were two: the nuclear family and the household.

There are fragmentary data on the size and composition of families
and households in areas of the New England colonies. Several studies
report an average of eight or nine, children born to families, although at
any one time, nuclear families averaged only about six persons.[33] There
often were, in addition, single persons, indentured servants, and unrelated children living with the family. As sons married, the laws of inheritance favored the eldest son bringing his bride to the home of his
parents. Adopting the English precedent, the New England colonies
followed modified primogeniture, in which the eldest son received a
double portion. Settlement in the southern colonies was more often on
farms and plantations, the self-sufficiency of which encouraged the development of large households. At the center were the plantation owners and operators who accumulated a large number of indentured servants and black slaves; beyond this elite were an undetermined number
of ordinary farmers and "poor whites."

In all colonies, the household size was increased by the emphasis on
marriage and large families. From England, came the tradition of trans-

33. John Demos, *A Little Commonwealth: Family Life in Plymouth Colony*, New York:
Oxford University Press, 1970, p. 68; Philip J. Greven, Jr., "Family Structure in Seventeenth Century Andover, Massachusetts," in Michael Gordon, *ed., The American Family
in Social-Historical Perspective*, New York: St. Martin's Press, 1973, p. 81; and Barbara
Laslett, "Social Change and the Family." *American Sociological Review* 42 (April
1977), pp. 269-91.

mitting property intact to one's heirs. The frontier and farming made economic assets of children, and marriage was protection against immorality. New England colonies, in particular, discouraged adults from remaining single and imposed restrictions on those who did. In Pennsylvania, single men paid double taxes, and in Hartford, "the selfish luxury of solitary living" was taxed 20 shillings per week. In some areas, single persons were required to live with families who were licensed and who would be responsible for their morals.

Colonial families performed almost every service for their members. With help, the men and boys built the house they lived in. Farm buildings, tools, implements, and furniture similarly were provided. Most families provided some of their own food, with the women processing and storing it. Thread was spun, cloth was woven, clothing was sewn, candles were poured, soap was made, and so on. The family was nearly an independent economic unit. It was an educational agency, with the skills of farming or trade and those of housewifery taught at home. Even where there were schools, some education in the three R's often was given at home. The family was both an educational unit and a religious unit. In the North, the orientation was Puritan; in the South, it was Anglican. But in both cases, the family was a religious unit organized around the father, who directed reading of scriptures, family prayers, and hymn singing.

Patriarchy

English common law was brought to the colonies. Over the centuries, the settling of disputes without clear precedent or explicit legislation had given way to the accumulation of court decisions and a body of parliamentary law. According to these precedents, women and children were held under the power of the husband.

Women held no property unless it was specifically given them by their husbands for personal use; even the wife's personal property and clothing belonged to the husband. On the other hand, husbands were legally responsible for their wives, were obligated for their support, and were even responsible for her debts incurred both before and after marriage.[34] A wife also had a dower interest in the husband's real property that could not be disposed of without her concurrence.[35] If the husband

34. The fact that the husband was responsible for his wife's debts incurred before marriage led, in scattered locations, to the custom of smock marriages, in which the couple would be married in the open countryside, with the bride clad only in a slip. This ceremony symbolized the wife's coming to her husband unencumbered and to free him from the obligation to pay debts that she might owe.
35. This right is recognized today in the requirement that signatures of both the husband and wife appear on any transfer of real estate. Otherwise, if the husband died, the wife might reclaim her dower interest.

died first, the wife gained control of her own property. If the wife died first, the husband was granted a "courtesy interest" in her property for the rest of his life. The question of whether unmarried women could own land early arose. In New England, the practice was discouraged. In the middle and southern colonies, however, women often held land in their own names.

The status of women varied from the North to the South. In New England, early Christian notions of the inferiority of women were prominent. In the south women were scarce during the early decades and had high status. The plantation economy also encouraged a high status for upper class women by providing slaves to do the menial labor and freeing women to develop social graces. The feudal practice of elevating women to high status resulted in an American form of chivalry.

American men were not permitted to beat their wives and could not even tongue-lash them too freely. "Cruelty" as grounds for legal action against the spouse emerged early and protected both husband and wife from too great abuse by the other. The power of the father over his children was great, but not so great as in the past. He was their legal guardian and could make many decisions concerning them. Laws in Massachusetts and Connecticut even provided that persistently disobedient youth might be put to death. There is no indication of youth actually having been slain under these laws, but the influence of the old Hebrew traditions is clearly there.

Parents sometimes arranged marriages for their children, and under the common law, boys could be married at 14 and girls at 12. Furthermore, a young man could not call on a young woman without her father's consent. With all this, child marriages appear to have been uncommon; young people were granted considerable freedom and girls could refuse to marry the young men their fathers had selected.[36] They were, however, undoubtedly influenced by the wishes of their parents.

---

36. For recent analyses, summarizing data that cast doubt on many myths concerning colonial families, see Herman R. Lantz, Margaret Britton, Raymond Schmitt, and Eloise C. Snyder, "Pre-Industrial Patterns in the Colonial Family in America: A Content Analysis of Colonial Magazines," *American Sociological Review* 33 (June 1968), pp. 413–26; Herman R. Lantz, Jane Keyes, and Martin Schultz, "The American Family in the Preindustrial Period: From Base Lines in History to Change," *American Sociological Review* 40 (Feb. 1975), pp. 21–36; Herman R. Lantz, Raymond L. Schmitt, and Richard Herman, "The Preindustrial Family in America: A Further Examination of Early Magazines," *American Journal of Sociology* 79 (Nov. 1973), pp. 566–88; Herman R. Lantz, Martin Schultz, and Mary O'Hara, "The Changing American Family from the Preindustrial to the Industrial Period: A Final Report," *American Sociological Review* 42 (June 1977), pp. 406–21; and Rudy R. Seward, *The American Family: A Demographic History*, Beverly Hills, Calif.: Sage Publications, 1978.

Courtship, Betrothal, and Marriage

The contradictory conditions of rigid control and considerable premarital freedom applied to young people. On the one hand, a young man had to secure the consent of a girl's father to call on her. But on the other hand, young men and women traveled to and from dances unescorted and even traveled from town to town together. Towns often were far apart, and the journey often took more than one day. There is evidence, too, of young couples frequenting taverns together.

The word *courtship* had definite meaning. Young men were not supposed to pay attention to a girl unless they had marriage in mind. If considerable freedom was granted the young couple, it was also expected that they should not delay marriage for long.

An intriguing custom was that of bundling. This practice, imported from Europe, took place in New Amsterdam and the New England colonies. It permitted the couple to retire to bed together fully clothed, or almost so, to carry on the courtship under the covers.[37] The custom was more remarkable when one considers that the northern attitude toward sex was harsh and that persons guilty of fornication might be compelled to marry or be fined, whipped, or forced to stand in the stocks. When a child was born within seven months of marriage, the couple also were forced to make public confession of premarital intercourse.

Defenders of bundling claim that it was quite innocent: the couple were fully clothed, there often was a bundling board between them, and the girl's parents often were asleep in the same room. More cynical persons agree with the observation of Washington Irving that, "To this sagacious custom, therefore, do I chiefly attribute the unparalleled increase of the . . . Yankee tribe; for it is a certain fact, well authenticated by court records and parish registers, that wherever the practice of bundling prevailed, there was an amazing number of sturdy brats annually born unto the state, without the license of the law, or the benefit of clergy." Assuming that the endocrinological makeup of men and women then was comparable to what it is now, we might conclude that the custom was more compatible with short courtships than long ones.

Bundling was more common among lower economic groups and was an adjustment to frontier conditions. Bundling permitted the couple to carry on their "conversations" after the family retired without wasting fuel and light. The custom faded as living conditions improved.

Again in New England, formal betrothal, called *precontract* (analo-

37. For a light-hearted account of the practice of bundling, see Henry R. Stiles, *Bundling: Its Origin and Decline in America*, New York: Book Collector's Association, 1934.

gous to *beweddung*) existed. Precontract required parental consent and was solemnized before two witnesses. It was a promise to marry and was often followed by the preaching of a sermon. Precontract changed the legal and the social status of the couple. Because they were "almost married," they were likely to begin sexual intercourse, and the laws punishing fornication were softened, with the penalties prescribed generally being half those imposed on other couples.

In all the colonies, the arrangement of marriage often hinged on economic considerations. Single living was discouraged, and both men and women found it socially and economically advantageous to marry. Financial bargaining appeared most unabashedly among widows and widowers. Widows with children were somewhat preferred marriage partners. The children provided a labor force and the widows often owned property or had a life interest in the property left to them by their first husbands.

Although early writers believed that the colonists married young, more recently tabulated data indicate that the average ages at marriage were higher then than now. Men appear to have been 24 or 25 years old, women 22 or 23 years old.[38]

The colonies hedged marriage with legal restrictions. In general, they required that (1) parental consent be secured, (2) notice of intention to marry be given, (3) the marriage ceremony be performed by an authorized officiant, and (4) the marriage be officially registered.

Because each colony had its own laws, there was no uniformity from one colony to another. Before long, however, virtually all colonies provided either for the publication of banns or the securing of a license. The banns were either posted or read on three successive Sundays at the church or meetinghouse. As an alternative, most colonies permitted the securing of a license from the governor or from the court. Then as now exceptions were made for certain religious groups such as the Quakers, who were permitted to post notice of marriage according to their traditional customs.

In only one colony, New York, did failure to post banns or secure a license render a marriage void. All of the other colonies provided punishment for disobeying the law, but they did not invalidate illegal marriages. In New York, too, failure to have a licensed officiant rendered the marriage invalid; in other colonies, lesser penalties were provided. Distrust in New England of the established church resulted in ministers being prohibited from performing marriages. All ceremonies had to be performed by justices of the peace or magistrates. In the South, where

---

38. Demos, *op. cit.,* p. 275; Greven, *op. cit.,* p. 83; and Seward, *op. cit.,* p. 54.

the Church of England was established, the opposite situation prevailed, only religious ceremonies were permitted. The middle colonies followed a middle course, accepting both religious and civil marriages.

The registration of marriages was carefully controlled. In more closely settled areas of the North, the town clerk registered marriages, births, and deaths. Failure to register a marriage resulted in a heavy fine. Parish ministers often were responsible for registration of marriages in the South, gradually being replaced by elected officials. In the middle colonies, intermediate arrangements prevailed.

Almost from the beginning and in spite of careful regulation, self-marriage crept into the colonies. As we have seen, self-marriage in words of the present tense was firmly established in Europe. In America, the practice emerged mostly in the rural South and on the frontier. In those areas, ministers and civil officials were scarce. Ministers often were circuit riders who visited isolated communities infrequently. In the interim when a couple wished to marry, they might simply say their vows at a gathering of friends and live together until a preacher appeared to formalize the relationship. In some cases, the couple were so habituated to the marital state that a religious ceremony seemed unnecessary. In isolated sections, even the saying of marriage vows before witnesses was omitted. Colonial laws generally did not declare such marriages invalid, and subsequent court decisions upheld them. Thus, common-law marriage was established in the United States.

The colonies also regulated mate selection. Minimum ages for marriage and the necessity for parental consent already have been discussed. Prohibitions for relationships within specified degrees of consanguinity and affinity were established. Queen and Habenstein report that in some instances there were 30 classes of kinsmen who were forbidden as mates.[39] Persons in New England who married within the prohibited degrees sometimes were punished by being required to wear a large "I" (for incest) sewn prominently on their clothing.

Prohibitions on interracial marriages appeared before 1700. Bardis reports that Chester County, Pennsylvania, prohibited black-white marriages in 1698 and that Massachusetts forbade black-white and mulatto-white marriages in 1705.[40] White-Indian marriages also were widely forbidden. The southern colonies forbade all interracial marriages.

Divorce

The Puritan rebellion against the Church of England included recognition of absolute divorce. Practices varied from one colony to another.

39. Queen and Haberstein, *op. cit.*, p. 321.
40. Bardis, *op. cit.*, p. 452.

Massachusetts first granted jurisdiction over divorces to the Court of Assistants but transferred it to the governor and Council before 1700. In many cases, suits were heard by colonial legislatures, each divorce requiring a separate act of the legislature. Only Connecticut administered divorce proceedings solely through the courts.

Grounds for divorce also varied. In general in New England, however, the grounds were fairly liberal and discriminated in favor of men. Men could divorce wives for adultery, desertion, and cruelty. Women, on the other hand, were not entitled to divorce on grounds of adultery alone—only if it was accompanied by desertion or failure to provide. Some colonies provided that the woman might be granted alimony if she was unjustly divorced by her husband.

There are few data on the incidence of divorce in these early days, but Calhoun presents some illustrative figures.[41] Between 1639 and 1692 in Massachusetts, 25 divorces were granted. From 1692 to 1739, there are no pertinent records. During the next 20 years, from 1739 to 1760, there were only 3 divorces, 2 separations from bed and board, and 5 annulments were granted.

Interestingly, more suits for divorce were brought by women than by men. Our history of the Western family has shown that divorce rules almost always favored men. Yet the first time that figures became available more divorces were granted to women. Would this also have been true among the ancient and medieval periods, one might wonder, or was this an American innovation? There are at least two plausible explanations. One is that, although there is male domination, the family is everywhere more central to the lives of women, and in spite of legal disabilities, women more often seek relief from intolerable circumstances. Another possibility, tracing from the chivalric period, is that men more often permit wives the face-saving alternative of being the seeker of the divorce even when they themselves wish the marriage to be terminated.

The middle and southern colonies were not so liberal in their attitudes toward divorce. The church did not recognize absolute divorce; it permitted only separation from bed and board for adultery and cruelty. The southern colonies became even more conservative because, although they accepted the church, they refused to establish church courts. The result was that no organization could hear divorce suits and neither absolute divorce nor legal separation was granted. Some couples separated anyway, of course, and some southern courts heard requests for alimony from persons thus separated.

The middle colonies followed divorce policies closer to those of the southern colonies than to those of the New England colonies. Few abso-

41. Arthur W. Calhoun, *A Social History of the American Family from Colonial Times to the Present,* New York: Barnes and Noble, 1945, V. II, pp. 332–66.

lute divorces were granted in New York or Pennsylvania. The middle colonies generally failed to grant jurisdiction over divorce to the courts, and what few suits there were, were heard by the legislatures.

The Colonial Attitudes Toward Sex

New England took its attitudes toward sex from the Hebrew-Christian tradition. Sex was inherently evil, and all sex other than for procreation was sinful. The colonies went to great lengths to discourage premarital and extramarital sexual activity. Yet there were overtones of interest that belied the official norms. Premarital sex relationships were punishable by fines, whipping, or being forced to marry. The offenders might also be forced to stand in the stocks and to be branded on the cheek. The woman who bore a child out of wedlock might be imprisoned. Even couples who bore a child within seven months of marriage were punished. After the birth of the infant, the couple was required to make public confession of their sin before the entire congregation of the church. Church attendance increased substantially for such events and the sensationalism may actually have promoted sexual immorality.

Most New England colonies actually permitted adulterers to be put to death, and some death sentences were meted out. More commonly, the punishment was whipping, branding, and being required to wear the scarlet letter A, for adulterer. Women were more strictly punished than men, but one unfortunately eager sea captain was forced to stand in the stocks for the "crime" of kissing his wife in public and on Sunday after returning home from a three-year voyage. Queen and Habenstein present data indicating that between 1726 and 1780 in one Massachusetts county, 160 married couples, 31 wives, and 523 single women were punished for sexual offenses.[42] In one Groton church, approximately one third of the parents of first-born children confessed to having had premarital intercourse.

The situation in the South was different. A landed aristocracy combined with a shortage of women and an abundance of women slaves to produce one standard for men and another for women. Legal provisions in the South were less strict than those in the North. The laws did prohibit fornication and adultery, and punishments—including fines and whipping—sometimes were provided. No stocks were used however; there were no scarlet letters; and physical punishment was carefully restricted. More important, the laws were not systematically enforced.

Upper class women occupied a special position. A chivalry not unlike that of medieval England was shown toward them. Unlike medieval women, however, upper class southern women were carefully guarded

42. Queen and Habenstein, *op. cit.*, pp. 285–86.

against sexual involvement before marriage and against extramarital affairs. The fiction was maintained, and it often may have become a self-fulfilling prophecy[43] that genteel women generally viewed sex in terms of duty rather than personal fulfillment. Upper-class men, by contrast, enjoyed great freedom, both before marriage and after. If they were victims of their own expectations concerning upper-class women, it was also expected that they would meet their sexual needs wherever they could. With an enslaved population of black women available, there was widespread violation of the miscegenation statutes. Many white men used black and mulatto women at their convenience, but there also were numerous liaisons in which men acknowledged their illegitimate offspring and accorded special status to their mistresses. The double standard operated between men and women and also between blacks and whites. The keeping of mistresses by wealthy white men was so open that two state governors saw no need to conceal their extramarital relationships. Censure actually fell on the wife if she failed to accept the situation graciously. And at the time time that white men openly exploited black women, any hint of sexual interest in a white woman by a black man was cause for him to be put to death.

THE TRANSITION TO THE PRESENT

It is a far cry from colonial days to twentieth-century America. From the original 13 colonies, we have become a nation of 50 states and over 230 million people. Whereas, at the time of the first United States Census in 1790, the population was 95 percent rural, in 1980 it was 75 percent urban. A volume could be written on the changes in family patterns that have accompanied the development of this country. To some extent, the remainder of this book contrasts the family structure of today with that of colonial times. It remains in the closing section of this chapter to indicate a few of the major forces operating to transform the colonial family into that of the 1980s.

The Influence of the Frontier

Even in colonial days, there was little elaboration of kinship structure. The household had replaced the clan and the extended family as the basic unit of society. Households were large. Ties to the land and a

43. The phrase *self-fulfilling prophecy* refers to a "false definition of the situation evoking a new behavior which makes the originally false conception come true. The specious validity of the self-fulfilling prophecy perpetuates a reign of error, for the prophet will cite the actual course of events as proof that he was right from the beginning." See Robert K. Merton, *Social Theory and Social Structure*, Glencoe, Ill.: The Free Press, 1957, p. 423.

tendency toward primogeniture encouraged the formation of stem families, and unmarried kin often had no choice but to attach themselves to existing households. Even then, however, nuclear families often were entire household units. The frontier operated to sever ties from both kin and land and to increase the isolation of the nuclear family.

Following the Revolution, the growing population spread westward, across the Appalachians, to the Mississippi, to the Pacific Ocean. Young men took their nuclear families with them or they sought wives and built families after they had left the settled communities of the East. The grandparental generation most often was left behind; it had its ties, and the settlement of the frontier was arduous work.

The effects of this migration on family structure hardly could have been imagined. First, it caused the further decline of patriarchal control. Throughout history, strong patriarchies have been associated with extended families. Children on the frontier never knew the direct authority of their grandfathers and, consequently, never learned to expect to control their own future grandchildren. True, their father was the final authority in the family, and it was to be many years before women gained legal equality with men. But the isolation and rigor of life on their frontier produced a hardy breed of women who had a de facto equality with men. The future could bring only an increasing democratization of relationships within the family.

Equally drastic were the effects on inheritance. As extended families broke up and spread over the countryside, parents disposed of their property by will. Instead of being held intact for future generations, property was broken up and sold. As the colonies became the United States, the democratic ideology on which they were founded refused to sanction inherited inequality among siblings, and the various state constitutions outlawed the practice of entail. The tradition developed that all children, girls included, should inherit equally. The immortality of the extended family system was waning. In its place there emerged a conjugal family system without much family tradition and without economic or sentimental ties to a wide array of kin.

The Effects of Large-Scale Immigration

The U.S. population grew through natural increase and immigration. Up to now, we have dealt only with the dominant English tradition. But the number of migrants from other areas far exceeded those from England for most of two centuries. The United States became a heterogeneous nation with heterogeneous family patterns.

Little attention is paid, ordinarily, to the fact that the largest migration to America, before 1800 was of black slaves. The number probably falls between 10 and 20 million people. By contrast, the migrants from all of Europe during the same period was not over 5 million. The conditions of slavery before the Civil War and the varied conditions since have produced family patterns that are both like and unlike their white counterparts. At the present time, there are over 26 million people in the United States who are defined as black. The distinctive family patterns of this largest American minority will be treated in detail in a later chapter.

After 1800, mass migration from Europe got under way. During the nineteenth century, approximately 19 million people came, chiefly from northwestern Europe—Great Britain, Ireland, Germany, and France. Beginning about 1890, the countries of origin shifted from northwest Europe to southern and eastern Europe. Between 1890 and 1930, an additional 22 million people came, mostly from Italy, Austria-Hungary, and Russia. In 1930, there were more than 14 million foreign-born persons living in the United States. Since then, a restrictive immigration policy has drastically limited the number of migrants and the number and proportion of foreign-born in the population has been declining.

The peak migration between 1890 and 1920 differed from earlier ones in several ways. First, the migrants were not so often farmers. Second, they found the country largely settled and rather than spreading out over the countryside, they created ethnic enclaves in the larger eastern cities. Third, a large proportion of the immigrants was Roman Catholic.

These new migrants were not altogether hospitably received. They reacted to prejudice and discrimination by turning inward, preserving their traditional languages and customs. Their family patterns varied by nationality, religion, and economic status. For generations, they resisted assimilation. They became sources of the preservation of old world family patterns in the new world. In the 1970s, they are not nearly so conspicuous as they were a generation earlier. But even today, they provide significant variations on the major American family theme.

Urbanization and Industrialization

Industrialization got under way shortly after 1800. Cities grew up around the new factories, and there were several effects on family organization. First, the family ceased to be a principal unit of production, becoming transformed basically into a consumption unit. Instead of father, mother, and children working together in an integrated economic enterprise, the father now went out of the home to earn the family's living.

Second, factory employment freed young adults from direct dependence on their families. As their wages made them financially independent, the authority of the head of the household weakened further.

Urbanization brought the development of hotels and rooming houses, restaurants, bakeries, grocery stores, and laundries, making it possible for people to live apart from families. This situation had special significance for women, who no longer had to marry to have a place to live and who no longer had to stay married simply because there was no alternative. The divorce rate began to rise.

Finally, children ceased to be economic assets and became liabilities. Although there was a period of the use and abuse of child labor, legal regulation gradually removed children from the job market. At the same time, educational requirements increased, lengthening dependence on parental support. Living space in the cities was crowded and expensive; child care was demanding. The birthrate began to fall.

So we come to the contemporary American family. To compress 3000 years of history into one chapter obviously produces oversimplification. We have not presented a detailed history of the Western family but have traced threads that are relevant to understanding the family system of today. Some "meaning" has been implicit and explicit in this discussion. A few sociologists have confronted this problem of meaning more directly and have formulated comprehensive theories of family structure and family change. Before turning to the modern American family, we shall examine several of these theoretical analyses.

SUMMARY

The pastoral Hebrew family was patriarchal, patrilineal, patrilocal, polygynous, and extended. Larger kin groups included the sib, the clan, and the tribe. The patriarch could marry off his children at will, sell them into slavery, or even kill them. Only widowed mothers were free of male control, and wives could be killed for adultery.

Minimum ages for marriage were 13 for boys and 12 for girls. Betrothal took two forms: *kaseph*, involving the transfer of money, and *kiddushin*, which required a written instrument. Marriage was a private matter involving the signing of the *ketubah*, or marriage deed. Marriage was highly valued for producing sons and included the practice of the levirate. Primogeniture was practiced.

Patriarchs could divorce their wives through handing them a bill of divorcement. Wives had no divorce rights. As the rabbis gained power, husbands' rights of divorce were restricted and wives gained the right to divorce for certain specified causes.

The ancient Greek family also was patriarchal, patrilineal, patrilocal, and extended. The patriarch was trustee of the family estates and priest in the practice of ancestor worship. Athenian women had low status, being defined as inherently inferior to men. The father could expose infants, sell children's labor, and could bestow them in marriage. *Agnation*, or tracing descent only through males, and primogeniture were practiced.

Betrothal was essentially a business contract; marriage was a private family matter. Marriage was a sacred obligation. Monogamy with concubines was the norm. Husbands early gained the right to repudiate their wives. Only later did wives gain limited divorce rights.

The pre-Punic War Roman family was the most complete patriarchy ever known. The power of a father over his children was called *potestas*, and that of a husband over his wife, *manus*. Nevertheless, women had high status. There were two principal marriage forms, *matrimonium justum* and *matrimonium nonjustum*. Husbands could repudiate wives, with divorce for specified causes emerging gradually.

This family system began to disintegrate after the Punic Wars. Women became powerful and marriage without *manus* became common. *Potestas* declined. Government efforts to limit celibacy, childlessness, divorce, and abortion failed.

The Christians gradually assumed control of family matters. Reaction to Roman excesses resulted in lowering the status of marriage, lowering the status of women, and defining sex as evil. Remarriages were discouraged, and the indissolubility of marriage proclaimed. Broad prohibitions to marriage were established.

The Christians accepted Teutonic family customs, just as they had the Roman ones. The Germanic and English peoples practiced double descent and had extended kin groups called the *sippe* and the *maegth*. Patriarchy continued, but the power of fathers and husbands was limited. *Beweddung* was betrothal and private marriage, *gifta*, was deeply entrenched. A double standard of morality existed. Gradually, the church eliminated absolute divorce, permitting only *divortium a vinculo matrimonii* (annulment) and *divortium a mensa et thoro* (separation).

Feudalism emphasized warfare and lowered the status of women again. Primogeniture and entail emerged to hold estates intact; marriages were arranged to build estates. With the absence of husbands, upper class women became powerful, and the romantic tradition of chivalry developed. Romantic love was regarded as incompatible with marriage.

In wresting control of marriage from laymen, the church unwittingly encouraged clandestine marriage in words of the present tense. The attempt to distinguish valid from legal marriage failed. Other scandals emerged around the celibate priesthood and the granting of annulments. The Reformation defined marriage as a civil contract and recreated absolute divorce. Most impediments to marriage were removed. The *maegth* declined, but otherwise the English family changed little from the sixteenth to the eighteenth century.

The colonial American family was organized around the nuclear unit and the household. It was a stable system in which the family performed many functions. Patriarchy continued, with the wife's property belonging to the husband and women not being the legal guardians of their children. The common-law minimum ages for marriage were 14 for boys and 12 for girls. Marriage often was based on economic considerations, with haggling occurring over dower and dowry. Parental consent, notice of intention to marry, performance by an authorized officiant, and the registration of marriages all were required. The northern colonies favored civil marriages and permitted divorce, whereas the southern colonies favored religious marriages and prohibited divorce.

With time, the influence of the frontier and geographic mobility further weakened the patriarchal tradition and broke up the family estates. Equal inheritance by all children was encouraged. Heterogeneous family patterns were encouraged by large-scale immigration, with black and ethnic family patterns appearing. Industrialization and urbanization transformed the family into a consumption unit. Work and home became separated, and alternatives to family living became feasible.

SUGGESTED READINGS

Degler, Carl N., *At Odds: Women and the Family in America from the Revolution to the Present*, New York: Oxford University Press, 1980. Presents a historical account of women's situation in relation to the family.

Gordon, Michael, ed., *The American Family in Social-Historical Perspective*, New York: St. Martin's Press, 1973. An excellent collection of essays, covering different facets of the history of American family life.

Hareven, Tamara K., ed., *Family and Kin in Urban Communities, 1700–1930*, New York: New Viewpoints, 1977. A series of essays that relate the family process to the urban process.

Lantz, Herman R., *Marital Incompatibility and Social Change in Early America*, Beverly Hills, Calif.: Sage Publications, 1976. A monograph reporting research into marital incompatibility in eighteenth-century America.

Laslett, Peter, ed., *Household and Family in Past Time*, London: Cambridge University Press, 1972. The most comprehensive collection of reports on research into family history that has yet appeared in print.

QUESTIONS AND PROJECTS

1. Describe the ancient Hebrew patriarchy. What restrictions existed on the power of the father over his children? On the husband over his wife?

2. What was the purpose of marriage among the Hebrews? How were polygyny and concubinage consistent with that purpose?

3. How did the Greek patriarchy differ from the Hebrew? Describe the sources of patriarchal power and the status of women?

4. What is the kinship system known as agnation?

5. Detail the progressive character of Roman family patterns. What parallels existed among the Hebrews and Greeks?

6. Define: *matrimonium justum, potestas, manus, confarreatio, coemptio, usus, diffarreatio.*

7. Why did the early Christians take the positions they did on marriage, sex, and the status of women? What were the church attitudes on divorce and remarriage?

8. Describe the kinship system of the Anglo-Saxon and Teutonic peoples during the Middle Ages. What was the role of the *sippe* or *maegth?*

9. What were the influences of feudalism on family life? Of chivalry?

10. What family-related problems plagued the church during the Middle Ages? How did the Reformation deal with these problems?

11. Describe the family system in the American colonies. What variations existed from North to South?

12. How did the frontier encourage emphasis on the nuclear family? How did immigration increase the heterogeneity of family patterns? What were the effects of urbanization and industrialization?

David Strickler, Monkmeyer

7
Conceptual Approaches in Family Study

The United States, as well as the other countries of western Christendom, will reach the final phases of a great family crisis between now and the last of this century. By that time the social consequences of this crisis will approach a maximum. This crisis will be identical in nature to the two previous crises in Greece and Rome. The results will be much more drastic in the United States because, being the most extreme and inexperienced of the aggregates of western civilization, it will take its first real "sickness" most violently.

Efforts to meet this situation in the United States will probably be very exaggerated. We will probably try all the "remedies" suggested or tried in Greek and Roman civilization, profiting perhaps but little from the mistakes already made in those periods. The violence and abruptness of the changes will probably be extreme indeed.[1]

The husband-father, in holding an acceptable job and earning an income from it is performing an essential function or set of functions for his family (which of course includes himself in one set of roles) as a system. The status of the family in the community is determined probably more by the "level" of job he holds than by any other single factor, and the income he earns is usually the most important basis of the family's standard of living and hence "style of life. . . ." He has other very important functions in relation both to wife and to children, but it is fundamentally by virtue of the importance of his occupational role *as a component of his familial role* that in our society we can unequivocally designate the husband-father as the "instrumental leader" of the family as a system.[2]

This study of the patterns of personal relationships in family life led directly

1. Carle C. Zimmerman, *Family and Civilization*, New York: Harper & Bros., 1947, p. 798.
2. Talcott Parsons and Robert F. Bales, *Family, Socialization and Interaction Process*, Glencoe, Ill.: The Free Press, 1955, p. 13.

to the conception of the family as a unity of interacting persons. By a unity of interacting personalities is meant a living, changing, growing thing. I was about to call it a superpersonality. At any rate the actual unity of family life has its existence not in any legal conception, nor in any formal contract, but in the interaction of its members. For the family does not depend for its survival on the harmonious relations of its members, nor does it necessarily disintegrate as a result of conflicts between its members. The family lives as long as interaction is taking place and only dies when it ceases.[3]

The quotations above indicate that there exist a number of competing views about the family. The ultimate goal of any discipline is the development of one broad theory to explain every aspect of a particular phenomenon. That is, of course, a difficult, if not impossible, task. Scholars in all disciplines bring to their research certain assumptions, concepts, and approaches they believe can best organize and explain the phenomenon under study. The same is true for the family. Although some may view the family as an institution existing passively or actively with other institutions, others may concentrate on the ways in which family members influence each other's behavior. Still other scholars may delineate the various stages a family goes through in its lifetime to understand family behavior, and so on. No one of these approaches is "right" or "best"; they act merely as conceptual tools that aid sociologists in understanding, organizing, and presenting their research topics. These various approaches to the study of the family are called *conceptual frameworks*. Each approach "frames," in an organized and general way, assumptions and concepts for studying various aspects of the family.

The effort to identify and delineate competing conceptual frameworks has been underway for over two decades. The classic work by Hill and Hansen[4] in 1960 identified the underlying assumptions and concepts of five conceptual frameworks: interactional, structural-functional, institutional, situational, and developmental. Since then, these approaches have been refined and others have been added.[5] In 1966, Nye and Berardo delineated 11 approaches.[6] They included the social-psy-

3. Ernest W. Burgess, "The Family as a Unity of Interacting Personalities," in Donald J. Bogue, *ed.*, *The Basic Writings of Ernest W. Burgess*, Chicago: Community and Family Study Center, 1974, pp. 144–45.
4. Reuben Hill and Donald Hansen, "The Identification of Conceptual Frameworks Utilized in Family Study," *Marriage and Family Living* 22 (Nov. 1960), pp. 299–311.
5. See Harold T. Christensen, ed., *Handbook of Marriage and the Family*, Chicago: Rand McNally, 1964; Reuben Hill, "Contemporary Developments in Family Theory," *Journal of Marriage and the Family* 28 (Feb. 1966), pp. 10–26; and Roy H. Rodgers, "Toward a Theory of Family Development," *Journal of Marriage and the Family* 36 (Aug. 1964), pp. 262–70.
6. F. Ivan Nye and Felix M. Berardo, *eds.*, *Emerging Conceptual Frameworks in Family Analysis*, New York: Macmillan, 1966.

chological, economic, legal, and anthropological approaches to family study. Work in the area continues, with other frameworks emerging and some going out of vogue.[7] We have chosen 5 representative approaches to present: the institutional, structural-functional, developmental, interactional, and conflict frameworks. General background, underlying assumptions, conceptual properties, and illustrations will be presented for each.

THE INSTITUTIONAL APPROACH

General Background

The institutional framework was one of the first approaches used in family studies, originating with eighteenth-century anthropologists and early nineteenth-century sociologists. In its original form, the family was likened to an organism that developed through time in an evolutionary fashion toward perfection. Later, this notion was abandoned as it became clear that change did not occur in a linear fashion, nor did it equate with progress.

The contemporary institutional approach uses a historical or cross-cultural approach. An entire society is examined at some point in history to understand how the family institution both fulfills specialized functions for its members and interweaves with other societal institutions. Institutions are viewed as arising in conjunction with human needs and values. This approach to the family is largely descriptive. It is concerned mainly with changes over time in family functions and the causes and effects of these changes on the family and other institutions.

Underlying Assumptions

As with other conceptual frameworks, the institutional approach is based on a number of underlying assumptions. Generally, most institu-

7. See Joan Aldous, "Strategies for Developing Family Theory," *Journal of Marriage and the Family* 32 (May 1970), pp. 250–57; Carlfred B. Broderick, "Beyond the Five Conceptual Frameworks: A Decade of Development in Family Theory," *Journal of Marriage and the Family* 33 (Feb. 1971), pp. 139–59; Wesley R. Burr, Reuben Hill, F. Ivan Nye, and Ira L. Reiss, eds., *Contemporary Theories About the Family*, Vols. I and II, New York: Macmillan, 1979; Thomas B. Holman and Wesley R. Burr, "Beyond the Beyond: The Growth of Family Theories in the 1970s," *Journal of Marriage and the Family* 42 (Nov. 1980), pp. 7–19; Raymond J. R. King, ed., *Family Relations: Concepts and Theories*, Berkeley, Calif.: Glendessary Press, 1969; John F. Klein, Gene P. Calbert, T. Neal Garland, and Margaret M. Poloma, "Pilgrim's Progress I: Recent Developments in Family Theory," *Journal of Marriage and the Family* 31 (Nov. 1969), pp. 677–87; Betty Ruano, James Bruce, and Margaret McDermott, "Pilgrim's Progress II: Recent Developments in Family Theory," *Journal of Marriage and the Family* 31 (Nov. 1969), pp. 688–98; and Robert F. Winch, "Theorizing About the Family," *Journal of Comparative Family Studies* 3 (Spring 1972), pp. 5–15.

tionalists believe that institutions arise from human needs and that they change in accord with changes in individual and group needs over time. The various societal institutions are seen as interdependent structures so that change in one may serve to transform one or more of the other institutions. This approach also assumes that social control and social order are impossible without the existence of institutions. Institutionalists acknowledge that the forms an institution may take are culturally and historically relative and must be examined in these terms. Because this approach examines trends and changes over time, it may be possible to foresee future changes in certain aspects of institutions.

Conceptual Properties

The institutional approach is largely concerned with social change on a grand scale over time. As noted in Chapter 1, an *institution* is a system of social norms organized around the fulfillment of certain societal needs. Although the form an institution takes may vary both historically and from society to society, all societies have five major institutions: economic system, family, government, education, and religion. *Social change* is defined as the differences found in an institution or a society as a whole when compared at two different time periods. Often, some aspects of culture change more rapidly than others (*culture lag*), resulting in what may seem to be social disorganization or the breakdown of society.

Some concepts employed by institutionalists will be found in other frameworks we discuss in this chapter. A *function* is an activity carried out by an institution to serve a societal need. Closely aligned with function is *structure*, which is the means through which a societal need is served. A *status* is a position an individual holds in society (e.g., father or teacher) that serves to identify that person in relation to other individuals and groups. Each of the statuses an individual holds carries with it certain role expectations. *Roles* are patterns of expected behavior that are societally imposed according to one's status position.

Illustrations

Carle C. Zimmerman is perhaps the best known advocate of a cyclical theory of family structure and change.[8] Throughout Western history, he finds that there have been three main family types—the trustee family, the domestic family, and the atomistic family.[9] These three types

---

8. Zimmerman, *op. cit.* Zimmerman's thesis was anticipated in Europe by Frédéric Le Play. See Pierre Guillaume Frédéric Le Play, *Les Ouvriers européens*, Tours: 1879.
9. Zimmerman explicitly states that these are ideal family types rather than empirical family types, *op. cit.*, p. 120.

are defined according to the amount of power vested in the family, the width of its field of action, and the amount of social control it exercises.

In the *trustee family*, living members of the family are not *the family* but are only living trustees of its name, its property, and its blood. The family itself is immortal. There is virtually no concept of individual rights, and questions of individual welfare are subordinated to the welfare of the group. The authority of the husband and father, delegated to him in his role as trustee, often gives him power of life and death over family members. Families are organized into *gentes*, and these combined families make up the state. There is little organized power outside the family; what little government there is does not interfere in family matters. Absolute divorce virtually does not exist. What does exist is the right to repudiate a spouse (wife) who fails to support the integration of the group.

The *domestic family* is an intermediate type that evolves from the trustee family. As the state gains power, the control of the family over its members is weakened. The state does not replace the family but comes to share power with it, restricting the right of the family to punish its members and creating a concept of individual rights to be maintained against family authority. The *gens* tends to disappear. The family remains strong, maintaining a balance between familism and individualism. Conceptions of absolute divorce emerge, but divorce is uncommon. The characteristic device for alleviating marital difficulties is legal separation, *divortium a mensa et thoro*.

The *atomistic family* represents the other extreme. Familism is replaced by individualism. The power and authority of the family are reduced to a minimum, and the state becomes an organization of individuals. Marriage becomes a civil contract rather than a sacrament, and it is often broken by divorce. The sacredness now attached to the individual results in the blurring of distinctions between legitimate and illegitimate children; whereas the trustee family tends to destroy illegitimate children as a threat to itself, the state declares illegitimate children to have full rights in the atomistic family. Other evidence of rampant individualism is to be found in feminist movements, childlessness, youth problems, and so on. The atomistic family loses the capacity to carry out necessary family functions and cannot satisfy the growing demands of individualism.

Zimmerman traces Western history from approximately 1500 B.C. to the present. Change is alleged to occur in giant historical cycles. The great cycles of change in Greek, Roman, and medieval civilization followed a common pattern. Each emerged in a relatively primitive state. Order and stability were achieved through the family, which emerged as the trustee type. The authoritarian character of the trustee family, however, led to the limitation of its power by state and church. The trustee family gradually evolved into the domestic type, which with its balance between individualism and familism, permitted each civilization to achieve greatness. The changes already set in motion, however, led the state to assume greater control until the domestic family was replaced by the atomistic one. In each case, the atomistic family was associated with moral degeneration. Goals of self-sacrifice and creativity in every field gave way to the demands of relentless hedonism.

Zimmerman's erudite analysis of nearly 4000 years of history carries with it a rather pessimistic view for the future. He believes the United States is destined to experience the last stages of a great family crisis by the end of the twentieth century. Unless the government and the church make great efforts toward reviving the familism to be found in the domestic cycle, modern society is destined for decay. It appears unlikely that our civilization will handle the crisis more effectively than earlier civilizations did.[10]

The work of William F. Ogburn also illustrates the institutional approach. His publications spanned more than three decades, the first published in 1922[11] and the last in 1955.[12] He viewed the family not as an active causal agent in social change, but as being acted on from outside, passively adapting to changes in the larger society. Looking outside the family for the primary source of social change, Ogburn found it in the increasing rate of invention in a technologically oriented society. The range of data used by Ogburn was much narrower than Zimmerman's. He confined his analyses of the family to America, using the preindustrial family as an informal baseline and tracing the changes that occurred during the nineteenth and twentieth centuries.

A sharp distinction between material culture (factories, machines, munitions, clothing, and so on) and nonmaterial culture (values, attitudes, customs, institutions, etc.) was central to Ogburn's thinking. He emphasized the different ways in which material and nonmaterial culture change. Change in material culture, he says, tends to be cumulative and directional, whereas change in nonmaterial culture is not characterized by any such regularity.

The difference between material inventions and customs lies in the fact that there are generally agreed-on standards that are used to evalu-

10. For reaffirmation and extension of this position, see Zimmerman's recent publications: "The Atomistic Family: Fact or Fiction," *Journal of Comparative Family Studies* 1 (Autumn 1970), pp. 5–16; "The Future of the American Family II. The Rise of the Counter-Revolution," *International Journal of Sociology of the Family* 2 (March 1972), pp. 1–9; and "The Future of the Nuclear Family," *International Journal of Sociology of the Family* 2 (Sept. 1972), pp. 109–20.
11. *Social Change*, New York: Viking Press, 1922.
12. *Technology and the Changing Family*, Boston: Houghton Mifflin, 1955.

ate material inventions. Thus, an engine may be evaluated in terms of the horsepower it produces, the fuel it consumes, its durability, and so on. With the standards agreed on, a better engine is soon produced, and so on. Change in material culture is rapid and accelerates with time.

In nonmaterial culture, on the other hand, there are few accepted standards. In the arts, for example, who is to determine the merits of Brahms over Mozart or Picasso over Gainsborough? As a consequence of lack of agreement, change in institutions tends to be both slow and without continuing direction. And in the uneven rates of change between material and nonmaterial culture are to be found the sources of culture lag.

The culture-lag hypothesis holds that change in one part of culture requires that corresponding adjustments be made in other related parts. Such adjustments, however, frequently are made only after a lag of months, years, or decades. The intervening period is one of maladjustment or disorganization. During the period of culture lag, the attitudes and customs passed down from previous generations seem to have lost their effectiveness, and there is widespread personal and group distress.

Culture lag is found in the family. Before industrialization, the family was adjusted to agricultural conditions. It possessed economic, educational, recreational, religious, and protective functions along with its biological functions. Marriage was a business arrangement, and divorce was serious. With the development of the factory system, production was taken out of the home. Women who formerly played an important economic role now found themselves forced either to go out of the home to work or to accept an essentially nonproductive role. Children were transformed from economic assets into liabilities. There were not proper places for them to play, and their supervision became onerous for parents and children alike.

Empirical evidence that developments in technology stripped the American family of traditional functions is found in a report prepared for President Hoover's Research Committee on Social Trends and published in 1934.[13] In that report, Ogburn discussed major functions of the family before modern times and the changes that occurred in these functions with rapid advances in technology. The report stated that the economic, protective, religious, recreational, educational, and status-conferring functions once found within the family setting had been displaced largely to agencies outside of family control.

According to Ogburn, disorganization resulted from the loss of these family functions. Symptoms included rising divorce rates, illicit sexual

13. William F. Ogburn and Clark Tibbitts, "The Family and Its Functions," Report of the President's Research Committee on Social Trends, in *Recent Social Trends in the United States,* New York: McGraw-Hill, 1934, pp. 661–708.

activity, family desertion, and juvenile delinquency. Ogburn did not pursue the analysis of family disorganization beyond this point, but he was social scientist enough not to fall victim to the temptation to equate defunctionalization of the family with imminent catastrophe.

Although Ogburn saw the family as losing many of its once-important functions, he also saw the remaining functions strengthened. Emotional satisfaction in marriage and the family came to be emphasized for all family members. As the family ceased to be a productive unit, husbands, wives, and parents were also free to cultivate relationships. Couples became concerned with happiness, seeking personal growth and fulfillment. Parents sought not only food, clothing, and shelter for their offspring but increasingly emphasized the children's social and emotional development. Thus, according to Ogburn, the family has fewer functions today, but it may be performing those few functions better than in the past.[14]

THE STRUCTURAL-FUNCTIONAL APPROACH

General Background

The structural-functional approach had its beginnings with early twentieth-century anthropologists and sociologists and remained a dominant framework through the 1960s. In structural-functional analysis, society is viewed as a dynamic system of interconnected parts. In analyzing this system, one repeatedly asks, "What are the consequences of each part of the system for every other part and for the system as a whole?" In this approach, systems exist at several levels: the individual (personality development), institutional (in this case, family), and societal (the whole social system). Analysis of the family may concentrate on the functions the family performs for its members such as socialization into adult roles and the relationship between the family and other institutional systems. The division of labor between the sexes, the interrelationship of family structure and the occupational system, and personality development in children are major emphases of this approach.

Underlying Assumptions

The structural-functional approach assumes that there are basic functional requisites that must be met in any society for its survival. Subsystems develop to fulfill these requirements. In every known society, past or present, some form of the family has fulfilled at least one of

14. Burgess and Locke call the modern, egalitarian-based family the *companionship* family. See Ernest W. Burgess and Harvey J. Locke, *The Family: From Institution to Companionship*, New York: American Book Co., 1945.

these functional requisites. Hence, the family is believed to be a universal phenomenon.

This approach also assumes that the individual acts in accord with an internalized set of norms and values learned through socialization that fulfills the system's needs; independent action is rare and asocial. Subsystems also work toward maintaining boundaries and an equilibrium, or a regulated internal structure.

Conceptual Properties

As with the institutional approach, the structural-functional approach employs the concepts of *structure, function, status,* and *role.* Although the emphasis of this approach is on the functions necessary for the survival of the system, it acknowledges that not all activities have positive or intended consequences. An activity may have a *manifest function*—recognized and intended consequences, or a *latent function*—unrecognized and unintended consequences. An activity may also be *dysfunctional* to the system; it may carry negative consequences.

Within the family, there is *role differentiation,* dependent on such factors as age and sex. The division of labor and role responsibilities are allocated on the basis of these positional factors, or *statuses.* This approach holds that there are primarily two domains of role responsibility within the family: the *instrumental* and the *expressive.* The instrumental domain centers around a leadership position and is primarily concerned with achievement, resource attainment, and interaction with the occupational system: the breadwinner role. This domain traditionally has been associated with the husband-father role. The expressive domain centers around a supportive position and is primarily concerned with nurturance, emotional satisfactions, and the integration of the family. This domain traditionally has been associated with the wife-mother role.

Illustrations

The most systematic application of structural-functional theory to the family probably has been made by Talcott Parsons.[15] Parsons's analysis begins with emphasis on the American family system as open, multilineal, and conjugal. Isolation of the nuclear family from larger kin groups

15. Parsons's most comprehensive work on the family is one written with Bales, *op. cit.* See also Talcott Parsons, "The Social Structure of the Family," in Ruth N. Anshen, ed., *The Family: Its Function and Destiny,* New York: Harper & Bros., 1949, pp. 241–74; "Age and Sex in the Social Structure of the United States," *American Sociological Review* 7 (Oct. 1942), pp. 604–16; and Hyman Rodman, "Talcott Parsons' View of the Changing American Family," in Hyman Rodman, ed., *Marriage, Family and Society,* New York: Random House, 1965, pp. 262–86.

is built into the family structure. At marriage, each person is partially removed from one kinship unit (nuclear family) and creates one new family. Ego is the only common member of the families of orientation and procreation, the spouse shares the same family of procreation but not the same family of orientation—and so on for each member of the family.

There is a poverty of kinship terms in the American family system. We really have only the term *family*, which usually refers to the nuclear family, and the term *relatives*, which does not refer to a kinship unit but includes all of the other people to whom a person is regarded as related. The monogamous character of the system is shown by the fact that the terms *mother, father, husband,* and *wife* apply to only one person at a time. All brothers and sisters are called by the same term. Contrast this with the Chinese system, in which older and younger brothers are called by separate terms.[16]

Parsons's analysis of the family also focuses on the open and multilineal nature of the system. He uses the term *multilineal* to emphasize that no kin groups based on lines of descent tend to develop. Each generation selects its mates from outside the circle of relatives and without consideration for cementing ties with kin of earlier generations. Thus, there are no preferred marriage partners. Moreover, there are strict norms that militate against favoritism to either the husband's or the wife's family line. Arrangements often are made to guarantee equal treatment on both sides, and parents are expected to treat their offspring equally in terms of gifts and inheritance.

Parsons describes marriage as the structural keystone of our kinship system. Unlike the situation in most societies, Americans have no kinship unit in which they retain membership throughout life. Instead, at marriage, they assume loyalties to spouses and children that outweigh loyalties to parents and siblings. Adjustment between the spouses is paramount, and relationships with other kin are largely irrelevant. Integration of the couple into a larger kin group may even be dysfunctional to the marriage. Moreover, residence is neolocal. Young married couples are expected to take up residence apart from the location (and influence) of both parental families.

Consistent with the structural and geographic isolation of the conjugal family unit, parents are not expected to play a significant role in mate selection. Contrary to the arranged-marriage system of other soci-

16. For illustrations of the research use to which kinship terminology and terms of address may be put, see Lionel S. Lewis, "Terms of Address for Parents and Some Clues About Social Relationships in the American Family," *Family Life Coordinator* 14 (April 1965), pp. 43–46; and Jay D. Schvaneveldt, "The Nuclear and Extended Family as Reflected in Autobiographical Dedications: A Comparative Study," *Journal of Marriage and the Family* 28 (Nov. 1966), pp. 495–97.

eties, American mate selection is expected to be freely made on the basis of romantic love. Love is also seen to be the primary reason for staying married. Large kin groups typically discourage romantic love because attraction between spouses would threaten the priority of their loyalties to parents and to the group. Where the large kin group is absent, however, romantic love serves as a substitute for detailed role prescriptions. The emotional attraction between partners in the conjugal unit is the functionally equivalent substitute for the large kinship group in conflict resolution and problem solving. Romantic love as the basis for marriage provides a strong bond and at the same time makes a variety of role relationships possible.

According to this analysis, the family system cannot be understood without reference to its ties to the occupational system. Parsons asserts that the status of the American family is bound up with the husband's occupation through the income, prestige, and style of life that derive from it. If one had to construct a picture of what any family is like from the answer to a single question, the most useful question probably would be, "What does the husband do for a living?" His occupation and the perquisites that go with it heavily influence where a family will live, their values and aspirations, how they are regarded by others, their material possessions, the nature of the children's education, and so on.

In preindustrial economies, there often is a direct integration between the family and occupational systems. The father works around the home, and other family members assist him. With the appearance of industry, this is no longer possible. The husband must go outside the home to earn a living. The world of business and the world of the family are structured on two entirely different sets of criteria that must not impinge on each other. This creates a dilemma in terms of role enactment that is resolved through the segregation of familial and occupational roles.[17] The world of the family and the world of the job are fairly completely separated.

According to Parsons, only the man usually plays a fully competitive role in the occupational system. The segregation of occupational and familial roles isolates the nuclear family and protects it against destructive internal rivalries. It also permits the social and geographic mobility required by the system. Whereas in an agricultural economy, the son remains on the farm and at the same social level as his father, the requirements of an industrial economy are different. Children can be suc-

17. For accounts of how family and occupational roles impinge on one another, see Joan Aldous, "Occupational Characteristics and Males' Role Performance in the Family," *Journal of Marriage and the Family* 31 (Nov. 1969), pp. 707–12; and John Scanzoni, "Occupation and Family Differentiation," *Sociological Quarterly* 8 (Spring 1967), pp. 187–98.

cessful in the economy only by moving with their jobs, acquiring technical skills, and developing new attitudes and values.

Parsons states that the isolated nuclear family is found most extensively among white, urban, middle-class Americans. The isolated nuclear family is presented as the prototypical American Family. It is the family portrayed and admired through TV, the movies, radio, and so on.

Parsons's emphasis on the apparent isolation of the nuclear family has caused difficulty. The theory assumes, but does not prove, that nuclear families are socially and physically more isolated than they were during the preindustrial era. Data have been amassed in recent years that cast doubt on this assumption. However, Parsons maintains, and his point appears valid, that the theory and data are not necessarily contradictory. The explanatory power of the concept of isolation lies principally in the context of anthropological comparisons with other societies, not in the context of the history of our own society.

THE DEVELOPMENTAL APPROACH

General Background

The developmental approach was first introduced in the early 1930s by family sociologists. Originally employed by rural sociologists, it later became prominent among home economists and those interested in child growth and development. This life-span approach currently enjoys wide usage by scholars in a number of family subspecialties.

The developmental framework focuses both on the individual within the family setting and the family as a whole unit. It views the family in a succession of developmental stages that begin at marriage and end with the death of the last spouse. As an organism grows, develops, and changes with time, so it is with the family. This approach adopts the premise that at each stage within the family life cycle, there are certain tasks that must be accomplished if the family is to function as a secure and healthy unit. This approach might focus on such topics as the changes that occur within the household on the birth of the first child or spousal interaction after all children have left the "nest."

Underlying Assumptions

The developmental approch assumes that the family unit (the nuclear family) is affected both by the interaction between family members and by the external social environment. The family unit and individuals change in accord with these two ongoing processes. Within each developmental stage, there are certain tasks that must be accomplished to prepare the family for change and for competency in the familial and social worlds. These tasks could more realistically be defined as goals toward which a family strives rather than requisite functions that *must* be accomplished. It is possible for a family to move from one stage to another without having completed the tasks of the earlier stage. This approach also assumes that human behavior is the result of both inter-action among family members and experience with the external social environment.

Conceptual Properties

The family is held to be a *semiclosed system*, neither wholly dependent on, nor independent from other social systems. This approach focuses on the *family life cycle*, which is composed of a series of critical stages through which the family passes as it expands, grows, and diminishes over time. As the family constellation changes (e.g., children are born, enter the teen years, leave home), role expectations, obligations, and responsibilities also change. Family interaction is influenced by the age and sex composition of its combined membership.

With each subsequent stage in the family life cycle come a series of *developmental tasks* that must be successfully accomplished to satisfy both human and cultural needs and to pave the way for future tasks. These may include a child's need to learn motor skills, establishing a new home, or the gaining of competence in raising children. Each family is a unique unit, different from all others in its age-sex composition, its exposure and reaction to impositions from the external social world, and its ability to accomplish the various development tasks before it.

Illustrations

The effort toward explaining family behavior through a series of developmental stages began in the early 1930s. Evelyn Millis Duvall, however, was the first scholar to consolidate earlier efforts into a comprehensive work on the developmental life-span approach to family living.[18]

18. Evelyn Millis Duvall, *Family Development*, Philadelphia: J. B. Lippincott, 1957. The present discussion closely follows this work. See also Duvall's "Conceptions of Parenthood," *American Journal of Sociology* 52 (March 1946), pp. 193–203; and "Implications for Education Through the Family Life Cycle," *Marriage and Family Living* 20 (Nov. 1958), pp. 334–42. For other provocative analyses of the family life cycle concept, see Sylvia Clavan, "The Family Process: A Sociological Model," *Family Coordinator* 18 (Oct. 1969), pp. 312–17; Frances A. Magrabi and William H. Marshall, "Family Developmental Tasks: A Research Model," *Journal of Marriage and the Family* 27 (Nov. 1965), pp. 454–58; Steven L. Nock, "The Family Life Cycle: Empirical or Conceptual Tool?" *Journal of Marriage and the Family* 41 (Feb. 1979), pp. 15–26; Arthur J. Norton, "Family Life Cycle: 1980," *Journal of Marriage and the Family* 45 (May 1983), pp. 267–75;

In 1957, she depicted the family life cycle and its accompanying developmental tasks in a series of eight stages:

Stage I   Beginning Families (married couple without children)

Stage II   Childbearing Families (oldest child, birth to 30 months)

Stage III   Families with Preschool Children (oldest child 2½ to 6 years)

Stage IV   Families with School Children (oldest child 6 to 13 years)

Stage V   Families with Teenagers (oldest child 13 to 20 years)

Stage VI   Families as Launching Centers (first child gone to last child leaving home)

Stage VII   Families in the Middle Years (empty nest to retirement)

Stage VIII   Aging Families (retirement to death of one or both spouses)

Although every family constitutes a unique, individual unit, there are certain general developmental tasks that face family members within each life-span stage.

According to Duvall, Stage I of the family life cycle (Beginning Families) entails the period of time from the marriage of the couple until the birth of the first child. She divides this stage into two phases: the establishment phase and the expectant phase. The establishment phase begins with the marriage of the couple and continues until they become aware of the wife's pregnancy. The time period involved in this phase varies, of course, from couple to couple. Duvall lists nine developmental tasks that face couples in this phase of their marriage. Couples work toward establishing (1) a home of their own; (2) an income and outgo of money; (3) patterns of who does what and who is accountable to whom; (4) a mutually satisfying sexual relationship; (5) systems of intellectual and emotional communication; (6) workable relationships with relatives; (7) patterns of interaction with friends, associates, and the community; (8) a workable philosophy of life as a couple; and (9) the expectation of, and planning for, children. Along with these familial tasks, there are developmental goals that the couple face as individuals in their new roles as husband and wife.

The second phase of Stage I, the expectant phase, lasts from the time the couple becomes aware of the pregnancy until the time of the baby's birth. This phase presents the couples with new tasks they must face, including reorganizing the household to prepare for the new baby; acquiring knowledge about and planning the specifics of pregnancy, child-

---

Roy H. Rodgers, op. cit.; and Graham B. Spanier, William Sauer, and Robert Larzelere, "An Empirical Evaluation of the Family Life Cycle," *Journal of Marriage and the Family* 41 (Feb. 1979), pp. 27–38.

birth, and parenthood; and informing relatives, friends, and associates about the impending birth and reorienting relationships accordingly.

Stage II (Childbearing Families) of Duvall's life-span perspective begins with the birth of the baby and continues until the child is 30 months of age. At this stage, family life becomes more complex as the couple take on the new roles of mother and father and reorient their household to include a third member. They face the developmental tasks of their family unit and the tasks of their new roles. The young mother must balance her attention to the child with her attention to her husband and at the same time maintain her own identity as an individual. She must care for the child with competence and love and acclimate herself to the pressures and strains that usually mark the early months of child care. She must also closely attend to the child's physical, emotional, and developmental needs. The new father usually faces the responsibility of earning the family's income and providing the resources for the family's style of life. He must also maintain a satisfying relationship with the wife and encourage the child's development by conforming to new regimens suitable to a young family. During this stage of its life, the child is also facing a series of tasks, many hours in the learning, that prepare it for future development. The child must learn sleep patterns, how to suck from a nipple and later to take solid foods, how to adjust to other people, motor skills and coordination, systems of communication, and how to manipulate the physical environment. This is a period of intense learning for the child.

Stage III of Duvall's life-cycle perspective (Families with Preschool Children) lasts from the time the child is 2½ to 6 years of age. As the child moves through this preschool stage, he or she is faced with many new tasks to learn and accomplish. It must master toilet training and the physical skills appropriate to its stage of motor development. The child must also put impulsive behavior aside in favor of behavior appropriate to others' expectations. Good sleeping and eating habits are important also. The child during this period is also learning to associate with adults other than parents and to play and get along with other children. Often during this period of time, the family has added a second child, and all members are adjusting interaction patterns to encompass the growing family and the developmental tasks that face them.

The next stage (Families with School Children) begins when the oldest child enters school and lasts until that child is a teenager. Often, during Stage IV, the family also has preschool children at home. The tasks that face the child during this time are complex and often may entail much responsibility. Entering and progressing successfully through school requires the mastery of new intellectual and emotional skills. The child must also learn how to handle money, relationships with the opposite sex, new physical skills requisite to certain sports, and behavior appropriate to his or her own sex role. The prepubescent period brings rapid bodily changes, which must be accepted, and a self-image as a future adult, which can be used to guide behavior. Children are also learning to be active members within the family unit, cooperating and participating in home maintenance tasks and (often) decision-making discussions. Parents during this stage are also facing new tasks, one of which is allowing the older child the freedom to pursue relationships and interests outside the family sphere. Cooperation is also necessary to ensure that all the things a burgeoning family requires are secured and that everything that must get done is done. The parents must, of course, also continue to interest and satisfy each other as married partners.

Stage V of Duvall's schema (Families with Teenagers) begins when the oldest child is around 13 years of age and continues through the end of the teen years. The teenager continues to explore emotional and physical maturity and independence from parental constraints. During this time, the teenager is starting to examine educational and occupational options while discovering the intimacy of opposite-sex relationships through dating. Dating also provides the opportunity to discover what traits are desirable in a future spouse. Teenagers also use this time to gain competence and confidence in future adult roles. During this time, parents work toward providing good role models for their teenagers, help them with money matters, serve as guides in the emotional aspects of opposite-sex relationships, and work toward maintaining lines of effective communication as their teenagers move through what may be a very difficult period in their lives.

Stage VI (Families as Launching Centers) finds the once-expanding family now contracting in size as the oldest child leaves the home. The oldest child is now either pursuing college, beginning a career, serving in the military, or moving into marriage. Within each of these options, there are a new set of competencies that the adult child must now master. In terms of marriage, the adult child must first go steady, discover appropriate ways of expressing and accepting love, become engaged, and either propose or accept a marriage pact. When an adult child marries, the parents must widen their circle to accept the new spouse and in-laws. They must also find lines of communication and assistance that are appropriate to the new situation without becoming interfering parents. They must reaffirm their own relationship as the children who once bound them together begin to leave the home. They must also practice treating adult children as adults to minimize conflict between the generations.

Stage VII (Families in the Middle Years) begins when all children have left the "nest" and continues until retirement. The couple once again find themselves alone in the household without children. Many of the tasks that now face the couple center around adjusting to life without children to care for. The husband and wife must discover and develop as individuals their mutual relationship and their personal identities. Middle-aged parents work toward maintaining a good relationship with their adult children and with their own aged parents. They must accept and adjust to the physical changes that their bodies go through during this time. The husband, and particularly the wife, seek out new activities and new ways to spend their leisure time. This is also the period of adjustment to the grandparent role.

The eighth and final stage of Duvall's schema (Aging Families) covers the time from retirement until the death of one or both spouses. This is generally a period of slowing down and adjusting to the changes that come with advancing age. The couple, particularly the husband, must adjust to the realities of retirement and the style of life that a retirement income brings. The maintenance of ties with children, grandchildren, relatives, and friends as well as civic activities are also important during this period of life. The aging couple must be ready to adjust to the changes in their bodies and often to the infirmities that come with advancing age. On the death of one spouse, the remaining spouse must cope with bereavement and life without the loved one. Often widowhood, the frailty of old age, and impending infirmity mean that the remaining spouse must give up the family home and seek residence in a new location or with a family member. A new home at this stage of life brings with it a series of adjustments with which the aged person must cope.

THE INTERACTIONAL APPROACH

General Background

The interactional approach, or symbolic interactionism, is the framework most widely used by family scholars today. It received its major impetus from the work of early philosophers and sociologists such as Georg Simmel, William James, Charles Horton Cooley, and George Herbert Mead. It was previously believed that the understanding and explanation of human behavior was founded in a set of instincts peculiar to the human organism. With these pioneering scholars, however, came the belief that people rather than being bound by evolutionary instincts instead have the capacity to use and manipulate symbols and to think freely and creatively. Because of this, individuals have the capacity to attach meanings to phenomena in the environment and to share these meanings with others. These meanings, or shared symbols, are learned

through interaction with others and have their greatest impact and significance within the family unit. The interactional approach holds that
the key to understanding family behavior lies in the interaction between
family members and the interpretations that individuals attribute to
these interactions. Because family members constantly influence each
other's behavior, the family is a growing, changing, dynamic unit.

Underlying Assumptions

This approach assumes that an infant is neither social nor antisocial but
rather asocial: a *blank slate*. Infants become social beings through interaction with others. The primary source of this socialization is the family, through which the child learns norms, values, symbols, and meanings. Individuals are actors as well as reactors. Through the process of
socialization, people learn to *take the role of the other* and imagine how
their own interaction will affect and be received by other people. They
develop a self-consciousness: how they are seen through the eyes of
others, what Cooley calls the *looking-glass self*. Dependent on the situation at hand and how that situation is interpreted, the individual will
choose from a cluster of roles the appropriate role to play. The student, for example, presents himself or herself differently, depending on
whether the interaction is with a parent, a teacher, a friend, or a sibling.
The individual personality is made up of many facets or roles that are
played out day by day.

Conceptual Properties

This framework focuses primarily on human interaction, which is the
process by which communication of any kind between two (or more)
persons serves to modify the behavior of those involved. Humans learn
to interact effectively through *role-taking* and *role-playing*. Individuals
take the role of the other when they anticipate how they will be received
by another and modify their behavior in accord with these perceptions.
Role-playing is the enactment of a pattern of behavior in line with group
expectations.

    Infants become humans capable of interaction through *socialization*
in the family home. This *primary group* is characterized by a high degree of intimacy and intense face-to-face communication. Because family members are constantly modifying each other's behavior through interaction, the family is a growing, changing, dynamic unit. The socialized
person learns to interpret the *symbolic environment*—composed of norms,
values, and shared meanings—of the *reference groups* with whom that
individual shares some identification.

Illustrations

One of the first textbooks that viewed the family within the interactional framework was written by Willard Waller in 1938.[19] This work was revised and expanded by Reuben Hill in 1951.[20] From an interactional perspective, Waller and Hill trace personality development, habit formation, love, courtship and mate selection, marriage and parenthood, and family breakdown.[21]

The family as an intimate primary group serves as the infant's first introduction to the social world. It is within this setting that the infant first faces restrictions on behavior and learns the processes of interaction that construct a social being. By the time the child encounters nonfamily influences, a repertoire of actions and reactions have been absorbed, internalized, and rehearsed. The child has learned cooperation in the fulfillment of personal and others' needs and the cultural components peculiar to his or her group. The interdependence of family members and the special emotional quality of the family unit serves to make this early socialization particularly impactful on the individual.

Within Waller and Hill's interactional framework, this period of early socialization involves not only the influence of parents on children but also the reciprocal effects of children on parents. The interactions of the various members within the family unit affect and modify the behavior of all. Just as children need to receive love and nurturance from their parents to thrive, so do parents need to provide this emotional bonding in fulfillment of their parental roles. The relationships are reciprocal, and because family members are ever changing, the family unit is in a constant state of flux: a dynamic unit.

It is within the family setting that the child first learns a consciousness of *self*. Interaction requires a degree of predictability; one must be able to predict, within a range of behaviors, the sort of actions and reactions that one's presence will elicit. Through the cumulative process of positive and negative feedback from associations within the home, the child learns what is acceptable behavior and what is not. Through the prac-

19. Willard Waller, *The Family: A Dynamic Interpretation*, New York: Cordon, 1938.
20. Willard Waller and Reuben Hill, *The Family: A Dynamic Interpretation* (rev. ed.), New York: Dryden Press, 1951. The present discussion focuses on this work.
21. Other works utilizing the interactional approach to the family include William J. Goode, "A Theory of Role Strain," *American Sociological Review* 25 (Aug. 1960), pp. 488–96; Bernard I. Murstein, "Stimulus–Value–Role: A Theory of Marital Choice," *Journal of Marriage and the Family* 37 (Aug. 1970), pp. 465–81; F. Ivan Nye *et al.*, *Role Structure and Analysis of the Family*, Beverly Hills, Calif.: Sage Publications, 1976; Sheldon Stryker, "Symbolic Interaction Theory: A Review and Some Suggestions for Comparative Family Research," *Journal of Comparative Family Studies* 3 (Spring 1972), pp. 17–32; and Ralph H. Turner, *Family Interaction*, New York: John Wiley & Sons, 1970.

tice of imagining how they appear to other people, *taking the role of the other,* children learn to modify their behavior in the presentation of a favorable self-image. The emergence of this *social self* also requires the effective transmittal to the child of the communicative process—the symbols, gestures, and meanings relative to the culture.

According to Waller and Hill, not only are the dynamics of socialization and personality growth relative to the cultural milieu but love, courtship, and mate selection are subject to these cultural forces as well. Although commonly attributed to fate, to the gods, or to a bolt out of the blue, love is actually a cultural product that results from interaction and is carefully constrained in line with cultural expectations. Romantic love is a Western notion and a fairly recent phenomenon. Western culture calls for love before marriage, heterosexual love, and love for only one individual for a lifetime. Contrast this with the ancient Greek ideal of love between an older, experienced man and a young boy or today's polygamous marriages, which are based on economic and social status.

Waller and Hill believe that love is a carefully conditioned social product. People fall in love because they are trained to do so. When in love, one tends to idealize the loved one, to create a picture of that person as a unique, perfect individual. There is a period of euphoria during which even conflicts and adjustments may be seen as pleasurable.

On the basis of these feelings, a mate is chosen. Waller and Hill believe that people do not marry others who will make the best spouses but rather those with whom they can most easily fall in love. The selection of a marriage partner and subsequent married life are largely influenced by experiences in the parental home. Feelings of love, affection, and dependency learned in the family unit may be carried over into adult life so that individuals construct a picture of the ideal marriage or ideal mate. Partners may even be chosen on the basis of their physical or emotional resemblance to a parent. Few ever meet, though, let alone marry, their vision of the ideal person. Usually concessions or modifications of the ideal image are made when evaluating a potential mate and traits not previously part of the image become desirable.

The beginning of a new marriage is a period of time in which patterns of interaction that will influence the marriage are being tested and defined. Because the marital situation is for the couple an as yet unexplored situation, the mates are testing their new roles and tentatively forming new habits as a married couple. They are extremely sensitive to each other's moods and needs. As time goes by, the euphoria and idealization that characterized the engagement and early marriage give way to reality, and the partners may have to deal with disappointment, disillusionment, and the realization that one has promised a lifetime to someone who is just an ordinary person. Personality changes may occur as the couple settle into their roles as husband and wife, and some may alarmingly find themselves paralleling their own parents' lives. The sources of conflict that may strain the marital bond during this period are many—sexual adjustment, clashing egos, role conflict, the realization that the spouse has annoying or disgusting habits, in-law problems, and so on.

The ways in which conflicts emerge and are handled can have a profound effect on the marriage. Although conflict is an inevitable outcome as the two partners adjust to, and grow in, their marital situation, it can be put to either productive or destructive purposes. Waller and Hill state that destructive quarreling is directed at the whole person rather than issues in an attempt at demoralizing the individual and the little fictions about each other that form the foundation of the marriage. These tend to accelerate with time and often end by alienating the couple and putting severe strains on the marriage. These marriages often end in early divorce. Productive quarreling is issue related and limited in duration. Often the outcome of this type of quarreling is new insights and understandings that serve to fortify and preserve the relationship.

Along with the sources of potential conflict within the marital bond are those forces that work toward couple solidarity. There is, first of all, the couple's expectation that their marriage will be a success. The partners make adjustments, concessions, and special efforts toward making their marriage work. The idea that if their marriage ends, they will somehow have failed may serve to impel an unhappy couple to work out their differences and preserve the marriage. There is also the cultural expectation that people should marry and stay married. Marriages are expected to be happy and if not, there is still the expectation that they will be long lasting. Social participation is also geared toward couple solidarity. The partners, together as a couple, usually attend parties, sporting events, dinners, and so on. Attendance by only one partner may be taken by others to mean unhappiness or estrangement in the relationship. Factors internal to the family unit may also strengthen the marital bond. With time comes acclimation to each other's habits, intimate rapport, shared empathy, and emotional and sexual interdependence.

With the birth and rearing of children comes a new series of adjustments as the number of persons interacting increases. The spouses must adjust to their new roles as mother and father, and children learn the adjustments that come with the socialization process. Because all the members of the family unit are constantly interacting within the structure of their respective family roles, the potential to affect and modify each other's behavior is ever present. For this reason, the family is always in a state of flux, constantly changing and growing as the various personalities intermesh.

THE CONFLICT APPROACH

General Background

In its application to the family, the conflict approach is a relatively new framework. Although Engels[22] in 1902 wrote of the capitalist family as the source of women's oppression, it was not really until the turbulent decades of the 1960s and 1970s that the conflict approach took hold.[23] It was given enormous impetus by the visibility of black leaders and women activists rallying for change in the familial and social structures.

Unlike some of the other conceptual approaches that view conflict as a pathological threat to the stability of the family, this framework views it as a natural, normal outcome of human interaction. Because of this, the emphasis of the approach is on conflict management and the allocation of power and resources among family members. Studies utilizing the conflict framework might focus on such topics as spouse abuse, the ways in which families solve problems, and marital dissolution.

Underlying Assumptions

The conflict approach assumes that conflict management, avoidance, and resolution are normal and ongoing processes within the family system. Because members occupy different status positions by virtue of their age and sex, the family composes a hierarchy of authority. This hierarchy results in a perpetual system of inequality; family members have differential access to power and resources. The inherent inequality forms the basis of conflict as family members bargain and compete for those things of value. Although the potential for competition and conflict is ever

22. Friedrich Engels, *The Origin of the Family, Private Property, and the State*, Chicago: Charles H. Kerr and Co., 1902.
23. See, for example, Bruce Glick, "Marital Interaction and Marital Conflict: A Critical Evaluation of Current Strategies," *Journal of Marriage and the Family* 37 (Aug. 1975), pp. 505-12; William J. Goode, "Force and Violence in the Family," *Journal of Marriage and the Family* 33 (Nov. 1971), pp. 624-36; Bernadette Gray-Little, "Marital Quality and Power Processes Among Black Couples," *Journal of Marriage and the Family* 44 (Aug. 1982), pp. 633-46; George Levinger, "Marriage Cohesiveness and Dissolution: An Integrative Review," *Journal of Marriage and the Family* 27 (Feb. 1965), pp. 19-28; John Scanzoni, *Sexual Bargaining*, Englewood Cliffs, N.J.: Prentice-Hall, 1972; John Scanzoni and Karen Polonko, "A Conceptual Approach to Explicit Marital Negotiation," *Journal of Marriage and the Family* 42 (Feb. 1980), pp. 31-44; and Irving Tallman, "The Family as a Small Problem Solving Group," *Journal of Marriage and the Family* 31 (Feb. 1970), pp. 94-104.

present, common goals and mutual affection serve to solidify family members. This approach also assumes that conflict can have positive as well as negative consequences for the family unit and that suppression of conflict can often be detrimental for the members. The absence of conflict does not necessarily ensure family happiness and success.

Conceptual Properties

Conflict occurs within the family as members struggle for scarce *resources:* those things considered to be of value such as money, attention, authority, and role competence. They may also *negotiate* or *bargain* for competing goals. Conflictual interaction can range from verbal manipulations to overt physical force. *Consensus*, or the agreement on an issue by all parties concerned, is one means of managing conflict. *Power*, or the ability to influence interactions and outcomes, is a major directive force within the family unit.

Illustrations

Through a series of articles, sociologist Jetse Sprey presents the family as a system in which conflict rather than harmony is the norm.[24] Unlike scholars who view the family analogously as an organism that strives toward equilibrium, Sprey views the family as an arena in which conflicting interests and personalities intermesh. Peace within the family unit is the outcome of effective negotiations that are continually subject to change.

Whereas other sociologists view the family as a haven for individuals from the stresses and pressures of the outside world, Sprey proposes the reverse as equally possible. The cool impartiality of the outside world, represented by work, casual associations, and friendships, may mediate the intimate hostilities of the family bond. The concept of voluntary participation in family life is important for understanding the nature of family hostilities. Although our mate-selection system is such that it appears, on the surface, to be a system free from external constraints, this is not actually the case. The societal expectation that one should marry and the lack of a socially approved life alternative make a strict norm. People enter marriage, consciously or unconsciously, because of the societal

24. Jetse Sprey, "Family Disorganization: Toward a Conceptual Clarification," *Journal of Marriage and the Family* 28 (Nov. 1966), pp. 398–406; "The Family as a System in Conflict," *Journal of Marriage and the Family* 31 (Nov. 1969), pp. 699–706; "On the Management of Conflict in Families," *Journal of Marriage and the Family* 33 (Nov. 1971), pp. 722–31; and "Conflict Theory and the Study of Marriage and the Family," in Wesley R. Burr, Reuben Hill, F. Ivan Nye, and Ira L. Reiss, *eds.*, *Contemporary Theories About the Family*, V.II, New York: The Free Press, 1979, pp. 130–59.

expectation that they should be married. This lessens the salience of marriage as a voluntary system. And also, of course, children do not choose the family into which they are born. These factors set the stage for competing interests.

Sprey rejects the conventional research question that asks how conflict arises within the family setting and asks instead how it is that cooperation is possible among family members. The answer to this question lies in the fact that it is possible for individuals to have different goals, ideas, and interests and still respect each other's stance in a mutually cooperative relationship. This can happen only in the instance in which there exists a set of mutually shared and understood procedural rules of interaction. Problematic interaction occurs when these rules are missing, haphazardly applied, or accepted by only one member. Marital problems occur not because of the differences between partners, as these occur normally, but rather because of the inability of the partners to live with each other's differences. These ever-present differences are handled effectively in successful marriages. Sprey contends that marriages that work are the ones in which members negotiate conflict in a mutually satisfying manner. Marriages that dissolve tend to have had partners who handled conflict differently from successful ones and in ways that served to alienate the members. Poor management of conflict and alienated family members do not always mean that the unit will dissolve in divorce however. It is possible for this type of marriage to last a lifetime. Most probably, however, the members will be neither satisfied nor happy with their marital situation. Marriages that succeed develop a system of procedural rules that are used effectively to negotiate conflictual issues that arise in the marriage and that are flexible enough to accept change and renegotiation as needs and interests change.

SUMMARY

Conceptual frameworks are useful tools for organizing and clarifying research ideas. This chapter presents the general backgrounds, underlying assumptions, conceptual properties, and illustrations of five conceptual frameworks: the institutional, structural-functional, developmental, interactional, and conflict approaches.

The institutional framework uses a historical or cross-cultural approach and is concerned with social change on a grand scale over time. Institutions arise from human needs and change in accord with changing needs. The forms an institution may take must be examined in culturally and historically relative terms. Institutions are seen as interdependent structures so that change in one may serve to transform one or more of the other institutions. Often, some aspects of culture change more rapidly than others, and it may appear that society is breaking down or becoming disorganized.

In structural-functional analysis, society is viewed as a dynamic system of interrelated parts. Subsystems develop to fulfill certain functional prerequisites that are essential for societal survival. Because the family fulfills at least one of these requirements in every known society, it is believed to be a universal phenomenon. This approach is also concerned with the ways in which these systems maintain boundaries and work toward equilibrium. All activities are held to have some function, whether manifest or latent. Activities may be dysfunctional as well as functional for the system.

The developmental framework examines the effects of internal and external forces on the family. This life-span approach follows the family from the time of marriage until the death of one or both spouses. During this time, the family moves through a series of stages that change as the family grows and contracts. Within each stage, there are a series of developmental tasks that face each individual member and the unit as a whole. These tasks must be successfully accomplished and mastered to ensure healthy functioning and to prepare for future tasks.

The interactional approach focuses on the internal workings of the family by observing interactions between members. The family is seen as a dynamic unit, constantly changing as family members influence and modify each other's behavior. Infants become social beings through interaction and the socialization process within the primary group. Successful interaction is the outcome of learning how to take and play roles. The human personality contains the potential for enactment of many roles within a single day.

The conflict approach views conflict as a natural rather than pathological outcome of human interaction. Family interaction consists of managing, avoiding, and resolving conflict. Families compose hierarchical systems of authority in which access to resources is inherently unequal. The struggle to gain valued resources results in constant bargaining, competition, cooperation, and negotiation. Although the potential for competition and conflict is ever present, common goals and mutual affection serve to solidify family members.

SUGGESTED READINGS

Bahr, Stephen J., ed., *Economics and the Family*, Lexington, Mass.: Lexington Books, 1980. A highly readable collection of papers on the uses of economic theory in relation to the family.

Duncan, Otis Dudley, ed., *William Ogburn on Culture and Social Change*,

Chicago: University of Chicago Press, 1964. A collection of Ogburn's writings, including selections on the concept of culture lag.

Morgan, D. H. J., *Social Theory and the Family*, London: Routledge & Kegan Paul, 1975. Critique of functionalist theory applied to the family, and a proposal for the substitution of Marxist and existentialist perspectives.

Nye, F. Ivan, *ed., Family Relationships: Rewards and Costs*, Beverly Hills, Calif.: Sage Publications, 1982. Examines a number of commonly used theoretical orientations and proposes a social choice theory to explain family interaction more adequately.

Reiss, David, *The Family's Construction of Reality*, Cambridge, Mass.: Harvard University Press, 1981. Develops from 15 years of background research a theoretical model to explain family decision making and problem solving.

FILMS

The Decision (National Film Board of Canada, 1251 Avenue of the Americas, 16th Floor, New York, N.Y. 10020), 30 minutes. Under the pressures of rising prices, competitive markets, and rising production costs, more and more farmers are being forced to abandon farming as a way of life. A father and son—the father holding to old ways, the son favoring the new—resolve difficulties to enable them to keep abreast of developments in agriculture.

Hazel and David (National Film Board of Canada, 1251 Avenue of the Americas, 16th Floor, New York, N.Y. 10020), 29 minutes. A husband insulates his family from his job. David feels that what happens at work should not bother his family. Hence, when his job is in doubt, his wife discovers it by accident. In the discussion, there is promise of improved communication in the family.

Our Changing Family Life (McGraw-Hill, Text-Film Division, 1221 Avenue of the Americas, New York, N.Y. 10020), 22 minutes. A farm family in 1880 is an integrated unit. Three generations live under one roof. Religion, recreation, and the sharing of work play roles in holding the family together. Since 1880, industrial expansion, urbanization, and the emancipation of women have changed family life. The farm family has become less important. The roles of husband and wife have changed, and companionship has become more important.

QUESTIONS AND PROJECTS

1. What is meant by the term *conceptual frameworks?* Why are conceptual frameworks useful to sociologists?
2. Define: institution, social change, culture lag.
3. Describe Zimmerman's theory of social and family change. Make explicit the interaction between family and society at each stage.

4. What are the assumptions underlying the structural-functional approach? How do these differ from the assumptions underlying the institutional approach?
5. How is marriage "the structural keystone of our family system"? How is marriage based on romantic love consistent with such a system?
6. What developmental tasks face a newborn infant? Newlyweds? Retired couples?
7. Describe the developmental tasks facing your own family at the present time. At what stage is your own family in the developmental life cycle?
8. Define role taking and role playing. Why are these skills important to human interaction?
9. Describe the factors that solidify the marital bond. Describe the factors that strain the marital bond.
10. What are the assumptions underlying the conflict approach? Why is conflict a natural outcome of family interaction?
11. Which conceptual frameworks focus primarily on the internal workings of the family? Which frameworks combine internal and external influences on the family?
12. Make a list of 10 research topics relating to marriage and the family. Decide which conceptual framework would best organize each topic.
13. Define: status, role, atomistic family, latent function, semiclosed system, power.

III
Contemporary American Families

Sam Falk, Monkmeyer

8
The Influence of Social Class

In almost every home on the wall in a prominent position is the family tree, appropriately framed. Many families have a crest, which is also framed, and which is used on stationery, rings, and so forth. The *Social Register,* a book containing only the names of people who are considered upper-upper class, is used as the telephone directory. Very seldom does anyone in the family find it necessary to use the regular telephone directory. Outsiders are made to see that they are not wanted. Money has *nothing* to do with getting into the *Social Register.* The criterion used is the family background. If the family dates back for many generations, if the members belong to exclusive clubs . . . the family is considered upper class.[1]

There is one cause for which middle-class parents try their very best to save: a college education for the children. Most middle-level parents sincerely want their children to improve on their (the parents') socioeconomic position, and a college degree is widely believed to be the instrument of improvement. While the upper and upper-middle classes may send a greater proportion of their children to college, it is the middle class that makes the most sacrifices.[2]

Even in the most consistently stable families, . . . the first and fundamental fact of most of their lives was that they were poor. Not one person, even those from the most stable and integrated homes, failed to mention growing up poor—some worse off than others, to be sure, but all whose dominant experience of childhood was material deprivation.

It matters little that these families may not have been poor by some arbitrary definition set by a governmental agency. What counts is the experience

1. Ruth Shonle Cavan, *The American Family* (4th ed.), New York: Thomas Y. Crowell, 1969, p. 101.
2. William M. Kephart, *The Family, Society, and the Individual* (4th ed.), Boston: Houghton Mifflin, 1977, p. 403.

of the people who lived those lives. For them, the deprivation was real—real when they knew parents had trouble paying the rent, when they didn't have shoes that fit, when the telephone was shut off, when the men came to take the refrigerator away. That fact alone colors every dimension of life and, for both parents and children, contributes powerfully to a world filled with pain, anger, fear, and loneliness.[3]

The consequences of social class touch all aspects of family life. The values upheld, the goals sought, the person one will marry, even the friends with whom one associates are largely influenced by one's social-class position. Although the lines of demarcation between the classes are not always clear, each has its own identifiable pattern of family life. Kahl very simply sums up the emergent characteristic of each: the upper class is noted for "graceful living"; the upper-middle class for "career-mindedness"; the lower-middle class for "respectability"; the working class for "getting by"; and the lower class for "apathy."[4]

Just what factors constitute a social class has been a subject of controversy among social scientists for generations. Occupation, income, education, life style, or some combination of these factors are the usual criteria, although disagreements still rage over which factors are *the* most important.[5] Another controversy surrounds the number of social classes in the United States. Although most people are used to thinking in terms of three classes (upper, middle, or lower), some researchers have delineated five, six, or as many as nine classes. This chapter will present the life styles and family patterns of three social classes: the upper-upper class, the middle class, and the working class.

UPPER-UPPER-CLASS FAMILIES

If the United States could be said to have an aristocracy, it would be found among the members of the upper-upper class. Although they compose only about 1 percent of the population, they control a highly significant portion of the country's wealth, power, and influence.[6] They are the possessors of a distinct way of life, which they seek to protect against the inroads of the spreading middle-class life style.

The upper-upper class is most discernible in the old cities of the urban Northeast and the Deep South. In less bold relief it is found in some cit-

3. Lillian Breslow Rubin, *Worlds of Pain: Life in the Working-Class Family*, New York: Basic Books, 1976, pp. 29–30.

4. Joseph A. Kahl, *The American Class Structure*, New York: Holt, Rinehart & Winston, 1957, pp. 187–210.

5. Luther B. Otto, "Class and Status in Family Research," *Journal of Marriage and the Family* 37 (May 1975), pp. 315–32.

6. W. Lloyd Warner and Paul S. Lunt, *Social Life of a Modern Community*, New Haven, Conn.: Yale University Press, 1941, p. 203.

ies of the midwest and far west. Because they carefully guard their style of life from outside encroachment and shield themselves from public scrutiny, there is little in the way of empirical research on this social class. However, the small amount of data gathered on the family patterns of the very wealthy indicate that they are set apart from other social classes by distinct cultural differences.

The Family's Value System

A distinguished American ancestry, income from inherited wealth, and residence in the community for several generations are criteria for membership in this class. In the East, emphasis is placed on establishment of the family in America during the colonial period and the accumulation of the family fortune prior to the Civil War. Careers in government, business, and the professions are followed by the men, after education at Ivy League schools. The families are of old English stock and few Catholics or Jews are to be found among them. In the South, the background is either English or French. The family history is traced to pre–Civil War days and to gracious plantation living.

Upper-class families in eastern cities generally have established themselves in the community for eight or nine generations. In the Midwest only four or five generations in the community are sufficient to confer upper-class status, whereas in the Far West, the time may be shorter still. The longer the family history, the greater the emphasis placed on illustrious forebears; the shorter the history, the more essential is significant accomplishment by recent generations.

The structure of the upper-class family suggests the trustee family of ancient times. The present members of the family are not *the family*, but only its current representatives. They guard the status and wealth created by earlier generations, and they are obliged to pass it on intact or enhanced to their successors. The timelessness of the family is emphasized in its material possessions, its style of life, and even in the selection of family names. Treasured heirlooms, family portraits, diaries, oral histories, and other symbols of the family are passed through the generations in reverence to the accomplishments of ancestors.

Upper-class families are not conspicuous consumers. The conscious show of wealth is considered pretentious and vulgar. They do not often live in spreading ranch houses, drive new Cadillacs, or indulge in fads. They consider such spending patterns a mark of the nouveau riche, whose recently acquired wealth without the requisite family lineage is looked on with disdain. Instead they live in ancestral family homes surrounded by furnishings and possessions handed down over the generations. The automobiles are expensive but sedate—and, for the older members, often chauffeur driven. Their wealth supports, not extravagant purchases, but indulgences in charity, the sponsoring of favorite projects, and (perhaps) travel abroad.

McNamara believes membership in exclusive and highly prestigious clubs and associations truly marks the individual's position on the upper-class social ladder.[7] Acceptance into the Daughters of the American Revolution, the Society of Mayflower Descendants, or the Acorn and Yale Clubs of Philadelphia more impressively identifies one's station in life among the upper class than probably any other single factor. There is a high degree of sex segregation found among these associations. In fact, the more exclusive the club, the greater the likelihood that the membership will be composed of only one sex.

Another factor peculiar to the upper class is residential stability. Whereas the middle class tends toward a high rate of geographic mobility in response to occupational needs, the upper class tends to remain firmly ensconced in a particular community for generations. This makes sense when we stop to consider that the length of time a family has held a position of leadership in a community partly determines its prestige and status. Residential mobility is so uncommon among the upper class that families have come to be associated with particular areas of the country, for instance, the Lowells of Boston, the Du Ponts of Wilmington, and the Roosevelts of New York City.

Both given names and surnames have a significance unmatched at other class levels. The surnames of earlier branches of the family frequently are used as given names to emphasize family continuity. Henry Cabot Lodge, for example, exemplifies the ties between two of Boston's upper-class families. Similarly, Franklin Delano Roosevelt represented ties to both the Franklins and the Delanos. The names Nathaniel, Richard, and Leverett appear recurrently in the Saltonstall family, and there were Josiahs in four generations of the Quincy family.[8]

Mate Selection and Marriage

Mate selection and marriage operate differently among the upper class. First, there is an attempt to raise young people in relative isolation from

7. Charles H. McNamara, "Social Register, Philadelphia 1969," in Saul D. Feldman and Gerald W. Thielbar, *Life Styles: Diversity in American Society*, Boston: Little, Brown, 1972, p. 107.
8. Cleveland Amory, *The Proper Bostonians*, New York: E. P. Dutton, 1947, p. 19, cited in Ruth Shonle Cavan, *The American Family* (4th ed.), New York: Thomas Y. Crowell, 1969, p. 87. Contrast this situation with that described for middle-class families by Alice Rossi, "Naming Children in Middle-Class Families," *American Sociological Review* 30 (Aug. 1965), pp. 499–513.

the children of other classes. After being under the care of nurses or governesses, they are sent to private schools where they associate only with upper-class children and where upper-class attitudes and behavior are carefully cultivated. In both school and college, sex-segregated schools often are preferred to coeducational ones. The interaction of the sexes is often restricted to formal events such as cotillions or balls designed to foster the acquisition of proper manners and social graces.

Carefully arranged relationships among small groups of men's colleges and women's colleges protect young people against "unfortunate involvement" with unsuitable persons. Blumberg and Paul assert that daughters are much more restricted in their dating partners than are sons.[9] Parents of upper-class girls exert a great deal of pressure on daughters to limit their interactions to upper-class boys. Private schools also carefully control the behavior of upper-class girls. Boys, on the other hand, are allowed more freedom to interact with girls from different social classes. These relationships, however, are expected to be casual; if they become too serious, families exert pressure to bring the errant boy back into line. When the time for marriage approaches, coming-out parties introduce eligible young men and women to each other.

Upper-class men and women marry relatively late. Although national data are not available, Warner and Lunt's research in Yankee City showed an average age at marriage three to four years older than for the general population.[10] Unlike the middle class, who often encourage innovation in the wedding ceremony, upper-class families favor formal church weddings with traditional dress, attendants, guests, ceremonies, and receptions.[11] Women are expected to be virgins when they marry, but it is expected that men will have had some discreet sexual experience before marriage. The media coverage given to Lady Diana's virginity on her marriage to Prince Charles points to the value given to women's sexual innocence among the upper class.

Marriages among the very wealthy tend to be patriarchal. Women are expected to be wives and mothers and to devote their free time to clubs or charitable organizations. Blumberg and Paul's study found that only 20 percent of the brides mentioned an occupation, and several brides said they would quit on marriage.[12] Baltzell's finding that upper-upper-class women are twice as likely to be married as lower-upper-class

9. Paul M. Blumberg and P. W. Paul, "Continuities and Discontinuities in Upper-Class Marriages," *Journal of Marriage and the Family* 37 (Feb. 1975), pp. 63–77.
10. Warner and Lunt, *op. cit.*, p. 423.
11. Blumberg and Paul, *op. cit.*, p. 64.
12. *Ibid.*, p. 73.

women points to the importance given to the mother and wife roles among this elite group.[13] He attributes the difference in marriage rates between the two groups to a very low divorce rate among upper-upper-class people and to the fact that few women opt for careers instead of marriage.

Childrearing

The anticipatory socialization practices of the middle class are virtually absent in the elite class. Upper-class children have no need to anticipate success because they are born into a style of life already at the top. They are, in fact, encouraged not to strive or ostentatiously to display symbols of success or wealth. Children grow up without the financial concerns common to most people and often have little conscious awareness of money or how much things actually cost.

The socialization of children focuses primarily on upholding the social positions into which they are born and representing and enhancing the family lineage. Relations among family members are often formal, encouraging the acquisition of manners and social skills requisite among adults. Rituals such as dressing for dinner instill ideas of correct behavior that will be carried over into adulthood. The family life of the elites, unlike that of the middle class, tends to be adult centered. Children are regarded not so much as children as they are young ladies and young gentlemen.

Kinship Relations

The integration and continuity of upper-class families also are illustrated by widespread intermarriage among them and by a large group of kin with whom close ties are maintained. Cavan describes them as nuclear families closely connected by blood, marriage, history, and the current joint ownership of property.[14] The marriage of cousins once or twice removed is common enough that kin ties pervade the whole upper-class community. Aunts, uncles, and cousins are members of the family, and the ties among them are reinforced by living on adjacent estates and by common interests in both real and industrial property.

Although upper-class families are not true extended families, there is

13. E. Digby Baltzell, *Philadelphia Gentlemen: The Making of a National Upper Class*, Glencoe, Ill.: The Free Press, 1958, p. 161.
14. Cavan, *op. cit.* See also August B. Hollingshead, "Class Differences in Family Stability," in Reinhard Bendix and Seymour M. Lipset, *Class, Status and Power*, Glencoe, Ill.: The Free Press, 1953.

more prominence given to generational ties and the larger kin group than among middle-class families. The prominence of extended family relationships traces to the position of elders as holders of family income and property and as bearers of family traditions. Older members often control the income of younger family members, sometimes making provision through trusts for the distribution of wealth two or three generations in the future. Consequently, middle-aged couples with half-grown children may remain financially dependent on their parents. Ceremonially, the position of the elders is analogous to that in the Chinese gentry family: as the closest living connections with the ancestors, they derive special status as bearers of the family traditions.

Technically, descent is bilateral, but there is a pervasive bias in favor of the husband's family. Wealth and power tend to be passed through the male line, sons tend to follow in the occupations of fathers and grandfathers, and boys are more often named for the father's relatives than for the mother's. Ironically, the person around whom family activities revolve frequently is a woman. Women usually outlive their husbands, with the result that the oldest person in the family is a grandmother. Again as among the Chinese, by the time a woman reaches this position, she is so thoroughly socialized that she represents her husband's family almost as he would do.

The careful restriction of marriage partners to other members of the upper class provides for the smooth incorporation of the couple into the larger kinship group. The young wife is required to take her place as a family member as well as a wife. Obligations to the larger family group usually take precedence over nonfamily social demands. In those rare instances when a person does marry outside the class, the couple may face ostracism and there may be ill-concealed hope that the marriage may break up in favor of a more appropriate one.

It cannot be emphasized enough that the primary reference group for this upper class is the class itself. It does not accept the mass-consumption, mobility-oriented, middle-class model as an ideal; indeed, it perpetuates its status partly through deliberate rejection of that ideal. Marriage is subordinated to perpetuation of the family traditions. Married love must compromise with the suitability of the relationship. Children are born to benefit the family; the family does not exist for the children.

These upper-class patterns, significant beyond the number of people involved, represent a holdout against the middle-class model. Whether this group will be able to maintain its aloof position in the future is uncertain. There are signs of incipient breakdown. The segregation of younger members of the group is a special problem. As education becomes increasingly coeducational and as young people of varied backgrounds are thrown together, the landed aristocracy may be yielding to a jet set that mirrors the middle-class model in exaggerated form.

MIDDLE-CLASS FAMILIES

The boundaries of the middle class are amorphous. Most people, when asked, label themselves as middle class rather than upper class, working class, or lower class. They identify with what they perceive to be a broad middle-class life style. To some degree, that life style character-izes most of the population. Although there are significant racial and ethnic variations of it, the family patterns of the middle class tend to be readily identifiable.

The Family's Value System

Middle-class people are committed to equality of the sexes. Old stereo-types of man's work and woman's work are being reassessed in favor of a flexible division of tasks based on the personal preferences of the cou-ple. As more women work outside the home, husbands tend to partici-pate more fully in housework and child care. Democracy extends to the relationships between parents and children. Discipline ceases to be an end in itself, with the differential status and power of parents and chil-dren being minimized.

Improvements in the level of living have freed adolescents from the labor market, increased their leisure, and encouraged casual association between the sexes. Youth use their freedom to meet and evaluate pro-spective marriage partners. Ultimately, they choose for love and com-panionship rather than because of family background, religion, and other traditional criteria.

Change in sexual norms has occurred. Both men and women have the right to enjoy sex. Moreover, these rights extend into the premarital pe-riod, when participation increases according to the level of emotional involvement. Increasing numbers of parents and offspring alike sanction sexual activity in relationships where a high degree of affection is present.

Although emphasis is on the conjugal unit, ties with extended kin—particularly grandparents and grandchildren—are highly valued. Grand-parents, when they are able, are expected to provide financial and moral support to the young families of their offspring—and in a fashion that does not imply financial or emotional dependence. In turn young par-ents and children are supposed to encourage participation of the grand-parents in the life of the family. Distance often requires interaction by mail and telephone, supplemented by occasional visits. As the grandparents grow older and dependent, younger family members are expected to increase the amounts and types of their support.

The permanence of marriage or the stability of family relationships have virtually ceased to be ends in themselves. Marriages are expected to promote the personal growth and well-being of the partners. When this does not happen, middle-class couples often seek professional help. Both partners should work to eliminate the problems, but if they are unable to do so, divorce is preferable to continuation of an unhappy marriage. Similarly, parent-child relations are expected to be rewarding to both generations. Marriage and parenthood are intended for the satisfaction they bring to the participants.

Many middle-class families have few geographic roots and move from city to city and region to region as their jobs and personal preferences dictate. Approximately, one family in every five in the United States moves each year. Not that the same families move year after year of course; some families set up a household at marriage and remain there for the rest of their lives. And some families of migratory workers are on the move constantly. However, for a vast intermediate segment of the population, occasional changes of house and community occur as part of the normal demands of many occupations, as an accompaniment of occupational advancement, and as families seek congenial atmospheres in which to fulfill themselves and raise children.

Census data are revealing at this point. Mobility is highest among young adult groups and declines steadily as people get older. Mobility is also highest at middle-income levels, indicating that much of it is a feature of the middle-class style of life. Considerable mobility characterizes young college-educated families who form the technical and management base of the nation's large organizations. Historically, the moves have been tied to the husband's occupational advancement. One national moving firm reports that of 60 companies responding, 14 move their employees every two years, 16 every three years, and 10 every five years.[15] Such "organization men" typically move across the country

15. Several studies have shown that frequent moves are not perceived as too stressful for middle-class families. See Curtis L. Barrett and Helen Noble, "Mothers' Anxieties Versus the Effects of Long Distance Moves on Children," *Journal of Marriage and the Family* 35 (May 1973), pp. 181–88; Edgar W. Butler, Ronald J. McAllister, and Edward J. Kaiser, "The Effects of Voluntary and Involuntary Residential Mobility on Females and Males," *Journal of Marriage and the Family* 35 (May 1973), pp. 219–27; Stella B. Jones, "Geographic Mobility as Seen by the Wife and Mother," *Journal of Marriage and the Family* 35 (May 1973), pp. 210–18; Judson R. Landis and Louis Stoetzer, "An Exploratory Study of Middle-Class Migrant Families," *Journal of Marriage and the Family* 28 (Feb. 1966), pp. 51–53; and Ronald J. McAllister, Edgar W. Butler, and Edward J. Kaiser, "The Adaptation of Women to Residential Mobility," *Journal of Marriage and the Family* 35 (May 1973), pp. 197–204.

from suburb to suburb, moving physically but taking the same way of life with them from place to place. As Whyte put it, "With each transfer, the *decor*, the architecture, the faces, and the names may change; the people, the conversation, and the values do not."[16]

Recently, the pattern has changed somewhat for those middle-class families in which the wife also has some career commitment. Research shows that families in which the wife works are less likely to make long-distance moves than families in which the wife does not work; but they are more likely to make short-distance moves. Apparently, the husband's mobility and his occupational advancement are hindered somewhat by the demands of the wife's job. At the same time, the income from her job probably also enables the family to improve its standard of living, including moves to better housing in the same geographic area. It should also be pointed out that although both partners' occupational advancements are hindered by restrictions on their mobility, the wife's career probably suffers more than the husband's.[17]

The family life style of the middle class is widely lived and even more widely imitated. There is a large and growing segment of the population that has the financial means to afford this life style and encourage their children to embrace it. This group has discretionary income. They are not wealthy in the traditional sense, but they have significant amounts of money left over after the basic necessities of life are provided for. This leftover income may be saved or it may be used to provide whatever luxuries are consistent with a given family's life style.

About 25 million families, or roughly two out of every five families, had reached this level by 1980. Young corporate executives' families comprise one large segment of this group. Another segment has attained this income level largely through the efforts of wives in gainful employment. More than half of all mothers with children under 18 are in the labor force.[18]

Middle-class family life styles vary considerably, but they are almost all characterized by the possession of, or seeking after, a common set of material goods—automobiles, furniture, television, radios, refrigerators, and standard brands of food and clothing. These possessions are called the *standard package.*"[19] Almost all middle-class families have these pos-

16. William H. Whyte, Jr., *The Organization Man*, Garden City, N.Y.: Doubleday, 1956, pp. 298–305.
17. Larry H. Long, "Women's Labor Force Participation and the Residential Mobility of Families," *Social Forces* 52 (March 1974), pp. 342–48.
18. Linda J. Waite, "U.S. Women at Work," *Population Bulletin* 36 (May 1981), p. 5.
19. David Riesman and Howard Roseborough, "Careers and Consumer Behavior," in Lincoln H. Clark, *ed.*, *Consumer Behavior*. Vol. 2: *The Life Cycle and Consumer Behavior*, New York: New York University Press, 1955, pp. 1–2. See also John Scanzoni, *The Conjugal Family and Consumption Behavior* (Occasional Paper Series No. 1), Bryn Mawr, Penn.: McCahan Foundation, n.d.

sessions and can easily transport them as they move about the country and up the occupational ladder.

The key to the universality of the standard package is found in the preparation of children and adolescents to want and expect to possess it when they reach adulthood. It begins early in life when, by means of television and the movies, children learn what the components of the package are and witness their parents' desires to own them. The children undergo what sociologists call *anticipatory socialization*, a process of role playing and fantasy that leads them to anticipate the conditions of adulthood and to respond to those conditions in a predetermined way.[20]

The significance of anticipatory socialization lies in the fact that children are, thus, prepared to live in ways that their parents have not really lived. In fact, they are prepared to live as no one has yet lived: to expect not only the standard package of today but to anticipate the additions that will be made to it from 10 to 20 years in the future.

Many middle-class parents who have collected the standard package required many years to do so. In their youth, they learned to save for years to acquire the amenities. Their children, however, having had most of the package and having their tastes further upgraded in adolescence, are not so often disposed to wait. They do not wait for marriage, but often marry before they are established in occupations and, thus, are without material possessions. Once married, even though their incomes are adequate by most standards, they use installment buying to spend beyond their incomes and more quickly acquire the standard package. They begin marriage almost at the economic and status level it took their parents 20 years to achieve.

Parent-Child Interaction

Parent-child interaction is bound up intimately with the nature of the interaction between the parents, particularly with the striving pattern in which they are caught up. For although the incomes of such young families are adequate by most standards, the incomes are usually inadequate to meet the demands that these young parents feel have been placed on them by their upbringing. Pregnancy and childbearing require substantial amounts of money that might otherwise be spent on social and occupational advancement. Nor is the problem one of money alone. Childbearing and childrearing consume time and energy. The

20. Robert K. Merton and Alice S. Kitt, "Contributions to the Theory of Reference-Group Behavior," in Robert K. Merton and Paul S. Lazarsfeld, *eds., Continuities in Social Research: Studies in the Scope and Method of "The American Soldier,"* Glencoe, Ill.: The Free Press, 1950, pp. 87–89.

wife especially finds herself physically tied to the household and unable to join her husband in the pursuit of other goals. Because most activities for middle-class people are engaged in by couples, the husband's freedom is limited too.

Under these circumstances, it would not be surprising if childbearing was regarded as a burden. Actually the reverse is true. Middle-class people accept, perhaps more than any others, the ideas that childbearing is to be sought, that children are lovable, and that parent-child relationships are sources of continual joy. Middle-class people, too, seem to hang on tenaciously to the idea that there is some mysterious parental instinct that results in people having unmixed feelings of love for their children, no matter how troublesome they may be. The contemporary middle-class household is a child-centered setting.

Parsons traces many features of middle-class childrearing practices to the smallness and relative isolation of the conjugal family. These conditions result in the child becoming dependent on, and vulnerable to, the parents. Unlike the situation in a large family, in which the child has protection against the wrath of a parent in the love of grandparents, aunts, cousins, and so on, the middle-class American child has no one else to turn to. From birth, the child's welfare is overwhelmingly tied up with the parents.

This complete dependence on the parents results in the children becoming sensitive to any actual or threatened withdrawal of approval by the parents; the children's need for the parents' love becomes unconditional. When the children begin to participate in the outside world, however, they find that playmates and neighbors make judgments, not according to family standards but according to the standards of the larger society. They must compete for affection and approval. They quickly learn that their parents are judged by others according to the kind of job(s) they have, the house they live in, the automobile(s) they drive, and so on.[21] Moreover, the child is judged by his or her own achievements. If the child is a bright, alert youngster who accomplishes more than his or her contemporaries, the child fares well. If the child lags behind, he or she fares badly. The child learns not only that it must

---

21. Students will see that the success-striving middle-class person is illustrated by Sinclair Lewis's *Babbitt* (1922). It should be remembered, however, that Babbittry is only one form of success striving. Not all middle-class people have automobiles, boats, houses, and so on. In fact, some people who are especially striving eschew conspicuous consumption. Striving can just as readily take the form of being knowledgeable about music or art, traveling widely, or giving time and money to charity. College professors, who are often thought to be seeking refuge from the business world and who sometimes glory in their lack of concern for material things, frequently engage in vicious competition for status among their peers.

compete in the outside world for approval, but also that love and approval from one's parents are contingent on performance. For although the parents are conspicuously committed to love their child regardless, they, too, have needs that must be met partly through the child.

Middle-class parents have difficulty showing aggression toward children. The widespread preoccupation over whether children should be spanked may reflect fear of hitting the child. Many middle-class parents use more subtle techniques of punishment that are more effective and more devastating. In one way or another, they threaten to withdraw love and approval. Middle-class parents may, thus, deal a heavier blow with a softly spoken sentence or with a raising of an eyebrow than could be dealt with a strong arm. The effectiveness of withholding love depends on the child's extreme dependence on the parents. Because it is so dependent, the threat of parental rejection is almost overwhelming. One might expect that many children would respond with anxiety and aggression against the parents. Some children do; but often most of the aggression is repressed and the child becomes conforming instead.

The Kin Network

Although the family system in the American colonies was clearly conjugal, without larger kin units such as clans, the evidence points to complex and continuing relationships between generations that suggests an informal kin structure—the kin network.[22] We shall view the kin network of the middle class in terms of relationships between married couples and their in-laws, visiting with relatives, and mutual aid between related conjugal families.

In-law Relationships. Relationships between young married couples and their parents on both sides are a source of strain in the American family system. Young people bristle at any intimation of parental interference, and parents shake their heads sadly or bristle in turn at their offspring's seeming obstreperousness.

Evelyn M. Duvall did a study involving men and women from all over the United States who were married from a few weeks to more than 40 years. Of the 5020 people sampled, 75 percent had one or more in-law problems.[23] John L. Thomas, studying 7000 broken Roman

22. Gary R. Lee, "Kinship in the Seventies: A Decade Review of Research and Theory," *Journal of Marriage and the Family* 42 (Nov. 1980), pp. 193–204.
23. Evelyn Millis Duvall, *In-laws: Pro and Con*, New York: Association Press, 1954, pp. 187–88.

Catholic marriages, found that in-laws were the most frequent single cause of marital breakup during the first year of marriage.[24] Judson T. Landis found that about 10 percent of 409 happily married couples had not achieved satisfactory in-law relationships even after 20 years of marriage.[25] Finally, a recent study found that the birth of a first child tends to strengthen the bonds between mothers and adult daughters but tends to put more strain on the relationships between mothers-in-law and daughters-in-law.[26]

In a study of 544 couples in the early years of marriage,[27] 67 percent of those who reported excellent adjustment to in-laws also reported their marriages to be very happy. Of those who indicated fair or poor adjustment to in-laws, however, only 18 percent reported very happy marriages. This is not to say that good in-law adjustments cause marital happiness. In-law adjustment is one part of total marital adjustment. Where there are excellent adjustments reported, it may be that there is a halo effect operating. People whose marriages are happy may tend to overestimate their relationships with in-laws and vice versa. People who report good relationships with in-laws are more likely to report that their marriages are happy than people who report poor in-law relationships.

The structure of the American family system appears to produce a particular range in in-law difficulties. First, parents and their married offspring are primarily concerned about the quality of their interpersonal relationships. They guard against meddling, interference, and dependence. Dependence usually is defined more in emotional terms than in economic ones. To be sure, young people complain if their parents are either too stingy or too lavish in their support of the young marriage; but the complaint is against the lack of love shown or the determination to control the young marriage rather than against financial support as such. What makes financial support acceptable or unacceptable is the conditions under which it is given.

The need of young middle-class adults to be independent of parents traces back to conditions within the nuclear family and the requirement that people become independent of the family at marriage and at entry into the occupational system. During childhood, physical and emotional dependence on the parents are relatively complete. During

24. John L. Thomas, "Marital Failure and Duration," *Social Order* 3 (Jan. 1953), pp. 24–29.
25. Judson T. Landis, "Adjustments After Marriage," *Marriage and Family Living* 9 (May 1947), pp. 32–34.
26. Lucy Rose Fischer, "Mothers and Mothers-in-law," *Journal of Marriage and the Family* 45 (Feb. 1983), pp. 187–92.
27. Judson T. Landis and Mary G. Landis, *Building a Successful Marriage*, Englewood Cliffs, N.J.: Prentice-Hall, 1968, pp. 329–43.

adolescence, the adolescent revolt symbolizes the attempt to free one-self both from parents and from one's own need to remain in a state of childlike dependence. Not all youngsters have remained so dependent that they need to rebel, of course, and not all of those who need to rebel are able to do so. It seems fair to say that a substantial proportion of young people approach adulthood with their needs for emotional de-pendence less than completely resolved.

The hold of many young married persons on their independence is precarious. They react strongly to actual or presumed threats to that independence. Parents are likely to have difficulties in this area too. After having had offspring dependent on them for 20 years—after hav-ing organized their lives around their children—they often do not give up those relationships without ambivalence. Parents are reluctant to let go, and their offspring—although they deny it—are often equally reluc-tant. Often, some time is required for emotional dependence to give way to the emotional give and take appropriate to parent-adult offspring relationships.

Visiting with Kin. Many studies show that a large proportion of con-jugal middle-class families are in regular communication with relatives and that they visit with kin frequently. Studies in Detroit, Los Angeles, and San Francisco all showed about 50 percent of families see relatives at least once a week and that an additional 25 percent see them as often as once a month.[28] A study of the kin relationships of 161 Boston-area families produced lower figures but still showed 14 percent interacting with kin at least once a month.[29] It appears that the Boston sample had fewer kin in the metropolitan area than was true for any other of the samples. Support for this interpretation is provided by a study of 133 migrant black women in Philadelphia; it showed that of 56 percent who had relatives living in Philadelphia, 46 percent visited with relatives at least once a week.[30]

A study of 731 married women in Detroit tested relationships be-tween the frequency of interaction with kin and marital adjustment, finding that interaction with kin up to about once a week is associated

28. Morris Axelrod, "Urban Structure and Social Participation," *American Sociological Review* 21 (Feb. 1956), p. 16; Wendell Bell and Marion Boat, "Urban Neighborhoods and Informal Social Relations," *American Journal of Sociology* 62 (Jan. 1957), pp. 391–98; Scott Greer, "Urbanism Reconsidered: A Comparative Study of Local Areas in a Metropolis," *American Sociological Review* 21 (Feb. 1956), p. 22; Aida K. Tomeh, "Informal Participation in a Metropolitan Community," *Sociological Quarterly* 8 (Win-ter 1967), pp. 85–102.
29. Paul J. Reiss, "The Extended Kinship System: Correlates of and Attitudes on Fre-quency of Interaction," *Marriage and Family Living* 24 (Nov. 1962), pp. 333–39.
30. Leonard Blumberg and Robert R. Bell, "Urban Migration and Kinship Ties," *Social Problems* 6 (Spring 1959), pp. 328–33.

with good adjustment. Interaction more frequently than that appears to interfere with marital adjustment.[31]

Finally, there is conflicting evidence over whether ties are closer with the husband's or the wife's kin. Sweetser summarized several studies that show a bias in favor of the wife's family,[32] and a recent study of 800 midwestern adults showed that women report more close kin than men do.[33] A carefully designed study of 530 working-class couples, however, found that these apparent relationships may be illusory. These researchers found that each spouse provides the linkage with his or her family of orientation and that when kin are not seen jointly by the couple, each spouse sees his or her own kindred separately.[34]

Mutual Aid Among Kin. Not only is visiting with kin very common, but there is an elaborate pattern of mutual aid among parental families and those of their married children. An early study of relationships among 97 middle-class, white, Protestant parental couples in Cleveland and their 195 married children living away from home found that the parents wanted to help their married children and wished in return to remain a part of their children's lives. For their part, the young married couples wanted the friendly encouragement and assistance of their parents. These wishes were realized in an extensive pattern of financial aid that flowed from parents to children. In 154 of the 195 cases, the parents were giving either direct financial support or help and service. The parents were quite definite that they did not expect their children to support them in turn.[35]

The existence of an elaborate mutual-aid network was confirmed by a study in Detroit, where approximately 70 percent of all couples both gave aid to, and received aid from, relatives.[36] The most frequent types of help were baby-sitting and help during illness. Next most common was financial aid. Help with housework was given frequently. Other aid such as giving business advice, helping to find a job, and the giving of valuable gifts were found less often. The distinctive contribution of

31. Robert O. Blood, "Kinship Interaction and Marital Solidarity," *Merrill-Palmer Quarterly* 15 (April 1969), pp. 171–84.
32. Dorrian A. Sweetser, "Intergenerational Ties in Finnish Urban Families," *American Sociological Review* 33 (April 1968), pp. 236–46.
33. Alan Booth, "Sex and Social Participation," *American Sociological Review* 37 (April 1972), pp. 183–93.
34. George S. Rosenberg and Donald F. Anspach, *Working Class Kinship*, Lexington, Mass.: D. C. Heath, 1973.
35. Marvin B. Sussman, "The Help Pattern in the Middle Class Family," *American Sociological Review* 18 (Feb. 1953), pp. 22–23.
36. Harry Sharp and Morris Axelrod, "Mutual Aid Among Relatives in an Urban Population," in Ronald Freedman, Amos Hawley, Werner Landecker, Gerhard Lenski, and Horace Miner, *eds.*, *Principles of Sociology: A Text with Readings*, New York: Holt, Rinehart & Winston, 1956, pp. 434–35.

this study was to show the pattern of aid according to the age of the persons involved. It is primarily younger women who receive baby-sitting help. In fact, help received, in each of the four major categories, declines steadily with age. Apparently, younger couples who have just begun their families are more in need of help from kin than are older, more established families. A surprising thing, however, is the relative constancy of aid given over the life cycle. With the exception of aid with housework, which undoubtedly reflects the diminishing physical capacity of the older woman, the aid extended to relatives remains at a high level up to the age of retirement. The pattern also appears to ex-tend to situations in which elderly parents require help from their mid-dle-aged children.[37]

Still other studies have confirmed this network of aid from parents to their children. Christopherson, Vandiver, and Krueger, studying married college students, found financial subsidies ranging from 5 to 80 percent of the students' total money income were being received by 38 percent of the student families.[38] Thus, in many locations and among a variety of samples, the same general finding obtains. Young people at marriage generally establish themselves apart from their parents, and both parents and children accept that they should be financially inde-pendent as well. Nevertheless, a widespread, intricate pattern of mutual aid exists. Many nuclear families are not so isolated, emotionally or financially, as they appear. Rather, they are embedded in an inconspicu-ous kin network in which there is considerable continuity from one generation to the next.

The Modified Extended Family. The American nuclear family is not so isolated as structural-functional theory might lead us to believe. Instead we find a network of visiting, mutual aid, and emotional support, which in some ways is reminiscent of the classical extended family. It may be, of course, that a more isolated nuclear family was characteristic of the early stages of industrialization. When the extended family was still strong, young people may have been more constrained to sever ties with it completely than they are today. There may have been no happy medium; to maintain ties at all may have been to accept subordination to parents and kin. Too, both transportation and communication were less efficient than today. A distance of 50 miles between the young

37. Victor C. Cicirelli, *Helping Elderly Parents: The Role of Adult Children,* Boston: Auburn House, 1981; Abigail M. Lang and Elaine M. Brody, "Characteristics of Mid-dle-Aged Daughters and Help to Their Elderly Mothers," *Journal of Marriage and the Family* 45 (Feb. 1983), pp. 193–202; and Ethel Shanas, "Social Myth as Hypothesis: The Case of the Family Relations of Old People," *Gerontologist* 32 (Feb. 1979), pp. 3–9.
38. Victor A. Christopherson, Joseph S. Vandiver, and Marie N. Kreuger, "The Mar-ried College Student, 1959," *Marriage and Family Living* 22 (May 1960), pp. 126–27.

couple and their kin may have been nearly insurmountable. It may have taken longer to travel that 50 miles than it takes to travel 300 today.

That there may have been more isolation of nuclear families from one to several generations ago seems plausible. By the very nature of the thing, it is impossible to verify that plausibility empirically.

It is also plausible that recent changes should have made the continuance of intergenerational contacts easier. First, as the classical extended family waned, the threat of parental domination of young marriages may also have lessened. Contemporary norms favoring equal status for all adults in the family may make it easier for young people to continue relationships with parents and yet to retain their independence. Second, transportation and communication have improved tremendously. Air mail and inexpensive long-distance telephone service have made it easier to stay in close contact. High-speed highway and air travel have effectively lessened distances and lowered barriers to the maintenance of interpersonal relationships.

Third, the development of huge, diversified urban centers may have reduced the need for young people to migrate to put their specialized training to use. When most families lived in small communities, getting a college education and putting it to use almost necessitated migration to an urban center. Now, however, three fourths of the population is urban. In areas like New York, Philadelphia, Chicago, Los Angeles, and dozens more, almost any technical or professional skill may be put to use right in the area. The young couple can remain in the midst of the kin group and still seek occupational advancement.[39]

Whether there was a stage when the nuclear family was more isolated than it is today or whether there has been a fairly elaborate kin network all along may never be answered. What is clear is that another concept is needed to describe the incorporation of the nuclear family into the kin network. This is the concept of the modified extended family.

The concept of the modified extended family assumes that cohesion of the extended family in the United States is prohibited neither by occupational nor by geographic mobility.[40] Instead extended family relations can exist in a mature industrial economy and may, for bureau-

---

39. Marvin B. Sussman and Lee Burchinal, "Kin Family Network: Unheralded Structure in Current Conceptualizations of Family Functioning," *Marriage and Family Living* 24 (Aug. 1962), pp. 231–40. See also Bartolomeo J. Palisi, "Ethnic Generation and Family Structure," *Journal of Marriage and the Family* 28 (Feb. 1966), pp. 49–50.

40. Eugene Litwak, "Occupational Mobility and Extended Family Cohesion," *American Sociological Review* 25 (Feb. 1960), pp. 9–21; and "Geographic Mobility and Extended Family Cohesion," *American Sociological Review* 25 (June 1960), pp. 385–94. See also Eugene Litwak and Ivan Szelenyi, "Primary Group Structures and Their Functions: Kin, Neighbors, and Friends," *American Sociological Review* 34 (Aug. 1969), pp. 465–81.

cratic occupations at least, actually promote occupational and geographic mobility.

Litwak describes the modified extended family as follows:

. . . The modified extended family structure . . . consists of a coalition of nuclear families in a state of partial dependence. Such partial dependence means that nuclear family members exchange significant services with each other, thus differing from the isolated nuclear family, as well as retain considerable autonomy (that is, not bound economically or geographically), therefore, differing from the classical extended family.[41]

Thus, we have a concept of extended family relationships that is consistent with the demands of an industrial economy.[42] Perhaps until this generation—and remnants are to be found today—there existed explicit verbal norms to the effect that young people should become economically self-sufficient at marriage. If they could not be self-sufficient, they had no right to marry. If parents were required to support their children after marriage then the children were, by definition, immature, and the parents had the right to say how their money was used. The reverse aspect of this problem was that there was economic dependency in old age. Before Social Security and company retirement plans became widespread, the plight of many aging parents was serious. Unable to save enough money for retirement out of their modest incomes, their security often lay in the possibility of moving in with or being supported by their married children. Under these circumstances, giving and accepting

41. Eugene Litwak, "Extended Kin Relations in an Industrial Democratic Society," in Ethel Shanas and Gorden F. Streib, eds., *Social Structure and the Family: Generational Relations*, Englewood Cliffs, N.J.: Prentice-Hall, 1965, p. 291. For additional evidence concerning the character of the modified extended family, see Bartolomeo J. Palisi, "Patterns of Social Participation in a Two-Generation Sample of Italian-Americans," *Sociological Quarterly* 7 (Spring 1966), pp. 167–78.

42. Although this discussion focuses on the United States, there is evidence of a modified extended family in other countries. See Everett D. Dyer, "Upward Social Mobility and Nuclear Family Integration as Perceived by the Wife in Swedish Urban Families," *Journal of Marriage and the Family* 32 (Aug. 1970), pp. 341–50; Guenther Leuschen, Robert O. Blood, Michael Lewis, Zachary Staikof, Veronica Stolte-Heiskanen, and Conor Ward, "Family Organization, Interaction and Ritual: A Cross-Cultural Study in Bulgaria, Finland, Germany and Ireland," *Journal of Marriage and the Family* 33 (Feb. 1971), pp. 228–34; James R. Mapstone, "Familistic Determinants of Property Acquisition," *Journal of Marriage and the Family* 32 (Feb. 1970), pp. 143–50; Helgi Osterreich, "Geographical Mobility and Kinship," *International Journal of Comparative Sociology* 6 (March 1965), pp. 131–44; Leonard I. Pearlin, *Class Context and Family Relations: A Cross-National Study*, Boston: Little, Brown, 1971; Ralph Piddington, "The Kinship Network Among French Canadians," *International Journal of Comparative Sociology* 6 (March 1965), pp. 145–65; and Colin Rosser and Christopher Harris, *The Family and Social Change: A Study of Family and Kinship in a South Wales Town*, New York: Humanities Press, 1965.

help from kin was fraught with hazards. Much of the bad reputation of in-law relationships may have stemmed from this situation.

The economic situation has changed drastically. A large proportion of middle-class parents have income for their old age and need no longer fear dependency on their children. In addition, levels of living have risen to the point where many parents can subsidize offsprings' marriages with no hardship to themselves. Under these new conditions, the norms governing parental aid to married children have changed appreciably.

WORKING-CLASS FAMILIES

Working-class families occupy what is regarded as the upper-lower rung of the social-class ladder. A portrait of the working-class person would most closely resemble that of the common man. Hard working and fiercely loyal to the traditional notions of the American value system, members of the working class are nonetheless constrained by general patterns of low educational attainment, occupational prestige, and income.

The working class is composed mainly of blue-collar workers, service workers, semiskilled factory workers, and tradespeople. Their income generally is earned by the hour, the piece, the day, or the week. Although some blue-collar workers such as plumbers earn much more than middle-class workers, their life style typically resembles the working-class family pattern.

The Family's Value System

Working-class people typically hold to the traditional notions of marital roles. There is a high degree of sex segregation within the family, with the result that task allocation is rigidly divided into "man's work" and "woman's work." The husband's world revolves around the provider role, whereas the house and children are the domain of the wife. Husbands as the primary breadwinners are very concerned with making a living and fulfilling the responsibilities of this role. Working-class families, however, are very seldom able to save money and must usually concentrate on just getting by. There is very little opportunity for upward mobility and because of the possibility of layoffs, illnesses, accidents, and so on, the role of the breadwinner is fraught with insecurity. Because of these circumstances, the working class emphasizes security and maintenance of the status quo rather than the risks that upward striving would entail.[43] Komarovsky reports that husbands' reluctance to pursue upward mobility is one source of strain in working-class families because the wives frequently hold higher mobility aspirations than their husbands.[44]

The high degree of sex segregation that characterizes working-class marriages is accompanied by a lack of communication between the spouses and a lack of consensus as to what makes a good marriage.[45] The spouses generally do not confide in each other nor seek each other's advice. The husbands do not talk about their jobs with their wives, but instead expect to find the house tidy, the children clean, and dinner waiting for them when they return from work. Wives who work outside the home maintain primary responsibility for the domestic sphere and do not discuss the minute details of their daily lives with their husbands, except when disciplinary action of an errant child is required. Lopata's study of housewives found that working-class wives consider themselves lucky if their husbands are good to them, bring home their paychecks, and do not use physical violence.[46]

Working-class families value hard work, conscientiousness, loyalty, and obedience. Creativity or innovative thinking are not encouraged. These values parallel the occupational requirements of the blue-collar world. Whereas most middle-class occupations focus on the manipulation of ideas and symbols that require creativity, working-class occupations focus on the manipulation of objects. These jobs are usually subject to direct supervision by others and standardization that calls for conformity and obedience to rules and regulations.

Children are expected to conform to the same values their parents hold. Parents and adults are to be obeyed and respected.[47] The working

43. Ely Chinoy, "The Tradition of Opportunity and the Aspirations of Automobile Workers," *American Journal of Sociology* 57 (March 1952), pp. 453–59; and *Automobile Workers and the American Dream*, Boston: Beacon Press, 1955; see also Nathan Hurvitz, "Marital Strain in the Blue-Collar Family," in Arthur B. Shostak and William Gomberg, *eds.*, *Blue-Collar World*, Englewood Cliffs, N.J.: Prentice-Hall, 1964.

44. Mirra Komarovsky, *Blue Collar Marriage*, New York: Random House, 1962.

45. Elizabeth Bott, *Family and Social Network: Roles, Norms, and External Relationships in Ordinary Urban Families*, London: Tavistock Publications, 1951; Alan C. Kerckhoff, "Status-Related Value Patterns Among Married Couples," *Journal of Marriage and the Family* 34 (Feb. 1972), pp. 105–10; Teresa Donati Marciano, "Middle-Class Incomes, Working-Class Hearts," in Arlene Skolnick and Jerome Skolnick, *eds.*, *Family in Transition*, Boston: Little, Brown, 1977, pp. 465–76; John H. Scanzoni, *Opportunity and the Family*, New York: The Free Press, 1970; and Irving Tallman and Gary Miller, "Class Differences in Family Problem Solving: The Effects of Verbal Ability, Hierarchical Structure, and Role Expectations," *Sociometry* 37 (Jan. 1974), pp. 13–37.

46. Helena Znaniecki Lopata, *Occupation: Housewife*, New York: Oxford University Press, 1971, p. 122.

47. S. M. Miller and Frank Reissman, "The Working Class Subculture: A New View," *Social Problems* 9 (Summer 1961), pp. 86–97.

class tends to have more children than the middle class, but children are subordinate to their parents' will, especially that of the father. Boys and girls are taught to be self-sufficient and uncomplaining. The working-class household tends to be adult-centered; children are rigidly constrained by parental expectations.

Unlike middle-class parents who stress educational achievement for their children and who sacrifice to ensure this, working-class parents expect their children to fulfill only the minimum legal requirements.[48] This comes partly from a distrust of higher education and new ideas that might be disruptive to family, kin, and peer-group relationships. Success or failure is more likely to be attributed to luck rather than to any personal skills or talent.

Working-class fathers tend to produce working-class sons.[49] Economic necessity causes many young men to begin working at an early age. This combined with the general distrust of education serves to keep most young people at the same class level as their parents. Unlike the middle class who experience high rates of geographic mobility in response to occupational opportunities, working-class youths usually take their first job in the same general locale as their fathers.[50] They are usually hired in the same factory or apprenticed in the same trade as a relative or family friend. There, surrounded by blue-collar family, friends, and kin, working-class values are reinforced. Lack of geographic mobility means that the young people, through lack of exposure to other family norms, internalize the "rightness" of traditional ways and parallel the life style of their parents.

Mate Selection and Marriage

Working-class men begin sexual relationships at an earlier age and tend to have a higher frequency of sexual experience than do either middle- or upper-class men.[51] Because male and female worlds are so segregated, females are often viewed as sexual targets for male exploitation. Gaining a wide and varied range of sexual experience at a young age is one way that blue-collar males gain status as "men." Although sexual experience

48. Ibid.
49. Peter M. Blau and Otis D. Duncan, The American Occupational Structure, New York: John Wiley & Sons, 1967; and John C. Goyder and James E. Curtis, "A Three-Generational Approach to Trends in Occupational Mobility," American Journal of Sociology 81 (Jan. 1975), pp. 129-38.
50. Gerald Handel and Lee Rainwater, "Persistence and Change in the Working-Class Life Style," in Arthur B. Shostak and William Gomberg, eds., Blue-Collar World, Englewood Cliffs, N.J.: Prentice-Hall, 1964, pp. 36-41.
51. Alfred S. Kinsey, Wardell B. Pomeroy, and Clyde E. Martin, Sexual Behavior in the Human Male, Philadelphia: W. B. Saunders, 1948, p. 381.

generally cuts across class lines for females, Gagnon and Simon believe that a minority of women, primarily from the working and lower classes, serve as sexual targets not only for the working class but for middle class men as well.[52]

Working-class people tend to marry young. Because they are likely to live at home until they wed, marriage serves both as a liberation from parental authority and as a way to gain adult status.[53] Many just drift into marriage because the opportunity is there or because they believe the time is right to start a family. Rubin asked the 50 working-class couples in her study how it was that they decided to marry.[54] The typical answers given by husbands and wives reflect both the stereotypical notions underlying male and female motives for marriage and the wide sex segregation of the working class. Wives spoke of romantic dreams of happiness, love, and security under the protection of benevolent husbands. Their husbands, on the other hand, intimated that they were "caught" by their wives or that they married because it was expected of them.

Unlike middle-class couples who highly value partner companionship, working-class couples rarely rely on each other for friendship and companionship. Wives tend to maintain close ties with relatives, whereas husbands continue premarital peer-group associations.[55] Both men and women believe that friendships are more likely among members of the same sex than between spouses. The marital bond revolves around sexual union and the completion of complementary tasks. Rubin sees the working class as the "most divorce prone segment of the population."[56] The relatively young age at time of marriage for working-class couples is one contributing factor. Scanzoni found that age at time of marriage is the critical factor in divorce, followed closely by education, occupation, and income.[57] The generally low patterns of educational attainment, occupational prestige, and income levels common among the working class strain marital bonds already emotionally loose.

52. John H. Gagnon and William Simon: *Sexual Conduct: The Social Sources of Human Sexuality*, Chicago: Aldine, 1973, pp. 224–225.
53. Komarovsky, *op. cit.*, p. 264; Lillian Rubin, *Worlds of Pain: Life in the Working-Class Family*, New York: Basic Books, 1976, p. 49.
54. Rubin, *ibid.*, p. 54.
55. Bennett Berger, *The Working Class Suburb*, Berkeley: University of California Press, 1960; Alan F. Blum, "Social Structure, Social Class, and Primary Relationships," in Arthur B. Shostak and William Gomberg, *eds.*, *Blue-Collar World*, Englewood Cliffs, N.J.: Prentice-Hall, 1964; and Lee Rainwater, Richard P. Coleman, and Gerald Handel, *Working Man's Wife*, New York: Macfadden Books, 1962.
56. Rubin, *op. cit.*, p. 225.
57. John H. Scanzoni, *Sexual Bargaining: Power Politics in the American Marriage*, Englewood Cliffs, N.J.: Prentice-Hall, 1972, pp. 6–28.

Parent-Child Interaction

Research into social-class differences in childrearing patterns got underway just after World War II. One of the first studies was done in Chicago of the childrearing practices of 48 middle-class and 52 lower-class mothers. This study found that middle-class parents were more rigid in infant-care practices than were lower-class parents; they were more likely to feed on a schedule, to wean early, and to toilet train early. Differences were more pronounced by social class than by race, with middle-class white and black practices being more similar than were the practices of either middle-class group to either lower-class group. The researchers concluded that middle-class parents were generally stricter than lower-class parents and that "middle-class children were subjected earlier and more consistently to the influences which make a child an orderly, conscientious, responsible and tame person." Middle-class children were seen as suffering more frustration of their impulses than were lower-class children.[58]

At about the same time, Duvall studied 433 Chicago members of mothers' groups, finding that middle-class mothers defined a "good" child as one who is happy and contented, loves and confides in his or her parents, shares and cooperates with others, and is eager to learn. Working-class mothers placed less emphasis on these traits and emphasized instead that the child should be neat and clean, that it should respect and obey adults, and that it be honest, polite, and fair.[59]

Over the next decade or so, a whole series of studies were done, some that yielded findings consistent with those of the two earlier studies and some that showed flatly contradictory findings.[60] One study of 375 Boston-area mothers found middle-class mothers were not more rigid but were more lenient than lower-class mothers. The middle-class

---

58. Allison Davis and Robert J. Havighurst, "Social Class and Color Differences in Child-rearing," *American Sociological Review* 11 (Dec. 1946), pp. 698–710.

59. Evelyn Millis Duvall, "Conceptions of Parenthood," *American Journal of Sociology* 52 (Nov. 1946), pp. 190–92. See also Rachel A. Elder, "Traditional and Developmental Conceptions of Fatherhood," *Marriage and Family Living* 11 (Summer 1949), pp. 98–100, 106; and Ruth Connor, Helen F. Greene, and James Walters, "Agreement of Family Members' Conceptions of 'Good' Parent and Child Roles," *Social Forces* 36 (May 1958), pp. 353–58.

60. Walter E. Boek, Marvin B. Sussman, and Alfred Yankhauer, "Social Class and Child Care Practices," *Marriage and Family Living* 20 (Nov. 1958), pp. 326–33; Ethelyn H. Klatskin, "Shifts in Child Care Practices in Three Social Classes Under an Infant Care Program of Flexible Methodology," *American Journal of Orthopsychiatry* 22 (Jan. 1952), pp. 52–61; Richard A. Littman, Robert A. Moore, and John Pierce-Jones, "Social Class Differences in Child-rearing: A Third Community for Comparison with Chicago and Newton," *American Sociological Review* 22 (Dec. 1957), pp. 694–704; and Martha S. White, "Social Class, Child-Rearing Practices, and Child Behavior," *American Sociological Review* 22 (Dec. 1957), pp. 704–12.

mothers were more permissive in toilet training, dependency, sex train-ing, and the expression of aggression. Middle-class mothers also were less punitive, less restrictive in activity permitted in the home, and more permissive of free-ranging activity outside the home.[61]

The conflict over whether middle-class parents are more permissive or more strict than lower-class parents was resolved by Bronfenbrenner, who reanalyzed data from earlier studies. He made the social-class groupings more consistent from study to study and estimated the ap-proximate dates at which the findings had been secured. In so doing, he found that there had been a gradual shift in child-care practices. Before World War II, it did appear that middle-class mothers were more rigid. By the end of World War II, however, the situation had reversed and middle-class mothers were more permissive.[62]

The shift in middle-class and working-class childrearing practices occurred within the context of a general shift toward permissiveness at all social levels. It will be recalled that Western society has a long his-tory of children being under the domination of their parents, particu-larly of their fathers. Even in the immediate premodern era, parents were supposed to be strict disciplinarians whose duty it was to break the will of the child, to make it submissive, and to train it in the denial of its innate evil impulses. Early in the present century, there began to appear a massive child-guidance literature, which by the 1930s was advocating more permissive childrearing. Parents were urged to assume friendly, loving roles and to allow their children to develop "naturally" and at their own pace. Bronfenbrenner's analysis showed a close corre-spondence between the trend toward permissiveness and childrearing and the practices recommended in the child-care literature.[63]

Differences between the middle and working classes in the charac-teristics believed desirable in children have persisted throughout the general trend toward permissiveness. In more recent studies, Kohn found that middle-class mothers valued happiness, considerateness, and self-control in their children, whereas mothers in the lower classes were more likely to value neatness, cleanliness, and obedience.[64]

61. Robert R. Sears, Eleanor E. Maccoby, and Harry Levin, *Patterns of Child-Rearing,* Evanston, Ill.: Row, Peterson, 1957.
62. Urie Bronfenbrenner, "Socialization and Social Class Through Time and Space," in Eleanor E. Maccoby, Theodore M. Newcomb, and Eugene L. Hartley, eds., *Readings in Social Psychology,* New York: Holt, 1958, pp. 400–424. See also Donald G. McKinley, *Social Class and Family Life,* New York: The Free Press, 1964; and William H. Sewell, "Social Class and Childhood Personality," *Sociometry* 24 (Dec. 1961), pp. 340–46, 358–61.
63. Bronfenbrenner, *ibid.* See also Gerald R. Leslie and Kathryn P. Johnsen, "Changed Perceptions of the Maternal Role," *American Sociological Review* 28 (Dec. 1963), pp. 919–28; and Martha Wolfenstein, "The Emergence of Fun Morality," *Journal of Social Issues* 7 (1951), pp. 15–25.
64. Melvin L. Kohn, "Social Class and Parental Values," *American Journal of Sociology*

The most provocative thesis explaining recent changes in childrearing patterns assumes that there is an increasingly dominant middle-class way of life and that the way in which the family is integrated into the economic structure is a major influence on the family's childrearing philosophy.[65] Particularly, the values and way of life of the parents are molded by their experiences in that part of the economic structure within which the father works. The characteristics or traits that are rewarded in this setting are emphasized in childrearing. The parents treat their children the same way they treat themselves and others, in line with their values and expectations.[66]

SUMMARY

The influence of social class touches all aspects of family life. The upper-upper-class family resembles the trustee system of ancient Greece, preserving heirlooms, names, and estates as symbols of the family's status. Family lineage is the primary criterion for inclusion in this class. Authority is often wielded by the oldest living generation in an extended family context. Mate selection is regulated carefully, and there is emphasis on socializing new spouses. It is becoming increasingly difficult for this class to preserve the social isolation in which it has flourished, and there is evidence of change in the younger generation.

The middle-class family life style is the most widely lived one in America. It is emulated by many who are not explicitly middle class. That life style is built on values of equality, democracy, person-centered mate selection, emphasis on the conjugal family, maintaining extended kin ties, and the professionalization of marital and parental roles.

---

64 (Jan. 1959), pp. 337–52; and "Social Class and Parent-Child Relationships: An Interpretation," *American Journal of Sociology* 68 (Jan. 1963), pp. 471–80; see also Viktor Gecas and F. Ivan Nye, "Sex and Class Differences in Parent-Child Interaction: A Test of Kohn's Hypothesis," *Journal of Marriage and the Family* 36 (Nov. 1974), pp. 742–49. For needed cautions in the conduct of research in this area, see Kathryn P. Johnsen and Gerald R. Leslie, "Methodological Notes on Research in Child-Rearing and Social Class," *Merrill-Palmer Quarterly* 11 (Oct. 1965), pp. 345–58.

65. Daniel R. Miller and Guy E. Swanson, *The Changing American Parent*, New York: John Wiley & Sons, 1958.

66. See Grace F. Brody, "Socioeconomic Differences in Stated Maternal Child-Rearing Practices and in Observed Maternal Behaviors," *Journal of Marriage and the Family* 30 (Nov. 1968), pp. 656–60; Glen H. Elder, "Structural Variations in the Child-Rearing Relationship," *Sociometry* 25 (Sept. 1962), pp. 241–62; Melvin L. Kohn, "Social Class and the Exercise of Parental Authority," *American Sociological Review* 24 (June 1959), pp. 352–66; Melvin L. Kohn and Eleanor E. Carroll, "Social Class and the Allocation of Parental Responsibilities," *Sociometry* 23 (Dec. 1960), pp. 372–92; and Bernard C. Rosen, "Social Class and the Child's Perception of the Parent," *Child Development* 35 (Dec. 1964), pp. 1147–54.

Middle-class families are a highly mobile group. Much of this mobility is occupationally related and helps create a fairly homogeneous middle-class life style. Middle-class children and adolescents undergo lengthy anticipatory socialization—learning from parents, the mass media, and colleges—to begin married life in possession of the standard middle-class package of consumer goods.

A large proportion of families have kin nearby, and up to half visit with kin at least once a week. Visiting up to that level appears associated with good marital adjustment; beyond that, it implies overdependence. There may be bias shown in favor of the wife's kin or each spouse may take the lead with his or her own kin. Mutual aid is widespread, with aid flowing from parents to married children. The aid is arranged carefully so as not to interfere with the independence of either family.

The working-class family is characterized generally by patterns of low education, occupational prestige, and income. Honesty, obedience, and conscientiousness are highly valued; creativity and innovation are discouraged. These traits parallel the occupational requirements of the blue-collar world. Children are trained to obey and respect parents in the adult-centered home.

Married life in the working class is characterized by a high degree of sex segregation. The emphasis is on the sexual union and complementary task completion. Wives retain close relationships with kin, whereas husbands continue premarital peer-group associations. The divorce rate is high in the working class because couples tend to marry at young ages. Marital bonds are also strained by factors difficult to change.

SUGGESTED READINGS

Baltzell, E. Digby, *Philadelphia Gentlemen: The Making of a National Upper Class*, Glencoe, Ill.: The Free Press, 1958. A study of the American upper class in Philadelphia, Boston, and New York.

Bane, Mary Jo, *Here to Stay: American Families in the Twentieth Century*, New York: Basic Books, 1977. Refutes the contention that the American family is in decline. Cautions against social policies that might inadvertently weaken the family.

Belle, Deborah, *ed.*, *Lives in Stress: Women and Depression*, Beverly Hills, Calif.: Sage Publications, 1982. Examines a variety of special stresses that face low-income families. Special attention is paid to the value of support systems among friends and relatives.

Klatzky, Sheila R., *Patterns of Contact with Relatives*, Washington, D.C.: American Sociological Association, 1973. This doctoral dissertation is the methodologically most rigorous analysis that has yet been done of the effects of distance on contacts with relatives outside the family of procreation.

Scanzoni, Letha, and Scanzoni, John, *Men, Women, and Change: A Sociology of Marriage and Family*, New York: McGraw-Hill, 1976. A basic textbook that emphasizes stability and change in the family.

FILMS

The Cage (National Film Board of Canada, 1251 Avenue of the Americas, 16th Floor, New York, N.Y. 10020), 27 minutes. Questions whether getting that important job and keeping up with the Joneses are worth the strains and tensions that go with them.

Marriage Is a Partnership (Coronet Films, 65 E. South Water Street, Chicago, Ill. 60601), 20 minutes. Analyzes adjustments of a young married couple. Shows that the resolution of their problem is a function of the young people's attitudes.

You Haven't Changed a Bit (Association Films, 866 Third Avenue, New York, N.Y., 10022), 15 minutes. A young couple come to realize that their personal growth hinges on their growth together in marriage.

QUESTIONS AND PROJECTS

1. In what ways do the upper class attempt to isolate itself from intrusion from the other classes?
2. How does the upper class go about trying to control the dating and mate-selection processes of its young people?
3. Is it accurate to describe the upper-upper class as a trustee family? Why or why not? How is that family changing?
4. Why is residential stability an important factor to upper-class families? Compare the geographic mobility patterns of the upper, middle, and working classes. How are they similar? How are they different? Why?
5. Describe the value system of the middle-class family. To what extent are these values held by most American families?
6. Define the concept of anticipatory socialization. How are middle-class youths conditioned to develop high-success drives? Do they necessarily strive for financial success?
7. What emotional and financial strains plague upwardly mobile young couples? How do these strains affect their relationships with their children?
8. How frequently do urban families visit with relatives? What patterns of mutual aid exist? How do these vary over the life cycle?
9. What is the modified extended family? How does it differ from the classical extended family?
10. Might there have been a stage in the development of Western society

when the nuclear family was more isolated than it is today? What recent changes have made it easier for families to maintain contact with kin?

11. Why is it that both the upper class and the working class are patriarchal, whereas the middle class tends toward egalitarianism? Do these spousal patterns overlap childrearing practices?

12. Why is upward mobility difficult for members of the working class?

13. What trends have been occurring in American childrearing patterns over the past three or four decades? What social class differences existed in the past? At present?

Paul Conklin, Monkmeyer

9
The Influence of Race: Black Families

To America's . . . blacks, the 1980s seem light-years from the exuberance of the civil-rights push in the 1960s and its battle hymn, "We Shall Overcome." That campaign was carried out despite white violence in the South and black rioting in the North's big cities. Yet it won many court actions, staged freedom marches and secured the passage of a succession of laws to solidify civil rights for blacks and other victims of discrimination. It was an era that revolutionized a community almost unchanged since the Reconstruction Era—largely isolated from the American mainstream and shaped over generations by its rural Southern origins and centuries of rigorous white supremacy. Today, as "blacks" instead of as "Negroes," this racial community is becoming a largely urban constituency of political and economic importance across the nation.[1]

Black people make up the largest racial or ethnic minority in the United States—over 26 million people. They also have a unique history. Both that history and the heterogeneity of so large a population must be taken into account in our description of black family patterns and the degree to which they conform to and differ from white middle-class family patterns.

FAMILY PATTERNS UNDER SLAVERY

The first blacks arrived in Virginia in 1619. Purchased from a Dutch ship, they had the same status as white indentured servants.[2] After they

---

1. *U.S. News & World Report,* March 1, 1982, p. 63.
2. E. Franklin Frazier, *The Negro in the United States,* New York: Macmillan, 1957, pp. 22–26; Alphonso Pinkney, *Black Americans,* Englewood Cliffs, N.J.: Prentice-Hall, 1969, p. 1.

had worked to earn their purchase, they were released from servitude. This happened in some cases and free blacks in the United States existed almost from the beginning. Under demands for a permanent, cheap labor supply, however, slavery was not long in emerging. The slave status of blacks in Virginia became fixed by law in 1670. At the first United States census in 1790, there were about 700,000 slaves; before the Civil War, the number had increased to almost 4 million.

A striking feature of black American family life from the beginning was the almost complete absence of influence from African culture. The English, Poles, Italians, and others transported many of their traditional patterns to the United States. The conditions of slavery, however, effectively prevented blacks from doing this. Before shipment to America, members of various African cultures often were mixed to prevent the development of resistance among them. Then in the New World, the process continued in the sale and training of slaves. The newcomers had to learn a new language, adopt new habits, and assume, in some form, the customs in their new environment. The children born into this situation never learned much of their African heritage and, almost within a generation, the old ways were lost.[3]

Early sexual, marital, and family practices also were influenced by a grossly disproportionate sex ratio. Although precise data are not available, the early shipments of slaves were heavily male and not until around 1840 did the number of black women approach that of black men. Not surprisingly, many informal sexual liaisons developed—first between indentured black men and indentured white women, later on between slaves and indentured white women. Miscegenation may have been proportionately more frequent during those early decades than it has ever been since.

The unbalanced sex ratio contributed also to casualness of sexual contact between many black women and men. The primary factors were the attitudes and policies of white slaveowners. Some owners literally considered their slaves as livestock and sought to breed them in comparable fashion. Strong, healthy males were used as studs, and the formalities of marriage often were dispensed with. Too, fathers were sold or traded without their wives and children, and vice versa. Under these circumstances, whatever tendency there was to seek sexual satisfaction without assuming further obligations was greatly intensified.

Conditions on the plantations were not everywhere alike nor even similar for all slaves on a given plantation. Some owners apparently

3. W. E. B. Du Bois, *The Negro American Family*, Atlanta: Atlanta University Press, 1908; and E. Franklin Frazier, *The Negro Family in the United States*, New York: Dryden Press, 1948, pp. 15–17.

treated their slaves with kindness and consideration and encouraged the development of a stable family life among them. In these instances, the family patterns that emerged were not significantly different from those that existed among whites and free blacks.[4]

On the same plantations, there often were differences between the family patterns of house slaves and field hands. The house servants were exposed intimately to the ideas and manners of their owners; black women assumed much of the care and training of white children, and the family lives of owners and slaves became intertwined. The family patterns of the house slaves often did not differ significantly from those of their owners. Often, there was great social distance between house slaves and field hands. The house servants reinforced their superiority by identifying with their owners, whereas the field hands were cut off from such opportunities and frequently were brutalized in the process.

Field hands typically were under the supervision of an overseer whose only interest was in production and who was prone to treat them as chattel. The harshest effects of slavery were found in this context, and what has come to be considered the ideal-typical slave family was that of the field hands. It was among field hands that the husband and father sometimes became a shadowy figure in the family. The field hands were most likely to be used as breeding stock, and emphasis was placed on the mother-child unit. Marriages seldom were regularized, and when families were split up there was a tendency to keep small children with their mother. Many owners reinforced the primary position of the mother and sabotaged the father by assigning to the woman the cabin in which she and her children lived and by issuing to her the rations of food. Men were not encouraged to assume responsibility for wives and children, and many did not. Thus, under slavery there emerged a mother-centered family that was to continue in modified form into the postslavery period.

---

4. For analyses supporting the thesis that the slave family structure was basically nuclear, see Robert W. Fogel and Stanley L. Engerman, *Time on the Cross: The Economics of American Negro Slavery*, Boston: Little, Brown, 1974; Eugene Genovese, *Roll, Jordan, Roll: The World the Slaves Made*, New York: Pantheon Books, 1974; and Herbert Gutman, *The Black Family in Slavery and Freedom, 1750–1925*, New York: Pantheon Books, 1976. A recent analysis of black family patterns in the South after the Civil War presents data indicating that both Du Bois and Frazier and their recent critics probably were partly correct. See Barbara Finlay Agresti, *Household and Family in the Postbellum South: Walton County, Florida, 1870 and 1885* (Ph.D. dissertation): University of Florida, 1976. See also Barbara Finlay Agresti, "The First Decades of Freedom: Black Families in a Southern County, 1870 and 1885," *Journal of Marriage and the Family* 40 (Nov. 1978), pp. 697–706; and Herbert Gutman, "Persistent Myths About the Afro-American Family," in Michael Gordon, *ed., The American Family in Social-Historical Perspective* (2nd ed.), New York: St. Martin's Press, 1978, pp. 467–89.

Black family life was further complicated by miscegenation. In the beginning, miscegenation was two-way, with intercourse between black men and white indentured women sometimes being encouraged by owners who wished to increase their numbers of indentured servants. As the "principles" of white domination and racial integrity became fixed, however, laws were enforced against unions between black men and white women. Although there are no precise data, relationships between white men and black women continued to be widespread.

Relationships between white men and black women ranged from the completely casual to those in which the female slave was emancipated and made a legal wife. In some instances, slave-mistresses were later sold and their mulatto children with them. Often, however, the slave-mistress received special consideration and the children were treated with affection. The woman sometimes was brought directly into the household and sometimes had her own small house near by. The children often were freed and occasionally were sent to college. Nor was miscegenation confined to plantations. There were, in cities like New Orleans, Charleston, and Mobile, large mixed-blood populations as well as free blacks. Attractive mulatto, quadroon, and octoroon women were sought after by well-to-do-men, with all the results that characterized such relationships in rural areas. Because the children of such unions were free, they helped to swell the ranks of free blacks in the United States.

By 1860, there were nearly half a million free blacks. Frazier reports that more than one third, as compared to an estimated one twelfth, of the slave population was probably of mixed blood.[5] Among these free blacks, another family pattern emerged. These families sometimes were almost patriarchal, with the husband and father wielding more power than in corresponding white families. For one thing, the free black man often purchased his wife from slavery and, where she had children, purchased them too. Thus, we have the anomaly of slaveowning blacks. There is even evidence of husbands selling their wives back into slavery when the marriages did not work out.[6]

On the whole, the families of free blacks prior to the Civil War appear to have been quite stable. Their members frequently were former house slaves who had adopted the attitudes and customs of upper-class whites. Many free blacks became landowners and assumed responsible places in their communities. These free blacks began a pattern, which continues today, in which social class or economic status is far more closely associated with variations in family life than is race.

5. Frazier, *Negro in the United States, op. cit.,* p. 67.
6. Frazier, *Negro Family in the United States, op. cit.,* p. 139.

EMANCIPATION

The effects of emancipation on black families were as diverse as the family forms that preceded it. In fact, emancipation seemed mostly to sharpen trends already evident. The families of previously free blacks and of those who had achieved stability under slavery were not affected greatly. They continued to live much as they had lived, with the father moving into a position of full responsibility for the support of his family and acquiring the authority that goes with it.

Where family ties were less secure, they often broke under the stresses that followed emancipation. Many men who were not formally married to women whose children they had fathered simply left their homes to test the limits of their newly acquired freedom. They clustered about Union army posts, went to the cities, and roamed aimlessly. Some women, chiefly those without children, did the same thing. Many people struggled to achieve family stability under very difficult societal conditions, sometimes succeeding and sometimes failing. The failure of given marriages seldom produced disillusionment with family living in general, however, and frequent marriages following marital breakups produced something approximating serial monogamy.

The instability of much family life following emancipation further emphasized the mother-child relationship. Women without children and men were free to come and go. But the woman with children could not be free of responsibility. She had to pretty much stay in one place; she had to find some means of economic livelihood; and she had to accept men, if at all, on their own terms. To have a man even temporarily was to have some affection and some security.

MIGRATION AND URBANIZATION

Free blacks even before the Civil War were concentrated in urban areas. At the first census in 1790, 10 percent of the populations of New York and Baltimore were black. The majority of blacks, however, lived in the rural South. After the war, a trek toward southern cities, then to northern cities, and finally to the West got under way.

From 1860 to 1870, the black population of 14 southern cities increased by 90 percent and the black population of 8 northern cities increased by 50 percent. After this first postwar surge into urban areas, the migration slowed down somewhat and consisted chiefly of movement into southern cities. By 1910, 70 percent of the urban black population still was in the South.

The large-scale migration of blacks northward got under way during

World War I. The southern economy was in serious decline and a major labor shortage developed in northern cities. Labor recruiters toured the South, offering transportation to those who would go, and northern black newspapers urged their brethren to escape from southern tyranny. Over 1 million blacks migrated north during the war.[7] All northern cities, except Pittsburgh and Kansas City, increased their black populations by over 50 percent. Philadelphia's black population increased by 59 percent; New York's increased by 80 percent; Chicago's by nearly 150 percent; and Detroit's blacks increased by over 600 percent.

The influx of blacks into northern cities changed the pattern of race relations there and created problems that plague whites and blacks today. Before the war, Chicago, for example, was considered a model example of black-white relations.[8] Over half the blacks lived on the South Side on amicable terms with their white neighbors.[9] Then thousands of uneducated, unskilled black migrants moved into the area. Homes and apartments were subdivided and then subdivided again. The dilapidated areas where rents were lowest were seized on first, then the human tide spilled over into adjacent middle-class areas. A huge and expanding black belt was exploited by unscrupulous realtors who frightened whites away with threats of loss of property values, and then increased rents and prices to incoming black people. The resulting tensions culminated in race riots, and a pattern of rigid residential segregation was established.

Migration to the urban North intensified family problems. The extreme overcrowding in residential areas made normal family life difficult. In 1930, over 40 percent of the black families in New York's Harlem had from one to four lodgers living with them. And, in 1939, one single Harlem block had a population of 3871 people and was reputed to be the most crowded living area in the world. Much of the irregularity of black family life and much social and personal disorganization may be traced to inadequate living quarters and the inability to find decent housing.[10]

Studies have also shown that the urbanization of black people has been accompanied by more family disorganization, higher proportions of broken marriages, higher proportions of families with female heads,

7. E. Franklin Frazier, "Ethnic Family Patterns: The Negro Family in the United States," *American Journal of Sociology* 53 (May 1948), p. 436.
8. St. Clair Drake and Horace Cayton, *Black Metropolis*, New York: Harcourt and Brace, 1945, p. 73.
9. Robert C. Weaver, *The Negro Ghetto*, New York: Harcourt and Brace, 1948, p. 31.
10. Otis D. Duncan and Beverly Duncan, *The Negro Population of Chicago*, Chicago: University of Chicago Press, 1957, p. 84.

more quasi-families, and larger numbers of unrelated members in households than before the movement to the cities. Although black family life in the rural south was sometimes irregular, it was at least governed by a host of personal controls and was accommodated to the environment. Illegitimacy, for example, was not as much of a problem. Illegitimate children and their mothers were accepted with less stigma, often being incorporated into a maternal household. Little money was required to provide the minimum of food and clothing expected, and the household group pooled its resources to provide these. With migration north, however, illegitimacy became a major problem. Mothers and children were stigmatized, and the failure of the father to provide produced a crisis. A vast, shifting group of homeless men, women, and children was created, dependent on public welfare and confused in their attempts to cope with an anonymous, impersonal urban world.

The migration northward continued and during and after World War II spread to the West. With few exceptions, blacks settled in the central cities, and white city residents moved to the suburbs. Between 1940 and 1950, 1.3 million blacks migrated to the central cities. Between 1940 and 1960, the black populations of Philadelphia and New York doubled, those of Detroit and Chicago tripled, and that of Los Angeles increased by 500 percent. Between 1960 and 1970, black people continued to move north and west at the rate of about 140,000 per year. The peak was reached during that decade, and from 1970 to 1980, the tide actually reversed. More blacks left the Northeast than entered it, whereas the Midwest and the South had about the same number of blacks moving out as moving in.

CONTEMPORARY FAMILY PATTERNS

There are over 26 million black Americans. It stands to reason that there are no one, two, or even three family patterns among them. Over 70 percent of these blacks live in urban areas, but the term *urban areas* includes southern cities, northern cities, and cities of 5000 as well as with those of 5 million. More than 6.5 million black people live in non-metropolitan areas; and 1 million live on farms. That differences exist from south to north and from rural to urban is certain. Undoubtedly, there are still other differences. But there is one dimension that is the most relevant of all to an analysis of black-family patterns—socioeconomic status. Black families vary more according to their position in the occupational structure than according to any other variable.

Variations by Social Class

Black people are not yet fully integrated into the American economy. In 1981, 34 percent of the black population lived in officially defined poverty, whereas only 11 percent of the white population did so.[11] Moreover, the trend during the 1960s for the income levels of black people to rise in relation to those of whites has not been sustained. In 1950, for example, the median income of blacks was 61 percent of that of whites. In 1981, the median family income of blacks was 56 percent of that of whites.

Economic discrimination against black people can be shown in other ways. Although blacks are about 11 percent of the working-age population black men hold only 2 or 3 percent of the top professional jobs. Furthermore, black women make up about 32 percent of those employed in household domestic work. The jobless rate for blacks as late as 1982 was more than twice that of whites. Black teenagers were the hardest hit, with almost 50 percent being unemployed.

If black people as a whole are making few gains toward income equality with whites, some younger, well-educated black people are making significant progress. The proportion of nonwhites earning $10,000 or more, to take one illustration, rose from 22 percent in 1966 to 33.7 percent in 1972. Young black families (husband under 35) with both husband and wife working had a median income of $16,715 in 1976, compared with $16,691 for similar white families.[12] If income equality has been reached here, however, it should be remembered that such black families are only 16 percent of all black husband-wife families in the country and only 10 percent of all black families. The other 90 percent continue to be unequal.[13]

Some of the difficulties in any attempt adequately to characterize contemporary black families may be gleaned from Figure 9.1, which is a somewhat impressionistic portrayal of the distribution of black people

11. In 1981, the official poverty level was $9,287 for a nonfarm family of four. John Reid, "Black Americans in the 1980s," *Population Bulletin* 37 (Dec. 1982), p. 30. For other evidence of racism, see Kenneth C. W. Kammeyer, Norman R. Yetman, and McKee J. McClendon, "Family Planning Services and the Distribution of Black Americans," *Social Problems* 21 (June 1974), pp. 674–90; and Melvin L. Oliver and Mark A. Glick, "An Analysis of the New Orthodoxy on Black Mobility," *Social Problems* 29 (June 1982), pp. 511–23.
12. Associated Press, June 19, 1979.
13. See Noel A. Cazanave, "Middle-Income Black Fathers: An Analysis of the Provider Role," *Family Coordinator* 28 (Oct. 1979), pp. 583–93; Sharon M. Collins, "The Making of the Black Middle Class," *Social Problems* 30 (April 1983), pp. 369–82; and Wayne Villemez and Alan R. Rowe, "Black Economic Gains in the Sixties: A Methodological Critique and Reassessment," *Social Forces* 54 (Sept. 1975), pp. 181–93.

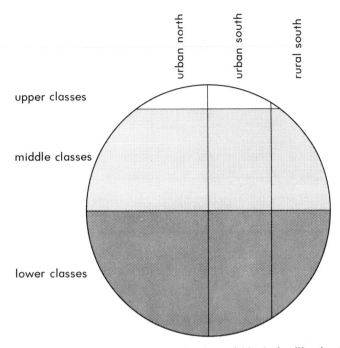

Figure 9.1. The urban and regional distribution of black families in the United States

Source: Andrew Billingsley, *Black Families in White America.* © 1968, p. 7. Reprinted by permission of Prentice-Hall, Inc., Englewood Cliffs, N.J.

in the United States by social class and by rural-urban residence. Roughly half of all black people live in the urban north, one fourth live in the urban south, and one fourth live in the rural south. Similarly, one half of all black people are lower class, some 40 percent are middle class, and approximately 10 percent upper class.[14]

Andrew Billingsley, who is responsible for this schematic, indicates that it is important to compare black families not only with white fam-

14. Furious debate among both black and white scholars, rages over the most accurate and useful way to classify black people by social class. As indicated in Figure 9.1, Billingsley classifies some 40 percent as middle class. A recent, widely publicized analysis argues that "a slight majority" of black Americans can now be considered as middle class: see Ben J. Wattenberg, and Richard M. Scammon, "Black Progress and Liberal Rhetoric," *Commentary* 55 (April 1973), pp. 35–44. Many black scholars insist, however, that the most appropriate criterion is the income level the government says is needed for an urban family of four to enjoy an intermediate standard of living. By this standard, only about 25 percent of the black population is middle class: see *The Social and Economic Status of the Black Population in the United States, 1972,* Washington, D.C.: U.S. Government Printing Office.

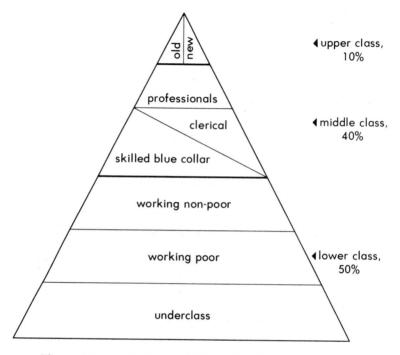

Figure 9.2. The social class distribution of black families

Source: Andrew Billingsley, *Black Families in White America.* © 1968, p. 123. Reprinted by permission of Prentice-Hall, Inc., Englewood Cliffs, N.J.

ilies but also to compare them by social class and to link them to their urban or rural moorings. Of these dimensions, social class is most salient, and the class structure of the black population is complex.[15] Emphasizing that biases in social science blocked the studying of black social structure adequately and have caused scholars to misperceive what they have found, Billingsley classifies black Americans into three broad social classes—upper, middle, and lower—and then subdivides each of these—shown in Figure 9.2.

The upper class is composed of two fairly distinct groups, differentiated according to how long they have enjoyed upper-class status. Adults of the "older" upper class had parents who also were either middle class or upper class—businessmen, executives, college presidents, judges, physicians, dentists, and so on. In some cases, high status can be traced back to pre–Civil War days when the ancestors were either house slaves or free blacks. Well-known families in this group would include

15. Andrew Billingsley, *Black Families in White America,* Englewood Cliffs, N.J.: Prentice-Hall, 1968, p. 8.

those of Supreme Court Justice Thurgood Marshall, Senator Edward Brooke, former Secretary of the Department of Housing and Urban Development Robert Weaver, former UN official Ralph Bunche, Mayor Maynard Jackson of Atlanta, Congressman Julian Bond, the Reverend Martin Luther King, Jr., and many others. There are family histories of college educations, professional occupations, financial success, and family stability.

The "new" upper class is composed of families who have risen from obscurity to great achievement in a single generation. Included would be present or former mayors of six of our major cities: Kenneth Gibson of Newark; Walter Washington of Washington, D. C.; Carl Stokes of Cleveland; Coleman Young of Detroit; Richard Hatcher of Gary, Indiana; and Thomas Bradley of Los Angeles. Other examples include the Reverend Ralph Abernathy, Roy Innis, Henry Aaron, and the Reverend Jesse Jackson, to name only a few. All of these families have substantial incomes and can afford comfortable housing, travel, and college educations for their children.

Billingsley divides the black middle class into three subgroups: professional, clerical, and skilled blue collar. These terms are almost self-explanatory. The professions are those that do not rank as high as those that bring upper-class status—schoolteaching, accounting, social work, nursing—or the heads of the families have still not quite made it in the major professions—young attorneys, ministers of small congregations, and so on. The line between upper-class and middle-class professionals is not sharp. The incomes of middle-class clerical workers and of skilled blue-collar workers may be as high, sometimes higher, than those of the professionals. Skilled blue-collar workers may also have job security through union membership. Family life tends to be stable, with egalitarian marital relationships and achievement aspirations instilled in children from an early age. Compared to their white middle-class counterparts, these families have lower incomes, less job security, and wives are more likely to have to work outside the home.

The lower class again is divided into three subgroups: the working nonpoor, the working poor, and the underclass. The highest of the groups, the working nonpoor, is composed of the families of men who work at steady jobs in the industrialized sector of the economy—factory workers, truck drivers, and so on. Again, the line between this group and the skilled blue-collar workers of the middle class often is blurred.

The working-poor families are headed by men who work hard and steadily at their jobs—janitors, porters, unskilled factory workers, and service workers—but who cannot earn enough money to escape poverty. They lack job security and are the first to be laid off or fired in times of recession. Billingsley estimates that they compose as much as one third of all black families. In spite of the problems they face, most of these families are intact families with father and mother present, and most manage to scrape by without accepting public welfare.

The final lower-class group, the underclass or the nonworking poor, constitutes 15 to 20 percent of black families, in which the adults generally were school dropouts, have few salable skills, and work sporadically, if at all. They live in such poverty that Billingsley maintains they should be considered as outside and below the formal class structure rather than as part of it. Dependent largely on support by relatives and public welfare, this is the group that receives most attention in the press. Here, family disorganization prevails. Most states literally coerce family disorganization by prohibiting welfare payments if there is a man in the home. The specific conditions of life vary from the rural south to the urban south to the urban north, but the consequences probably range from severe malnutrition to outright starvation. Problems of family organization yield to the problem of sheer survival.[16]

Types of Black Families

Black scholars maintain that white social scientists, reflecting the values of the racist society in which they live, have long distorted the nature of black family patterns. In addition to the social class variation described, black family patterns may be classified into three basic types: nuclear, extended, and augmented. These types in turn are divisible into subtypes, shown in Table 9.1.

Nuclear Families. The nuclear family is the familiar unit of husband, wife, and children. Billingsley's division of nuclear families into incipient, simple, and attenuated subtypes acknowledges that there is a pre-childbearing period during which the married couple constitute an *incipient* nuclear family. It also acknowledges that separation, divorce, military service, distant employment, imprisonment, hospitalization, death, and other conditions occasionally remove one parent from the home, leaving the other parent and the children as an *attenuated* nuclear family.

The importance of this classification derives from the unconscious assumption that the majority of white families are simple nuclear families and the frequently quoted statistics concerning the large proportion of broken black families. The assumption about white families is wrong,

16. *Ibid.*, pp. 137–42. For a devastating analysis of how the public welfare system has failed black children, see Andrew Billingsley and Jeanne M. Giovannoni, *Children of the Storm: Black Children and American Child Welfare*, New York: Harcourt Brace Jovanovich, 1972.

Table 9.1. The structure of black families

Types of Family	Household Head		Other Household Members		
	Husband and Wife	Single Parent	Children	Other Relatives	Non-relatives
Nuclear Families					
I: Incipient nuclear family	X				
II: Simple nuclear family	X		X		
III: Attenuated nuclear family		X	X		
Extended Families					
IV: Incipient extended family	X			X	
V: Simple extended family	X		X	X	
VI: Attenuated extended family		X	X	X	
Augmented Families					
VII: Incipient augmented family	X				X
VIII: Incipient extended augmented family	X			X	X
IX: Nuclear augmented family	X		X		X
X: Nuclear extended augmented family	X		X	X	X
XI: Attenuated augmented family		X	X		X
XII: Attenuated extended augmented family		X	X	X	X

Source: Andrew Billingsley, *Black Families in White America.* © 1968, p. 17. Reprinted by permission of Prentice-Hall, Inc., Englewood Cliffs, N.J.

and the alleged facts about black families are misleading. *Simple* nuclear families, with both parents and children living in the home, are a minority among both races; if there are any differences in the proportions of blacks and whites with such arrangements, they are relatively small. Billingsley indicates that about 36 percent of all black families, more than 1.5 million, are of the simple nuclear type.[17] Another 20 percent of black families, about 1 million, are incipient nuclear families: either married couples who have not yet produced children or older couples whose children are grown and gone.

Attenuated families, commonly referred to as broken or one-parent families—contrary to the prevailing stereotype—constitute only 6 percent of black families. Over 90 percent of these families are headed by women, providing much of the factual support for the widespread conception of a contemporary matricentric black family. It should not be

17. Billingsley, *Black Families in White America, op cit.,* p. 18. This section continues to draw heavily on Billingsley's work.

overlooked, however, that nationwide values and judicial practice both support children remaining with their mothers in separation or divorce, regardless of whether the families are black or white. The tendency of welfare regulations to force the fathers of poor families out of the home was also discussed in our analysis of social-class variations.

Almost two thirds of all black families, in summary, are nuclear families of one of these three subtypes. Roughly one fourth of all black families are extended families and around 10 percent are augmented families.

Extended Families. In earlier chapters, we have used the term *extended family* in the conventional way to refer to residential units of three or more generations. The usage here to analyze black family structure is somewhat looser and includes all families where other relatives live with a nuclear family. An *incipient extended* family is one in which a husband and wife without children at home have other relatives living with them. The *simple extended* family includes other relatives along with the parents and children. *Attenuated extended* families consist of one parent with his or her children in addition to other relatives in the home.

The "other relatives" who live with nuclear families fall into four categories. First, they may be minors such as grandchildren, nieces, nephews, and cousins. Second, they may be peers of the parents in the home: siblings, cousins, or other adult relatives. Third, they may be grandparents. Fourth, they may be other elderly relatives such as aunts and uncles. There may, of course, be various combinations of these living with given families.

Billingsley estimates that about 15 percent of black families have minor relatives living with them and that over 25 percent have adult relatives in the home. A majority of female-headed attenuated families care for other relatives. Many families, of course, have both adult relatives and children living with them. In an independent analysis, Robert Hill found that four times as many black incipient nuclear families as white incipient nuclear families, proportionately, have minor relatives living with them. Among female-headed attenuated nuclear families, the disparity is even greater: 41 percent of the black families compared to only 7 percent of the white families care for minor relatives.[18]

Augmented Families. The concept of augmented families was developed to include families who take nonrelatives—roomers, boarders,

---

18. Robert B. Hill, *The Strengths of Black Families*, New York: Emerson Hall, 1971, p. 5. For additional supporting evidence, see William C. Hays and Charles H. Mindel, "Extended Kinship Relations in Black and White Families," *Journal of Marriage and the Family* 35 (Feb. 1973), pp. 51–57.

lodgers—into the home on a long-term basis. Such nonrelatives may be taken in either by nuclear families or extended families. Consequently, there are six types of augmented families, shown in Table 9.1. The number of augmented families is unknown, but Billingsley reports almost a half million black people living with family groups to whom they are not related. Two thirds of these are men; one-third are women. Most are adults and a considerable number are older people.

Thus, the structure of American black families obviously is much more complicated than generally is known.[19] The basic family type is that of the nuclear unit. There are many incipient nuclear families who represent early and late stages in the family life cycle. Many families have relatives or nonrelatives or both, living with them. Attenuated, or broken, families are not so common as believed. These facts call into question the old assumptions that black families are disorganized, deteriorating, or caught up in a tangle of pathology.[20]

THE STRENGTHS OF BLACK FAMILIES

The phrase "the strengths of black families" was originated by the Research Director of the National Urban League to title a research report in 1971. In that report, he presented data showing that five characteristics of black families have been functional for their stability and survival in a hostile social environment: strong kinship bonds, strong work orientation, adaptable roles, strong achievement orientation, and strong religious orientation.[21]

Strong Kinship Bonds

Black families experience a higher rate of marital disruption than the general population and the situation is worsening. Although over two thirds of all black families had both parents present in 1970, the 1980

19. For evidence that black families are even more complex, see Suzanne M. Bianchi and Reynolds Farley, "Racial Differences in Family Living Arrangements and Economic Well-being: An Analysis of Recent Trends," *Journal of Marriage and the Family* 41 (Aug. 1979), pp. 537-51; Wade W. Nobles," Toward an Empirical and Theoretical Framework for Defining Black Families," *Journal of Marriage and the Family* 40 (Nov. 1978), pp. 679-90; Marta Tienda and Ronald Angel, "Headship and Household Composition Among Blacks, Hispanics and Other Whites," *Social Forces* 61 (Dec. 1982), pp. 508-31; and J. Allen Williams and Robert Stockton, "Black Family Structures and Functions: An Empirical Examination of Some Suggestions Made by Billingsley," *Journal of Marriage and the Family* 35 (Feb. 1973), pp. 39-49.
20. Daniel P. Moynihan, *The Negro Family: The Case for National Action*, Washington, D.C.: U.S. Government Printing Office, 1965.
21. Hill, *op. cit.*

figure stands at just over 50 percent. In the general population, over 80 percent of families in 1980 had both parents present in the home.[22]

The well-known greater frequency of female-headed families among blacks than among whites is real. It is not only being perpetuated but is actually increasing as more whites escape poverty and as poverty is increasingly associated with blackness. In 1950, for example, some 17 percent of black families were headed by women. In 1960, the figure had climbed to 22 percent, and in 1980 to 31 percent. The figure for whites has hovered around 9 percent over the 20-year period.

Even among poor blacks, however, family life is amazingly cohesive, with a remarkable capacity to care for children and other relatives. Six times as many black women as white women without husbands are caring for relatives under 18 years of age. In part, this is due to the fact that black people have been denied access to public adoption agencies and, whereas white families have placed children for adoption, black families have had to care for their own. Moreover, the burden on black families has been proportionately greater because of their lower incomes. In 1980, more black children under 18 were living with their mothers than with two parents.

Black families place a great deal more emphasis on the extended family as a source of aid and support than do white families.[23] Moreover, these strong kinship bonds transcend social-class lines.[24] The family, in all its forms, is a source of strength and mutual support for members of the black population.

Strong Work Orientation

Although white society has long rationalized discrimination against black people by saying that blacks either are too lazy to work or are emotionally alienated from work, systematic data show a strong work orientation among blacks. Hill points out, for example, that poor black people are more likely than poor whites to be employed. In 1969, 59 percent of the heads of poor black families were gainfully employed, whereas

22. Reid, *op. cit.*, p. 21.
23. See Richard E. Ball, "Marital Status, Household Structure, and Life Satisfaction of Black Women," *Social Problems* 30 (April 1983), pp. 400–409; and "Family and Friends: A Supportive Network for Low-Income American Black Families," *Journal of Comparative Family Studies* 14 (Spring 1983), pp. 51–65; see also Harriette P. McAdoo, "Stress Absorbing Systems in Black Families," *Family Relations* 31 (Oct. 1982), pp. 479–88; and Lena Wright Myers, "Elderly Black Women and Stress Resolution: An Exploratory Study," *Black Sociologist* 8 (Fall Summer 1978–1979), pp. 29–37.
24. Harriette P. McAdoo, "Factors Related to Stability in Upwardly Mobile Black Families," *Journal of Marriage and the Family* 40 (Nov. 1978), pp. 762–78.

only 53 percent of the heads of poor white families were employed.[25] In 1980, 40 percent of black workers were employed in white-collar jobs, up from just 11 percent in 1960.

This strong commitment to work also is apparent at both ends of the economic scale and in both intact and attenuated families. Among relatively prosperous young black families whose incomes exceed $10,000, wives are more likely to be employed than in comparable white families. Moreover, almost two thirds of the women who head black families also work outside the home. Most of them work full time.

The most crucial data on work orientation come from federal studies of the effects of a guaranteed minimum income on work behavior. Not all of these people were black, of course, but many were. The data involved 725 families in five cities in Pennsylvania and New Jersey and 450 families in rural Iowa and North Carolina that were given income supplements. Each family faced a break-even point at which subsidies were reduced to that the family could retain no more income by working than by relying on the income supplement alone. Few recipients withdrew from the labor market but some quit their unskilled jobs to train for better jobs. In addition, preliminary analyses of the data indicate that black people who received the income supplements earned more money while working than did a control group of black people who did not receive the extra income.[26]

Adaptable Roles

Several studies show that husband-wife relationships in most black families are equalitarian.[27] Three separate studies of national samples of the population showed both black and white husbands to have slightly more influence than their wives in family decision making, but these studies also implied that most decisions are made by the partners jointly.[28] Black husbands also share significantly in the performance of household tasks. In both low-income and middle-income families, the picture that emerges

25. Hill, *op. cit.*, p. 9.

26. Irene Lurie, *ed., Integrating Income Maintenance Programs*, New York: Academic Press, 1976. See also Robert Staples, "Public Policy and the Changing Status of Black Families," *Family Coordinator* 22 (July 1973), pp. 345–51.

27. Vicky L. Cromwell and Ronald E. Cromwell, "Perceived Dominance in Decision-Making and Conflict Resolution Among Anglo, Black, and Chicano Couples," *Journal of Marriage and the Family* 40 (Nov. 1978), pp. 749–59; and Charles V. Willie and Susan L. Greenblatt, "Four 'Classic' Studies of Power Relationships in Black Families: A Review and Look to the Future," *Journal of Marriage and the Family* 40 (Nov. 1978), pp. 691–94.

28. Reported in Hill, *op. cit.*, pp. 18–19.

is one of active, involved husbands and strong, but not dominant, women.

The situation concerning female-headed families was analyzed earlier, and there is no need to repeat it here. Contrary to the impression that these families are caught up in a tangle of pathology, many of them show impressive stability under difficult circumstances. Moreover, although it is widely assumed that being reared in one-parent homes has a negative impact on children, it has not been demonstrated by research.[29] The *quality* of relationships with the parent or parents present appears to be more influential than *how many* parents are present.

Strong Achievement Orientation

Social science has shown that middle-class youth have higher educational aspirations than lower-class youth. It is also well known that most black youth have been lower class. From these facts, many writers have jumped to the unwarranted conclusion that black youth is not highly motivated to succeed educationally. The data show instead that most lower-class youth have college aspirations. Moreover, because there are so many lower-class black youth, the number of such youths attending college may be greater than the number of middle-class black youths attending college. In 1980, the median number of years completed in school for blacks (12.0 years) nearly equaled that for whites (12.5 years).[30] Finally, research indicates that parental influence to complete college may be greater among lower-class blacks than among lower-class whites. In one study, 80 percent of the black parents exerted such influence, whereas only 64 percent of the white parents did so.[31]

Strong Religious Orientation

The church probably has been the most conspicuous organization in most black communities. Not only has it been a source of solace for a downtrodden people and a steady source of moral standards in an almost anarchic social environment but it also has served as a vehicle for rebellion and social advancement. During slavery, rebellions often were organized with the aid of ministers; churches aided runaway slaves on their journeys north. More recently, churches and ministers were deeply involved in the development of the civil rights movement of the 1960s. Names such as those of Dr. Martin Luther King, Jr., the Rev-

29. Elizabeth Herzog and Cecelia E. Sudia, *Boys in Fatherless Families*, Washington, D.C.: Office of Child Development, 1970.
30. Reid, *op. cit.*, p. 25.
31. Reported in Hill, *op. cit.*, p. 31.

erend Ralph Abernathy, and the Reverend Jesse Jackson will go down in history. The role of the church in promoting family solidarity among black people is obvious enough, but most of the history of this relationship remains to be written.

SUMMARY

Although the first black people came to America as indentured servants, slavery soon appeared. Under slavery, all traces of African culture were deliberately expunged, and a variable family system, reflecting the division of labor among blacks and the policies of the white owners, emerged. Field hands frequently were discouraged from developing stable families. Whether or not there was a deliberate policy of breeding slaves, the primacy of the mother-child unit was emphasized in the assignment of living quarters and the distribution of food supplies. Men were sold or traded without their families; there was little opportunity for the development of responsibility by men. The family patterns of house slaves often were modeled on those of the owners. Stability and morality were emphasized; the father played a more prominent role. A father-centered family in which miscegenation figured prominently, also appeared among a growing class of free black people.

Emancipation seemed generally to heighten trends already present in black families. Stable, father-centered families remained stable, and the husband acquired increased responsibility. Families that were disorganized before, disintegrated further. The disorganized mother-centered family became recognizable in both urban and rural areas.

After the Civil War, a large-scale migration of black people, first to the cities and then northward began. The northward movement received impetus during World War I and resulted in strict residential segregation, overcrowding in black areas, and the intensification of family problems. Informal norms of casual sexual contact and illegitimate births created havoc in the urban situation where black people were deprived of their old primary group supports. The present status of black family patterns reflects the fact that black people are not yet fully incorporated into the occupational system. What differences exist appear to be more closely linked to socioeconomic status than to race.

One classificatory system divides black families into upper, middle, and lower classes, but it attaches special meanings to those labels and further subdivides the three classes. The upper class is divided into "old" and, "new" families, depending on when eminence was achieved. Some "old" upper-class families have histories of achievement and stability that extend back before the Civil War. Others have become prominent more recently, but all have had upper-class status for at least two generations. The "new" upper-class by contrast, has acquired wealth and status within the past generation.

The middle class is composed of three subclasses: the professional, the clerical, and the skilled blue collar. These terms are fairly self-explanatory. The middle-class professions are those that do not have enough prestige to warrant upper-class status: school teachers, accountants, nurses, and social workers for example. Some are young attorneys, ministers, and the like, who may eventually acquire upper-class status. Middle-class clerical workers cover the whole range from file clerks and typists to supervisors and office managers. The skilled blue-collar workers may not have as much prestige as some of the clerical workers, but their incomes often are higher.

The line between upper-class and middle-class black families often is not a sharp one. The incomes of middle-class clerical workers and those of blue-collar workers may be as high as, sometimes higher than, those of the professionals. The skilled blue-collar workers may also have job security through union membership. Family life tends to be stable, with egalitarian marital relationships and high aspiration levels instilled in children.

The black lower class again is divided into three subclasses: the working nonpoor, the working poor, and the underclass. The working nonpoor overlap significantly with the middle class. Typical occupations include those of truck driver, equipment operator, and factory worker—stable occupations in the industrialized sector of the economy. The working poor are fairly steadily employed at jobs such as service workers, porters, and janitors that yield incomes too low to permit their holders ever rising out of poverty. The underclass, which constitutes only about 15 to 20 percent of the black population, is the one around which most popular stereotypes of black families are built.

Black families may be divided into nuclear, extended, and augmented types, and these may be further subdivided. Such a classification shows that most black families are intact nuclear families and differ little from most white families. Extended black families offer testimony to the adaptability of black families under conditions of adversity. Augmented families show a similar capacity of black people to care for nonrelatives in a family situation.

Social scientists have focused far too much on the problems faced by black families and have paid too little attention to evidences of strength and resiliency in the system. The strength of kinship bonds is shown in the great reliance on the extended family and in the apparent stability of low-income, mother-headed families. A strong work orientation among black people is reflected in the high percentage of gainfully employed men, in the high proportion of working wives, and in the results of income-maintenance experiments. Role flexibility is shown in the preponderance of egalitarian marital relationships, and in significant participation of husbands and fathers in household duties. The attitudes of both parents and youth, and aspirations for college educations, demonstrate a strong achievement orientation. Finally, a strong religious orientation has a long history and is related to the church's continuing involvement in the struggle for equality.

SUGGESTED READINGS

Blackwell, James E., *The Black Community: Diversity and Unity*, New York: Dodd, Mead, 1975. The black family is described and analyzed in the larger context of black society.

Engram, Eleanor, *Science, Myth, Reality: The Black Family in One-Half Century of Research*, Westport, Conn.: Greenwood Press, 1982. Critiques 50 years of research on the black family, covering such topics as family theory, mate selection, childrearing, and marital disruption.

Gary, Lawrence E., *ed., Black Men*, Beverly Hills, Calif.: Sage Publications, 1981. A collection of 18 articles that reflect the position of the black man in contemporary society.

Heiss, Jerold, *The Case of the Black Family: A Sociological Inquiry*, New York: Columbia University Press, 1975. Report of a major research project into the structure of black families in major metropolitan areas.

Kennedy, Theodore R., *You Gotta Deal with It: Black Family Relations in a Southern Community*, New York: Oxford University Press, 1980. Insightful study of extended black families in an environment of poverty, prejudice, and hopelessness.

McAdoo, Harriette P., *Black Families*, Beverly Hills, Calif.: Sage Publications, 1981. Examines the diversity in lifestyles among blacks and compares black families with their white counterparts.

Martin, Elmer P., and Martin, Joanne Mitchell, *The Black Extended Family*, Chicago: University of Chicago Press, 1978. A unique study of 30 extended black families that includes over 1000 persons and covers large geographic areas.

Scanzoni, John H., *The Black Family in Modern Society*, Boston: Allyn & Bacon, 1971. A systematic and perceptive monograph based on information gathered from 400 black households in Indianapolis.

Staples, Robert, *ed., The Black Family: Essays and Studies*, Belmont, Calif.: Wadsworth, 1971. A comprehensive set of readings on many aspects of the family life of black people.

FILMS

The Black Woman (Audio-Visual Center, Indiana University, Bloomington, Ind. 47401), 52 minutes. Black women discuss the role of black women in modern society, and the problems they confront. Includes the relationships of the black women with black men and black women in the liberation movement.

Diary of a Harlem Family Audio-Visual Center, Indiana University, Bloomington, Ind. 47401), 20 minutes. Poignant view of the plight of a Harlem family through the photographs of Gordon Parks. Shows the impotence of poverty agencies and others to help.

"*Hey Mama*" (Vaughn Obern, 501 Bay Street, Apt. B, Santa Monica, Calif. 90405), 18 minutes. The offspring of one black woman in a stark documentary of lives in a black ghetto that might be anywhere.

Lay My Burden Down (Audio-Visual Center, Indiana University, Bloomington, Ind. 47401), 60 minutes. The plight of black tenant farmers and their families in the South. Their only hope is the recently obtained right to vote.

QUESTIONS AND PROJECTS

1. What is the difference between indentured servitude and slavery? How did indentured servitude influence the development of black-family patterns in the United States?

2. Describe black-family patterns under slavery. Describe the differences between the patterns of house servants and field hands.

3. How did emancipation influence black-family patterns? How did it increase the prominence of the matricentric family?

4. Describe the urban and northern migration of black people after the Civil War. What was the impact on family life?

5. What evidence is there that black people are not yet fully integrated into the economy? What gains, if any, have been achieved over the past two decades?

6. How are social class and rural-urban residence important in the analysis of black-family patterns? Which of these two factors do you believe to be more important? Why?

7. What is the difference between the "old" and the "new" black upper class? Why is it difficult to describe the patterns of the "new" upper class?

8. What variations exist within the black middle class? Within the black lower class? Comment on the effects of widespread emphasis on the family patterns of the black underclass.

9. Define the following concepts as they apply to black families: nuclear families, extended families, augmented families. What subtypes exist within each classification?

10. What is the most common family type among black people? What authority relationship (patriarchal-egalitarian-matriarchal) is most common? What kind of division of labor exists within the black home?

11. What evidence is there on the work orientation and the achievement orientation of black people?

12. What do you understand by the phrase, "the strengths of black families"? Take several "facts" about black family life and show how they can be interpreted either as indications of strength or weakness in black families.

Copyright © Jean Shapiro

10

The Influence of Ethnicity

Just as blacks thrust themselves into center stage in the 1960s by flexing their muscles and winning dramatic political, social and economic gains, another minority group has put the nation on notice: The 1980s will be theirs—the decade of the Hispanics.

Latin leaders paint a picture of a people on the move—young, aggressive and hungry for their rightful share of the American dream. Pointing to a Hispanic population that has grown by more than 60 percent in the last decade to nearly 15 million—a faster increase than any major ethnic group— these same standard bearers talks of a storehouse of "brown power" pent up for years and ready to break loose.

"Hispanics spent the '70s deciding by what name we ought to be called," notes former New Mexico Governor Jerry Apodaca. "Our call in the '80s is to educate our children and recognize our power as a political force."[1]

This vignette and the possibly apocryphal story of President Franklin D. Roosevelt welcoming a convention of the Daughters of the American Revolution during the 1930s with the statement, "Welcome, fellow immigrants!" should remind us again that contemporary American family patterns have developed at the confluence of a number of cultural streams. The dominant Western European influences were detailed in Chapter 6 and black American family patterns were described in the chapter that precedes this one. We now pursue further the idea of variability in American family patterns.

It will be recalled that, beginning about 1890, migration to the United States shifted substantially from northwestern Europe to southern and eastern Europe. Between 1890 and 1920, 22 million people came, mostly from Italy, Austria-Hungary, and Russia. Restrictive immigration poli-

1. *U.S. News & World Report*, August 24, 1981, p. 60.

cies after 1920 greatly reduced the number of migrants, caused the proportion of foreign-born in the population to decline, and encouraged assimilation toward a common American family pattern.

The Immigration Act of 1965 changed the situation drastically again. Under the new law, about 400,000 immigrants have been coming to the United States annually. In 1977, the largest single group, over 114,000, came from the West Indies, with over 69,000 coming from Cuba. Over 44,000 came from Mexico, more than 39,000 came from the Philippines, 31,000 came from Korea, and almost 20,000 came from China.[2] Immigration recently has been accounting for almost 20 percent of the growth in the population.

The last two decades have seen a new emphasis on various ethnic groups seeking to preserve their cultural heritages. Whereas, formerly, there had been attempts to rid themselves of traits that set them apart from "native Americans," many groups now endorsed a cultural pluralism that emphasized the contributions that their ways of life had made and could continue to make to a fuller and richer American culture. Our portrayal of contemporary American family patterns would not be complete without description of these family systems. We cannot describe them all, but we shall take a few representative ones. In this chapter, we shall analyze Italian American families, Mexican American families, Japanese American families, and Cuban American families.

ITALIAN AMERICAN FAMILIES

Italians have been selected to represent migrants from southern and eastern Europe around the turn of the century because they were the largest of these groups.[3] Their assimilation also was complicated by language differences, Roman Catholic religious affiliation, a low level of occupational skills, and stereotyping by the host population as dirty, ignorant, and generally undesirable.

Most of the migrants were from southern Italy and Sicily where they lived in small villages and farmed for a living. Life was organized around the family and village, which were characterized by suspiciousness and hostility toward outsiders. When they migrated to the United States, they located in northern cities and clustered in neighborhoods composed primarily of people from their own and neighboring villages. In many cities, these ethnic settlements came to be known as "Little Italy."

Italians in the United States received a less than enthusiastic recep-

2. U.S. Bureau of the Census, *Statistical Abstract of the United States, 1978*, Washington, D.C., p. 101.
3. Michael Lalli, "The Italian-American Family: Assimilation and Change, 1900–1965," *Family Coordinator* 18 (Jan. 1969), pp. 44–48.

tion. Set apart by differences in language, religion, and dress—and usually of low economic status—the immigrants were shunned by most residents of the cities into which they moved. They reacted by clustering even more tightly together in residential enclaves. They sought out their own kind and sought to preserve the old ways. They spoke Italian, read Italian newspapers, patronized Italian stores and businesses, preserved traditional foods and styles of clothing, and developed social organizations to provide recreation and reinforce ethnic solidarity.

The family system they brought was more patriarchal than that of the "old Americans." It revolved around the father, who ruled with something ranging from benevolent despotism to outright tyranny. He was the chief provider, but he also controlled incomes earned by other family members. He dominated his wife and controlled his children. When it came time for the children to marry, he helped to select their marriage partners. And, as in the old country, the norms were clearly spelled out. If the system was oppressive, people knew just where they stood.[4]

Assimilation

In America, assimilation tended to proceed by generations. The term *first generation* describes the immigrants themselves—the young husband and wife who spoke a foreign tongue and who were isolated from the mainstream of American culture. It was they who located in an ethnic enclave and began to raise a family.

As a general rule, assimilation proceeded slowly. The father had to accommodate to the society to some degree to get and hold a job. His foreign tongue was a handicap and he began to learn English. In the ethnic settlement at the end of the day, however, he reverted to the old language and the old ways. His wife might not even make this much concession. Bewildered by the strange ways and repelled by indifference or hostility from outsides, she was likely to seek security in the time-honored ways. Often, she avoided learning English and confined her activities to the ethnic group. As her husband's halting efforts toward

4. This section draws on a number of sources: see Paul J. Campisi, "Ethnic Family Patterns: The Italian Family in the United States," *American Journal of Sociology* 53 (1948), pp. 443–49; Francis X. Femminella, "The Italian-American Family," in Meyer Barash and Alice Scourby, eds., *Marriage and the Family: A Comparative Analysis of Contemporary Problems*, New York: Random House, 1970, pp. 127–39; Herbert J. Gans, *The Urban Villagers: Group and Class in the Life of Italian-Americans*, New York: The Free Press, 1962; Francis A. J. Ianni, "The Italo-American Teen-Ager," *Annals of the American Academy of Political and Social Science* 338 (Nov. 1961), pp. 70–78; Bartolomeo J. Palisi, "Ethnic Generation and Family Structure," *Journal of Marriage and the Family* 28 (Feb. 1966), pp. 49–50; and "Patterns of Social Participation in a Two-Generation Sample of Italian-Americans," *Sociological Quarterly* (Spring 1966), pp. 167–78.

assimilation created a gulf between them, she often responded by clinging more desperately to ethnic customs. Primarily, it was she who
dressed her children in the traditional way and who taught them to
speak the old language.

If the first generation was resistant to change, their children could not
often resist it. Even before school, the children were likely to have contacts outside the ethnic group and to learn from their more Americanized peers how funny their clothes were, how shameful it was to speak
a foreign language, and how bad it was to be different.

Perhaps the primary agent of assimilation was the school. School
teachers were likely to be middle class and often were, themselves, attempting to reject their ethnic origins. The official language was English, and the school taught that to be successful, as everyone should,
one must adopt middle-class ways. The schools also taught values of
democracy, egalitarianism, and individualism that conflicted with the
values of the parents and subverted the old form of family organization.

Children responded by refusing to speak anything but English, by
protesting against being different from their peers in any way, and by
adopting the attitudes of the larger society toward their parents and
their ways. The parents' ways were "old-fashioned" and a barrier to the
young person's need to belong.

A crisis often developed in adolescence. Resistance to parental ways
approached open defiance. Whereas the parents' lower-class lives were
conforming and stable, their children turned to the streets to show their
contempt for the adult world. With the street gang as their primary
reference group, they frequently sought status in gang warfare, delinquency, and sexual experience. To the adult world, the situation appeared
to be one of complete unregulation; but among the youth, the governing normative structure was quite clear. William F. Whyte shows this
clearly in an analysis of a slum sex code that sanctioned sexual intercourse with sexually experienced girls but that strictly forbade it with
virgins.[5]

Conflict developed between parents and their adult children over income and the selection of marriage partners. By parental standards, the
income earned by the young people was to be turned over to the father
who would dole out an allowance. Some young people accepted such an
arrangement only eventually to rebel against it; some rebelled from the
first. Parents' hopes that their children would marry within the group
often were frustrated as their children found Americanized young people to be more attractive than those who clung to the ethnic traditions.

For all the complications in their lives, many of those young people

5. William Foote Whyte, "A Slum Sex Code," *American Journal of Sociology* 49 (July
1943), pp. 24-31.

fared well as they moved into marriage and the occupational world. The school had performed its acculturation function well; except for the family name (and often it was changed—e.g., Capobianco became White-head, Campagnia became Bell), few traces of ethnic status remained. Although the parents generally worked at unskilled jobs, their offspring frequently were equipped to come into the white-collar and skilled-labor worlds. Their rejection of ethnic ways led them to locate their families of procreation in nonethnic middle-class areas. When they had children, the children were likely to be reared to seek full participation in the mass-consumption middle-class world.

Distinctive Italian American Patterns

By the middle of the twentieth century, the assimilation of many of the Italians in the United States was virtually complete. Several qualifications must be added however. First, the identity as Roman Catholics still separates many Italian-Americans from much of the non-Catholic population. Some of the implications of this will be analyzed in the chapter on mate selection. We should note that the Roman Catholic value system continues to strengthen the authority of the father, and the fact that children frequently are unplanned alters the relationship of parents to them. There is less emphasis on meeting the emotional needs of children and developing them into rounded adults. Care for the children and their education are both provided within a context of firm parental discipline.

Among many second-generation and some third-generation families, there also are differences in husband-wife relationships from those of other Americans. Tracing back to the strong patriarchy in Italy and the necessity for wives to control husbands unobtrusively (if at all), role relationships between second-generation immigrant husbands and wives tend to be segregated, with a clear division of labor defining women's work and men's work and with a minimum of joint decision making and sharing of activities and interests. There is less communication, less conversation, and less emphasis on gratification of the spouse's emotional needs than in the dominant middle-class family pattern.[6]

Still a third way in which Italian American family patterns remain distinctive derives from pressures to adapt to the Italian community and yet to become full-fledged members of the American community. The conflict thus generated has been heightened as the concept of ethnic pride has spread among Italian Americans and other ethnic groups. Tomasi has described three patterns of reaction to this conflict.

6. Lydio F. Tomasi, *The Italian American Family*, New York: Center for Migration Studies, 1972, p. 32.

The Rebel Reaction. Rebels seek to solve the nationality problem by rejecting their Italian heritage and becoming fully assimilated. They seek as spouses either people who are not Italian or who, like themselves, are seeking to escape ethnic identification. They rebel against turning over their pay to the father and, after marriage, they limit their contacts with their parents, brothers, and sisters. Further, they advocate egalitarian husband-wife relationships and democratic relationships between parents and children. Because of the psychological costs to the individuals involved, Tomasi believes this pattern to be uncommon.

The Ingroup Reaction. Those who choose this pattern seek to confirm their identities as Italians as they gradually structure their families in accord with prevailing American norms. They date Italians and non-Italians, but generally marry within the group. Having continued to accept parental authority themselves, they insist on it with their own children. The acceptance as Americans that they seek is not simply personal acceptance for themselves but is acceptance for Italians as a group. This appears to be the most common adjustment pattern, and it reinforces ethnic solidarity.

The Apathetic Reaction. In this form of adjustment, people seek to escape conflict over assimilation by deemotionalizing the whole issue and denying its importance. They show no preferences in the opposite sex either for Italians or non-Italians, perhaps marrying other Italians only because the similarity of background makes them more comfortable. There is considerable intermarriage, and the families of these apathetic persons remain marginal to the cultural worlds of both Italians and other Americans. Tomasi believes this adjustment pattern to be quite rare. The events of the last decade probably have made it even more uncommon than before.

Only time will tell whether the tendency toward complete assimilation has been halted permanently and whether a distinct family type is emerging. Ethnic bonds are stronger today than they were a few years ago. Still there is prejudice against those who are different, and the temptation to escape discrimination by conforming is strong.

MEXICAN AMERICAN FAMILIES

The Original Spanish Settlers

The first Mexican Americans became part of the United States through annexation rather than through immigration; the Mexicans were here when what is now Texas, New Mexico, Arizona, and California were incorporated into the Union. The land they occupied was huge, and the original settlers were scattered, numbering not more than 75,000 in 1860. Quite distinct social patterns existed, however, among them.[7]

Cattle ranching dominated the economy in Texas throughout the nineteenth century, and as land ownership rather than cattle became the determining factor, the Mexicans became a depressed class, working the land and running cattle for the Anglos. An exception existed along the Rio Grande where middle-class Mexican communities prospered in towns like Brownsville and Laredo. During the last decades of the century, cotton farming invaded the area, creating demand for cheap labor, and new Mexican immigrants joined the old Mexican settlers to fill the need. The suppression of Mexicans became complete and the stereotypes of Mexicans as ignorant, shiftless people solidified.

The situation in New Mexico was very different. Here, where there were some 60,000 Mexican settlers by 1850, there were relatively few Anglos, and Spanish-speaking ranchers both dominated the economy and controlled the legislature. Intermarriage between Mexican and Anglo families occurred frequently, and the two groups lived in relative harmony. Gradually, depletion of the lands through overgrazing, the invasion of the railroads, and the diversion of lands into mining shifted the balance of power toward the Anglos, and much of the Mexican minority concentrated in towns where they worked as laborers.

The few Spanish-speaking residents of what is now Arizona lived mostly in Tucson during the middle of the nineteenth century, where they clustered for protection against the Apache Indians. Soon the railroads brought an Anglo invasion, and the land was opened for mining. The Anglos gained control, operated the mines, and encouraged the immigration of Mexicans to work them. Discrimination against the Mexican workers was more drastic than in either Texas or New Mexico. Company stores often offered the only shopping, and physical brutality was the likely reward of workers who challenged the system.

Geographic isolation was instrumental in structuring the situation in California, where wealthy and powerful Mexican *rancheros* dominated the southern and central part of the state. The discovery of gold in the central region changed the situation drastically, bringing in hordes of Anglo miners and massive migrations of Mexicans. The elite and genteel culture of the native Castilians clashed with the crude and aggressive ways of the miners. The Anglo miners fought the Mexicans and made no distinctions in their hatred between lower-class Mexican miners and wealthy and cultured landowners. As mining withered, agriculture developed, and Anglos simply settled on, and appropriated large portions

7. This discussion follows closely the treatment of Joan W. Moore with Harry Pachon, *Mexican Americans*, Englewood Cliffs, N.J.: Prentice-Hall, 1976.

of, the old Mexican land grants. The wresting of the land from the Mexicans followed at a slower pace in southern California. But it proceeded inexorably. Los Angeles, settled by a mixture of lower-class Mexicans, Indians, Chinese, and Anglos became a center of racial and ethnic violence.

By the dawn of the twentieth century, only in New Mexico did Spanish-speaking people retain some economic and political power. Elsewhere, the dominant Anglo majority stereotyped all people of Spanish descent as "Mexicans" and forced most of them into manual labor, poverty, and subjection.[8]

Immigration

No reliable figures on the extent of Mexican migration to the United States are available for earlier than 1910, and even after that, one must distinguish between legal and illegal migrants. Statistics are available to assess legal immigration only. In 1910, nearly 18,000 legal immigrants came, with the figure dropping to a low of 11,000 and rising to 29,000 over the next decade. During the 1920s, the pattern was erratic but higher, averaging almost 50,000 per year. Mexican immigration dropped off to almost nothing during the Depression of the 1930s, remained low during World War II, and then began to climb again during the 1950s. During the 1960s, the rate fluctuated above and below 40,000, the 1970 figure being almost 45,000.

Although accurate estimates are not possible, some authorities believe that, in some years at least, three times as many Mexicans have entered the United States illegally as legally. From early in the twentieth century, agricultural and mining enterprises in the border states required large amounts of cheap labor, and by World War I Mexicans provided about the only supply. Special immigration regulations admitting "temporary" workers were instituted in 1917, with the result that most of the so-called temporary residents admitted remained permanently in the United States.

Migrants, both legal and illegal, came into the country fairly easily during the 1920s, but with the onset of the Depression, the Immigration Service sought the deportation of illegal aliens on a large scale. The Mexican and U.S. governments cooperated in schemes to expel persons of Mexican descent from the United States but were not overly careful to exclude persons who were U.S. citizens. The combination of deportation and lessened immigration during the 1930s lowered the number of Mexicans in the United States from 639,000 in 1930 to 377,000 in 1940.

8. *Ibid.*, pp. 11–20.

As World War II drained manpower into the armed forces, U.S. immigration policies changed again, and Mexican laborers (*braceros*) were actively recruited. Farm owners encouraged the illegal immigration of *wetbacks* also, for although unauthorized immigration was illegal, the employment of illegal aliens was not. Illegal immigrants may have outnumbered legal ones by four to one. The Immigration Service continued to expel illegal aliens in large numbers, sometimes promptly readmitting them as *braceros* and maintaining the fiction that the policies were rational and humane. This disgraceful situation continued through the 1940s and 1950s, generating distrust and hatred of the authorities in many Mexican American communities.

Organized labor in the United States had opposed the large-scale immigration of Mexicans since the end of World War II, with little effect until the early 1960s. In 1963, the Department of Labor established an informal quota by requiring that before a Mexican immigrant could be admitted, a state employment agency must certify that he or she would not take a job that would "adversely affect domestic wages or working conditions" or a job for which there were American applicants. The very next year, the *bracero* program was discontinued. The Immigration Act of 1965 limited the number of immigrants from the whole Western Hemisphere to 120,000 and was expected to curtail Mexican immigration still further. To date, however, the administration of the law has permitted Mexico to furnish over 40,000 people annually.[9]

Demographic Characteristics

There are almost 9 million people of Mexican descent in the United States, most of them in the four states of original settlement plus Colorado. In those five states, they are the largest minority, constituting 12 percent of the population. Mexican Americans are heavily concentrated in Texas and California. The Los Angeles area alone has over two thirds of a million. There has been some limited dispersal over the country, there are now small communities of Mexican Americans in Illinois, Kansas, Michigan, and Wisconsin.

Within Texas and California, Mexican Americans also are concentrated in certain areas. In Texas, south Texas, along the Rio Grande is the area of greatest concentration. In California, the concentration is in and around cities in the southern part of the state.

In many cities, Mexican Americans live in segregated neighborhoods called *barrios*. These are comparable to the "Little Italys" and other ethnic settlements of the northeast and midwest, except that, in this

9. *Ibid.*, pp. 38–44. See also Alejandro Portes, "Return of the Wetback," *Society* 11 (March/April 1974), pp. 40–46.

case, the Mexicans were the original settlers and the Anglos moved in around them. Many *barrios* adjoin the original plaza that has continued as the "Mexican Downtown." In other cities, Mexican Americans are not segregated and, literally, dominate the city. Laredo, Texas, may be the largest such city, but the pattern exists in many small towns in southern Texas and northern New Mexico. Finally, despite rapid migration to the cities, many Mexican Americans still reside in rural areas. No other minority group has such highly varied living conditions.

The nativity patterns of Mexican Americans have varied as a consequence of vacillating immigration policies. Most Mexican Americans became U.S. citizens by treaty in 1848. Then, large-scale immigration increased the number and proportion of foreign born. Early in this century, the native-born population became dominant again and now immigration is increasing the foreign-born again.

First-, second-, and third-generation Mexican American experience may be compared to that of European immigrants. Most of the first generation, of course, have been unskilled laborers of low economic status. Incomes rise among the second generation but, probably as a result of discrimination, do not show significant increase again among the third generation. Third- and subsequent-generation Mexican Americans generally are better educated, less likely to work at manual occupations, and more likely to intermarry with Anglos. The evidence on divorce rates is somewhat contradictory. Most analyses indicate that third-generation families are more stable and that, following divorce, they are more likely to remarry than are more recent migrants. An analysis of 1960 census data showed Mexican American divorce rates to be higher than those of Anglos and approaching those of blacks.[10] When the 1970 figures for Mexican Americans were compared with those of Anglos and blacks in the same five southwestern states, however, the Mexican American divorce rates were lower than those for either Anglos or blacks.[11]

A high birthrate among Mexican Americans is linked to a low average age. Mexican American families average 4.8 persons compared to

10. Peter Uhlenberg, "Marital Instability Among Mexican Americans: Following the Patterns of Blacks?" *Social Problems* 20 (Summer 1972), pp. 49–56.
11. Isaac W. Eberstein and W. Parker Frisbie, "Differences in Marital Instability Among Mexican Americans, Blacks, and Anglos: 1960 and 1970," *Social Problems* 23 (June 1976), pp. 609–21; and W. Parker Frisbie, Frank D. Bean, and Isaac W. Eberstein, "Recent Changes in Marital Instability Among Mexican Americans: Convergence with Black and Anglo Trends?" *Social Forces* 58 (June 1980), pp. 1205–20. See also, Frank D. Bean, Russell L. Curtis, and John P. Marcum, "Familism and Marital Satisfaction Among Mexican-Americans: The Effects of Family Size, Wife's Labor Force Participation, and Conjugal Power," *Journal of Marriage and the Family* 39 (Nov. 1977), pp. 759–67; and Marta Tienda, "Familism and Structural Assimilation of Mexican Immigrants in the U.S.," *International Migration Review* 14 (Aug. 1980), pp. 383–408.

4.5 persons for black families in the same region and 3.4 persons in comparable Anglo families. The median age among Mexican Americans is 21.3 years, almost 10 years younger than among Anglos. More than 40 percent of all Mexican Americans are under 15 years of age.[12]

Variation in Family Patterns

Mexican American family patterns are not simply a function of rural-urban status and social class; that would imply a uniform pattern of assimilation, which simply does not exist. There is, for example, great variation from one area to another. Generally, families in California, particularly in the larger cities, are more completely assimilated than are families in Texas. The more rural the Texas environment, the more traditional is the family system. At the other extreme, some old-family Mexican Americans in Colorado and New Mexico show virtually no tendencies toward assimilation. They may speak Spanish exclusively, follow traditional occupations, and appear to have totally resisted the forces of change.

Lower-Class Rural Families. Large numbers of poor people live in the *barrios* of agricultural towns. These segregated enclaves appear to continue almost unchanged from generation to generation. They maintain that appearance through the outmigration of numbers of young people and elders who have aspirations toward another way of life. Spanish is the principal language, and there are a few professional people such as doctors and lawyers as well as retail business people such as storekeepers and filling station operators.

In this setting, the extended family is *the* important institution. Relationships are traced outward on both sides of the family, and family rights and responsibilities are clearly defined. The man is the unquestioned head of the family, and his *machismo* (masculinity) is demonstrated through the production of children, through imposing himself sexually on his wife, and through extramarital liaisons. He is supported in these activities by a peer group of other men.[13]

---

12. Joan W. Moore, *op. cit.*, pp. 52–57.

13. Two studies show more egalitarianism than expected between spouses in farm-labor families. See Glenn R. Hawkes and Minna Taylor, "Power Structure in Mexican and Mexican-American Farm Labor Families," *Journal of Marriage and the Family* 37 (Nov. 1975), pp. 807–11; and Vicky L. Cromwell and Ronald E. Cromwell, "Perceived Dominance in Decision-Making and Conflict Resolution Among Anglo, Black, and Chicano Couples," *Journal of Marriage and the Family* 40 (Nov. 1978), pp. 749–59. For further analyses of variability in Mexican-American Families, see Alfredo Mirandé, "The Chicano Family: A Reanalysis of Conflicting Views," *Journal of Marriage and the Family* 39 (Nov. 1977), pp. 747–56; and "A Reinterpretation of Male Dominance in the Chicano Family," *Family Coordinator* 28 (Oct. 1979), pp. 473–79.

The wife-and-mother role in the family is modeled after the Madonna. Women are expected to be paragons of virtue, subordinating themselves completely to their husbands and other male relatives, eschewing sexuality, and devoting themselves to their children. Daughters are raised to continue the pattern. Different branches of the family often have their homes located close to one another, and warm, affectionate relationships among the women are a major source of solidarity.

A special kinship device that promotes continuing close relationships among extended families is that of *compadrazgo* (godparenthood). A man and a woman are chosen to be godparents for each child, committing themselves to see that it is brought up in the church, and implicitly obligating themselves to care for it if something should happen to the parents. Special ties develop between a man and his godson, who are referred to as *compadres*. Godparenthood also is a way of establishing ties with higher status families when the godfather is a boss, or *patrón*.

Middle-Class and Upper-Class Rural Families. Rural middle-class Mexican Americans, particularly in Texas, live better than their lower-class counterparts; they patronize physicians rather than faith healers; they use attorneys rather than priests for legal counsel; and they may send their children to college. But like lower-class people, they remain almost isolated from Anglo society, and their lives continue to center on a traditional kinship group. Again in comparison with what has often been reported for middle-class black people, they live the middle-class life style even more enthusiastically than most other middle-class people do.

There is also a small Mexican American upper class in some of the towns of the Rio Grande Valley. Some of these people have business interests on both sides of the border, and some who are U.S. citizens live in Mexico and commute to their American places of business. By and large, they have escaped the castelike isolation of middle-class and lower-class Mexican Americans and associate freely with Anglos. They sometimes belong to Mexican country clubs, and their sons and daughters may intermarry with upper-class Mexican families across the river.[14]

Urban Families. Unlike the situation among most immigrants of European origin, the residential segregation of Mexican Americans in U.S. cities does not decrease regularly by generation. As a general rule, segregation has broken down most rapidly in large California cities such as

14. Jaime Sena-Rivera, "Extended Kinship in the United States: Competing Models and the Case of La Familia Chicana," *Journal of Marriage and the Family* 41 (Feb. 1979), pp. 121–29.

Los Angeles, which has more residents of Mexican descent than any other city in the United States and more than any Mexican city, except for Mexico City. We shall discuss here the general impact of urban living on the traditional Mexican American family patterns.

First, extended family relationships become much less prominent. Few people are willing to double up families in the same household, and the existence of welfare services and health services relieve other family members of most obligations to support and care for the poor, the sick, and the disabled. Another symptom of change is the lessened importance and the changed character of *compadrazgo*. Although it has by no means disappeared, it is less common and has taken on political overtones as it is used to forge ties among unrelated adult men.

The roles of men in the cities have changed more than those of women. The trend is away from arbitrary male domination and toward an equality in which important decisions are reached jointly by the married pair. As extended family relationships diminish in importance and frequency, marital relationships become more important, with men no longer requiring their wives to be subservient and with men sharing in household duties and child care. Nevertheless, women still function primarily as wives and mothers; few Mexican American women attend college, and most men still disapprove of their wives working outside the home. Those families in which the wives are gainfully employed, however, do tend to be more egalitarian.[15]

It is in the cities that Mexican American families come to share most of the value system of other middle-class Americans. They strive to get ahead financially and to climb occupationally. At the same time, they continue to value deference to elders and to emphasize the importance of children. Their birthrates are beginning to drop as they hesitantly experiment with family planning.

The Chicano Movement

A vigorous Mexican American political action movement emerged around 1966 among young, urbanized, Anglicized, middle-class youth and spread rapidly to include both urban and rural, middle class and lower class, young people and adults. The movement challenges the stereotyped perceptions of Mexicans that have been held by the Anglo majority and by many Mexican Americans. It uses both conventional political tactics such as voting and direct confrontation of established authority to accomplish such goals as changing the public school system to provide more opportunities for Mexican American youth and to

15. Lea Ybarra, "When Wives Work: The Impact on the Chicano Family," *Journal of Marriage and the Family* 44 (Feb. 1982), pp. 169–78.

increase the numbers of older youth in colleges and universities. It includes the struggles to secure adequate unionization of farm workers. But most of all, it seeks to restore the Mexican American biological and cultural heritage as sources of pride, and it emphasizes the contributions of Mexican culture to contemporary American culture.

The Chicano movement has created divisions within the Mexican American population as the predominantly younger group presses for rapid change and articulates a radical rhetoric. Many older Mexican American leaders have disassociated themselves from the movement and denounced it as irresponsible. The division is clearest over the desirability of assimilation. Young Mexican Americans oppose this, and they are a very large proportion of the Mexican American population. As of this writing, the movement has not yet become articulate about how its values might impinge on family patterns. Militant young people who demand the right of self-determination for others as well as themselves also demand respect for Mexican values, which included a traditional authoritarian family system.[16]

JAPANESE AMERICAN FAMILIES

Although there were differences, the family system of traditional Japan was a strong, stable, extended one, comparable to that of China.[17] Japan was also rigidly stratified and by the nineteenth century, there were four principal classes: the *samurai* (warrior) upper class, an agricultural middle class, a class of artisans and artists, and the lower, merchant class. Unlike other migrations, the Japanese who migrated to the United States were mostly middle-class persons of some formal education and with experience in the ownership and management of land.

Immigration

The first significant migration of Japanese to the United States began around 1890. Most of the early migrants were young men who became farm workers or who worked in or established their own small businesses. The men were soon followed by women of comparable middle-class background who were brought to be their marriage partners.[18]

These early immigrants had the misfortune to come at a time when

16. See Robert Staples and Alfredo Mirandé, "Racial and Cultural Variations Among American Families: A Decennial Review of the Literature on Minority Families," *Journal of Marriage and the Family* 42 (Nov. 1980), pp. 157–73.
17. For an account of the contemporary family in Japan, see Ezra F. Vogel, *Japan's New Middle Class*, Berkeley: University of California Press, 1963.
18. This discussion follows the treatment in Harry H. L. Kitano, *Japanese Americans: The Evolution of a Subculture*, Englewood Cliffs, N.J.: Prentice-Hall, 1976.

California was in reaction against the wave of Chinese immigration that had followed the gold rush of 1849. The Chinese were widely hated because of their willingness to work for low wages, because of religious differences, and because they were slow to assimilate.

Some 28,000 Japanese came to the United States between 1890 and 1900, most finding work in the lower-paid areas of railroading, mining, canning, and meat packing. Another 59,000 came between 1900 and 1910, most of whom had agricultural backgrounds and, by 1910, about 30,000 Japanese Americans were working on farms. Thriftiness, hard work, and expertise in the intensive cultivation of crops permitted many of them to either lease land or acquire it outright. The Japanese became agricultural competitors to white farmers, and the white-dominated government retaliated through legislation.

The California Alien Land Act of 1913 prohibited aliens from either leasing land for more than three years or bequeathing it. The law was never too effective because by then many Japanese had children or American friends in whose names they could place their land. The demands of World War I lessened the pressure, and the hold of Japanese people on agriculture expanded. After the war, a second wave of reaction set in, and a revised alien land law in 1920 prohibited first-generation Japanese from acting as guardians for the land of native-born minors. The amended law was more effective, and Japanese farms in California declined from over 5000 in 1920 to under 4000 by 1930. The denials to Japanese of the right to citizenship and of the right to own land were serious blows, only slightly less devastating than what was to come with World War II.

After the very earliest period, Japanese immigrants faced less serious discrimination in the cities than in agriculture. They established small businesses—restaurants, laundries, barbershops, dry goods stores, and so on—that catered to both Japanese and non-Japanese. The almost assured Japanese clientele aided these establishments; organized pools of money and credit (*tanomoshi*) provided banking services. Many of these efforts were organized by members of the same *ken*, or Japanese state, and some of the *ken* specialized in certain businesses such as insurance and barbering. Incipient white boycotts of Japanese businesses were thwarted through threat of counterboycotts by the well-organized Japanese. Of increasing importance up to, and after, World War II was contract gardening, in which skilled Japanese workers assumed the management of urban estates, lawns, and gardens.

That Japanese were ineligible to become citizens has already been mentioned. The Alien Land Acts discriminated against the Japanese further, and other efforts were made to discourage Japanese businesses and to isolate Japanese residents. In 1921 and 1924, restrictive immigration acts virtually cut off Japanese migration to the United States. The full effects of these policies may never be known, but they may have contributed directly to the Japanese attack on Pearl Harbor in 1941. The restrictive immigration laws of the 1920s involved unilateral repudiation of the "Gentleman's Agreement" between the governments of Japan and the United States in 1908 whereby both nations agreed to restrict migration and both agreed that neither would enact discriminatory legislation against the other.[19]

By 1940, there were almost 127,000 Japanese residing in the U.S. mainland, with 157,000 more in Hawaii. When war broke out, first the West Coast and then the nation were engulfed in hysteria fed by long-standing racial prejudice. Mass arrests of Japanese Americans and curfews were followed, early in 1942, by removal of more than 110,000 people from the entire West Coast. More than two thirds of these people were second and third generation and were U.S. citizens.

The effects of relocation were drastic. Families had their property confiscated or stolen. Many were ruined financially. The humiliation suffered and the damage done to individual and group self-concepts can scarcely be imagined today. Family structure was profoundly affected. The authority of the first-generation immigrants was undermined. Husbands could no longer be effective wage earners. Dormitory living and having meals in mess halls almost removed any family privacy. There was provision for individual security clearances and for leaving the relocation camps to resettle away from the Western Defense Area.

Some 35,000 younger, predominantly second-generation people managed eventually to resettle in the Midwest and the East. These young people were freed from family authority as never before. Even in the camps, the absence of dominant non-Japanese residents both permitted and forced Japanese into positions of leadership in all areas of life.

This shameful period came to an end in 1946 when the camps closed down. Many Japanese Americans returned to the West Coast where, after initial hostility toward them, the government made token attempts at compensation for confiscated property. The otherwise reactionary McCarran-Walter Immigration Act of 1962 at least permitted first-generation Japanese to undergo naturalization and provided them a token immigration quota. Second- and third-generation Japanese Americans on the West Coast and in the Midwest and the East resumed the climb toward occupational success and, today, have as large a proportion engaged in professional occupations as does the native white population. Income and educational levels have risen correspondingly. A growing influence in recent decades has been the *Kai-sha* Japanese, the

19. *Ibid.*, pp. 10–29.

American representatives of large Japanese corporations. Most of these corporations are on the East Coast and have both Oriental and Caucasian employees.[20]

Family Patterns

The traditional Japanese family was patriarchal and extended, with the clan providing linkage between the family and the larger society. Age was venerated, and there were special terms of address for elders. Men dominated women, and because males continued the family line, the father-son relationship was especially important. Filial duty was emphasized and go-betweens aided parents in selecting proper spouses for their offspring. Occasionally, a man married a woman from a family with daughters only, assumed her family's name and continued the family line.

The Issei Family. The term *Issei* refers to first-generation immigrants, most of whom came to the United States between 1890 and 1920. Death is taking its toll rapidly of this generation, and those who remain are elderly, mostly in retirement. Many live with, or near, their children where they are accorded prestige and honor, both as symbols of the traditional order and because of the sacrifices they have made for their children and grandchildren. For their part, they rest comfortably in the security of their families, but reflect somewhat sadly on the apparent breakdown of time-honored ways.[21]

The original migrants were overwhelmingly young men, many of whom expected, one day, to return to their homeland. Facing hostility in the new environment, being isolated by cultural differences, and being accustomed to arranged marriages, most selected mates who were sent to them from Japan. The mates were from the same *ken*, and most of the Japanese in California lived in rooming houses inhabited by a group of families from the same *ken*. Thus, small communities were created, ethnic enclaves, in which traditional ways were perpetuated and assimilation hindered. These immigrant families followed the traditional patriarchal model, the chief difference being that there was no grandparental generation present to provide direct ties with the ancestors and to serve as models for indoctrinating the young in the traditional ways.

When children came, they acquired the American citizenship that was denied their parents. Too, because of alien land laws, many of the

20. *Ibid.*, pp. 47–51.
21. For an analysis of the ways in which massive industrial growth in contemporary Japan is affecting the patriarchal system, see Marvin B. Sussman and J. C. Rameis, "Willingness to Assist One's Elderly Parents: Responses From United States and Japanese Families," *Human Organization* 41 (Fall 1982), pp. 256–59.

second generation (*Nisei*) became land owners early. Although the parents remained tied to the traditional ways, their children adopted the values and norms of mainstream American society. The gap between the two generations also widened because of limited communication among family members, particularly from parents to children. Parents typically gave orders that the children were expected to obey unhesitatingly. There was little discussion of problems and no consideration of the well-being of individuals apart from the family group.

Under these circumstances, youthful rebellion against parental controls and against the "funny ways" of the Japanese community would have seemed to be a likely possibility. It did not happen however. Instead indoctrination of youth with the idea that discredit on one Japanese discredited them all was extraordinarily effective. *Nisei* children generally were models of obedience and conformity, a source of pride to their parents, and the envy of most American parents who knew them.

If sacrifice was required of children, they had role models for it in their parents. Most adults viewed their marriages not as sources of happiness but as networks of obligation and duty, beginning with "contracts" between brides and grooms who did not even know one another and continuing as combined obligations to ancestors, children, and the Japanese community. Although many *Nisei* were aware of lack of harmony between their parents, separation and divorce were rare. There was also much unacknowledged sacrifice by parents for the welfare and education of the children. Few parents were prosperous when their children were young, and good clothes and shoes for them often meant old and worn clothes for the parents. Many parents deprived themselves severely so that their children might receive university educations.

What *Issei* remain today still are almost completely unassimilated. In fact, they appear in many ways to be more traditionally Japanese than present-day adults living in Japan. Japan has been changing very rapidly, and life in her larger cities is thoroughly modern. *Issei* who return to visit, expecting that they will be returning to the world they left years ago, often hurry back to the United States to their traditional families here.

The Nisei Family. The Nisei, or second-generation Japanese Americans, were born for the most part between 1910 and 1940. Unlike their parents, they were citizens and could own property. Much of the property accumulated by the *Issei* in the names of their children was lost in internment, but the *Nisei* recovery from that has been remarkable. Today, Japanese Americans are better educated and have higher incomes than any other minority group in the United States. Moreover, the U.S. government is of late beginning to make reparations to those families who lost property during internment.

The *Nisei* occupy an intermediate position on an assimilation continuum. Habituated to American values and customs, they still confine most of their contacts to other Japanese Americans. Many Japanese consider them to be American, but most Americans still regard them as Japanese. There has been little intermarriage with white Americans, and although some successful *Nisei* have moved into suburban areas, there is still marked residential segregation, with most *Nisei* living on the fringes of slum areas and in racially mixed neighborhoods.

As a group, the *Nisei* now are middle aged and generally affluent. There appears to be a correlation between Americanization and financial prosperity; Americanization may contribute to success and vice versa. The marriages of the *Nisei*, like those of most other Americans, are judged increasingly in terms of personal happiness, and although the evidence is far from satisfactory, it appears that some rise in divorce is occurring. As when they were children, the *Nisei* appear to be socially and emotionally well adjusted, but the presence now of a few Japanese psychiatrists in Los Angeles attests to the price to be paid for assimilation to American patterns.

The Sansei Family. It is somewhat premature to write of the third-generation Japanese American family because its character is not yet fully evident. Most *Sansei* have been born since World War II and few have yet completed childbearing. The most we can do is to make some inferences from their early life experiences.[22]

To the slight dismay of their parents, the *Sansei* appear virtually to have completed assimilation. If they still are better behaved than most other American children when they are with their parents, they shed their inhibitions at school and in peer-group situations. Teachers complain that they have become distressingly like other children. There is still some structural isolation, with the *Sansei* continuing to belong to Japanese groups and organizations. In college, for example, patterns vary from membership in strictly ethnic fraternities and sororities to membership in fully integrated ones. Many *Sansei* reject and resent any reference to themselves as other than American.

Ties to the family still are strong, and most *Sansei* appear to be remaining on the West Coast and engaging in predominantly Japanese-run businesses. There has been some Japanese penetration of the higher man-

22. For comparison of *Nisei* and *Sansei* patterns in Hawaii, see Colleen Leahy Johnson, "Interdependence, Reciprocity and Indebtedness: An Analysis of Japanese American Kinship Relations," *Journal of Marriage and the Family* 39 (May 1977), pp. 351–63.

agement echelons of corporations however, particularly among those who have migrated to the Midwest and the East. Intermarriage is on the increase, particularly for Japanese women. Residential segregation seems to be breaking down rapidly on the West Coast as well as elsewhere.

A logical conclusion to this account would be that assimilation will continue until the Japanese Americans will soon no longer exist as an identifiable minority. Perhaps so. Japanese Americans have not displayed much of the ethnic militance that has characterized other groups in recent years. In-marriage, however, is still the rule rather than the exception, and national and group pride has been strong. It remains to be seen whether a plateau in assimilation has been reached.

CUBAN AMERICAN FAMILIES

The Cubans are among the most recent of the many migrant groups in the United States, having come generally since the revolution of 1959. Thus, the majority of Cuban families have been here for less than a single generation, very little time for there to have been marked changes in family patterns. We begin with the family in Cuba, turn to the immigration to the United States, and finally to Cuban families in this country.

The Family in Cuba

The dominant tradition in premodern Cuba was that of feudal Spain, a consequence of the settlement of Cuba by sixteenth-century *conquistadores*. Spanish law and institutions, including the Roman Catholic Church, were firmly established, and the native Indian population was virtually exterminated before the year 1600. The importation of slaves from Africa was begun in 1517, and more than 1 million black people were brought to the island before slavery ended in 1886. As a result of extensive miscegenation, a large mulatto population developed, and accurate racial classification of much of the population became almost impossible. By the early twentieth century, perhaps one half of the population was white, approximately one fourth was black, and one fourth was mixed.[23]

The family system of the Spanish elite was firmly patriarchal, the father dominating his wife and children. Women could not appear in court without their husbands' permission, could not make major financial transactions, and were required to follow the husband to whatever residence he chose. Divorce was forbidden by the church, but civil au-

---

23. *Problems of the New Cuba: Report of the Commission on Cuban Affairs*, New York: Foreign Policy Association, 1935, pp. 28–29.

thorities permitted the divorce of wives for adultery. Men could be divorced for adultery only if it was flagrant, resulting in public scandal or neglect of the wife.[24]

Social changes militated against the perpetuation of this elite colonial family type far into the present century. Feudal estates were never firmly established in Cuba, and legal changes were steadily in the direction of increasing equality for women and children. Too, the black population under slavery suffered ravages of family life comparable to those encountered by black people in the United States. Although most black Cuban families by the 1930s were legally sanctioned families, a substantial minority lived in consensual unions, the problems of which were aggravated by poverty. Finally, there were no legal barriers to racial intermarriage, and this blurred differences between the racial groups.

By the middle of the twentieth century, the principal variables influencing Cuban family patterns had become those of social class and rural-urban residence. These two variables operated in combination because most of the rural population also was lower class. For our purposes, three main family patterns may be described: the upper-class family, the urban lower-class family, and the rural farm family.

The Upper-Class Family. This is the immediate descendant of the elite colonial family. The father is a business or professional man or a wealthy farmer. The household includes servants, wife, and children, and the father is dominant over them all. The wife leads a life of relative ease secluded from most public contacts, and she is submissive. Young children are cared for by nursemaids, and older children are chauffeured about. They attend private schools and have few responsibilities. There may also be grandparents present, and wealthy families are expected to assist siblings who may have fallen on hard times as well.

In a less prosperous variant of the upper-class family, financial restrictions limit the number of servants to one, there may be no automobile, and there is great emphasis on keeping up appearances. Children are likely to come more directly under the care of the mother and to assume regular duties around the home.

The Urban Lower-Class Family. Many families of manual workers live in *solares*, which are alleys in wealthy sections of town that are lined with one-room shacks. Father and mother work in a desperate and frequently unsuccessful effort to make ends meet. The wives usually are servants for upper-class families, requiring them to be away for long

24. Lowry Nelson, *Rural Cuba*, Minneapolis: University of Minnesota Press, 1950, pp. 174–79.

hours and to leave their children without adequate supervision. Although there are compulsory school attendance laws, many children drop out after a few years because of boredom with school and the need to earn money. They shine shoes, run errands, and take odd jobs. There are never enough jobs and their earnings are meager. The obvious differences in wealth move many of them to panhandle upper-class persons and foreigners and to engage in petty thievery.

Women are likely to marry young, and consensual unions are common. Men may be three or four years older than their wives. Birthrates are relatively high, Cuban families being one fourth larger than others in the United States. Because the children of consensual unions technically are illegitimate, official counts of illegitimacy are very high.

Relationships between husbands and wives are complicated by *machismo*, a concept of masculinity that ties a man's feelings of self-worth to his ability to father children, to continue to father them, and to his success in extramarital liaisons. Lower-class wives are not so subordinate to their husbands as upper-class wives are, but the tradition of patriarchy still is strong, and wives are caught in a continuing, self-defeating cycle of childbearing. The crowded and unstable conditions of living in the *solares* encourage extramarital liaisons as too many children make life increasingly difficult, as communication between spouses breaks down, and as men and women need outside support for their sagging egos.

Although the family ideals are those of traditional Catholicism, the everyday influence of the church is not strong. The relatively limited and unsuccessful use of birth control, for example, appears to be more a function of poverty, ignorance, and lack of motivation than of religious taboo.[25] The religious prohibition may play a direct role in keeping the divorce rate down, although here too, the low rate may be at least as much a function of consensual marriage and the proclivity to terminate marriages as informally as they were established originally.

The Rural Farm Family. Farm families vary in financial status, ranging from wealthy sugar, coffee, and tobacco planters and cattlemen to impoverished peasants. In general, their family patterns correspond to those of the urban social classes they parallel. One obvious difference in family structure is the greater preponderance of actual or modified stem families in rural areas. Where finances permit, the eldest son is likely to

25. For an analysis linking high Latin American birthrates to female unemployment and illiteracy, see Nora S. Kinzer, "Priests, Machos and Babies: Or Latin American Women and the Manichaean Heresy," *Journal of Marriage and the Family* 35 (May 1973), pp. 300–312.

bring his bride to the parental home where the son is groomed to assume the father's position and possessions at his death or retirement. Even where limited resources do not permit the full development of a stem family, there is more continuity from generation to generation than among comparable urban families. Male dominance exists in this setting also. This is illustrated by the fairly common practice of women serving meals to the men but not sitting down to eat with them. Fathers also dominate their children rather completely, and even grown sons defer to their fathers at least until they are married.

Immigration to the United States

The large-scale Cuban migration to the United States began after Fidel Castro came to power in 1959. That revolution, which was supported initially by significant proportions of virtually all elements of the Cuban population, eventually proved to be more of a revolution than many people expected. As Premier Castro openly espoused economic socialism and as power was transferred more and more to lower-class and predominantly nonwhite segments of the population, large numbers of prosperous, light complexioned Cubans began to flee the country with Miami, Florida, as their principal destination.

The migrants came in three main waves. The first lasted from January 1959 to October 1962, during which commercial airline flights were available. Then from October 1962 through December 1965 when there was no regular air transportation, people came any way they could—by small boat, for example, and through third countries such as Mexico. The third stage began in 1965 when the Cuban government authorized twice-daily airline flights. This continued until April 1973.

We do not know exactly how many migrants from Cuba there were. Some came, originally, as tourists, others as residents. Some came through third countries, obscuring their points of origin. In 1980, it was estimated that there were 430,000 Cubans in metropolitan Miami and approximately 800,000 in the United States.[26] Today, only Havana has more Cubans than does Miami.[27]

As already indicated, upper economic groups are overrepresented among the migrants. Persons of professional and semiprofessional backgrounds are overrepresented by a factor of 5, whereas people from agriculture and fishing are underrepresented by a factor of 16. Educationally, 4 percent of the Cuban population in 1953 had completed the 12th

26. Cary Davis, Carl Haub, and JoAnn Willette, "U.S. Hispanics: Changing the Face of America," *Population Bulletin* 38 (June 1983), p. 12.
27. *U.S. News & World Report*, Sept. 27, 1982, p. 12.

grade; in 1963, 36 percent of the refugees had at least that much education. Adults and older age groups are overrepresented too. Nonwhites
are underrepresented. The distribution of the sexes is approximately
equal.

The assimilation of the migrants has been complicated by the expectation of many that they would, one day, return to their homeland and
by their legal statuses. There are three legal groups. First, "immigrants"
are those who were admitted as permanent residents, having acquired
that status before leaving Cuba or acquired it in other countries. Second,
are the "nonimmigrants." This group includes all others (students, tourists, etc.) who were granted indefinite voluntary departure dates on the
expiration of their entry permits. Finally, there are the "parolees." The
parolees include all refugees who sought asylum in the United States
without having secured entry visas. They are ineligible for permanent
alien registration until they have been in the United States for two
years, and they are barred from categories of employment that require
at least resident alien status.

In a time period ranging from a few months to 15 to 20 years, there
are outward signs of substantial assimilation. Although the largest number of Cubans still reside in Florida, there are substantial numbers in
approximately 20 other states. Most of the Cubans reside in metropolitan
areas, with large concentrations in New York, New Jersey, California,
and Illinois. Between 1951 and 1970, almost 69,000 persons of Cuban
origin became naturalized citizens.

A study of the assimilation of 48 Cuban families in Milwaukee in 1969
produced several indicators of fairly rapid integration and assimilation.
For example, 58 percent of the husbands declared themselves to be quite
satisfied with their present lives in the United States; an additional 31
percent were somewhat satisfied. Too, 35 percent stated that they would
not return to Cuba even if the Castro government should fall; 19 percent
more were undecided. Of these families, 42 percent preferred that their
children also assume American identities and follow American customs,
whereas only 35 percent preferred their children to retain a Cuban
identity and to preserve Cuban customs.[28]

Finally, the Cuban migrants have already reached income levels close
to U.S. averages. In 1979, their median family income was $17,538 com-
pared to $20,502 for white families. Family incomes are significantly
affected by whether wives work outside the home, another indirect
measure of assimilation. As might be expected, fewer of the wives of
families who have remained in the Miami area than those who live elsewhere work. By March 1972, 54 percent of all women of Cuban origin

28. Alejandro Portes, "Dilemmas of a Golden Exile: Integration of Cuban Families in
Milwaukee," *American Sociological Review* 34 (Aug. 1969), pp. 505–18.

were in the work force, and high rates of participation were maintained even among women with children.[29]

Cuban Families in Miami

Because the vast majority of Cuban families have been in the United States for less than one generation, there has not been much time for major changes in family structure. Nor has there yet been much research on this matter. One study, however, of 120 Cuban wives in Miami and of 30 of their husbands has shown that changes are occurring.[30]

The families were young, the mean age of the husbands being 35 years and that of the wives being 32 years. The modal number of children was two, with 10 percent having only one child and another 10 percent having five children; 60 percent of the children were preadolescent. The husbands were relatively well educated, over 45 percent having either university or professional degrees. Fewer wives had received higher educations, but over three fourths had completed secondary school. Over two thirds of the husbands and almost half of the wives had at least a conversational knowledge of English. Reflecting their recent arrival in this country and the difficulties associated therewith, the husbands' occupational and income levels were below those appropriate to their educational backgrounds. Almost three fourths were skilled blue-collar, clerical, or sales workers, earning $550 per month or less. Also, 55 percent of the wives worked outside the home.[31]

The study measured assimilation in terms of the degree of departure from ideals of male dominance and the amount of independence granted to children. Both variables showed substantial assimilation, the amount of assimilation depending on other social factors.

Of the factors studied, the amount of contact with native Americans seemed most important; those who had frequent and regular contact were most assimilated; those who remained within the Cuban commu-

29. Rafael J. Prohías and Lourdes Casal, *The Cuban Minority in the U.S.: Preliminary Report on Need Identification and Program Evaluation, Final Report for Fiscal Year 1973*, Boca Raton: Florida Atlantic University, 1973, p. 25.

30. Marie L. Richmond, *Immigrant Adaptation and Family Structure Among Cubans in Miami, Florida* (Ph.D. dissertation): Florida State University, 1973; see also Marie L. Richmond, "Beyond Resource Theory: Another Look at Factors Enabling Women to Affect Family Interaction," *Journal of Marriage and the Family* 38 (May 1976), pp. 257–66.

31. Richmond, "Immigrant Adaptation," pp. 54–55, 166–69. In 1970, the median income of Cuban families in the United States was $8091. See Susan Jacoby, "An Immigrant Success Story," *New York Times*, Sept. 29, 1974; and Kenneth L. Wilson and W. William Martin, "Ethnic Enclaves: A Comparison of the Cuban and Black Economies in Miami," *American Journal of Sociology* 88 (July 1982), pp. 135–60.

nity were least assimilated. Other factors associated with assimilation were the length of residence in the United States, knowledge of English, higher education, the possession of job skills, and the wife's working. As had been found in studies of earlier immigrant groups, wives were somewhat less assimilated than husbands, being more likely to accept traditional ideas of male dominance.

One finding that surprised the researcher, which is consistent with the experience of other ethnic groups, is that the younger men held more tenaciously to the ideology of male dominance than did the older men. Although this could be the result of the younger men being more recent migrants, it could also be the effect of a consciousness of ethnic pride and a determination not to lose their ethnic identity.

SUMMARY

The Italian Americans, Mexican Americans, Japanese Americans, and Cuban Americans are some of the prominent ethnic groups who have brought distinctive family patterns to this country. Each group has accommodated itself to the dominant middle-class family life style in its own way. The general trend is toward assimilation and the minimization of cultural differences. In recent years, however, there has been a resurgence of ethnic pride, and many younger adults are seeking to preserve and strengthen their cultural heritages.

Italian Americans have had assimilation complicated by language, religious differences, and lack of occupational skills. Mainly farm people from southern Italian villages, they settled in northern cities in ethnic enclaves widely known as "Little Italys." Hostility from older Americans reinforced their cultural isolation and hindered assimilation.

The patriarchal family system came under strain as the migrants' children emulated their American peers and adopted the standards of their middle-class teachers. Assimilation proceeded, generally, by generations, becoming virtually complete among many of the third generation. Some third-generation Italian Americans, however, have sought to reconfirm their ethnic identities.

Spanish settlers were living in much of the southwestern United States before the Anglos. Many were cattle ranchers. Some were wealthy and held vast tracts of land. With the exception of small groups in New Mexico and California, virtually all were dominated by invading Anglos and were reduced to manual laborers in the fields, mines, and industries.

Immigration from Mexico was erratic from 1910 through the 1950s, reflecting U.S. policies and economic conditions. The fiction was maintained that many people were admitted as temporary workers; still more came illegally. During periods of slack demand for labor, the government shamelessly rounded up Spanish-speaking people and shipped them back to Mexico. Today, there are over 19 million people with Spanish surnames in the United States, the largest minority in the southwest.

The assimilation of Mexican Americans has proceeded unevenly, and there is considerable variation in family patterns. Lower-class rural families are nominally extended and traditional. *Machismo* thwarts effective husband-wife communication. Women are subservient, organizing their lives around home and family. *Compadrazgo* (god-parenthood) cements ties between families. Middle-class rural families live better than lower-class families but still remain generally isolated from Anglo society. A small rural upper class intermingles freely with Anglos, often having businesses and ties on both sides of the border.

Assimilation is most complete in the cities, particularly in California. Extended families are uncommon, welfare agencies have assumed many former family functions, and many marriages are rather egalitarian. Birthrates are dropping, divorce rates are increasing. The family style approximates that of other urban Americans. The Chicano movement is concentrated in the cities, but it also includes attempts to improve the economic situation for farm laborers. It opposes assimilation, apparently without being prepared to resurrect the traditional family system.

Most Japanese migrants to the United States were middle-class people with some formal education and experience with land ownership. Substantial migration began around 1890, the first migrants being young unattached men. By about 1910, they were perceived as a major threat to other American farmers, and discriminatory legislation covering the ownership and leasing of land was initiated. The resourceful Japanese coped with the problem by putting land in the names of their American-born children. Small Japanese businesses in the cities prospered; the *ken* provided financing and a guaranteed clientele.

Harshly restrictive immigration policies initiated during the 1920s were one of the factors leading to World War II, and war led to further discrimination against Japanese Americans and eventually to their forced relocation. The camp life during the war helped to break down the authority of the first generation (*Issei*). Some of the younger, second-generation people (*Nisei*) secured individual security clearances and migrated to the Midwest and to the East. After the war, most Japanese Americans returned to the West Coast.

The last of the *Issei* remain traditional in their beliefs about proper family life, often more so than people of the same age still in Japan. They raised their children to be obedient and respectful and regard changes in family life as symptoms of breakdown. Most of the *Nisei* generation today is adult, middle aged, and reasonably prosperous. Although most have accepted American values and are not distinguishable behaviorally from other Americans, they remain residentially segregated and confine most of their contacts to other Japanese Americans. Their children, the *Sansei* (third generation), have moved further toward complete assimilation. Generally, however, they are still too young for the character of their family patterns to have become fully evident.

The major Cuban migration to the United States began in 1959. Colonial Cuba was dominated by the Spanish who intermingled with more than 1 million black slaves, creating a considerably mixed population. The family system of the Spanish elite was a traditional patriarchy, subordinating women and children and forbidding divorce. By the present century, however, families varied chiefly by rural-urban residence and social class. Upper-class families remained rather traditional, whereas lower-class families struggled for survival. *Machismo* complicated relationships at all levels. Modified stem families were common in rural areas.

There now are more than 600,000 persons of Cuban parentage in the United States, most having been here for less than a decade. Already, however, the old pattern of male dominance is lessening, and children are being granted more independence. Some younger people are beginning to oppose these trends and to value their ethnic identity.

SUGGESTED READINGS

Gallo, Patrick J., *Old Bread, New Wine: A Portrait of the Italian Americans*, Chicago: Nelson-Hall Publications, 1981. Examines various aspects of the lives of Italian Americans.

Kitano, Harry H. L., *Japanese Americans: The Evolution of a Subculture*, Englewood Cliffs, N.J.: Prentice-Hall, 1976. This well-informed account of the Japanese experience in the United States includes analysis of family patterns in Japan and in the United States both in the early period and at present.

Levine, Gena M., and Rhodes, Robert C., *The Japanese-American Community: A Three Generation Study*, New York: Praeger, 1981. Compares the life styles and life experiences of the Japanese in the United States.

Mindel, Charles H., and Habenstein, Robert W., eds., *Ethnic Families in America: Patterns and Variations* (2nd ed.), New York: Elsevier, 1981. Contains descriptions of 15 different ethnic family systems in the United States.

Murguia, Edward, *Assimilation, Colonialism and the Mexican American People*, Austin: University of Texas Press, 1975. Examines the past, present, and future of Mexican Americans in terms of assimilation and cultural pluralism.

Richmond, Marie L., *Immigrant Adaptation and Family Structure Among Cubans in Miami, Florida"* (Ph.D. dissertation): Florida State University, 1973. Study showing less male domination and more child independence among Cuban immigrant families than in traditional Latin American families. A principal source used in the writing of this chapter.

FILMS

Mama (Soho Cinema, Ltd., 225 Lafayette Street, New York, N.Y. 10012), 30 minutes, color. A Sicilian woman's journey to New York that lasts 69 years. Shows her experience as one of the first Italian Americans, her marriage and family.

A Mexican-American Family (Atlantis Productions, Inc., 850 Thousand Oaks Boulevard, Thousand Oaks, Calif. 91360), 16 minutes. Provides insight into the life of a Mexican American family: their traditions, their warmth and closeness, and their difficulties.

North from Mexico (Greenwood Press, 51 Riverside Avenue, Westport, Conn. 06880), 20 minutes, color. Follows the route of Coronado along the Rio Grande into New Mexico. Brings Anglo-Hispanic relations into historical perspective and examines the basis for the current Chicano movement.

QUESTIONS AND PROJECTS

1. What factors hindered the assimilation of Italian immigrants to the United States? What kinds of family problems were thus created?
2. Describe the adjustment patterns of Italian Americans that have been labeled rebel, ingroup, and apathetic.
3. Explain and qualify the statement that, "Mexican Americans are a conquered rather than an immigrant group." Trace the subjugation of the Spanish minority in each of the southwestern states.
4. Trace the policies of the U.S. government in relation to the immigration of Mexicans. How have these policies influenced assimilation?
5. Describe the varied family patterns of Mexican Americans today, using the concepts of *machismo* and *compadrazgo*.
6. Contrast the Mexican and Japanese migrations to the United States. How were they similar? How were they different?
7. What was the effect of relocation during World War II on Japanese American family patterns?
8. Describe the family patterns of the *Issei*, the *Nisei*, and the *Sansei*. What changes would you predict during the next generation? Why?
9. Detail the influences of the Spanish and of the black population on the family system in Cuba. What changes appear to be occurring in Cuban American family patterns?
10. Search among your classmates for people who are not more than third-generation Americans. Get as many different backgrounds as possible and arrange a panel discussion that focuses on the changes in their families from their grandparental generation to their own.
11. It has been said that the United States is a melting pot. Is this true or is the United States really a plurality of ethnic identities living more or less compatibly? What evidence can you gather to debate this controversy?

Michael Kagan, Monkmeyer

II
The Influence of Religion

In a country like the United States no group of people is deliberately forced to change its religion, customs, or value orientations. But it is nonetheless a fact that where progress is a major goal of society, the differences among people tend to disappear. Different languages, races, customs, and ways of thinking usually merge into one dominant culture. The Amish, as a distinct cultural group that has been in the United States for over two centuries, still stand out sharply as a people who have maintained strong group identity.[1]

Though without real power, Mormonism made a desert productive and filled it with tens of thousands of settlers, all by using the supernatural as the chief organizing power for every major activity and rituals as the chief instruments for securing material success. Starting off as a religious utopia, Mormonism grew into a genuine theocracy, governed not from police, armies, surpluses, and plutocratic, aristocratic, or democratic election—none of which existed at the time in Utah—but mainly from the fact that everybody believed in the same version of the supernatural.[2]

The United States is a nation composed of a plurality of religions, all living more or less harmoniously with each other. Long considered a haven of religious freedom, the United States houses Jews, Catholics, Protestants, Hare Krishnas, Buddhists, born-again Christians, snake worshippers, and countless other faiths. For some groups, religion is but a part of their lives; for others, it is the major influence. In this chapter, we examine the ways in which theological beliefs interweave with the family patterns of two religious groups: the Old Order Amish and the Mormons.

1. John A. Hostetler, *Amish Society* (rev. ed.), Baltimore: Johns Hopkins University Press, 1970, pp. 158–59.
2. Mark P. Leone, *Roots of Modern Mormonism*, Cambridge, Mass.: Harvard University Press, 1979, pp. 3–4.

OLD ORDER AMISH FAMILIES

Old Order Amish families residing in the United States today are descendents of the Mennonite-Anabaptists of sixteenth-century Switzerland. A schism developed among the Mennonites in the late sixteenth century when Jacob Amman, a devoutly religious bishop, discovered that many of the Mennonite districts were not enforcing the *Meidung*. The *Meidung* was a punishment for those who strayed from strict religious doctrine; it called for the errant member to be shunned or virtually avoided by all others, including family members. Controversy over enforcement of the *Meidung* grew to such a pitch that the membership split into two groups. Those who followed Amman's support of shunning became the Amish; those who did not, stayed within the Mennonite fold.[3] Among the Old Order Amish living in the United States today, the *Meidung* remains a powerful motivation for religious adherence. The Old Order Amish are among the most conservative of Amish groups.

Seeking freedom from religious persecution in Europe, the Amish immigrated to the United States in two waves. Those among the first wave settled in Pennsylvania from about 1730 to 1790. The second wave of immigration occurred from 1815 to 1860, bringing the Amish to New York, Ohio, Indiana, and Illinois. Although the estimated 80,000 Amish in the United States can today be found in 20 states, the great majority live in only three—Pennsylvania, Ohio, and Indiana.[4] Virtually no Amish reside in Europe today. The Old Order Amish of Lancaster County, Pennsylvania, compose the most widely studied Amish community, and it is this group to which we shall refer in this chapter.

The Old Order Amish are distinguished by social patterns, clothing, and a religious devoutness that virtually have remained unchanged since the seventeenth century. The use of automobiles, electricity, telephones, indoor plumbing, modern technology, and other marks of the "English" (non-Amish) world are forbidden. Although surrounded on all sides by an encroaching technologically oriented world, the Old Order Amish cling fervently to the "simple life." By avoiding things of a worldly nature, the Amish show their devotion to God.

3. William M. Kephart, *Extraordinary Groups: The Sociology of Unconventional Lifestyles* (2nd ed.), New York: St. Martin's Press, 1982, p. 49. See also Arnold Snyder, "The Monastic Origins of Swiss Anabaptist Sectarianism," *Mennonite Quarterly Review* 57 (Jan. 1983), pp. 5–26.
4. Julia A. Ericksen, Eugene P. Ericksen, John A. Hostetler, and Gertrude E. Huntington, "Fertility Patterns and Trends Among the Old Order Amish," *Population Studies* 33 (July 1979), pp. 255–77.

The Family's Value System

All aspects of Amish culture revolve around the home and family life. Unlike modern American families, described by William F. Ogburn in Chapter 7 as having lost many of their traditional functions to external structures, Amish families compose the primary social structure within the community and are the center of economic, religious, and educational functioning. Behavior in the community is governed by the *Ordnung*, which is a set of rules dictated by the church and handed down through time. The Amish employ intensive instruction to socialize young members into the Amish culture and the rules of the *Ordnung*. Curiously, they rely almost entirely on oral instruction and oral history to accomplish this, for the rules of the *Ordnung* are not written down. Because communities are small, members are able informally to keep a watchful eye on the behavior of others and chastise those who wander too far from doctrine. In this way, innovation is kept to a minimum.

All Amish communities are rural and most families are involved in an intensive farming economy.[5] A burgeoning population and the unavailability of new land, however, has meant that increasing numbers of Amish adults are becoming involved in occupations other than farming. Nonetheless, these occupations such as carpentry, blacksmithing, carriage making, and beekeeping are geared toward the Amish way of life.

Sex roles in the Amish family are very firmly defined and follow from biblical scripture. Men are the heads of their families and women are subject to their husbands' authority. To Amish women, however, God comes first; husbands, second. If a husband transgresses in the eyes of the church, the wife will join the community in shunning him until he repents. This includes abstaining from sexual relationships until the punishment is lifted.[6] Women are extensions of their husbands, not possessions.

Even though family authority is vested in the man, husbands and wives are equal partners in the marriage. Women play an extremely important economic role in Amish families. In these intensive farming communities, wives help butcher animals and preserve meat; can fruits and vegetables, which they themselves produce; and may also help with the farming. Also because of the strict avoidance of things modern, the women make most of the family's clothing, quilts, and soap along with

5. Eugene P. Ericksen, Julia A. Ericksen, and John A. Hostetler, "The Cultivation of the Soil as a Moral Directive: Population Growth, Family Ties, and the Maintenance of Community Among the Old Order Amish," *Rural Sociology* 45 (Spring 1980), pp. 49–68.
6. Gertrude E. Huntington, "The Amish Family," in Charles H. Mindel and Robert W. Habenstein, eds., *Ethnic Families in America: Patterns and Variations* (2nd ed.), New York: Elsevier, 1981, p. 306.

performing their everyday household duties. They also bear the large
numbers of children characteristic in Amish homes, without whom the
large farms could not be maintained. Because of their essential economic
roles in the Amish community, women's status is higher than might be
expected in such a conservatively religious group.[7] Huntington states
that farms are owned in the names of both husbands and wives and that
all important decisions are made jointly.[8] Women's position in the family parallels their position in the church—they have an equal voice but
not an equal vote. Desertion is extremely rare among the Amish, and no
divorces have yet been reported. The Amish marry for life.

The Amish place great value on hard work, plain living, and isolation
from the non-Amish contemporary world.[9] Because their lives are tied
so closely to the rural farming economy, they are able to put their values into practice on a daily basis. Because machinery and the tools of the
modern world are forbidden, the work is hard and time consuming. The
profits from cash crops such as tomatoes, tobacco, and potatoes are small
and put back into the land and the farm. Because Amish families are essentially self-sufficient units, providing for almost all of their own daily
needs, they are able to keep their dependence on the outside world to a
minimum. Amish farms are acknowledged to be among the best in the
world, and the fervor of their devotion to the soil nearly matches their
devotion to the Scriptures. Both endeavors are pursued with a sober,
unwavering will.

The Old Order Amish practice adult baptism and, surprisingly, there
are no churches to be found within the community. Rather, church services are held within the members' homes on a rotating basis. For this
reason, the homes are very large and quite sturdy. Birth control of any
kind is forbidden and the Old Order Amish have one of the highest
fertility rates in the developed world.[10] Not only does the average family have between 6 to 8 children living under the same roof, but usually
several generations of family members live in the home as well. A home-
stead will remain in the family for many generations, so it is little wonder they build and maintain their homes and farms with such diligence
and care.

7. Julia Ericksen and Gary Klein, "Women's Roles and Family Production Among the
Old Order Amish," *Rural Sociology* 46 (Summer 1981), pp. 282–96; and Richard A.
Wright, "A Comparative Analysis of Economic Roles Within the Family: Amish and
Contemporary American Women," *International Journal of Sociology of the Family* 7
(Jan. 1977), pp. 55–60.
8. Huntington, *op. cit.*, p. 306.
9. Ericksen, Ericksen, and Hostetler, *op. cit.*, p. 50.
10. Ericksen, Ericksen, Hostetler, and Huntington, *op. cit.*, p. 255; and Gerald E.
Markle and Sharon Pasco, "Family Limitation Among the Old Order Amish," *Population Studies* 31 (July 1977), pp. 267–80.

Courtship and Mate Selection

The dating and courtship activities that today's college students are familiar with and take almost for granted are virtually unknown to Amish youth. Remember that Amish communities have no movie theaters, health spas, football stadiums, bars, or beaches. Ownership of automobiles is forbidden by the *Ordnung,* so the recreational activities associated with them are noticeably lacking. Also because Amish youth attend school only in fulfillment of compulsory requirements, those over the age of 16 spend long hours working either with their fathers in the fields or with their mothers in the home. One may wonder how it is, with all these seemingly insurmountable obstacles, that Amish boys and girls ever manage to get together. The fact is, however, that practically all Amish teenagers date, court, and eventually marry.

The Sunday evening "singings" provide the best opportunity for young people to meet on dates.[11] Sitting on opposite sides of a long table, the unmarried boys and girls of the community sing hymns and engage in friendly conversation. When the singing ends at around 10 o'clock, they may gather to talk and joke in pairs for another hour or so. Along with the eagerly awaited singings, periodically there are husking bees, weddings, and picnics that provide occasions for fun and relaxation.

The young are rather limited in their choice of dating and marriage partners. The Amish are an *endogamous* group and do not allow their children to date or marry people who do not belong to the Amish faith. To do so would mean immediate excommunication. For young people seeking partners, this rule limits them to their own small district or other Amish districts within easy traveling distances. This might not seem too great an obstacle until we stop to realize that each district averages only about 200 members.[12] And because automobiles are forbidden, the boys can travel only as far as a horse and buggy can carry them in an evening.

Amish youth court with marriage in mind. Physical attraction is not, to any great degree, the motivating factor in choosing partners. All of the boys dress exactly alike, as do the girls; even their hairstyles are identical. Jewelry and ornaments of any kind are forbidden. Until they are married, men are not allowed to grow any facial hair, then only beards are permitted. Mustaches are never allowed. Amish boys and girls look like younger versions of their parents. The men wear low-crowned, broad-brimmed hats and coats without lapels or pockets. Trousers are always worn with suspenders and never have creases or cuffs. Belts and sweaters are forbidden and, no matter how cold the weather may be-

11. Hostetler, *op. cit.,* pp. 158–59.
12. Kephart, *op. cit.,* p. 64.

come, gloves are never worn. Women keep their heads covered at all times, usually with a black bonnet when outdoors. Dresses are of a dark solid color, long, and covered in front by an apron. Black stockings and low-heeled black shoes are worn. All women wear their hair in a characteristic coiled braid.

Amish youth look for qualities in partners that are compatible with the farming life such as industriousness and reliability. Dating begins at about age 16 for boys, when it is customary for their fathers to buy them a "courting buggy." Girls begin dating at around 14 years of age. Dating and courtship is a very secretive matter for Amish youth. Typically, if a boy and girl are interested in each other, the boy will drive his buggy over to her home after her parents are asleep. Both the boy and the girl will vehemently deny any interest in each other, if asked, because a positive response will open them to relentless taunting and jeering. There is some speculation that "bundling," the practice of lying fully dressed together in bed, occurs, but this is another aspect of courting that is seldom discussed.[13]

Amish youth marry at about the same ages as the non-Amish: women on the average marry at around 21 to 23 years of age; 22 to 24 years is usually the age range for men.[14] Weddings are joyous occasions for the Amish, frequently involving the whole community. Food is plentiful and often the guests must be fed in shifts to accommodate everyone. The majority of weddings take place in the winter when the year's harvest is completed. Huntington reports that over 90 percent of the weddings in Lancaster County, Pennsylvania, occur in November and December.[15]

Weddings, though large, are not elaborate. No engagement ring is given and wedding rings are not exchanged. Remember, wedding rings are jewelry and the Amish consider jewelry to be "worldly." Women come to the marriage with a dowry provided by their parents, usually consisting of quilts, bedding, furniture, and livestock. Honeymoons do not consist of two weeks in Hawaii or a European tour. Instead the newly married couple spend their honeymoon traveling around the district visiting family and friends. At the end of this time, they either move in with the husband's parents or into their own new farmstead, bought with substantial parental help. Parents and their married children almost always live in close proximity. This factor contributes to the strong feelings of community and closeness found among the Amish.

13. Hostetler, *op. cit.*, pp. 160–61.
14. Kephart, *op. cit.*, p. 72.
15. Huntington, *op. cit.*, p. 302.

Parent-Child Interaction

Amish families almost always include large numbers of children. The birth of a child is a joyful occasion not only because it is considered a gift from God but also because it means a new worker has joined the family. It is the duty and responsibility of parents to instruct their children in the ways of the Amish, and this includes instilling in them the value of hard work.

For their first two years of life, Amish children are indulged and smothered with affection from parents, brothers and sisters, grandparents, and other relatives. At about two years of age, they begin to be firmly yet fairly guided toward the moral dictates of the faith. Children are taught to obey absolutely the authority of their parents and to show respect for all adults. It is the parents' duty to set good examples for their children. By so doing, a dual socializing effect occurs. Not only do children learn to become good Amish people but their parents also strive to improve themselves in the process.

Children learn very early that being Amish means being different from the "English." They will never have the toys or the clothes that non-Amish children have. They will never ride in cars, see movies, or go to college. Yet rather than feeling deprived, they are proud to imitate the lives of their parents and feel a special security in being "different." It is in fact quite rare for an Amish child to even question this way of life.[16] Years of admonitions from parents about the dangers and evils lurking outside the community in the "English" world serve to ensure that grown children will choose to remain close to the family and the faith. It must work, for the Amish are remarkably successful in keeping their members within the fold.[17] Those who do leave usually join Amish communities that are more liberal in their interpretation of the Bible and *Ordnung* regulations.

Along with the transferral of moral and religious values, parents are also expected to give their children a reading knowledge of German. This is usually done on Sundays when along with the regular devotional, the family gathers around to read sections of the German Bible. Even children as young as four practice the language by repeating words as they are spoken by the father. A German dialect known as Pennsylvania Dutch is spoken among community members.

By the age of four or five, children begin contributing their labor to the family. They may help to feed the livestock or chickens or perform simple chores around the house. Older children usually have the responsibility of caring for the younger ones who in turn are expected to obey

16. Hostetler, *op. cit.*, p. 154.
17. Huntington, *op. cit.*, p. 301.

their older brothers and sisters. Daughters are expected to defer not only to their parents but to their brothers as well. By the time children are in their teens, they are actively involved in the duties of the farm and the house. Chores are usually segregated by sex, but it is not unusual for children to perform whatever jobs need to be done at the time.

It is during the teenage years that Amish youth, particularly boys, experience the most freedom and privacy away from parents. The Amish realize that this is usually a period of rebellion, and so they loosen a bit the tight controls over their children's behavior. The more adventuresome youth may ride in cars, dress in "English" clothes while in town, or try alcohol during this time. Baptism at age 16 or 18 is a voluntary choice, and the Amish believe that young people should satisfy their curiosity about the worldly things they will be giving up. Once a person chooses the Amish faith and is baptized, he or she comes under the strict province of the *Ordnung*. Behavior tolerantly treated as youthful enthusiasm before baptism is excised as the threat of the *Meidung* and community censure becomes a reality.

Although Old Order Amish communities appear to be worlds unto themselves, they are nonetheless subject to state laws. Until recently, the Amish were often at odds with state authorities because they refused to send their children to public schools, fearful of worldly influences. Although specific educational laws differ among the states, compulsory education requires that children attend school until the age of 16. Some states have worked out a compromise whereby Amish children aged 15 may apply for a farm work permit or attend a farm vocational school rather than attend high school.[18]

Many Amish communities now have their own schools that their children attend. These schools epitomize our common notion of the little one-room schoolhouses of preindustrial America. They function without electricity, indoor plumbing, or heat. Generally, enrollment numbers around 30 students who are all taught by the same teacher in the same room. Amish teachers do not have college degrees and many have not even completed high school. Generally, their credentials include correspondence courses and a one-year teaching internship before they are given their own classrooms.

Amish schools concentrate on the basics of education woven into the fabric of Amish values. Kindness and cooperation are considered more important than competitiveness. Because talent is considered to be God-given, the slowest child is treated no differently than the brightest. The singular aim of Amish schools is to produce young men and women who will carry on the traditions of the faith.

18. Kephart, *op. cit.*. pp. 80–81.

Kinship Relations

The Amish way of life revolves around the family. When asked how many members comprise a community, the Amish will reply not in terms of individual members but in terms of the number of families.

The Old Order Amish have lived in the same locale for hundreds of years, have large numbers of children, and do not marry outside the faith. They do not allow first cousins to marry, but second- and third-cousin marriages are plentiful. Consequently, virtually all of the present Amish membership of Lancaster County can trace their roots back to the original followers of Jacob Amman.

Because of the long history of inbreeding among the Amish, districts are composed of large kinship groupings. Kephart finds that only about a dozen surnames are to be found among the Amish of Lancaster County.[19] In Indiana, only three family names—Miller, Yoder, and Bontrager—make up about 50 percent of the Amish membership. These same three names comprise over 50 percent of the Amish population in Ohio. Moreover, the Amish tend to give their children biblical first names such as John, Daniel, Mary, and Sarah. To deal with the obvious confusion that would ensue from having, say, 30 John Fishers living in the same district, the Amish make elaborate use of nicknames. These nicknames usually identify individuals by some characteristic that differentiates them from anyone else such as Curly-Top Joe or Shy Lizzie. In conversation, a person may be identified by his or her relationship to others. Samuel King, for example, might be referred to as "Menno and Katie King's oldest boy Samuel."

Members of Amish communities often work cooperatively together as groups. They meet often to participate in quilting bees, husking bees, weddings, and barn raisings.[20] Amish men have been known to construct totally in one day a barn that has burned to the ground. Community support is always available in times of need. Also, there is quite an extensive pattern of visiting among Amish families. Almost all of the parents in Lancaster County see their grown children at least once a month.[21] In the Amish community, there is little time or inclination toward leisure-time activities, but as much time as possible is spent traveling to see family and friends.

The Old Order Amish take care of their own. There are no old age homes, hospitals, social service agencies, or welfare recipients to be

19. *Ibid.*, p. 77.
20. An interesting science fiction novel written in the 1950s that deals with life after a nuclear holocaust closely parallels the Amish way of life. See Leigh Brackett, *The Long Tomorrow*, Garden City, N.Y.: Doubleday, 1955.
21. Huntington, *op. cit.*, p. 307.

found in Amish communities. They also refuse to accept Social Security benefits from the federal government, which finally exempted them from paying into the fund after years of conflict.

The old and the infirm are cared for in the home, among family members. There is no mandatory retirement. Generally, parents continue working on the farm until they are no longer able. Gradually, the work is taken over by the younger couples; the grandparents retain a position of advice-givers in the family. Children care lovingly for their aged parents.

Births and deaths are family matters, and both events find much support from family and relatives. Americans, being far removed from the ritual of death, tend to fear it. Not so the Amish. Children become quite used to the fact of death because it occurs in the home, not in faraway hospitals. The Amish view death as "the final rite of passage into a new and better life."[22] At the time of death, men and women are dressed in white, symbolizing a purification of the body and the soul. There is a calm acceptance of death and its meaning. Family members gather to lend support, aid, and comfort to the bereaved. Death is openly discussed so that family members may anticipate and plan for the feelings and problems that may ensue with the death of a loved one. The high level of community support for a bereaved family is continued for at least one year following a death, and Bryer reports that the remarriage rate among the Amish is one of the highest in the country.[23]

MORMON FAMILIES

Mormonism is a distinctly American religion, having had its origins in the western part of New York State during the early nineteenth century. This area was known as the "burned-over district" because for a period of time it was a beehive of religious fervor and activity.[24] Evangelists, preachers, spiritualists, and their followers, all touting their own message of divine inspiration, converged, mingled, and parted with a rapidity that has not been seen since. Out of this tumult came a religion that has survived until now with an amazing strength and vitality: Mormonism.

The founder of modern-day Mormonism was a young teenager named Joseph Smith. Surrounded on all sides by this cornucopia of religious opinion, he was naturally confused about which was the

22. Kathleen B. Bryer, "The Amish Way of Death: A Study of Family Support Systems," *American Psychologist* 34 (July 1979), pp. 255–62.
23. *Ibid.*, p. 259.
24. James B. Allen and Glen M. Leonard, *The Story of the Latter Day Saints*, Salt Lake City: Deseret Book Co., 1976, p. 11.

"right" and "true" religion. To find truth out of all this muddle, he fled alone to the contemplative atmosphere of the woods to ponder, meditate, and pray on his questions. There, he experienced the first of a series of revelations that were to provide the backbone of his new religion. His first revelation took the form of a visitation from God the Father and his son, Jesus Christ, who informed the 15-year-old Smith that none of the existing churches was the true one; therefore, he should not give his allegiance to any. His excitement over this visitation led him to attempt to spread its meaning to the people, who in turn ignored and ridiculed him. This reaction to the message of Joseph Smith was to continue for many years.

Three years later, the man who would become known as the Prophet Joseph by his adherents experienced a second visitation, this time from the Angel Moroni in the year 1823. This visitation would lay the foundation of the new religion. During this and subsequent visits, the Angel Moroni revealed to young Smith the location of the true book of the Gospel. He was told that this book was written on a series of gold plates and could be translated with the aid of a device buried in the same location.[25] God's great mission for Smith would be as translator of the plates and leader on earth of the true word of God. He translated the work at the age of 23, producing the Book of Mormon. When the Book of Mormon was published in 1830, it became an important tool for gaining new adherents through missionary work. Although the events leading to its writing remain a source of controversy among scholars,[26] this book remains the scriptural guide for the millions of Mormons living today in the United States and around the world.

On publication of the book, Smith set out with some loyal followers in 1830 to organize his Church of Christ. Because one of the tenets of the faith is belief in the second coming of Christ, the official name of the church became the Church of Jesus Christ of Latter-Day Saints, although it is more commonly referred to as Mormonism.

Smith was a charismatic leader and soon had quite a following, with branches of the church springing up in New York, Pennsylvania, and Ohio. He also had a large contingent of detractors and enemies. In 1831, he moved the church from Palmyra, New York, to Kirtland, Ohio, to find for his people more room and freedom from harassment.

Once in Kirtland, Smith began an experiment common to utopian ventures of the day. Called the United Order of Enoch, this experiment

25. Klaus J. Hansen, *Mormonism and the American Experience*, Chicago: University of Chicago Press, 1981, p. 5.
26. See Fawn M. Brodie, *No Man Knows My History: The Life of Joseph Smith the Mormon Prophet* (2nd ed.), New York: Alfred A. Knopf, 1971; Howard A. Davis, Donald R. Scales, and Wayne L. Cowdrey, *Who Really Wrote the Book of Mormon?* Santa Ana, Calif.: Vision House, 1977; and Mark P. Leone, *op. cit.*

sought to ensure an equality of resources for all members.[27] To do this, the income of wealthy adherents was redistributed to the poor, ensuring that all members would have equal access to the necessities of life. Soon, however, the leaders of the faith found that without profit as an incentive, individual initiative waned. Smith then instituted a practice that remains strong in the contemporary Mormon church: tithing. Tithing requires that members contribute 10 percent of their incomes to the church, no matter how much or how little they earn. In this way, everyone is free to use the great bulk of their income however they choose and the church is assured of being able to care for the needy.

Their time in Ohio was not long, for they encountered hostility and violence from the Gentiles (non-Mormons) there. Their trek continued westward, from Ohio to Missouri and Illinois. In each state, persecution, raids, and attacks by mobs continued. Finally, an event occurred that shook the foundations of the church—the Prophet Joseph was shot to death by an angry and bloodthirsty mob in the jail cell where he and three other Mormon leaders were being held. The year was 1844.

Brigham Young and the Move to Utah

The death of a leader would have marked the demise of many a young religion. The Mormon faith is notable, however, for its body of strong leaders who were able to carry on Smith's work and lead the Mormon people to freedom. Central to these figures of authority was Brigham Young, who today is most closely associated with the origins of Mormonism.

For almost two years after the death of the Prophet Joseph, the Mormons remained in Illinois. By this time, however, it was obvious that they could not live in peace with the Gentiles, who subjected them to raids and mob violence and who set their temples ablaze. Unlike so many religious groups who sought respite from persecution inside the boundaries of the United States, the original Mormon followers sought freedom by leaving it.

Moving slowly westward, blazing new paths, they left the settled states and pushed on across the Rockies into largely unsettled areas of the country. Under the leadership of Brigham Young, more than 10,000 followers settled in the Great Salt Lake Valley, which at that time was still owned by Mexico. There they found what they had been seeking since the early days in Palmyra: freedom to build their Church and practice their chosen faith. In 1849, the United States went to war with

27. Leonard J. Arrington, *Great Basin Kingdom*, Cambridge, Mass.: Harvard University Press, 1958, p. 7.

Mexico and acquired all the land west to California. But even after Utah became a territory of the United States, the Mormons retained for decades an isolation from outside intervention that allowed a growth of community and strength of faith that remains to this day.

Polygamy

Although several Mormon practices were sources of controversy, none became so great an issue as did polygamy.[28] The practice was begun, secretly at first, in 1842 by Joseph Smith. Smith experienced a divine revelation during which he was told by God that it was the duty of righteous men to bring as many children into the world as possible.[29] For this, many wives were needed. For almost a decade, the practice was kept as much a secret as possible, with only the top-ranking church leaders taking plural wives. The suspicion of outsiders concerning what they considered to be a great immorality was one reason for the persecution of Mormons.

Because most states had bigamy laws, it was only after the membership was safely ensconced in the Utah Territory that the pronouncement could be publicly made. In 1852, Brigham Young announced to the followers what was revealed to the Prophet Joseph. Because of their isolation from outside control and because of the membership's total faith in the revelations of its leaders, polygamy flourished among the Mormons for almost 50 years.[30]

Although the ideal relationship was polygamous, the great majority of Mormon marriages were monogamous.[31] Estimates vary, but it is generally agreed that only around 10 percent of the eligible men had plural wives.[32] These men were usually the older, more prosperous men or the leaders of the community. There were no limits to the number of wives allowed each man. Brigham Young himself had 27 wives and 56 children.

Living arrangements varied among the families. In some cases, the wives maintained separate households along with their children; husbands visited their wives on a rotating schedule. In other polygamous

---

28. Although *polygamy* may refer either to the taking of plural wives or husbands, among Mormons the practice was restricted to the marriage of one husband and two or more wives. This practice is more properly referred to as *polygyny*.

29. Bruce L. Campbell and Eugene E. Campbell, "The Mormon Family," in Mindel and Habenstein, eds., *op. cit.*, p. 393.

30. Kephart, *op. cit.*, p. 245.

31. See Nels Anderson, "The Mormon Family," *American Sociological Review* 2 (Oct. 1937), pp. 601–8; and Kimball Young, *Isn't One Wife Enough?* New York: Holt, 1954.

32. The sex-ratio and economic issues discussed in Chapter 2 apply equally well to the Mormon situation.

households, all the wives and children lived with the husband in the same house. To ease tensions, it was not unusual for a man to marry sets of sisters. And although all wives were supposed to have equal status, it was generally true that the first wife wielded the most power because she was the only *legal* wife.[33]

Polygamy was accepted as a dictum from God and, so, flourished within the Mormon community, but pressures from the outside world soon came to bear on the practice. Already persecuted in the press for their religious beliefs, Mormon polygamy was seized on and sensationalized in the newspapers. The public became inflamed with horror at the immoral goings-on of these strange people. In 1862, President Abraham Lincoln declared polygamy illegal in the territories of the United States, and federal agents began rooting out and arresting practitioners. Many of the leaders went into hiding and many spent time in jail. Some of the leaders spent years incarcerated rather than give up their beliefs.

Although most members remained resolute in their practice of polygamy, it became obvious that the principle was doomed to oblivion when, in 1887, the Edmunds-Tucker Law was passed. This law resulted in the disincorporation of the church and a loss of over $50,000 in payment to the government.[34] It also resulted in the loss of certain rights; only those who pledged loyalty to antipolygamy laws could vote, hold office, or serve on juries. When the Supreme Court upheld the Edmunds-Tucker Law as constitutional in 1890, the members realized that to fight further was futile. They also realized that the practice had to be discontinued before Utah could become a state. Mormon President Wilford Woodruff then issued what has become known as the Manifesto, an official pronouncement marking the end of polygamy. The Manifesto was issued and accepted as a revelation from God.

Although the Latter-Day Saints, or Mormons, oppose the practice of polygamy, they still today believe in it as divine revelation. Because of the negative connotations associated with it, the Mormon Church has made great efforts to disassociate itself from identification with polygamy. This is difficult, however, because there is evidence that descendants of those dissatisfied with the Manifesto practice polygamy to this day.[35] Scattered throughout a number of western states, it is impossible to know how many of these "fundamentalist" families exist. Once in a while, however, newspapers bring to light stories of men with many wives, causing great embarrassment to the leaders of the modern Mormon Church.

33. Campbell and Campbell, *op. cit.,* p. 395.
34. Hansen, *op. cit.,* p. 145.
35. Kephart, *op. cit.,* pp. 271–72.

Mormon Families Today

The Church of Jesus Christ of Latter-Day Saints has survived with an amazing strength and vitality that will undoubtedly continue. Church membership stands today at almost 3.5 million.[36] Although scattered throughout a number of states, the highest concentration of members remains in Utah, accounting for over 70 percent of that state's population.[37] Like the Amish, Mormons consider the family unit as the primary social structure around which everything else revolves.

The Family's Value System

The Mormons' belief in the family is so strong that it extends beyond mere existence on earth. A primary tenet of the faith teaches that the family composes *the* social structure in the Kingdom of God. According to doctrine, a married couple may continue their marriage in Heaven throughout eternity if both the husband and wife are Mormon and if they are married in a Mormon temple. This is called a *celestial marriage* and is the highest state of existence to which Mormons may strive. The Mormon faith teaches that God Himself lives in a family with a wife, producing spiritual children who become the mortals of earth. The attainment of Godhood is possible for humans who pass through the many levels of heaven. The highest level cannot be reached without the marriage and family unit.[38] By producing as many children as they can on earth, Mormons believe that they are providing homes for God's children. Anything that interferes with this goal such as abortion, contraception, premarital and extramarital relations, is frowned on by the Church.

Certain requirements must be met before couples are allowed marriage ceremonies in Mormon temples. In addition to the requirement that both partners be of the Mormon faith, they must be members of the Church in good standing, be sexually pure, tithe 10 percent of their income to the Church, and obey the Word of Wisdom.[39] The Word of Wisdom, handed down in revelation from Joseph Smith, requires that members abstain from tobacco, alcohol, tea, and coffee. If these requirements are met, couples may form eternal families, producing spiritual

36. Charles Austin, "Decline in Church Membership May Be Ending," *New York Times*, July 2, 1983.
37. John Willis, "Mormon Fertility and the Americanization Hypothesis: Some Further Comments," *Social Biology* 22 (Fall 1975), pp. 282–84.
38. Arland Thornton, "Religion and Fertility: The Case of Mormonism," *Journal of Marriage and the Family* 41 (Feb. 1979), pp. 131–42.
39. Kephart, *op. cit.*, p. 391.

children in their life after death. Not all couples meet these requirements, of course, but they serve as a powerful means of social control
of members' behavior.

Like the Amish, Mormon families are patriarchal in nature. Wives
are expected to be subservient to their husbands, just as they are in the
Church. Mormon husbands preside over their families and compose the
Church hierarchy. All worthy male members of the Church are ordained to the priesthood at age 12; from then on, they are given increased responsibilities in the Church. Mormon fathers perform for
their families all of the functions that are usually the domain, in other
religions, of ministers, priests, or rabbis. They bless and baptize children,
bless sick family members, ordain their sons as priests, and lead their
families in prayer at meals and on special occasions.

Women are not allowed the priesthood in the Mormon faith, and
most are satisfied to occupy a subordinate position in the family structure. Scripture places men in the dominant position both in the Church
and family structures, and most wives are content to obey what they
believe is divine revelation. Any activities that take women away from
the home and children are frowned on and discouraged. Not surprisingly, Mormon leaders vehemently oppose both the feminist movement
and passage of the ERA (Equal Rights Amendment) even though a
number of Mormons favor both. Sonia Johnson, a vocal supporter of
the ERA and a Mormon, was excommunicated from the Church when
she opposed the leadership's stand on this issue.[40] Until a short time ago,
blacks, although welcomed as members in the Church, were not allowed priesthood. Charges of racism and discrimination plagued the
leaders of the Church for years. In 1978, Mormon President Spencer W.
Kimball reported a divine revelation that instructed him that all worthy
male members could be ordained to the priesthood, regardless of race
or color. This revelation soothed the charges of racism but, of course,
did not speak to the exclusion of women from the Church hierarchy.

Although birthrates are declining among Mormons, they still tend to
want and have more children than other Americans.[41] In 1970, Utah

---

40. Sonia Johnson, "The Woman Who Talked Back to God and Didn't Get Zapped,"
in Laurel Richardson and Verta Johnson, eds., *Feminist Frontiers: Rethinking Sex,
Gender, and Society*, Reading, Mass.: Addison-Wesley, 1983, pp. 97–103. See also Marilyn
Warenski, *Patriarchs and Politics: The Plight of the Mormon Woman*, New York:
McGraw-Hill, 1978.
41. See Donald Hastings, Charles H. Reynolds, and Ray Canning, "Mormonism and
Birth Planning: The Discrepancy Between Church Authorities' Teachings and Lay
Attitudes," *Population Studies* 26 (Jan. 1972), pp. 19–28; and Armand L. Mauss, "Saints,
Cities, and Secularism: Religious Attitudes and Behavior of Modern Urban Mormons,"
Dialogue: A Journal of Mormon Thought 7 (Summer 1972), pp. 8–27.

had the highest fertility rate of any state in the country.[42] It appears, though, that Mormon families are not immune to the pressures of urbanization and modern life. There is increasing evidence that many Mormons are now turning to contraception in an effort to limit family size. According to Thornton, if present trends continue, there will be a convergence of birthrates between Utah and the rest of the United States. This will take about 150 years to happen though.[43]

Mormons generally oppose intermarriage with non-Mormons, mainly for reasons of religious doctrine. Mixed marriages cannot be performed in a temple and, hence, the marriage is for life only and not for eternity. Although the rates of intermarriage for this group are unknown, the great majority of Mormans do marry other Mormons.[44]

Not surprisingly, the Mormon faith opposes divorce. Although the divorce rate for Utah is nearly identical to the rate for the United States, it appears that those couples who have temple marriages have a lower probability of divorce than those Mormons not married in the temple. The reasons for this are not entirely clear. It may be that couples who meet the requirements for a temple marriage are more compatible in outlook and life values. They may view divorce as more sinful than other persons. Or because of the strong prescription put on family life by the Mormon faith, they may overlook sources of dissension that would tear other marriages apart.[45]

Mormons value hard work and human enterprise, and these values have turned it into one of the richest churches in the world.[46] The practice of tithing has allowed the Church to make financial investments in a multitude of businesses. They own hotels, radio and TV stations, newspapers, ranchlands, plantations, factories, and farms. The list of their holdings around the world could go on and on. The revenues generated from these investments are used to maintain and expand the Church.

Needy Mormon families rarely need to turn to public relief or welfare programs. Mormon families contribute to a special welfare fund that is used to supply goods and foodstuffs to other, less fortunate families. Large amounts of money are collected each month and members of the Church hierarchy are constantly in touch with recipient families.

Mormons also value education and a good part of the monies collected from membership tithes go toward supporting higher education

42. Willis, *ibid.*, p. 282.
43. Thornton, *op. cit.*, p. 136.
44. Brent A. Barlow, "Notes on Mormon Interfaith Marriages," *Family Coordinator* 26 (April 1977), pp. 143–50.
45. Campbell and Campbell, *op. cit.*, p. 402.
46. Kephart, *op. cit.*, p. 273.

for their young people. The Mormons founded both the University of Utah and Brigham Young University. Brigham Young University is the largest church-related university in the United States, enrolling over 25,000 students each year.[47] Because the university is supported almost entirely from tithing revenues, tuition is low and there are no mortgages on the university or its holdings.

Parent-Child Interaction

Mormon families center around the children. Couples produce children very early in their marriages and have large families. Mothers particularly are actively involved in socializing their children to become good citizens and worthy members of the Church. Socialization practices do not appear to be much different from the ways in which other Americans raise their children.[48] The emphasis in Mormon families is on the end results of proper socialization, not the means through which this is achieved.

The Mormon regard for the sanctity of the family is strengthened and reinforced by the Church. Along with various programs designed to teach parents how to be successful in raising their children, the Church in 1964 instituted a program called "family home evening." On Monday evenings, entire families stay within their homes and devote their time to learning about the gospel and sharing activities as a family group. Church services are suspended on these evenings specifically for the purpose of encouraging family interaction. Although not all families participate in this program, it is enthusiastically endorsed by most and points to the primacy of the family in Mormon life.

Both the Church and parental control serve to guide the activities of young people into acceptable realms of behavior and, for the most part, children expect and appreciate these controls. There are indications, however, that some teenagers are experimenting with drugs and sex, against both of which the Mormon Church has taken a strong stand. But even though the Mormon leadership is vehemently opposed to the use of drugs, Utah was one of the first states in the country to enact a law reducing the charge for a first-time possession-of-marijuana offense from a felony to a misdemeanor.[49]

In terms of premarital sexuality, most Mormon teenagers find necking

47. *Ibid.*, p. 276.
48. Philip R. Kunz, "Religious Influences on Parental Discipline and Achievement Demands," *Marriage and Family Living* 24 (May 1963), pp. 224–25. See also Melvin L. Wilkinson and William C. Tanner III, "The Influence of Family Size, Interaction and Religiosity on Family Affection in a Mormon Sample," *Journal of Marriage and the Family* 42 (May 1980), pp. 297–304.
49. Campbell and Campbell, *op. cit.*, p. 408.

and petting the extent of acceptable behavior. And although the rates of premarital intercourse have been rising over the last several decades, Christensen found that Mormons active in the Church had a much lower rate of reported sexual intercourse than did inactive Mormons.[50] The inactive Mormons had rates of premarital intercourse similar to non-Mormons in the same locale.

No discussion of Mormon youth would be complete without an examination of the Church's missionary program. The Church sends out about 28,000 missionaries each year to places all around the world.[51] One of the reasons for the enormous growth of the Mormon Church is its active program; about half of its annual growth consists of converts.

Acceptance into the missionary program is considered a high honor by young Mormons (most are 19 or 20) who must be deemed worthy by Church officials. About 90 percent of the missionaries are young men who devote up to two years of their lives in the territory that is chosen for them by the Church.[52] They must be able to support themselves during this time because they receive no money from the Church for their work. Those who are chosen must meet strict requirements: they must be sexually pure, obey the Word of Wisdom, comply with standards of dress and deportment, and be willing to work wherever they are placed. And they do work! Kephart states that it is not unusual for these young missionaries to spend 8 to 10 hours a day, seven days a week, visiting the homes of potential converts and discussing with them the beliefs of Mormonism.[53] The strength of the Mormon Church is particularly evident in these young people who put aside their own lives for two years to spread the word of the faith. They are not even allowed to date during this period of time. They are amazingly successful in their efforts, bringing around 80,000 new converts into the church each year.[54]

Kinship Relations

The Mormon emphasis on, and enjoyment of, family life extends to their kinship relations as well. Because families tend to be very large, the extended kin network can include hundreds of people. This notwithstanding, Mormons make great efforts toward maintaining active relationships with kin members. The summer is usually the time of many a

50. Harold T. Christensen, "Some Next Steps in Mormon Family Research," in Philip R. Kunz, *ed.*, *The Mormon Family*, Provo, Utah: Brigham Young University Family Research Center, 1977, pp. 1–12.
51. Leone, *op. cit.*, p. 1.
52. Campbell and Campbell, *op. cit.*, p. 407.
53. Kephart, *op. cit.*, p. 265.
54. *Ibid.*, p. 265.

family reunion, bringing hundreds of family members together from all over the country.

The feelings of closeness and camaraderie intrinsic to Mormon family relations extend to the community as well. There are numerous activities, organizations, and events in which community members are encouraged to participate. Mormons feel very strongly the bonds of their common faith. They almost always refer to each other as sister or brother and to the membership as brethren.[55]

The Mormon conception of kinship extends beyond the living and embraces relatives who have already died. They believe that only those who have heard the gospel and been baptized can travel through the levels of heaven and reach Godhood. Because Mormonism was founded in the early nineteenth century, this means that the majority of Mormon ancestors did not have the opportunity to be confirmed within the Church. Mormons are taught that they are obligated to research their genealogy to locate as many of their ancestors as possible. They may then, by proxy, seek baptism and other sacred rites for the deceased. Kephart reports that the number of proxy ceremonies has today reached over 50 million![56] This "work for the dead," as it is called, has resulted in one of the most extensive genealogical library systems in the world.[57] The Mormon Genealogical Society, located in Salt Lake City, and its branches scattered throughout the United States and abroad, are open free of charge to the public interested in researching their roots. These extensive records and microfilms have also contributed invaluable information to scholars around the world.

SUMMARY

The Old Order Amish settled in the United States during the eighteenth century after a schism developed among the Mennonites of Switzerland. They live much the same today as they did hundreds of years ago. The Amish live in rural communities and have an intensive farming economy. Behavior is governed by the *Ordnung*, and the *Meidung*, or shunning, is an effective means of social control. Automobiles, electricity, telephones, and other markings of the modern world are forbidden. Everyday life is simple; hard work and devotion to God is stressed.

Old Order Amish families are patriarchal, but husbands and wives are considered equal partners in marriage. Birth control of any kind is

55. Robert Mullen, *The Latter-Day Saints: The Mormons Yesterday and Today*, Garden City, N.Y.: Doubleday, 1966, p. 27.
56. Kephart, *op. cit.*, p. 260.
57. Campbell and Campbell, *op. cit.*, p. 392.

forbidden, and families tend to have large numbers of children. Children are expected to be obedient to their parents and older siblings. Education is devalued, and most children attend school only in fulfillment of compulsory education laws.

Amish communities are small, do not allow exogamous marriages, and do not seek converts. Hence, communities tend to be inbred, with only a few family names comprising entire communities. Extended family and community relations are very close. There are no old age homes, hospitals, or social service agencies within the Amish districts. All of the community's needs are taken care of within the family units. Isolation from the outside world is a very important part of Amish life.

Mormonism, or the Church of Latter-Day Saints, is a distinctly American religion. Founded by Joseph Smith in the early nineteenth century, Mormonism is today one of the fastest growing religions in the world.

Their scriptural guide is the Book of Mormon, said to be translated by Joseph Smith from a set of golden plates. Facing persecution from non-Mormons, Brigham Young eventually led his followers to Utah after the murder of the Prophet Joseph. The practice of polygamy, an integral part of Mormon doctrine, flourished in Utah for a number of years before public and governmental pressures effectively forced its end.

The core of Mormon existence centers around the family. Those who are married in a Mormon temple achieve celestial marriage, a union that lasts throughout eternity. By doctrine, Mormons are expected to produce as many children as possible, and anything that interferes with this such as abortion or contraception is frowned on. The family structure is patriarchal, and all worthy males are ordained as priests in the Church at age 12.

The practice of tithing allows the Mormon Church to make financial investments in the United States and abroad. The Church is one of the richest in the world. Tithing also allows for the support of needy families and the maintenance of university systems.

Their active missionary program accounts for a large part of the growth in Mormon membership. Young men spend up to two years in designated areas spreading the word of the faith. Acceptance into the program is considered a high honor and missionaries must comply with stringent rules.

Kinship relations are extensive and include all of one's ancestors. It is the duty and obligation of every Mormon family to research their family tree and receive baptism and sacred rites for those who died without receiving the gospel. The Mormon Genealogical Society holds one of the most extensive collections of genealogical records in the world.

SUGGESTED READINGS

D'Antonio, William, and Aldous, Joan, *eds.*, *Families and Religions: Conflict and Change in Modern Society*, Beverly Hills, Calif.: Sage Publications, 1983. Examines contemporary social issues in the context of various religious and family types.

Foster, Lawrence, *Religion and Sexuality: Three American Communal Experiments of the Nineteenth Century*, New York: Oxford University Press, 1981. Includes one of the finest analyses of Mormon polygamy yet available.

Hostetler, John A., and Huntington, Gertrude Enders, *Children in Amish Society: Socialization and Community Education*, New York: Holt, Rinehart & Winston, 1971. A fascinating account that depicts the lives of Amish children by two acknowledged authorities in the field.

Kern, L. J., *An Ordered Love: Sex Roles and Sexuality in Victorian Utopias: The Shakers, the Mormons, and the Oneida Community*, Chapel Hill: University of North Carolina Press, 1981. A historical investigation of the sexual ideologies and behaviors of three nineteenth-century communities.

Merrill, Melissa, *Polygamist's Wife*, Salt Lake City: Olympus, 1975. Discusses polygamy in the context of Mormon life. Written by a woman who is a member of a polygamous marriage.

Meyer, Carolyn, *Amish People*, New York: Atheneum, 1976. Focuses on the ways in which a people are molded by their religious beliefs.

FILMS

The Amish: A People of Preservation (Britannica Educational Corporation, 425 North Michigan Avenue, Chicago, Ill. 60611), 53 minutes. An ethnographic documentary that explores the value systems of Amish residents of Lancaster County, Pennsylvania.

The Older Order Amish (Modern Talking Picture Service, 2323 New Hyde Park, N.Y. 11040), 32 minutes. This film deals with the origins of the Pennsylvania Amish and their day-to-day lives in contemporary times.

The Religious Revolution and the Void (Association Films, 866 Third Avenue, New York, N.Y. 10022), 34 minutes. Examines a cross-section of American life in an attempt to understand why young people are drifting away from religion.

QUESTIONS AND PROJECTS

1. Trace the origins of the Old Order Amish. Why have their social patterns remained essentially unchanged for hundreds of years?
2. Why is isolation from the outside world so important to the Amish? How do they ensure their independence from the outside world?

3. What is the *Meidung?* Why is it so effective as a means of social control in Amish communities?

4. Describe sex-role patterns in Amish families. How is it possible for Amish women to have equal status with their husbands in a patriarchal society?

5. Describe the dating and courtship activities of Amish youth. What structural components of the Amish life style encourage endogamous marriages?

6. How does Amish childhood differ from that in other American homes? How do parents ensure their children will stay within the fold?

7. Why is Mormonism a distinctly American religion? Trace the origins of Mormonism from its inception to the final settlement in Utah.

8. What is celestial marriage? What is the connection between celestial marriage and polygamy? Why did the practice of plural marriage end in Utah?

9. What is the purpose of tithing? What does the Mormon Church do with the revenues from tithing?

10. Why do the leaders of the Mormon Church oppose the ERA? How do they deal with members who oppose them on this issue? What is the current status of black members in relation to the priesthood?

11. Why do Mormons "work for the dead"? Describe the relationship between "working for the dead" and the Mormon Genealogical Society.

12. Compare Amish and Mormon practices concerning the following issues: birth control, education, converts to the faith, intermarriage, finances, kinship relations.

13. How has your own religion influenced your family patterns? Debate the question: "Is God dead"?

IV
The Family Life Cycle

Copyright © Jean Shapiro

12
Premarital Interaction

From the minute a newborn baby girl is wrapped in a pink blanket and her brother in a blue one, the two children are treated differently. The difference starts with the subtle tone of voice of the adults cooing over the two cradles, and continues with the father's mock wrestling with his baby boy and gentler play with his "fragile" daughter. Researchers have observed sex differences in behavior of male and female babies at amazingly young ages, most of it directly traceable to parents' differential treatment of boys and girls.[1]

Despite the widespread belief that dating practices are changing rapidly in the United States, psychologists report that traditional patterns remain: The anxiety associated with dating is still preponderantly the problem of men, and men still initiate dates in the vast majority of instances. At the same time, new research has begun to suggest why some men have more trouble than others in opposite-sex relationships.[2]

Sex without love is not acceptable or not enjoyable to 44 percent of the women and 29 percent of the men who responded to a magazine survey on love and romance. . . . Loss of desire seemed to go together with lack of love and romance.[3]

Separate phones were a "must," and with them a rule that each answer only his or her own phone. One couple actually had six phones in their home, two in each kitchen, bedroom and loft, largely for their (separate) convenience. Separate mail boxes were also sometimes used, and because most apartment

1. Lenore J. Weitzman, "Sex-Role Socialization," in Jo Freeman, *ed., Women: A Feminist Perspective* (2nd ed.), Palo Alto, Calif.: Mayfield, 1979, p. 156.
2. Marilyn Machlowitz, "Dating's Unchanged: Men Still Have Most Problems," *New York Times*, May 13, 1981.
3. Associated Press, June 23, 1983.

complexes provided one mailbox, one cohabitor sometimes rented a post office box; otherwise one name was removed from the apartment box.[4]

Socialization into masculine and feminine roles begins almost from the moment of birth and has a profound effect on the relationships of men and women. In this chapter, we explore the interactions between the sexes before marriage. Beginning with an analysis of sex-role socialization, we examine the experiences of men and women in their dating, sexual, and cohabiting relationships.

SEX-ROLE SOCIALIZATION

"Is it a boy or a girl?" Invariably, this is the first question asked of new parents and the answer will usually influence how the child is treated. Boys and girls tend to be treated differently from the moment of birth. Some of the differences such as using the color blue for boys and pink for girls are trivial. Others, however, cumulate systematically to produce different personality patterns in males and females. Males are encouraged to become assertive, active, and goal oriented whereas females are encouraged to become passive, dependent, and relationship oriented. Thus, boys are prepared for lives of competition in the world of work. Girls are prepared to become wives and mothers.

This differential socialization by sex during the early years occurs primarily in the relationship with the parents. Two basic processes are involved. First, parents treat sons and daughters differently. Second, further differentiation occurs as the child comes to identify with the parent of the same sex.

Differential Treatment

Differential treatment comes first in time.[5] Parents have explicit views of what little girls and little boys should be like and do not hesitate to share these views with their children. They reward sex-appropriate behavior and punish sex-inappropriate behavior. Boys are encouraged to strenuous outdoor activity; girls are encouraged to more sedentary pursuits.

4. Patrick G. Jackson, "On Living Together Unmarried: Awareness Contexts and Social Interaction," *Journal of Family Issues* 4 (March 1983), p. 45.
5. Jeanne H. Block, "Assessing Sex Differences: Issues, Problems, and Pitfalls," *Merrill-Palmer Quarterly* 22 (Oct. 1976), pp. 283–308; John Condry and Sandra Condry, "Sex Differences: A Study of the Eye of the Beholder," *Child Development* 47 (Sept. 1976), pp. 812–19; Beverly I. Fagot, "The Influence of Sex of Child on Parental Reactions to Toddler Children," *Child Development* 49 (June 1978), pp. 459–65; Jeffrey Z. Rubin, Frank J. Provenzano, and Zella Luria, "The Eye of the Beholder: Parents' Views of Sex of Newborns," *American Journal of Orthopsychiatry* 44 (June 1974), pp. 512–19; and Caroline Smith and Barbara Lloyd, "Maternal Behavior and Perceived Sex of Infant: Revisited," *Child Development* 49 (Dec. 1978), pp. 1263–65.

Punishment for sex-inappropriate behavior is probably stricter for boys than for girls.[6] Girls may receive mild censure for tomboy behavior or they might not even experience that. They can wear jeans or other pants and they may indulge in a certain amount of roughhousing.[7] Boys, however, cannot dress in feminine attire and are strongly discouraged from playing with dolls, tea sets, and the like. For a boy to be labeled a "sissy" is perceived a threat both to him and his parents. Some analysts believe that this difference is linked to fear on the part of the parents that sons who are permitted so-called feminine qualities may develop homosexual tendencies. Some researchers believe that the avoidance of the sissy label leads some males, in adult life, to become hostile toward and contemptuous of women and anything feminine.[8]

That boys and girls are treated differently seems certain. That these differences stem solely from the attitudes of parents, however, is an oversimplification. Parents act not only on their own, they also react to what they perceive as the dispositions and responses of their children. Fathers may focus on assertive behavior in their sons as much because they perceive assertiveness already in them as because they wish the boys to become assertive. Similarly, parents may talk more to their daughters because the daughters talk more to them. The process of cause and effect is complex, involving action and reaction on the part of both parents and children.

Identification

Ordinarily, by about age three, the child has formed a firm sense of self as being either male or female. Up to that point, the personality structure is relatively flexible and the child may make identification with either parent. Some analysts believe that both boys and girls tend to identify originally with the mother both because of more frequent and

6. Elaine F. Currant, Andrew L. Dickson, Howard N. Anderson, and Patricia J. Faulkender, "Sex Role Stereotyping and Assertive Behavior," *Journal of Psychology* 101 (March 1979), pp. 223–28; Beverly I. Fagot, Sex-Related Stereotyping of Toddler's Behavior and Parental Reaction," *Developmental Psychology* 10 (July 1974), pp. 554–58; Sheila Fling and Martin Manosevitz, "Sex Typing in Nursery School Children's Play Interests," *Developmental Psychology* 7 (Sept. 1972), pp. 146–52; Leonard M. Lansky, "The Family Structure also Affects the Model: Sex-Role Attitudes in Parents of Preschool Children," *Merrill-Palmer Quarterly* 13 (April 1967), pp. 139–50; Robert R. Sears, "Development of Gender Role," in Frank A. Beach, *ed., Sex and Behavior*, New York: John Wiley & Sons, 1965; and Shirley Weitz, *Sex Roles: Biological, Psychological, and Social Foundations*, New York: Oxford University Press, 1977, p. 65.
7. Bryce Nelson, "Men Found More Aggressive, but Women Are Catching Up," *New York Times*, July 5, 1983.
8. See Ruth E. Hartley, "Sex Role Pressures and Socialization of the Male Child," *Psychological Reports* 5 (March 1959), pp. 457–68; and Diane Herman, "The Rape Culture," in Freeman, *op. cit.* pp. 41–63.

intimate association with her and because the father is more often absent from the home.

Boys do learn, however, of the value attached to maleness by society. They learn that men are bigger and stronger than women and that their occupational activities are highly valued. Gradually, they assume a male-gender identity, seeking approval and the development of a positive self-concept through doing those things that society says males ought to do. Similarly, girls' early identification with their mothers is reinforced by rewards accruing to them through their association with the mother in her nurturant, childrearing role. Not surprisingly, in households where the mother works outside the home, children tend to have less stereotyped sex-role perceptions.[9] Similarly, in homes where there are high levels of sex-role flexibility in both parents, children tend less to be tied to rigid sex-role divisions.[10]

Both boys and girls actually are involved in a very complex pattern of interaction with both parents, learning different aspects of role behavior from each. From the parent of the same sex, they learn the behavior in which they are expected to engage. From the parent of the opposite sex, they learn the behaviors to which they are expected to respond.

School and Peer Influences

It is widely known that most school curriculum materials emphasize the achievements of males, either ignoring women or relegating them to essentially support roles as wives and mothers.[11] This is true from the picture-book stories children use in the early grades to the interpretations of civics and history taught to high school seniors. There is also systematic sex typing in the counseling of girls into courses such as home economics and typing, whereas boys are directed into courses in shop, science, and mathematics. Once again, though, more censure is directed toward the choices of boys. It probably would not be too difficult for girls to enroll in shop or auto mechanics classes, but boys seeking entrance into cooking or sewing classes would most likely face

9. Richard Perloff, "Some Antecedents of Children's Sex-Role Stereotypes," *Psychological Reports* 40 (March 1977), pp. 463–66.
10. Jacob L. Orlofsky, "Parental Antecedents of Sex-Role Orientations in College Men and Women," *Sex Roles* 5 (Aug. 1979), pp. 495–512.
11. Elizabeth Fennema, "Women and Girls in the Public Schools: Defeat or Liberation"? in Joan I. Roberts, *ed., Beyond Intellectual Sexism: A New Woman, a New Reality*, New York: David McKay, 1976, pp. 343–52; Florence Howe, "Sexual Stereotypes Start Early," *Saturday Review*, October 16, 1971, p. 76; Marjorie B. U'Ren, "The Image of Women in Textbooks," in Vivian Gornick and Barbara K. Moran, *eds., Woman in Sexist Society: Studies in Power and Powerlessness*, New York: Basic Books, 1971, pp. 318–28; and Lenore J. Weitzman, Deborah Eiffler, Elizabeth Hokada, and Catherine Ross, "Sex-Role Socialization in Picture Books for Pre-School Children," *American Journal of Sociology* 77 (May 1972), pp. 1125–50.

ridicule from their friends and discouragement from their teachers and counselors.

If the conservative influences of the schools on sex-role socialization are widely known, it is not so often recognized that children's peer groups often exert a similar influence. Lever found six systematic differences in the play activities of boys and girls.[12] Betty Harragan argues that the types of play activities to which boys are encouraged prepare them for life in the corporate sphere.[13] The quiet, sedentary, cooperative play activities of girls discourage the competitive qualities that the business world requires.

By the age of 20 months, boys and girls know which toys are appropriate to their sex and seem to prefer them.[14] The toys considered appropriate for boys encourage far more activity, creativity, and imagination than do the toys for girls. Advertisers reinforce gender appropriateness in the selection of toys. It is rare to see a picture of a girl displayed on the packaging for chemistry sets or baseball bats. The only dolls usually sold to boys are geared toward war and combat. Studies show that girls have more interest in boys' toys and activities than the reverse.[15] The freewheeling, enthusiastic appeal of tree climbing, foot races, baseball games, and the like, is often much more exhilarating to healthy, exuberant little girls than is serving tea to a tableful of dolls.

A recent study found that children are less rigid in their notions of appropriate toys if they are exposed to examples of more flexible choice.[16] In this study, a group of children examined picture books showing boys and girls playing with sex-appropriate toys. When given toys of their own to play with, they chose sex-appropriate ones too. Later, they examined picture books showing children playing with non-stereotypical toys. Again, they were given a range of toys from which to choose. This time, however, they were more flexible in their choices and were not tied to stereotypical sex-specific toys. Karpoe and Olney[17]

12. Janet Lever, "Sex Differences in the Games Children Play," *Social Problems* 23 (April 1976), pp. 478–87; and "Sex Differences in the Complexity of Children's Play and Games," *American Sociological Review* 43 (April 1978), pp. 471–83. See also Donna Elder and Maureen T. Hallinan, "Sex Differences in Children's Friendships," *American Sociological Review* 43 (April 1978), pp. 237–50.

13. Betty Harragan, *Games Mother Never Taught You*, New York: Warner Books, 1972.

14. Greta Fein, David Johnson, Nancy Kosson, Linda Stork, and Lisa Wasserman, "Sex Stereotypes and Preferences in the Toy Choices of 20-Month-Old Boys and Girls," *Developmental Psychology* 11 (July 1975), pp. 527–28.

15. Mirra Komarovsky, *Women in the Modern World*, Boston: Little, Brown, 1953; and William D. Ward, "Variance of Sex-Role Preference Among Boys and Girls," *Psychological Reports* 23 (Oct. 1968), pp. 467–70.

16. Eleanor Ashton, "Measures of Play Behavior: The Influence of Sex-Role Stereotyped Children's Books," *Sex Roles* 9 (Jan. 1983), pp. 43–47.

17. Kelly P. Karpoe and Rachel L. Olney, "The Effect of Boys' or Girls' Toys on Sex-typed Play in Preadolescents," *Sex Roles* 9 (April 1983), pp. 507–18.

found that when children are limited to either boys' toys (trucks) or girls' toys (dolls), the ways in which they play and the stories they compose about their play reflect the gender associations of the toys rather than their own sex. Rarely, though, are children so limited in their choice of toys, and when given a choice, most prefer those considered appropriate to their own sex. Boys tend to be more rigid than girls in their choice of toys and games.

Thus, the influences of parents, schools, and peer groups all reinforce, in some way, the traditional masculine and feminine roles in our society. Although some of this influence may be conscious and intended, most of it is probably unintended and unrecognized. These childhood influences are further acted on as boys and girls move into adulthood.

Adult Sex-Role Expectations

Any line drawn between childhood and adult sex-role expectations would be both thin and arbitrary. Expectations develop gradually through the teen years and extend into early adulthood. Perhaps no other area of family relationships has been more widely researched in recent years than that of the marital-role expectations of men and women. Attention has concentrated on the changing expectations of women.

For most men and women, marriage remains a desirable adult option. But although marriage was once the primary and singular concern of young women, it now appears that many envision combining careers with marriage and parenthood. A 1975 Gallup poll found that 45 percent of women aged 18 to 24 believe that marriage, children, and a full-time job will lead to the most satisfying and fulfilling type of life.[18] A study of 1063 first-year women at the City University of the City of New York found that almost half want occupational careers along with marriage and children.[19] Although parenthood is still a desirable option

18. "Women in America," *Gallup Poll Index*, Report 128 (March 1976), p. 30.

19. Gilda F. Epstein and Arline L. Bronzaft, "Female Freshmen View Their Roles as Women," *Journal of Marriage and the Family* 34 (Nov. 1972), pp. 671–72. See also Laurie Davidson Cummings, "Value Stretch in Definitions of Career Among College Women: Horatia Alger as Feminist Model," *Social Problems* 25 (Oct. 1977), pp. 65–74; Marie S. Dunn, "Marriage Role Expectations of Adolescents," *Marriage and Family Living* 22 (May 1960), pp. 99–104; William G. Dyer and Dick Urban, "The Institutionalization of Equalitarian Family Norms," *Marriage and Family Living* 20 (Feb. 1958), pp. 53–58; Charles W. Hobart, "Orientations to Marriage Among Young Canadians," *Journal of Comparative Family Studies* 3 (Autumn 1972), pp. 171–93; Alver H. Jacobson, "Conflict of Attitudes Toward the Roles of the Husband and Wife in Marriage," *American Sociological Review* 17 (April 1952), pp. 146–50; Theodore Johannis, Jr., "Roles of Family Members," in *Family Mobility in Our Dynamic Society*, Ames: Center for Agricultural and Economic Development, Iowa State University Press, 1965, pp. 69–79; William F. Kenkel and Dean K. Hoffman, "Real and Conceived Roles in

among young women, for many it will be delayed until their careers are launched.[20]

Not only are women including careers as part of their adult role expectations, many are also preparing for careers in occupations that once were the domain of men. The number of women in law, medical, veterinary, and graduate schools has risen dramatically in the last few years and the trend is expected to continue.[21] Studies have shown that young women whose mothers have worked outside the home and whose perceptions of themselves have been influenced by college professors and other professional people are more likely to expect to work outside the home themselves.[22] In 1971, women's education and age at marriage had the most influence on their earnings; in the last few years sex-role attitudes have become an important factor too.[23]

Several studies have shown that women's role expectations have changed substantially over the past decade and that there has been much less change in men's role expectations. A study at Rutger's University, for example, showed a marked shift toward feminist attitudes among young women but little change in the women's perceptions of men's attitudes.[24] A much larger study, employing data from five surveys, reported substantial changes in women's sex-role attitudes between 1964

Family Decision Making," *Marriage and Family Living* 18 (Nov. 1956), pp. 311–16; Debi D. Lovejoy, "College Student Conceptions of the Roles of the Husband and the Wife in Family Decision Making," *Family Life Coordinator* 9 (March–June 1961), pp. 43–46; Alvin J. Moser, "Marriage Role Expectations of High School Students," *Marriage and Family Living* 23 (Feb. 1961), pp. 42–43; and Genevieve M. Wise and Don C. Carter, "A Definition of the Role of Homemaker by Two Generations of Women," *Journal of Marriage and the Family* 27 (Nov. 1965), pp. 531–32.

20. Patricia Kain Knaub, Deanna Baxter Eversoll, and Jacqueline Holm Voss, "Is Parenthood a Desirable Adult Role? An Assessment of Attitudes Held By Contemporary Women," *Sex Roles* 9 (March 1983), pp. 355–62.

21. Linda J. Waite, "U.S. Women at Work," *Population Bulletin* 36 (May 1981), p. 38.

22. Elizabeth M. Almquist and Shirley S. Angrist, "Career Salience and Atypicality of Occupational Choice Among College Women," *Journal of Marriage and the Family* 32 (May 1970), pp. 242–49; and "Role Model Influences on College Women's Career Aspirations," *Merrill-Palmer Quarterly* 17 (July 1971), pp. 263–79. See also Sheila K. Korman, "The Feminist: Familial Influences on Adherence to Ideology and Commitment to a Self-Perception," *Family Relations* 32 (July 1983), pp. 431–39; Harold C. Meier, "Mother Centeredness and College Youths' Attitudes Toward Equality for Women: Some Empirical Findings," *Journal of Marriage and the Family* 34 (Feb. 1972), pp. 115–21; Charles W. Mueller and Blair G. Campbell, "Female Occupational Achievement and Marital Status: A Research Note," *Journal of Marriage and the Family* 39 (Aug. 1977), pp. 587–93; and Gillian Stevens and Monica Boyd, "The Importance of Mother: Labor Force Participation and Intergenerational Mobility of Women," *Social Forces* 59 (Aug. 1977), pp. 575–85.

23. Alan C. Acock and John N. Edwards, "Egalitarian Sex-Role Attitudes and Female Income," *Journal of Marriage and the Family* 44 (Aug. 1982), pp. 581–89.

24. Ann P. Parelius, "Emerging Sex-Role Attitudes, Expectations, and Strains Among College Women," *Journal of Marriage and the Family* 37 (Feb. 1975), pp. 146–53.

and 1974. This study also found that the changes had occurred equally among high-status and low-status women.[25]

Rexroat and Shehan analyzed longitudinal data from surveys first taken in 1968.[26] The women in these surveys, aged 22 to 24 in 1968, were asked whether or not they expected to be employed when they were 35 years old. Only 37 percent answered yes to this question at that time. Years later, when they became 35 years old, 63 percent of them actually were in the labor force. Moreover, the authors found that the women anticipated the changes in their work roles at age 35 because the percentage who planned to be full-time housewives declined steadily from 63 percent in 1968 to 34 percent in 1975.

Studies assessing male sex-role attitudes indicate that men who favor role equality for men and women simply may be paying lip service to liberal attitudes.[27] Although the college men in these studies favored equality for women in occupational, economic, and social spheres, the majority of them expect their own wives to be traditionally oriented women whose main concerns are the home and family.

These studies indicate that the differing sex-role expectations of men and women carry the potential for strain in the marital relationship. As we shall see, this potential is evident even in premarital relationships. We turn now to an exploration of the dating, sexual, and cohabiting experiences of young men and women.

DATING

Students may be surprised to learn that dating is a relatively recent phenomenon in the United States. It is believed to have originated in the 1920s when urban living, the automobile, and increases in coeducational colleges gave young men and women the freedom and opportunity to participate in leisure-time activities before marriage.

25. Karen Oppenheim Mason, John L. Czajka, and Sara Arber, "Change in U.S. Women's Sex-Role Attitudes, 1964–1974," *American Sociological Review* 41 (Aug. 1976), pp. 573–96. See also Gary Lee Bowen and Dennis K. Orthner, "Sex-Role Congruency and Marital Quality," *Journal of Marriage and the Family* 45 (Feb. 1983), pp. 223–30; Donna Brogan and Nancy G. Kutner, "Measuring Sex-Role Orientation: A Normative Approach," *Journal of Marriage and the Family* 38 (Feb. 1976), pp. 31–41; and Ruth C. Cronkite, "The Determinants of Spouses' Normative Preferences for Family Roles," *Journal of Marriage and the Family* 39 (Aug. 1977), pp. 575–85.
26. Cynthia Rexroat and Constance L. Shehan, "Expected Versus Actual Work Roles of Women," *American Sociological Review*, forthcoming.
27. Mirra Komarovsky, "Cultural Contradictions and Sex Roles: The Masculine Case," *American Journal of Sociology* 78 (Jan. 1973), pp. 873–84; and Marie Withers Osmond and Patricia Yancey Martin, "Sex and Sexism: A Comparison of Male and Female Sex-Role Attitudes," *Journal of Marriage and the Family* 37 (Nov. 1975), pp. 744–58. See also Brent S. Roper and Emily Labeff, "Sex Roles and Feminism Revisited: An Intergenerational Comparison," *Journal of Marriage and the Family* 39 (Feb. 1977), pp. 113–19.

The Traditional Dating System

As far back as the 1940s, young children had boy friends and girl friends, and they "dated" in imitation of the somewhat more sophisticated patterns of adolescents. Several studies showed, for example, that the more adventurous youngsters of both sexes began dating by the ages of 10 to 12.[28] Arbitrarily, we shall refer to the activities of these youngsters and those through high school as early dating.

Norms Governing Early Dating. Many students may be surprised to learn that parents a generation ago had as many misgivings concerning the dating of their children as today's parents have about premarital sex and living together. Parents saw the less desirable aspects of dating and viewed it both as risky and as poor preparation for marriage. Young people themselves often acted in terms of two conflicting sets of norms, one set explicit and the other set implicit.

Insight into how the system worked may be facilitated by pointing out that most boys and girls faced dating with some trepidation. Studies demonstrated that up to two thirds of the members of both sexes were shy, self-conscious, ill at ease, and felt inadequate as dating partners.[29]

Consciously, most young people sought to use dating to become widely acquainted with members of the opposite sex and to develop standards for what they would desire eventually in marriage partners. Studies showed, for example, that the traits desired in dating partners were essentially the same ones that their parents believed to be important. They included such things as being dependable, trustworthy, considerate, and pleasant; taking pride in one's appearance; desiring a normal family life; acting one's own age; and being clean in speech and action.[30] Thus, the formal norms reflected a conscious awareness of the relationship between early dating, later pairing off, and marriage.

28. Alan E. Bayer, "Early Dating and Early Marriage," *Journal of Marriage and the Family* 30 (Nov. 1968), pp. 628–32; Carlfred B. Broderick and Stanley E. Fowler, "New Patterns of Relationships Between the Sexes Among Preadolescents," *Marriage and Family Living* 23 (Feb. 1961), p. 29; William J. Cameron and William F. Kenkel, "High School Dating: A Study in Variation," *Marriage and Family Living* 22 (Feb. 1960), pp. 74–76; and S. Parvez Wakil, "Campus Dating: An Exploratory Study of Cross-National Relevance," *Journal of Comparative Family Studies* 4 (Autumn 1973), pp. 286–94.

29. Warren Breed, "Sex, Class and Socialization in Dating," *Marriage and Family Living* 18 (May 1956), p. 144; Carlfred B. Broderick, and Jean Weaver, "The Perceptual Context of Boy-Girl Communication," *Journal of Marriage and the Family* 30 (Nov. 1968), pp. 618–27; and John R. Crist, "High School Dating as a Behavior System," *Marriage and Family Living* 15 (Feb. 1953), p. 25.

30. Harold T. Christensen and Kathryn P. Johnsen, *Marriage and the Family*, New York: Ronald Press, 1971, pp. 160–63; and Lester E. Hewitt, "Student Perceptions of Traits Desired in Themselves as Dating and Marriage Partners," *Marriage and Family Living* 20 (Nov. 1958), pp. 344–49.

Alongside these explicit norms, however, was another implicit set, the function of which was to facilitate competition for status within each sex and between the sexes. Young people competed not only for grades and possessions but also for success with the opposite sex. Even then, long before the youth counterculture, the values of youth deviated substantially from those of their parents. Boys could acquire status by dating the prettiest, most popular, most wholesome girls in the class, but they might acquire even more status by dating the girls who liked to neck and with whom they might score. Similarly, girls competed with other girls to date the outstanding boys in the class, but they also gained status by showing that they could date "dangerous" boys and handle them without giving in.[31]

College Dating. The most perceptive analyst of traditional dating patterns among young adults, particularly college students, was Willard Waller. First of all, Waller distinguished between dating and courtship.[32] Dating, he said, allowed a period of dalliance and experimentation between the sexes. Couples were encouraged to associate under all of the conditions that, in other times and places, had led directly into marriage. The norms governing dating, however, defined it as an end in itself. Fun rather than marriage was the intended outcome.

Prominent in dating was the seeking of what Waller called "thrills," physiological stimulation, and the release of tension. Settings and activities conductive to thrill seeking included dancing, petting, necking, the automobile, the amusement park, and drinking and attending the movies. The thrills sought were alleged to vary somewhat between the sexes. Beyond the general excitement widely sought by the young, men were inclined to seek thrills in sex. College-age women were less often interested in sex for its own sake. They had been taught that they must resist involvement in it. Women often were intensely interested in dating itself and in other rewards that dating brought them.

What frequently developed was a more or less explicit bargaining relationship. The man provided the woman with the satisfactions she wanted from dating, in the expectation that she would reward him with equivalent necking and petting on the way home.

31. See Jerold S. Heiss, "Variations in Courtship Progress Among High School Students," *Marriage and Family Living* 22 (May 1960), pp. 165–70; Robert D. Herman, "The 'Going Steady' Complex: A Re-Examination," *Marriage and Family Living* 17 (Feb. 1955), pp. 36–40; Charles W. Hobart, "Emancipation from Parents and Courtship in Adolescents," *Pacific Sociological Review* 1 (Spring 1958), pp. 25–29; E. A. Smith, *American Youth Culture: Group Life in Teenage Society*, New York: The Free Press, 1962; and James S. Wittman, Jr., "Dating Patterns of Rural and Urban Kentucky Teenagers," *Family Coordinator* 20 (Jan. 1971), pp. 63–66.
32. Willard Waller, "The Rating and Dating Complex," *American Sociological Review* 2 (Oct. 1937), pp. 727–34.

What women wanted from dating was to advance themselves in the competition for status with other women and to form relationships with more desirable men. The achievement of these aims required the man to spend money. He needed an automobile if he was to take the woman to fashionable dating places and in a fashion that would attract the desired attention. Both the car and the dating cost money; and the most desirable dating activities usually cost the most money. Although to make it explicit would have called forth a stout denial from both parties, the implicit assumption was that the more money the man spent (the better time he showed the girl), the more disposed the girl should be to show him affection later on.

Implicit in this bargaining relationship was a certain latent antagonism between the dating partners. Each sought the best bargain possible and—to a degree—each distrusted the other. This antagonism was illustrated by some of the stereotypes each sex held of the other. Thus, women often likened men to the octopus—all arms and hands seeking to intrude and overwhelm. In turn men stereotyped women as gold diggers—selfish, grasping creatures interested only in the money that they could induce their dates to spend. These stereotypes lurked below the surface and threatened to come out whenever either partner got the worst of it.

According to Waller, the bargaining worked out equitably in many cases and became the basis for a series of commitments that transformed dating into courtship and eventually led to marriage. Often, however, the bargaining was not equal and led to exploitation of one partner.

If the man had more bargaining power than his date, he was in a position to exploit her sexually. He demanded necking and petting; the woman could either acquiesce or give up the relationship. Similarly, if the woman had superior bargaining power, she could induce her date to take her where she wanted to go, when she wanted to go, and to spend money. Moreover, she was relatively free to concentrate on attracting men who were more desirable than her present dating partner.

Waller formalized this competitive-exploitative dating into what he called the "rating and dating complex." The rating and dating complex described the classification of students according to their desirability as dating partners, the pairing off among them, and the resulting interaction on dates. The desirability of men was determined by such things as fraternity membership, a car, spending money, being a good dancer, dressing well, and being smooth in manners and appearance. Fraternity men ranked higher than nonfraternity men, and the fraternities themselves carried different status, with some fraternities ranking higher than others. Similarly, having an automobile was better than not having access to one. A new car was better than an old one, and a new sports car was better yet. The more the man approximated the campus ideal,

the higher his status; and the more money at his disposal, the more successfully he could compete.

The traits establishing the desirability of women were similar. Sorority membership helped, and a top sorority was better than a lower one.
Appearance and physical beauty were more important for women; the
prettier and more shapely the woman, the more desirable she was as a
date. She, too, should be a good dresser and able to dance well. Perhaps
most important of all for women was their popularity. Men competed
to date the women other men wanted to date.

One further important characteristic for both sexes was the possession
of a good "line," a pattern of verbal banter used to flatter, tease, and
heighten the interest of the other. Each partner worked to induce the
other to become emotionally involved without himself or herself becoming involved in any way. The better one's line, the higher he or she
ranked on the dating desirability scale.

Rating in dating was not altogether an individual matter. Rather,
there existed an informal hierarchy on the campus, analogous to the
class system in the larger society. Some people ranked at the very top of
the dating desirability scale. Waller placed such men and women in a
hypothetical Class A. Somewhat farther down the scale, there was a
Class B, and then a Class C, Class D, and so on. At the bottom of the
scale were people who were socially and physically unattractive.[33]

The rating and dating system functioned most smoothly, according
to Waller, when people did date at their own levels.[34] In this instance,
the dating partners were likely to have approximately equal bargaining
power, reducing the probability that either partner would be in a posi-

33. See Mark Krain, Drew Cannon, and Jeffrey Bagford, "Rating-Dating or Simply Pres-
tige Homogamy? Data on Dating in the Greek System on a Midwestern Campus," *Jour-
nal of Marriage and the Family* 39 (Nov. 1977), pp. 663-74; Richard F. Larson and
Gerald R. Leslie, "Prestige Influences in Serious Dating Relationships," *Social Forces* 47
(Dec. 1968), pp. 195-202; Gene N. Levine and Leila A. Sussman, "Social Class and
Sociability," *American Journal of Sociology* 64 (Jan. 1960), pp. 391-99; Everett M.
Rogers and A. Eugene Havens, "Prestige Rating and Mate Selection on a College Cam-
pus," *Marriage and Family Living* 22 (Feb. 1960), pp. 55-59; and Eldon E. Snyder, "So-
cioeconomic Variations, Values, and Social Participation Among High School Students,"
Journal of Marriage and the Family 28 (May 1966), pp. 174-76.
34. Waller's theses provoked many attempts at empirical testing. See Robert O. Blood,
Jr., "Uniformities and Diversities in Campus Dating Preferences," *Marriage and Family
Living* 18 (Feb. 1956), pp. 37-45; Reuben Hill, "Campus Norms in Mate Selection,"
Journal of Home Economics 37 (Nov. 1945), pp. 554-58; John W. Hudson, and Lura F.
Henze, "Campus Values in Mate Selection: A Replication," *Journal of Marriage and the
Family* 31 (Nov. 1969), pp. 772-75; Marvin R. Koller, "Some Changes in Courtship Be-
havior in Three Generations of Ohio Women," *American Sociological Review* 16 (June
1951), pp. 366-70; Eleanor Smith and J. H. G. Monane, "Courtship Values in a Youth
Sample," *American Sociological Review* 18 (Dec. 1953), pp. 635-40; William M. Smith,
Jr., "Rating and Dating: A Restudy," *Marriage and Family Living* 14 (Nov. 1952), pp.
312-17; and S. Parvez Wakil, "Campus Mate Selection Preferences: A Cross-National
Comparison," *Social Forces* 51 (June 1973), pp. 471-76.

tion to exploit the other. Because they had equal bargaining power, each commitment to the relationship made by one partner was contingent on a compensating commitment made by the other partner, and the relationship progressed relatively rapidly toward marriage.

Not all dating, of course, took place within levels of the hierarchy; occasionally, people dated up or down. People who dated downward suffered loss of prestige for so doing, but they also placed themselves in a better competitive position vis-à-vis the dating partner. Thus, the high-status man who dated a lower-ranking woman could demand more sexual favors from her. If she wished to continue the relationship, she had to accede to his demands. In the same way, a high-status woman who dated a lower-status man was relieved of some of the obligation for necking and petting that she might otherwise feel. She could use her escort manipulatively to take her places, while she established a relationship with a higher-status man.

In brief, dating outside one's own level was conducive to exploitation of the lower-status partner. Waller formalized this idea as the "principle of least interest."[35] The principle of least interest holds that control in a relationship redounds to the one who has the least interest in continuing the relationship. Because this person has less to lose by discontinuing the relationship, demands can be made on the other partner. The partner who has more to lose by discontinuing the relationship often has no choice but to yield.

Lower-status partners who were exploited in a relationship might suffer personality damage as a result. Sooner or later, they had to face up to the fact that they were being exploited and revise their self-concepts downward. Even if they chose to break the relationship rather than to continue to submit to exploitation, they could not escape the definition that they were used by the other partner.[36] Some of the man haters or woman haters on any campus probably were people who had reacted

35. See also Kenneth N. Eslinger, Alfred C. Clarke, and Russell R. Dynes, "The Principle of Least Interest, Dating Behavior, and Family Integration Settings," *Journal of Marriage and the Family* 34 (May 1972), pp. 269-72; and James K. Skipper, Jr., and Gilbert Nass, "Dating Behavior: A Framework for Analysis and an Illustration," *Journal of Marriage and the Family* 28 (Nov. 1966), pp. 412-20.

36. The patterns used by the sexes in confronting exploitation differed and reflected the different operation of the masculine and feminine subcultures. The man who had to face the fact that his date had been using him was likely to go to his peer group and share his anguish with them. His friends were likely to identify with his plight, to sympathize, and to afford him catharsis. He felt better for having gotten it off his chest, in finding that his buddies had similar experiences, and in having reestablished solidarity with them. His buddies, in addition to sharing his contempt for the girl, might decide that it was their collective obligation to revenge themselves on her.

In contrast, the girl who was sexually exploited was less free to seek the support of girl friends. The traditional feminine subculture did not blame the boy who did the exploiting, but the girl who permitted it. Thus, the girl was denied the group support the boy had.

to earlier exploitation by being defensive, thus protecting themselves against exploitation in the future. Their defensiveness testified to a low self-concept and also denied them the rewards of dating.

In one respect dating outside of one's own level proved quite functional for the individual and for the society at large. Such cross-class dating opened an avenue of upward social mobility to lower-status women. Men dated lower-status women—more often than women dated lower-status men—for the sexual advantages in such relationships. That college men dated town girls for this purpose was well known around many campuses.

At first, it appears that the advantages were all on the side of the man; and it is true that a great deal of sexual exploitation took place. However, some lower-status women more or less consciously risked exploitation in the hope that the men would become emotionally involved and that the relationships might lead to marriage. Because the social class of the couple was determined largely through the man, the woman had a great deal to gain in such relationships. It was not entirely unknown for women deliberately to become pregnant to make sure that the relationship led to marriage.

In the society at large, such cross-class dating helped to preserve the fluidity of the social-class system. If the rating and dating complex served perfectly to restrict dating to persons of the same class level, it would have worked to make class lines more rigid and to restrict opportunities for upward mobility. As it was, the risk of exploitation sometimes was weighed against the chance of marrying into a higher class.

Waller's analysis of dating and his analysis of emotional involvement were not separable. Courtship, he said, grows out of dating as one or both partners become emotionally involved. The dating game, it will be recalled, called for each partner to titillate the other's emotions but for both partners to resist involvement. Many relationships remained at this level for some time. Each partner, however, to some degree, pretended greater involvement than he or she actually felt. Especially did the man attempt to convince the woman that he had fallen in love with her and, by this pretense, invited her to reciprocate. Under these circumstances, either partner might actually become involved and, when they did, a different pattern of interaction ensued.

Emotional involvement tended to lead the other partner, whether deliberately or not, into being exploitative. This is consistent with the principle of least interest—whoever is least interested in the relation tends to control it. In the ideal situation, the same process was going on in both partners at the same time, only neither knew it. The artificiality of the "line" resulted in both partners being kept unsure of the other's true feelings. They continued in this fashion for a while, with each fear-ing to be exploited and hoping that they were not. Tension built until suddenly it came out in a lovers' quarrel—the essence of which was the open accusation of exploitation, the function of which was to redefine the relationship at a new level.

We should point out here that the young men and women who were caught up in this intrigue consciously sought trustworthiness, consideration, and dependability in their marriage partners. When either the man or woman was confronted with accusations of exploitation, they were likely to deny it—to themselves as well as to the partners. In lovers' quarrels, the cards probably were stacked in favor of both partners making further avowals of love and serious intent.[37]

With the resolution of this crisis, each partner gained security in the relationship, and the intimacy between the partners increased. The relationship moved along on a fairly even keel for a time until one or both partners again became fearful of the extent of the other's involvement. Another quarrel then ensued, the relationship was redefined at a deeper level of involvement, and so on and on until it reached marriage. Either partner might arrive at marriage without knowing quite how he or she got there or whether, indeed, he or she intended this outcome.

Central to Waller's analysis of courtship was the concept of "idealization." He believed that each partner tended to idealize the other; that under the influence of the "line," the partners created idealized images of others as they would have liked them to be. The man presented to the woman only that portion of his personality that was consistent with his idealized image of her. She in turn idealized him and behaved toward him selectively. Each reinforced the other's lack of objectivity, and they created a private world. Here emerges whatever truth there is in the cliché that "love is blind." Waller described love as sentiment formation overcoming objectivity. The couple's absorption in one another becomes an *egoisme à deux* that borders on *folie à deux*. Outsiders may see more clearly than the couple involved but, assuming that the rela-

---

37. An interesting question is the degree to which the involvement led to the quarrel, which then only made the involvement a matter of record, and the degree to which the involvement actually grew out of the quarrel and the subsequent avowal of love. It is not difficult to imagine, for example, that the man actually had been exploiting the woman sexually. In accord with the masculine subculture, he might have been somewhat aware of what he was doing. In accord with the norms of family and community, however, he might avoid being too conscious of this exploitation. When the woman confronted him in a lovers' quarrel with her suspicions that he was using her, what she really did was to reinforce the family and community norms. The surprised young man could hardly do other than to deny exploitation and to profess love. Later on, he might think to himself, "You know, until tonight, I never realized that I loved her." Or, if he was a bit more sophisticated, he might think, "I wonder if I really do love her." If this analysis is correct, it may help explain the lingering feelings of doubt that many young men and women had as they approached marriage.

tionship is a socially acceptable one, they ordinarily throw their support behind the relationship by treating the man and woman as a couple and helping to move them toward marriage.

Emerging Dating Patterns

Although the competitive and exploitative aspects of dating described by Waller may still occur in the contemporary dating scene, it is probable that traditional patterns are giving way to new sets of roles and norms. Little empirical information exists on dating in the 1980s, but there are indications that the dating relations between young men and women are becoming more friendship oriented and egalitarian.

To some degree, spontaneous group activity has replaced the formal dating patterns of earlier generations. Pairing off still occurs, however, and as people move into adulthood, there is more activity by pairs and more of what is recognizable as dating. Insight into the changes that have been taking place among college students is provided by a study of the Harvard University classes of 1964 and 1974.

Students were asked to rank six reasons for dating: recreation, having an understanding listener, sex, finding a wife, being seen with girls who would enhance one's reputation, and finding a woman friend. They were also asked to rate qualities of a good date such as being uninhibited, artistic, altruistic, and being intelligent and showing it. Finally, they rated dating activities as to importance. Activities rated included sitting around talking, watching TV, going to nightclubs, attending lectures, engaging in sports, taking walks, and making love.[38]

Based on responses of the class of 1964, four dating patterns were identified. In the *companion* pattern, emphasis was on informal pair activities and finding a friend and sympathetic listener. These were friendships in which the activities were private and intimate. *Instrumental* relationships approximated the traditional dating relationship, with emphasis on sexual conquest and the enhancement of one's reputation. The women were taken to dances, nightclubs, football games, and so on, where they could be seen and appreciated. In what researchers labeled the *traditional* pattern, the most important goal was to find a wife. Women of good reputation, sexual inhibition, and comparable social status were sought. Finally, the *intellectual* dating pattern may be most common at elite colleges. In it, emphasis was on finding a woman who was the man's intellectual equal and sharing intellectual discussions with her.

38. Rebecca S. Vreeland, "Sex at Harvard," *Sexual Behavior* (Feb. 1972), pp. 3–10.

The results from the class of 1974 showed that changes had occurred over the decade. The companion pattern still emphasized finding a friend, but the variety of activities had broadened; recreational activities of many sorts were now engaged in together. The intellectual dating pattern had not changed much, except that it now seemed to be less of a defensive mechanism for brilliant, but socially inadequate men.

The instrumental dating pattern had changed substantially. There was less emphasis on showing off conquests and more emphasis on political activities, taking drugs, and making love. The bad-girl syndrome was still there, but the emphasis was now on being swingers rather than studs. The traditional dating pattern had changed most of all, with men generally no longer being interested in socially acceptable women, but being attracted to women who are liberated and unconventional. They now wanted women who would support their own opposition to traditional social patterns.

These changes in the four dating patterns do not tell us what proportions of the men follow the various patterns and, indeed, the study does not provide us with hard data on that matter. We are told that the instrumental and intellectual patterns have not changed much in popularity, whereas the popularity of the companion pattern has increased greatly. The traditional pattern appears to have declined almost to zero.[39]

Other studies provide evidence that young people are becoming increasingly more egalitarian in their attitudes toward sex roles and the balance of power in dating relations.[40] Along with the shifts in attitudes toward dating and dating partners, there is evidence that norms concerning behavior patterns may be changing as well. The traditional dating system held that it was the prerogative of men both to initiate and pay the expenses of dates. The modern dating scene finds that women increasingly are participating in both these areas[41] and that men are even more supportive than women of females initiating and financing dates.[42]

39. *Ibid.*, p. 7.
40. Michael J. Gordon, "Was Waller Ever Right? The Rating and Dating Complex Reconsidered," *Journal of Marriage and the Family* 43 (Feb. 1981), pp. 67–76; Sally L. Hansen, "Dating Choices of High School Students," *Family Coordinator* 26 (April 1977), pp. 133–38; Letitia Anne Peplau, "Power in Dating Relations," in Freeman, *op. cit.*, pp. 106–21; and Zick Rubin, Charles T. Hill, Letitia Anne Peplau, and Christine Dunkel-Schetter, "Self-Disclosure in Dating Couples: Sex Roles and the Ethic of Openness," *Journal of Marriage and the Family* 42 (May 1980), pp. 305–17.
41. Sheila K. Korman, "Nontraditional Dating Behavior: Date Initiation and Date Expense Sharing by Feminists and Nonfeminists," *Family Relations* 32 (Oct. 1983), pp. 575–81; and Sheila K. Korman and Gerald R. Leslie, "The Relationship of Feminist Ideology and Date Expense-Sharing to Perceptions of Sexual Aggression in Dating," *Journal of Sex Research* 18 (May 1982), pp. 114–29.
42. Elizabeth Rice Allgeier, "The Influence of Androgynous Identification on Heterosexual Relationships," *Sex Roles* 7 (March 1981), pp. 321–30.

PREMARITAL SEX

Various aspects of human sexuality have long been sources of curiosity, speculation, titillation, wonder, and concern among the masses. One aspect of sexuality that has gained an enormous amount of attention in the last few decades is premarital sexual behavior.

Traditional Premarital Sexual Patterns

Most sexual involvements before marriage have occurred in the context of their broader associations in dating and courtship. These processes began, for many people, early in childhood and proceeded in fairly regular stages toward adult relationships and marriage.

Preadolescent Sexual Play. That some boys and girls display signs of sexual arousal almost from birth and engage in sexual behavior before puberty are now widely accepted. Over three decades ago, Kinsey reported that approximately 10 percent of boys were engaging in sex play by age 5, and more than 35 percent by age 10. Of older boys and men, 57 percent recalled sexual play before adolescence.[43] Among girls, he found that 4 percent were responding sexually by 5 years of age, 16 percent by age 10, and 27 percent before adolescence. Fully 14 percent of the girls had reached orgasm by age 13.[44]

Preadolescent sexual play can be solitary, homosexual, or heterosexual. Kinsey reported that about 20 percent of boys began to masturbate by age 12 and that during adolescence the figure rose to over 90 percent. Masturbation was the most common source of first ejaculation and remained the commonest source of sexual outlet during early adolescence.[45] Some 12 percent of Kinsey's female sample had masturbated to orgasm by age 12, and by age 15 the figure had climbed to 20 percent.

An interesting comparison, although it goes beyond preadolescence, is that the total incidence of female masturbation reached only 62 percent, compared to over 90 percent among males. Moreover, the proportion of males who masturbated was highest during the late teens and declined thereafter, whereas the proportion of females who masturbated increased up to middle age.[46] Masturbation was also the technique

43. Alfred C. Kinsey, Wardell B. Pomeroy, and Clyde E. Martin, *Sexual Behavior in the Human Male,* Philadelphia: W. B. Saunders, 1948, pp. 162–65.
44. Alfred C. Kinsey, Wardell B. Pomeroy, Clyde E. Martin, and Paul H. Gebhard, *Sexual Behavior in the Human Female,* Philadelphia: W. B. Saunders, 1953, pp. 103–5. See also Carlfred B. Broderick and George P. Rowe, "A Scale of Preadolescent Heterosexual Development," *Journal of Marriage and the Family* 30 (Feb. 1968), pp. 97–101.
45. *Ibid.,* p. 173.
46. *Ibid.* For more recent data, see Ibtihaj Arafat and Wayne L. Cotton, "Masturbation Practices of Males and Females," *Journal of Sex Research* 10 (Nov. 1974), pp. 293–307.

through which the highest proportion of women were able to reach orgasm. Of the 62 percent of women who ultimately masturbated, 58 percent also reached orgasm. No other technique, including marital coitus, produced such a high proportion of orgasmic response.[47]

Among preadolescent boys, homosexual play was actually more common than heterosexual play. Kinsey attributed this to the greater accessibility of boys to other boys than to girls, to young boys' disdain for girls, and to the greater curiosity of boys about their genitalia. The incidence of girls who experienced homosexual play before adolescence, 33 percent,[48] actually exceeded the proportion who reported sexual arousal before adolescence, and it reflects a fundamental fact about female sexual behavior: it need not reflect, or even be accompanied by, sexual arousal. At these early ages, the motivations often were those of simple nonerotic curiosity. Only a minority of boys or girls carried their homosexual experimentation into adolescence or adulthood.

In all, Kinsey found preadolescent heterosexual play in about 40 percent of his male histories and in about 30 percent of his female histories. Much of this play, however, was not clearly separable from other forms of play in which children imitate adult behavior, and much of it was not overtly erotic. The doctor games, and mother and father games that were typical often were carried through without sexual arousal on the part of any of the participants. Such nonerotic play shaded off into frankly sexual play and attempts at intercourse.

Heterosexual Petting. In adolescence, male sexual play became geared toward sexual arousal and satisfaction. The incidence and nature of petting were found to be closely related to educational level, with 84 percent of grade-school-level males and 92 percent of high school and college-level males involved before marriage. Among the males with grade-school educations, petting tended to be a brief prelude to coitus, whereas among the better educated, it often was prolonged without ever resulting in intercourse. Orgasm from petting occurred among 16 percent of the grade-school-level males, 32 percent of the high school-level males, and 61 percent of the college-level males who were not married by the age of 30.[49]

The statistics on petting among females are not strictly comparable to those among males, but show the proportion of females who became involved to be related to age, and to the behavior of the men involved. Approximately 40 percent of Kinsey's female sample had petting experience by 15 years of age, between 69 and 95 percent had experience

47. Kinsey, Pomeroy, and Martin, *op. cit.,* p. 168.
48. Kinsey, Pomeroy, Martin, and Gebhard, *op. cit.,* p. 114.
49. Kinsey, Pomeroy, and Martin, *op. cit.,* p. 537.

by age 18, and almost 100 percent of the women petted before marriage.
That women sometimes participated to please their male companions
was shown by the fact that only 80 percent of the sample reported that
they had been erotically aroused in petting. Thirty-nine percent of the
women had achieved orgasm at least once.[50]

Petting by women was not related to educational level as among men,
but was related to age at marriage. The higher-educated women who
had more petting experience also married later. Finally, although there
was no relationship between petting experience and religious faith
(Catholic, Protestant, Jewish), religiosity did make a difference. Devout
Catholics and Protestants were less likely to become involved in petting
than were inactive members of either faith.[51]

Premarital Intercourse. Although the date is arbitrary, we shall use
the year 1965 as the dividing line between traditional and contemporary
patterns of premarital sexual intercourse. A score of major studies provide estimates of the incidence of premarital intercourse for men and
women from the 1920s to the 1960s. The Kinsey statistics, again, are the
most comprehensive available and are generally consistent with those
provided by other investigators.

As with petting, premarital intercourse among men was related to
educational level. Among men who went to college, only 67 percent had
intercourse before marriage; among those who did not go beyond high
school, the figure was 84 percent; and among those who stopped with
grade school, the proportion climbed to 98 percent. It appears that, at
lower social levels, coitus was considered to be the "normal" way to
pursue sexual interests, and most men became involved during their
teens. At the upper levels, however, where greater value was placed on
virginity, petting often served as a substitute for coitus.[52]

Although the proportions of men having premarital intercourse did
not change significantly over the 40 years under discussion, the proportion of women involved changed markedly, with the major change having occurred among women who reached adulthood at, or shortly after,
World War I. Between 1915 and 1930, the percentage of women who
had intercourse before marriage increased from approximately 15 percent to 30 to 35 percent. In Kinsey's total sample approximately 50
percent had intercourse before marriage. Most was confined to the year
or two just before marriage, and a good proportion was had with the
fiancé only. Kinsey reported that 46 percent had intercourse with the

50. Kinsey, Pomeroy, Martin, and Gebhard, *op. cit.,* p. 233.
51. *Ibid.,* p. 278.
52. Kinsey, Pomeroy, and Martin, *op. cit.,* p. 552.

fiancé only, 41 percent with the fiancé and other men, and 13 percent with some other man, not the fiancé.[53]

Again, we find a relationship with religious background. Religiously inactive women were more likely to become involved than were the devout. Among those who had not married by age 35, over 60 percent of inactive Protestants and Jews and 55 percent of inactive Catholics were involved. The corresponding figures for the devout were about 30 percent for Protestants, 24 percent for Catholics.[54]

Beyond providing statistics on premarital intercourse, other studies related sexual experience to dating patterns and love involvement. One study of 1157 students at the University of Florida, for example, found that although most men and women tended to date persons from their own social class and to have their most intimate sexual experience with those persons, of those who did date outside their own class, more of the men had their most intimate experiences with women of a lower social class, whereas most of the women had theirs with men of the same or a higher class.[55] These general findings were confirmed in another study at a midwestern university: the incidence of premarital intercourse was highest among couples where the husband came from a higher social class than his wife, was intermediate where they were of the same social class, and was lowest where the wife was from the higher social class.[56]

The Florida research also classified dating relationships into those with acquaintances, friends, and lovers; classified respondents according to the most intimate sex behavior they had experienced; and classified them according to "personal code" or the most intimate behavior they considered permissible with an acquaintance, friend, or lover. Far more

53. Kinsey, Pomeroy, Martin, and Gebhard, *op. cit.*, pp. 292-98.

54. *Ibid.*, p. 304. These general findings have been confirmed in other studies. See Jerry D. Cardwell, "The Relationship Between Religious Commitment and Premarital Sexual Permissiveness: A Five Dimensional Analysis," *Sociological Analysis* 30 (Summer 1969), pp. 72-81; Richard R. Clayton, "Religious Orthodoxy and Premarital Sex," *Social Forces* 47 (June 1969), pp. 469-74; Jean Dedman, "The Relationship Between Religious Attitude and Attitude Toward Premarital Sex Relations," *Marriage and Family Living* 21 (May 1959), pp. 171-76; Eugene J. Kanin and David H. Howard, "Postmarital Consequences of Premarital Sex Adjustments," *American Sociological Review* 23 (Oct. 1958), pp. 556-62; Frank Lindenfield, "A Note on Social Mobility, Religiosity, and Students' Attitudes Toward Premarital Sexual Relations," *American Sociological Review* 25 (Feb. 1960), pp. 81-84; E. R. Mahoney, "Religiosity and Sexual Behavior Among Heterosexual College Students," *Journal of Sex Research* 16 (Feb. 1980), pp. 97-113; Alfred J. Prince and Gordon Shipman, "Attitudes of College Students Toward Premarital Sex Experience," *Family Life Coordinator* 6 (June 1958), pp. 57-60; Howard J. Ruppel, Jr., "Religiosity and Premarital Sexual Permissiveness: A Response to the Reiss-Heltsley Debate," *Journal of Marriage and the Family* 32 (Nov. 1970), pp. 647-55; and Gordon Shipman, "The Psychodynamics of Sex Education," *Family Coordinator* 17 (Jan. 1968), pp. 3-12.

55. Winston W. Ehrmann, *Premarital Dating Behavior*, New York: Holt, Rinehart & Winston, 1959, pp. 144-45.

56. Kanin and Howard, *op. cit.*, p. 558.

men had had intercourse with friends and acquaintances (56 and 60 percent, respectively) than had done so with women they loved. Moreover, far more men considered coitus acceptable with friends and acquaintances than with lovers. Among women, the pattern was reversed. Very few women had intercourse with friends or acquaintances (6 percent and 2 percent, respectively), whereas more (17 percent) had done so with men whom they loved. The women believed that intimacy is more acceptable in love relationships, and their behavior closely paralleled their standards.

Both dating and sexual relationships in the traditional system were complicated by these attitudinal differences between men and women and by their elaboration into a distinctive masculine subculture. This masculine subculture exercised an imperious force in most boys' lives, which most girls—because there was no truly feminine equivalent of it—seldom understood. The most prominent symbol of the masculine subculture among boys and young men probably was the bull session.

Although other things were discussed and other functions were served, the primary functions of young male bull sessions were three. First, they provided opportunity to participate vicariously in, and to receive erotic arousal from, one another's sex lives. A typical procedure was for each boy to tell of a sexual exploit, embellishing it with exciting detail. As the session progressed, each narrator tried to top his predecessor, making himself appear more experienced than the others. This, then, was the second function; to permit each boy to enhance his conception of himself as a male, at the expense of the others.[57]

It might be appropriate here to point out that the primary ingredient in most bull sessions really was "bull." Honesty was not one of the virtues of a bull session. Honesty would have seriously hampered the first function of providing erotic stimulation, for most of the boys had neither as many nor as exciting experiences as they reported. With frequent, intense participation in bull sessions, however, the experiences that were fabricated took on reality for the teller until, after a time, he was not sure himself where experience left off and fantasy began. Each boy was likely to be somewhat aware that he was not wholly honest but, unfortunately, his insight did not enable him to be equally critical of his fellows' accounts. One result was that even while he was enhancing his ego by exaggerating his experiences, he was acquiring an uncomfortable sense of inadequacy by listening to and believing the wilder tales of his companions.

57. For current data bearing on these phenomena, see David G. Berger and Morton G. Wenger, "The Ideology of Virginity," *Journal of Marriage and the Family* 35 (Nov. 1973), pp. 666–76; and Donald E. Carns, "Talking About Sex: Notes on First Coitus and the Double Sexual Standard," *Journal of Marriage and the Family* 35 (Nov. 1973), pp. 677–88.

Thus, the bull session's third function was brought into being. On the fringe of the session were likely to be one or more wide-eyed innocents. These honest boys' inability to get into the swing of things made them the logical scapegoats for the accumulating fears of inadequacy in other members of the group. One of the ringleaders might turn and say something like, "Hey, look at Joe. I'll bet he has never had any." Everyone then jumped on Joe and, by making him feel terribly inexperienced, they relieved somewhat their own feelings of inadequacy. The end result was to leave each boy with the idea that everybody else was making out better than he was and that not only should he get his share but he was not much of a man if he didn't.

One byproduct of the masculine subculture apparently was the sexual victimization of some women on dates. In one midwestern study the researchers distinguished five different degrees of erotic aggressiveness: attempts at necking, petting above the waist, petting below the waist, sexual intercourse, and attempts at sexual intercourse with violence or threats of violence. A total of 56 percent of the women reported that they had been offended by forceful attempts at intercourse and 6 percent by aggressively forceful attempts at intercourse that involved threats or the infliction of pain.[58]

Another finding was a significant association between offensiveness at a mild level of intimacy in casual dating relationships and offensiveness at more intimate levels in engaged relationships. Apparently, an emotional relationship between the man and woman is no protection against sexual aggression. Offenses at the petting levels tended on the average to be repeated twice and, in half of the cases, attempts at intercourse were repeated. Only when attempted intercourse was accompanied by threats or violence were the relationships likely to be broken off.

Less than 6 percent of the offenses were reported to parents or academic authorities. The women were more inclined to reason with and rebuke the offender, and they were more likely to keep secret the offenses at advanced intimacy levels. In a study of offenses at the high school level, Kanin found that women's proneness to sexual aggression was related to the absence of male siblings.[59] Presumably, girls with older brothers are more likely to have some insight into the masculine subculture and are more able to prevent aggression from occurring.

58. Clifford Kirkpatrick and Eugene Kanin, "Male Sex Aggression on a University Campus," *American Sociological Review* 22 (Feb. 1957), pp. 52–58. See also Eugene J. Kanin, "Male Sex Aggression and Three Psychiatric Hypotheses," *Journal of Sex Research* 1 (Nov. 1965), pp. 221–31.
59. Eugene J. Kanin, "Male Aggression in Dating-Courtship Relations," *American Journal of Sociology* 63 (Sept. 1957), pp. 197–204. See also Eugene J. Kanin, "Selected Dyadic Aspects of Male Sex Aggression," *Journal of Sex Research* 5 (Feb. 1969), pp. 12–28.

A study completed at a major southeastern university in 1979 showed that male sexual aggression continues to complicate college dating relationships. Korman found that 63 percent of her sample of 400 women had been sexually offended on dates.[60] Approximately 20 percent of these situations involved attempts at sexual intercourse. Although no data were collected on the number of forceful attempts at intercourse that were successful, it probably would be safe to say that date rapes or attempted rapes are not unknown on college campuses.[61]

Recent research also has found that physical violence between partners is a pervasive occurrence on dates. Makepeace found that approximately one-fifth of the respondents in his study had participated in episodes involving punching, slapping, pushing, and other forms of violence with their dates.[62] Moreover, almost two-thirds of the respondents knew personally someone who had been involved in this kind of interaction. Over 90 percent of the women involved in violent episodes reported themselves the victims of the abuse.

Bernard and Bernard found a slightly higher percentage of their respondents reporting involvement in courtship violence; the 30 percent reporting episodes of violence consisted of 19 percent of the men and 38 percent of the women.[63] The researchers add that a questionnaire administered anonymously resulted in 42 percent of their sample reporting involvement in courtship violence.

Emerging Sexual Norms

In distinguishing between traditional and emerging premarital sexual norms, we arbitrarily selected the year 1965 as the dividing point. Prior to 1965, the gradual increases in the number of young people having intercourse were largely the result of couples becoming involved soon before marriage. The dramatic increases that began to show up after 1965, however, reflected significant changes in public attitudes toward premarital sex. A Gallup Poll in August 1973, for example, compared atti-

60. Sheila K. Korman, *Perceived Offensive Male Sexual Aggression in Dating: Influences of Feminist Ideology and Exchange Relationships*, (Master's thesis): University of Florida, 1980, pp. 80–88.
61. Researchers studying rape and rape victims agree that the chances are better than 50 percent that the rapist will be someone the victim knows—including a date. See Menachim Amir, *Patterns in Forcible Rape*, Chicago: University of Chicago Press, 1971; and Susan Brownmiller, *Against Our Will: Men, Women, and Rape*, New York: Bantam Books, 1975.
62. James M. Makepeace, "Courtship Violence Among College Students," *Family Relations* 30 (Jan. 1981), pp. 97–102. See also James M. Makepeace, "Life Events Stress and Courtship Violence," *Family Relations* 32 (Jan. 1983), pp. 101–9.
63. M. L. Bernard and J. L. Bernard, "Violent Intimacy: The Family as a Model for Love Relationships," *Family Relations* 32 (April 1983), pp. 283–86.

tudes at that time with those reported four years earlier. In 1969, two out of three adults said that premarital sexual relations were wrong. By 1973, 48 percent said they were wrong, but 43 percent gave approval. Age and marital status were related to the opinions given. Only 29 percent of young people aged 18 to 29 said that premarital sex was wrong, and only 27 percent of single persons, compared to 51 percent of married persons, thought so.[64]

A Gallup Poll in 1972 found that most adults believe that teenagers should have access to birth control. More than 70 percent favored nationwide programs of birth control education in the high schools, and 54 percent approved of health programs to give free birth control to teenage girls who request it. Interestingly, Roman Catholics reported attitudes as favorable as those of non-Catholics.

Teenage Sexual Patterns. A study of 4220 Michigan high school students from the eighth grade through the twelfth grade found that 25 percent of the boys and 14 percent of the girls had already had coitus. Among the students who were 17 years old, 33 percent of the boys and 26 percent of the girls had had intercourse. This incidence is lower than Kinsey reported for 17-year-old boys, but more than twice as high as he reported for 17-year-old girls.[65]

Until recently, estimates of the incidence of intercourse among teenagers were suspect because of possible biases in the samples studied. In 1971, 1976, and again in 1979, however, a team of researchers studied national probability samples of never-married girls, age 15 to 19. These samples provided the first reliable national estimates.

The percentages of unmarried women reporting intercourse in 1976 and 1979, by race, are shown in Table 12.1. Almost 19 percent of the 15-year-old girls were sexually experienced in 1976 and, by age 19, the figure rose to over 59 percent. Three years later, in 1979, increases in coital activity can be seen for each age group. The number of sexually experienced 19-year-olds rose almost 10 percent from 1976 to 1979. Sharp differences at every age level appeared between the races, with

64. Gallup Poll, syndicated column, August 12, 1973. See also Danny E. Harrison, Walter H. Bennett, Gerald Globetti, and Majeed Alsikafi, "Premarital Sexual Standards of Rural Youth," *Journal of Sex Research* 10 (Nov. 1974), pp. 266–77.
65. Arthur M. Vener, Cyrus S. Stewart, and David L. Hager, "The Sexual Behavior of Adolescents in Middle America: Generational and American British Comparisons," *Journal of Marriage and the Family* 34 (Nov. 1972), pp. 696–705; and Arthur M. Vener and Cyrus S. Stewart, "Adolescent Sexual Behavior in Middle America Revisited: 1970–1973," *Journal of Marriage and the Family* 36 (Nov. 1974), pp. 728–35. See also Richard R. Clayton and Janet L. Bokemeier, "Premarital Sex in the Seventies," *Journal of Marriage and the Family* 42 (Nov. 1980), pp. 34–50; and Patricia Y. Miller and William Simon, "Adolescent Sexual Behavior: Context and Change," *Social Problems* 22 (Oct. 1974), pp. 58–76.

Table 12.1. Percentages of unmarried women, 15 to 19 years of age, who
have had coitus, by age and race, 1976 and 1979

Age	Black		White		Total	
	1976	*1979*	*1976*	*1979*	*1976*	*1979*
15	38.9	41.4	13.8	18.3	18.6	22.5
16	55.1	50.4	23.7	35.4	28.9	37.8
17	71.0	73.3	36.1	44.1	42.9	48.5
18	76.2	76.3	46.0	52.6	51.4	56.9
19	83.9	88.5	53.6	64.9	59.5	69.0
Total Sample	64.3	64.8	33.6	42.3	39.2	46.0
N	(376)	(455)	(350)	(478)	(726)	(933)

Source: Adapted from Melvin Zelnik and John F. Kantner, "Sexual Activity, Contraceptive Use and Pregnancy Among Metropolitan-Area Teenagers: 1971–1979," *Family Planning Perspectives* 12 (September–October 1980), p. 231. Adapted with permission from
Family Planning Perspectives, Volume 12, Number 5, 1980.

black girls being more experienced. For those aged 15 in 1976, almost
two fifths of black girls, compared to one eighth of white girls, had had
intercourse. By age 19, over four fifths of the black girls and almost
half of the white girls had had coitus.[66] Although discrepancies still
existed between the races in 1979, the growth in overall coital activity
is attributed primarily to increases in the sexual experiences of never-
married white girls. For the total sample, black girls increased their
coital activity by less than 1 percent in the three years from 1976 to
1979, whereas the rate for white girls rose almost 10 percent during the
same time period.

Although, at first glance, these percentages seem high and suggest possible teenage promiscuity, this is not the case. In 1976, almost half the
experienced girls, for example, had not had intercourse during the
month prior to the interview, and another 25 percent had had intercourse only once or twice.[67] There were no appreciable differences in
frequency between black girls and white girls. Moreover, half the girls
had had only one sex partner during their entire lives.

The evidence then shows an increasing incidence of sexual intercourse
among teenagers. It does not, however, support the stereotype of promiscuous, irresponsible behavior. Almost half of the young women used

66. Table 12.1 includes the rates of premarital intercourse for never-married girls only.
The percentages for married women, aged 15 to 19, who have had intercourse before
marriage are much higher: 91.2 percent for blacks and 86.2 percent for whites in 1979.
All figures in this table are for girls living in metropolitan areas only.
67. Melvin Zelnik and John F. Kantner, "Sexual and Contraceptive Experience of
Young Unmarried Women in the United States, 1976 and 1971." *Family Planning Perspectives* 9 (March–April 1977), pp. 55–71.

some method of contraception with their first intercourse and were in relationships that carried mutual commitment between the partners.[68] About 6 in 10 young women reported that they had been engaged to, or were going steady with, their first sexual partner.[69]

College Sexual Patterns. Although the younger girls in the national study were high school girls, many of the 18- and 19-year-olds were college students. Hence, our distinction between teenage and college sexual patterns is blurred. Nevertheless, we should note that the shifts in attitudes toward, and participation in, premarital intercourse already demonstrated for the general population are especially pronounced among college students.

One study gave an attitude scale to college students in 1968 and then gave it to comparable groups of students again in 1972, finding that both sexes showed considerably more liberal attitudes toward premarital coitus in 1972.[70] Other studies showed behavioral changes got under way about 1965. One study compared students at a southern university in 1975 with students at the same university in 1970 and 1965. The three waves of the study showed that the increases in heavy petting and sexual intercourse that were evident between 1965 and 1970 continued through 1975. The increases were larger among women than among men. The percentages engaging in heavy petting, for example, were 71

68. Melvin Zelnik and Farida K. Shah, "First Intercourse Among Young Americans," *Family Planning Perspectives* 15 (March–April 1983), pp. 64–70.

69. One interesting study suggests that pregnancy often is the result of the unavailability of contraceptives and that well-meaning parents who oppose premarital sex hoping to protect their daughters against pregnancy may actually be making them more vulnerable to it. See Frank F. Furstenberg, Jr., "Birth Control Experience Among Pregnant Adolescents: The Process of Unplanned Parenthood," *Social Problems* 19 (Fall 1971), pp. 192–203.

70. James W. Croake and Barbara James, "A Four Year Comparison of Premarital Sexual Attitudes," *Journal of Sex Research* 9 (May 1973), pp. 91–96. For other supporting data, see Robert R. Bell and Jay B. Chaskes, "Premarital Sexual Experience Among Coeds, 1958 and 1968," *Journal of Marriage and the Family* 32 (Feb. 1970), pp. 81–84; William F. Eastman, "First Intercourse," *Sexual Behavior* (March 1972), pp. 22–27; Frank W. Finger, "Changes in Sex Practices and Beliefs of Male College Students Over 30 Years," *Journal of Sex Research* 11 (Nov. 1975), pp. 304–17; Robert A. Lewis, "Parents and Peers: Socialization Agents in the Coital Behavior of Young Adults," *Journal of Sex Research* 9 (May 1973), pp. 156– 70; Eleanore B. Luckey and Gilbert D. Nass, "A Comparison of Sexual Attitudes and Behavior in an International Sample," *Journal of Marriage and the Family* 31 (May 1969), pp. 364–79; Peter O. Peretti, "Premarital Sexual Behavior Between Females and Males of Two Middle-Sized Midwestern Cities," *Journal of Sex Research* 5 (Aug. 1969), pp. 218–25; Ira E. Robinson, Karl King, Charles J. Dudley, and Francis J. Clune, "Change in Sexual Behavior and Attitudes of College Students," *Family Coordinator* 17 (April 1968), pp. 119–23; B. K. Singh, "Trends in Attitudes Toward Premarital Sexual Relations," *Journal of Marriage and the Family* 42 (May 1980), pp. 387–93; and Graham B. Spanier, "Sexualization and Premarital Sexual Behavior," *Family Coordinator* 24 (Jan. 1975), pp. 33–41.

percent for men in 1965 and 80 percent in 1975. Among women there was an increase from 34 percent to 73 percent. The proportions of men with coital experience increased from 65 percent in 1965 to 74 percent in 1975. Among women, there was an increase from 29 percent to 57 percent.[71] A more recent study put the figure for women at over 63 percent.[72]

Most premarital intercourse for women before 1965 appears to have been the result of relationships between soon-to-be-married couples, and much premarital sex today still is of that variety. The dramatic increase since 1965, however, appears to be more the result of intercourse in relationships of affection and intimacy, but where there is no formal or informal commitment to marriage. This was the conclusion of investigators who found that the proportion of nonvirgins at one western university increased from 48 percent to over 60 percent between 1965 and 1970.[73]

The most dramatic and comprehensive findings come from a survey of 2026 people in 24 urban areas conducted for the Playboy Foundation in 1973. They found that premarital intercourse is beginning earlier in life and is occurring more frequently. For men, the chief differences were in age of initiation. More than half of the men with some college education had experienced coitus by age 17, twice as many as Kinsey reported a generation earlier. For single women under 25, about 75 percent had had coitus compared to only 33 percent in Kinsey's day. Among the youngest married women (ages 18 to 24), fully 80 percent had had intercourse before marriage.[74]

NONMARITAL COHABITATION

Even the most casual observer can scarcely avoid knowing that many unmarried couples around college and university campuses these days are living together. The openness with which they do so and the degree

71. Karl King, Jack O. Balswick, and Ira E. Robinson, "The Continuing Premarital Sexual Revolution Among College Females," *Journal of Marriage and the Family* 39 (Aug. 1977), pp. 455–59. For evidence of comparable changes among Canadian students, see Charles W. Hobart, "Sexual Permissiveness in Young English and French Canadian Students," *Journal of Marriage and the Family* 34 (May 1977), pp. 292–303.

72. Ira E. Robinson and Davor Jedlicka, "Change in Sexual Attitudes and Behavior of College Students from 1965 to 1980: A Research Note," *Journal of Marriage and the Family* 44 (Feb. 1982), pp. 237–40.

73. Marvin B. Freedman and Marjorie Lozoff, "Some Statistical Background," *Sexual Behavior* (Nov. 1972), pp. 30–32.

74. *Time*, Oct. 1, 1973, pp. 63–64. For similar findings at a major southern university, see Karl E. Bauman and Robert R. Wilson, "Sexual Behavior of Unmarried University Students in 1968 and 1972," *Journal of Sex Research* 10 (Nov. 1974), pp. 327–33; and J. Richard Udry, Karl E. Bauman, and Naomi M. Morris, "Changes in Premarital Coital Experience of Recent Decade of Birth Cohorts of Urban American Women," *Journal of Marriage and the Family* 37 (Nov. 1975), pp. 783–87.

to which university officials, landlords, and others ignore the matter stands in marked contrast to the situation just a few years ago. It has become so commonplace today that a recent Gallup poll found almost 60 percent of the nation's teenagers approving of people living together before marriage.[75] There are no comprehensive statistics available on how many couples live together, but scattered evidence indicates that the number is sizable and growing.

On the national level, the U.S. Census Bureau reports that the number of single adults living with a member of the opposite sex approximately tripled between 1970 and 1982. In 1982, there were almost 1.9 million such households involving 3.8 million persons. About 25 percent of these couples had one or more children living in the home. Almost half of these people had never been married, and in 63 percent of couples, both partners were under 35 years of age. Lest the proportion of people living together appear greater than it is, it should be pointed out that these households constitute only about 4 percent of all couples. It should be emphasized, too, that some of these people are not lovers, but are roomers, employees, and others.[76]

In a national study of cohabitation, a probability sample of 2510 men between the ages of 20 and 30 were interviewed. Of these men, 18 percent had lived with a woman for six months or more. Only 5 percent were living with someone at the time of the interview. Because many of these men were still young and unmarried, their lifetime figures of cohabitation without marriage probably will be considerably higher.[77]

Careful study has been done of the incidence of dynamics of couples living together around university campuses. One study of 762 students at a large urban northeastern university in 1971 found that approximately one fifth of them were living with a member of the opposite sex. More surprising is the fact that almost four fifths would enter such an arrangement if they had the opportunity. Men and women expressed equally favorable attitudes, whereas older students and those with strong religious backgrounds were less favorable.[78]

At the other end of the country, 29 percent of the men and 18 per-

75. George Gallup, "More Teenagers Accept 'Trial Marriage' Concept," *Gallup Youth Survey*, July 7, 1982.
76. U.S. Bureau of the Census, "Marital Status and Living Arrangements: March 1982," *Current Population Reports*, Series P-20, No. 380 (May 1983), p. 7. See also Judith L. Lyness, Milton E. Lipetz, and Keith E. Davis, "Living Together: An Alternative to Marriage," *Journal of Marriage and the Family* 34 (May 1972), pp. 305-11; and Graham B. Spanier, "Married and Unmarried Cohabitation in the United States: 1980," *Journal of Marriage and the Family* 45 (May 1983), pp. 277-88.
77. Richard R. Clayton and Harwin L. Voss, "Shacking Up: Cohabitation in the 1970s," *Journal of Marriage and the Family* 39 (May 1977), pp. 273-83. See also Paul C. Glick and Graham B. Spanier, *op. cit.*, pp. 19-30.
78. Ibtihaj Arafat and Betty Yorburg, "On Living Together Without Marriage," *Journal of Sex Research* 9 (May 1973), pp. 97-106.

cent of the women in a random sample of 300 southwestern university
students had cohabited. Moreover, almost 60 percent of the men and 35
percent of the women answered yes to the question, "Would you want
to?"[79] Back northeast again, data from two samples of Cornell University students showed 28 percent and 34 percent already having lived together and that 40 percent or more would do so before completing college.[80] Finally, a survey of 1191 students at state universities in seven
different geographic regions showed that about 25 percent, 34 percent
of the men and 23 percent of the women, had lived with someone. Few
regional differences were evident.[81]

Reasons for Living Together

At the most general and idealistic level, young people are disenchanted
with the superficiality of traditional dating and the exploitation of sex.
They strive for realism in their relationships, without the complications
of marriage.[82] Part of it simply is a matter of expediency; the couple
already are having intercourse, and it is too much trouble for one of
them to get up late at night and return home. Other practical reasons
include the fact that it is less expensive, one partner has no place to go
because someone else is living with his or her roommate, there is curiosity about what it would be like, and there is a desire to test the relationship.

Two studies found motivations to vary by sex. In one, 36 percent of
the men said that their primary motivation was sex,[83] and the other study
reported that women are more faithful in living-together arrangements
and are more satisfied with them.[84] Of the women at the northeastern
university, 30 percent reported their primary motivation was marriage;
if they didn't live with him, someone else would. Overall, 80 percent of
the men and over 67 percent of the women said that eventual marriage
was not their goal. What few men did given marriage as a reason were
cynical about it: "You wouldn't buy a new car without trying it out

79. John W. Hudson and Lura F. Henze, "A Note on Cohabitation," *Family Coordinator* 22 (Oct. 1973), p. 495; and "Personal and Family Characteristics of Cohabiting and
Noncohabiting College Students," *Journal of Marriage and the Family* 36 (Nov. 1974),
pp. 722–27.
80. Eleanor D. Macklin, "Heterosexual Cohabitation Among Unmarried College Students," *Family Coordinator* 21 (Oct. 1972), pp. 463–72.
81. Donald W. Bower and Victor A. Christopherson, "University Student Cohabitation:
A Regional Comparison of Selected Attitudes and Behavior," *Journal of Marriage and
the Family* 39 (Aug. 1977), pp. 447–53.
82. David H. Olson, "Marriage of the Future: Revolutionary or Evolutionary Change?"
Family Coordinator 21 (Oct. 1972), pp. 383–93.
83. Arafat and Yorburg, *op. cit.*, p. 101.
84. Hudson and Henze, *op. cit.*

first!" About two thirds of both sexes said that they were not sure of their original motives, and slightly over half did not know whether they would eventually marry one another.[85]

Circumstances of Living Together

Living together is less the result of deliberate planning than of gradually drifting into it. Among the Cornell couples, staying together one night at a time was followed by spending weekends together and then by adding one or more nights in between. The researcher classified couples as living together when they spent four or more nights a week together for three consecutive months.[86]

Most often, the girl partially moves in with her boyfriend in an apartment or house he shares with others. Usually, she keeps her own quarters, keeps some of her clothes there, receives her mail, and eats some meals there. This helps conceal the relationship from her parents, helps her maintain relationships with other women, and provides a refuge when the relationship with the boyfriend is not going well. Among Cornell couples, about half spent seven nights a week together and in the other half, the woman spent occasional nights at her own residence.

When asked about their relationships with the men with whom they were living, about half the Cornell women said that theirs was a strong and exclusive affectionate relationship. They resisted the idea that they were going steady. About one third of the women said that they were also interested in other dating relationships. About 10 percent were tentatively or formally engaged. Most women intended to continue the relationships as long as they were mutually rewarding, many thought of marriage as an ultimate possibility, but most resisted the idea of a definite commitment to marriage.

Few couples fully share finances. The man generally keeps his income, the woman hers, sharing some expenses of food and entertainment. This arrangement symbolizes and ensures the woman's independence. Some household chores such as doing the laundry and shopping are shared, but women still do most of the cleaning and cooking and some of them resent it.[87] Another study found that cohabiting women

---

85. Arafat and Yorburg, *op. cit.*, pp. 101–2.
86. Eleanor D. Macklin, *op. cit.* For a study using a more flexible definition of living together, see Dan J. Peterman, Carl A. Ridley, and Scott M. Anderson, "A Comparison of Cohabiting and Noncohabiting College Students," *Journal of Marriage and the Family* 36 (May 1974), pp. 344–54.
87. See Rebecca Stafford, Elaine Backman, and Pamela Dibona, "The Division of Labor Among Cohabiting and Married Couples," *Journal of Marriage and the Family* 39 (Feb. 1977), pp. 43–57.

compared to noncohabitating women see themselves at a power disadvantage in their relationships.[88]

Advantages and Problems. Most participants in these relationships believe them to be successful, maturing, and pleasant. Even couples especially conscious of problems in their relationships emphasize how much emotional growth they have produced. Most also state that they would not consider marriage without having lived together first.

Many couples also are frank about their problems. Among the Cornell couples, the major emotional problem was the tendency for one or both partners to become overinvolved, overdependent on the relationship, and isolated from other friends. Some people felt "trapped," and others believed that they were being "used" by their partners. Over two thirds of the couples reported no such problems however, and no guilt. Where guilt was found, it most often stemmed from having to conceal the relationship from parents.

About two thirds of the women encountered some sexual problems. Differing degrees of, or periods of, sexual disinterest were reported most frequently, followed closely by lack of orgasm. Fear of pregnancy, in spite of almost universal contraception, was reported in over two fifths of the cases. In spite of the sexual problems, however, more than three-fourths of the women described their relationships as sexually satisfying.

In virtually all studies, relationships with parents are a major problem. Fear of discovery, guilt over deceiving the parents, and ultimatums from parents who learn of the situation, all are common. Over two thirds of the Cornell women had tried to conceal their relationships from parents by not telling them everything, distorting the truth, or by using elaborate schemes to prevent discovery. About half of the women believed that they had been successful in concealing cohabitation, about one fourth were sure their parents knew, and the other one fourth were unsure whether their parents knew. The men's parents were much more likely to know and were less likely to cause problems over it.

Some young people argue that living together permits them to test for compatibility in marriage and that breakups from these relationships are far less traumatic than divorces would be. They maintain that, in the long run, living together may be increasing the quality of marriage. One recent study of 309 married couples in Florida casts doubt on this assertion. DeMaris found that couples who had cohabited before marriage scored significantly lower on a marital adjustment scale than couples

88. Barbara J. Risman, Charles T. Hill, Zick Rubin, and Letitia Anne Peplau, "Living Together in College: Implications for Courtship," *Journal of Marriage and the Family* 43 (Feb. 1981), pp. 77–83.

who had not lived together prior to marriage.[89] Watson, with similar findings, attributes the lower marital adjustment scores of cohabitors to the longer durations of their relationships.[90] Because of their longer experience of shared living, cohabitors may simply be experiencing the decline in marital satisfaction common to married couples beyond the honeymoon phase. Research on these assertions is just beginning, and no definite statements can be made as yet.[91]

SUMMARY

The differential socialization of boys and girls occurs first through the parents and involves both differential treatment and imitation. Both mothers and fathers treat boys and girls differently, reflecting their own conceptions of what boys and girls should be like and responding to cues from the children themselves. It is an interactive situation rather than simply a matter of parents imposing their conceptions on children. By about age three, children have developed a firm sense of themselves as either male or female and identify with the parent of the same sex. Children learn to enact the role appropriate to their own sex and to respond to the role of the opposite sex.

The parental influences are reinforced in school as teachers use sex-stereotyped curriculum materials and as they track boys into certain subjects and girls into others. Even the playground activities of children tend to perpetuate traditional masculine and feminine roles. Research shows systematic differences between boys' and girls' play. Researchers conclude that boys' play prepares them to be successful in the occupational world, whereas girls' play prepares them more for domesticity.

Considerable research has been done on the sex-role expectations of college and university students. Research shows that about half of college women expect to combine occupational careers with marriage and motherhood. Many of these plan careers in nontraditional fields and expect to delay marriage and parenthood until their careers are launched.

89. Alfred DeMaris, *The Influence of Premarital Cohabitation with Future Spouse on Subsequent Marital Quality* (Ph.D. dissertation): University of Florida, 1982.
90. Roy E. L. Watson, "Premarital Cohabitation vs. Traditional Courtship: Their Effects on Subsequent Marital Adjustment," *Family Relations* 32 (Jan. 1983), pp. 139–47.
91. See Burton E. Bernstein, "Legal Problems of Cohabitation," *Family Coordinator* 26 (Oct. 1977), pp. 361–66; Jeffrey M. Jacques and Karen M. Chason, "Cohabitation: A Test of Reference Group Theory Among Black and White College Students," *Journal of Comparative Family Studies* 9 (Summer 1978), pp. 147–65; Paul R. Newcomb, "Cohabitation in America: An Assessment of Consequences," *Journal of Marriage and the Family* 41 (Aug. 1979), pp. 597–603; and Carl A. Ridley, Dan J. Peterman, and Arthur W. Avery, "Cohabitation: Does It Make for a Better Marriage?" *Family Coordinator* 27 (April 1978), pp. 129–36.

Studies also show that women's role expectations have been changing rapidly in recent years, whereas men's expectations, both for themselves and for their wives, lag behind. The potential for conflict in relationships is obvious.

The traditional dating system in the United States emerged from the 1920s into the 1940s. Early dating was governed by explicit norms that emphasized its use for becoming acquainted with members of the opposite sex in eventual preparation for the selection of marital partners and by implicit norms that focused on competition for success and the enhancement of self-esteem.

College dating patterns were analyzed by Waller, who distinguished between dating, a dalliance relationship, and serious courtship. Dating was characterized by a quest for thrills, men bargaining for sexual favors, whereas women sought to be sought after. When bargaining power was unequal, exploitation of the less successful partner often resulted. This status system was conceptualized as the rating-and-dating complex, in which such characteristics as fraternity or sorority membership, dressing well, having smooth manners and a car were important. Physical attractiveness was also important for women. For both sexes, the possession of a good line"—verbal banter designed to titillate the other—was important.

Courtship developed when the partners began to succumb to one another's blandishments. If uneven, the involvement might be accompanied by exploitation of the more involved partner, according to the principle of least interst. The balance between the partners tended to be restored through lovers' quarrels, which produced increasing commitment to the relationship and led to marriage. Involvement was accompanied by idealization of each partner by the other.

It appears that modern dating patterns are becoming more friendship oriented and egalitarian. Students tend to favor an equal balance of power between dating partners and women increasingly are becoming involved in date initiation and expense sharing.

Data a generation or more ago showed that some boys and girls display sexual interest from an early age and that numbers of both sexes engage in sex play before puberty. Most preadolescent sex play is masturbation, some of which is motivated as much out of curiosity as out of definite erotic interest. Beginning in adolescence, petting becomes prominent, and the goals are explicitly sexual arousal and satisfaction.

Drastic changes in premarital sex began to appear around 1965, with more intercourse occurring and there being less public condemnation of it. Among young teenagers, the portrait emerges of young girls in serious heterosexual relationships, usually rather monogamous, with steps being taken toward contraception. Comparable increases in intercourse have occurred among college students, whose dating includes less emphasis on conquest and more emphasis on sharing and making love.

The trend of unmarried students living together, on campus or off, also is an emerging pattern. Several studies show sizable proportions of men and women having this experience before graduation. Participants consider it less artificial than traditional dating and do not see it culminating, automatically, in marriage. Men are motivated more by sex and women are motivated more by the possibility of further development of the relationship. Most describe their relationships as very satisfactory and report problems not too different from those of young married couples.

SUGGESTED READINGS

Bell, Robert R., *Worlds of Friendship*, Beverly Hills, Calif.: Sage Publications, 1981. Explores all aspects of male-female and same-sex friendship patterns, using research from a variety of disciplines.

Eekelarr, John M., and Katz, Sanford N., eds., *Marriage and Cohabitation in Contemporary Societies: Areas of Legal, Social and Ethical Change*, Scarborough, Ontario: Butterworth, 1980. This massive compilation of articles represents the state of the art of what is known about cohabitation and marriage. Authors' contributions reflect scholarship from 22 countries.

Hill, Reuben, and Aldous, Joan, "Socialization for Marriage and Parenthood," in David A. Goslin, ed., *Handbook of Socialization Theory and Research*, Chicago: Rand McNally, 1969, pp. 885–950. An excellent summary of the state of theory and research. Contains sections on dating, going steady, and engagement.

Lantz, Herman R., and Snyder, Eloise C., *Marriage: An Examination of the Man-Woman Relationship*, New York: John Wiley & Sons, 1969, chs. 6, 7, 9, and 10. These chapters on the nature of heterosexual love and dating and courtship in middle-class America are perceptive and constructive.

Morrison, Eleanor S., and Borosage, Vera, eds., *Human Sexuality: Contemporary Perspectives*, Palo Alto, Calif.: National Press Books, 1973. Various articles deal with the development of human sexuality, masculinity and femininity, and adult heterosexual behavior.

Richmond-Abbott, Marie, *Masculine and Feminine: Sex Roles Over the Life Cycle*, Reading, Mass.: Addison-Wesley, 1983. Examines sex-role socialization and male-female relations from birth to death.

Tittle, Carol Kehr, *Careers and Family: Sex Roles and Adolescent Life Plans*,

Beverly Hills, Calif.: Sage Publications, 1981. Values underlying the marriage, parenthood, and career plans of 600 high school students in New York are examined and analyzed.

FILMS

Achieving Sexual Maturity (John Wiley & Sons, 605 Third Avenue, New York, N.Y. 10016), 21 minutes. Deals with the sexual anatomy, physiology, and behavior of both sexes from conception through adulthood. Uses explicit live photography to explain anatomy.

How to Make a Woman (Polymorph Films, 331 Newbury Street, Boston, Mass. 02115), 58 minutes. Forceful presentation of the problem of male-female relationships from a strongly feminist perspective.

Joe and Roxy (National Film Board of Canada, 1251 Avenue of the Americas, 16th Floor, New York, N.Y. 10020), 30 minutes. Analyzes going steady, planning for a secure future, and seeing education in proper perspective. Shows how the inadequate home lives of Joe and Roxy fail them during adolescent adjustment.

Sex Role Development (Pennsylvania State University Audio Visual Services, University Park, Pa. 16802), 23 minutes. The transmission to children of sex-role stereotypes. Explores alternative approaches to socialization by one family and by educators.

Teenage Pregnancy (Sterling Educational Films, 241 East 34th Street, New York, N.Y. 10016), 14 minutes. The discovery that a teenage daughter is pregnant causes upheaval in a family. The frantic mother tries to restore unity.

QUESTIONS AND PROJECTS

1. What two processes are involved in parental influences on the sex-role development of their children? Describe how each works.
2. What role do the schools play in the development of sex-role expectations? Do you think this role is changing? If so, how?
3. What factors appear to influence women to have occupational careers? What do studies show about recent changes in women's role expectations?
4. How much change has there been in the expectations of men for their roles and those of their wives. What implications does this have for marital conflict?
5. Take a poll of the class. Determine what marital-role expectations the students hold. Are there differences by sex? Are there differences by the work experience of the students' mothers?
6. Outline Waller's theory of rating and dating in the college context. Specify the relationship between bargaining and exploitation. Are there any positive effects of cross-class dating and exploitation?
7. What does research show about the involvement of preadolescents in

sexual play? What generalizations can be made? What variation exists?

8. How does the masculine subculture condition boys toward the pursuit of nonmarital sex? What proportion of girls can accept nonmarital sex?

9. What proportion of U.S. teenagers are having sexual intercourse? How promiscuous are these relationships?

10. What changes have occurred in college dating patterns over the past decade or so? Speculate about the impact of these changes on marital relationships.

11. How widespread is male sexual aggression in dating relationships? Is it confined to casual relationships? How prevalent is premarital violence?

12. How common is living together around college campuses? Why do couples say they live together? What advantages do they find in such arrangements? What problems? What implications does cohabitation have for the future of marriage in the United States? Why?

Copyright © Jean Shapiro

13
Mate Selection

The family is the oldest institution of the human race. Other institutions have always depended on it and I think people will go right on doing this. But if we would take a look at the modern world, we would realize that people today are taking extraordinary risks. Young people are marrying across wide expanses of the world, choosing partners of other classes, other religions, other races. And people who are taking these risks ought to realize that they are doing something different, but that they take the risk because they feel it is worth it—because they care about differences, because they care about contrast, because they care about intensity. If you are not going to marry the boy next door—and if you do you may die of boredom—then you have got to work much harder.[1]

It should come as no surprise that most American teenagers responding in the latest Gallup Youth Survey indicated a desire for marriage. . . . Eight in 10 teenagers (82 percent) believe they will get married someday. By comparison, 87 percent in 1981 and 84 percent in 1977 expressed a similar intention. The proportion of young people who plan to remain single remains constant at 9 percent, but those who are not certain about marriage has risen in 1983 to 9 percent.[2]

All societies have mechanisms for controlling who gets married to whom. In this chapter, we shall look systematically at the ways in which mates are sorted in American society.

1. Margaret Mead, "We Must Learn to See What's Really New," *Life Magazine* (Aug. 1968), p. 34. © Time Inc., 1968.
2. George Gallup, "Most Youths Plan Marriage But Want Smaller Families," *Gallup Youth Survey*, August 3, 1983.

HOMOGAMY

Marriage based on romantic love is the norm in America and is spreading rapidly over the world. No society, however, leaves falling in love solely to the whims of the young. The general regulation of mate selection is subsumed under the concepts of endogamy and exogamy; people are required to select spouses from within certain groups and are forbidden to choose them from certain groups. These norms may be formalized into law or they may be largely implicit and, thus, studied only through analysis of who actually marries whom.

Comparatively, America has few exogamous norms. The incest taboos extend outward roughly to first cousins, but there are no clans or other kinship structures within which mate selection is prohibited. Endogamous norms are more pervasive. It will be recalled that Christianity has a long history of forbidding marriage with outsiders. Early in colonial days, interracial marriage also was forbidden. In few other respects are there laws requiring people to marry within their own groups. There is, however, evidence of a widespread tendency for people to marry others who are like themselves in ways that are not subject to formal regulation. This tendency for like to marry like is called *homogamy*.

Hundreds of studies have been done of homogamy. They embrace homogamy by age and marital status, social status, religion, ethnic affiliation, race, and a host of other social and personal characteristics. Only a small portion of this research can be presented here.

Age and Marital Status

Laws concerning age at marriage are intended to assure reasonable maturity in the contracting parties and to make certain that they are old enough to give valid consent. Under the old English common law, the minimum ages were 14 for boys and 12 for girls, with parental consent. Virtually all of the states in the United States subsequently passed laws setting minimum ages for marriage with and without parental consent.[3] The most common provision permits men and women 18 years old to marry without parental consent. With parental consent, the most common ages are 18 for men and 16 for women.[4] In some states, both men

3. The Constitution reserves the area of domestic relations laws to the states, so each of the 50 states and the District of Columbia has its own laws, and the laws vary widely from one jurisdiction to another.
4. A Utah district court, in 1975, ruled that such laws are unconstitutional because they discriminate against men: Associated Press, October 11, 1975. Until and unless the Supreme Court rules on the matter, most states probably will continue to enforce existing statutes.

and women must be 21 to marry without parental consent; in a few others, 12-year-olds may marry with parental consent. In many states, courts may grant special permission for underage couples to marry when the girl is pregnant.

From the last part of the nineteenth century until 1960, the average ages at marriage for both men and women moved downward. In 1890, for example, the median ages at first marriage were 26.1 for men and 22.0 for women. By 1960, these averages had dropped to 22.8 and 20.3. Then they began to rise again. They climbed to 23.2 and 20.8 in 1970 and rose further to 24.4 for men and 22.1 for women in 1979. The 1982 figures indicate further that age at marriage is climbing to heights reminiscent of the early decades of this century: 25.2 for men and 22.5 for women.

Although about 90 percent of Americans eventually do marry, a trend toward delaying marriage has been evidenced among young people over the past two decades. Thornton and Freedman attribute the rise in delayed marriage to the growing acceptance of singlehood as a legitimate life style and the desire on the part of many people, particularly women, to finish their educations and gain work experience before marriage.[5]

The trend toward delayed marriage today also can be seen by examing the age range within which most people marry. In 1965, Mogey reported that all first marriages occurred within a four- or five-year period and that 75 percent occurred within three or four years on either side of age 21.[6] By 1982, 75 percent of men were married for the first time by age 29 and 75 percent of women by age 26.[7]

Homogamy in age at marriage is indicated by the relative ages of brides and grooms. On the average, brides are 2.5 years younger than their grooms; in 10 percent of all cases, they are the same age. In three fourths of all cases, brides are younger; in one case out of seven, the bride is older than the groom.

Homogamy, by age, holds for all groups in the population that have been studied. Hollingshead compared the ages of black and white couples in first marriages and remarriages.[8] In all four types and within both

5. Arland Thornton and Deborah Freedman, "Changing Attitudes Toward Marriage and Single Life," *Family Planning Perspectives* 14 (Nov.–Dec. 1982), pp. 297–303.
6. John Mogey, "Age at First Marriage," in Alvin W. Gouldner and S. M. Miller, *eds.*, *Applied Sociology: Opportunities and Problems*, New York: The Free Press, 1965, pp. 248–59.
7. U.S. Bureau of the Census, "Marital Status and Living Arrangements: March 1982," *Current Population Reports*, Series P–20, No. 380 (May 1983), p. 3.
8. August B. Hollingshead, "Age Relationships and Marriage," *American Sociological Review* 16 (Aug. 1951), pp. 492–99.

races, the correlations were high. Glick verified age homogamy at different occupational levels, ranging from professionals to laborers.[9]

The age-homogamy norms are themselves a function of age; they operate most strongly at youthful ages and become less effective as people grow older. At age 20, men marry women of median age 19—only 1 year's difference. By age 25 there is 3 years' difference, by age 30 there is nearly 5 years' difference, and by age 60, there is almost 10 years' difference. Women, of course, typically choose husbands who are older, but the pattern fluctuates widely with the age of the woman. Girls who marry at age 15 choose men almost 5 years their seniors. By age 20 the difference has dropped to less than 3 years, and by age 30 there is less than 1 year's difference. Beyond age 30 the difference begins to increase again. After age 30, women tend to marry men who are from 2 to 4 years older than they are.[10]

Age is related to whether people are marrying for the first time. Bowerman studied these relationships in Seattle and reached the following conclusions. First, single persons as marriage partners are younger, on the average, than persons who have been married; among the previously married, widows are older than divorcées. These generalizations hold regardless of the age, sex, and previous marital status of the person. Second, as men get older they marry increasingly younger women. The age differences are least when men marry widows. As women get older, on the other hand, they marry men more nearly their own age, the age differences being greatest when they marry widowers. Finally, those who are remarrying do not differ significantly in the age difference from their mates who are marrying for the first time.[11]

In summary, these data show homogamy by age, but that the effectiveness of the norms varies by age and previous marital status. There are several possible explanations. First, age differences seem greater to the young; at age 20, a difference of two years may loom larger than a difference of five years at age 40. Second, the range of association with persons of different ages probably becomes greater as one grows

9. Paul C. Glick and Emmanuel Landau, "Age as a Factor in Marriage," *American Sociological Review* 15 (Aug. 1950), pp. 517–29.

10. For discussions of age differences between spouses at marriage, see Felix M. Berardo, Hernan Vera, and Donna H. Berardo, "Age Discrepant Marriages," *Medical Aspects of Human Sexuality* 17 (Jan. 1983), pp. 57–76; William R. Bytheway, "The Variation with Age of Age Differences in Marriage," *Journal of Marriage and the Family* 43 (Nov. 1981), pp. 923–27; and William F. Kenkel, "Black-White Differences in Age at Marriage Expectations of Low Income High School Girls," *Journal of Negro Education* 50 (Fall 1981), pp. 425–38.

11. Charles E. Bowerman, "Age Relationships at Marriage, by Marital Status and Age at Marriage," *Marriage and Family Living* 18 (Aug. 1956), pp. 231–33; see also Gillian Dean and Douglas T. Gurak, "Marital Homogamy the Second Time Around," *Journal of Marriage and the Family* 40 (Aug. 1978), pp. 559–70.

older. Third, the opportunities for selecting a mate at one's own age level become more restricted with increasing age; most of one's age mates already are married. If one wishes to marry, one may have to be more flexible in one's age requirements. The competitive situations of men and women differ here. Although this can be overemphasized, the initiative in mate seeking tends to rest with men, and men seek physical attractiveness in women. As men get older, frequently their economic status improves and they are able to attract younger women. As women get older, however, they face a declining market and have to accept, for the most part, marriage with older men or with men their own ages who have been married before.[12]

Age Relationships and Marital Success. A number of early studies showed that age at marriage is related to marital happiness,[13] with marriages under the age of 20 being most hazardous. The same pattern was discovered when divorce rates were related to age at marriage; young marriages had the highest divorce rates.[14]

A recent study in this area was of the marital experience of 5442 white, ever-married women under age 45, in the 1970 National Fertility Study. Of these women, 15 percent were separated from or had divorced their first husbands. Again, women who married before age 20 had considerably higher rates of marital disruption than those who married at older ages. Moreover, these higher rates were found not to be due to interrupted educations or to premarital pregnancy. Heterogamous marriages by age had higher marital disruption rates when the age differences were large (wives 14 to 17 married to husbands 25 and older), and when wives were older than their husbands.[15]

12. Davor Jedlicka, "Sex Inequality, Aging, and Innovation in Preferential Mate Selection," *Family Coordinator* 27 (April 1978), pp. 137-40.
13. Ernest W. Burgess and Leonard S. Cottrell, Jr., *Predicting Success or Failure in Marriage*, New York: Prentice-Hall, 1939; Judson T. Landis and Mary G. Landis, *Building a Successful Marriage*, Englewood Cliffs, N.J.: Prentice-Hall, 1973, pp. 106-7; and Lewis M. Terman, *Psychological Factors in Marital Happiness*, New York: McGraw-Hill, 1938.
14. Paul C. Glick and Arthur J. Norton, "Marrying, Divorcing, and Living Together in the U.S. Today," *Population Bulletin* 32 (Oct. 1977); Landis and Landis, *op. cit.*, pp. 108-9; Harvey J. Locke, *Predicting Adjustment in Marriage: A Comparison of a Divorced and a Happily Married Group*, New York: Holt, 1951, pp. 101-2; and Thomas P. Monahan, "Does Age at Marriage Matter in Divorce?" *Social Forces* 32 (Oct. 1953), pp. 81-87.
15. Larry L. Bumpass and James A. Sweet, "Differentials in Marital Stability: 1970," *American Sociological Review* 37 (Dec. 1972), pp. 754-66. See also Gary R. Lee, "Age at Marriage and Marital Satisfaction: A Multivariate Analysis with Implications for Marital Stability," *Journal of Marriage and the Family* 39 (Aug. 1977), pp. 493-504; and A. Wade Smith and June E. G. Meitz, "Cohort, Education, and the Decline in Undisrupted Marriages," *Journal of Marriage and the Family* 45 (Aug. 1983), pp. 613-22.

The logic underlying these findings, of course, is that age is related to emotional and social maturity,[16] persons who marry after age 20 are less likely to be rebelling against authority, are less likely to be forced into marriage by pregnancy,[17] are less likely to be broken up by parents, and encounter fewer financial hardships than those who are younger. That many marriages of high school-age youth do encounter these special problems seems inescapable.[18]

Part of the public attention given to young marriages today may be accounted for by the fact that the public schools are changing their policies in dealing with such marriages. Before World War II, young people who married while still in high school were dropped from school almost automatically. Many schools, either formally or informally, still have such policies. An increasing number, however, are attempting to keep such youngsters in school.[19]

16. Lee G. Burchinal, "Adolescent Role Deprivation and High School Age Marriage," *Marriage and Family Living* 21 (Nov. 1959), pp. 378–84; J. Ross Eshleman, "Mental Health and Marital Integration in Young Marriages," *Journal of Marriage and the Family* 27 (May 1965), pp. 255–62; Floyd M. Martinson, "Ego Deficiency as a Factor in Marriage," *American Sociological Review* 20 (April 1955), pp. 161–64; Floyd M. Martinson, "Ego Deficiency as a Factor in Marriage—A Male Sample," *Marriage and Family Living* 21 (Feb. 1959), pp. 48–52; and J. Joel Moss and Ruby Gingles, "The Relationship of Personality to the Incidence of Early Marriage," *Marriage and Family Living* 21 (Nov. 1959), pp. 373–77.

17. Of all girls who marry while still in high school, from one third to one half are pregnant. Half to three fourths of the high school-age boys who marry are involved in premarital pregnancies. See Lloyd Bacon, "Early Motherhood, Accelerated Role Transition, and Social Pathologies," *Social Forces* 52 (March 1974), pp. 333–41; Lee G. Burchinal, "Comparison of Factors Related to Adjustment in Pregnancy-Provoked and Non-Pregnancy-Provoked Youthful Marriages," *Midwest Sociologist* 21 (July 1959), pp. 92–96; Elwood Carlson, "Family Background, School and Early Marriage," *Journal of Marriage and the Family* 41 (May 1979), pp. 341–53; Rachel M. Inselberg, "Marital Problems and Satisfaction in High School Marriages," *Marriage and Family Living* 24 (Feb. 1962), pp. 74–77; Martin L. Norris, "Teenage Marriages: Facts and Figures." Paper presented at the Indiana Council on Family Relations, March 24, 1962; and Mark W. Roosa, Hiram E. Fitzgerald, and Nancy A. Carlson, "A Comparison of Teenage and Older Mothers: A Systems Analysis," *Journal of Marriage and the Family* 44 (May 1982), pp. 367–77.

18. Josephina J. Card and Lauress L. Wise, "Teenage Mothers and Teenage Fathers: The Impact of Early Childbearing on the Parents' Personal and Professional Lives," *Family Planning Perspectives* 10 (July–Aug. 1978), pp. 199–205; Sandra L. Hofferth and Kristin A. Moore, "Early Childbearing and Later Economic Well-Being," *American Sociological Review* 44 (Oct. 1979), pp. 784–815; see also Alan C. Kerckhoff and Alan A. Parrow, "The Effect of Early Marriage on the Educational Attainment of Young Men," *Journal of Marriage and the Family* 41 (Feb. 1979), pp. 97–107; and Kristin A. Moore and Linda J. Waite, "Early Childbearing and Educational Attainment," *Family Planning Perspectives* 9 (Sept.–Oct. 1977), pp. 220–25.

19. See Wayne J. Anderson and Sander M. Latts, "High School Marriages and School Policies in Minnesota," *Journal of Marriage and the Family* 27 (May 1965), pp. 266–70; Glenn C. Atkyns, "School Administrative Policy Related to Motherhood, Pregnancy, and Marriage," *Family Coordinator* 17 (April 1968), pp. 69–73; B. B. Brown, "Married

The divorce rate among high school-age marriages is estimated at two to four times that among marriages of persons after the age of 20, part of which is accounted for by the fact that young marriages are concentrated among high divorce-rate groups: those of low educational levels, low socioeconomic levels, and those who are premaritally pregnant.[20] Even when the influence of these factors is partialed out, however, the disadvantage remains. Those who marry very young appear more likely to marry out of dysfunctional emotional needs and to encounter a disproportionate set of "outside" problems.

One writer has criticized the condemnation of young marriages. Doress argues that such criticism ignores the large number of apparently successful young marriages and questions whether couples who marry in their late 20s and early 30s may not have developed individual patterns of living that are scarcely affected by marriage. The stability of these later marriages, he says, may be largely due to the fact that they do not involve the deep commitments of young marriages. There may be less welding, less joining together, less *egoisme à deux*.[21]

Unquestionably, disapproval of young marriages has much to do with their high failure rate. If society were to support young marriages with enthusiasm, the present negative effects of emotional immaturity might be largely overcome. This does not change things, however. There are few signs that society will became more accepting of youthful marriages in the near future. Society is more tolerant of marriages occurring later than of those occurring earlier.

Students in Public High Schools: A Texas Study," *Family Coordinator* 21 (July 1972), pp. 321–24; Vladimir de Lissovoy, "High School Marriages: A Longitudinal Study," *Journal of Marriage and the Family* 35 (May 1973), pp. 245–55; Vladimir de Lissovoy and Mary Ellen Hitchcock, "High School Marriages in Pennsylvania," *Journal of Marriage and the Family* 27 (May 1965), pp. 263–65; June M. Henton, "The Effects of Married High School Students on Their Unmarried Class Mates," *Journal of Marriage and the Family* 26 (Feb. 1964), pp. 87–88; Wilson Ivins, "Student Marriages in New Mexico Secondary Schools: Practices and Policies," *Marriage and Family Living* 22 (Feb. 1960), pp. 71–74.
20. Although early studies showed a relationship between premarital pregnancy and subsequent divorce, these studies did not control for related factors such as low economic status, youthful ages, low educational achievement, and so on. Recent controlled studies have cast doubt on the long-term effects of premarital pregnancy. See Larry L. Bumpass and James A. Sweet, *op. cit.*, p. 758; and Phillips Cutright, "Timing the First Birth: Does It Matter?" *Journal of Marriage and the Family* 35 (Nov. 1973), pp. 585–95.
21. Irving Dorass, "The Problem of Early Marriage," *Bulletin on Family Development* 2 (Spring 1961), pp. 20–23.

Social Status

Data in the last chapter showed both that people tend to date at their own status levels and that dating outside one's level is associated with sexual involvement, exploitation, and the hope of marriage on the part of the lower-status partner. These data should lead us to expect both status homogamy and status heterogamy in marriage; and, indeed, this is what we find.

Early studies found mixed evidence. Burgess and Wallin found that 1000 engaged couples tended to select persons of similar family background.[22] Centers, using a national sample, found that men and women marry persons from their same occupational level more often than they marry persons from any other one occupational stratum. He also found, however, that fewer than 50 percent marry within their own occupational level and that, despite the endogamous tendency, more men of each occupational level are married to women of strata other than their own than are married to women of it.[23] In Connecticut, Hollingshead discovered that men and women tend to marry persons from the same class of residential area and from the same educational level.[24] Hunt, using data on marriages occurring in Massachusetts, however, failed to find much evidence for status endogamy.[25] Only women from the lowest status levels made mostly endogamous marriages. At all other status levels, there was no uniform tendency for the selection of partners from any status level.

Leslie and Richardson studied students who married while they were in college. These researchers reasoned that, although status endogamy may operate in the larger society, it might not be effective in a group virtually all of whom were middle class. They reasoned further that, if parents tend to pressure their offspring toward endogamous marriages, such pressure might be less effective when students marry while they are away at college and subject to the democratic norms found on most campuses. They discovered only a slight tendency toward homogamy among students who married someone whom they had known at home before attending college, and none at all among couples who met and married while on campus.[26] They concluded that the campus situation,

22. Ernest W. Burgess and Paul Wallin, "Homogamy in Social Characteristics," *American Journal of Sociology* 49 (Sept. 1943), pp. 117–24.

23. Richard Centers, "Marital Selection and Occupational Strata," *American Journal of Sociology* 54 (May 1949), pp. 530–35.

24. August B. Hollingshead, "Cultural Factors in the Selection of Marriage Mates," *American Sociological Review* 15 (Oct. 1950), pp. 619–27.

25. T. C. Hunt, "Occupational Status and Marriage Selection," *American Sociological Review* 5 (Aug. 1940), pp. 495–504.

26. Gerald R. Leslie and Arthur H. Richardson, "Family Versus Campus Influences in

by encouraging the association of persons of diverse backgrounds and through its formal democratic norms, favors heterogamous pairings. Direct group pressures operating at the time of marriage appear to be at least as influential as homogamy-oriented norms internalized earlier in life.

Coombs, studying married couples at the University of Utah, supported the idea that campus norms favor status heterogamy, whereas community norms favor status endogamy. He found that status homogamy was much higher when both parties to the couple lived at home during courtship than when neither lived at home.[27]

These data suggest that status homogamy might be declining with the passage of time, at least in some segments of the population. This interpretation is supported by the data on 5442 women from the 1970 National Fertility Study. Using education as the measure of social status, this study found that marital-disruption rates did not differ significantly between homogamous and heterogamous marriages unless the differences in background were large. Disruption rates were highest for college women who had married high school dropouts.[28]

The Mating Gradient. Just as patterns of dating and premarital sex involvement led us to expect both status homogamy and status heterogamy in marriage, they should also lead us to expect certain patterns in heterogamous marriages. The data showed that men more often date below their social levels, whereas women often date above theirs. In fact, there seems to be a tendency for men to wish to marry at their own levels or below on a wide range of characteristics. The men tend to marry down in terms of age was shown in the preceding section. Early studies also demonstrated that men tend to marry down in education and IQ. This tendency for men to marry downward has been labeled the *mating gradient.*

Most studies on status homogamy have shown the operation of the mating gradient. The data suggest further that, except at the very top and bottom, men have wider mate choice than women do.[29]

Relation to Mate Selection," *Social Problems* 4 (Oct. 1956), pp. 117–21. At least one study indicates that some apparent homogamy may develop as a function of interaction between the couple. See Eloise C. Snyder, "Attitudes: A Study of Homogamy and Marital Selectivity," *Journal of Marriage and the Family* 26 (Aug. 1964), pp. 332–36.

27. Robert H. Coombs, "Reinforcement of Values in the Parental Home as a Factor in Mate Selection," *Marriage and Family Living* 24 (May 1962), pp. 155–57.

28. Bumpass and Sweet, *op. cit.,* p. 762. See also Leonard I. Pearlin, "Status Inequality and Stress in Marriage," *American Sociological Review* 40 (June 1975), pp. 344–57.

29. Some methodological difficulties in getting a definitive test of the mating gradient are analyzed in the following articles: Zick Rubin "Do American Women Marry Up?" *American Sociological Review* 33 (Oct. 1968), pp. 750–60; John F. Scott, "A Comment

An interesting implication of the mating gradient is that it works to keep some of the highest-status women and the lowest-status men from marrying. Women at the highest levels have a smaller pool of potential mates to begin with because it is not generally acceptable for them to marry downward. In addition, these high-status women must compete both against one another and against women from other status levels for high-status men. To the extent that high-status men marry downward, they leave high-status women without partners. Among men, the reverse obtains. The lowest-status men generally are not eligible to marry higher-status women; yet higher-status men may select lower-status spouses. Thus, unmarried women may be, disproportionately, high-status women, and unmarried men may be, disproportionately, low-status men.

Racial Background

Nowhere are homogamy norms more widely held to than in the area of race. For over 20 years, the courts have tended to strike down laws forbidding miscegenation and intermarriage and, in 1967, the Supreme Court declared Virginia's law unconstitutional, thereby nullifying similar prohibitions in the 16 other states that still had them.

Although persons of different races may now legally marry, the intermarriage rate is still so low as virtually to defy reliable measurement. Studies of intermarriage rates in various states and cities up to 1960 showed rates of 0.50 to 1.50 percent. The first census reporting of data on the races of married persons in the United States occurred in 1960, with the result that 0.44 percent of the over 40 million couples reported themselves interracially married.

By 1970, the percentage had increased to 0.70 percent, and by 1977 it had increased to approximately 1 percent of all married couples.[30] Of the 421,000 interracially married couples, 125,000 were black-white couples. Three fourths of the black-white marriages involved black husbands and white wives.[31] These figures probably do not mean that white

---

on 'Do American Women Marry Up?'" *American Sociological Review* 34 (Oct. 1969), pp. 725–28; J. David Martin, "A Comment on Whether American Women Do Marry Up," *American Sociological Review* 35 (April 1970), pp. 327–28; Norval D. Glenn, Adreain A. Ross, and Judy Corder Tully, "Patterns of Intergenerational Mobility of Females Through Marriage," *American Sociological Review* 39 (Oct. 1974), pp. 683–99; and Richard C. Rockwell, "Historical Trends and Variations in Educational Homogamy," *Journal of Marriage and the Family* 38 (Feb. 1976), pp. 83–95.

30. Ernest Porterfield, "Black-American Intermarriage in the United States," *Marriage and Family Review* 5 (Spring 1982), pp. 17–34.

31. U.S. Bureau of the Census, "Perspectives on American Husbands and Wives," *Current Population Reports*, Series P-23, No. 77 (December 1978), pp. 7–10.

men do not form sexual associations with nonwhite women, but only that such relationships do not tend to lead to marriage.

Intermarriage rates also are reported for several minority groups. Among American Indians, 33 percent of the men have white wives; 24 percent of the Filipino men, 8 percent of the Japanese men, 8 percent of the Chinese men, and 2 percent of black men have white wives. The numbers of white men with American Indian wives and white men with Japanese wives appear to be increasing.[32]

In spite of the small number of people involved—or perhaps because of it—there is an almost morbid curiosity about the kinds of people who intermarry. Several studies have sought to specify some of the social and emotional characteristics of the racially intermarried.

Studies by Golden and by Pavela found that persons in interracial marriages are older at marriage than are those who enter racially homogamous marriages. There is some evidence that these higher ages at marriage are associated with the persons having previously been married. More than one third of the black grooms interviewed in Philadelphia, and almost one fourth of the brides, had been previously divorced. In Indiana, Pavela found that 29 percent of black brides and 25 percent of black grooms had been divorced; the corresponding percentages among the white brides and grooms were 18 percent and 21 percent.[33]

The personal and emotional characteristics of those who intermarry are more difficult to get at. It is widely believed that interracial marriages must be highly selective in terms of personal characteristics. Both Golden and Pavela demonstrated that families and friends of both races exert strong pressures against such marriages.

The study going into the greatest depth may be that of Freeman, who studied interracial couples in Hawaii.[34] All of his respondents described

32. *New York Times*, Feb. 15, 1973. See also Delores P. Aldridge, "The Changing Nature of Interracial Marriage in Georgia: A Research Note," *Journal of Marriage and the Family* 35 (Nov. 1973), p. 641; Harry H. L. Kitano and Wai-tsang Yeung, "Chinese Interracial Marriage," *Marriage and Family Review* 5 (Spring 1982), pp. 35-48; Robert C. Schmitt, "Recent Trends in Hawaiian Interracial Marriage Rates by Occupation," *Journal of Marriage and the Family* 33 (May 1971), pp. 373-74; and John N. Tinker, "Intermarriage and Assimilation in a Plural Society: Japanese-Americans in the United States," *Marriage and Family Review* 5 (Spring 1982), pp. 61-74.
33. John H. Burma, "Research Note on the Measurement of Interracial Marriage," *American Journal of Sociology* 57 (May 1952), pp. 587-89; Joseph Golden, "Characteristics of the Negro White Intermarried in Philadelphia," *American Sociological Review* 18 (April 1953), p. 178; and Todd H. Pavela, "An Exploratory Study of Negro-White Intermarriage in Indiana," *Journal of Marriage and the Family* 26 (May 1964), pp. 209-11.
34. Linton Freeman, "Homogamy in Interethnic Mate Selection," *Sociology and Social Research* 39 (July-Aug. 1955), pp. 369-77. The unique situation in Hawaii has been studied extensively. See, for example, Paul H. Besanceney, "On Reporting Rates of Intermarriage," *American Journal of Sociology* 70 (May 1965), pp. 717-21; Andrew W.

early feelings of rejection, frequently tracing back to parent-child relationships. All respondents also reported poor social adjustment in grade school and high school. The backgrounds of rejection produced frustration and hostility toward the individuals' ethnic groups. They desired to escape identification with the ethnic group and turned toward deviant behavior to do so. Exposure to other ethnic groups led to idealization of opposite-sex members of those groups, dating, and, often, marriage. Many of the interethnic dating relationships were short lived and, when marriage occurred, adjustment was a long, difficult process in which the rebelliousness abated.

Although Freeman's conclusions are widely shared, Burchinal argues that interracial marriages may occur disproportionately among a very different class of youth.[35] In cities, especially among students and professional people, he says, racial egalitarianism and integration are widely supported. Interracial dating occurs with increasing frequency and interracial marriage becomes increasingly likely.

In support of this argument, Blood and Nicholson found that acquaintances with students from other nations were almost universal on campus and that almost half of the women had dated foreign students. Of those who had not dated, most said that they would if they were asked.[36] Moreover, international dating was not related to rebellion or to any crusade against prejudice. The women reported satisfaction with their experiences, their women friends were sympathetic, and their parents and American boy friends typically were neutral.[37]

Lind, "Interracial Marriage as Affecting Divorce in Hawaii," *Sociology and Social Research* 49 (Oct. 1964), pp. 17-26; Margaret A. Parkman and Jack Sawyer, "Dimensions of Ethnic Intermarriage in Hawaii," *American Sociological Review* 32 (Aug. 1967), pp. 593-607; Robert C. Schmitt, "Demographic Correlates of Interracial Marriage in Hawaii," *Population Index* 30 (July 1964), pp. 312-13; and Margaret M. Schwertfeger, "Interethnic Marriage and Divorce in Hawaii: A Panel Study of 1968 First Marriages," *Marriage and Family Review* 5 (Spring 1982), pp. 49-59.
35. Lee G. Burchinal, "The Premarital Dyad and Love Involvement," in Harold T. Christensen, ed., *Handbook of Marriage and the Family*, Chicago: Rand McNally, 1964, p. 648.
36. Robert O. Blood, Jr. and Samuel O. Nicholson, "The Attitudes of American Men and Women Students Toward International Dating," *Marriage and Family Living* 24 (Feb. 1962), pp. 35-41. For evidence that these attitudes are shared by teenagers generally, see *Gallup Youth Survey*, March 26, 1980.
37. Robert O. Blood, Jr., and Samuel O. Nicholson, "International Dating Experiences of American Women Students," *Marriage and Family Living* 24 (May 1962), pp. 129-36. See also Ann Baker Cottrell, "Cross-National Marriages as an Extension of an International Life Style: A Study of Indian-Western Couples," *Journal of Marriage and the Family* 35 (Nov. 1973), pp. 739-41; Harrop A. Freeman and Ruth Freeman, "Dating Between American and Foreign College Students," *Journal of Sex Research* 2 (Nov. 1966), pp. 207-14.

Racial Heterogamy and Marital Success. Many people believe that interracial marriages are fraught with hazard and doomed to failure. Research, however, shows the situation to be anything but simple.

One perceptive study was made of marriages between American service men and Japanese women in the 1950s. The couples were living in the Chicago area. The study challenged the assumption that Oriental-Caucasian marriages are subject to greater strains than the ordinary marriage, contending that, as in other marriages, the strains that occur in mixed marriages are patterned and predictable. Some Japanese-American marriages, the researcher says, are likely to be quite stable and to involve fewer strains than many American marriages.[38]

These husbands were mostly semiskilled or skilled laborers, professional soldiers, or white-collar workers; not upwardly mobile. Some had married without their parents' knowledge, but most had received either enthusiastic or grudging approval. Their wives had married at an average age of 22, they were usually urban working girls, and their marriages to Americans frequently were opposed by their parents. The couples faced the usual adjustment problems with food, sex, play, work, finances, and so on. In addition, they faced problems of learning how to communicate, of handling the women's parents, and of becoming parents. By the time of interview several years later, however, differences of age, class, religion, and education did not cause strain. There were strains in these marriages still however. Some were more serious and some of them less so than in most marriages.

The strains involved in leaving the parental family were different from typical in-law problems, but not automatically more or less severe. Few women had much stress over having left their parents or Japan. There was some nostalgia to see their parents and country again, and a few wives were attempting to get their husbands to return to Japan.

Few couples experienced strong institutional pressures. They had few organizational affiliations and were not usually deeply religious. A few brides had become Catholic, thus avoiding sharp differences between themselves and their husbands. Much of their recreation took place in their own homes or those of friends. Their problems in this area seemed to be fewer than in many American marriages.

There was a fairly complete separation of home and work. The women were satisfied with their husbands' incomes and did not pressure them; similarly, the husbands did not expect their wives to have careers, although some of them worked. These couples seemed satisfied on steady, modest incomes.

38. Anselm L. Strauss, "Strain and Harmony in American-Japanese War-Bride Marriages," *Marriage and Family Living* 16 (May 1954), pp. 99–106.

Relationships with the husbands' families generally were good, and the in-laws often helped the bride learn American ways. When in-law conflict did develop, there was severe strain as in comparable American marriages. Relationships with friends also appeared good, but selective; much interaction was with other interracially married couples. It would be interesting to speculate whether this pairing off of interracially married couples reflected common interests or rejection by other couples.

Presumably, the strains involved in Oriental-Caucasian marriages may be less than those in black-white marriages. Data on black-white marriages also reveal the situation to be complicated.

At least three in-depth studies of black-white marriages have been completed: in New York, in Philadelphia, and in Indianapolis.[39] The number of couples was small: 22, 50, and 9, respectively. All couples were carefully interviewed. Although there were differences of location and time span, the three studies present a rather consistent picture of what such marriages are like.

The evidence suggests that many people who enter intermarriages are relatively isolated from their families to begin with. Often, the family of the white partner at least does not know of the courtship, which tends to be carried on with some secrecy. In some cases, the secrecy is continued after the marriage. Golden found that some white spouses avoided contacts with their parents and former white friends. On the other hand, not all white parents oppose the marriages. Pavela found both some opposition and some support among white parents. Both Golden and Pavela found much less opposition from black parents; acceptance or rejection of the white partner was more likely to be based on his or her personal characteristics than on the mere fact of race.

No couple was completely ostracized by both races. They tended to live in borderline residential areas, with more couples living in all-black areas than in all-white areas. Relations with neighbors usually were amicable but not intimate. Friends were most often black than white; relatively few had extensive contacts with other interracial couples. Some of Smith's New York couples even reported that they probably had more social contacts than similar white or black couples.

Many couples did report special difficulties. Being stared at in public places was emphasized by New York and Philadelphia couples. Some white spouses had lost jobs when their employers learned of their marriages; others concealed the fact from employers and fellow employees. Some couples were discriminated against in housing, a problem sometimes solved by sending the white partner to inspect the property and

39. Golden, "Patterns of Negro-White Intermarriage," *op. cit.;* Pavela, *op. cit.;* and Charles E. Smith, "Negro-White Intermarriage—Forbidden Sexual Union," *Journal of Sex Research* 2 (Nov. 1966), pp. 169–78.

sign the lease. In general, the problems encountered by interracial couples were those typically met by black couples.

Over half the Philadelphia and Indianapolis couples had children, and none of the New York couples had decided against having children. If they had fewer children than average, this may be related to their older age at marriage. Relatively little discrimination against the children was experienced at the hands of blacks, but virtually all parents acknowledged that their children would be raised as blacks. Many couples longed for the day when prejudice would not be a problem.

Golden reported that 34 couples out of 50 had been married five years or longer. He concluded that these marriages have a good chance of survival. Pavela's conclusion is consistent with Burchinal's analysis of the changing nature of interracial marriage. Pavela says: "In many respects, the Negro-white marriages studied contradict the picture of such marriages in the public mind or even in much sociological literature. It would appear that such intermarriage now occurs between persons who are, by and large, economically, educationally, and culturally equal and who have a strong emotional attachment, be it rationaliaztion or real. The external pressures faced by interracial couples are often great, but certainly do not appear to be overwhelming."

National data on the stability of interracial marriages are limited and generally confined to black-white marriages. These data indicate that black-white marriages are more likely to end in divorce than either homogamous black or homogamous white marriages. The proportion of black-white marriages that had occurred in the 1950s and were still intact in 1970, for example, was lower than the corresponding percentages of couples who were of the same race: 90 percent of the white marriages and 78 percent of the black marriages were still intact, whereas only 63 percent of mixed marriages with black husbands and 47 percent of those with white husbands had survived.[40]

Religious Affiliation

The norms supporting religious homogamy in the United States have long been strong—only slightly less strong than those supporting racial homogamy. In 1950 in New Haven, Connecticut, for example, Hollingshead reported that 97 percent of Jewish marriages, 94 percent of Catholic marriages, and 74 percent of Protestant marriages were religiously homogamous.[41] Other studies have challenged the existence of ex-

40. Hugh Carter and Paul C. Glick, *Marriage and Divorce: A Social and Economic Study*, Cambridge, Mass.: Harvard University Press, 1976, pp. 414–15.
41. *Op. cit.*

treme religious endogamy, however, and have shown that even the computation of rates of religious homogamy is very complicated.

Thomas, for example, gathered data for Catholic dioceses in different sections of the country and reported mixed-marriage rates ranging from 10 percent in El Paso to 70 percent in Raleigh and Charleston.[42] The mixed-marriage rate for one half of the Catholic dioceses in the United States was about 30 percent. For Connecticut, Thomas estimates that the rate probably is about 50 percent.

If taken at face value, the figures reported by Hollingshead for New Haven and by Thomas for all of Connecticut appear to be in serious conflict. Part of the discrepancy is to be accounted for by the fact that these are not comparable rates. The rate reported by Hollingshead is a mixed-marriage rate for individuals, whereas Thomas's rate is a rate for marriages. A *mixed-marriage rate for individuals* refers to the percentage of married persons (in any category) who enter mixed marriages; a *mixed-marriage rate for marriages*, in contrast, refers to the percentage of marriages (in any category) that are mixed.[43] Making Thomas's figures comparable to Hollingshead's, his rate for Connecticut turns out to be 33.3 percent.

Even after the data are rendered comparable, Thomas's point that the New Haven data are not representative appears well taken. Burchinal and Chancellor found individual mixed-marriage rates in Iowa to range from 9 to 24 percent.[44] In New York City, Heiss found 18 percent of Jews, 21 percent of Catholics, and 34 percent of Protestants to be intermarried.[45] Finally, Rodman's computations yield individual mixed-

42. John L. Thomas, "The Factor of Religion in the Selection of Marriage Mates," *American Sociological Review* 16 (Aug. 1951), pp. 487–91.
43. The importance of distinguishing between mixed-marriage rates for individuals and for marriages has been pointed out by Rodman, who also provided the following illustration. If there are 6 homogamous Catholic marriages and 4 mixed marriages, the mixed-marriage rate can be either 40 percent or 25 percent. Four of the 10 marriages are mixed, but only 1 out of 4 of the Catholics is involved in a mixed marriage. Hyman Rodman, "Technical Note on Two Rates of Mixed Marriage," *American Sociological Review* 30 (Oct. 1965), pp. 776–78.
44. Lee G. Burchinal and Loren E. Chancellor, "Ages at Marriage, Occupations of Grooms, and Interreligious Marriage Rates," *Social Forces* 40 (May 1962), pp. 348–54. There have been numerous other studies of the incidence of interfaith marriages in various groups. See, for example, Donald H. Bouma, "Religiously Mixed Marriages: Denominational Consequences in the Christian Reformed Church," *Marriage and Family Living* 25 (Nov. 1963), pp. 428–32; and David M. Heer, "The Trend of Interfaith Marriages in Canada: 1922–1957," *American Sociological Review* 27 (April 1962), pp. 245–50; and Thomas P. Monahan, "Some Dimensions of Interreligious Marriages in Indiana, 1962–67," *Social Forces* 52 (Dec. 1973), pp. 195–203.
45. Jerold S. Heiss, "Premarital Characteristics of the Religiously Intermarried in an Urban Area," *American Sociological Review* 25 (Feb. 1960), pp. 47–55.

marriage rates of 3.7 percent for Jews, 4.5 percent for Protestants, and 12.1 percent for Catholics.[46]

If prohibitions against religious intermarriage were effective through the 1950s, intermarriage rates increased during the 1960s and 1970s. With several studies showing the individual mixed-marriage rate for Catholics to be about 30 percent, Pope Paul VI, in 1970, dropped the requirement that the non-Catholic partner to a mixed marriage promise to raise the children as Catholics and ruled that local bishops may grant dispensation "for serious reasons" from the requirement that the marriage ceremony be performed by a priest. Even more drastic change has occurred in Jewish-Gentile marriages. A study by the Council of Jewish Federations and Welfare Funds reported that one third of the American Jews who married between 1966 and 1972 had non-Jewish spouses, more than double the rate of the preceding five years, and more than four times the pre-1960 rate. The same study showed that one fifth of Reform rabbis would perform mixed marriages without conditions and that an additional one fifth would do so when the couple pledged to raise the children as Jews.[47]

A recent study by Glenn combined data from six national surveys conducted from 1973 to 1978.[48] From these data, he estimates that from 15 to 20 percent of marriages in the United States are between spouses with different religious preferences. By denomination, 18 percent of Catholics, almost 12 percent of Jews, and about 7 percent of Protestants marry persons of different faiths. Also, some degree of religious homogamy among couples, particularly Jewish couples, is due to the fact that a number of them convert to their spouse's religion either before or after the marriage.

One factor closely associated with variation in intermarriage rates is the proportion that the religious group is of the community; the larger the proportion that the group is of the total community, the lower the intermarriage rate. In Iowa, a correlation of .66 was found between the proportion of Catholics in county populations and the proportion of homogamous Catholic marriages.[49] This general finding has been borne

46. U.S. Bureau of the Census, *Current Population Reports*, "Religion Reported by the Civilian Population of the United States: March, 1957," Series P-20, No. 79 (1958), as reported in Rodman, *op. cit.*, p. 777.

47. *New York Times*, Feb. 11, 1973, p. E8.

48. Norval D. Glenn, "Interreligious Marriage in the United States: Patterns and Recent Trends," *Journal of Marriage and the Family* 44 (Aug. 1982), pp. 555–66. See also Bernard Farber and Leonard Gordon, "Accounting for Jewish Intermarriage: An Assessment of National and Community Studies," *Contemporary Jewry* 6 (Spring–Summer 1982), pp. 47–75; and Bernard Lazerwitz, "Jewish-Christian Marriages and Conversions," *Jewish Social Studies* 43 (Winter 1981), pp. 31–46.

49. Lee G. Burchinal and Loren E. Chancellor, "Proportions of Catholics, Urbanism,

out by studies using data from the *Official Catholic Directory*,[50] and from the Dominion Bureau of Statistics in Canada.[51]

Interreligious marriages also vary inversely with the cohesiveness of the ethnic group; the more integrated the group, the lower the intermarriage rate. Research shows that ethnic bonds weaken first—marriages occurring across nationality lines but still within the major religious groups.[52] One study of Polish and Italian residents of Buffalo showed in-group marriages among the Poles falling from 79 percent to 35 percent between 1930 and 1960 and in-group Italian marriages falling from 71 percent to 27 percent. The decreases were particularly great after 1940.[53]

A study of religiously intermarried New York City residents casts light on the influence of early family experiences. Heiss found that intermarried Catholics were more likely to have nonreligious parents, expressed greater dissatisfaction with their parents when young, reported greater early strife with their parents, and were more emancipated from parents at the time of marriage. The relationships for the Protestant intermarried were smaller, but in the same direction. None of the relationships held for Jews except for the strength of their family ties while young and at the time of marriage.[54]

Religious Heterogamy and Marital Success. As with racial intermarriages, religious intermarriages are widely believed to be associated with marital failure. A number of studies of the divorce rates of mixed and nonmixed religious marriages bear this out.

Studies show divorce rates to be lowest among Catholics and Jews, somewhat higher among Protestants, higher still in mixed marriages, and highest of all where there is no religious affiliation.[55]

---

and Mixed-Catholic Marriage Rates Among Iowa Counties," *Social Problems* 9 (Spring 1962), pp. 359–65.

50. Harvey J. Locke, Georges Sabagh, and Mary Margaret Thomes, "Interfaith Marriages," *Social Problems* 4 (April 1957), pp. 329–33.

51. Heer, *op. cit.*

52. Ruby Jo Reeves Kennedy, "Single or Triple Melting Pot? Intermarriage Trends in New Haven, 1870–1940," *American Journal of Sociology* 49 (Jan. 1944), pp. 331–39. See also Richard D. Alba and Ronald C. Kessler, "Patterns of Interethnic Marriage Among American Catholics," *Social Forces* 57 (June 1979), pp. 1124–40; and Brent A. Barlow, "Notes on Mormon Interfaith Marriages," *Family Coordinator* 26 (April 1977), pp. 143–50.

53. B. R. Bugelski, "Assimilation Through Intermarriage," *Social Forces* 40 (Dec. 1961), pp. 148–53.

54. *Op. cit.*

55. Alan Booth, David Johnson, and John N. Edwards, "Measuring Marital Instability," *Journal of Marriage and the Family* 45 (May 1983), pp. 387–93; Judson T. Landis, "Marriages of Mixed and Non-mixed Religious Faith," *American Sociological Review* 14 (June 1949), pp. 401–7; and Bumpass and Sweet, *op. cit.,* pp. 758–65.

Table 13.1. Rank order of marital survival rates, by religious affiliation types

Religious affiliation types	Marital survival rates
Homogamous Catholic	96.2
Mixed Presbyterian	94.6
Homogamous Lutheran	94.1
Residual specified Protestant	94.0
Mixed Lutheran	93.0
Mixed Methodist	92.9
Homogamous Methodist	91.4
Homogamous Presbyterian	91.0
Catholic-Lutheran	90.5
Mixed Baptist	90.0
Catholic-Presbyterian	89.8
Homogamous Baptist	89.8
Catholic-residual specified Protestant	89.1
Homogamous Protestant	86.2
Catholic-Methodist	83.8
Mixed unspecified Protestant	82.7
Catholic-Baptist	81.6
Catholic-interreligious	77.6
Homogamous unspecified Protestant	35.0
Catholic-unspecified Protestant	28.7
Total Population	87.6

Source: Lee G. Burchinal and Loren E. Chancellor, "Survival Rates Among Religiously Homogamous and Interreligious Marriages," *Social Forces* 41 (May 1963), p. 360.

One of the more definitive studies of divorce rates in interfaith marriages was done for the state of Iowa, using data for a seven-year period. This study, which imposed controls for age and social status, partly confirmed the results of earlier studies and partly called their findings into question. It did show the divorce rate in homogamous Catholic marriages to be lower than in marriages where Catholics were married to denominationally affiliated Protestants. The differences, however, were considerably reduced, and there were no differences according to whether the Catholic spouse in the mixed marriages was husband or wife. The researchers concluded that the smaller differences did not justify generalizations of considerably greater marital difficulties facing Catholics who marry outside their faith, providing the person they marry is identified with a Protestant denomination.[56]

A special contribution of this study was the computation of marital-survival rates for many types of religiously homogamous and heterogamous marriages. Several factors stand out in the data in Table 13.1.

56. Lee G. Burchinal and Loren E. Chancellor, "Survival Rates Among Religiously Homogamous and Interreligious Marriages," *Social Forces* 41 (May 1963), pp. 353–62.

First, the survival rates almost form a continuum without sharp breaks until the last two categories are reached. Second, although homogamous Catholic marriages had the highest survival rate, a number of other homogamous and mixed marriage types had survival rates nearly as high. Third, many of the rates ranged within a single percentage point of one another. Fourth, the lower-middle segment of the table includes homogamous Protestant marriages, marriages of Catholics with Methodists or Baptists, and the total for all interreligious marriages.

Of particular interest is the fact that Presbyterians, Methodists, and Baptists married to other Protestants had higher marital survival rates than members of those same denominations who were homogamously married. Moreover, the data indicated that the marital survival rates were influenced more by age at marriage and social status than by the fact of religious differences. Marital survival rates were consistently higher among marriages involving older brides and couples marrying at higher status levels.

In summary, we conclude that in spite of the apparently higher divorce rates among some types of mixed marriages, the data are somewhat equivocal. Some authors have gone further, and argued that the frequent admonitions concerning the hazards of mixed marriages reflect a widespread bias against such marriages as much as they reflect data on divorce rates. Vernon, for example, states that family-life educators should be taken to task for presenting only one side of the question. The statistics on the proportion of each type of each marriage that endure are ignored, he says, in the usual presentation of data.[57] Vincent makes a similar point and claims that data on divorce rates could as easily be used to indicate that the problem is not so much one of intermarriage as it is the persistence of religious differences.[58]

At best, divorce rates are a crude index of marital success or failure. We cannot even assume that all of the marriages that result in divorce are unhappy marriages. Among some groups, divorce may be sought whenever the advantages appear to outweigh those involved in remaining married. At the other extreme, divorce may not be acceptable to some no matter how great the unhappiness. No one knows what proportion of religiously homogamous marriages may survive simply because the church condemns divorce.

A number of studies of religiously heterogamous marriages have been

57. Glenn M. Vernon, "Bias in Professional Publications Concerning Interfaith Marriages," *Religious Education* 55 (July–Aug. 1960), pp. 261–64.
58. Clark K. Vincent, "Interfaith Marriages: Problem or Symptom?," in Marvin B. Sussman, *ed., Sourcebook in Marriage and the Family*, Boston: Houghton Mifflin, 1963, pp. 349–59.

made; again, the evidence is far from one-sided. One part of Heiss's study in New York City, for example, included comparisons between matched samples of intermarried and intramarried couples. The findings showed intermarried Catholics to be more dissatisfied, to worry more about marriage, to be in poorer mental health, to have fewer children, and to have more problems with their children. Differences between intermarried and intramarried Jews were smaller and less consistent, but Heiss concluded that intermarried Catholics and Jews may carry something of an additional burden. The pressures on intermarried Protestants were not quite so great.[59]

Two other studies present the other side of the picture. In a study of 194 interfaith marriages, Prince found that nearly half of the spouses were the offspring of interfaith marriages. Moreover, more than half reported themselves either very much satisfied or entirely satisfied with their marriages. Fewer than 10 percent reported any dissatisfaction.[60]

Dyer and Luckey made carefully controlled comparisons among the marriages of 522 former University of Minnesota students and concluded that there was no relation between religious affiliation and marital happiness. This was true in both denominationally homogamous and heterogamous marriages. In testing the relationship of personality variables and marital happiness, no differences were found. The researchers pointed out that these were young couples who had hardly embarked on parenthood and who might encounter difficulties later. On the other hand, they believe that their results may reflect a trend to accept and deal with heterogamous marriages more adequately.[61]

RESIDENTIAL PROPINQUITY

Years ago, sociologists discovered that many people select their marriage partners from among those who live near them geographically. This tendency to select partners from those near at hand is called *residential propinquity*.

The first study of propinquity, in Philadelphia, showed that one sixth of 5000 pairs applying for marriage licenses lived within 1 city block

59. Jerold S. Heiss, "Interfaith Marriage and Marital Outcome," *Marriage and Family Living* 23 (Aug. 1961), pp. 228–33.
60. Alfred J. Prince, "A Study of 194 Cross-Religion Marriages," *Family Life Coordinator* 11 (Jan. 1962), pp. 3–7. For evidence that intermarriage does not change things very much, see Rudolf K. Haerle, Jr., "Church Attendance Patterns Among Intermarried Catholics: A Panel Study," *Sociological Analysis* 30 (Winter 1969), pp. 204–16.
61. Dorothy T. Dyer and Eleanore B. Luckey, "Religious Affiliation and Selected Personality Scores as They Relate to Marital Happiness of a Minnesota College Sample," *Marriage and Family Living* 23 (Feb. 1961), pp. 46–47.

of each other. One third lived within 5 blocks, and half lived within 20 blocks.[62] Bossard concluded that the proportion of marriages decreases markedly as the distance between the parties increases.

Several other studies verified the fact that people select marriage partners disproportionately from those who live nearby, but they did not substantiate the *steady* decrease with increasing distance that Bossard had hypothesized.[63] Rather than concentrate on couples selecting mates from within 1-block, 5-block, and 10-block distances, these researchers focused on whether the general findings would hold up in increasingly controlled studies and on developing theoretical explanations for residential propinquity.

The propinquity studies have assumed that distance is related to mate selection through the opportunities that people have to become acquainted. Clarke tested this assumption in Columbus, Ohio, by securing the addresses of the partners at the time of their first date as well as at marriage. He found that nearly half of the sample had changed addresses between the time of the first date and the application for a marriage license. Some couples moved closer and some moved farther away, with the result that the proportion residing within 16 city blocks remained approximately the same.[64] He did find that the proportions reporting the same address or living within 4 city blocks increased by the time of applying for the license.

Having established that propinquity does not emerge simply from courtship interaction, we turn to two major theoretical interpretations. Katz and Hill propound a norm-interaction theory. Briefly, that theory holds that (1) mate selection is normatively regulated; (2) within eligible groups of potential spouses, the probability of marriage varies directly with the probability of interaction; and (3) the probability of interaction is governed by distance and by the segregation of racial, religious, economic, and other groups in the community.[65] According to

62. James H. S. Bossard, "Residential Propinquity as a Factor in Marriage Selection," *American Journal of Sociology* 38 (Sept. 1932), pp. 219–24.

63. Ray H. Abrams, "Residential Propinquity as a Factor in Marriage Selection: Fifty Year Trends in Philadelphia," *American Sociological Review* 8 (June 1943), pp. 288–94; Alfred C. Clarke, "An Examination of the Operation of Residential Propinquity as a Factor in Mate Selection," *American Sociological Review* 17 (Feb. 1952), pp. 17–22; Alan C. Kerckhoff, "Notes and Comments on the Meaning of Residential Propinquity as a Factor in Mate Selection," *Social Forces* 34 (March 1956), pp. 207–13; Marvin R. Koller, "Residential Propinquity of White Mates at Marriage in Relation to Age and Occupation of Males. Columbus, Ohio, 1938 and 1946," *American Sociological Review* 13 (Oct. 1948), pp. 613–16; and Barrie S. Morgan, "A Contribution to the Debate on Homogamy, Propinquity, and Segregation," *Journal of Marriage and the Family* 43 (Nov. 1981), pp. 909–21.

64. *Op. cit.*

65. See Alvin M. Katz and Reuben Hill, "Residential Propinquity and Marital Selection:

this theory, groups that are most segregated residentially will be the most propinquitous; and where the homogamy norms are strong there will be more propinquity.

This norm-interaction theory is useful in explaining the variations in propinquity that have been found. However, Catton and Smircich, using data from Seattle, find that the most useful model is one that interprets distance gradients as reflecting economy of time and energy rather than competition between near and remote courtship opportunities or the operation of norms.[66] They suggest that the number of "meaningful" mate-selection opportunities that most people have are rather few; most people simply do not become intimately acquainted with many eligible persons of opposite sex. The probability that any one person of opposite sex will be included among that small number probably depends on the time and energy costs in traveling.

The Catton and Smircich theory has not been adequately tested as yet. It is important, however, because it implies that norms in mate selection may not be as important as we think. It holds instead that propinquity may lead to homogamous marriages and that the familiarity of homogamous marriages leads to the development of homogamy norms.

THE THEORY OF COMPLEMENTARY NEEDS

The discussion of homogamous norms in mate selection was confined to homogamy in *social* characteristics. This does not mean that there are no homogamous tendencies in the area of *personal* characteristics, for there are. Early studies showed similarity between husbands and wives in physical traits, attractiveness, intellectual ability, attitudes, and temperament. More recently, Schellenberg studied the similarity in values among engaged and married couples and found more similarity than in a group of artificially paired couples.[67] Kerckhoff and Davis, studying consensus on family values, found it to increase as dating couples moved toward more permanent relationships.[68]

A Review of Theory, Method, and Fact," *Marriage and Family Living* 20 (Feb. 1958), pp. 27–35.

66. William R. Catton, Jr. and R. J. Smircich, "A Comparison of Mathematical Models for the Effect of Residential Propinquity on Mate Selection," *American Sociological Review* 29 (Aug. 1964), pp. 522–29.

67. James A. Schellenberg, "Homogamy in Personal Values and the Field of Eligibles," *Social Forces* 39 (Dec. 1969), pp. 157–62. For similar findings with regard to empathy, see Norman Goodman, and Richard Ofshe, "Empathy, Communication Efficiency, and Marital Status," *Journal of Marriage and the Family* 30 (Nov. 1968), pp. 597–603.

68. Alan C. Kerckhoff and Keith E. Davis, "Value Consensus and Need Complementarity in Mate Selection," *American Sociological Review* 27 (June 1962), pp. 295–303. Snyder

The evidence in favor of homogamy in personal characteristics is not so convincing, however, as that on homogamy in social characteristics. There were, even among the early studies, some that suggested that people may choose marriage partners who have traits opposite from their own. Kretschmer found such a pairing of opposites among 170 married couples, and Gray found the mating of complementary types rather than the mating of homogamous personality types.[69]

Formulation of a theory of mate selection in terms of complementary personality needs and the partial testing of that theory were accomplished by Winch and associates.[70] This theory holds, first, that human behavior is oriented toward the gratification of needs. Important needs become organized in the personality and give pattern to behavior. Not all of these needs are always conscious, so people are aware of some of their needs, partly aware of others, and completely unaware of some.

Needs are learned in personality development and, so, become subject to normative regulation. They must be expressed within the general endogamous and exogamous norms of the group. The endogamous and exogamous norms define for people the "field of eligibles"—those persons from among whom they are permitted to select mates.

Building on these assumptions, Winch describes how love and mate selection operate. He defines love as the positive emotion expressed by one person in a relationship when the second person meets certain important needs of the first or manifests or appears to manifest personal qualities highly valued by the first. In mate selection then each person selects from within the field of eligibles that person who gives greatest promise of providing the maximum need gratification. The partners' need patterns, consequently, will be complementary rather than similar. Further, the complementariness was hypothesized to be either of two

---

found, however, that homogamy in self, social, and total adjustment, and in IQ existed among 20 couples prior to their selection of one another as marital partners. See Eloise C. Snyder, "Marital Selectivity in Self-Adjustment, and I.Q.," *Journal of Marriage and the Family* 28 (May 1966), pp. 188–89.

69. This literature is summarized in Clifford Kirkpatrick, *The Family: As Process and Institution*, New York: Ronald Press, 1963, pp. 335–36.

70. The research appeared in a series of articles. See Thomas Ktsanes, "Mate Selection on the Basis of Personality Type: A Study Utilizing an Empirical Typology of Personality," *American Sociological Review* 20 (Oct. 1955), pp. 547–51; Robert F. Winch, "The Theory of Complementary Needs in Mate Selection: A Test of One Kind of Complementariness," *American Sociological Review* 20 (Feb. 1955), pp. 52–56; Robert F. Winch, "The Theory of Complementary Needs in Mate Selection: Final Results on the Test of the General Hypothesis," *American Sociological Review* 20 (Oct. 1955), pp. 552–55; Robert F. Winch, Thomas Ktsanes, and Virginia Ktsanes, "Empirical Elaboration of the Theory of Complementary Needs in Mate Selection," *Journal of Abnormal and Social Psychology* 51 (Nov. 1955), pp. 508–13.

kinds. First, the needs of the one spouse may be different in kind from
the needs of the second spouse. Or second, the needs of the one spouse
may differ in degree or intensity from those of the other.

The research that sought to verify these hypotheses was very complex and used a very limited sample. Lengthy "need" interviews and
case history interviews were supplemented through the use of projec-
tive testing. Ratings of personality needs were then based on content
analysis of the need interview and case history materials, summarized
and evaluated at conferences of the investigators.

The sample from whom these data were secured were only 25 under-
graduate, childless couples at Northwestern University. The results generally supported the hypotheses. An early test, for example, supported
the notion that the assertive-receptive dimension is important in mate
selection; high assertives tended to marry high receptives. Similarly, it
was found that when the same traits in husband and wife were correlated (abasement with abasement, hostility with hostility, dominance
with dominance, and so on), the relationships were generally negative.
They found little evidence of personality homogamy. When the husbands' hostility scores were correlated with the wives' abasement scores,
by contrast, the relationship was positive; their needs were complementary.

The results required careful qualification. Winch acknowledged that
they were not as compelling as they might have been. He concluded,
however, that the bulk of the data supported the theory of complementary needs. Moreover, that portion of the results that did not clearly
support the theory of complementary needs did not support the idea of
homogamy in personal needs either; they simply showed little relationship among the variables.

The theory of complementary needs attracted considerable attention.
If subsequent research should establish its validity, it would contribute
greatly to our knowledge of mate selection. It is not surprising that
there have been several attempts to test the theory.

At least five studies attempted to test Winch's findings directly, using
the Edwards Personal Preference Schedule to measure personality needs
and complementariness. One study used 60 college couples who either
were regular dating partners or were engaged;[71] one used 36 unmarried
couples and 64 married couples;[72] one used an accidental sample of 50

71. Charles E. Bowerman and Barbara R. Day, "A Test of the Theory of Complementary
Needs as Applied to Couples During Courtship," *American Sociological Review* 21 (Oct.
1956), pp. 602–5.
72. James A. Schellenberg and Lawrence S. Bee, "A Re-examination of the Theory of
Complementary Needs in Mate Selection," *Marriage and Family Living* 22 (Aug. 1960),
pp. 227–32.

relatively well-adjusted married couples;[73] one used 62 couples who were either dating, going steady, or engaged;[74] and the fifth used 258 Swedish couples who had published the banns.[75] In all five studies, the results were essentially negative; no real support was found for the theory of complementary needs.

It should be pointed out that these studies were not strictly comparable to Winch's study. The instruments and procedures differed. Moreover, the samples were small and selective. The theory of complementary needs cannot be said to have been either adequately established or refused. Perhaps the most valuable contribution so far has been to encourage attempts to improve the theory itself.

Rosow pointed out that the theory of complementary needs is oversimplified. He maintains that there are at least four kinds of complementarity that affect marital cohesion: (1) the relations strictly between the couple, as studied by Winch; (2) the relations that involve either partner acting for the couple with outsiders; (3) relations between the couple, as a couple, with outsiders; and (4) relations in which each partner separately seeks, within the marriage, to balance satisfactions or frustrations encountered outside the family. Rosow points out, too, that needs exist as organized patterns and that the importance of these patterns in an individual life may change over time.[76]

Udry suggested, further, that we react to others on the basis of our perceptions of them and that perception may or may not coincide with measured personality traits. He found that mates' perceptions of one another exaggerate personality differences and involve projection of their own traits. One implication is that an adequate theory of complementary needs will need to be more complex than the existing theory.[77]

Finally, Bolton introduced balance into theories of mate selection by arguing that, although both homogamy and complementary theories have utility, mate selection must be studied not only in terms of variables brought by the partners to the courtship situation, but also in

73. John A. Blazer, "Complementary Needs and Marital Happiness," *Marriage and Family Living* 25 (Feb. 1963), pp. 89–95.

74. Jerold S. Heiss and Michael Gordon, "Need Patterns and the Mutual Satisfaction of Dating and Engaged Couples," *Journal of Marriage and the Family* 26 (Aug. 1964), pp. 337–39.

75. Jan Trost, "Some Data on Mate Selection: Complementarity," *Journal of Marriage and the Family* 29 (Nov. 1967), pp. 730–38.

76. Irving Rosow, "Issues in the Concept of Need-Complementarity," *Sociometry* 20 (Sept. 1957), pp. 216–33. See also Ellen S. Karp, Julie H. Jackson, and David Lester, "Ideal-Self Fulfillment in Mate Selection: A Corollary to the Complementary Need Theory of Mate Selection," *Journal of Marriage and the Family* 32 (May 1970), pp. 269–72; and Jan Trost, "Some Data on Mate Selection: Homogamy and Perceived Homogamy," *Journal of Marriage and the Family* 29 (Nov. 1967), pp. 739–55.

77. J. Richard Udry, "Complementarity in Mate Selection: A Perceptual Approach," *Marriage and Family Living* 25 (Aug. 1963), pp. 281–89.

terms of the process by which their relationship moves toward marriage. There are many turning points and commitments.

A DEVELOPMENTAL APPROACH TO MATE SELECTION

The development of a courtship is not mechanically predetermined by either social or personality variables. Instead the outcome is the product of a long series of advances and retreats, changing definitions of the situation and the resolution of tensions. Bolton describes five different types of developmental processes:[78]

Type I: *Personality meshing developmental processes.* The predominant characteristic of this type is the mutual perception of personality "fit," bringing into meshing the existing personality orientations of the two parties and providing the qualities of experience that serve as indexes of a marriageable relation. Couples tend to be homogamous in background and values but complementary in personality needs and organization. Attraction is felt early, the developmental tempos of the pair are in close rhythm and interactions increase in frequency with erotic interaction, empathy, and idealization important. These relations correspond fairly closely to romantic expectations.

Type II: *Identity clarification developmental processes.* The central theme is the clarification or change of one or both individuals' identities. Although the two individuals may differ initially about values, interaction brings about increasing agreements along with a role pattern tending to be egalitarian. The assumption of compatibility either is made early or emerges out of interaction about identity problems. Identity problems are precipitated by interaction such as through conflict with parents or threat to defenses against intimate involvement. The relationship cannot progress to marriage until the identity problems are resolved. The importance of interpersonal strategies is great, turning points are frequent; and shared understandings of considerable depth are built up. There is a withdrawal into the relationship away from outside influences.

Type III: *Relation-centered developmental processes.* The central theme is the building up of images of the other, amorous identifications and bonds that lead the couple to marriage. Personalities do not spontaneously mesh; their "fit" remains in doubt throughout the premarital period. Adjustments, shared understandings, and com-

78. Charles D. Bolton, "Mate Selection as the Development of a Relationship," *Marriage and Family Living* 23 (Aug. 1961), pp. 234–40. See also Robert G. Ryder, John S. Kafka, and David H. Olson, "Separating and Joining Influences in Courtship and Early Marriage," *American Journal of Orthopsychiatry* 41 (April 1971), pp. 450–64.

mitments are consciously built up, although they may not have much depth. There is initial superficial commitment; then one or both parties begin having questions and the theme becomes the viability of the relation. There are more ups and downs, breaks, rivals, and outside pressures to maintain the relationship than in any other developmental type.

Type IV: *Pressure- and intrapersonal-centered developmental processes.* The two parties are similar and traditional in background, and they dislike conflict. Their personalities, however, decidedly do not mesh. One party uses direct, frontal pressure, whereas the other depends on subtle manipulation. One is relatively free of blocks, whereas the other has personality barriers to intimate involvements. Several themes emerge: (1) one member, being under pressure to marry, falls in love quickly and pressures the other for marriage, but the resisting member blocks; (2) a concentration directly on marriageability and on securing commitments; (3) a dependence of one or both members more on the relationship per se than on one another; and (4) importance of fantasy for one or both members. Identity problems are avoided, except at crises—and then interaction halts short of efforts at resolution—and even amorous identifications are built up primarily in intrapersonal processes. The lack of congruity of definitions is met by fantasy and tactical maneuvering. There is an emphasis on formality, romanticism, and role playing, with avoidance of the directly erotic. Often crucial developments come by correspondence, where the inhibited member feels freer and ambiguity is harder to maintain.

Type V: *Expediency-centered developmental processes.* The relationship centers on a strongly felt pressure to marry on the part of one or both members, in the context of a basic personality problem or identity crisis. Where this pressure characterizes only one partner, the other is inexperienced in heterosexual relationships, highly suggestible, or apathetic. If expediency exists at the outset, the process is short; if it emerges after a casual relationship is in progress, there are sharp turning points and tactical maneuvers through which the relationship quickly moves toward marriage. Personality "fit" and mutuality of values are only superficially considered, although some fantasy is important.

Whether or not these five types cover all of the processes whereby future spouses are selected, their construction displays a broad, perceptive knowledge of personality and courtship. They indicate the importance of personal, interpersonal, and situational variables within the general context imposed by social homogamy.

A STIMULUS-VALUE-ROLE THEORY

One final theory of mate selection has been developed by Murstein who holds that most couples pass through three stages before they marry: the stimulus stage, the value stage, and the role stage.[79]

This theory holds that people are first attracted to one another by their perceptions of their attractive qualities. This is the stimulus stage. The attractive qualities are both physical and social: good looks, strong, tall, petite, jovial, considerate, aggressive, and so on. Without being wholly aware of it, each partner prepares a mental balance sheet, comparing the other's attractive and unattractive features, which are then compared with his or her own. If the one partner is substantially more or less attractive than the other, the relationship is likely to be broken off by the more attractive partner.

If the couple are fairly evenly matched, the relationship may develop on into the value stage. Now the partners talk. They discuss their attitudes toward men's and women's roles and toward marriage. They discuss such abstract subjects as politics and religion and such intimate ones as practicing birth control and having children. The more similar the discovered values, the stronger their attraction to one another becomes and the more time they spend together. They are falling in love.

Some couples marry at this point, but most move on into the role stage. Now the pair's association is so continuous that they not only hear one another's expressed values, but they see how those values are expressed in real-life situations. They see whether the other partner is cheerful or moody, dependable or erratic, generous or selfish, punitive or forgiving, and so on. The more they interact, the more they perceive what it would be like to be married to one another. Again, the concept of the hypothetical balance sheet applies. If the bargain continues to be favorable and fairly equal, marriage is likely to be the outcome.

The stimulus-value-role theory along with developmental theory and complementary-needs theory all help us to understand how couples sorted originally by homogamy and propinquity move on toward marriage.

Finally, it should at least be questioned whether we overrationalize the process of mate selection. Our emphasis on free marital choice seems to imply that one chooses a mate as rationally as one buys a garden tool or a tube of toothpaste. At the same time, it seems apparent that at about a certain age strong cultural pressures are generated for

79. Bernard I. Murstein, "A Theory of Marital Choice and Its Applicability to Marriage Adjustment," in Bernard I. Murstein, ed., *Theories of Attraction and Love*, New York: Springer, 1971, pp. 100–151.

people to find mates and they do just that—telling themselves all the while how carefully their choices are being made. Some writers have suggested that although the percentage of marriages that are purely of the supply-and-demand variety may be small, possibly most marriages embody some element of chance.

SUMMARY

Homogamy, the tendency for like to marry like, reflects endogamous norms. Homogamy has been verified for age, marital status, social status, race, religion, and ethnic background.

Although the age at marriage is rising, most Americans marry young and marry persons of nearly their own age. Age-homogamy norms become less effective in remarriages. Studies show that age at marriage is related to marital success, with those marrying very young having poorer chances of achieving marital happiness. The divorce rate among such young marriages is estimated at from two to four times that among persons who marry after 20 years of age. The high divorce rate is related to low educational levels, low economic levels, premarital pregnancies, and possibly to personality difficulties. Whether young marriages that remain intact are of higher or lower quality than other marriages is unknown.

Status homogamy operates by occupational level, educational level, and class of residential area. When status homogamy does not hold, however, the general pattern is for men to marry downward. This mating gradient may leave high-status women and low-status men among the unmarried. Status homogamy may be declining with time.

Traditionally, the norms requiring racial endogamy have been strong. Perhaps no more than 1 percent of all marriages are interracial, although the intermarriage rate is increasing. There is great interest in that small proportion of the population that does intermarry.

Studies show that spouses in interracial marriages tend to be older than those entering homogamous marriages, that they may have been married before, and that they may have histories of rejection by parents and their own racial group. On the other hand, egalitarian norms may be leading groups to contemplate interracial dating and marriage without the historically associated conditions of rebellion and nonconformity.

Interracial marriages are widely believed to be doomed to failure. Studies of war-bride marriages and black-white marriages do not bear out the belief however. Instead studies show that strains are patterned and predictable, just as they are in racially homogamous marriages. The strains in black-white marriages include isolation from parental families, particularly the white family, and having to raise children as black. Discrimination may be encountered in housing, employment, and in public encounters. Nationally, black-white marriages have higher divorce rates than either homogamous black or homogamous white marriages.

Studies of religious homogamy have shown wide variation in inter-marriage rates. In general, the larger the proportion a religious group is of the community, the lower its intermarriage rate and vice versa. Intermarriage also varies inversely with the cohesion of the ethnic group. Religious intermarriage rates are increasing.

Research shows divorce rates to be higher in marriages where Catholics marry non-Catholics than in Catholic-Catholic marriages. The differences are smaller than generally believed however, and do not cover all types of religious mixed marriages. Martial-survival rates are influenced more by age and social status than by religious differences. Studies of adjustment in interfaith marriages have produced conflicting findings. Some studies show special problems of adjustment, some do not. Society may be becoming increasingly accepting of interfaith marriages.

Residential propinquity refers to the tendency of persons to select marriage partners who live near to them. Propinquity operates at the first date and at marriage. Theories explaining propinquity have emphasized residential segregation, homogamous norms, the relation between distance and the likelihood of interaction, and the sheer time and energy costs involved in traveling.

The evidence for homogamy in personal characteristics is not so strong as that in social characteristics. In fact, there is some evidence that people seek marital partners who complement themselves in personality. A theory of complementary needs has received some empirical support; subsequent testing failed to confirm the original findings however. Efforts to develop the theory continue. Full understanding of mate selection requires that relationships be viewed developmentally in addition to the perspective provided by homogamy, propinquity, and complementary needs. The development of courtship is not completely predetermined but involves a series of advances and retreats, changing definitions of the situation, and commitments.

Finally, mate selection is not yet fully explained. There may be fortuitous factors operating. Few instances of mate selection can be ascribed wholly to chance, but some chance elements may enter into most relationships.

SUGGESTED READINGS

Carter, Hugh, and Glick, Paul C., *Marriage and Divorce: A Social and Economic Study*, Cambridge, Mass.: Harvard University Press, 1976. A rich compilation of data, from federal sources, on marriage patterns in the United States.

Johnson, Robert A., *Religious Assortative Mating in the United States*, New York: Academic Press, 1980. Complex mathematical and demographic analysis of mate selection and marriage among various religious groups.

Rubin, Lillian B., *Intimate Strangers: Men and Women Together*, New York: Harper & Row, 1983. An insightful examination of the differing needs of men and women.

Tseng, Wen-Shing, McDermott, John F., Jr., and Maretzki, Thomas W., eds., *Adjustment in Intercultural Marriage*, Honolulu: University Press of Hawaii, 1977. Nine essays focusing on intermarriage in Hawaii where such marriages are the cultural norm.

Weitzman, Lenore J., *The Marriage Contract: Spouses, Lovers, and the Law*, New York: The Free Press, 1981. A scholarly presentation of the laws concerning marriage and the uses of prenuptial contracts for marital and cohabiting partners.

FILMS

Are You the One? (Educational Media Services, Brigham Young University, Provo, Utah 84601), 24 minutes. Through analysis of one couple, pinpoints some of the issues to be considered in selecting a mate.

Marriage: What Kind for You? (Educational Media Services, Brigham Young University, Provo, Utah 84601), 25 minutes. An engaged couple view different couples at an office party. Makes sharp contrasts between healthy and deteriorating relationships.

Never a Bride: Preparing for Marriage (Educational Media Services, Brigham Young University, Provo, Utah 84601), 22 minutes. A self-seeking girl discovers that it is more important to be the right person than to find the right person for marriage.

QUESTIONS AND PROJECTS

1. What is meant by homogamy? How are homogamous norms related to endogamy and exogamy?

2. What is the pattern of homogamy by age? How is it related to marital status?

3. What trends have been evident in very youthful marriages? What factors are related to success or failure of such marriages? Can you see any elements of a self-fulfilling prophecy operating?

4. Does homogamy operate by status levels in the society? What is the evidence? Is there any evidence that status homogamy may be weakening?

5. What is meant by the mating gradient? What influence does it have on determining what groups are likely to remain among the unmarried?

6. How much interracial marriage is there in the United States? How rapidly is the rate increasing?

7. What are the consequences of interracial marriages? Are these in accord with traditional stereotypes? What do we know about the personality needs of those who intermarry? What change may be occurring?

8. How much religious homogamy is there in the United States? What factors are related to intermarriage rates? Is intermarriage increasing? What do studies show of attitudes toward intermarriage?

9. What is the relation between religious heterogamy and divorce rates? Is the relationship a simple one? What does research show about the relationship between marital happiness and interfaith marriage?

10. Define residential propinquity. How does it operate? What explanations have been proposed for it?

11. Explain the theory of complementary needs. What does research show? Is further development of the theory needed?

12. How may mate selection be conceived of as a developmental process? Relate this concept to Waller's theory of dating and courtship.

Mimi Forsyth, Monkmeyer

14
Marital Adjustment

Now marriage is, in actual fact, just a way of living. We don't expect life to be all sunshine and roses, or even beer and skittles. But somehow we do expect marriage to be that way. People who are accustomed to bickering with everyone else are shocked when they find that they bicker with their wives. Women who have found everything somewhat disappointing are surprised and pained when marriage proves itself no exception. Most of the complaints about the institution of holy matrimony arise not because it is worse than the rest of life, but because it is not incomparably better.

There are reasons for this almost universal feeling of disillusionment about marriage. One is that we are taught to expect too much from it. . . . But even if we have become profoundly cynical about marriage in general we are apt to be disillusioned about our own, because most of us marry while we are in love. . . . The sexual excitement, the uncertainties and novelties of the new relationship actually lift us out of ourselves for a time. With the best will in the world we cannot during the falling-in-love stage show ourselves to our beloved as we really are, nor see her in her everyday personality. We are quite genuinely not our everyday selves at this period. We are more intense, more vital than usual. Moreover we see ourselves through the eyes of our beloved. Unconsciously we match our feeling about ourselves with the glorified impression she has formed of us.

This excited state of mind cannot endure the protracted association of marriage. The thrilling sexual tension which normally keeps engaged couples in a state of fervid and delighted expectation abates with frequent, satisfying intercourse. The element of uncertainty is dissipated—and there is no doubt that a goal we have not yet won is more intriguing than one which is wholly ours. . . . Sooner or later, when flamboyant anticipations of betrothal give way to the sober satisfactions of marriage, we lapse back into our ordinary selves. Fortunately, we can surpass ourselves during emotional crises without seriously depleting our reserves. We can run from a bear very fast indeed, but if we made that speed habitual we would soon collapse entirely. Walking is the most practicable gait for common use, and marriage too must be paced at the rate of our usual temperament. This inevitable change of pace is what we call disillusionment. Our disillusionment does not proceed wholly, or perhaps even primarily, from the unromantic facts we learn about our partner in the course of daily observation. It comes largely from our bored recognition of the same old self within our own breast. Our own newfound charm and prowess and glamour evaporate when we can no longer read them in a worshipping gaze, when we are no longer stimulated by the desire for conquest.[1]

The last two chapters have shown that the routes whereby couples approach marriage are multiple and varied. It seems likely that some persons exercise rationality in their selection of spouses and approach marriage with realistic expectations. At the other extreme are couples caught up in overwhelming attraction for one another. Some of these relationships develop essentially without exploitation and involve intense idealization of each partner by the other. In others, one partner is clearly dominant, with the disadvantaged partner more or less successfully concealing the already present pain the relationship produces. Some couples are trapped into marriage by pregnancy. Some appear to result primarily from the pressures exerted by partners and friends and the lack of a better alternative. Some defy explanation.

We cannot even list all of the qualities of relationships and all of the courtship processes that lead to marriage. It is obvious, however, that the adjustments required in marriage are related to the relationships on which marriages are based; the adjustment of 22-year-old college graduates with parental approval and adequate finances will differ from that of high school students trapped by pregnancy. Moreover, the adjustment of an aggressive, unattractive 25-year-old bride and a divorced man will differ from both. Processes of marital adjustment are unlikely to be fewer or simpler than those of courtship.

No one has yet succeeded in developing a fully adequate theory of marital adjustment. In fact there is scarcely a satisfactory definition of marital adjustment. In this chapter, we shall look first at some common patterns of interaction in early marriage and then subject the concept of marital adjustment to critical scrutiny.

THE DYNAMICS OF MARITAL ADJUSTMENT

Marriage may or may not involve a drastic change in living arrangements. Clarke, for example, found that 10 percent of the couples he

1. John Levy and Ruth Munroe, *The Happy Family*, New York: Alfred A. Knopf, 1948, pp. 65–67.

studied reported the same address on the marriage-license application form.[2] Some of this might be accounted for by couples reporting the address to which they were moving rather than where they had previously been living. Some of these couples, however, already were living together.

Other evidence indicates that whether the couple already are having intercourse influences their early marital adjustments. Kanin and Howard found that couples who were having premarital intercourse were less likely to take wedding trips, were less likely to practice contraception early in marriage, and were more likely to report both sexual satisfaction and aspiration toward better sexual adjustment in marriage.[3]

Honeymoon Interaction

For most couples, marriage represents a sharp break with conditions of prior living. The marriage ceremony endorses whatever relationship already exists and, often, propels them into a 24-hour-a-day physical and emotional intimacy for which they are not wholly prepared. Marriages seldom are scheduled to coincide with readiness for full intimacy but are arranged instead in terms of less relevant criteria such as graduation from college, attaining the minimum legal age, having the harvest in, and so on. It should not be surprising if the sudden transition occasioned by the wedding ceremony were accompanied by both bliss and strain for most young couples.

A perceptive analysis of early marital adjustment has come from Willard Waller. It cannot be said that he described the adjustment processes in all young marriages but something approaching some of the conditions he describes may appear in most of them.[4]

Waller describes the early weeks of marriage as suffused with erotically tinged euphoria. To the degree idealization has developed during courtship, each partner carries into marriage a romanticized conception of what the other is like. It seems wonderful to be marrying such an extraordinary person as the partner appears to be and, if the partner is so exceptional, then one must also be special to merit such a partner.

Many forces operate in the premarital period to enhance the egos and general well-being of the couple. To have found a partner at all represents success in the competition for mates. To have found such an ideal

2. Alfred C. Clarke, "An Examination of the Operation of Residential Propinquity as a Factor in Mate Selection," *American Sociological Review* 17 (Feb. 1952), pp. 17–22.
3. Eugene J. Kanin and David H. Howard, "Postmarital Consequences of Premarital Sex Adjustments," *American Sociological Review* 23 (Oct. 1958), pp. 556–62.
4. The following discussion draws heavily on Willard Waller and Reuben Hill, *The Family: A Dynamic Interpretation* (rev. ed.), New York: Dryden Press, 1951, pp. 253–321.

partner produces something akin to a mild, continuing intoxication. Then, as the sex relationship progresses, there is the overwhelming desire for complete fulfillment. As with other forms of fulfillment, the anticipation, fantasy, and accompanying feelings probably are as important as the achievement itself. Finally, the approval and vicarious participation of family and friends in the relationship brings psychic rewards. One's position has shifted a little closer to the center of the universe, and one experiences emotions that surely are denied most ordinary people.

This heady euphoria continues into the early weeks of marriage. Moreover, it is reinforced by the excitement of the new married status, acquiring new possessions, moving into new quarters, and establishing new routines. According to Waller, this anesthetizes each partner against the too-early and too-violent intrusion on preexisting habit patterns of the nonmeshing habits of the partner. Thus, a man, fussy about food can eat the undercooked eggs without the gastrointestinal spasms they would otherwise produce. Similarly, the young wife who finds that her husband wears his underwear for three days and then throws it under the bed is not immediately overcome with revulsion. Locked in one another's arms, in their fantasies, in their new status, and in the interest and approval of others, most couples experience—whether or not they take a wedding trip—an initial blissful adjustment that merits the sentimental term *honeymoon*.

Even during this early period, however, the couple move toward a *modus vivendi*. Our system does not provide rigidly structured roles into which husband and wife must fit, but it depends on the attraction between the couple to see them through the development of roles appropriate to their situation, ones that will enhance their social and economic status. There are large areas of behavior that must be defined in a short time.

Paradoxically, the so-called honeymoon period also is characterized by unusual sensitivity of each spouse to the behavior of the other. The euphoria alternates with periods of excessive hurt and shock at actual or alleged slights. If idealization frequently accompanies courtship, so does doubt—of self, of partner, and of the relationship. To the degree to which love serves as a rationalization of the movement toward marriage, the partner who has these feelings may react violently to their confirmation in the marriage. The first time, for example, that the husband comes home too tired to go out with his wife may constitute irrefutable proof that he does not love her. The first time that the wife crawls into bed and goes promptly to sleep may signal to the husband that he should have heeded his doubts about getting married in the first place.

The opportunities for rebuffs and slights in early marriage are legion. Moreover, marriage forces on people in intimacy that is not all erotic. Husbands cannot escape confrontation with the paraphernalia attending menstruation or with hair curlers and the washing of lingerie. Many wives must handle dirty socks and underwear and clean up the bathroom, which has been turned into a swamp during their husbands' showers. Both sexes must contend with messy toothpaste tubes and catsup bottles—rendered that way by inconsiderate partners.

Waller defined the honeymoon as that period in the psychic adjustment of the couple while illusion lasts. Eventually, he thought, the opposition between idealization, on the one hand, and the intrusion of humdrum reality, on the other, yields to reality. Inherent in this is some disillusionment, both with the partner and with oneself. If the partner is not so different from others, then the special desirability that was imputed to oneself must be illusory also. The shattering of dreams is painful and the onset of disillusionment sets the stage for conflict.

There is some empirical support for the idea of generalized disillusionment early in marriage. Hobart reports a study of 258 couples ranging from "favorite date" to "married" at a West Coast college. He found strong evidence of disillusionment in the transition from engagement to marriage. The data indicated more disillusionment among men than among women and more tendency among men for disillusionment to be associated with prior romanticism.[5] What is particularly striking is the implication that disillusionment may occur early in marriage even where there has not been excessive unreality in courtship.

Indirect evidence of disillusionment in early marriage also is provided by separation and divorce rates. Landis, studying 544 college couples who had been married about two years, found that one fifth of them had considered separation.[6] In Oregon, Johannis found that one third of 54 college couples married three years had considered separation. For the country as a whole, there are more separations during the first year of marriage than in any year after the fourth year. Moreover, the highest divorce rates occur during the second and third years of marriage.[7] Many of these couples have separated after only a few months of living to-

5. Charles W. Hobart, "Disillusionment in Marriage, and Romanticism," *Marriage and Family Living* 20 (May 1958), pp. 156–62; Peter C. Pineo. "Development Patterns in Marriage," *Family Coordinator* 18 (April 1969), pp. 135–40. For additional evidence on the tendency toward higher levels of romanticism among men, see Zick Rubin, Letitia Anne Peplau, and Charles T. Hill, "Loving and Leaving: Sex Differences in Romantic Attachments," *Sex Roles* 7 (Aug. 1981), pp. 821–25.
6. Judson T. Landis, "On the Campus," *Survey Midmonthly* 84 (Jan. 1948), pp. 17–19.
7. Theodore B. Johannis, Jr., "The Marital Adjustment of a Sample of Married College Students," *Family Life Coordinator* 4 (June 1956), p. 29.

gether. Although these rates do not automatically testify to disillusionment, they indicate that many couples undergo severe stress in the early
months and years of marriage.

When disillusionment occurs, conflict develops. No one enjoys being
hurt and the marriage partner is not only the most available target but is
also, by a perverse sort of logic, responsible for one's plight. What is
more natural than to attack?

The Emergence of Conflict

The incidents that set off conflict more often than not are trivial. The
same undercooked eggs that one gamely ate before now become intolerable. The messy catsup bottle, the messy bathroom, lack of enthusiasm
for going to the movies or making love—all produce rage. Often, of
course, one's partner is undergoing comparable frustrations and meets
rage with rage. Even when a spouse is not disposed to quarrel, he or she
seldom is prepared to withstand hostile attacks from the partner. Whatever doubts and anxieties surround oneself and the relationship become
the focus of attention. Without intending to, and without wanting to,
many young couples test their relationships severely.

Waller and Hill emphasize the potential destructiveness of quarreling.
They point out that ordinarily people, in general, and spouses, in particular, handle carefully the little fictions, rationalizations, and half-
truths according to which people order their lives and protect their self-
concepts.[8] A woman may know and her husband may know that she is
not very attractive. Usually, however, she emphasizes her good points
such as wavy hair or well-shaped legs. Her husband, too, emphasizes
her good features. There is a tacit conspiracy in which each protects the
other and both protect the relationship. As long as they get along well,
it works just fine. Even in marriage, each partner preserves some of the
adoration so carefully cultivated in courtship.

When conflict develops, this breaks down. Each partner is hurt and
wishes to inflict hurt in turn. How better to do it than to attack where
the other is vulnerable? Say, for example, that a husband's occupational
success is important. The degree to which he is a success depends on
many factors, not the least of which is his wife's ability to play the
hostess and companion. Even if she is extraordinarily adroit at further-

8. Waller and Hill, *op. cit.*, p. 301. See also Wells Goodrich, Robert G. Ryder, and
Harold L. Raush, "Patterns of Newlywed Marriage," *Journal of Marriage and the Family* 30 (Aug. 1968), pp. 383–91; Robert G. Ryder, John S. Kafka, and David H. Olson,
"Separating and Joining Influences in Courtship and Early Marriage," *American Journal of Orthopsychiatry* 41 (April 1971), pp. 450–64; and Jetse Sprey, "The Family as
a System in Conflict," *Journal of Marriage and the Family* 31 (Nov. 1969), pp. 699–706.

ing her husband's career, usually she plays it down and basks in his success. When he tells her how astutely he put over a program, she tells him what a wonderful executive he is. Not until they come into serious conflict will she point out that much of his success depends on the friendship that she has cultivated with the boss and the boss's wife. Only then will she tell him that most people think of him as only an average boy who was fortunate to marry a talented woman.

The example could be multipled hundreds of times and turned against the husband and wife equally. The point is that, under provocation, each partner sets out to destroy the little fictions that are so important to maintaining the self-concept. And, in these bitter attacks on one anoher, they may soon destroy the basis on which their relationship is built. In the illustration, the husband who has been confronted by his wife will find it difficult to share his successes with her in full enthusiasm again. Once it has been said, neither of them can assume the full pretense that operated before. If he is to adjust benignly, the husband may seek approval more from his coworkers. In that case, his marriage suffers only by attrition. In more destructive forms, the husband may cherish the adoration bestowed on him by a secretary, a girl he picks up in a bar, or even the attentive ear of a bartender.

Overt Conflict

There are many ways to conceptualize conflict. One way is to describe it in terms of acute, progressive, or habituated forms.

Acute conflict is most characteristic of early marriage and stems from the many undefined situations that exist at that time. Its function is to permit the couple to work out a joint pattern of life in which the frustrations that accompany early disillusionment are worked through. The question, of course, is whether accommodation will be achieved before quarreling has destroyed the foundation on which it must rest. As the particular problems that a couple face are resolved, acute conflict tends to disappear from the marriage. It may reappear, however, whenever any basic change in conditions produces a new undefined situation. Acute conflict, for example, may reappear when the first child is born, and continue until techniques for handling the accompanying changes are worked out. Similarly, a promotion, a move to another city, the marriage of one's children, and having to care for one's aged parents all may provoke new outbursts of acute conflict.

Acute conflict involves intense explosions of hostility with great emotional involvement by both spouses. It is the kind of conflict in which each party sets out to inflict maximum damage on the other. Its potential for disruption of the relationship is great. Apparently most couples resolve most basic issues before too much damage is done. And having eliminated most acute conflict from a marriage apparently improves the chances that subsequent outbursts will also be handled successfully. Some marriages do break down, however, after 10, 20, or 30 years of marriage. Some of these probably have proved to be ultimate victims of the inability to resolve acute conflict.

Unless couples learn rather quickly to resolve conflict, the probability is great that the conflict will take a directional form; it will become progressive. When acute conflict is not resolved, each quarrel leaves a residue of hard feeling and an area in which the couple cannot communicate effectively. Then each time a quarrel develops, there is not only the new issue to solve, but the hard feelings and unresolved issues from earlier quarrels too. The conflict spirals, with the disagreement becoming wider and the feelings more bitter. Too much of this may produce estrangement—a condition in which the partners are permanently alienated. Unless the couple is irrevocably committed to the permanence of marriage, movement toward separation and/or divorce may follow.

The tendency for acute conflict to become progressive may help explain the large number of couples who separate during the first year. What is not known is whether marriages that remain intact involve less conflict. At present, it appears that most intact marriages that survive do show less conflict; it also appears that some intact marriages continue in spite of marked estrangement between the spouses.

In the "best" of marriages, there may be little apparent conflict after the initial adjustments are worked out. In the "worst" of marriages, husband-wife interaction, except for conflict, virtually may not exist. Most marriages probably fall in between. In most areas they have worked out a reasonably satisfactory adjustment, but there also remain areas where they have reached only tentative compromises or where they cannot agree. This may happen in the areas of in-law relationships and money management. In spite of our equal-treatment norms, either spouse may be unable to accept the in-laws completely. They may avoid contact with them and may lash out at the spouse whenever he or she is tactless enough to force the issue. Similarly, after the budget, insurance payments, and all the rest have been worked out, one spouse may consistently overspend or underspend as compared to the partner's expectations. The situation may generally be kept under control, with open conflict emerging only at the time the bank statement is received, say, or when the couple run out of money before the end of the month.

Such areas of conflict that crop up again and again, with a stable accommodation never quite being achieved, may be labeled habituated.

Habituated conflict differs from acute conflict, in that there is not the same emotional investment in it; it is less explosive. In early marriage, when a husband sleeps on the living room sofa; it may throw his wife into an unreasoning rage. After a stable adjustment has been reached, he may continue to nap on the sofa and his wife may mutter with some disgust that he is a lazy slob, but neither she nor he is greatly upset. Habituated conflict also differs from progressive conflict, in that it does not become worse. The wife may even reach the point where she refers to her husband as a lazy slob with some overtones of affection.

Marriages vary widely in the amount of habituated conflict in them and in the amount of such conflict that they can tolerate. In some there may be very little, whereas in others there may be little else. The dynamics of marital accommodation may be as variable as the personality structures of husbands and wives, as the interests that they do and do not share, and as the patterns of interaction that led them into marriage.

Physical Violence

Although most marital conflicts occur as quarrels, researchers have learned in recent years that couples engage in a surprising amount of physical fighting. One survey of 385 college students, for example, reported that 16 percent of them were aware of recent episodes of violence between their parents.[9] These were couples who had been married for many years. A second study of 80 married couples reported 55 percent of them had had at least one incident of physical violence.[10] The National Commission on the Causes and Prevention of Crime and Violence estimated that between one fourth and one fifth of all adult Americans believe that it is acceptable for spouses to hit one another under certain circumstances.

In one of the most revealing studies to date, Steinmetz secured 78 questionnaires from college students and their older friends. Of these families, 30 percent had used physical aggression to resolve marital conflicts. Among them, Steinmetz classified four basic types of problem solvers. The first type, labeled *screaming sluggers* were couples who made both verbal and physical attacks on one another. The second type, the *silent attackers* avoided quarreling, but eventually released their frustrations through physical assault. *Threateners* attacked verbally and threatened the use of violence, but did not resort to it. Finally, the last

9. Murray Straus, "Leveling, Civility, and Violence in the Family," *Journal of Marriage and the Family* 36 (Feb. 1974), pp. 13–29.
10. Richard J. Gelles, *The Violent Home: A Study of Physical Aggression Between Husbands and Wives*, Beverly Hills, Calif.: Sage Publications, 1972.

type, who were called *pacifists*, were able to resolve issues without either verbal or physical attack.[11]

The first data from a national survey of a representative sample of U.S. husbands and wives were collected by Straus and by Gelles. These 2143 interviews indicated that, during the course of one year, 28 percent of the husbands had acted violently against their wives. Some 3.8 percent of the wives had been severely attacked (hit with a fist, kicked, bitten, beaten up, or attacked with a weapon).

The number of attacks varied widely. Approximately one third of the attacked wives were attacked only once. Another one third, however, were attacked five times or more. Attacks occurred among couples at all social levels. The more severe attacks, however, were twice as common among blue-collar couples as among white-collar couples.

The study showed, also, that almost as many wives use physical violence against their husbands. Moreover, the violent wives used force more frequently than the husbands did, and they also used severe violence somewhat more frequently.[12]

If the violence is frequent and severe, it becomes spouse abuse and often leads to separation or divorce.[13] A number of studies have found that wives who remain in abusive marriages do so because of economic dependence on their husbands.[14] One group of researchers estimate that almost 4 million Americans inflict some sort of physical violence on their spouses each year.[15] Although this figure may seem high, it undoubtedly underrepresents the incidence of spouse abuse occurring today among American families. Moreover, almost 1 million children annually are victims of physical abuse, sexual abuse, or neglect. The psychological effects on children who are witnesses to violence between spouses is almost impossible to measure.

11. Suzanne K. Steinmetz, "The Use of Force for Resolving Family Conflict: The Training Ground for Abuse," *Family Coordinator* 26 (Jan. 1977), pp. 19–26.

12. Herbert Yahraes, "Physical Violence in Families," in *Families Today*, Vol. 2, National Institute of Mental Health: Washington, D.C., 1979, pp. 553–76. See also Ursula Dibble and Murray A. Straus, "Some Social Structure Determinants of Inconsistency Between Attitudes and Behavior: The Case of Family Violence," *Journal of Marriage and the Family* 42 (Feb. 1980), pp. 71–80; and Murray A. Straus, "Victims and Aggressors in Marital Violence," *American Behavioral Scientist* 23 (May–June 1980), pp. 681–704.

13. Richard J. Gelles, "Abused Wives: Why Do They Stay?" *Journal of Marriage and the Family* 38 (Nov. 1976), pp. 659–68.

14. Debra S. Kalmus and Murray A. Straus, "Wife's Marital Dependency and Wife Abuse," *Journal of Marriage and the Family* 44 (May 1982), pp. 277–86; and Kersti Yllo, "Sexual Equality and Violence Against Wives in American States," *Journal of Comparative Family Studies* 14 (Spring 1983), pp. 67–86.

15. Murray A. Straus, Richard J. Gelles, and Suzanne K. Steinmetz, *Behind Closed Doors: Violence in the American Family*, Garden City, N.Y.: Doubleday (Anchor), 1980.

Covert Conflict

So far, we have dealt with marital conflict as though it were synonymous with open fighting. We have assumed that quarreling is normal in marriage as it is in the rest of life and that most couples learn to handle quarreling in marriage as they do elsewhere. To conceive of marital conflict in such limited terms, however, is to miss some of the most significant and devastating ways in which people struggle against one another.

Throughout this book we have assumed that behavior occurs at varying levels of awareness. Some behavior may best be understood as fully conscious and rational. In other instances, people act in ways that do not make sense unless one is willing to assume that certain functions of the behavior are different from the apparent ones. We saw how this operates in dating and mate selection. Now we observe it in marriage.

The pervasiveness of covert conflict in marriage is difficult to estimate. By definition it is hidden and cannot be observed directly. Only through psychotherapeutic evaluation can it often be definitely established. Yet there is widespread agreement that there is a whole series of "emotional withholdings" in many relationships that reveal undercover hostility. Some would say that some conflict is inherent in all relationships and that, if a couple does not at least occasionally disagree openly, one is sure to find evidences of unknowing sabotage in the relationship.

Perhaps the most widely recognized forms of emotional withholding in marriage are in the sexual area. Lack of sexual responsiveness in wives and impotence in husbands are examples. This is not to say that there may not be occasional instances where there are organic problems or that there may not be deep-seated psychological factors operating in other cases. The incidence of sexual dysfunction is far greater than can be accounted for in these terms however. What better way for a spouse, who cannot show hostility openly, to hurt his or her partner than to fail to respond sexually?

Short of total unresponsiveness, husbands and wives even more commonly contest with one another by being "too tired" for sex. The seriousness of such conflict is difficult to estimate because often there are legitimate reasons for being too tired. All fatigue cannot be interpreted as covert conflict. However, when the fatigue is recurrent and cannot be accounted for medically, there is a strong presumption of problems in a relationship. On the basis of impressionistic evidence and the testimony of psychotherapists, such conflict is widespread.

There are other forms of withholding—ways of making one's partner suffer without appearing to do so. The spouse who is hypochondriacal often unwittingly uses illness to control the partner and to deny the partner the full joy of living; the ill one must be cared for and catered to, but cannot be expected to be a satisfying sexual partner and companion. At less extreme levels, the whole range of psychosomatic symptoms—rashes, allergies, headaches, ulcers, obesity, almost any unexplained symptom—may represent marital conflict. In very minor form, such problems may plague all marriages.

One problem is that one cannot always be certain that psychosomatic symptoms trace to marital problems. The underlying problems may derive more from conditions at work than at home. They may stem from frustrations encountered outside the home; they may be tied to problems with parents or children. Given the central role that marriage plays in the life of American adults and the interpenetration of family with the occupational and community spheres, however, many such conditions may either reflect or cause problems in the marriage.

Mental hygienists affirm that covert conflict is potentially more damaging than is open fighting. When people quarrel, they are at least aware of a problem. The chances are good that they will find some sort of solution. When the problem is masked as something else, however, it may take its toll without the difficulty ever being discovered. The loss of efficiency and personal satisfaction stemming from covert conflict may be greater, in some ways, than open conflict that leads to marital dissolution.

On the other hand, some marriages may become stabilized around covert conflict. There is the possibility that the personal and social costs of organizing some marriages around an ulcer or migraine headaches may be less than the costs of confronting those couples with the neurotic character of their interaction. Few reasonable people would deny that many ulcerous parents have had outwardly successful marriages and raised apparently healthy, successful children.

The Role of Insight

This brings up the whole question of what factors are linked with the successful resolution of marital conflict. And, in all candor, it must be acknowledged that even though we can describe typical processes of conflict, we know little about the ways in which conflicts are limited or eliminated or why some couples apparently do it better than others.

One important factor—but which, unfortunately, operates in very complex fashion—is the kind and amount of insight each partner develops into his own behavior and that of his or her spouse. Some people appear totally incapable of comprehending underlying motivations for either their own or others' behavior, whereas others shrewdly anticipate one another and quickly recognize the long-term consequences of given courses of action. This capacity for insight is not an all-or-none matter. Probably people can be ranged along a continuum according to how insightful they are. Differences among them are of degree rather than differences in kind.

In general, insight probably increases harmony in marriage. Many attacks that marital partners make on one another are motivated out of hurt or fear. When one realizes that one's partner is only retaliating for injury or is afraid that he or she will be rejected, it becomes easier to react in ways that will lessen the hurt and fear rather than to leap to the attack oneself. Once the process of understanding instead of hurting becomes established, the interaction takes on spiral form. Here we have the reverse of progressive conflict. An insightful, constructive response from one partner calls forth a constructive response from the other partner, and so on. There may be critical points early in most marriages where the interaction takes on spiral form. If it spirals negatively, estrangement soon results. If it spirals as a function of insight development, the areas of sharing may rapidly be enlarged.

This assumes, of course, that both partners show some insight development. In some cases, undoubtedly, they do. Many couples are unequal in their capacities for insight, however, just as they are unequal in other regards. What happens when they are unequal in insight is less certain and leads to less optimistic conclusions.

If both partners are somewhat insightful, the more insightful partner is in a position to control the relationship. By anticipating more quickly and more accurately, he or she may be able to influence the partner. That power may be exercised either in the interests of both partners and the relationship or it may be used to profit the one partner at the expense of the other.[16] Some exploitation of the less insightful partner may be a frequent occurrence.

In some instances the partners' capacities for insight may differ markedly, leading to the domination of the more insightful spouse by the less insightful one. Particularly, if the less insightful spouse is rigid to begin with, he or she may continue the conflict regardless of the ultimate harm done. The more insightful spouse, foreseeing the outcome, may yield rather than destroy the relationship or the partner.[17] This is not a very comforting thought to those who believe that the possession of insight is accompanied by power.

16. For evidence that altruism is not always associated with good marital adjustment, see Jack V. Buerkle, Theodore R. Anderson, and Robin F. Badgley, "Altruism, Role Conflict and Marital Adjustment: A Factor Analysis of Marital Interaction," *Marriage and Family Living* 23 (Feb. 1961), pp. 20–26.

17. Darwin L. Thomas, David D. Franks, and James M. Calonico, "Role-Taking and Power in Social Psychology," *American Sociological Review* 37 (Oct. 1972), pp. 605–14.

There has also been speculation on the quality of marriages in which the more insightful partner is dominated by the less insightful one. It stems from doubt that perceptive persons can endure continued domination and continue to invest themselves fully in the marriage. What appears plausible is that the insightful partner may gradually withdraw emotionally from the relationship. Outwardly, the marriage may be quite stable, but emotionally it may be hollow. Outsiders may be totally unaware that the marriage is unfulfilling for one or both of the partners.

There is relatively little research bearing directly on these problems. One project did show that satisfaction in marriage is related to the wife's accurate perception of her husband's self-concept but that satisfaction was not related to the accuracy of the husband's perception of his wife's self-concept. This difference between the sexes may reflect the fact that wives are required to make the greater adjustments in marriage.[18] The findings are in accord with the widely accepted generalization that subordinate persons and groups tend to be more insightful than those who are able to control through the open use of power.

At least three studies failed to establish any relation between insight and marital adjustment. Corsini studying 20 volunteer couples concluded that there is no evidence that happiness in marriage is a function of understanding the mate.[19] Udry, Nelson, and Nelson studied 34 couples married from 1 to 10 years and found that agreement between husband and wife was not associated with frequency of interaction or length of time married. In addition, there was no relationship between "understanding" and either the frequency of interaction or the length of time married. The couples with the least "togetherness" could predict the responses of their spouses as well as those who spent the most time together, and those married for only a short time could predict their spouses' reactions as well as those who had been married for years.[20] Garland's study of 19 couples found that those trained in listening skills became more accurate in their perceptions of their spouses' attitudes and feelings, but this greater accuracy had no relation to marital adjustment.[21]

18. Eleanore B. Luckey, "Marital Satisfaction and Congruent Self-Spouse Concepts," *Social Forces* 39 (Dec. 1960), pp. 153–57.

19. Raymond Corsini, "Understanding and Similarity in Marriage," *Journal of Abnormal and Social Psychology* 52 (May 1956), pp. 327–32.

20. J. Richard Udry, Harold A. Nelson, and Ruth Nelson, "An Empirical Investigation of Some Widely Held Beliefs About Marital Interaction," *Marriage and Family Living* 23 (Nov. 1961), pp. 388–90.

21. Diana R. Garland, "Training Married Couples in Listening Skills: Effects on Behavior, Perceptual Accuracy and Marital Adjustment," *Family Relations* 30 (April 1981), pp. 297–306.

Development of Communication

It is a truism that happily married couples are able to talk to one another more effectively than unhappily married couples can. They have fewer problems and deal with those problems more effectively.

Surprisingly, rather little research has been done either on the improvement of communication in marriage or on the different styles of communication that married couples use. Two studies, however, are worthy of discussion here.

Gary Birchler, a clinical psychologist, has been studying the communication patterns of happily and unhappily married couples for several years. He finds that both in laboratory problem-solving situations and in real-life problem solving, happily married couples are much more positive in their behaviors toward their mates. They cooperate more, compromise more, and say "please" and "thank you" more. Interestingly, the unhappy couples, when paired with persons other than their spouses in the laboratory situation, also became much more positive in their behaviors: they listened better, smiled more, and interrupted less.[22]

Birchler, who is a therapist, believes that counseling can turn about two thirds of the unhappy marriages into happy ones in less than a year. The therapy consists of extinguishing negative behaviors by refusing to reward them and encouraging positive behaviors by rewarding them systematically.

A study of a random sample of 171 Indianapolis couples focused on the communication styles that the couples preferred to use. The researchers began with the hypothesis that communication styles would be a function of social class. They defined four different communication styles: conventional, controlling, speculative, and contactful. The conventional and controlling styles they describe as *closed*, in that they minimize the contributions of the partner. The speculative and contactful styles, by contrast, are *open*, in that they attach importance to the partner's needs and feelings.

The types also differed in the levels of disclosure that they involved. The controlling and contactful types tended to reveal the speaker's feelings, intentions, and interpretations, whereas the conventional and speculative types were low on disclosure. The diagram illustrates the four types on the two dimensions.

The researchers anticipated that higher-status couples would prefer open communication styles but that lower-status couples would prefer closed styles. The class differences discovered were small however. The speculative style, which involves talking things over calmly, was pre-

22. Herbert Yahraes, "Improving Communication in Marriage," in *Families Today*, Vol. 1, National Institute of Mental Health: Washington, D.C., 1979, pp. 233-47.

	Closed	*Open*
Low disclosure	conventional	speculative
High disclosure	controlling	contactful

ferred at all social levels. Similarly, the controlling style was soundly rejected at all social levels. All couples favored patterns of communication that involve both partners in the intimacy that stems from the respectful confrontation of feelings, their own and one another's.[23]

ESTIMATES OF MARITAL HAPPINESS

Noting that some conflict normally develops in early marriage may suggest that marital adjustment is seldom very satisfactory. It would be surprising, however, if this were the case, for the American ethos places great emphasis on the achievement of success in various aspects of life. If the majority of people did not define their marriages as successful, serious strain would be placed on the system and would be felt by the spouses.

Studies seeking to determine the proportions of various samples who define themselves as happily married have been conducted irregularly over the past 40 years. The findings have been remarkably consistent. Burgess and Cottrell, studying 526 couples in the mid-1930s, found that 63 percent reported their marriages to be "very happy."[24] Terman's study of 792 California couples reported a whopping 85 percent of the marriages to be very happy.[25] In 1965, a study of 1738 respondents from 10 metropolitan areas found that 60 percent of the marriages were rated as "very happy."[26] The most recent of these studies, using modified probability samples of the adult population of the United States, in the years 1973, 1974, and 1975, found that 68 percent of the respondents reported their marriages to be "very happy."[27]

23. James L. Hawkins, Carol Weisberg, and Dixie L. Ray, "Marital Communication Style and Social Class," *Journal of Marriage and the Family* 39 (Aug. 1977), pp. 479–90; and "Spouse Differences in Communication Style: Preference, Perception, Behavior," *Journal of Marriage and the Family* 42 (Aug. 1980), pp. 585–93.
24. Ernest W. Burgess and Leonard S. Cottrell, Jr., *Predicting Success or Failure in Marriage*, New York: Prentice-Hall, 1939, p. 32.
25. Lewis M. Terman, *Psychological Factors in Marital Happiness*, New York: McGraw-Hill, 1938, p. 78.
26. Susan R. Orden and Norman M. Bradburn, "Dimensions of Marriage Happiness," *American Journal of Sociology* 73 (May 1968), pp. 715–31.
27. Norval D. Glenn and Charles N. Weaver, "A Multivariate Multi-survey of Marital Happiness," *Journal of Marriage and the Family* 40 (May 1978), pp. 269–82. See also Glenn and Weaver, "A Note on Family Situation and Global Happiness," *Social Forces* 57 (March 1979), pp. 960–67.

Even allowing for people to report more happiness than they actually experience, these figures are impressive. They strongly suggest that, early in marriage at least, the majority of couples find their marriages to be pretty satisfactory.

THE MEASUREMENT OF MARITAL ADJUSTMENT

Sociologists have not been content with simple estimates of marital happiness and have long sought to develop measures of marital adjustment. In the process, problems inherent in various concepts of marital adjustment have emerged strongly.

The earliest comprehensive study of marital adjustment was that by Burgess and Cottrell. These authors, who developed a scale to predict marital success, distributed lengthy questionnaires to nearly 7000 couples and received 526 completed ones from Illinois couples who had been married from one to six years.

The questionnaires contained items on the premarital backgrounds of the husband and wife and items on their postmarital attitudes and experiences. Each couple was asked to rate the happiness of their marriage. Then an index of marital adjustment was constructed from the answers to 27 items on the questionnaire. In constructing this scale of marital adjustment, Burgess and Cottrell assumed that a well-adjusted marriage is one in which the husband and wife (1) agree on critical issues in their relationship, (2) share common interests and joint activities, (3) share demonstrations of affection and mutual confidences, (4) have few complaints about the marriage, and (5) are not bothered with feelings of loneliness, irritability, and miserableness. Scores on the marital-adjustment scale correlated satisfactorily with the marital happiness ratings. From then on in the research, individual items were tested to determine how well they correlated with total marital-adjustment scores.

A large number of social background factors proved to be associated with marital adjustment. Some of the more significant include:

1. The greater the similarity in family backgrounds, the larger was the proportion of couples in the very-high-adjustment class.
    a. The husband's family background appeared more closely related to adjustment than did the wife's family background.
    b. The economic and social status of the parents seemed less important for marital success than did other factors.
    c. Rural backgrounds for persons who migrated to the city were more favorable than a childhood spent in either town or city.
    d. Differences in educational background or religious affiliation showed no relation to marital adjustment. Church attendance, however, was associated with marital success.

2. The domestic happiness of the parents was correlated with the marital adjustment of their children.
    a. Closeness of attachment and absence of conflict between parents and son showed a small positive relationship to marital adjustment.
    b. Size of family also was more important for the adjustment of the husband than for that of the wife. Two- to five-child families were more favorable than only-child families.
3. Several factors relating to the couple's social type were found to be related to marital adjustment.
    a. Marriage between 28 and 30 years of age for men was found to be favorable. Very early marriages were unfavorable.
    b. Marriage-success scores were positively associated with increased educational achievement for both spouses.
    c. Going to Sunday School until age 19 was associated with marital success. Marriage in a church also was favorable.
    d. Having several friends of both sexes and belonging to organizations was associated with good adjustment.
    e. Residence in a suburb was more favorable than residence in an apartment or rooming house area.
    f. The longer the period of intimate association before marriage, the greater were the chances for marital success.
    g. Security and stability of occupation were more important than income level.
    h. The desire for children was associated with good adjustment.

Burgess and Cottrell emphasized that the correlations between single items and marital success scores were very low. To be used for prediction, a large number of items had to be combined in a scale. The scale they developed has been used in further research and in clinical work.

Probably the greatest significance of the Burgess and Cottrell research is the general concept of marital adjustment that emerged from it. Good adjustment—defined in terms of husband-wife agreement, common interests and activities, sharing of affection and confidences, few complaints, and absence of loneliness—was found to be associated with similarity of the couple's background, happiness in the parental family, and a fairly conventional adjustment in other areas of life.

At the time the Burgess and Cottrell research was under way, Lewis Terman was searching for personality factors associated with marital adjustment. Questionnaires were filled out by 792 middle- and upper-middle-class urban California couples who had been married (on the average), about 11 years. Precautions were taken to see that there was no collaboration between husbands and wives in filling out the questionnaires.

Terman derived total marital happiness scores from questions dealing with common interests, agreements and disagreements, methods of handling disagreements, frequency of regretting marriage, whether one would marry the same person again, contemplation of divorce or separation, rating of marital happiness, length of unhappiness, and number of complaints about the marriage. Then 300 happily married couples and 150 unhappily married couples were compared for age, years married, schooling, and occupation. These groups were used to test the general idea that a large proportion of incompatible marriages are so because of a predisposition to unhappiness in one or both of the spouses.

In all, 132 items discriminated between happily married and unhappily married persons. Following is a portrait of the husbands and wives:

Husbands

Happy: emotionally stable, cooperative, egalitarian in ideals, extroverted, responsible, methodical, and conservative.

Unhappy: moody, neurotic, feel inferior and insecure, domineering and radical.

Wives

Happy: kindly, cooperative, methodical, meticulous, conservative, conventional, self-assured, and optimistic.

Unhappy: emotionally unstable, feel inferior, rivalrous, overactive, radical, and egoistic.

Terman does not claim that all unhappy marriages can be explained in terms of basic personality problems, but he does believe that such factors play a large causal role.

Terman also used a number of social-background-factor items from the Burgess and Cottrell research and included items on premarital sex experience. Soome of the general findings in these areas were:

1. For men to marry under age 22 and for women to marry under age 20 was slightly unfavorable. Relationships where the husband was 10 or more years older or younger than his wife were slightly favorable.
2. Wives of husbands of inferior mental ability tended to be unhappy, whereas their husbands were happy. Markedly superior husbands tended to be unhappy, but their wives were happy. Both spouses had the best chances for marital happiness where husband and wife were equal in ability or the husband was slightly superior.
3. There was an association between length of acquaintance and length of engagement and marital success.

4. Marital happiness was correlated with happiness of the parents' marriages.
5. Happiness was associated with attachment to, and lack of conflict with, parents.
6. Childhood happiness and firm but not harsh discipline were favorable.
7. A number of items relating to sexual education, attitudes, and premarital experience were favorable for marital happiness.
    a. Frank parental responses to sexual curiosity, without evasion.
    b. Indifference to, or pleasant anticipation of, the sex relationship on the part of the man. Both passionate longing and aversion were unfavorable.
    c. No petting before marriage for the wife appeared favorable.
    d. Wife's admission of present or past desire to be of the opposite sex was unfavorable.
    e. For husbands, premarital intercourse with wife was not unfavorable. Wives who had premarital intercourse with men other than the husband had low happiness scores.
8. Some items relating to marital sexual experience also were associated with marital happiness.
    a. Happiness ratings of wives who found their first sexual experiences disgusting were lower than those of wives who found them enjoyable.
    b. Husbands above average in sexual desire had lower happiness ratings, whereas wives above average in desire had higher ratings.
    c. Where the spouses were equal or the wife was slightly less passionate, the happiness ratings of both spouses were highest.
    d. Wife's orgasm capacity was highly correlated with happiness scores of both spouses.

In spite of the relationships found, Terman concluded that happiness could be predicted almost as well from personality and background factors as from those factors and the sexual factors combined. Most sexual maladjustment was seen as stemming from personality and background factors, with little unhappiness resulting from biological sexual incompatibility.

The Burgess and Cottrell and Terman studies were done in different parts of the country and used different samples and techniques of data collection. One emphasized background factors; one emphasized personality and sexual factors. Their results, however, were surprisingly consistent. Where items were similar, their findings were similar. They found that mature, stable, conventional, conforming people from untroubled family backgrounds scored high on marital success and happiness.

Several investigators sought to test these findings and to improve the prediction of marital success. Kelley used Terman's background and personality items with 300 unmarried couples whom he checked for adjustment after two years of marriage.[28] King used the Burgess and Cottrell items with a southern black sample;[29] Stroup used them with a random sample in Akron, Ohio.[30] Locke used items from both early studies in comparing happily married with divorced couples in Indiana,[31] and Karlsson did a similar study in Sweden.[32] Although these studies used different samples and varied their techniques, the general findings were highly confirmatory.

The most comprehensive study of marital prediction was made by Burgess and Wallin as a follow-up to the study of Burgess and Cottrell and in response to recognized limitations in the early studies. Those studies were not truly predictive because the adjustment and prediction scales were built on couples who were already married.

Burgess and Wallin secured questionnaires from 1000 engaged couples in the Chicago area; almost one fourth of the couples also were interviewed. Data were then collected from those couples after they had been married for at least three years. Some couples had not married, some already were divorced, and some could not be located, but marital adjustment questionnaires were secured from 666 of the original couples.

For predicting marital success, three groups of premarital items were used: (1) social background items similar to those used by Burgess and Cottrell, (2) personality items similar to Terman's, and (3) items about the couple's engagement history. A group of "contingency" items also were used, in which husband and wife were asked to anticipate such conditions of their marriage as whether the wife would work, the number of children they expected to have, and where they would live. The general findings were quite consistent with those of Burgess and Cottrell and Terman.

28. E. Lowell Kelley, "Concerning the Validity of Terman's Weights for Predicting Marital Happiness." *Psychological Bulletin* 36 (1939), pp. 202–3.

29. Charles E. King, "The Burgess-Cottrell Method of Measuring Marital Adjustment Applied to a Non-white Southern Urban Population," *Marriage and Family Living* 14 (Nov. 1952), pp. 280–85.

30. Atlee L. Stroup, "Predicting Marital Success or Failure in an Urban Population," *American Sociological Review* 18 (Oct. 1953), pp. 558–62. King and Stroup's interest in the utility of the Burgess and Cottrell scale with persons of different social-class backgrounds was extended in Julius Roth and Robert F. Peck, "Social Class and Social Mobility Factors Related to Marital Adjustment," *American Sociological Review* 16 (Aug. 1951), pp. 478–87.

31. Harvey J. Locke, *Predicting Adjustment in Marriage: A Comparison of a Divorced and a Happily Married Group*, New York: Holt, 1951. See also James L. Hawkins, "The Locke Marital Adjustment Test and Social Desirability," *Journal of Marriage and the Family* 28 (May 1966), pp. 193–95.

32. Georg Karlsson, *Adaptability and Communication in Marriage: A Swedish Predictive Study of Marital Satisfaction*, Uppsala: Almqvist & Wiksell, 1951.

An index of engagement success proved to be the best single predictor of subsequent marital-adjustment scores. Apparently, a better guess about marital adjustment can be made on the basis of how a couple gets along during engagement than on the basis of any combination of background or personality factors.[33]

A variety of studies extend our measurement of marital adjustment.[34] Buerkle and Badgley, for example, constructed items to get at role taking in marital interaction, which measured new dimensions of adjustment and indicated need for further conceptual analysis.[35] Work on indirect measures of marital adjustment that would eliminate the tendency for persons to overstate their marital happiness has been reported by Kirkpatrick, by Taves, and by Frumkin.[36] Finally, a different approach to the measurement of marital adjustment has been tried by Farber, who used a consensus index and a role-tension index.[37]

33. Ernest W. Burgess and Paul Wallin, *Engagement and Marriage*, Philadelphia: J. B. Lippincott, 1953. Several investigators have done follow-up work to this study. See Purnell Benson, "Familism and Marital Success," *Social Forces* 33 (March 1955), pp. 277–80; and "The Common Interest Myth in Marriage," *Social Problems* 3 (July 1955), pp. 27–34; Charles E. Bowerman, "Adjustment in Marriage: Overall and In Specific Areas," *Sociology and Social Research* 41 (March–April 1957), pp. 257–63; Raymond J. Corsini, "Multiple Predictors of Marital Happiness," *Marriage and Family Living* 18 (Aug. 1956), pp. 240–42; Nathan Hurvitz, "The Significance of Discrepancies Between the Scores of Spouses on a Marital Adjustment Scale," *Alpha Kappa Deltan* 29 (Spring 1959), pp. 251–55; Benjamin J. Keeley, "Value Convergence and Marital Relations," *Marriage and Family Living* 17 (Nov. 1955), pp. 342–45; Eugene Litwak, Gloria Count, and Edward M. Haydon, "Group Structure and Interpersonal Creativity as Factors which Reduce Errors in the Prediction of Marital Adjustment," *Social Forces* 38 (May 1960), pp. 308–15; and Harvey J. Locke and Robert C. Willamson, "Marriage Adjustment: A Factor Analysis Study," *American Sociological Review* 23 (Oct. 1958), pp. 562–69.

34. Millard J. Bienvenu, Sr., "Measurement of Marital Communication," *Family Coordinator* 19 (Jan. 1970), pp. 26–31; Hawkins, *op. cit.* pp. 193–95; Richard A. Hunt, "The Effect of Item Weighting on the Locke-Wallace Marital Adjustment Scale," *Journal of Marriage and the Family* 40 (May 1978), pp. 249–57; Douglas K. Snyder, "Multidimensional Assessment of Marital Satisfaction," *Journal of Marriage and the Family* 41 (Nov. 1979), pp. 813–23; and Michael J. Sporakowski, "Marital Preparedness, Predictions and Adjustment," *Family Coordinator* 17 (July 1968), pp. 155–61.

35. Jack V. Buerkle and Robin F. Badgley, "Couple Role Taking: The Yale Marital Interaction Battery," *Marriage and Family Living* 21 (Feb. 1959), pp. 53–58. See also Jack V. Buerkle, "Self Attitudes and Marital Adjustment," *Merrill-Palmer Quarterly* 6 (Jan. 1960), pp. 114–24.

36. Robert M. Frumkin, "The Kirkpatrick Scale of Family Interests as an Instrument for the Indirect Assessment of Marital Adjustment," *Marriage and Family Living* 15 (Feb. 1953), pp. 35–37; Clifford Kirkpatrick, "Community of Interest and the Measurement of Marriage Adjustment," *Family* 18 (1937), pp. 133–37; Marvin J. Taves, "A Direct vs. an Indirect Approach in Measuring Marital Adjustment," *American Sociological Review* 13 (Oct. 1948), pp. 538–41.

37. Bernard Farber, "An Index of Marital Integration," *Sociometry* 20 (June 1957), pp. 117–18.

Other studies related marital satisfaction to the ways in which spouses perceive themselves, one another, and their parents. Luckey reported that better adjusted persons agree on (1) perception in regard to self and the perception of self by spouse, (2) perception of self and the parent of the same sex, (3) perception of spouse and parent of the opposite sex, and (4) perception of one's ideal mate and of one's spouse.[38] Other findings that generally support these findings have been reported by Katz and associates and Stuckert.[39]

The effort to measure marital adjustment and to predict marital success goes on.[40] In recent studies, there is an attempt not only to improve the measurement, but also to arrive at a more adequate concept of marital adjustment. Scholars are becoming more sensitive to ethical implications of a general concept of marriage adjustment unwittingly carried forward from the early studies. That concept of marital adjustment emphasizes the prosaic nature of ordinary human beings who are tacitly urged toward making conventional, conforming, stable marriages by selecting their partners from within their own race, nationality, religion, and social class. Thus, the very existence of norms governing mate selection, it is suggested, have come to be used to reinforce an anti-individualistic, antipersonal-freedom bias in American society.

CRITIQUE OF THE CONCEPT OF MARITAL ADJUSTMENT

The most effective critic of the concept of marital success implicit in the marital adjustment studies has been Kolb. In two provocative pa-

38. Eleanore B. Luckey, "Marital Satisfaction and Its Association with Congruence of Perception," *Marriage and Family Living* 22 (Feb. 1960), pp. 49–54; and "Perceptional Congruence of Self and Family Concepts as Related to Marital Interaction," *Sociometry* 3 (Sept. 1961), pp. 234–40.
39. Irwin Katz, Judith Goldston, Melvin Cohen, and Solomon Stuckers, "Need Satisfaction, Perception, and Cooperative Interactions in Married Couples," *Marriage and Family Living* 25 (May 1963), pp. 209–13; and Robert P. Stuckert, "Role Perception and Marital Satisfaction—A Configurational Approach," *Marriage and Family Living* 25 (Nov. 1963), pp. 415–19.
40. David B. Brinkerhoff and Lynn K. White, "Marital Satisfaction in an Economically Marginal Population," *Journal of Marriage and the Family* 40 (May 1978), pp. 259–67; Kevin C. Donohue and Robert G. Ryder, "A Methodological Note on Marital Satisfaction and Social Variables, " *Journal of Marriage and the Family* 44 (Aug. 1982), pp. 743–47; Mary Lou Larson McNamara and Howard M. Bahr, "The Dimensionality of Marital Role Satisfaction," *Journal of Marriage and the Family* 42 (Feb. 1980), pp. 45–55; Graham B. Spanier. "Measuring Dyadic Adjustment: New Scales for Assessing the Quality of Marriage and Similar Dyads," *Journal of Marriage and the Family* 38 (Feb. 1976), pp. 15–28; and Graham B. Spanier and Linda Thompson, "A Confirmatory Analysis of the Dyadic Adjustment Scale," *Journal of Marriage and the Family* 44 (Aug. 1982), pp. 731–38.

pers,[41] he developed the thesis that there are implicit value judgments in the criteria used to define successful marriage. These value judgments lend support to a family structure that is in basic conflict with democratic values and with ideals of personal growth and freedom. Moreover, the family structure that results from the use of these criteria is one which is unsatisfactory even in terms of ensuring conventionality and stability.

Kolb presents a composite picture of the "successful" marriages emerging from the marital-adjustment studies. First, he says, the spouses in such marriages describe themselves as happy. Second, they agree on what decisions need to be made. Third, the couple agree on leisure-time preferences and engage in outside interests together. Fourth, there is affection and confidence. Finally, they are satisfied with their marriage. In addition, they expect the marriage to be permanent, that it will conform to community expectations, and that it will involve interdependence between husband and wife.

A major problem with this concept of marital adjustment is that it does not specify what the people are happy about, what they are adjusted to, what goals are at the center of family stability, and what value content is at the center of family integration. In some cases, Kolb says, these factors will be associated with other goals that we value and in some cases they will not.

A duel image of the "happy," "adjusted" family emerges from the literature. Which of the two images fits a given family may depend on the vantage point from which it is viewed. In Kolb's words:

One [image] is that of a family characterized by absence of conflict, the prevalence of accommodative habits, mutual affection, the middle-class para-

41. William L. Kolb, "Sociologically Established Family Norms and Democratic Values," *Social Forces* 26 (May 1948), pp. 451–56; and "Family Sociology, Marriage Education, and the Romantic Complex: A Critique," *Social Forces* 29 (Oct. 1950), pp. 65–72. See also Vernon H. Edmonds, "Marital Conventionalization: Definition and Measurement," *Journal of Marriage and the Family* 29 (Nov. 1967), pp. 681–88; James L. Hawkins and Kathryn Johnsen, "Perception of Behavioral Conformity, Imputation of Consensus, and Marital Satisfaction," *Journal of Marriage and the Family* 31 (Aug. 1969), pp. 507–11; Mary W. Hicks and Marilyn Platt, "Marital Happiness and Stability: A Review of the Research in the Sixties," *Journal of Marriage and the Family* 32 (Nov. 1970), pp. 553–74; Edwin L. Lively, "Toward Concept Clarification: The Case of Marital Interaction," *Journal of Marriage and the Family* 31 (Feb. 1969), pp. 108–14; Graham B. Spanier, "Further Evidence on Methodological Weaknesses in the Locke-Wallace Marital Adjustment Scale and Other Measures of Adjustment," *Journal of Marriage and the Family* 34 (Aug. 1972), pp. 403–4; Graham B. Spanier and Robert A. Lewis, "Marital Quality: A Review of the Seventies," *Journal of Marriage and the Family* 42 (Nov. 1980), pp. 96–110; Alexander B. Taylor, "Role Perception, Empathy, and Marriage Adjustment," *Sociology and Social Research* 52 (Oct. 1967), pp. 22–34; and Robert N. Whitehurst, "Premarital Reference Group Orientations and Marriage Adjustment," *Journal of Marriage and the Family* 30 (Aug. 1968), pp. 397–401.

phernalia of status, i.e., an owned home, radios, bathtubs, and automobiles, social conservatism and conformity, discreet and cautious extramarital adventures, and the unending struggle for success. . . . The other image contains the above characteristics, . . . but emphasizes the structure of this family as the breeding ground of neurosis and conflict. It pictures the role of the . . . wife as empty, stultifying, and confused; the role of the husband as that of the individual subjected to all the pressures of the struggle for success; and the role of the child as determined by the ambivalent attitudes of his parents toward one another and toward him.[42]

Remember that this grim portrayal is of couples who do well on marriage-adjustment scales; it does not describe unhappy relationships. It criticizes the concept of marital adjustment as being negative—as defining marriage in terms of absence of conflict and accommodation to the status quo rather than in terms of the achievement of positive goals. No matter how much "adjustment," "happiness," and "integration is present," such marriages are seen as stunting the personal growth and development of the partners. Without defining personality growth—which is an extremely difficult idea to define adequately—it is argued that personality growth "cannot mean the extreme concentration upon status and economic struggle which is characteristic of the middle-class family."

Kolb does not argue that the concept of marital adjustment should be discarded. He knows the role that normative regulation of mate selection and marital interaction play in maintaining order and stability in the society. He does propose that goals of new experience and personality development should be part of the test of a "happy" marriage. He also concludes that major changes in the social, political, and economic structure of American society may be necessary before such marriages become a reality.

TWO PROVOCATIVE ANALYSES OF MARITAL ADJUSTMENT

Most sociologists share Kolb's dissatisfaction with the conventional concept of marital adjustment. Most of them know that the image of couples existing in a state of cowlike contentment is too simple. It fails to encompass the richness of love and hate, exultation and sorrow, boredom and excitement that are part of the lives of even outwardly drab persons. Yet efforts to develop a more vital concept of marital adjustment are few and far between. Few among us show any flair for conceiving of marriage in any but conventional terms. Let us look briefly at

42. Kolb, "Sociologically Established Family Norms," p. 454.

two analyses of marital adjustment, unconventional enough to be some-what frightening in their implications, but based on perceptive studies of real people.

Presented here are typologies of marital adjustment that have stemmed from research. Neither of the two projects was methodologically very rigorous. Neither of the authors would argue that he or she was dealing with a representative sample, that the methods were foolproof, or that the findings can be generalized to all couples. Each did, however, gather data systematically and then exercise a fertile mind in developing a com-posite picture of what the marriages studied were like. To say the least, the findings provide food for thought.

Carolyn (Levy) Cline and her students at the University of Kansas City conducted 112 interviews with people married from 1 to 46 years. All were at least high school graduates, most were white, and they were estimated to vary from upper-lower to upper-middle class. The respond-ents were classified according to basic themes observed running through the interviews. The themes are not mutually exclusive, and more than one theme sometimes was apparent in a given marriage. Five themes around which these 112 marriages appeared to be organized were la-beled (1) mass-produced marriages; (2) inside-out romantic complex marriages; (3) I've grown accustomed to my fate marriages; (4) mar-riage makes estranged bedfellows marriages; and (5) she and empathy marriages.

We can do no better than to describe these five types of marriages in Cline's words:

Mass-produced Marriages. The "mass-produced marriage" refers to the marriage of those who seem to marry because that is what is done and seem likely to stay married because that is what is done. They refer to their spouses more nearly as room-mates of the other sex rather than partners in the intimacy of marriage. They seem to view unhappy marriages with little more than a mild curiosity and explain happiness or unhappiness in terms such as, "If people would just do what they're supposed to do, everything would be all right." They use themselves as the yardstick and, being con-formists themselves—often without being aware of conforming—almost by definition are apt to have fewer problems of which they are aware. They seem not to verbalize or recognize problem areas.

Perhaps it will more clearly state the case if we designate this theme of mass-produced marriage as mass-producing marriage, for such may be the products, members of masses, not individuals. We might call them "omni-directed." For the omni-directed there are many alternatives, but all of them seem so similar. All the mass media, offering so many variations of choices seem still to offer, all of them essentially the same thing. And more than that, the whole society seems to the omni-directed to be in agreement on that same thing. The omni-directed, then, do not have, like Riesman's other-directed, a sensitive radar mechanism to follow a varying lead of others. Instead, they see themselves as following "all"—since the mass media say to them, "Everybody's doing whatever you're doing."

These omni-directed (or automatons of the mass-mesmerizing media) often may appear to be the well integrated, upright citizens who "get things done" and are always "Johnny on the spot." But omni-directed action must be differentiated from autonomous action. Living in a world where there are many alternatives does not mean that the individual, even when aware of them, is able to implement alternatives in his own decision-making process.

Inside-out Romantic Complex Marriages. Although the "inside-out romantic complex" theme was not as prevalent as the "mass produced" in these interviews, it might account for many of the marriages in that group. It differs from the "mass-producing" marriages in that the individuals are aware of and are, at least verbally, attempting to deal with the stereotypes of marriage as conveyed by the mass-mesmerizing media. Many respondents, and most poignantly, the teenagers said, "We want to prove we can make it work." They not only did not mention "love" or any of its grammatical relatives as a reason for getting married, but also they attempted to show a picture of themselves as being "not romantic" adolescents. This stance can be summed up by the statement, "What Hollywood, we won't." This is tantamount to the partners in the marriage saying, "We are not going to ask that our marriage be the all and end all of being; we are not going to be led down that primrose path to divorce. We, on the other hand, are going to imitate the going version of adult (middle-age and routinized) marriage behavior and ask, and settle for, a marriage of accommodation along the competitive lives of a push-pull arrangement . . . and thereby show that we are responsible individuals and have our feet on the ground."

I've Grown Accustomed to My Fate Marriages. [This] theme is typified by the woman who after twenty years of wondering why her husband wished to remain married to her and finally ended up divorcing him said, "I think he wanted a Mother, and that was not the kind of love I had to offer. I don't know what it is, but things happen to me that don't seem to happen to other people. I've had an awful lot of trouble; I guess some people are just born luckier than others. I'm one of the unlucky ones." Another wife said, "At first I kept saying, 'Well, it'll be different after we get more used to one another.' But it didn't. I kept hoping he'd change, or I would, but we didn't. Now it doesn't seem to matter much."

These are people who distrust themselves as choosers. Perhaps they even "will to lose." They feel themselves to be pawns in a completely deterministic life. Everyone else is a pawn too and even the knights and kings and queens move in their directed ways.

Marriage Makes Estranged Bedfellows. [This] theme is illustrated in the following quotations:

A wife reported, "During the first years we had sex so often I would have been ashamed for anyone to know how often. We still do more than other people who are 'old married couples.' The only time we don't argue is in bed."

Another wife said, "I cried a lot during the first year. Nothing was the way I expected. In bed it was just matter-of-fact. Still is. But I don't cry anymore."

And a husband stated estrangement directly. "Sometimes it's like living with a stranger—without the excitement. But she never did really enjoy it—and I can get my kicks elsewhere, if you know what I mean."

While in these interviews no effort was made to probe sexual compatibility and incompatibility, the theme of estrangement either assuaged or reinforced in sexual relations appears not to be uncommon.

She and Empathy Marriages. [This] category . . . is most nearly opposite to that of the "mass-produced" marriage theme. And, just as the mass-produced theme seems to be most frequently found in these interviews, this romantic emphasis upon understanding and insight is rarely found. People in this category seem (1) acutely aware of the state of their marriage (especially the women, and even more poignantly so, the teen-aged women), and (2) ready to act to do something about the marriage. More women than men fall into this category and, also, more romanticists. One wife said:

"The best thing about our marriage is that we can talk. We always could—and get through to each other."

Her husband said, "It's relaxing with her—sometimes I think about other women—prettier, smarter, maybe—and think, wouldn't it be fun—but then I think, fun okay but what else? Of course I feel guilty too."

Another wife said, "I was very much in love with him when we were married, couldn't get enough of him. Loved him more than he did me. But I could see he felt kind of smothered. It hurt me, but I learned to handle it."[43]

The emphasis in this research was on the development of types, so no figures are given on how many couples fell into each category. It is clear that the mass-produced and inside-out romantic complex marriages were the most common and that the she and empathy marriages—those that most closely fit the American ideal of what marriage should be like—were the least numerous.

The author points out that the validity of these themes has not been established. She maintains, however, that the results are highly suggestive. The outcome of mass-produced marriages, she says, may be predictable after the first few months of marriage. The inside-out romantic complex operating early in a marriage may indicate a mass-producing marriage in the future. Unsatisfactory relationships at the beginning of

43. Carolyn (Levy) Cline, "Five Variations on the Marriage Theme: Types of Marriage Formation," *Bulletin on Family Development* 3 (Spring 1962), pp. 10–13.

marriage may suggest a future phrased in terms of "I've become accustomed to my fate." Estrangement may develop either early in marriage or later. Among the most significant of the author's suggestions is the possibility that romanticism early in a marriage may be predictive of a warm empathic relationship later on. Romanticism may not be simply a sign of emotional immaturity, but it may be associated with achievement of the finest that marriage has to offer.

A second classification of marriages derives from a study of 437 persons, 35 to 55 years of age. Although single, divorced, and widowed persons were interviewed also, the analysis reported here is based on couples who had been married at least 10 years and who had never seriously considered separation or divorce. They were upper-middle-class, highly educated, widely traveled, articulate, financially successful people who had been exposed to a variety of emancipating experiences. None displayed signs of gross emotional maladjustment.

Cuber and Harroff presented descriptions of five general themes pervading marriage relationships:

Conflict-Habituated Relationships. In this husband-wife configuration there is much tension and conflict—although largely "controlled." At worst, there is some private quarreling, nagging, and "throwing up the past" of which members of the immediate family, and more rarely even close friends and relatives, have some awareness. At best, the couple is discreet and polite, "genteel about it" when in the company of others, but rarely succeeds completely in concealing it from the children—although the illusion is common among them that they do. The essence, however, is that there is awareness by both husband and wife that incompatibility is pervasive, conflict is ever-potential, and an atmosphere of equilibrated tension permeates their lives together. These relationships are sometimes said to be "dead" or "gone" but there is a more subtle valence here—a very active one. So central is the necessity for channeling conflict and bridling hostility that these imperatives structure the togetherness. Some psychiatrists have gone so far as to suggest that it is precisely the conflict and the habituated need to do psychological battle with one another which constitutes the cohesive factor which ensures continuity of the marriage. Possibly so, but from a less psychiatric point of view, the overt and manifest fact of habituated attention to handling tension, keeping it chained, and concealing it, becomes the overriding life force. And it can, and does for some, last for a lifetime.

Devitalized Relationships. Here the relationship is essentially devoid of zest. There is typically no serious tension or conflict and there may be aspects of the marriage which are actively satisfying, such as mutual interest in children, property, or family tradition. But the interplay between the pair is apathetic, lifeless. There is no serious threat to the marriage. It will likely continue indefinitely, despite its numbness. It continues, and conflict does not

occur in part because of the inertia of "the habit cage." Continuity is further
ensured by the absence of any engaging alternatives, "all things considered."
Perpetuation is also reinforced, sometimes rather decisively, by legal and ecclesiastical requirements and expectations. These people quickly explain that
"there are other things in life," which are worthy of sustained human effort.
But the relationship *between the pair* is essentially devoid of vital meaning,
essentially empty, by comparison to what it was when the mating began and
what was then considered to be its *raison d'être*.

This kind of relationship is exceedingly common. Many persons in this
circumstance do not accurately appraise their position because they frequently make comparisons with other pairs, many of whom are similar to
themselves. This fosters the illusion that "marriage is like this—except for a
few odd balls or pretenders who claim otherwise."

While these relationships lack vitality, there is "*something* there." There
are occasional periods of sharing at least of something, if only memory.
Formalities can have meanings. Anniversaries can be celebrated, even if a
little grimly, for what they once commemorated. As one said, "Tomorrow
we are celebrating the anniversary of our anniversary." Even clearly sub-
standard sexual expression is said by some to be better than nothing, or better
than a clandestine substitute. A "good man" or "good mother for the kids"
may "with a little affection and occasional companionship now and then, get
you by."

Passive-Congenial Relationships. This configuration seems roughly about
as prevalent as the preceding one. There is little suggestion of disillusionment
or compulsion to make believe to anyone. Existing modes of association are
comfortably adequate—no stronger words fit the facts. There is little conflict. They tip-toe rather gingerly over and around a residue of subtle resentments and frustrations. In their better moods they remind us that "there are
many common interests" which they both enjoy. When they get specific
about these common interests it typically comes out that the interests are
neither very vital things nor do they involve participation and sharings which
could not almost as well be carried out in one-sex associations or with comparative strangers. "We both like classical music"; "We agree completely on
religious and political matters"; "We both love the country and our quaint
exurban neighbors"; "We are both lawyers."

We get the strong feeling when talking with these people that they would
have said the same things when they were first married—or even before.
When discussing their decisions to marry, some of them gave the same ra-
tionales for that decision that they do now for their present relationship,
some twenty or thirty years later. This is why we have said that they seem
to be passively content, not disillusioned even though, as compared to the
next type, they show so little vitality and so little evidence that the spouse is
important—much less indispensable—to the satisfactions which they say they
enjoy.

Vital Relationships. It is hard to escape the word, vitality, here—vibrant and exciting sharing of some important life experience. Sex immediately comes to mind, but the vitality need not surround the sexual focus or any aspect of it. It may emanate from work, association in some creative enterprise, child rearing, or even hobby participation. The clue that the *relationship is vital* and significant derives from the *feeling of importance about it* and *that that importance is shared*. Other things are readily sacrificed to it. It is apparent, even sometimes to the superficial observer, that these people are living for something which is exciting; it consumes their interest and effort, and the particular man or woman who shares it is the indispensable ingredient in the meaning which it has.

Total Relationships. The total relationship is like the vital relationship with the important addition that it is *multi-faceted*. This kind of man-woman relationship is rare in marriage or out, but it does exist and undoubtedly could exist more often than it does were men and women free of various impediments. One will occasionally find relationships in which all important aspects of life are mutually shared and enthusiastically participated in. It is as if neither partner had a truly private existence. Cynics and the disillusioned scoff at this, calling it "romance" and usually offering an anecdote or two concerning some such "idyllic" relationship which later lost its totality, if not its vitality too. This should not be taken to mean, however, even if accurately interpreted and reported, that the relationship had not been total at the prior time. Or it may simply be evidence of the failure of the observer to be more discriminating in the first place.

Relationships are not *made* vital, much less total, by asserting them to be so, by striving to make them so, or by deceiving the neighbors that they are so. This is not to deny, however, that the total relationship is particularly precarious; precisely because it is multi-faceted, it is multi-vulnerable as circumstances change.[44]

Cuber and Harroff do not indicate how many relationships fell into each type, but it is clear that the majority ranged from conflict-habituated to passive-congenial. Total relationships are rare; vital relationships presumably are more common. Like Cline, these authors make no claim for the validity of their types. In fact, they state that their findings should not be generalized beyond the upper-middle-class segment of the society from which the couples came.

The findings of these two studies are sobering; they suggest that the majority of marriages may be routinized and unexciting. They also suggest that the marriages that rank high on marital-adjustment scales may include many mass-produced, passive-congenial relationships. If Cline, Cuber, and Harroff are guilty of presenting a pessimistic picture of marital adjustment, perhaps it is because they set their aspirations high.

44. John F. Cuber and Peggy B. Harroff, "The More Total View: Relationships Among Men and Women of the Upper Middle Class," *Marriage and Family Living* 25 (May 1963), pp. 140–45.

SUMMARY

The early weeks of marriage often are suffused with an erotically tinged euphoria that provides protection for each partner while the initial adjustments are being made. This is the *honeymoon period*. Under the pressure of 24-hour-a-day living, however, idealization breaks down. Extraordinary sensitivity to the moods of the partner brings the honeymoon to an end and brings conflict into the relationship.

Middle-class couples fight with words, which they use with devastating effect. Instead of protecting the partner as in the past, each spouse becomes hurt and sets out to inflict pain in return. Overt conflict may be classified into three types. First, there is acute conflict, the function of which is to enable the couple to work out a *modus vivendi*. If acute conflicts are not resolved, they cumulate in a worsening spiral; the conflict becomes progressive. Even after most of the basic issues have been solved, some touchy areas remain and become the source of intermittent, habituated conflict. Recent research shows physical fighting to occur among married couples much more commonly than was formerly recognized.

Conflict may also be covert. In this case, couples who are not fully aware of their resentments resort to emotional withholdings such as frigidity, impotence, and physical illness, or they develop other unexplained symptoms, one result of which is to sabotage the relationship with the spouse. Mental hygienists emphasize that covert conflict is dangerous because its true nature is disguised.

Insightful understanding of the spouse should be an aid in adjustment. Whether insight will be used for the benefit of the relationship or to control it, however, is not predetermined. Where the spouses are greatly unequal in insight, the relationship may be controlled by the less insightful partner whose insensitivity makes him or her a formidable antagonist.

Most couples, when asked about the happiness of their marriages, report them to be relatively happy. One fifth or less report their marriages to be unhappy. Even when measuring devices are used, the pattern holds. Most middle-class people report satisfactory marriages.

A general concept of marital adjustment has emerged out of research designed to predict and measure adjustment. In general, well-adjusted marriages are described as relatively free of conflict, the husband and wife are in relative agreement on major issues, they enjoy the same leisure interests, and they show affection for one another. Well-adjusted spouses are mature, stable, conventional, conforming people who come from untroubled family backgrounds.

This concept of marital adjustment has been criticized for implicit value judgments. It is maintained that these value judgments support a family structure that is in conflict with basic democratic values of personal growth and freedom. What traditionally have been defined as successful marriages may emphasize stability and conventionality at the expense of vitality in the husband-wife relationship and may stunt the emotional growth of children.

A satisfactory alternative concept of marital adjustment has yet to be developed. Two provocative studies have produced typologies of marriages that suggest that the average "successful" marriage may be devoid of zest. Although these studies are less optimistic than the early marital-adjustment studies, they also find evidence of the existence of a minority of marriages that are deeply satisfying to the people involved and that contribute to the full joy of living.

SUGGESTED READINGS

Burgess, Robert L., and Ted L. Huston, *eds., Social Exchange in Developing Relationships,* New York: Academic Press, 1979. Uses the framework of exchange theory to analyze the development and the dissolution of pair relationships.

Gottman, John, *Marital Interaction: Experimental Investigations,* New York: Academic Press, 1979. Develops a theoretical model for the study of marital interaction and tests it through a variety of studies.

Leslie, Gerald R., and Elizabeth McLaughlin Leslie, *Marriage in a Changing World,* New York: Wiley, 1980. A functional textbook in preparation for marriage. Four chapters analyze various aspects of early marriage adjustments.

Straus, Murray A., Richard J. Gelles, and Suzanne K. Steinmetz, *Behind Closed Doors: Violence in the American Family,* New York: Anchor, 1980. This national survey of 2143 families finds violence a prevalent occurrence in American homes.

Straus, Murray A., and Gerald T. Hotaling, *eds., The Social Causes of Husband-Wife Violence,* Minneapolis: University of Minnesota Press, 1980. Shows that violence is produced by social arrangements rather than being a personality pattern. Points toward social change to reduce or eliminate violence.

FILMS

Battered Women: Violence Behind Closed Doors (MTI Teleprograms, 4825 N. Scott Street, Suite 23, Schiller Park, Ill. 60176), 24 minutes. Explores how love is replaced by fear and fisticuffs, and why women tolerate the abuse.

Being in Love (NET Film Service, Indiana University, Bloomington, Ind. 47401). Film opens with two brothers meeting in a restaurant. One brother plans to divorce his wife to marry a woman he has met in business. Psychotherapist discusses the possibilities of success for such a second marriage and questions whether the man is mature in his attitude.

Jealousy (McGraw-Hill, Text-Film Division, 1221 Avenue of the Americas, New York, N.Y. 10020), 16 minutes. Incidents from the life of a young couple demonstrate the unfortunate results of a treacherous imagination and lack of faith and understanding in a marriage relationship. Stresses the importance of continuous self-appraisal and indicates that a change of attitude often is necessary to combat jealousy.

A Wedding in the Family (New Day Films, P.O. Box 315, Franklin Lakes, N.J. 07417), 22 minutes. Explores the atitudes, behaviors, and feelings of people involved in a wedding-to-be. Sometimes funny, sometimes painful analysis of two generations' changing expectations for men and women.

QUESTIONS AND PROJECTS

1. How can the honeymoon, as distinguished from the wedding trip, be defined in terms of emotional dynamics?
2. What factors during the honeymoon bring about disillusionment with self and partner? What evidence is there for such disillusionment?
3. Describe three major types of overt conflict in marriage. What is the significance of each? Contrast overt with covert conflict. Give examples of, and estimate the significance of, covert conflict.
4. How may insight into self and spouse influence marital adjustment? May the possession of insight be related to the power structure that develops? How may the less insightful partner dominate a marriage?
5. How do most middle-class people rate the happiness of their marriages? What proportions acknowledge that their marriages are unhappy?
6. Describe the early Burgess and Cottrell study of marital adjustment. What concept of marital adjustment was used? Summarize the findings relating social background factors to marital adjustment.
7. Compare Terman's study of happiness with the Burgess and Cottrell study of marital adjustment. How do the studies compare?
8. How did the Burgess and Wallin study differ from the two earlier ones? What was the best single predictor of marital success?
9. What criticism has been offered of the concept of marital adjustment deriving from prediction studies? How valid is this criticism? Why?
10. Recall the typologies of marital adjustment developed in the two studies reported in this chapter. Do these give cause for optimism? Why?
11. Suppose you wanted to reconcile some of the apparent contraditions in

research findings on marital adjustment, what methods or techniques could you devise to get at what marriages are really like?

12. Arrange a panel discussion among married students in the class. Draw out various concepts of marital adjustment. Have the panel react to the concepts of adjustment developed in this chapter. See whether a typology of marital adjustment makes sense for these students.

Mimi Forsyth

15
Sexual Adjustment in Marriage

After at least a decade of the famous Sexual Revolution, it is often assumed that most Americans have entered a state known as the New Morality. It is a condition in which pleasure is the principle, living in sin is no sin and more or less anything, between consenting adults, goes. Yet although some observers have proclaimed the revolution triumphant, new battles keep breaking out. . . .

In St. Paul, where Planned Parenthood opened a new headquarters and a clinic for abortions and birth control, the building was doused with gasoline and set afire. . . .

Los Angeles, once in the vanguard of public hedonism, has imposed a temporary moratorium on new sex movie theaters, pornographic bookstores and massage parlors. . . .

After an era of revolution, is a counterrevolution under way? Is it even possible that the revolution never really succeeded, that much of America watched the New Morality—voyeuristically—without abandoning the Old Morality? . . .

"Intellectually, I think it's fine to sleep around,' says Linda Gams, 25, a teacher who lived with her husband, Bob, for a year before marrying him two years ago. "But emotionally I'd be very upset if Bob slept with another woman. I wish I could be more liberated about this. I always felt I had conquered this until I started living with Bob and got dependent on him. It's a definite split in me."[1]

As shown in the chapter on premarital involvement, most couples have begun sexual adjustment before marriage. Their interest in, and readiness for, sexual relationships in marriage, however, usually are not equal.

1. *Time*, The Weekly News magazine, Nov. 21, 1977, p. 111; Copyright © Time Inc., 1977, Reprinted by permission

The pattern that develops tends to be a compromise, with varying satisfactions and frustrations for each partner.

FREQUENCY OF INTERCOURSE
AND SEXUAL ADJUSTMENT

Married couples vary enormously in their frequency of coital activity. A recent study of a random sample of people married five years or less centered around this issue. Subjects were asked how many times per month they had intercourse with their spouses during their first year of marriage. Responses ranged from one episode of intercourse per month all the way up to 45 times per month![2] Obviously, there is no magic normative number against which married couples may gauge their own sexual activity. Some may consider themselves oversexed if they have intercourse more than once a week, whereas others may feel deprived with less than one orgasm a day. Still the issue of how many times per week or month is "proper" remains a concern with many couples. Keeping up with the Joneses may involve not only new cars, fine furnishings, and larger swimming pools, but Olympian sexual efforts as well.

Research on the frequency of marital intercourse has been going on for about 30 years, since the time of Kinsey's original work. Although the frequency of intercourse tends to decline steadily with age, there are indications that overall rates of married intercourse are on the rise. According to the Kinsey research, the 1965 National Fertility Study, and a national survey in 1972, married couples in their teens have intercourse nearly 3.0 times per week on the average (see Table 15.1).[3] This drops to about 2.0 times a week at age 30, and 1.5 times per week at age 40. A study based on two national samples of women aged 15 to 44 examined rates of marital intercourse for the years 1965 and 1970. The researcher found that average frequencies of marital coitus had increased over 20 percent during this time period—from 6.8 times per month in 1965 to 8.2 in 1970.[4] By 1975, the coital rate had increased to 8.9 times per month.[5] Although there is a steady decline in the frequency of in-

2. Cathy Stein Greenblat, "The Salience of Sexuality in the Early Years of Marriage," *Journal of Marriage and the Family* 45 (May 1983), pp. 289–99. See also W. H. James, "Variation Between Couples of Human Coital Rates," *Journal of Biosocial Science* 13 (April 1981), pp. 151–56.
3. The median is used because it is less affected by extreme cases near the ends of the distribution. If arithmetic mean figures were used, they would be slightly higher than those reported here.
4. Charles F. Westoff, "Coital Frequency and Contraception," *Family Planning Perspectives* 3 (Summer 1974), pp. 136–41.
5. James Trussell and Charles F. Westoff, "Contraceptive Practices and Trends in Coital Frequency," *Family Planning Perspectives* 12 (Sept.–Oct. 1980), pp. 246–49.

Table 15.1. Reports of frequency of marital intercourse at various ages

Age group	Median frequencies per week (Kinsey)		Mean frequencies per month	
	Men	Women	1965 Study	1972 Study
16–20	2.6	2.8	10.3	
21–25	2.3	2.5	8.1	
26–30	2.0	2.1	7.3	9.4
31–35	1.8	1.9	6.7	7.4
36–40	1.6	1.5	5.9	
41–45	1.3	1.2	5.1	6.1
46–50	0.9	0.9		
51–55	0.7	0.8		4.1
56–60	0.6	0.4		

Source: Alfred C. Kinsey, Wardell B. Pomeroy, Clyde E. Martin, and Paul H. Gebhard, *Sexual Behavior in the Human Female*, Philadelphia: W. B. Saunders, 1953, p. 77; Leslie A. Westoff and Charles F. Westoff, *From Now to Zero: Fertility, Contraception and Abortion in America*, Boston: Little, Brown, 1971, p. 24; and Robert R. Bell and Phyllis L. Bell, "Sexual Satisfaction Among Married Women," *Medical Aspects of Human Sexuality*, Dec. 1972, p. 141.

tercourse after the first year of marriage, it is the rate of coital activity during the first year that seems to influence subsequent sexual activity in marriage. Allowing for the expected decline, sexual activity during the first year has the strongest effect on the frequency of sexual activity during the later years of marriage. Increases in marital coitus since the time of Kinsey's work parallel increases in the incidence of premarital sexuality and are associated, to a large degree, with the effectiveness of the contraceptive methods used.[6]

As significant as the figures on frequency of coitus are the discrepancies between the figures reported by men and by women (see Table 15.1). The median figures reported by men are slightly lower than those reported by women, suggesting the possibility of relative satiation of the women and deprivation of men. Some women who would prefer less sexual intercourse may overestimate the actual frequency whereas men who would prefer more may underestimate the actual frequency.[7] From the beginning of marriage, differential interest in sex is a problem for many couples.

6. Trussell and Westoff, *op. cit.;* Westoff, *op. cit.*
7. Research shows that husband and wife agree more closely in their estimates of sexual aspects of their relationship than of other aspects. See Bruce Thomason, "Extent of Spousal Agreement on Certain Non-sexual and Sexual Aspects of Marital Adjustment," *Marriage and Family Living* 17 (Nov. 1955), pp. 332–24.

Table 15.2. Spouse who desires sex more frequently (in percent)

Desire	Husband's report (N = 207)	Wife's report (N = 205)
Husband much more frequently	37.2	34.6
Husband somewhat more frequently	41.6	38.1
Husband and wife the same	13.0	20.0
Wife somewhat more frequently	6.8	6.3
Wife much more frequently	1.5	1.0
Totals	100.1	100.0

Source: Adapted from F. Ivan Nye et al., Role Structure and Analysis of the Family, Beverly Hills, Calif.: Sage Publications, 1976, p. 108.

The existence of wide differences in sexual desire between husbands and wives was verified by Nye in a study of 210 couples in the state of Washington (see Table 15.2): (1) about four fifths of both husbands and wives report that the husbands desire sex more frequently, (2) 13 percent of the husbands and 20 percent of the wives report that their desires are equal, (3) the percentages stating that the wives desire sex more frequently are small and approximately equal, 8.3 percent as reported by the husbands and 7.3 percent as reported by the wives.[8]

One might hypothesize a relationship between mutual high sexual desire of husband and wife and good marital adjustment. Research shows, however, that it is not that simple. Wallin and Clark found that maritally satisfied husbands perceived their wives to be similar to themselves in preferred frequency of coitus more often than did maritally dissatisfied husbands. The relationship did not hold equally well for wives however.[9] Further light was thrown on this situation by Adams in a study of 150 women who had been married for an average of eight years. He found that wives' sexual adjustment was related to their marital happiness but that the relationship between the wives' sexual responsiveness and marital happiness was low.[10] Thus, the relationship between fre-

8. F. Ivan Nye et al., Role Structure and Analysis of the Family, Beverly Hills, Calif.: Sage Publications, 1976, pp. 27, 107-8.
9. Paul Wallin and Alexander Clark, "Marital Satisfaction and Husbands' and Wives' Perception of Similarity in Their Preferred Frequency of Coitus," Journal of Abnormal and Social Psychology 57 (Nov. 1958), pp. 370-73. See also George Levinger, "Systematic Distortion in Spouses' Reports of Preferred and Actual Sexual Behavior," Sociometry 29 (Sept. 1966), pp. 291-99.
10. Clifford R. Adams, An Informal Preliminary Report on Some Factors Relating to Sexual Responsiveness of Certain College Wives, 1953. Mimeo. See also John N. Edwards and Alan Booth, "Sexual Behavior In and Out of Marriage: An Assessment of Correlates," Journal of Marriage and the Family 38 (Feb. 1976), pp. 73-81.

quency of desire for coitus, sexual adjustment, and marital adjustment is more complicated among women than among men. For both men and women, however, the greater the frequency of orgasm, the higher the ratings of sexual satisfaction.[11]

Although most men desire intercourse more frequently than their wives do, there are cases where the reverse is true. Moreover, with the trend toward equality between the sexes, the number of women who are highly responsive probably is increasing. Wallin and Clark studied 604 couples to determine the relative acceptability of marriages in which the husbands' sex drives were stronger, the drives of the partners were equal, and in which the wives' sex drives were stronger. They found that equality of sex drive in husband and wife or a stronger drive in the husband are acceptable but that a stronger drive on the part of the wife is not.[12] Apparently, husbands want their wives to be responsive, but not to have more drive than they do.

One measure of the satisfaction of women in intercourse is the regularity with which they experience orgasm. Table 15.3 presents Kinsey statistics that show the proportions of marital coitus leading to orgasm during the 1st, 5th, 10th, 15th, and 20th years of marriage. The table shows that, during the first year, 75 percent of the women reached orgasm at least some of the time and about half reached it at least 60 percent of the time. Approximately 4 women out of 10 almost always

Table 15.3. Percentage of marital coitus leading to female orgasm, by length of marriage

Percent of coitus with orgasm	Year of marriage				
	1st	5th	10th	15th	20th
None	25	17	14	12	11
1–29	11	13	14	16	13
30–59	13	15	13	11	12
60–89	12	15	17	16	17
90–100	39	40	42	45	47
Number of cases	2244	1448	858	505	261

Source: Alfred C. Kinsey, Wardell B. Pomeroy, Clyde E. Martin, and Paul H. Gebhard, Sexual Behavior in the Human Female, Philadelphia: W. B. Saunders, 1953, p. 408.

11. Stuart D. Perlman and Paul R. Abramson, "Sexual Satisfaction Among Married and Cohabiting Individuals," Journal of Consulting and Clinical Psychology 50 (June 1982), pp. 458–60.
12. Paul Wallin and Alexander Clark, "Cultural Norms and Husbands' and Wives' Reports of their Marital Partners' Preferred Frequency of Coitus Relative to Their Own," Sociometry 21 (Sept. 1958), pp. 247–54.

experienced orgasm. In subsequent years, the proportion of women experiencing coital orgasm increased. During the 20th year, almost 90 percent of women were reaching coital orgasm at least some of the time. The proportion of women almost always having orgasm rose with length of time married. For those married at least 20 years, Kinsey found almost half reported reaching orgasm most or all of the time.[13]

Some recent statistics indicate that the proportion of women who almost always experience orgasm during intercourse is rising. Bell and Bell report that the number of women in this category may now be between 50 and 60 percent.[14] A survey conducted by *Redbook* magazine in 1974 brought responses from 100,000 women concerning their sexual experiences.[15] Although this sample was voluntary and probably not representative of all American women, the results indicate that the frequency of coital orgasm among women is indeed rising: 63 percent of the women reported reaching orgasm most or all of the time. Only 7 percent of the women reported never reaching orgasm during intercourse. Hunt also found that only about 7 percent of his female subjects never experienced coital orgasm.[16]

The data show that orgasm in marital coitus is related to the decade of the woman's birth, her father's occupational class, and her educational level. The likelihood of experiencing orgasm at all, the likelihood of having orgasm within any five-year period, and the proportion of marital intercourse producing orgasm all are higher among women born in more recent decades, among those whose fathers followed upper-white-collar or professional occupations, and among those with more formal education.[17] The widely held stereotype that regards lower-class women as being sexually more responsive appears simply to be wrong.

A retabulation of the Kinsey data on 1026 women in intact marriages and a national study of 2372 women married an average of 13 years showed a correlation between the regularity with which the wives ex-

13. A study of marital adjustment among blacks yielded similar findings. King found that 131 out of 418 black wives reported that they always had orgasm in marital intercourse; 160 said that they usually did, 107 said they sometimes did, and 20 reported that they never experienced orgasm. See Charles E. King, "The Sex Factor in Marital Adjustment," *Marriage and Family Living* 16 (Aug. 1954), pp. 237–40.
14. Robert R. Bell and Phyllis L. Bell, "Sexual Satisfaction Among Married Women," *Medical Aspects of Human Sexuality,* Dec. 1972, p. 142. See also *Time,* October 1, 1973, p. 63.
15. Carol Tavris and Susan Sadd, *The Redbook Report on Female Sexuality,* New York: Delacourt, 1977.
16. Morton Hunt, *Sexual Behavior in the 1970s,* Chicago: Playboy Press, 1974.
17. See Marilyn Peddicord Whitley and Susan B. Poulson, "Assertiveness and Sexual Satisfaction in Employed Professional Women," *Journal of Marriage and the Family* 37 (Aug. 1975), pp. 573–81.

perienced orgasm and their marital happiness.[18] Approximately 60 percent of the Kinsey wives who reported reaching orgasm from 90 to 100 percent of the time also reported their marriages to be very happy. At the other extreme, only 4 percent of the wives who never reach orgasm reported very happy marriages, and 19 percent of the no-orgasm group said that their marriages were very unhappy. Gebhard concludes that the strong correlation between female orgasm and marital happiness probably is causal in both directions; more responsive women are happier and regular orgasm brings happiness.

Gebhard also found that female orgasm during coitus is associated with the amount of time indulged in foreplay. When couples engaged in only 1 to 10 minutes of foreplay prior to intercourse, only about two fifths of the wives in his sample reached orgasm nearly all the time. When foreplay lasted 21 minutes or more, nearly three fifths of the women reached this orgasm rate.[19]

Although it is clear that not all women experience orgasm during intercourse, it is important to remember that human sexuality encompasses a wide range of intimate behaviors. Most studies on marital orgasm have focused on coitus and neglected the incidence of orgasm in women through means other than penile penetration. Women may have any number of orgasms through manual or oral stimulation, yet be tallied as unresponsive because these orgasms are not experienced through intercourse. For many women, the stimulation received during coitus with their husbands is insufficient for their orgasmic needs and not indicative of any lack of responsiveness.

Up to now, our discussion of sexual adjustment in marriage mainly has focused on women. Indeed, much of the research conducted on marital sexuality over the past few decades primarily has centered on women and women's sexual "problems": low sex drive, unresponsiveness, orgasmic incapacity, and so on. Peterson and Peterson recently reviewed 24 popular sex and marriage manuals and found that women far more frequently than men are seen as the "cause" and "cure" of sexual problems.[20]

What is implicit in the lack of concentration on men's sexuality is that all men are equally desirous of, and successful in, experiencing sexual satisfaction. Part of this stems from traditional notions of the dualistic nature of sexuality in men and women; men are seen as inherently

18. Bell and Bell, *op. cit.*; and Paul H. Gebhard, "Factors in Marital Orgasm," *Journal of Social Issues* 22 (April 1966), pp. 88–95.
19. Gebhard, *Ibid.*
20. Gail Beaton Peterson and Larry R. Peterson, "Sexism in the Treatment of Sexual Dysfunction," *Family Coordinator* 22 (Oct. 1973), pp. 397–404.

more sexually aggressive, and, hence, are expected to desire sex more than women. This idea has predisposed some researchers to focus on female sexuality and neglect the problematic aspects of male sexuality. From this, one might get the impression that all men achieve erections on demand, sustain them literally for hours, and ejaculate at that precise moment chosen for orgasmic ecstasy. Nothing could be further from the truth. The variation among men in drive, ability, and satisfaction is great and also is a contributing factor to sexual adjustment in marriage.

Many people are dissatisfied with their sexual lives in marriage, not necessarily because of problems but because they believe the sex lives of other people are better. Shaver and Freedman recently surveyed over 50,000 adults and found that over half of the men and a third of the women believed that their peers were more satisfied with sex than they were.[21] Although much of the sexual dissatisfaction in marriage may be attributable to unfavorable comparisons with others, there remains a segment of the population who suffer very real sexual dysfunctioning of either psychological or physical origin. It is to the issue of sexual dysfunction that we now turn.

SEXUAL DYSFUNCTION

Masters and Johnson estimate that as many as 50 percent of all couples have some sort of sexual inadequacy or dysfunctioning on the part of the husband, the wife, or both spouses.[22] Although this estimate may be questionable, it is undoubtedly true that there are a variety of sexual problems that human flesh is heir to. Because people with sexual dysfunction usually do not seek help unless the problem is chronic or acknowledged as a problem that can be remedied and because they usually are seen only by clinicians, it is impossible to know with any certainty how many people are affected.

Sexual dysfunction takes many forms. Among males, chronic sexual problems usually center around erectile dysfunction, premature ejaculation, or retarded ejaculation; among females, orgasmic dysfunction, dyspareunia, or vaginismus are the most common complaints.

21. Phillip Shaver and Jonathon Freedman, "Your Pursuit of Happiness," *Psychology Today* 10 (Aug. 1976), pp. 26–29.
22. William H. Masters and Virginia E. Johnson, *Human Sexual Inadequacy*, Boston: Little, Brown, 1970, p. 342.

Erectile Dysfunction

The inability to achieve or maintain a penile erection is indicative of erectile dysfunction. Although synonymous with impotence, erectile dysfunction is now the preferred term. It may take one of two forms: primary or secondary dysfunction. Masters and Johnson state that a man has primary erectile dysfunction if he never has been "able to achieve or maintain an erection quality sufficient to accomplish successful coital connection."[23] A man who does not experience erection in at least 25 percent of his sexual attempts can be diagnosed as having secondary erectile dysfunction. This is far more common than primary dysfunction. Of the 277 patients treated by Masters and Johnson for erection problems, only 12 percent had never been able to achieve and maintain an erection at least once.

There are few men who have not at some time in their lives experienced difficulties with erection. Because they may be unaware that often there are medical reasons for the problem, some men unfortunately may believe it marks the end of their sexual lives or is an indication that their masculinity is questionable. The fact is, though, organic reasons for erectile problems may even outweigh psychological factors.[24] One side effect of many medications is difficulty in achieving or maintaining penile erections. Various drugs such as those used to treat heart problems, high blood pressure, gastrointestinal disorders, hormone imbalances, and so on, may lead to impotence or a loss in sexual desire. Common ailments such as allergies, muscle spasms, ulcers, depression, and high blood pressure are treated with medications that may produce as a side effect libidinal changes in men and women. Moreover, the use and abuse of many recreational drugs such as alcohol, cocaine, marijuana, and amphetamines may also take their toll on the sexual aspect of people's lives. Other factors contributing to erectile dysfunction include diseases such as diabetes or multiple sclerosis, glandular deficiencies, vascular disorders, surgical traumas, and even dietary deficiencies.

Kaplan estimates that at least half of the male population has experienced occasional episodes of erectile difficulty.[25] For some men, however, the psychological implications of this experience may turn it into an endless cycle of fear and anxiety. Men who feel a loss of self-esteem when difficulties arise usually have a large psychological investment in

23. *Ibid.,* p. 137.
24. Jane E. Brody, "Drug Side Effects Interfering with Sex Lives of Many," *New York Times,* October 14, 1983.
25. Helen Singer Kaplan, *The New Sex Therapy,* New York: Times Books (Quadrangle), 1974, p. 255.

their ability to perform. The first time they experience difficulties in achieving or sustaining erections may cause them to be anxious about their sexual abilities in subsequent attempts. The fear and anxiety associated with sex may create a self-fulfilling prophecy; because they believe themselves to be impaired, the anxiety associated with the belief impairs the erectile function, thus "proving" and reinforcing the belief.

The psychological causes of erectile dysfunction are endless. Some men may feel angry toward a dull, boring, or unattractive spouse and may come to look on sex as a chore rather than a pleasure. Some may resent being expected to bring an unappreciative partner to five or six orgasms before they are allowed to have their single orgasm. If they are having sex on the sly with other women, guilt may impair their functioning with their wives. Or, as is very often the case, simple fatigue or boredom may interfere with sexual responsiveness.

Premature Ejaculation

Premature ejaculation probably is the most common complaint of men and their partners. Just what marks premature ejaculation, however, is difficult to define. Some clinicians hold that men are premature ejaculators if they experience orgasm either before, or within 10 seconds after, penetration. Others believe that men must be able to thrust for 5 or 10 minutes before ejaculating. Masters and Johnson define prematurity as the inability to satisfy the woman 50 percent of the time in intercourse, regardless of the time required. Obviously, this definition is not satisfactory either because women vary enormously in the time required to experience orgasm in intercourse. And, as we noted earlier, some women who are orgasmic through other means simply do not have orgasms through intercourse. Perelman believes that the critical factor in premature ejaculation is the lack of a learned ability to delay orgasm once sexually aroused, regardless of time.[26]

It appears that premature ejaculation is, for the most part, tied to psychological rather than physical causes. In Chapter 12, we found that the emphasis within the masculine subculture is on the quantity rather than the quality of sexual experiences. For many young men, their first sexual experiences involve masturbation among a group of boys to see who can "come first." The emphasis is on a rapid orgasm and those boys who can do this before the others in the group are the ones on whom status is conferred. An association then may be made between rapid

26. Michael A. Perelman, "Treatment of Premature Ejaculation," in Sandra R. Leiblum and Lawrence A Pervin, *Principles and Practice of Sex Therapy*, New York: Guilford Press, 1980, p. 201.

arousal, orgasm, and sexual competence. For some men, this association may be carried over into the marriage bed, and they may not understand wives who complain of sexual frustration and anger.

In other instances, the fear of being caught doing something "wrong" may push young adolescents toward a quick finish. Sex in the back seat of a car or on the family sofa before the parents come home does not usually allow for long, leisurely love making. Masturbating in the bathroom while waiting for a knock at the door also places an emphasis on speed. The guilt and fear associated with these early experiences may also carry over into the marriage bed.

Some men ejaculate quickly as a means of expressing anger or resentment toward a partner. Some may be unaware or uncaring about their partner's need for prolonged intercourse for satisfaction. Also, with advancing age, a man's ability to sustain lengthy intercourse may diminish.

Retarded Ejaculation

Retarded ejaculation involves an inability to ejaculate while the penis is in intromission or an inability to ejaculate at all. In this instance, the man might be able to thrust for an hour or more but be unable to ejaculate. Retarded ejaculation, or ejaculatory incompetence, as it is called, is relatively rare. Of the 510 couples treated by Masters and Johnson, only 17 suffered from this form of sexual dysfunction.[27]

Few organic causes have been implicated in retarded ejaculation. Undetected diabetes may affect ejaculation, but it most usually affects erectile functioning. The use of some drugs such as those used in treatment of psychosis or high blood pressure may produce dry ejaculation (ejaculation without the expulsion of seminal fluid) or impede ejaculation entirely. These are rare cases however; retarded ejaculation is most usually tied to psychological factors.

Intercourse without ejaculation may be the means through which some men hold back from their wives or express anger or resentment over some conflict. It may be the means of wielding control or power in an unhappy marriage. Some men may even think their ejaculate is dirty or polluted and may fear bespoiling their partners with it.[28] Some may have had an unfortunate experience with an unwanted pregnancy and fear it happening again. Although the underlying reasons for retarded ejaculation are many, it should be pointed out again that this type of sexual dysfunction is rare.

27. Masters and Johnson, *op. cit.*
28. Kaplan, *op. cit.*, p. 327.

Orgasmic Dysfunction

Orgasmic dysfunction is the most common complaint of women seeking sex therapy. It may take one of two forms: primary or secondary orgasmic dysfunction. Women who have primary orgasmic dysfunction have never experienced orgasm by any means. Kaplan estimates that only about 8 to 10 percent of sexually active women never experience orgasm.[29] With secondary orgasmic dysfunction, women experience orgasm in some situations, not in others. This is also called situational dysfunction.

The causes of orgasmic dysfunction are most commonly psychological in origin. Women who have been taught their whole lives that sex is dirty or shameful may be unresponsive in marriage. They may feel guilt or shame about their own sexual feelings or be unwilling to let themselves go in sexual settings. Some may feel concerned with how their bodies look naked and take on a spectator role during sex. Some may have a general distrust of men or feel hostile toward their partners. Often, women may be able easily to experience orgasms through oral or manual means but cannot climax during intercourse because their partners cannot sustain thrusting long enough to satisfy them. For many couples, sex is synonymous only with intercourse, so, they may put the greatest emphasis on the ability to experience orgasm during intromission. Many women receive sexual satisfaction through other types of sexual play, but because prowess is most usually concentrated on intercourse, they may feel failure as "real women" or be labeled frigid if they cannot climax during it. Also, because of the concentration on intercourse as sexual expression, many couples simply do not devote enough time to foreplay, afterplay, or play in general.

Dyspareunia

Dyspareunia is pain during intercourse. Pain during sex can have many physical causes. It can be indicative of undetected infections of the cervix, ovaries, or other reproductive organs. Cysts or polyps may be present or there may be tears in the ligaments that secure the uterus. Some women may experience allergic reactions to contraceptive creams and foams, douches, or feminine hygiene products.

Pain during intercourse also may have psychological causes. It may be associated with tension, fear, or guilt concerning sex and one's own body. It may also indicate insufficient arousal or lack of vaginal lubrica-

29. *Ibid.*, p. 380.

tion when intercourse is attempted. A strict religious upbringing or the fear of acting like an "animal" may interfere with arousal and cause penetration to be painful.

Vaginismus

In cases of dyspareunia, intercourse is painful but possible. With vaginismus, intercourse is impossible. Anatomically, the genitalia of vaginismic women are normal but whenever penetration is attempted, involuntary spasms of the vaginal sphincter make intercourse impossible. Not only may attempts at coitus prove painful, frightening, and frustrating, but very often even gynecological examinations must be done under anesthesia. Vaginismus understandably is very troubling for couples involved and can lead to marriages of long duration never consummated in intercourse.

Many women suffering from vaginismus enjoy sexual activity, experience arousal, and even orgasm—as long as it does not entail intercourse. Vaginismus is most usually associated with a prior history of trauma or pain in connection with sexuality such as in cases of rape or incest. Attempts at intercourse for women with unremitting hymens may induce vaginismus during subsequent attempts. Physical ailments such as endometriosis, pelvic tumors, or childbirth traumas may not directly affect the vaginal sphincter but may indirectly lead to vaginismus because of the fear of additional pain and discomfort.

Although it is undoubtedly true that many couples experience problems in sexual adjustment or unresponsiveness at some time, it must be emphasized that sexual dysfunction is indicative of chronic problems that probably affect only a minority of couples. The fact remains, however, that for most couples the sexual aspects of marriage change as they move out of the honeymoon years and settle into married life together. For many, this includes finding additional outlets for sexual expression.

ADDITIONAL OUTLETS

The frequency of intercourse is highest at younger ages and declines steadily. For husbands, this has manifold significance. To some degree the decreasing frequency reflects physiological aging and decreased frequency of sexual activity of any sort. Kinsey found that male sexual activity reaches its peak in adolescence and then drops steadily with increasing age. Psychological causation operates too. Fatigue, boredom, and lack of interest in the spouse may have many causal factors. In addition, there is loss of interest in endlessly repeating the same sexual experience. The opportunities for trying new techniques, new positions, and new situations must eventually end.

The decrease in frequency of marital intercourse often represents more than physiological and psychological fatigue however. Many males whose sexual urges are quite strong find additional outlets. The commonest is masturbation. At lower educational levels, 30 to 40 percent of married men masturbate at some time, whereas among those who have attended college almost 70 percent do so. These college-educated married men may masturbate as often as once or twice per week.

Almost as widespread as masturbation is extramarital intercourse. Kinsey estimated the proportion of men who become involved at about 50 percent. Again, differences are found by educational level. The highest incidences for those with less formal education appear at younger ages and decrease steadily with age. Among college-educated men, on the other hand, not more than 15 to 20 percent are involved at younger ages. The proportion who are involved increases steadily until approximately 27 percent are having extramarital intercourse by age 50. Among these same college-educated men, the frequencies of extramarital intercourse are not more than once every two or three weeks between 16 and 30 years of age, but climb to almost once a week at age 50.[30]

Obviously, marital intercourse accounts for only part of the sexual activity of married men. Among college-educated men, it supplies about 85 percent of the outlet during the early years of marriage but, by age 55, it is accounting for only 62 percent. Apparently, college-educated men as they grow older may conclude that the restraints on their early sexual involvements were not justified and frequently deal with their frustrations by finding other partners.

The situations of wives are different. Their interest in sexuality increases as they become more experienced. Kinsey estimated that women reach a peak of responsiveness at about 30 years of age and that this higher level of sexual interest is then maintained until the 50s or 60s. At some point, the desires of the wife surpass in frequency those of the husband. Some wives find alternate sources of sexual satisfaction.

The proportion of women who are active in masturbation at given ages is much higher at higher educational levels. The active incidence of masturbation to orgasm by married women between the ages of 21 and 25 is close to 30 percent for women with college and postgraduate educations. By age 31 to 35, it has climbed to 34 percent among college-educated women and to 40 percent among those with some graduate education. The percentages continue to climb at least through age 36 to

30. Alfred C. Kinsey, Wardell B. Pomeroy, and Clyde E. Martin, *Sexual Behavior in the Human Male*, Philadelphia: W. B. Saunders, 1948, p. 587.

40, with a high of 48 percent of graduate-school-educated women masturbating in the period from 41 to 45 years.[31] Many of these women are now being forced to seek sexual satisfaction that they cannot get from their husbands. Many even experience their first orgasms in marriages of long duration through masturbation.

Many women also have extramartial intercourse. Relatively few are involved during their teens and early 20s, and the majority who do become involved early are women from lower educational levels. The proportion of women who have extramarital coitus rises from 7 percent in the teens to 16 percent by age 30, 23 percent by age 35, and to a maximum of 26 percent by age 40. The proportion who are having such relationships during any one age period is, of course, somewhat lower. Between 16 and 20 years of age, only 6 percent are actively involved; the percentage climbs to 9 percent between 21 and 25 years, to 14 percent between 26 and 30, and to 17 percent between 31 and 35. It then remains relatively constant to about age 45.[32]

There are differences by educational level (see Table 15.4). Not until age 25 have college-educated women become involved in as large numbers as women of less formal education. By age 35, more college-educated women have become involved and the gap continues to widen through age 45. The percentage of college-level women who have had

Table 15.4. Percentage of women with experience in extramarital intercourse, by educational level and age

		Educational level		
Age	Total sample	9–12	13–16	17+
18	8	6	6	
19	7	8	4	
20	6	7	6	6
25	9	10	10	7
30	16	16	16	17
35	23	21	26	25
40	26	24	31	27
45	26	22	29	27

Source: Alfred C. Kinsey, Wardell B. Pomeroy, Clyde E. Martin, and Paul H. Gebhard, *Sexual Behavior in the Human Female*, Philadelphia: W. B. Saunders, 1953, p. 440.

31. Kinsey, Pomeroy, Martin, and Gebhard, *op. cit.*, p. 181.
32. A poll funded by *Playboy* magazine indicates that more young married women are having affairs (24 percent by age 25). How representative this sample may be is open to question. See *Time*, October 1, 1973, p. 63.

extramarital coitus reaches a high of 31 percent at age 40.[33] Thus, both men and women at higher educational levels are more likely to become involved in extramarital relationships after several years of marriage.[34] It is ironic that among the couples who should be most able to communicate with one another, noncommunication in the sexual area should be so pervasive.

In spite of widespread interest in the topic, relatively little research has assessed the impact of extramarital affairs on marriages. Kinsey reported that the extramarital activities not infrequently led to emotional involvements that interfered with their relationships with their husbands. Difficulty was least likely when the husbands did not know of the relationships, and crises often developed when the spouses learned of the affairs.[35]

The situation with regard to sexual adjustment may be likened to that involving total marital adjustment. Most couples report their sexual adjustment to be good. In the Burgess and Wallin study, 75 percent of the husbands and 61 percent of the wives reported receiving complete relief from sexual desire through marital coitus.[36] Yet, along with these reassuring reports must be considered the steadily decreasing frequency of intercourse as marriages continue, orgasm incapacity in women, and the resort of spouses to other sources of sexual satisfaction. The communication between many husbands and wives about sexual matters leaves something to be desired and that, if anything, the communication becomes poorer as marriages continue.

33. Kinsey, Pomeroy, Martin, and Gebhard, *op. cit.*, pp. 439–40. See also Lynn Atwater, "Women and Marriage: Adding an Extramarital Role," in Howard Robboy, Sidney L. Greenblatt, and Candace Clark, *eds.*, *Social Interaction*, New York: St. Martin's Press, 1979, pp. 510–20.
34. Research shows that college students who have premarital coitus are likely to anticipate having extramarital coitus. See Lee H. Bukstell, Gregory D. Roeder, Peter R. Kilmann, James Laughlin, and Wayne M. Sotile, "Projected Extramarital Sexual Involvement in Unmarried College Students," *Journal of Marriage and the Family* 40 (May 1978), pp. 337–40; Ira L. Reiss, Ronald E. Anderson, and G. C. Sponaugle, "A Multivariate Model of the Determinants of Extramarital Sexual Permissiveness," *Journal of Marriage and the Family* 42 (May 1980), pp. 395–411; and David L. Weis and Michael Slosnerick, "Attitudes Toward Sexual and Nonsexual Extramarital Involvement Among a Sample of College Students," *Journal of Marriage and the Family* 43 (May 1981), pp. 349–58.
35. See also Robert R. Bell, Stanley Turner, and Lawrence Rosen, "A Multivariate Analysis of Female Extramarital Coitus," *Journal of Marriage and the Family* 37 (May 1975), pp. 375–84; John N. Edwards, "Extramarital Involvement: Fact and Theory," *Journal of Sex Research* 9 (Aug. 1973), pp. 210–24; Phillip L. Elbaum, "The Dynamics, Implications and Treatment of Extramarital Sexual Relationships for the Family Therapist," *Journal of Marital and Family Therapy* 7 (Oct. 1981), pp. 489–94; and Minako K. Maykovich, "Attitudes Versus Behavior in Extramarital Sexual Relations," *Journal of Marriage and the Family* 38 (Nov. 1976), pp. 693–99.
36. Ernest W. Burgess and Paul Wallin, *Engagement and Marriage*, Philadelphia: J. B. Lippincott, 1953, p. 669.

SWINGING

The above discussion of extramarital intercourse focuses on the solitary, generally secretive adventures either of the husband or the wife. Whether one-night stands or affairs are involved, the participating spouse usually conceals the activity from the partner; in this context, the joint participation of husband and wife is not even considered.

Yet joint extramarital sexual participation is not new, nor has it been particularly rare. During the 1940s and 1950s, for example, there existed organized extramarital activities that were referred to as wife swapping, and there were persistent rumors, in most communities of the existence of key clubs.

Key clubs were the predecessors of today's swinging. Although the techniques of pairing off varied, the term *key club* stemmed from the technique of having all of the women place their keys in a hat. The men then drew keys, spending the night with the woman whose keys they had drawn. The number of key clubs was unknown because they were highly secretive. Apparently, they were also very unstable. The initiative usually was taken by a few of the husbands, and some wives participated reluctantly. Public censure would follow discovery, jealousies developed, and many participants believed that there must be something seriously wrong with them or their marriages or else that their spouses would not want to participate in such behavior.

Wife swapping differed from key clubbing as much in attitude as in technique. In wife swapping, there often were only two couples and the switch of partners might continue irregularly for a time. The very term *wife swapping*, however, has sexist connotations, implying that wives are property whose favors might be traded. Wife swapping was less egalitarian than key clubbing, and the potential for conflict was greater. Public knowledge of the arrangements often emerged when one of the partners sought separation or divorce.

Swinging as a distinct phenomenon appeared on the American scene in the early 1960s. Approximately 50 magazines that carried advertisements inviting contacts for sexual purposes sprang up—and they had substantial circulations.[37]

The essence of swinging is the joint participation of husband and wife in sexual activity with at least one other person, usually with other mar-

---

37. See Duane Denfeld and Michael Gordon, "The Sociology of Mate Swapping: Or the Family that Swings Together Clings Together," *Journal of Sex Research* 6 (May 1971), pp. 85–100; Richard M. Stephenson, "Involvement in Deviance: An Example and Some Theoretical Implications," *Social Problems* 21 (Fall 1973), pp. 173–90; Carolyn Symonds, "A Vocabulary of Sexual Enticement and Proposition," *Journal of Sex Research* 8 (May 1972), pp. 136–39; and Mary L. Walshok, "The Emergence of Middle-Class Deviant Sub-cultures: The Case of Swingers," *Social Problems* 18 (Spring 1971), pp. 488–95.

ried couples. The sexual activity is an end in itself, and both partners are willing to accept sexual intercourse with strangers.

There are no reliable estimates of how many couples swing. The most extravagant estimate comes from a sample of 407 swinging couples, only 4 percent of whom placed or replied to ads in swingers' magazines. Because almost 70,000 couples did use the magazines, the investigators estimated the total number of swinging couples at 8 million.[38] From another study of 350 Chicago couples, another researcher estimated that there are 8000 swinging couples within a 200 mile radius of that city.[39] The most trustworthy generalization comes from Robert Bell, who concluded that "there are more swingers than non-swingers believe, but not as many as swingers think."

Because we do not even know how many swingers there are, we cannot know their social characteristics. The groups who have been studied are primarily middle class, many having some college education. Many follow white-collar or professional occupations. Most appear to be relatively young. Interestingly, except in the sexual area, they seem to be conventional and conservative people. They conceal their swinging from their children and friends, and they are committed to swinging as a means of improving their marital adjustment.

An explicit set of social norms governs the behavior of swingers. First, there is no double standard. What is right for the husband is also right for the wife. No jealousy or private restrictions on the spouse's behavior are accepted. Second, sex among swingers must be kept strictly physical and impersonal. No "dates" outside the swinging sessions are permitted. Third, no one may be pressured into sexual activity. Women are free to reject overtures. Fourth, no moral judgments are permitted; one may choose not to participate in oral intercourse or in homosexual intercourse, for example, but one may not disapprove of such activities in others.

Swingers maintain that swinging actually improves their marriages. They argue that most nonswingers are hung-up on the idea of sexual possessiveness and that they have poor marriages as a result. By keeping sex with their spouses based on emotional as well as physical desire and by satisfying their physical needs in shared, nonhypocritical fashion, they believe that their marriages are happier and stronger than most.

Few objective studies of swinging have yet been done. One of the best studies involved questionnaires filled out by 965 marriage counselors,

38. William Breedlove and Jerrye Breedlove, *Swap Clubs*, Los Angeles: Sherbourne Press, 1964.
39. Gilbert D. Bartell, *Group Sex: A Scientist's Eyewitness Report on the American Way of Swinging*, New York: Peter H. Wyden, 1971.

of whom 473 had counseled couples who had tried swinging but had given it up. Among the 1175 couples reported on, 109 stated that they had problems of jealousy resulting from swinging. The men tended to be jealous of their wives' popularity or sexual performance. The women feared they would lose their husbands. There were 68 couples who reported fights and hostilities developed between them; as a result, their marriages were threatened. In 53 cases, emotional attachments to swinging partners developed, and 29 couples actually separated or divorced. Other problems reported were disappointment and boredom with swinging, fear of discovery, and the wife's "inability to take it."[40]

A Canadian study, in which 25 women swingers were interviewed by a woman researcher, focused on how couples reached the decision to swing and reported that the man made most of the decisions and that swinging is not the nonsexist, egalitarian arrangement it is reputed to be.[41] Dodson also reports that she found the same problems at orgies that occur in marital bedrooms, for example, women not having orgasms and the operation of the double standard.[42]

CESSATION OF MARITAL INTERCOURSE

Ordinarily, married couples have sexual intercourse. Researchers analyze how often they have coitus and how satisfactory it is. We know, of course, that these things vary over time and that various conditions, including fighting and quarreling, absence from the home, and illness, may interfere with marital sexual activity. Until recently, however, no one has stopped to inquire whether interruptions in the sexual lives of married couples may be common and prolonged.

One study of 221 women and 144 men, some of whom were married to one another, inquired into whether they had ever discontinued intercourse for any reason other than pregnancy. The couples had been married for an average of 11 years and three fourths of them were between 20 and 39 years old.

One third of the respondents indicated that they had stopped having intercourse for at least one period of time. The median length of time was eight weeks.

40. Duane Denfeld, "Dropouts from Swinging," *Family Coordinator* 23 (Jan. 1974), pp. 45–49. For an analysis that reported lack of harmful results from swinging, see Charles L. Cole and Graham B. Spanier, "Comarital Mate-Sharing and Family Stability," *Journal of Sex Research* 10 (Feb. 1974), pp. 21–31.
41. Anne-Marie Henshel, "Swinging: A Study of Decision Making in Marriage," in Joan Huber, ed., *Changing Women in a Changing Society,* Chicago and London: University of Chicago Press, 1973, pp. 123–29.
42. Betty Dodson, "Playboy Panel: New Sexual Life Styles," *Playboy,* Sept. 1973, p. 85.

Table 15.5. Reasons for cessation of marital intercourse

Reason	Men (N = 46)	Women (N = 80)	Total (N = 126)
Marital discord	35%	42%	40%
Illness	21	19	20
Decreased interest in sex	13	11	12
Surgery	13	9	10
Psychiatric impairment	9	8	8
Menstruation	4	4	4
Birth control procedures	0	5	3
Geographic separation	5	2	3

Source: Adapted from John N. Edwards and Alan Booth, "The Cessation of Marital Intercourse," *American Journal of Psychiatry* 133 (Nov. 1976), p. 1336. © 1976, the American Psychiatric Association. Reprinted by permission.

The reported reasons for discontinuing intercourse are shown in Table 15.5. Marital discord was far and away the most frequent cause. Moreover, at least part of the instances of psychiatric impairment and decreased interest in sex probably either cause or reflect mental discord. Thus, up to 60 percent of the cases may involve other kinds of problems in the marriage relationship. The only other reports of any magnitude involved medical problems, either illness or surgery.[43]

These data are enough to indicate that interruptions of marital intercourse owing to other marital problems are a common occurrence. They do not tell us whether they tend to be repeated. More research is needed to assess their impact upon marriages.

SUMMARY

Married couples vary enormously in their frequency of coital activity. Frequency of intercourse tends to be high during the first year of marriage, with a steady subsequent decline. Influenced by effective contraceptive use, marital coitus has been on the increase since the time of Kinsey's early work. Husbands and wives differ in their desire for sexual intercourse and the percentage of women who experience coital orgasms rises with the duration of marriage. Frequency of female or-

43. John N. Edwards and Alan Booth, "The Cessation of Marital Intercourse," *American Journal of Psychiatry* 133 (Nov. 1976), pp. 1333-36.

gasm is related to the decade of the woman's birth, her father's occupational class, and her educational level. Orgasm in women also is associated with the time spent in sexual play.

When sexual problems are chronic, they may be labeled sexual dysfunction. Among men, these sexual dysfunctions include erectile dysfunction, premature ejaculation, and retarded ejaculation, Erectile dysfunction involves the inability to achieve or maintain a penile erection. Premature ejaculation is more problematic in its definition but is generally defined as an inability to satisfy a responsive partner, in intercourse, at least 50 percent of the time. Retarded ejaculation is the inability to ejaculate while in intromission.

Among females, sexual dysfunctions include orgasmic dysfunction, dyspareunia, and vaginismus. Orgasmic dysfunction is the inability either to experience orgasm at all or only in certain situations. Dyspareunia entails pain upon intercourse. With vaginismus, contractions of the vaginal sphincter make intercourse impossible. It has been estimated that as many as 50 percent of all couples experience some form of sexual maladjustment in marriage, but this is impossible to know with any certainty.

Men and women seek additional outlets for their sexual needs. These include masturbation and extramarital intercourse. Among men and women, frequency of masturbation is related to level of education. Involvement in extramarital relations is related to education and age.

Key clubs and wife swapping came into view during the 1940s and 1950s and were the predecessors of today's swinging. In the 1960s, specialized magazines appeared that featured advertisements for sexual contacts. There are no reliable estimates of how many couples swing.

SUGGESTED READINGS

Edwards, John N., ed., *Sex and Society*, Chicago: Markham, 1972. A comprehensive set of essays covering marital sex, extramarital sex, and sex among widows and divorcees.

Neubeck, Gerhard, ed., *Extramarital Relations*, Englewood Cliffs, N.J.: Prentice-Hall, 1969. A varied collection of essays on a formerly taboo topic. Contains a section on causes and effects of extramarital relations.

Offir, Carol Wade, *Human Sexuality*, New York: Harcourt Brace Jovanovich, 1982. A well-written textbook covering all aspects of human sexuality.

Pomeroy, Wardell B., *Dr. Kinsey and the Institute for Sex Research*, New Haven, Conn.: Yale University Press, 1982. A personal account of the

man who shocked the world with his reports on human sexuality by one
who was closely associated with him for many years.

Strean, Herbert S., *The Extramarital Affair*, New York: The Free Press, 1980.
Reviews the major psychodynamics of men and women involved in extramarital affairs, from a psychoanalytic perspective.

FILMS

The Sexes (Visual Aids Service, University of Illinois, Champaign, Ill. 61820),
17 minutes. A discussion by Masters and Johnson of sexual malfunction.

Sexual Anatomy and Physiology: Male and Female (Focus International, 1776
Broadway, New York, N.Y. 10019), 43 minutes. Discusses the Masters
and Johnson four-stage model of sexual response.

To Love (Audio Visual Services, Pennsylvania State University, University
Park, Pennsylvania 16802), 25 minutes. Filmed in Yugoslavia, a husband
and wife who rarely have time together share a special picnic lunch.

Why Didn't You Tell Me? (Focus International, 1776 Broadway, New York,
N.Y. 10019), 11 minutes. A woman tells her lover of six months that she
has not had an orgasm with him. They discuss their sexual concerns.

QUESTIONS AND PROJECTS

1. What is the relationship between age and marital intercourse? What interpretation would you place on the discrepancies between husbands and
wives in reported frequencies of orgasm?

2. What factors are related to female coital orgasm? Why do you think
these particular factors affect women's ability to experience orgasm during intercourse?

3. Why is it difficult to know with any certainty how many couples in the
United States suffer sexual dysfunction?

4. Define: *erectile dysfunction, secondary orgasmic dysfunction, retarded
ejaculation, dyspareunia.*

5. What are some of the physical causes of erectile dysfunction? Some psychological causes?

6. What is the difference between dyspareunia and vaginismus? What kinds
of trauma are associated with vaginismus?

7. What associations are there between sexual frustration in marriage and
extramarital intercourse? Are these purely biological frustrations? Use
data by social class to show that they are not.

8. At what ages are men and women at their peak sexual responsiveness?

What implications do these differential responsiveness ages have for marriage in the later years?

9. Describe the normative structure that regulates swinging. Evaluate the available evidence on the effects of swinging on marriage.

10. What are some of the reasons for the cessation of intercourse in marriage? How likely is it that sexless marriages survive?

Mimi Forsyth, Monkmeyer

16

Family Planning and Childbearing

Morning sickness, backache, fatigue—these and other symptoms of pregnancy are more likely than not to afflict an expectant father, says a nurse-scientist who is researching the mysterious male reaction to the condition of pregnant wives that Western science knows as "couvade."

"Even abdominal swelling—all the men we've seen have experienced that, too," adds Dr. Jacqueline Clinton. . . . Clinton and two assistant professors of nursing, Rita Beck and Eileen P. Sheil, have interviewed 60 fathers-to-be in Milwaukee and plan to include 200 more in their study.

. . . More than half the expectant fathers in the Western world join their wives in suffering clear signs of pregnancy. The symptoms include headaches, depression, irritability, cravings for particular foods and weight gain. ". . . I think it would be a lot higher if men didn't hide what's happening to them—if they would 'fess up."[1]

Over 3.5 million babies were born in the United States in 1982.[2] Improvements in contraceptive methods have made it possible for couples effectively to plan both the number of children they want and when they want to have them. Most couples desire children and have them early in marriage. Nearly one out of every two couples produces a child within the first two years of marriage, and at least 90 percent of all couples produce at least one child eventually.[3]

1. Associated Press, August 7, 1983.
2. National Center for Health Statistics, *Monthly Vital Statistics Report* 32, September 21, 1983.
3. Anne R. Pebley, "Changing Attitudes Toward the Timing of First Births," *Family Planning Perspectives* 13 (July–Aug. 1981), pp. 171–75. See also Margaret Mooney Marini, "Effects of the Timing of Marriage and First Birth on Fertility," *Journal of Marriage and the Family* 43 (Feb. 1981), pp. 27–46; and Ronald R. Rindfuss and Craig St. John, "Social Determinants of Age at First Birth," *Journal of Marriage and the Family* 45 (Aug. 1983), pp. 553–65.

FAMILY PLANNING

Data on family size are available for about the last 100 years. They show that from 1860 to 1930 birthrates and the size of families steadily declined. The number of persons per household declined from 5.1 to 4.1. Birthrates stayed at low levels until the end of World War II when a rush of marriages deferred during the depression of the 1930s and the war years began to produce rapidly increasing numbers of births. The crude birthrate climbed to 25 in 1946. Since that time, advances in contraceptive techniques, concerns about overpopulation, and increased participation of women in the labor force have led to an enormous reduction in the number of children born to American women. The birthrate stood at around 15 in 1983.[4] A better indication than the crude birthrate of what happened is changing preferences in family size.

During the 1940s, a national sample of women was asked how many children they considered to be ideal. Again in 1955 and 1960, national samples of married women were asked the same thing. In all three periods, about 90 percent stated that they wanted two, three, or four children. The proportions wanting two children steadily declined, however, whereas the proportions wanting four children steadily increased. In 1960, the proportion wanting four children was higher than the proportion wanting any other number.[5]

By 1960, however, birthrates had started down, and expected family size changed drastically. By 1978, women expected to have an average of only 2.3 children each.[6] In 1982, women aged 18 to 24 reported that they expect to have an average of 2 children only.[7] Birth expectations vary according to level of education. Among women aged 18 to 34, those who have not completed high school expect an average of 2.3 children; those who have completed four years of college expect only 1.8 children. Among college-educated women, those with four years of college expect an average of 1.9 children, whereas those with five or more years expect only 1.7 lifetime births.

Trends in Family Size

In Chapter 13, we found that there is a growing trend among young people to delay marriage. One reason for this is the desire among some, particularly women, to complete their education and launch careers

4. National Center for Health Statistics, *op. cit.*
5. Pascal K. Whelpton, Arthur A. Campbell, and John E. Patterson, *Fertility and Family Planning in the United States*, Princeton, N.J.: Princeton University Press, 1966.
6. U.S. Bureau of the Census, "Fertility of American Women: June 1978," *Current Population Reports*, Series P–20, No. 341 (October 1979).
7. U.S. Bureau of the Census, "Fertility of American Women: June 1982," Series P–20, No. 379 (May, 1983). Advance Report.

before they settle into married life. Accompanying the rise in age at first marriage there are two trends that focus on childbearing: delayed parenthood and planned childlessness.

Delayed Parenthood. There is a growing tendency among American women to delay their childbearing to pursue careers. From 1973 to 1981, the number of women having their first child after the age of 30 dramatically rose from 58,000 to more than 100,000.[8] Women aged 30 to 34 accounted for a larger increase in the fertility rate in 1980 than did women in any other age group.[9] One study found that women who consciously delay childbearing are concerned with economic security and personal freedom.[10]

The effects of delayed parenthood on family size may be significant. The longer a woman postpones having her first child after marriage, the fewer children she will have or the less likely it is that she will be able to have children at all.[11] Although it is still too early to make any concrete predictions, it seems likely that the future may bring both a growing number of families raising only one child and couples who would like to be parents but find themselves unable to conceive.

Planned Childlessness. During the late 1960s and early 1970s, scattered groups of married couples received support from some sociologists for rejecting parenthood altogether. Bernard, for example, although acknowledging that childless marriages have higher divorce rates than those with children, pointed out that *surviving* childless marriages report higher marital-happiness ratings than marriages with children.[12] A study of over 5000 people in California found that couples currently raising children make lower marital-happiness scores.[13] Recent studies have confirmed that childless couples are happier and more satisfied with their lives than are couples with children.[14]

8. *New York Times,* July 24, 1983. See also Jane Price, "Who Waits to Have Children? And Why?" in Jeffrey P. Rosenberg, *Relationships: The Marriage and Family Reader,* Glenview, Ill.: Scott, Foresman, 1982, pp. 280–89.
9. "Fertility Rate Slows in 1980, but Large Increases Continue Among Older Mothers, Unmarried Women," *Family Planning Perspectives* 15 (Jan.–Feb. 1983), pp. 38–39.
10. Jane Riblett Wilkie, "The Trend Toward Delayed Parenthood," *Journal of Marriage and the Family* 43 (Aug. 1981), pp. 583–91.
11. "U.S. Women Expecting Small Families, Waiting Longer to Have Children," *Family Planning Perspectives* 13 (July–Aug. 1981), p. 191.
12. Jessie Bernard, *The Future of Marriage,* New York: World, 1972.
13. Karen Renne, "Correlates of Dissatisfaction in Marriage," *Journal of Marriage and the Family* 32 (Feb. 1970), pp. 54–67.
14. Victor J. Callan, "The Voluntarily Childless and Their Perceptions of Parenthood and Childlessness," *Journal of Comparative Family Studies* 14 (Spring 1983), pp. 87–96; and Karen A. Polonko, John Scanzoni, and Jay D. Teachman, "Childlessness and Marital Satisfaction: A Further Assessment," *Journal of Family Issues* 3 (Dec. 1982), pp. 545–73.

In 1971, a national organization, the National Organization for Non-parents (NON), was formed to promote childlessness as a superior way of life and to support couples who do not wish to have children. Of the approximately 600 people who joined NON during its first year or so, about one fourth were couples with children. Since that time, there has been a slow but steadily growing acceptance of childless marriages. Around 1 to 2 percent of currently married couples are voluntarily childless,[15] and it is estimated that if current trends continue, almost 30 percent of white women and 20 percent of nonwhite women will remain childless throughout their lives.[16]

Scholarly interest in planned childlessness has skyrocketed in recent years and probably will continue.[17] Those who plan to remain childless tend to have higher levels of education, higher incomes, and tend also to be nonreligious. Veevers reported on 52 voluntarily childless wives in Canada and found that they divided into two groups: those who decided on childlessness before marriage and those who decided later. The latter group decided first to postpone childbearing and gradually drifted into making the decision permanent.[18] Mosher and Bachrach, using data from a national survey of 17,000 women, found that 43 percent of voluntarily childless women had agreed with their spouses before marriage not to have children.[19] These same women used the most effective methods of birth control to prevent unwanted pregnancies.

Callan compared two groups of young single women: those who wanted children and those who wanted none.[20] The women who planned to remain childless wanted marriage partners who were more egalitarian and who would not expect total commitment from their wives. Those women who reported wanting children desired mates who would be more traditional in their attitudes. Feldman found that these expecta-

15. William D. Mosher and Christine A. Bachrach, "Childlessness in the United States: Estimates from the National Survey of Family Growth," *Journal of Family Issues* 3 (Dec. 1982), pp. 517–43.
16. "Predict More Than Two in Ten Young U.S. Women Will Remain Childless," *Family Planning Perspectives* 13 (July–Aug. 1981), p. 184.
17. See, for example, Sharon K. Houseknecht, "Reference Group Support for Voluntary Childlessness: Evidence for Conformity," *Journal of Marriage and the Family* 39 (May 1977), pp. 285–92; "Childlessness and Marital Adjustment," *Journal of Marriage and the Family* 41 (May 1979), pp. 259–65; and "Voluntary Childlessness: Toward a Theoretical Integration," *Journal of Family Issues* 3 (Dec. 1982), pp. 459–71; also see Dudley L. Poston, Jr. and Katherine Trent, "International Variability in Childlessness: A Descriptive and Analytical Study," *Journal of Family Issues* 3 (Dec. 1982), pp. 473–91.
18. J. E. Veevers, "Voluntarily Childless Wives: An Exploratory Study," *Sociology and Social Research* (April 1973), pp. 356–65; and "The Moral Careers of Voluntarily Childless Wives: Notes on the Defense of a Variant World View," *Family Coordinator* 24 (Oct. 1975), pp. 473–86.
19. Mosher and Bachrach, *op. cit.*, p. 531.
20. Victor J. Callan, "Childlessness and Partner Selection," *Journal of Marriage and the Family* 45 (Feb. 1983), pp. 181–86.

tions carry over into marriage.[21] Comparing parents with childless couples, he found that childless spouses have less traditional attitudes toward women and tend to interact more with each other than do couples who have children.

Contraception

Over 33 million women in the United States today practice some method of contraception. A 1982 national survey of women aged 18 to 44 questioned over 6700 women about their birth control attitudes and usage.[22] The results showed that contraceptive use has been spreading rapidly and that almost all couples now use contraceptives at some time during their married lives. Around 95 percent of the married women favor using some means to limit pregnancies, regardless of race, religion, or income.

The data collected from this survey were used to estimate contraceptive practices among U.S. women aged 15 to 44. Table 16.1 presents the estimated percentages of women currently using or not using contraception and the types of practices employed. The figures show that the percentage practicing contraception at any one time is about 61 percent. Of the nonusers, the majority either are not involved with a sexual partner, are pregnant, or trying to conceive. Some do not need contraception because their marriages are infertile, and only about 6 percent of those exposed to pregnancy risk are not using some means of birth control.

Among those using contraception, sterilization is the most popular method, accounting for almost 12 million women in the United States.[23] Over 20 percent of these women have had tubal sterilizations, whereas another 14 percent rely on their partner's vasectomies for protection from unwanted pregnancies. Women who depend on sterilization tend to be older than the average woman at risk; 79 percent of women relying on sterilization are 30 or older.

The second most popular method of birth control is the oral contraceptive, used by about 10 million women in the United States. Pill users tend to be younger than women using other methods; around 82 percent are under 30. The largest group of women using the pill are between

21. Harold Feldman, "A Comparison of Intentional Parents and Intentionally Childless Couples," *Journal of Marriage and the Family* 43 (Aug. 1981), pp. 593–600.

22. Jacqueline Darroch Forrest and Stanley K. Henshaw, "What U.S. Women Think and Do About Contraception," *Family Planning Perspectives* 15 (July–Aug. 1983), pp. 157–66.

23. *Ibid.* See also Frank D. Bean, Margaret Pruitt Clark, Gray Swicegood, and Dorie Williams, "Husband-wife Communication, Wife's Employment, and the Decision for Male or Female Sterilization," *Journal of Marriage and the Family* 45 (May 1983), pp. 395–403.

Table 16.1. Estimated current exposure to the risk of conception among U.S. women aged 15 to 44

Type of Exposure	Percentages
Percentage total	101.0
Exposed and using a method	61.0
Exposed and not using a method	6.0
Not exposed	34.0
Not having sex	14.0
Infrequent sex	5.0
Pregnant or trying to get pregnant	8.0
Infertile or menopausal	7.0
Contraceptive users	
Sterilization	34.8
Tubal	20.3
Vasectomy	14.5
Pill	29.9
Condom	13.4
IUD	6.9
Diaphragm	5.7
Spermicide	4.4
Withdrawal	2.8
Rhythm	1.7
Douche and other	0.4
Total users	100.0

Source: Adapted from Jacqueline Darroch Forrest and Stanley K. Henshaw, "What U.S. Women Think and Do About Contraception," *Family Planning Perspectives* 15 (July–Aug. 1983), p. 162. Adapted with permission from *Family Planning Perspectives*, Volume 15, Number 4, 1983.

20 to 24, around 4 million oral contraceptive users. Among married women over the age of 30, sterilization is the most popular method, regardless of family size. Among married women under the age of 30, sterilization is preferred only by those who have two or more children. Compared with married women, unmarried women are more likely to be using the pill.

The use of condoms and diaphragms has increased slightly during the past few years, probably as a result of complications people are encountering in the use of the pill and the IUD. Because of the opposition of the Roman Catholic Church to all methods of contraception other than rhythm, trends in the use of this method are especially interesting. Almost 7 percent of women were using the rhythm method in 1965; by 1975, the percentage had dropped to 2.8, and by 1982, only 1.7 percent of American women were relying on rhythm for birth control. Over two thirds of Catholic women use prohibited methods, and researchers predict that their birth control practices will be indistinguishable from those of non-Catholics in just a few years.[24]

PREGNANCY AND CHILDBEARING

At least 75 percent of all pregnancies are welcomed by the prospective parents. Under these circumstances, the pregnancy experience should be rewarding. Conversely, unplanned and unwanted pregnancies should be accompanied by problems. If this is true, however, it is later pregnancies rather than the first one that create problems for married couples.

The first pregnancies of 212 university students' wives were classified into those where the wives had not wanted the conception, those where they had not tried to achieve or avoid conception, and those where conception was sought. During the first trimester of pregnancy, there were more feelings of unhappiness and more emotional upset among those who had not wanted to conceive. But by the second trimester, these differences had virtually disappeared, indicating that most couples quickly make their peace with the first pregnancy, whether planned or not. The nausea experienced by the wives during pregnancy was not related to whether the child was planned, and there were no relationships between planning status and the ease or difficulty of delivery.[25] Brodsky, studying other student wives, found that the self-acceptance of pregnant women did not differ significantly from that of wives who were not pregnant.[26]

The first study showed that pregnancy often has some effect on sexual adjustment. Of the couples, 58 percent indicated that their sexual adjustment had not been affected, but 24 percent believed their adjustment had been adversely affected, whereas 18 percent stated that their adjustment had improved. In general, those who had good sexual adjustment before the pregnancy continued to have good adjustment. Where previously poor adjustment improved, the improvement might have occurred without the pregnancy or it might have been linked to the pregnancy. Some husbands and wives described themselves as more considerate of one another during the pregnancy. Where poorer adjustment devel-

24. Charles F. Westoff and Elise F. Jones, "The Secularization of U.S. Catholic Birth Control Practice," *Family Planning Perspectives* 9 (Sept.–Oct. 1977), pp. 203-7.
25. Shirley Poffenberger, Thomas Poffenberger, and Judson T. Landis, "Intent Toward Conception and the Pregnancy Experience," *American Sociological Review* 17 (Oct. 1952), pp. 616-20.
26. Stanley L. Brodsky, "Self-Acceptance in Pregnant Women," *Marriage and Family Living* 25 (Nov. 1963), pp. 483-84. See also Ralph LaRossa, "Sex During Pregnancy: A Symbolic Interactionist Analysis," *Journal of Sex Research* 15 (May 1979), pp. 119-28; William R. Rosengren, "Social Sources of Pregnancy as Illness or Normality," *Social Forces* 29 (March 1961), pp. 260-67; and "Social Instability and Attitudes Toward Pregnancy as a Social Role," *Social Problems* 9 (Spring 1962), pp. 371-78.

oped, it was frequently explained in terms of the added responsibilities that childbearing entailed; the wife sometimes became too busy and too tired to be interested in sex. There also was a tendency for the frequency of sexual desire of both husband and wife to decrease during pregnancy and to remain lower after the birth of the child. Fear of another pregnancy hindered sexual adjustment after the birth, and sexual adjustment was better where the wife had confidence in the contraceptive subsequently used.[27]

Studies of family planning and general knowledge would lead us to expect that the effects of subsequent pregnancies, particularly unwanted pregnancies, would be different. That this is true is verified by data collected by Kinsey. He found that some pregnancies at each birth order are terminated by induced abortion. Only about 10 percent of second pregnancies were so terminated, 16 percent of third pregnancies, 19 percent of fifth pregnancies, and 34 percent of sixth pregnancies ended in induced abortion.[28]

The abortion situation in the United States changed rapidly in the late 1960s and early 1970s as 17 states liberalized their abortion laws. Then in January 1973, the Supreme Court issued a landmark ruling that virtually wiped out both the old laws and most of the new ones. The court held that during the first trimester of pregnancy, the decision to have an abortion must be left solely to the woman and her physician. The only restriction permitted is that the abortion must be performed by a physician licensed by the state. During the second trimester, the state may impose regulations "reasonably related to maternal health," still not limiting the grounds for abortion but stating the qualifications of persons permitted to perform the procedure and specifying the nature of the facility—such as a clinic or hospital. After the fetus becomes viable (24 to 28 weeks) laws prohibiting abortion for the purpose of promoting the state's "interest in the potentiality of human life" are permitted, unless abortion is necessary for the preservation of the life or health of the mother, including her mental health.[29]

The number of legal abortions performed has risen spectacularly since about 1969. From 18,000 in 1968, the number climbed to 50,000 in 1969, 230,000 in 1970, 600,000 in 1971, 700,000 in 1972, about 1.3 million in 1977, and about 1.5 million in 1980. Almost 320,000 married women had abortions in 1980.[30]

27. Judson T. Landis, Thomas Poffenberger, and Shirley Poffenberger, "The Effects of First Pregnancy Upon the Sexual Adjustment of 212 Couples," *American Sociological Review* 15 (Dec. 1950), pp. 766–68.
28. Paul H. Gebhard, Wardell B. Pomeroy, Clyde E. Martin, and Cornelia V. Christenson, *Pregnancy, Birth and Abortion*, New York: Harper & Bros., 1958, p. 136.
29. The political struggle over abortion is not over. The legislatures of 15 states have called for a constitutional amendment that would prohibit abortion in the United States.
30. Stanley K. Henshaw and Kevin O'Reilly, "Characteristics of Abortion Patients in

Tentative findings suggest that these increases in legal abortions have been accompanied by lower birth rates, particularly of illegitimate births, falling morbidity and mortality rates, and diminished emotional consequences for the women involved. This is particularly significant in view of the fact that even at the time of the Kinsey studies, 82 percent of the married women who had been aborted reported no unfavorable consequences.[31]

Obviously, reactions to pregnancy vary with the number of pregnancies and whether the pregnancy is desired. Most early pregnancies appear to be wanted and produce only minor effect on the marriage. Later pregnancies, after the couple have had all the children they want, are more likely to have negative repercussions and to end in abortion.

If there is justification for conceiving of pregnancy as possibly crisis producing, there also is justification for reasoning that childbirth may sometimes produce a marital crisis. Le Masters studied 46 middle-class couples who were having their first child. He found that 38 of the 46 couples (83 percent) reported an "extensive" or "severe" crisis in adjusting to the birth of the child. Because 35 of these 38 children were "desired" or "planned," the crisis could not be attributed to unwanted pregnancy. Neither could the crisis be attributed to poor marital adjustment or psychiatric problems. Instead Le Masters concluded that these parents had romanticized parenthood and were unprepared for the reality of having a baby in the home. The mothers often complained of feeling tired, of being confined to their homes, and of having to give up social activities and employment. The fathers also complained of financial pressures, of worry about another pregnancy, and of lessened sexual interest on the part of their wives.[32]

Other studies have attempted to confirm or refute Le Masters's findings. Dyer studied 32 middle-class couples in Houston, Texas, and reached conclusions similar to those of Le Masters'. Of his couples 53 percent experienced extensive or severe crises after the birth of their first child. The crises often lasted for several months. Both Le Masters and Dyer found that the large majority of couples eventually made satisfactory recovery from the crises.[33]

the United States, 1979 and 1980," *Family Planning Perspectives* 15 (Jan.-Feb. 1983), pp. 5–16.

31. Kinsey, Pomeroy, Martin, and Gebhard, *op. cit.*, pp. 203–11. For analysis of change in attitudes toward abortion, see Helen Rose Fuchs Ebaugh and C. Allen Haney, "Shifts in Abortion Attitudes: 1972–1978," *Journal of Marriage and the Family* 42 (Aug. 1980), pp. 491–500. See also Barbara Finlay Agresti, "Sex Differences in Correlates of Abortion Attitudes Among College Students," *Journal of Marriage and the Family* 43 (Aug. 1981), pp. 571–81.

32. Ersel E. Le Masters, "Parenthood as Crisis," *Marriage and Family Living* 19 (Nov. 1957), pp. 352–55.

33. Everett D. Dyer, "Parenthood as Crisis: A Re-study," *Marriage and Family Living* 25 (May 1963), pp. 196–201.

Hobbs studied a broader sample of couples whose babies averaged only about 10 weeks of age and found that 87 percent experienced only a slight crisis and that only 13 percent experienced even a moderate crisis.[34] This study was replicated a decade later, in 1975, with essentially the same findings.[35] Another study of 300 Minneapolis couples whose babies ranged from 6 to 56 weeks of age produced similar findings.[36] Hobbs quotes Feldman as saying that the low proportion of couples experiencing crisis at this early period may be due to a "baby honeymoon." Feldman believes that couples experience early elation over parenthood but that after 4 to 6 weeks crisis begins to set in.[37] Most investigators agree that whatever trauma is involved in early parenthood is successfully resolved by most couples within a few years.[38]

INFERTILITY

There are many couples in the United States today who would gladly face the complications and crises that accompany parenthood. For these couples, the hope of having their own children is complicated by a problem that appears to be affecting a growing segment of the population: infertility on the part of the husband, the wife, or both partners. Infertility has been defined as "the failure of a couple to conceive after

34. Daniel F. Hobbs, Jr., "Parenthood as Crisis: A Third Study," *Journal of Marriage and the Family* 27 (Aug. 1965), pp. 367–72. See also Arthur P. Jacoby, "Transition to Parenthood: A Reassessment," *Journal of Marriage and the Family* 31 (Nov. 1969), pp. 720–27.
35. Daniel F. Hobbs, Jr. and Sue Peck Cole, "Transition to Parenthood: A Decade Replication," *Journal of Marriage and the Family* 38 (Nov. 1976), pp. 723–31; and Daniel F. Hobbs, Jr., and Jane Maynard Wimbish, "Transition to Parenthood by Black Couples," *Journal of Marriage and the Family* 39 (Nov. 1977), pp. 677–89.
36. Candyce Smith Russell, "Transition to Parenthood: Problems and Gratifications," *Journal of Marriage and the Family* 36 (May 1974), pp. 294–302.
37. Feldman also found that the advent of the first child begins a critical period in the marital relationship. See Harold Feldman, *Development of the Husband-Wife Relationship: A Research Report:* Cornell University, n.d., Mimeo.; see also Brent C. Miller and Donna L. Sollie, "Normal Stresses During the Transition to Parenthood," *Family Relations* 29 (Oct. 1980), pp. 459–65.
38. See Jay Belsky, Graham B. Spanier, and Michael Rovine, "Stability and Change in Marriage Across the Transition to Parenthood," *Journal of Marriage and the Family* 45 (Aug. 1983), pp. 567–77; Norval D. Glenn and Sarah McLanahan, "Children and Marital Happiness: A Further Specification of the Relationship," *Journal of Marriage and the Family* 45 (Aug. 1983), pp. 579–89; Steven D. McLaughlin and Michael Micklin, "The Timing of the First Birth and Changes in Personal Efficacy," *Journal of Marriage and the Family* 44 (Feb. 1982), pp. 63–77; Ralph LaRossa, "The Transition to Parenthood and the Social Reality of Time," *Journal of Marriage and the Family* 45 (Aug. 1983), pp. 579–89; Steven D. McLaughlin and Michael Micklin, "The Timing of the First Birth and Changes in Personal Efficacy," *Journal of Marriage and the Family* 45 (Feb. 1983), pp. 47–55; Katherine A. May, "Factors Contributing to First-Time Fathers' Readiness for Fatherhood: An Exploratory Study," *Family Relations* 31 (July 1982), pp. 353–61; and Holly Waldron and Donald K. Routh, "The Effect of the First Child on the Marital Relationship," *Journal of Marriage and the Family* 43 (Nov. 1981), pp. 785–88.

one or more years of continuous marriage during which contraceptives are not used.[39] About 15 percent of today's married couples are infertile; for many, the inability to conceive contributes to feelings of guilt, anger, depression, and marital dispute.

Until recently, the inability to conceive a child usually was attributed to barrenness on the part of wives. At one time, barrenness was even grounds for divorce in the United States. We know today, however, that only about 40 percent of infertility cases involve difficulties on the part of the women involved. Another 40 percent of cases involve reproductive problems among husbands, and in 20 percent of cases both spouses have some degree of fertility deficiency.[40] The causes of infertility are numerous, but an explosion of research in recent years has resulted in a number of treatments that are bringing new hope to couples where once there was none.

Causes of Infertility

Although it is still too early to know with any certainty, it is believed that cases of infertility may be increasing. One factor implicated in the rise is the proliferation of environmental pollutants that damage sperm or reduce the mobility of sperm. It is estimated that among males, nearly one fourth have sperm counts so low that they are considered "functionally sterile."[41] It is believed that toxic substances from the environment enter the body and accumulate in fatty tissue, eventually damaging and reducing the number of viable sperm. Noise pollution, found to affect the fertility of laboratory animals, may also take its toll on humans in an increasingly technological society. Not only pollution, but clothing styles also may result in faulty semen. Close-fitting underwear and tight jeans hold the testicles abnormally close to the body, where the warmth is too intense to keep sperm healthy. A common bacterial germ, *T mycoplasma*, has also been implicated in a number of infertility cases.[42]

Perhaps the most common cause of infertility in men is *varicocele*. In these cases, varicose veins in the scrotum block the production of sperm by raising the temperature of the testes. Exposure to venereal disease also may produce an obstruction of the vas deferens, the duct from the testes to the penis, thus blocking the exit of sperm during intercourse.

Exposure to venereal disease also is a contributory factor to infertility

39. William D. Mosher, "Infertility Trends Among U.S. Couples: 1965–1976," *Family Planning Perspectives* 14 (Jan.–Feb. 1982), pp. 22–27.
40. *Newsweek*, December 6, 1982, p. 102.
41. Lori B. Andrews, "Embryo Technology," in Ollie Pocs, *ed., Human Sexuality 83–84*, Guilford, Conn.: Duskin Publishing Group, 1983, pp. 89–94.
42. Associated Press, March 3, 1983.

in women, often producing tubal blocking and scarring. Having a variety of sexual partners may lead to low-grade infections that damage reproductive organs.[43] Although a point of controversial debate, the growing tendency on the part of women to delay childbearing may result in a diminished capacity to conceive.

In some women, long-term usage of oral contraceptives may result in an inability to ovulate even after their use is discontinued. IUDs have been the precipitating cause of pelvic infections in over 1 million women since 1970; in many cases, these infections cause so much damage that the women are rendered sterile.

About 20 percent of female infertility cases are the result of ovulatory disorders that arise from hormonal imbalances.[44] Endometriosis, the growth of uterine material outside the uterus, can block the reproductive tract and prevent fertilization of the ovum. Blockage of the fallopian tubes may result from infections, endometriosis, gonorrhea, and from other, unknown causes.

Treatments for Infertility

Hormone and ovulatory disorders in women were commonly treated with fertility drugs in the past, often resulting in multiple births among the families involved. Although an effective treatment for many infertile couples, fertility drugs, nonetheless, were often the only treatment available for couples who wished to give birth to children. Today, however, there are a number of treatments, some controversial, that are being used in the United States and around the world to cure infertility.

Artificial Insemination by Husband (AIH). More than 250,000 babies have been conceived through artificial insemination.[45] As the name implies, this method involves the artificial introduction of semen into the cervix of the female. In cases of AIH, sperm are obtained from the husband and deposited by syringe in the uterus. This procedure is repeated for several days to increase the probability of fertilization. Artificial insemination is used in cases in which the husband has a low sperm count. Sperm may be collected from repeated ejaculations and frozen until a count sufficient for impregnation is obtained. It is also used in cases of male sexual dysfunction and instances in which the mucosa covering the woman's cervix is too thick to allow entrance to sperm. Artificial insemination by husbands probably is the least controversial of

43. Andrews, *op. cit.*, p. 89.
44. *Newsweek, op. cit.*, p. 105.
45. Shirley L. Zimmerman, "Alternatives in Human Reproduction for Involuntary Childless Couples," *Family Relations* 31 (April 1982), pp. 233–41.

all infertility treatments; the children produced are the genetic off-spring of both the husbands and wives involved.

Artificial Insemination by Donor (AID). Although the procedure used in AID is the same as that described above, these cases involve the introduction into the cervix of sperm from men other than the husbands. In these cases, husbands are either sterile (*azoospermic*) or have very low sperm counts (*oligospermic*).[46] They may also have, or be, carriers of genetically transmitted diseases such as Tay-Sachs disease, which would prove harmful or fatal to offspring. Sperm are collected from donors who are paid a small fee and screened for genetic anomolies, venereal disease, and semen quality. Medical students most often are used as donors. This treatment for infertility has met with some controversy of late. Because the child produced by AID is the genetic offspring only of the mother, the controversy surrounds the question of paternity. Who is the legal father? If the child is born deformed, can the spouses demand of the donor financial support? In cases of divorce, can the woman be accused of infidelity? Can husbands be expected to pay child support for children not of their own genetic material? Although these and other questions can be answered only in the courts, they, un-doubtedly, will be the center of debate for some time to come.

In Vitro Fertilization (IVF). In vitro fertilization has received a great deal of public attention in the last few years. Children conceived through this method have been called test-tube babies even though no test tube is involved in the procedure. In vitro fertilization has been used in cases in which women, either because of tubal blockage or scar-ring, cannot pass ova through the fallopian tubes for fertilization. This method involves surgically removing an egg from the ovary and placing it in a petri dish (a small shallow dish of thin glass) filled with a special medium.[47] Semen is then introduced into the solution and once fertiliza-tion has occurred, the embryo is implanted in the hormonally ready uterus of the mother. The woman may then carry the baby to term.

The first in vitro baby, Louise Brown, was born in July 1978. Since that time, several hundred IVF babies have been born to couples and thousands more await the procedure.[48] Perhaps because it has received so much attention, IVF is the most controversial treatment for infer-tility. Specialists involved in the procedure often are accused of playing God. The Roman Catholic Church opposes the treatment because it is often necessary for several eggs to be extracted and fertilized; the

46. *Ibid.,* p. 234.
47. Andrews, *op. cit.,* p. 90.
48. *Newsweek,* op. cit., p. 103.

Church sees the rejection of a fertilized egg from the woman's body as destruction of life. Many infertility specialists using IVF have resorted to removing only one ovum at a time to satisfy this criticism.

Artificial Embryonation (AE). In cases of artificial embryonation, a woman other than the wife donates an egg for fertilization.[49] The donor woman is artificially inseminated with the husband's sperm after being screened for genetic anomalies and venereal disease. Insemination is repeated for several days to ensure fertilization of the egg. Several days after fertilization occurs, the fertilized ovum is flushed from the donor woman's uterus and implanted in the uterus of the wife. In these cases, the offspring will have the genetic material of the husband but not the wife even though it is she who will carry the child to term. Artificial embryonation is a relatively recent procedure and the legal implications have yet to be tested in court.

Surrogate Mothers. Surrogate mothers contract with an infertile couple to carry a child to term.[50] In these cases, wives may have uterine problems or genetic diseases that preclude carrying a child. The surrogate mother is inseminated with the husband's sperm and carries the child for the duration of the gestation period. The parents pay all doctor and hospital bills for the pregnancy in addition to paying a typical fee of $10,000 to $15,000 to the surrogate mother. It is estimated that over 100 babies have been born using surrogates.[51] The use of surrogate mothers also has met with a great deal of controversy. Donor women have been accused of baby selling. Lawyers handling the arrangements between the donor mothers and the infertile couples have been accused of turning childbirth into big business and quick get rich schemes. The use of surrogate mothers surfaced only about three years ago, so it is still too early to know fully the legal implications of this practice. In some states, the couples must adopt the babies with no cash payment to the surrogate other than her doctor and hospital costs.[52] Other states do allow the payment of a fee to the surrogate. As it stands today, however, if the surrogate mother changes her mind and decides to keep the child, the couple has no legal recourse.

SUMMARY

Most couples move quickly into childbearing. After an upsurge in desired family size from 1940 to 1960, the long-term downward trend in

49. Andrews, *op. cit.*, p. 91.
50. *U.S. News & World Report*, June 6, 1983, p. 76.
51. *Ibid.*
52. Zimmerman, *op. cit.*, p. 237.

birthrates resumed. Most couples today plan small families. There is also a growing trend among young couples to delay parenthood to seek economic security and personal freedom. Voluntarily childless couples now compose about 1 to 2 percent of all married couples. Scholars predict the trend to remain childless will continue and grow.

Virtually all couples try family planning. Among U.S. women of childbearing age, surgical sterilization is the most popular method of controlling fertility. The pill is most often used by unmarried, single women and married women who plan to have children. The use of condoms and diaphragms has increased in recent years, probably as a result of complications from the pill and the IUD. Differences between Catholics and non-Catholics in contraception are declining and appear destined to disappear.

The impact of pregnancy and childbearing on the marital relationship has been studied. Most first pregnancies among married couples are desired or quickly accepted. Few differences exist in the adjustment to pregnancy between couples who had planned the pregnancy and those who had not. Variable effects of pregnancy on sexual adjustment are reported; slightly over half of all couples report no effect, whereas some report improvement and some report deterioration. There is a tendency for the frequency of sexual intercourse to decrease during the latter part of pregnancy and to remain lower after the birth of the child.

Subsequent pregnancies are less often welcomed, and the proportion of couples resorting to abortion increases with succeeding pregnancies. Abortion laws began to liberalize in the late 1960s; in 1973, the Supreme Court barred virtually any interference with abortion during the first trimester of pregnancy. The number of legal abortions has increased spectacularly, with depressed birthrates, falling mortality and morbidity rates, and diminished emotional consequences for women being results.

Studies show that the birth of the first child often produces a crisis in the home. The new arrival forces the restructuring of marital roles and some time often is required to do this. Most couples do achieve such readjustment with time.

About one out of every six couples is unable to have children due to infertility. There are many causes for infertility, and it is believed to be a growing problem in the United States. New techniques have been developed in the last few years that allow infertile couples to produce offspring. These techniques include artificial insemination, in vitro fertilization, artificial embryonation, and the use of surrogate mothers.

SUGGESTED READINGS

Fox, Greer Litton, *ed.*, *The Childbearing Decision: Fertility Attitudes and Behavior*, Beverly Hills, Calif.: Sage Publications, 1982. A collection of

11 theoretical and methodological articles that cover a myriad of fertility-related issues.

Kamerman, Sheila B., and Hayes, Cheryl D., *eds.*, *Families That Work: Children in a Changing World*, Washington, D.C.: National Academy Press, 1982. Examines the implications of family work on the educational, social, and behavioral development of children.

Lerner, Richard M., and Spanier, Graham B., *eds.*, *Child Influences on Marital and Family Interaction: A Life-Span Perspective*, New York: Academic Press, 1978. A collection of 12 articles, compiled from conference proceedings that focus on the reciprocal influences of the child and the family.

McKee, Lorna, and O'Brien, Margaret, *eds.*, *The Father Figure*, London: Tavistock Publications, 1982. A series of articles examining the role of the father in family life.

Snowden, R., Michell, G. D., and Snowden, E. M., *eds.*, *Artificial Reproduction: A Social Investigation*, Winchester, Mass.: Allen & Unwin, 1983. Examines the social implications of artificial insemination by donor. Based on interviews with almost 900 couples who underwent the procedure.

Veevers, Jean E., *Childless By Choice*, Scarborough, Ontario: Butterworth, 1980. An analysis of childless marriages, how they get that way, what they are like, and the problems they encounter.

FILMS

Adapting to Parenthood (Polymorph Films, 331 Newbury Street, Boston, Mass. 02115), 20 minutes, color. The stress that results from the birth of a first baby and the effect on a marriage.

Birth (Filmmakers Library, 290 West End Avenue, New York, N.Y. 10023), 40 minutes, black and white. A *cinéma vérité* study of a young expectant couple, their hopes and expectations, and the actual birth of the baby, in which the husband takes an active role.

Each Child Loved (Planned Parenthood-World Population, 267 West 25th Street, New York, N.Y. 10011), 37 minutes, color. Scenes in a licensed clinic give viewers a view emphasizing the safety and simplicity of abortion when an unwanted pregnancy is terminated early. Shows the vacuum aspiration method.

It Happens to Us (New Day Films, P.O. Box 315, Franklin Lakes, N.J. 07417), 30 minutes, color. Women of different ages, marital statuses, and races speak candidly of their abortion experiences. Explores the problem of illegal versus legal, medically safe abortions.

You Can't Mean "Not Ever" (Audio-Visual Library Service, University of Minnesota, 3300 University Avenue, SE, Minneapolis 55414), 26 minutes. Portrays three social situations in which a fictional child-free couple experience pressures to have children. Following this, they demonstrate their growing confidence in their chosen life style.

QUESTIONS AND PROJECTS

1. Discuss the changes in family size that have occurred since the 1940s. What predictions can you make about family size in the near future?
2. What is the relationship between childlessness and marital happiness? How do childless couples differ from couples with children?
3. How widespread is the use of contraception among American women? What is the relationship between contraceptive use and voluntary childlessness? What group of women are most likely to be using oral contraceptives?
4. What does research show about the adjustment of couples to the first pregnancy? How do statistics on abortion indicate a different pattern of reaction to subsequent pregnancies?
5. What evidence is there for assuming that the birth of the first child is likely to produce a crisis in the marital relationship? What time sequence appears to be involved? Are most crises successfully resolved?
6. What is the percentage of U.S. couples affected by infertility? Why is it believed that infertility is on the rise?
7. Define: *artificial embryonation, varicocele, endometriosis, in vitro fertilization.*
8. What is the relationship between environmental pollution and male infertility? Gonorrhea and female infertility? Contraceptives and infertility?
9. Debate the following questions: Should fertility specialists be allowed to "interfere" with nature? Are they just "playing God"?
10. Define: *oligospermic, AID, azoospermic, petri dish, surrogate mother.*

Copyright © Jean Shapiro

17
Marriage in the Middle Years

By the year 2000, there will be many more two-income households in the United States and a greater sharing of family responsibilities between men and women, according to a study that predicts changes in the personal and professional lives of many Americans.

. . . Many women who are permanently committed to the work force still do all the same chores in the home that they did when they were not working. As dual-career families increase, which the study says will happen, families will have to modify their attitudes. . . . More men will be doing more housework. . . . Men will be spending more time with kids. . . . While men will be relieved of the pressures of having to be the sole breadwinner, women will be relieved of having to be the sole homemaker.[1]

Couples average only two years together before their first child is born, a half-dozen years in childbearing, about 20 years in childrearing, and almost 20 years more before retirement. The middle years of marriage, as we use the phrase here, refers not so much to one specific part of that time period as to the whole series of changes that occur over the middle part of the family life cycle. These include changes in marital adjustment, in the distribution of power between husband and wife, and in roles. We shall continue to pay special attention to the changing roles of women and the rising popularity of dual-career families.

MARRIAGE AS A DEVELOPMENTAL PROCESS

One analyst conceives of mate selection in terms of matching husband and wife in phases of development rather than in terms of particular

1. *New York Times,* September 21, 1983.

traits brought by the partners to the marriage.[2] He assumes that the matching of personalities is a continual process and that personalities change throughout adult life. He questions whether it is possible to determine, at marriage, whether a given match will prove to be a good or bad one. Changes that occur in the partners during the marriage itself may be just as important.

Foote cites several kinds of evidence to support this view. Studies of the stresses faced by couples undergoing enforced separation are a case in point. The separation of couples by military service strains their relationship and requires complex readjustments on reunion.[3] Other kinds of separation such as those required by migration, employment, and confinement in institutions have similar effects. In less drastic circumstances, the involvement of husband and wife in different groups in the community may provide them with experiences that they cannot satisfactorily share with one another in the few evening hours they have together.

The implication that there are forces encouraging couples to grow apart finds support in popular interpretations of causes for divorce. One frequently hears it said that one of the spouses outgrew the other. Their occupations frequently force them into new experiences and into extensive contact with members of the opposite sex who, in time, may come to share more aspects of their daily lives than does the spouse. This is one of the major challenges facing people in contemporary marriages, and one of which they are becoming more aware.

Although we emphasize the fact that more separations occur during the first year of marriage than in any other year, other averages suggest that marriages deteriorate over time.[4] The median length of marriages ending in divorce is about 3 years, whereas the mean length may be as long as 6 years. Some divorces occur even after 20 to 30 years. Such figures indicate that simple mismatching does not account for all divorces. "A better hypothesis would be that those who were sufficiently matched to marry became sufficiently unmatched to unmarry."[5]

An analogy may also be made between marriage and friendship.

2. Nelson N. Foote, "Matching of Husband and Wife in Phases of Development," *Transactions of the Third World Congress of Sociology, International Sociological Association* 4 (1956), pp. 24–34.
3. Reuben Hill, *et al., Families Under Stress: Adjustment to the Crisis of War Separation and Reunion,* New York: Harper & Bros., 1949; and Hamilton I. McCubbin, Barbara D. Dahl, Gary R. Lester, Dorothy Benson, and Marilyn L. Robertson, "Coping Repertoires of Families Adapting to Prolonged War-Induced Separations," *Journal of Marriage and the Family* 38 (Aug. 1976), pp. 461–71.
4. Thomas P. Monahan, "Is Childlessness Related to Family Stability?" *American Sociological Review* 20 (Aug. 1955), pp. 446–56.
5. Foote, *op. cit.,* p. 17.

Friendship is one component in marriage and marriage may improve or worsen as friendship between the partners prospers or withers. Significantly, there are, for most people, few lifelong friendships outside of marriage. Instead, friendships develop, change, and decline. It is plausible that friendship both in and out of marriage depends on shared interests; because interests change, the continuance of friendships rest in part on the development of new common interests. The more marriage comes to center on companionship and friendship, the more crucial it becomes that spouses share new common interests. This probably is little related to conventional social homogamy, but it may be related instead to some sequence of developmental stages in the individual.

The notion of developmental stages in marriage has been conceptualized by Farber, who describes the family as a set of mutually contingent careers. That people pass through a progression of statuses in their occupations is well recognized. It is also recognized that changes in occupational careers impinge directly on people's relationships with the family. Farber extends the notion of career to all members of the family, and he sees careers as being not only occupational but also familial, recreational, and so on. Significant changes then in any aspect of any career of any family member impinge on the careers of other family members. In this sense, the family is not only a set of careers but a set of intercontingent careers.[6]

Marriage as mutually contingent careers does not require that husband and wife both pursue careers outside the home, nor does it assume any other kind of invariant relationship between them. It regards personal happiness as an unsatisfactory criterion of marital success both because it is unstable and because happiness is affected by too many variables apart from the marital relationship. It hypothesizes that the spouses' judgments of their marriages may depend as much on prospects for the future as on the present relationship. If there is a single variable that predicts the future of a marriage, Foote believes that it is communication—the degree to which husband and wife are truly able to communicate when they are together.

Foote acknowledges that his conception of modern marriage is a demanding one. It is not necessarily discouraging however. He points out that the segment of the population that makes the most stable marriages—the professional class—is also the one in which the concept of marriage as a set of mutually contingent careers emerges most clearly. He implies that the number and proportion of stable, rewarding marriages may increase as the professionalization of the society continues.

6. Bernard Farber, *Family: Organization and Interaction*, San Francisco: Chandler, 1964, pp. 334–35.

THE TREND OF MARITAL ADJUSTMENT

Research has begun to assess the changes in marital adjustment that occur after the early years of marriage. Studies have appeared, based on a variety of populations, that trace the trend in adjustment over 5, 10, and 20 or more years of marriage. Without exception, they show that the high levels of commitment characteristic of early marriage are not commonly maintained. The data indicate that marriage as a set of mutually contingent careers may be more of an ideal than an accomplished fact. However marital adjustment is conceived, the long-term trend is apparently downward.

Longitudinal Studies of Marital Adjustment

The first longitudinal study of marital adjustment was Burgess and Wallin's study of 1000 engaged couples whom they attempted to follow through early marital adjustment and into middle life. Only 666 of the original couples married and were available after 4 to 6 years of marriage. Further losses occurred up to the point when 400 couples were restudied after they had been married up to 20 years.[7]

The results of the comparison of 400 couples after about 5 years of marriage and again after nearly 20 years of marriage showed a large and pervasive drop in marital adjustment.

The greatest losses are in the category labeled *marital satisfaction*. Pineo, who did the analysis, believes that this is a phenomenon of such magnitude that the phrase *loss of satisfaction* "is insufficient to express the fact that this . . . appears to be generally an inescapable consequence of the passage of time in a marriage."[8] He conceptualizes decreasing marital satisfaction as being "disenchantment." This disenchantment appears inevitable and need not have its roots in idealization of the partner prior to marriage. That it is a general process rather than a series of independent changes is indicated by two things. First, there is an association between the losses experienced by husbands and those experienced by wives. Second, changes on one score are associated with changes on other scores.

Pineo theorizes that disenchantment sets in after the early years of marriage, stating explicitly that personality changes in the partner and changes in the context in which marriage will operate cannot be deter-

7. Ernest W. Burgess and Paul Wallin, *Engagement and Marriage*, Philadelphia: J. B. Lippincott, 1953.
8. Peter C. Pineo, "Disenchantment in the Later Years of Marriage," *Marriage and Family Living* 23 (Feb. 1961), p. 6. For a comprehensive final report on the results of the third wave of interviews, see Jan Dizard, *Social Change in the Family*, University of Chicago, Community and Family Study Center, 1968.

mined before the wedding. What happens is that people marry on the basis of a good fit between them at the time. When they are already well matched, the changes that inevitably occur after marriage are more likely to worsen that fit than to improve it. As Pineo puts it, "The deviant characteristics which provided the grounds upon which the marriage was contrasted begin to be lost, as later changes tend toward the population mean and the couples become more and more like ones who married at random rather than by choice."[9]

One possibility, of course, is that the drop in marital adjustment might be a function of a drop in personal adjustment over the same period—a function of aging. The data, however, contradict this hypothesis. Some changes in personal adjustment were detected, but personal adjustment was as likely to improve as to worsen and there was no association between a drop in personal adjustment and a drop in marital adjustment.[10]

It should be pointed out that the drop in general marital adjustment does not mean that *all* couples suffered a drop in adjustment. Some couples actually improved their adjustment, many appeared not to have changed significantly, and some, of course, declined. Unfortunately, the researchers do not give us detailed figures on this point. They do indicate that 75 percent of the husbands maintained their early levels of adjustment, with only 25 percent changing significantly. Among those who changed, two thirds changed from high to low adjustment.

In addition to the drop in marital satisfaction, some other conclusions may be drawn from the data. For one thing, the greatest drop outside that in general marital adjustment occurs in the sharing of interests and activities. Because these couples had already been married a few years at the time of measurement, this drop cannot be attributed to marriage alone. It seems to be associated with childrearing and the many duties that childrearing imposes on parents.

Two other items, "traditionalism" and "dominance," indicate paradoxical shifts. There is a general decrease in the traditionalism of husbands and wives over time. Yet husbands also tend to become more dominant and wives more submissive. Couples give lip service to the ideal of egalitarian relationships, but as they grow older, relationships between them actually become more authoritarian. Both Pineo and Goode have analyzed this situation in terms of the power that accrues to middle-class husbands as a function of high incomes and occupational prestige.[11] Irony exists in the fact that lower-class couples who are more likely to

9. Pineo, *op. cit.*, p. 7.
10. *Ibid.*, p. 8; and Robert A. Dentler and Peter Pineo, "Sexual Adjustment, Marital Adjustment and Personal Growth of Husbands: A Panel Analysis," *Marriage and Family Living* 22 (Feb. 1960), pp. 45–48.
11. Pineo, *op. cit.*, p. 8; and William J. Goode, *World Revolution and Family Patterns*, New York: The Free Press, 1963, pp. 20–22.

endorse verbal norms of dominance and submission are actually more egalitarian because of the relatively greater economic power of the wife, whereas egalitarian-oriented middle-class couples actually have relationships based more on dominance and submission.

Finally, there were differences in several areas between couples who experienced a drop in marital adjustment and those who did not. Those who had dropped in adjustment were more likely to regret their marriages and to state they would not marry the same person again. They were also more likely to report decreases in kissing and confiding and to indicate less reciprocity in settling disagreements. The couples who did not suffer disenchantment showed no drops in these areas. Of these, 99 percent would marry the same person again and also reported no decrease in kissing; 99 percent continued to confide in their spouses; and 96 percent settled disagreements by give and take.

The couples studied by Burgess and Wallin were married in the late 1930s and early 1940s, and it could be that the drop in adjustment was characteristic of that particular generation. Changes in circumstances might not produce the same pattern in succeeding generations. To check that possibility, let us examine another study—done on a much smaller scale—that was completed in 1965.

Luckey studied two groups of 40 married couples each who were classified as satisfactorily or unsatisfactorily married on the basis of marital-adjustment-scale scores.[12] The couples had been married for a mean average of 7.7 years, and 6 years later, they were studied again. Responses were received from 36 wives in the satisfied group, 34 wives in the unsatisfied group, and 31 husbands from each of the two groups.[13] Changes in adjustment between the 7th and 13th years of marriage were measured by changes in adjustment-scale scores. When the two groups were analyzed together, both husbands and wives made lower scores in 1963 than they did in 1957. Thus, the results are consistent with those of the earlier, larger study.

The findings are presented separately for the originally satisfied and originally unsatisfied groups. The scores of the satisfied couples were more likely to decline over the six-year period, whereas for the originally unsatisfied couples the reverse was true; the scores of poorly adjusted couples increased. There are at least two possible explanations. First, the satisfied couples, by virtue of higher aspiration levels for their marriages, may be less likely to discover that their experience lives up to expectations. Second, the scores of the satisfied group are so high in

12. Eleanore B. Luckey, "Perceptional Congruence of Self and Family Concepts as Related to Marital Interaction," *Sociometry* 24 (Sept. 1961), pp. 234–50.
13. Bethel L. Paris and Eleanore B. Luckey, "A Longitudinal Study in Marital Satisfaction," *Sociology and Social Research* 50 (Jan. 1966), pp. 212–23.

the first place that they have only one direction to go. By the same token, the low scores of the unsatisfied group may have to increase if divorce is to be avoided. This interpretation is strengthened by the fact that three of the original unsatisfied couples had divorced during the six-year period.

Other Comparative Studies of Marital Adjustment

Other studies that involved studying couples married different lengths of time—rather than following the same couples through time—have yielded data that inferentially support the longitudinal studies. These studies include data from lower-socioeconomic groups and middle-class couples.

A study of 731 city families and 178 farm families in the Detroit area provides a variety of relevant data. These data were derived from interviewing wives who ranged from 21 to more than 60 years of age and who had been married from less than 1 to more than 40 years. The samples were representative of the Detroit area and covered virtually the whole range of socioeconomic and occupational statuses.[14]

The authors describe time as a corrosive influence, wearing away the strength of marriages. Of women married for two years or less, 52 percent described themselves as being very satisfied with their marriages and none said that they were notably dissatisfied. Among those married 20 years or longer, however, only 6 percent remained fully satisfied and 21 percent were conspicuously dissatisfied. Much dissatisfaction, according to the authors, reflects decreases in the things that spouses do for, and with, each other. Many husbands and wives permit their marriages to go to seed. Middle-aged people find satisfaction in children, in jobs, in friends, and elsewhere, but they seldom find as much satisfaction in one another.

More wives chose doing things with their husbands as the most valuable aspect of marriage than chose love, understanding, standard of living, or the opportunity to have children. For women, companionship apparently is the most important thing in marriage. However, companionship, too, tends to decline at least through the middle years of marriage. The mean satisfaction scores of wives for companionship with their husbands declined steadily during the honeymoon, the preschool stage, the preadolescent stage, the period when they had adolescent children, and the period when there were adult but still unmarried children in the home. One possible reason for the decline in satisfaction with companionship is the fact that husbands and wives tend to disagree on

14. Robert O. Blood, Jr., and Donald M. Wolfe, *Husbands and Wives: The Dynamics of Married Living*, Glencoe, Ill.: The Free Press, 1960, pp. 5–7, 263–73.

what they consider to be the important aspects of marriage.[15] Couples may turn away from each other because of this lack of consensus.

That wives tend, with time, to turn away from their husbands is illustrated by their responses to questions concerning how they handle small emotional crises. Blood and Wolfe asked, "After you've had a bad day, what do you do to get it out of your system?" Most often the wives coped with their problems by sitting down and relaxing, going to bed early, reading, watching television, or going for a walk. Only 8 percent of the city wives and 3 percent of the farm wives mentioned their husbands in their response to this question. And of the 8 percent of city wives, almost half attacked their husbands rather than turned to them for comfort. Some consolation may be gained from the fact that the wives who took out their frustrations on someone were also more likely to choose persons other than the husband for that purpose. The picture is softened, too, by the fact that one fifth of the wives reported that they almost always tell their husbands their problems and an additional one fourth or more usually do so.

A study of 58 marriages in which the husbands followed blue-collar occupations, had gone only through high school, and were under 40 years of age bears out some of Blood and Wolfe's findings. Komarovsky found that about one third of the husbands and wives could hardly be called friends because they did not share hurts, worries, and dreams with one another. When the wives were asked, "What helps you when you feel bad, unhappy or worried about something, or generally low?" they mentioned a total of 278 different aids but mentioned the husband only 22 percent of the time. Indeed, 44 percent did not mention their mates at all. High school graduates were more likely to share feelings with their spouses than were those with less formal education, and communication between mates declined with number of years married.[16] Komarovsky also found that two thirds of the wives had at least one person other than the husband in whom they confided. In 35 percent of the cases, these other confidants, most often kinswomen, shared some aspect of the wives' lives more fully than did the husbands.

Another study secured questionnaires from two samples of 120 couples each. These couples were well educated and middle or upper class. Most were in their first marriages, and most of the wives were not working outside the home. The findings on the trend of marital adjustment were as follows. Marital discussions are most frequent early in marriage,

15. Kathryn D. Rettig and Margaret M. Bubolz, "Interpersonal Resource Exchange as Indicators of Quality of Marriage," *Journal of Marriage and the Family* 45 (Aug. 1983), pp. 497–509.
16. Mirra Komarovsky, *Blue-Collar Marriage*, New York: Random House, 1964, pp. 140–86.

but decline with time. Couples, as they move into the middle years, may not need to communicate verbally because they understand one another without the necessity for talk, or they may find each other less interesting, or they may simply have less to talk about.[17]

A final report of the trend of marital adjustment comes from a study of 80 couples who had been married from 2 to 21 years. It found that marital-adjustment scores were negatively correlated with the number of years married and that the longer couples were married the less favorable personality qualities each partner saw in his or her mate. As Luckey phrased it, "subjects in happy marriages tended to see their spouses less admirably, while those in unhappy marriages tended to see their spouses as being more undesirable" with the passage of time.[18]

All of this evidence is impressive. Studies have yielded a remarkably consistent pattern, showing a tendency for marital adjustment to decline steadily from almost the beginning of marriage to at least the point where children are grown and leave home.[19] The conclusion seems inescapable that romance is closely linked to novelty in most relationships. On the other hand, it should not be overlooked that in almost all of the studies a sizable proportion of marriages continued to be characterized by closeness, affection, and effective communication. Some marriages even improve in communication and empathy as the years go by. A major task for future research is to determine what factors account for the ability of some marriages to withstand the corrosive effects of time.

Marriage, of course, does not typically end with the middle years, and there are data available on the trend of adjustment during the post-parental years. These data on the latter stages of the family life cycle will be presented in a later chapter.

---

17. Harold Feldman, *Development of the Husband-Wife Relationship: A Research Report,* Cornell University, n.d., p. 119. Mimeo. See also Wesley R. Burr, "Satisfaction with Various Aspects of Marriage Over the Life Cycle: A Random Middle Class Sample," *Journal of Marriage and the Family* 32 (Feb. 1970), pp. 29–37. For somewhat contrary views, see Boyd C. Rollins and Kenneth L. Cannon, "Marital Satisfaction Over the Family Life Cycle: A Re-evaluation," *Journal of Marriage and the Family* 36 (May 1974), pp. 271–82; Boyd C. Rollins and Harold Feldman, "Marital Satisfaction Over the Family Life Cycle," *Journal of Marriage and the Family* 32 (Feb. 1970), pp. 20–28; and Lynn K. White, "Determinants of Spousal Interaction: Marital Structure or Marital Happiness," *Journal of Marriage and the Family* 45 (Aug. 1983), pp. 511–19.

18. Eleanore B. Luckey, "Number of Years Married as Related to Personality Perception and Marital Satisfaction," *Journal of Marriage and the Family* 28 (Feb. 1966), pp. 44–48. See also Richard J. Estes and Harold L. Wilensky, "Life Cycle Squeeze and the Morale Curve," *Social Problems* 25 (Feb. 1978), pp. 279–92.

19. Eugen Lupri and James Frideres, "The Quality of Marriage and the Passage of Time: Marital Satisfaction Over the Family Life Cycle," *Canadian Journal of Sociology* 6 (1981), pp. 283–305; and James M. Medling and Michael McCarry, "Marital Adjustment Over Segments of the Family Life Cycle: The Issue of Spouses' Value Similarity," *Journal of Marriage and the Family* 43 (Feb. 1981), pp. 195–203.

MARITAL POWER

For approximately two decades, researchers have sought to relate marital adjustment to the distribution of power between husband and wife and to trace changes in marital power over the family life cycle. The Blood and Wolfe study of Detroit-area families provided some of the earliest data. They reported that the power of the husband over the wife is greater among white-collar families than among blue-collar families and that the husband's power increases directly with his income.[20] They also found that the husband's power varies by stage of the family life cycle and by whether the couple has children.

Interestingly, childless wives had more power for at least the first 22 years of marriage than did those with children. This was hypothesized to be linked to the fact that childless wives are more likely to continue working and to have more economic resources than do women with children. Among couples with children, becoming a mother appeared to increase the wife's dependence on her husband. As the children grew older, her dependence on her husband lessened somewhat and the husband's power declined slightly. For reasons that are not wholly understood, the husband's power increased slightly again after the children were grown. Perhaps the prospect of the husband's demise before his wife led the wife to defer more to the husband. The husband's retirement and associated loss of income led to a decline in his power again in the final stage of life.

The Blood and Wolfe research led to the formulation of what has been called the resource theory of marital power. In brief, the theory holds that the more resources a spouse possesses, the greater his or her power over the other spouse. Because more husbands than wives work and because the husbands usually have more income, they commonly dominate their wives to some degree.[21] A number of recent studies have found wives' decision-making power increases as they move from the home into the labor market.[22]

---

20. Blood and Wolfe, *op. cit.*, p. 31.
21. Stephen J. Bahr, Charles E. Bowerman, and Viktor Gecas, "Adolescent Perceptions of Conjugal Power," *Social Forces* 52 (March 1974), pp. 356–67; Denise B. Kandel and Gerald S. Lesser, "Marital Decision-Making in American and Danish Urban Families: A Research Note," *Journal of Marriage and the Family* 34 (Feb. 1972), pp. 134–38; Gerald W. McDonald, "Parental Power and Adolescents' Parental Identification: A Reexamination," *Journal of Marriage and the Family* 42 (May 1980), pp. 289–96; Sharon Price-Bonham, "A Comparison of Weighted and Unweighted Decision-Making Scores," *Journal of Marriage and the Family* 38 (Nov. 1976), pp. 629–40; and Darwin L. Thomas, David D. Franks, and James M. Calonico, "Role-Taking and Power in Social Psychology," *American Sociological Review* 33 (Oct. 1972), pp. 605–14.
22. Dana V. Hiller and William W. Philliber, "The Derivation of Status Benefits from

This resource theory of marital power has been challenged as being an oversimplification. Heer, for example, pointed out that in addition to their usually having more resources, widespread social norms hold that husbands should have greater power than their wives.[23] The major challenge to the resource theory comes from the work of Rodman who compared the correlates of marital power in the United States, France, Greece, and Yugoslavia. In France and the United States, the husband's power increased with higher occupational, educational, and income statuses; in Greece and Yugoslavia, however, men of higher occupation, income, and education exercised less power over their wives. Rodman concluded that in such developing countries, higher-status men are more likely to have been exposed to developing cultural norms favoring equality for women. Thus, they grant their wives more authority in spite of a traditional patriarchal culture.

This led Rodman to formulate a theory of "resources in cultural context" to explain marital power. He postulated that the balance of marital power is determined by the interaction of the comparative resources of the husband and wife and by the cultural or subcultural expectations about the distribution of marital power.[24] Theorizing continues. The

---

Occupational Attainments of Working Wives," *Journal of Marriage and the Family* 40 (Feb. 1978), pp. 63–69; Marie W. Osmond, "Reciprocity: A Dynamic Model and a Method to Study Marital Power," *Journal of Marriage and the Family* 40 (Feb. 1978), pp. 49–61; Mark A. Rank, "Determinants of Conjugal Influence in Wives' Employment Decision Making," *Journal of Marriage and the Family* 44 (Aug. 1982), pp. 591–604; and John Scanzoni, "Contemporary Marriage Types," *Journal of Family Issues* 1 (March 1980), pp. 452–61.

23. David M. Heer, "Dominance and the Working Wife," in F. Ivan Nye and Lois W. Hoffman, eds., *The Employed Mother in America*, Chicago: Rand McNally, 1963, pp. 251–62. See also, Maximiliane E. Szinovacz, "Role Allocation, Family Structure and Female Employment," *Journal of Marriage and the Family* 39 (Nov. 1977), pp. 781–91.

24. Hyman Rodman, "Marital Power and the Theory of Resources in Cultural Context," *Journal of Comparative Family Studies* 3 (Spring 1972), pp. 50–69. See also Marilyn H. Buehler, Andrew J. Weigert, and Darwin L. Thomas, "Correlates of Conjugal Power: A Five Culture Analysis of Adolescent Perceptions," *Journal of Comparative Family Studies* 5 (Spring 1974), pp. 5–16; Wesley R. Burr, Louise Ahern, and Elmer W. Knowles, "An Empirical Test of Rodman's Theory of Resources in Cultural Context," *Journal of Marriage and the Family* 39 (Aug. 1977), pp. 505–14; Ronald E. Cromwell, Ramon Corrales, and Peter M. Torsiello, "Normative Patterns of Decision Making Power and Influence in Mexico and the United States: A Partial Test of Resource and Ideology Theory," *Journal of Comparative Family Studies* 4 (Autumn 1973), pp. 177–96; Ronald E. Cromwell and Stephen G. Wieting, "Multidimensionality of Conjugal Decision Making Indices: Comparative Analysis of Five Samples," *Journal of Comparative Family Studies* 6 (Autumn 1975), pp. 139–52; Joyce E. Elliott and William Moskoff, "Decision-Making Power in Romanian Families," *Journal of Comparative Family Studies* 14 (Spring 1983), pp. 39–50; Greer Litton Fox, "Another Look at the Comparative Resources Model: Assessing the Balance of Power in Turkish Marriages," *Journal of Marriage and the Family* 35 (Nov. 1973), pp. 718–30; and Marie La Liberte Richmond, "Beyond Resource Theory: Another Look at Factors Enabling Women to Affect Family Interaction," *Journal of Marriage and the Family* 38 (May 1976), pp. 257–66.

more the concept of marital power is analyzed and the more research is conducted on it, the more complex the matter becomes. In addition to resources and cultural norms, the perceptions of husbands and wives and the nature of their attempts to control the relationship need to be taken into account.[25]

Several early studies asked whether husbands or wives exercise more power in family decision making and generally showed the husbands to have more influence. Then, in 1971, a group of researchers studied a sample of 776 husbands and wives in California, classifying them into four types (see Table 17.1). The greatest number of marriages, according to both men and women are *autonomic*, ones in which the husbands and wives have equal but independent decision-making power. The second most common type was the *syncratic*, one in which decisions are made equally and jointly by the spouses. Approximately 10 percent of the marriages were reported to be husband dominant, only 4 percent were said to be wife dominant.

The study also classified the four tyes of marriages according to the

Table 17.1. The distribution of power in 776 marriages as reported by husbands and wives

Power type	Husbands' reports	Wives' reports
Autonomic	70%	67%
Syncratic	16	20
Husband dominant	10	9
Wife dominant	4	4
Totals	100	100

Source: Adapted from Richard Centers, Bertram H. Raven, and Aroldo Rodrigues, "Conjugal Power Structure: A Re-examination," *American Sociological Review* 36 (April 1971), p. 271.

25. See Janet Bokemeier and Pamela Monroe, "Continued Reliance on One Respondent in Family Decision-Making Studies: A Content Analysis," *Journal of Marriage and the Family* 45 (Aug. 1983), pp. 645–52; Merlin Brinkerhoff and Eugen Lupri, "Theoretical and Methodological Issues in the Use of Decision Making as an Indicator of Conjugal Power: Some Canadian Observations," *Canadian Journal of Sociology* 3 (1978), pp. 1–20; George H. Conklin, "Cultural Determinants of Power for Women Within the Family: A Neglected Area of Family Research," *Journal of Comparative Family Studies* 10 (Spring 1979), pp. 35–53; David H. Olson and Carolyn Rabunsky, "Validity of Four Measures of Family Power," *Journal of Marriage and the Family* 34 (May 1972), pp. 224–34; Boyd C. Rollins and Stephen J. Bahr, "A Theory of Power Relationships in Marriage," *Journal of Marriage and the Family* 38 (Nov. 1976), pp. 619–27; Constantina Safilios-Rothschild, "A Macro- and Micro-examination of Family Power and Love: An Exchange Model," *Journal of Marriage and the Family* 38 (May 1976), pp. 355–62; and James L. Turk and Norman W. Bell, "Measuring Power in Families," *Journal of Marriage and the Family* 34 (May 1972), pp. 215–22.

Table 17.2. Percentages of marriages rated as very satisfactory by conjugal-power type

Conjugal-power type	Percentage very satisfactory
Autonomic	79%
Husband dominant	73
Syncratic	70
Wife dominant	20

Source: Adapted from Richard Centers, Bertram H. Raven, and Aroldo Rodrigues, "Conjugal Power Structure: A Re-examination," *American Sociological Review* 36 (April 1971), p. 274.

percentage of respondents reporting them to be "very satisfactory." Those data appear in Table 17.2. The autonomic type provided the highest percentage of very satisfactory marriages, followed rather closely by the husband-dominant type, then by the syncratic type. The vast majority of all three of these types were described as very satisfactory. Of the 4 percent of the marriages that were classified as wife dominant, only one fifth were rated as very satisfactory.[26]

WORKING WIVES AND MOTHERS

The percentage of married women living with their husbands and working outside the home has been increasing irregularly for the last 30 years. In 1940, the percentage was only 15 percent. By the end of World War II, it was approximately 20 percent, by 1960, it had climbed to 31 percent. Since 1960 the percentage has fluctuated upward, reaching a high of 56 percent in 1982.

Wives' participation in the labor force varies with age, education, income, and the presence or absence of children.[27] A full 58 percent of the youngest wives, those under 25, work outside the home. From ages 25 through 34, the proportion drops slightly as some women devote themselves, full time to childrearing. After age 35, the proportion of wives in the labor force rises again.

Education has considerable effect on whether wives work or not,

26. See also Stephen J. Bahr and Boyd C. Rollins, "Crisis and Conjugal Power," *Journal of Marriage and the Family* 33 (May 1971), pp. 360–67; Lois Pratt, "Conjugal Organization and Health," *Journal of Marriage and the Family* 34 (Feb. 1972), pp. 85–95; and Trudy M. Kolb and Murray A. Straus, "Marital Power and Marital Happiness in Relation to Problem-Solving Ability," *Journal of Marriage and the Family* 36 (Nov. 1974), pp. 756–66.

27. U.S. Bureau of the Census, "Perspectives on American Husbands and Wives," *Current Population Reports*, Series P–23, No. 77 (December 1978), pp. 23–24.

with better educated wives more likely to seek employment.[28] Only one third of wives who are not high school graduates hold jobs, while 69 percent of those who have more than four years of college are in the labor force. Of those wives who have more than four years of college, are under 45, and have no children under 18, a whopping 90 percent are either employed or seeking employment.

Women work for the same reasons that men do.[29] For most, economic necessity is the most compelling reason. Few families today can survive on one paycheck. Also, the last few years have found more women than ever before enrolled in colleges and universities, a factor that enables them to pursue more lucrative and attractive positions. Many women find satisfaction and fulfillment in the expansion of their roles outside the family. The stigma once attached to the working wife and mother has been loosening its hold as more and more women enter the labor force. The labor market itself has been a factor in the growth of gainfully employed wives. Since World War II, service occupations and industries that traditionally employ large numbers of women have seen tremendous growth. Women are also entering nontraditional occupations at an unprecedented rate.

Effects of Wife's Employment on Marital Adjustment

Several studies have sought the effects of the wife's employment on marital adjustment. Blood, reanalyzing data from the Detroit study in 1965, concluded that employment of the wife decreases her housekeeping duties and increases the husband's sharing in those duties. In some families, this produces conflict over marital roles. Working wives from low-income families reported more marital satisfaction than did nonworking wives. Where the husband's income was $5000 or more, however, the reverse was true; working wives reported less marital satisfaction.[30] Blood was not able to study the husband's reaction to his wife's employment.

28. Ronald R. Rindfuss, Larry Bumpass, and Craig St. John, "Education and Fertility: Implications for the Roles Women Occupy," *American Sociological Review* 45 (June 1980), pp. 431–47.
29. Nancy S. Barrett, "Women in the Job Market: Unemployment and Work Schedules," in Ralph E. Smith, *ed.*, *The Subtle Revolution: Women At Work*, Washington, D.C.: Urban Institute, 1979; Marianne A. Ferber, "Labor Market Participation of Young Married Women: Causes and Effects," *Journal of Marriage and the Family* 44 (May 1982), pp. 457–68; Henry A. Gordon and Kenneth C. W. Kammeyer, "The Gainful Employment of Women with Small Children," *Journal of Marriage and the Family* 42 (May 1980), pp. 327–36; and Dana Hiller and William W. Philliber, "Necessity, Compatibility and Status Attainment as Factors in the Labor Force Participation of Married Women," *Journal of Marriage and the Family* 42 (May 1980), pp. 347–54.
30. Robert O. Blood, "The Husband Wife Relationship," in Nye and Hoffman, *eds.*, *op. cit.*, pp. 282–305. See also Robert N. Whitehurst and Edward Z. Dager, "The Lower-

Nye collected data from 1993 mothers and found more conflict in marriages where mothers were employed. Not only did mothers report more conflict with their husbands, but adolescent children verified their mother's reports. Whether the criterion of conflict was the frequency of quarreling, having separated one or more times, or having considered divorce, the working mothers showed up poorest in every case.

Nye's findings contradict Blood's concerning variations in marital adjustment by socioeconomic status. Nye found that any adverse effect of maternal employment on adjustment is less among higher economic groups than among lower economic groups. The difference almost disappeared among the higher income and educational groups. Nye also found that dissatisfaction with the wife's employment by either spouse was associated with poor adjustment. He cautions that a husband's dissatisfaction may be either a cause of poor adjustment or a result of the poorer marital adjustment produced by the wife's working.[31]

More recent studies provide contradictory evidence. Using data from three national surveys, Glenn and Weaver found no significant differences in marital happiness between working wives and homemakers.[32] Wright, also, could find no consistent differences between these two groups.[33] Burke and Weir, on the other hand, studying 189 couples, found that working wives are more satisfied and healthier than wives who do not work outside the home.[34] Kessler and MacRae found that employment outside the home has positive effects on the mental health of wives.[35]

Data concerning the effects of wives' employment on husbands' adjustment also are contradictory. Some studies find that although employment brings positive benefits to wives, it is stressful on the husbands of these women.[36] Waite attributes the husbands' difficulties in this area to the fact that they receive less attention and care from wives, must

Class Working Mother: Some Findings from a Small Sample Comparison Study." Paper presented at the meeting of the National Council on Family Relations, Toronto, October 1965.

31. F. Ivan Nye, "Marital Interaction," in Nye and Hoffman, eds., op. cit., pp. 263–81.

32. Norval Glenn and Charles N. Weaver, "A Multivariate, Multisurvey Study of Marital Happiness," *Journal of Marriage and the Family* 40 (May 1978), pp. 269–82.

33. James D. Wright, "Are Working Women Really More Satisfied? Evidence from Several National Surveys," *Journal of Marriage and the Family* 40 (May 1978), pp. 301–313.

34. Ronald J. Burke and Tamara Weir, "Relationship of Wives' Employment Status to Husband, Wife, and Pair Satisfaction and Performance," *Journal of Marriage and the Family* 38 (May 1976), pp. 279–87.

35. Ronald C. Kessler and James A. MacRae, Jr., "The Effect of Wives' Employment on the Mental Health of Married Men and Women," *American Sociological Review* 47 (April 1982), pp. 216–27.

36. Burke and Weir, op. cit.; Kessler and MacRae, op cit.

increase their participation in the home, and may feel that their central position in the home is threatened.[37] Booth, however, studying a probability sample of Toronto families, reported that the husbands of employed women evidenced no more signs of marital discord and stress than did the husbands of homemakers.[38]

Spitze and Waite found that husbands change their attitudes toward working wives during the early years of marriage to conform to their wives' attitudes and preferences for work.[39] Approval for their own wives working, however, is given only for their current employment situation, not necessarily for long-term labor-force participation. Changes in the home situation may affect husbands' attitudes. Although they give approval for their wives' current employment, they do not necessarily favor equality in other sex-role related areas.[40]

Alper and Morlock conducted a longitudinal study of 1456 households in which either the husband held a second job or in which the wife was a second earner.[41] They found that the probability of women entering paid employment is high if the number of children in the home is small and the wife's potential income is high. The attitudes of both husbands and wives toward working women are important. The authors predict that fewer husbands will moonlight to supplement their families' incomes and more women will enter the labor market as family size continues to decrease.

Effects of Working Mothers on Children

The connection between maternal employment and problems of adjustment has contributed to widespread suspicion of working mothers as a social problem. There is also a series of alleged connections between maternal employment and undesirable effects on the children. It has been claimed that children of working mothers are likely to become

37. Linda J. Waite, "U.S. Women at Work," *Population Bulletin* 36 (May 1981), p. 20.
38. Alan Booth, "Wife's Employment and Husband's Stress: A Replication and Refutation," *Journal of Marriage and the Family* 39 (Nov. 1977), pp. 645–50. See also Leland J. Axelson, "The Marital Adjustment and Marital Role Definitions of Husbands of Working and Nonworking Wives," *Marriage and Family Living* 25 (May 1963), pp. 189–95; David A. Gover, "Socio-Economic Differential in the Relationship Between Marital Adjustment and Wife's Employment Status," *Marriage and Family Living* 25 (Nov. 1963), pp. 452–58; and Glenn S. Sanders and Jerry Suls, "Social Comparison, Competition and Marriage," *Journal of Marriage and the Family* 44 (Aug. 1982), pp. 721–30.
39. Glenna D. Spitze and Linda J. Waite, "Wives' Employment: The Role of Husbands' Perceived Attitudes," *Journal of Marriage and the Family* 43 (Feb. 1981), pp. 117–24.
40. Joan Huber and Glenna D. Spitze, "Wives' Employment, Household Behaviors, and Sex-Role Attitudes," *Social Forces* 60 (Sept. 1981), pp. 150–69.
41. Neil O. Alper and Mark J. Morlock, "Moonlighting Husbands or Working Wives: An Economic Analysis," *Journal of Family Issues* 3 (June 1982), pp. 181–98.

delinquent and that they are more anxious, more antisocial, and more likely to make a poor adjustment in school, and so on. Fortunately, a growing body of research permits us to put such generalizations to empirical test.

The research on the effects of maternal employment on children has been summarized by Hoffman, who points out that research does not show meaningful differences between the children of working and nonworking mothers. Scattered research has reported differences, but these probably are due to chance because they are so few among the many tests made and because they have not been verified in repeat studies.[42] Hoffman cautions against interpreting this to mean that maternal employment has no effects at all however. She argues instead that only research that imposes careful controls will reveal what relationships actually exist. She summarizes studies that have imposed controls by social class, by full-time versus part-time employment, by age and sex of child, and by the mother's attitude toward her employment.

Three studies find a relationship between maternal employment and juvenile delinquency among middle-class youth, but not among lower-class youth. Nye found that children of working mothers were more likely to be delinquent than children of nonworking mothers. Nye's sample was mostly middle class however, and the findings were found to hold only for the middle-class respondents.[43] Glueck and Glueck, using contact with the police as the criterion of delinquency and studying lower-class youth, found no relationship between full-time employment of the mother and delinquency.[44] In a third study, Gold compared the children of blue-collar and white-collar families and found a relationship only within the white-collar group.[45]

These statistical correlations do not answer, of course, the question of why maternal employment may be related to delinquency in the middle class and not in the lower class. Perhaps the nature and conditions of maternal employment are different in the two classes. Perhaps the effects on family structure are different. It remains for future research to tell.

---

42. Lois W. Hoffman, "Effects on Children: Summary and Discussion," in Nye and Hoffman, eds., op. cit., pp. 190–212. See also Claire Etaugh, "Effects of Maternal Employment on Children: A Review of Recent Research," Merrill-Palmer Quarterly 20 (April 1974), pp. 71–98; Walter R. Gove and Robert D. Crutchfield, "The Family and Juvenile Delinquency," Sociological Quarterly 23 (Summer 1982), pp. 301–19; and Anne Locksley, "On the Effects of Wives' Employment on Marital Adjustment and Companionship," Journal of Marriage and the Family 42 (May 1980), pp. 337–46.
43. F. Ivan Nye, "The Adjustment of Adolescent Children," in Nye and Hoffman, eds., op. cit., pp. 133–41.
44. Sheldon Glueck and Eleanor Glueck, "Working Mothers and Delinquency," Mental Hygiene 41 (July 1957), pp. 327–52.
45. M. Gold, A Social-Psychology of Delinquent Boys, Ann Arbor, Mich.: Institute for Social Research, 1961.

Research supports the position that part-time employment has a favorable effect on adolescent children. Four separate studies have found such an association.[46] It appears likely that the factors leading mothers of adolescents into part-time employment are quite different from those leading mothers of younger children into full-time employment. Whereas the latter group are likely to be of lower economic status and under pressure to work to help support their families, the former are more likely to work by choice. Women who work by choice and who are not under financial pressure may be likely both to derive satisfaction from their work and to compensate for working by presenting a positive role model to their children. The part-time employment presents less of a threat to the husband than full-time employment would, yet the status of the wife is raised. Such women, because they have outside interests, may be more likely to grant adolescents the increasing freedom they need.

Long-established belief has it that it is especially detrimental for mothers to work while their children are young. There is also evidence that the lot of working mothers of young children is hard: they are under financial pressure and their children require a good deal of care and supervision. By and large, however, research has failed to support the idea of adverse effects of maternal employment on young children.[47] Few significant differences have been found. Maternal employment during the child's preschool years has no observable effects at later ages, and the mother's work history makes little difference; no effects have been found whether the mother works continuously or intermittently.

The effects of maternal employment might be different for boys than for girls, and evidence indicates that this is so. A series of studies has shown that girls' concepts of themselves and their concepts of female roles differ when their mothers work. The daughters of working mothers make fewer differentiations between household tasks deemed appropriate for men and women to perform, see women as less restricted to their homes, and are more favorable to the employment of women. Such girls are also more likely to wish to work themselves when they have

---

46. Elizabeth Douvan, "Employment and the Adolescent," in Nye and Hoffman, *eds.*, *op. cit.*, pp. 142–64; F. Ivan Nye, "Adolescent-Parent Adjustment: Age, Sex, Sibling Number, Broken Homes, and Employed Mothers as Variables," *Marriage and Family Living* 14 (Nov. 1952), pp. 327–32; and "The Adjustment of Adolescent Children," *op. cit.*; see also Alice M. Propper, "The Relationship of Maternal Employment to Adolescent Roles, Activities, and Parental Relationships," *Journal of Marriage and the Family* 34 (Aug. 1972), pp. 417–21.

47. Lee G. Burchinal, "Personality Characteristics of Children," in Nye and Hoffman, *eds.*, *op. cit.*, pp. 106–21; and from the same source: F. Ivan Nye, Joseph B. Perry, Jr., and Richard H. Ogles, "Anxiety and Anti-social Behavior in Preschool Children," pp. 82–94; Kathryn S. Powell, "Personalities of Children and Child-Rearing Attitudes of Mothers," pp. 125–32; and Alberta E. Siegel, Lois M. Stolz, Ethel A. Hitchcock, and Jean Adamson, "Dependence and Independence in Children," pp. 67–81.

children.[48] Hoffman concludes that working mothers provide role models that their daughters admire and emulate.

The effects of maternal employment on sons are less clear. Although there is some pattern in the findings, the results have not achieved statistical significance. For this reason, the following should be considered more as hypotheses than as definite findings. One study indicates that lower-class sons of working mothers are least likely to name their fathers as the persons they most admire.[49] Because lower-class men are least able to support their families without assistance, the sons' low estimates may stem from the perceived inadequacy of the fathers rather than from effects of the mothers' employment. Both the mothers' employment and the sons' negative evaluations of their fathers may reflect lower-class conditions of life.

A second study found that the young sons of working mothers were more dependent and obedient, less self-reliant, less sociable, and more likely to seek succor from adults.[50] Hoffman also found that the sons of working mothers are more dependent on teachers,[51] and data from a study by Rouman suggest that sons of working mothers are more likely to be sent for counseling for withdrawal problems than for any other kind of problem.[52] Until further research modifies it, a tenable hypothesis appears to be that maternal employment is associated with positive self-concepts and achievement orientation among girls but with dependency and low achievement among boys.

Finally, the mother's attitude toward her employment appears to be important. Two studies show that when the mother is satisfied with her employment, the relationship between her and her children is likely to be warm and satisfying. There is some suggestion that mothers in this category may overindulge their children because they feel a little guilty about working. Among mothers who are dissatisfied with their employ-

48. Elizabeth M. Almquist and Shirley S. Angrist, "Role Model Influences on College Women's Career Aspirations," *Merrill-Palmer Quarterly* 17 (July 1971), pp. 263–79; and Brian Powell and Lola Carr Steelman, "Testing an Untested Comparison: Maternal Effects on Sons' and Daughters' Attitudes Toward Women in the Labor Force," *Journal of Marriage and the Family* 44 (May 1982), pp. 349–66. For analysis of effects on mate selection and childbearing, see John A. Bruce, "The Role of Mothers in the Social Placement of Daughters: Marriage or Work?" *Journal of Marriage and the Family* 36 (Aug. 1974), pp. 492–97; and Victor J. Callan and Cynthia Gallois, "Perceptions About Having Children: Are Daughters Different from Their Mothers?" *Journal of Marriage and the Family* 45 (Aug. 1983), pp. 607–12.

49. Douvan, *op. cit.* See also Karl King, Jennie McIntyre, and Leland J. Axelson, "Adolescents' Views of Maternal Employment as a Threat to the Marital Relationship," *Journal of Marriage and the Family* 30 (Nov. 1968), pp. 633–37.

50. Siegel, Hitchcock, and Adamson, *op. cit.*

51. Lois W. Hoffman, "Mother's Enjoyment of Work and Effects on the Child," in F. Ivan Nye and Lois W. Hoffman, eds., *op. cit.*, pp. 95–105.

52. J. Rouman, "School Children's Problems as Related to Parental Factors," *Journal of Educational Research* 50 (Oct. 1956), pp. 105–12.

ment, relationships with their children are less rewarding and the children are more likely to be burdened with too many household tasks.[53] Shehan found recently that employed mothers, to ease their feelings of guilt, express normative ideologies that emphasize the importance of the quality of time spent with children and the beneficial effects of maternal absence from the home.[54] Nonemployed mothers, on the other hand, justify their role behavior by emphasizing beneficial results of the quantity of time spent with children and the harmful effects of maternal absence caused by employment.

In summary, research contradicts the idea of significant differences between the children of working and nonworking mothers. Maternal employment operates in interaction with too many other variables to be studied alone. Scattered research indicates that there may be some relationships with juvenile delinquency at middle-class levels, that part-time maternal employment has a favorable effect on adolescent children, and that the effects on younger children may vary by sex. Any general conclusion that maternal employment is undesirable appears unwarranted.

DUAL-CAREER FAMILIES

A phenomenon that has received growing attention over the past few years is that of the dual-career family. There is no one precise definition of the dual-career family, but it seems to be mostly an upper-middle-class pattern that, while the couple raises a family, the wife also pursues an occupation that requires higher education and that has considerable personal salience for her. Only small-scale studies of such families have been done to date, but careful studies have been completed both in England[55] and the United States.[56]

The studies agree that dual-career families are not the result of any

53. Elizabeth Douvan, *op. cit.* See also Doris K. Katelman and Larry D. Barnett, "Work Orientations of Urban, Middle-Class, Married Women," *Journal of Marriage and the Family* 30 (Feb. 1968), pp. 80–88; and Constantina Safilios-Rothschild, "The Influence of the Wife's Degree of Work Commitment Upon Some Aspects of Family Organization and Dynamics," *Journal of Marriage and the Family* 32 (Nov. 1970), pp. 681–91.

54. Constance L. Shehan, *Normative Beliefs and Work Orientations of Employed and Nonemployed Mothers of Preschool Children*, (Ph.D. dissertation): Pennsylvania State University, 1981. See also Constance L. Shehan, "Wives' Work and Psychological Well-Being: An Extension of Gove's Social Role Theory of Depression," *Sex Roles*, forthcoming.

55. Rhona Rapoport and Robert Rapoport, *Dual-Career Families*, Harmondsworth, Engl.: Penguin Books, 1971; and Rhona Rapoport and Robert N. Rapoport, *Dual-Career Families Reexamined: New Integrations of Work and Family*, London: Martin Robertson, 1976.

56. Lynda Lytle Holmstrom, *The Two-Career Family*, Cambridge, Mass.: Shenkman, 1972; and Jeff B. Bryson and Rebecca Bryson, eds., *Dual-Career Couples*, New York: Human Sciences Press, 1978.

one conscious decision for the wife to continue her career after marriage and childbearing. Instead most of the women even before marriage consider their work important and depreciate being "just a housewife." By the birth of their first child, the wife is so committed to her job that modification of family roles seems more plausible than giving up her work.

One study of 14 dual-career couples sought factors in the women's backgrounds that might have disposed them to this form of adjustment, with the following results. First, a high proportion were an only child, and the majority of the others were the oldest child in the family. Second, the mothers of these women often were employed while the girls were growing up, and many of the mothers, both employed and unemployed, were ambitious for their daughters. Third, tension in the home was common, centering, often, on the father. Miscellaneous other disturbing experiences during childhood also were reported.

Interestingly, no differences appeared between the backgrounds of the dual-career husbands and the husbands in traditional families. Some husbands acquiesced in their wives' desires, saying: "I knew what I was getting into." Or, more often, they were supportive, espousing principles of fair play or wanting their wives to be happy and fulfilled.[57]

Sometimes, the theme is muted; sometimes, it is clear. But most studies agree that dual-career families experience special strains, originating both outside and within the marriage. Outside pressures are felt primarily in two areas: first, husbands and wives are uncomfortable having to delegate much childrearing to sitters, day care centers, schools, and so on; second, the demands of work and family are so great that social activities must be limited. The limitation of friendship circles does not appear to be particularly upsetting because the couple seek friends who also face severe time limitations. But relationships with the parental families are more troubling. Parents both resent the fact that their children's families do not have time for them and sometimes criticize the wives for apparent neglect of home and children.

Strains internal to the family are primarily of three sorts. First, there are problems of work overload for both husband and wife. Even with the husband sharing housework and child care, the demands of two careers, meal preparation, cleaning, caring for and enjoying children, and so on, leave most spouses without the time and energy to perform all

57. A. C. Bebbington, "The Function of Stress in the Establishment of the Dual-Career Family," *Journal of Marriage and the Family* 35 (Aug. 1973), pp. 532–33. See also Ronald J. Burke and Tamara Weir, "Some Personality Differences Between Members of One-Career and Two Career Families," *Journal of Marriage and the Family* 38 (Aug. 1976), pp. 453–59; and Dana V. Hiller and William W. Philliber, "Predicting Marital and Career Success Among Dual-Career Workers," *Journal of Marriage and the Family* 44 (Feb. 1982), pp. 53–62.

of their duties and responsibilities.[58] Second, some persons experience confusion in relation to traditional definitions of masculine and feminine spheres. In extreme instances, this may lead to psychological or physical problems. Finally, there are problems of role cycling associated with transition points in both career and family. The demands of the husband's career and the wife's career may conflict so that, for example, one must forego a sought-after promotion or transfer because of the potential interference with the other's career.[59] Childbearing, too, is often delayed or timed not to coincide with transitions in either partner's career. This may lead to having fewer children than the couple would like or having none at all.

We should not assume, however, that stress is higher in dual-career families than in traditional families or at least it is not clear that *these* families could solve their problems by the wife giving up her career. Dual-career wives receive as much satisfaction and fulfillment from their work as their husbands do. The dual-career couples studied do not appear to have unstable marriages or even to be less less happy than other couples. Perhaps the partners are unusually tolerant of stress or perhaps they have simply accepted the strains of dual-career living in order to escape, for them, the even greater strains of traditional living.

SUMMARY

This chapter focuses on changes in marital adjustment as couples move through the childrearing years, and beyond. Marital adjustment is seen as a process rather than a state, and the events of 5, 10, and 20 years after the marriage ceremony change it significantly. It is useful to conceptualize marriage as a set of mutually contingent careers in which couples may grow closer together or move farther apart.

Both longitudinal and cross-sectional studies of marital adjustment

---

58. Available evidence indicates that husbands of working wives contribute rather little time to housekeeping and childrearing duties and that they assist their wives no more than the husbands of nonworking wives. See Sharon Y. Nickols and Edward J. Metzen, "Impact of Wife's Employment upon Husband's Housework," *Journal of Family Issues* 3 (June 1982), pp. 199–216; Joseph H. Pleck, "The Work Family Role System," *Social Problems* 24 (April 1977), pp. 417–27; Ida Simpson and Paula England, "Conjugal Work Roles and Marital Solidarity," *Journal of Family Issues* 2 (June 1981), pp. 180–204; and Maximiliane Szinovacz, "Role Allocation, Family Structure and Female Employment," *Journal of Marriage and the Family* 39 (Nov. 1977), 781–91. This situation may be beginning to change. See Joseph H. Pleck, "Men's Family Work: Three Perspectives and Some New Data," *Family Coordinator* 28 (Oct. 1979), pp. 481–88.

59. See R. Paul Duncan and Carolyn Cummings Perrucci, "Dual Occupation Families and Migration," *American Sociological Review* 41 (April 1976), pp. 252–61; and Benson Rosen, Thomas H. Jerdee, and Thomas L. Prestwich, "Dual-Career Marital Adjustment: Potential Effects of Discriminatory Managerial Attitudes," *Journal of Marriage and the Family* 37 (Aug. 1975), pp. 565–72.

show a tendency for couples to grow farther apart with time. There is a gradual drop in marital-adjustment scores, in marital satisfaction, in the frequency of sexual intercourse, and in the adequacy of marital communication. Nor are these changes simply a function of aging, for there is no comparable drop in personal adjustment scores. What happens may be conceptualized as a process of disenchantment in which the "goodness of fit" that prevailed between the couple at marriage gradually diminishes. Not all marriages suffer this fate however. A smaller percentage of marriages appears to improve in communication and empathy as time goes by.

Early studies showed most marriages to be somewhat male dominated, with the husband's power being greater at higher-status levels. Husbands had more power in families with children, particularly during the childbearing years. The husband's power fell off in retirement and old age.

One theory holds that the power of husbands and wives reflects the relative resources they bring to the marriage. Another theory holds that resources can only be evaluated in a particular cultural context: that norms concerning the distribution of power influence the way in which resources are used.

Recent studies show most marriages to have a fairly equal distribution of power, with some couples emphasizing autonomous decision making and others emphasizing joint decision making. Surprisingly, husband-dominated marriages have about as many high-happiness ratings as do egalitarian ones. Wife-dominated marriages have a much smaller percentage of very satisfactory relationships. Marriages in which one partner dominates the other are few in number however.

The proportion of wives who work outside the home has been increasing irregularly over the past 30 years. The percentage of working wives drops off somewhat during the early childbearing years and then reaches a high point when wives are between 35 and 65 years of age. Research shows that the gainful employment of wives is associated with a slight increase in the sharing of household tasks and some conflict over marital roles.

Contrary to widespread belief, there appear to be few, if any, gross relationships between maternal employment and the adjustment of children. Carefully controlled studies have suggested a relationship between maternal employment and juvenile delinquency among middle-class children, but not among lower-class children. There is some evidence, also, that part-time maternal employment is positively correlated with the adjustment of adolescent children. Maternal employment appears to influence the self-concepts of both sons and daughters but in different ways. The daughters of working mothers appear likely to develop positive self-concepts, to make minimal distinctions between the household tasks deemed appropriate for men and women, and to anticipate employment themselves when they are older. The evidence concerning sons is less convincing but suggests that sons of working mothers have less admiration for their fathers, are more obedient, and less independent and self-reliant. An important variable is the mother's attitude toward her employment. When she is satisfied, the relationship between her and her children is likely to be warm and rewarding. When she is dissatisfied, the relationship with her children suffers.

Dual-career families, in which both partners pursue careers, appear to involve special strains, but no more than the couples can handle. Parents acknowledge some regret over having to delegate so much of the child-rearing function, and parental families resent not seeing more of their children and grandchildren. There also are problems of work overload, role confusion, and role cycling.

SUGGESTED READINGS

Aldous, Joan, ed., *Two Paychecks: Life in Dual-Earner Families*, Beverly Hills, Calif.: Sage Publications, 1982. Explores such topics as the effects of two careers on preschool children, role flexibility, economic and demographic characteristics, conflicts, and concessions.

Beer, William R., *Househusbands: Men and Housework in American Families*, New York: J. F. Bergin/Praeger, 1983. A study of 56 husbands who equally share the duties of running their homes with their wives.

Lopata, Helena Znaniecki, *Occupation: Housewife*, New York: Oxford University Press, 1971. A monograph reporting the findings of a series of studies of women in and around Chicago, and the ways in which they cope with the role of housewife.

Nye, F. Ivan, et al., *Role Structure and Analysis of the Family*, Beverly Hills, Calif.: Sage Publications, 1976. A report of research that interprets data systematically in the context of various aspects of marital and parental roles.

Rapoport, Rhona, and Rapoport, Robert N., eds., *Working Couples*, New York: Harper & Row, 1978. An exploration of the solutions that couples are finding to the problems of dual-breadwinner families.

Rubin, Lillian B., *Women of a Certain Age: The Midlife Search for Self*, New York: Harper & Row, 1979. A well-written and provocative analysis of the challenges facing middle-aged women in our society.

FILMS

A Family Affair (International Film Bureau, 332 S. Michigan Ave., Chicago, Ill. 01274), 30 minutes. The story of a middle-aged couple whose relationships are strained to the breaking point. Shows how the breaking up of a marriage can be averted with the help of a marriage counselor.

Careers and Babies (Polymorph Films, 331 Newbury Street, Boston, Mass. 02115), 20 minutes. Examines the different decisions that four women have made concerning careers and motherhood.

New Relations: A Film About Fathers and Sons (Plainsong Productions, 47 Halifax Street, Jamaica Plain, Mass. 02130), 34 minutes. As his son's first birthday approaches, a father reflects on his relationship with his child, his wife, and his own father.

The Weekend (Associated Films, 866 Third Avenue, New York, N.Y. 10022), 15 minutes. Confined to a hotel room by a rainstorm, a middle-aged couple decide to make a close, if painful, examination of their lives together.

QUESTIONS AND PROJECTS

1. What is meant by the phrase *marriage as a developmental process?* What are the implications for mate selection? How may marriage be conceived of as a set of mutually contingent careers?

2. What does research show about marital adjustment through the middle years? How does disenchantment describe what happens to most marriages? Do all couples decline in adjustment?

3. How does the power of husbands vary with socioeconomic status and with parental status? How does it vary over the life cycle?

4. How common, relatively, are autonomous, syncratic, wife-dominant, and husband-dominant decision-making patterns? What are the relationships between them and marital satisfaction?

5. What proportion of wives work outside the home? How does this vary with the ages of the women?

6. What are the reasons why wives work outside the home? Do you think the number will increase or decrease in the future?

7. What appear to be the major effects on marital adjustment of the wife's working outside the home? What inferences, if any, can be made about cause and effect?

8. What does research show about the effects of maternal employment on the adjustment of children? Are all of the effects of maternal employment known?

9. What are dual-career families? How do they differ from other families in which the wives work?

10. What special kinds of internal and external problems are experienced by dual-career families? Would these people have fewer problems in traditional families?

Irene Bayer, Monkmeyer

18
Divorce

A new method of dealing with troubled marriages—the do-it-yourself divorce—goes into effect this month in California. The plan may soon spread
to other states. The law goes far beyond the "no fault" divorce proceedings
that first appeared in California in 1970 and now have been adopted in 47
states.

"This could be called the 'no-lawyers, no-courts, no legal-hassles divorce,'"
says Georgia Franklin of the Women Lawyers' Association of Los Angeles.
"It makes divorce as simple as getting a marriage license."

Under the law, childless couples with limited property who have been
married less than two years can get a divorce by mail. Using this system
enables such couples to avoid all court appearances and lawyers' services.
Couples pay a fee of less than $50 to the state and take responsibility for
dividing any jointly owned property. The divorce is granted automatically
in six months—by mail.[1]

Children, always the primary victims of divorce, have a new problem to
worry about: even after custody is settled they are apt to be kidnapped by
the parent who loses out. Though statistics are unavailable, an estimated
25,000 to 100,000 youngsters are whisked away from home by a parent each
year. Since mothers routinely get custody in most states, the abductor is
usually the father, acting partly out of revenge, partly out of fear that the
child will be turned against him. . . .

Typically, the kidnapping is an angry, impulsive act: a parent decides on
the spot not to give the child back after a regular visit, usually after news of
a change in the ex-spouse's life, such as remarriage or plans to move out of
town. The child is almost always between the ages of three and twelve; children under three are too difficult for a working parent to care for alone, and
a teen-ager can always phone home or hop a bus and leave.[2]

1. *U.S. News & World Report*, Jan. 8, 1979, p. 8.
2. *Time*, July 14, 1980, p. 41.

These excerpts reflect two different aspects of the current divorce situation in the United States. The first is the continuing effort to simplify divorce procedures and to reduce the trauma for those caught up in it. The second is the particularly bitter struggle between divorced parents who are desperate to preserve their relationships with their children.

Virtually everyone has read that the United States has the highest divorce rate in the world. In that bald form the statement is false, but that doesn't stop it from being repeated and reprinted. Perhaps this is because the statement is often intended to convey a feeling rather than to communicate a fact. The feeling is that divorce rates in the United States are so high as to threaten the existence of the family.

INTERCULTURAL PERSPECTIVE ON DIVORCE

When people evaluate American divorce rates, they usually compare them with the rates of other large nations. It should not be forgotten, however, that most of the world's societies are small, preliterate ones and that they have something to teach us, too, about the range of family practices that is consistent with the overall stability of the system.

As with other family practices, useful data on divorce in preliterate societies have been assembled by Murdock. He points out that all societies have provisions for ending marriages and that divorce rates in about 60 percent of all preliterate societies are higher than those in the contemporary United States.[3]

Nor is there any particular relationship between divorce rates and other symptoms of social disorganization. High divorce rates can be, and are, associated with stable family systems where there are clear norms specifying what happens to husband, wife, and children after the divorce. It is generally provided that the husband and wife should be reabsorbed by their respective kin groups. The children continue to live with their lineage and do not suffer unduly from the separation of their parents.

Statements that the United States has the world's highest divorce rate generally have, as their referent, other large nations. Even within that context, however, the statement has not always been true. Some Moslem countries, for example, that still permit men to take up to four wives and to divorce any of them simply by saying three times, "I divorce thee," have had extremely high divorce rates. In 1900, the divorce rate in Algeria (the only Moslem country for which reliable data were avail-

3. George P. Murdock, "Family Stability in Non-European Cultures," *Annals of the American Academy of Political and Social Science* 272 (Nov. 1950), p. 197.

able then) was roughly four times as high as that in the United States. Algeria's rate has fallen since then, but a recent unofficial report indicates that, in 1970, Egypt had twice as many divorces (700,000) as marriages (325,000).[4] Premodern Japan also had high divorce rates associated with its patriarchal, patrilineal, extended family system. As in traditional China, divorce indicated that the young bride did not please her in-laws. As Japan urbanized, the divorce rate fell, a pattern opposite to what occurred in the United States.

In summary, divorce rates vary drastically from one society to another; in the same society, they may also vary drastically over time. There is no necessary relationship between divorce rates and either family or societal stability; high divorce rates may reflect family breakdown, or they may reflect societally prescribed ways of eliminating disruptive influences.[5] In world perspective, the United States falls in the large group of societies having relatively high divorce rates. Striking increases in U.S. divorce rates have accompanied urbanization, industrialization, and the shift to a conjugal family system.

THE DIVORCE RATE IN THE UNITED STATES

The Historical Trend

Statistics on the frequency of divorce in the United States became available only about a century ago. These statistics, a few of which are presented in Table 18.1, show an inexorable rise both in the number and rate of divorces. In 1860, there were fewer than 8000 divorces in all of the United States. By 1900 there were 55,000; in 1982, there were over 1 million divorces.

Part of the increase in the number of divorces, of course, is to be accounted for simply by the growth of the population. It would be quite possible, in a growing nation, for the number of divorces to climb without there being any increase in the probability that any given marriage would end in divorce. The right-hand column of Table 18.1, however, shows that the number of divorces per 1000 population in the United States also has been climbing. In 1940, there were only 2.0 divorces per 1000 population. By 1979, the rate was 5.3. In 1982, the number of divorces declined for the first time since 1962. Whether or not the decline will continue remains to be seen.

---

4. Reuters dispatch, Sept. 22, 1973.
5. William Moskoff, "Divorce in the USSR," *Journal of Marriage and the Family* 45 (May 1983), pp. 419–26.

Table 18.1. U.S. divorce and annulment rates, 1920–1982

Year	Number of divorces	Divorce and annulment rate per 1000 population
1920	171,000	1.6
1930	196,000	1.6
1940	264,000	2.0
1946	610,000	4.3
1950	385,000	2.5
1960	393,000	2.2
1970	715,000	3.5
1979	1,170,000	5.3
1982	1,180,000	5.1

Source: Historical Statistics of the United States, Colonial Times to 1957, Series B–29, p. 22; U.S. Bureau of the Census, Statistical Abstract of the United States: 1972, Washington, D.C., p. 63; National Center for Health Statistics, Monthly Vital Statistics Report, March 14, 1980, p. 2; and National Center for Health Statistics, Monthly Vital Statistics Report, October 5, 1983, p. 9.

The Influence of War and the Economy

Although the long-term trend in the divorce rate has been upward, the increases have not been uniform. The years 1930 and 1933 had lower rates than prevailed during the 1920s, and the years of 1945 and 1946 had higher divorce rates than either before, or for nearly 30 years after that time. These fluctuations suggest the influences of wars and recessions that more complete statistics would show in detail.

Wars tend to be followed by sharp increases in divorce rates and then by a return to the level of the prewar trend. As early as the Civil War this was evident. There were 7380 U.S. divorces in 1860. In 1862, the number was down to 6230. In 1865, the number was 10,090 and the peak of 11,530 divorces was reached in 1866. The number of divorces then dropped off and did not reach the 1866 level again until 1871.

A similar pattern followed World War I. From 116,254 divorces in 1918, the number jumped to 141,527 in 1919 and to 171,000 in 1920. The number in 1921 was back down to 56,580 and dropped further in 1922. World War I also demonstrated that this is not strictly an American phenomenon. England, France, and Germany all had relatively greater increases in 1919 and 1920 than the United States. All three countries also experienced decreases in divorces during the early 1920s.

World War II saw fluctuations in the number of U.S. divorces, but gradually increasing numbers until 1946, when a total of 610,000 divorces was recorded. The divorce rate in 1946 was 4.3 per 1000 population. By 1950, the divorce rate dropped back almost to immediate pre-

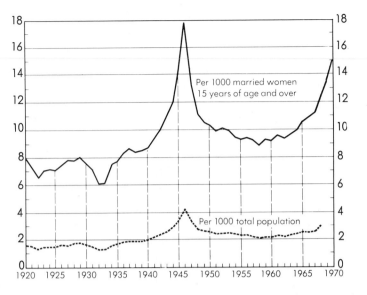

Figure 18.1. The influences of the Great Depression and World War II on U.S. divorce rates

World War II levels, where it hovered until 1963. Since 1963, it has been on the rise again.

Explanations for these relationships between war and divorce rates are not difficult to find. A major factor is the large number of marriages contracted after short acquaintance. Such marriages probably would produce many divorces even without the effects of war. The war itself, however, separates many couples for long periods. In some instances, couples, who formerly were close, simply grow apart. In other cases, wartime separation merely establishes separate existences for couples whose marriages had been held together only by inertia. In addition, many lonely spouses are thrown together with persons of the opposite sex under conditions that encourage involvement. Relatively few of these persons institute divorce actions while the war is in progress, but many do so when the war is ended and readjustment must be achieved. Finally, the strains of postwar reunion themselves often are great. Some formerly stable marriages break under this additional strain.[6]

In addition to war, economic depressions also have marked effects on divorce rates. The relative influences of a major depression and a major war shown in Figure 18.1, which covers the Great Depression of the 1930s and World War II. The Depression lowered divorce rates markedly, although not so much as World War II inflated them. Before the

6. Reuben Hill, *Families Under Stress*, New York: Harper & Bro., 1949.

stock market crash in 1929, there were 201,468 divorces, or 7.9 divorces per 1000 marriages. At the depth of the depression in 1933, there were 40,000 fewer divorces and the divorce rate had dropped to 6.1. From 1933 until the start of World War II, again both the number of divorces and the divorce rate climbed steadily.[7]

Explanations for the effect of depressions on divorce rates are, again, not hard to find. Securing a divorce is often costly and many people cannot afford it during a depression. Beyond that, divorce requires establishment of separate households, division of property, and establishment of specific terms for the support of children. These requirements tax most people's financial resources even during prosperity and often become prohibitive in bad times. Great financial hardship may draw together some couples who might otherwise become alienated; if it does, apparently the effect is short lived. For although divorce rates drop during the depression itself, they rise rapidly as the depression ends.

Present Status and Future Prospects

Popular concern with divorce rates often manifests itself in estimates of the probability that any given marriage will end in divorce. Just as the rate of divorce has been increasing, so have estimates of the probability of divorce for individual couples. In 1940, before World War II, there was 1 divorce for each 6 marriages contracted. There was 1 divorce for every 3.8 marriages in 1946, and by 1970 there was 1 divorce for every 3 marriages. Demographers estimate that about 40 percent of all first marriages occurring today will ultimately end in divorce.[8]

We have already seen that the long-term trend in American divorce rates is upward; although predictions are hazardous, the prospect is that the upward trend will continue for some time. The number of divorces will continue to climb if only because the population is growing. In all probability the divorce rate will rise also.

THE DISTRIBUTION OF DIVORCE

The probability of divorce is not spread evenly throughout the population. The significance of this difference will be pursued in the next

7. Paul H. Jacobson, *American Marriage and Divorce,* New York: Rinehart, 1959, pp. 89–91.
8. *New York Times Magazine,* Aug. 10, 1975, p. 13. See also J. Lynn England and Phillip R. Kunz, "The Application of Age-Specific Rates to Divorce," *Journal of Marriage and the Family* 37 (Feb. 1975), pp. 40–46; Paul C. Glick and Arthur J. Norton, "Marrying, Divorcing, and Living Together in the U.S. Today," *Population Bulletin* 32 (Dec. 1977); and Jay D. Teachman, "Methodological Issues in the Analysis of Family Formation and Dissolution," *Journal of Marriage and the Family* 44 (Nov. 1982), pp. 1037–53.

chapter on remarriages. Here, we shall analyze the influences of region, race, economic status, length of time married, and parental status on divorce rates.

Variations by Rural-Urban Status and by Region

In the decennial census, information is secured on the current marital status of persons enumerated. These data show that divorced persons are overrepresented in urban and underrepresented in rural areas. In part, these data reflect a higher probability of divorce under conditions of urban living; the lesser likelihood of divorce under rural, particularly farm, conditions has been pointed out earlier. In part also, however, these statistics reflect a tendency for rural persons to migrate to urban areas before, during, or after a divorce. There is little place for divorced persons, particularly women, in a farm economy, whereas life in cities caters more to married and unmarried persons alike.

Divorce rates also vary by region, increasing from east to west. The divorce rate is lowest in the northeast, followed by the north central region, then by the south and, finally, by the west. Several factors help to account for these regional variations, but a full explanation does not exist. One factor, undoubtedly, is a difference in attitudes and values; something of a frontier tradition that includes rootlessness lingers on in the west. The age distribution of the population varies, with more younger divorce-prone persons being found in the west. Finally, the ethnic and religious composition of the population has something to do with it; Roman Catholics particularly are overrepresented in northern and eastern sections of the country.[9]

Fenelon offers another explanation of these variations. He suggests that divorce rates are a function of the social costs involved. States having a large number of migrants in their populations may be characterized by a lower degree of social integration and there may be fewer effective sanctions against divorce. Analysis of state and regional variations in divorce rates supports his hypothesis.[10]

9. See Paul C. Glick, "Marriage Instability: Variations by Size of Place and Religion," *Milbank Memorial Fund Quarterly* 41 (Jan. 1963), pp. 43–55; and Kenneth L. Cannon and Ruby Gingles, "Social Factors Related to Divorce Rates for Urban Counties in Nebraska," *Rural Sociology* 21 (March 1956), pp. 34–40. See also Norval D. Glenn and Beth Ann Shelton, "Pre-adult Background Variables and Divorce: A Note of Caution About Overreliance on Explained Variance," *Journal of Marriage and the Family* 45 (May 1983), pp. 405–10; Tomoko Makabe, "Provincial Variation in Divorce Rates: A Canadian Case," *Journal of Marriage and the Family* 42 (Feb. 1980), pp. 171–76; and Kenneth P. Wilkinson, Reynolds R. Reynolds, Jr., James G. Thompson, and Lawrence M. Ostresh, "Divorce and Net Migration into the Old West," *Journal of Marriage and the Family* 45 (May 1983), pp. 437–45.
10. Bill Fenelon, "State Variations in United States Divorce Rates," *Journal of Marriage and the Family* 33 (May 1971), pp. 321–27. See also Henry Pang and Sue M. Hanson,

Variations by Race

Strange as it may seem, data on divorce rates by race are woefully inadequate. The decennial censuses report only the number of persons who are divorced or separated at the time of enumeration. Not only are these figures subject to error, but they do not include persons who divorced and got remarried. Nevertheless, the figures show higher percentages of divorced black males and black females than white females and white males.

Some comprehensive data come from the June 1975 marital history survey conducted by the Bureau of the Census, which reported that the incidence of divorce is uniformly higher for blacks than for whites. Of persons 35 to 44 years of age, 25 percent of the black men and women had been divorced. Only 19 percent of white men and 21 percent of white women had been divorced.[11] More recent data found that blacks had 220 divorced persons for every 1000 married persons living with their spouses in 1982 compared with 107 per 1000 for whites.[12]

Data from the Divorce Registration Area (DRA) are improving but still are woefully inadequate. The DRA is made up of 28 states in which local courts forward data on all divorces to their state health departments, which in turn send systematic samples of these records to the National Center for Health Statistics. Unfortunately for our purposes, many of these records omit information pertaining to race. Very fragmentary data for the period from 1939 through 1950 suggest that divorce rates may have been higher among whites than among blacks until 1942; then the relationship appears to have been reversed and black divorce rates came to average 20 percent higher than those of whites.

Why these relationships should have changed over time requires explanation, and a plausible explanation is available. It appears likely that black divorce rates recently have come to reflect more accurately than they did before the actual rate of marital disruption. The factors described in Chapter 9 that encouraged the use of desertion among blacks as a solution to family problems probably held down the divorce rate.

There is evidence, too, that black divorce rates are more sensitive to

"Highest Divorce Rates in Western United States," *Sociology and Social Research* 52 (Jan. 1968), pp. 228–36.

11. Arthur J. Norton and Paul C. Glick, "Marital Instability in America: Past, Present, and Future," in George Levinger and Oliver C. Moles, *eds., Divorce and Separation: Context, Causes and Consequences,* New York: Basic Books, 1979, pp. 14–15. For supporting evidence from another survey, see Richard J. Galligan and Stephen J. Bahr, "Economic Well-Being and Marital Stability: Implications for Income Maintenance Programs," *Journal of Marriage and the Family* 40 (May 1978), pp. 283–90.

12. Arlene F. Saluter, "Marital Status and Living Arrangements: March 1982," *Current Population Reports,* Series P-20, No. 380 (May 1983), p. 3.

economic conditions than are white rates. Blacks hold fewer middle-class jobs where employment is relatively secure, and they are more likely to be laid off or fired during economic recessions. Jacobson, using divorce rates for Virginia, demonstrated that nonwhite divorce rates were higher than white rates during the prosperous period between 1918 and 1928. During the depression decade from 1929 through 1940, by contrast, nonwhite divorce rates were lower than those among whites. The same reversal occurred in Mississippi. Jacobson concludes that the upsurge in black divorce rates after World War II also was associated with economic prosperity. Higher incomes permitted blacks to hire lawyers and to file formal divorce proceedings.[13]

Variations by Socioeconomic Status

At least four major studies have demonstrated an inverse correlation between socioeconomic status and divorce rates. Regardless of the criterion of socioeconomic status used, there are more divorces at the bottom of the structure, and the rate steadily declines as we move upward.

Hillman found that male private-household workers and service workers had the highest proportion of divorces; laborers had rates nearly as high. The proportion of divorces dropped through the middle-class, white-collar occupations and was lowest of all among professionals, managers, and proprietors. Farming was in a class by itself. As might be imagined, the divorce rate among farm owners and farm managers was less than half that among proprietors, managers, and officials.[14]

In a study of 425 Detroit-area women who had been divorced from 2 to 26 months, Goode calculated an index of proneness to divorce by the husbands' occupational status. The results were consistent with Hillman's findings. Divorce rates were lowest at the top of the occupational structure, with professionals and proprietors contributing barely more than half their proportionate share. Not until we drop down to semi-skilled and operatives did any group exceed its share. Finally, the unskilled had almost twice as many divorces as their share in the population.[15]

13. *Op. cit.*, pp. 102–3.
14. Farm laborers, interestingly, had high divorce rates like other laborers rather than low divorce rates like farm owners. See Karen G. Hillman, "Marital Instability and Its Relation to Education, Income, and Occupation: An Analysis Based on Census Data," in Robert F. Winch, Robert McGinnis, and Herbert R. Barringer, *eds.*, *Selected Studies in Marriage and the Family*, New York: Holt, Rinehart & Winston, 1962, pp. 603–8; and A. Wade Smith and June E. G. Meitz, "Cohorts, Education, and the Decline in Undisrupted Marriages," *Journal of Marriage and the Family* 45 (Aug. 1983), pp. 613–22.
15. William J. Goode, *After Divorce*, Glencoe, Ill.: The Free Press, 1956, pp. 46–47. See also Irving Rosow and K. Daniel Rose, "Divorce Among Doctors," *Journal of Marriage and the Family* 34 (Dec. 1972), pp. 587–98.

Goode's findings were confirmed in an independent study of 1434 Philadelphia divorce cases. Working from the divorce records, Kephart found that the upper occupational levels were underrepresented in divorce actions, the middle-level occupations were represented roughly in accord with their proportions of the population, and lower-level occupations were greatly overrepresented.[16]

Finally, Monahan analyzed 4449 divorce cases in Iowa and found evidence to support the three studies already cited. He found professional persons, officials, managers, and owners to contribute less than their share of divorces. The clerical and sales group contributed almost exactly their expected share, and laboring groups contributed up to four times their share. Farmers had the lowest rates of all.[17]

These four studies all used occupation as the index of socioeconomic status. Goode and Hillman, however, also used education and income as indexes and found the same inverse relationship between these measures and divorce rates. When education is used, however, some striking anomalies appear. Hillman found that the relationships hold for white males only, and Goode found that when education is used, the relationships are reversed for blacks and whites. Among blacks, the higher the educational level up to college graduation, the higher the divorce rate. Again, blacks who actually finish college have low divorce rates, approximating those of blacks who have little formal education. It may be that blacks with more formal education are more likely to use attorneys and courts in the solution of their marital problems and are less likely to resort to desertion. The low divorce rates among black college graduates may reflect the next stage in this process: the eventual tendency for middle-class norms to have more salience than those associated with race.

Comparison of data from the 1960 and 1970 censuses shows that differences in divorce rates by socioeconomic status generally are probably decreasing. Data from the 1975 marital history survey show that the trend continued at least through the first half of the last decade. The increases in divorce rates, so prominent over the past 15 years or so, have occurred more among higher-status than lower-status segments of the population.

16. William M. Kephart, "Occupational Level and Marital Disruption," *American Sociological Review* 20 (Aug. 1955), pp. 456–65. For a sophisticated analysis based on 1960 census data, see Phillips Cutright, "Income and Family Events: Marital Stability," *Journal of Marriage and the Family* 33 (May 1971), pp. 291–306.
17. Monahan found Iowa farm laborers to have very low divorce rates also. The conflict in findings here between Monahan's and Hillman's studies has not yet been reconciled. See Thomas P. Monahan, "Divorce by Occupational Level," *Marriage and Family Living* 17 (Nov. 1955), pp. 322–24.

Variations by Length of Time Married

One of the hazards in tracing changes in divorce rates is that there may be apparent increases in yearly rates without there being any long-term changes in the proportion of the population becoming divorced. This may happen if the average duration of marriages to divorce shortens. Earlier divorces would cause the yearly rates to show temporary increases. Unfortunately, available data on length of marriage to divorce are too fragmentary to show conclusively what has been happening.

A second problem is that the duration of marriage to the date of divorce is not so useful a measure as is the duration of marriage to the time of separation. The period of separation before a divorce decree is granted may vary from only a few weeks to many years.[18]

Several early studies showed that divorce rates are higher in the early years of marriage and are highest among those who marry young. These studies also suggested that the first year of marriage is the peak year for separations, the third year shows the highest number of divorces being granted, and the mean length of marriage to divorce is longer, at least six years. A recent tabulation of data by the National Center for Health Statistics showed that, in 1975, the median interval from marriage to divorce was 6.5 years.

One recent study was based on 77,491 Californian divorces. It also showed more divorces to be granted during the third year of marriage than any other and an inverse relationship between age at marriage and the likelihood of divorce. Men marrying at age 18 and women marrying at age 16 were more than twice as likely to be divorced as those marrying at ages 29 and 27.[19]

Variations by Parental Status

Crude statistics collected early in this century make it appear that the possibility of divorce was many times as great among childless couples as among couples with children. Cahen, for example, concluded that some 71 percent of childless marriages ended in divorce, whereas only 8 percent of marriages with children did so.[20] For some time, no one seriously questioned these extreme figures and the conclusion was widely accepted that childlessness and divorce are causally associated.

18. Thomas P. Monahan, "When Married Couples Part: Statistical Trends and Relationships in Divorce," *American Sociological Review* 27 (Oct. 1962), pp. 625–33.

19. Robert Schoen, "California Divorce Rates by Age at First Marriage and Duration of First Marriage," *Journal of Marriage and the Family* 37 (Aug. 1975), pp. 548–55.

20. Alfred Cahen, *Statistical Analysis of American Divorce*, New York: Columbia University Press, 1932, p. 113.

Gradually, however, flaws in the statistics became apparent. "Children" had been variously defined to refer to the number of children ever born to a marriage, the number of children living in the family, the number of minor children, the number of children affected by the decree, and so on. Moreover, it was discovered that the apparent childlessness of divorcing couples might be largely a function of the duration of marriage to divorce. Both childlessness and divorce are most common early in marriage, hence, the relationship between them might be spurious.

We do not know what the relationship between childlessness and divorce was several decades ago. Perhaps childbearing was more of a deterrent to divorce then than it is now. We do know that the more refined the statistics become, the less of a relationship appears. And we do know that the proportion of divorces granted to couples with minor children in the home has been increasing fairly rapidly.

Both the number of children affected by divorce and the proportion of divorces involving children have been increasing. In 1948, for example, there were an estimated 322,000 children involved in parental divorces. By 1965, the number had climbed to 630,000. It should be remembered that these increases were occurring during a period when the number of divorces was relatively stable. This means that both the proportion of couples with children and the number of children per divorce were rising.

The most recent data, for 1975, show that there were 1,123,000 children involved in parental divorces, an average of 1.08 children per divorce. Of all divorces 60 percent were granted to couples with children in the home. Thus, it seems quite clear that children are no longer—if they ever were—an effective deterrent to divorce. The effects of divorce on children will be dealt with in a later section of this chapter. Now we turn to a discussion of the divorce process itself.

THE DIVORCE PROCESS IN THE UNITED STATES

The divorce process may produce as much strife within families as does divorce itself. Divorce law in the United States is state law and there are as many sets of laws as there are jurisdictions—51, including all the states plus the District of Columbia. Divorce law and all of domestic-relations law is state law because the U.S. Constitution does not grant the power to enact such law to the federal government. All powers not specifically granted to the federal government by the Constitution are reserved to the states.

The Old Adversary System

Analysis of the divorce situation in the United States must be divided into two time periods: before 1970, and afterwards. Until 1970, the situation in all states involved a so-called adversary system. For a divorce to be granted, one spouse had to bring charges against the other, claiming that the accused spouse was guilty of one or more offenses that were legal grounds for divorce in that state. Legal grounds for divorce ranged from only 1, adultery, in New York State (until 1966, when the number of grounds was broadened to 5) to 20 grounds in Kentucky.

The vast majority of all divorces were granted on only two grounds, cruelty and desertion. The choice of these grounds, out of all those available, appears to have been based on the fact that they carried less stigma than other grounds, such as adultery. Not only did one spouse have to bring charges against the other, however, but for the divorce to be granted, the plaintiff (the spouse who brought the charges) could not himself or herself be guilty of any offense that was grounds for divorce. The law required that there be a guilty and an innocent party, a situation that seldom, if ever, occurs in marriage.

In truth, of course, people do not generally seek divorce because one of them has committed adultery or been cruel to the other; they seek divorce because they can no longer live together. By that time, it is likely that both spouses have treated one another in ways that constitute grounds for divorce and that both partners, if reluctantly, are agreed that a divorce should be sought. Yet if it was called to the attention of the judge that both partners had agreed to the divorce, this constituted collusion and the judge was legally bound to deny the divorce.

In practice, the legal requirements were winked at. More often than not, the husband and wife agreed to seek a divorce, their attorneys worked out the terms, presented a recommended settlement to the judge, and the judge accepted it with or without minor modification. Around 85 percent of U.S. divorces were uncontested; the defendant-spouse did not appear in court and was assumed to be guilty by default.

The significance of the adversary system—beyond the fact that it involved judge, attorneys, and the couple in a tacit conspiracy to ignore the law—was that, in spite of the efforts of all concerned to keep trauma to a minimum and to make the divorce as therapeutic as possible, it generated strife and bitterness. The husband and wife ordinarily agreed that divorce was necessary, but there were likely to be feelings of hurt, rejection, shame, and anger. The attorneys in turn were bound by legal ethics to obtain the best possible settlement for their clients. In addition to deciding which partner was to be charged with what offense and how that was to be proved in court, bargaining occurred over the house, furniture, automobile, and so on. Custody and support arrangements had to be worked out for children, and it had to be decided whether the wife was entitled to alimony. Before the negotiations were completed, what started out as an attempt by both partners to reach an equitable solution often degenerated into bitter conflict. Virtually all authorities agreed that much of the vindictiveness that has traditionally been associated with divorce was traceable to the hostilities engendered by the divorce process.

No-Fault Divorce

Beginning in 1969 with California, some states began doing something about it. The California legislation eliminated the term *divorce* and substituted *dissolution of marriage* to be granted on grounds of *irreconcilable differences* that have caused the irremediable breakdown of the marriage. The law also provides for the substantially equal division of property and bases alimony on the length of the marriage and the earning ability of both spouses.

Between 1969 and 1977, an additional 17 states passed a single no-fault ground for divorce. By 1983, only one state, South Dakota, had failed to substitute no-fault for traditional grounds.[21]

It is still too early to know in detail how these laws will work, but some trends already are evident. First, in spite of dire predictions to the contrary, experience with the California law failed to show that it increased divorce rates.[22] The divorce rate in California did increase, but it failed to keep pace with the national average. There was a significant increase in the number of husbands who filed for divorce.[23] Under the old adversary system, husbands more often bore the stigma of fault by allowing their wives to file for the divorces. Second, the administration of no-fault laws, so far, is quite uneven. Some judges accept the fact that the marriage is dead when one spouse testifies that he or she will no longer live with the other. Other judges still demand that detailed testimony be presented in which specific acts that have destroyed the marriage must be recounted.

21. Charles E. Welch III and Sharon Price-Bonham, "A Decade of No-fault Divorce Revisited: California, Georgia, and Washington," *Journal of Marriage and the Family* 45 (May 1983), pp. 411–18. See also Norman N. Robbins, "Have We Found Fault in No Fault Divorce?" *Family Coordinator* 22 (July 1973), pp. 359–62; and Marie W. Kargman, "There Ought to Be a Law! The Revolution in Divorce Law," *Family Coordinator* 22 (April 1973), pp. 245–48. See also Gerald R. Leslie and Elizabeth McLaughlin Leslie, *Marriage in a Changing World*, New York: John Wiley & Sons, 1980, pp. 340–41.
22. Ruth B. Dixon and Lenore J. Weitzman, "Evaluating the Impact of No-Fault Divorce in California," *Family Relations* 29 (July 1980), pp. 297–307.
23. Ruth B. Dixon and Lenore J. Weitzman, "When Husbands File for Divorce," *Journal of Marriage and the Family* 44 (Feb. 1982), pp. 103–15.

Another development that is intended to move more states in the direction of no-fault legislation was the promulgation by the National Conference of Commissioners on Uniform State Laws of the Uniform Marriage and Divorce Act of 1970. This act is not a law, but provides a model for state legislatures to use in revising their laws.[24]

Migratory Divorce

People have long sought to get around the strict divorce requirements of their own states by traveling to other states or countries with more lenient laws. Reno, Nevada, has long been famed as a divorce center, as has Juarez, Mexico. Reno's popularity dropped after the passage of the new California law, and Mexico recently went out of the divorce business. Haiti and the Dominican Republic leaped into the breech, however, and the migratory divorce pattern goes on.

The problem (or the solution if one happens to be seeking a migratory divorce) stems from the fact that divorce laws vary from one state to another and from the fact that the Supreme Court has held that the full-faith-and-credit clause in the Constitution applies to domestic relations as well as to business contracts. This clause, which was designed to prevent people from escaping contractual obligations by moving from one state to another, holds that any legal status that accrues to a person by virtue of residence in one state shall be legally binding in any and all states to which he or she may subsequently move. As applied in this case, it means that people who are legally divorced in Nevada or elsewhere must have their divorced status recognized by New York or any other state to which they subsequently move.

Confusion arises when people take up residence in states with short residence requirements for divorce for the specific purpose of securing a divorce under that state's more lenient laws. The traffic between New York, with its stringent divorce laws, and Nevada, with its six-weeks' residence requirement, has been widely publicized. Because there are many borderline cases and because no statistics are kept, it is not known exactly how much migratory divorce occurs. Jacobson estimates migratory divorces at somewhere between 3 and 5 percent of the total number of divorces.[25] In addition to Nevada and Idaho, disproportionately large numbers of divorces are granted in Florida; Alabama; Paris, France; and the Virgin Islands.

Most migratory divorces are binding simply because the parties agree

24. Kargman, *op. cit.* For a critical analysis of the act, see Thomas P. Monahan, "National Divorce Legislation: The Problem and Some Suggestions," *Family Coordinator* 22 (July 1973), pp. 353–57.
25. Jacobson, *op cit.,* p. 109.

to the divorce and no one challenges them. Occasionally, however, one spouse does bring suit in a court in the home state to have the migratory divorce secured by the partner declared invalid. A few cases have reached the Supreme Court, and it has held that courts in one state have the right to review court decisions in other states to determine whether those courts had jurisdiction under their own laws. The attempt obviously is to get away from establishing phony legal residence for purposes of divorce. The question has not yet been completely resolved. Most migratory divorces are binding simply because they go unchallenged. When suit is brought, most cases are resolved in state courts, and there is no unanimity of practice among these; certain migratory divorces may be accepted as binding in some states but not in others. Finally, the Supreme Court has not been consistent in its rulings. As a consequence, there are hundreds of thousands of people who have had migratory divorces whose marital statuses are potentially in legal jeopardy.

THE CONSEQUENCES OF DIVORCE

Most societies define divorce as undesirable, and the United States is no exception. On the one hand, there is the tendency to associate divorce with a threat to family stability and to the larger society. On the other hand, divorce is assumed to have grave consequences for men, women, and children. The first part of this concern was dealt with earlier and requires no further treatment here. The second part—the presumed effects on adults and children—has been extensively researched. We will first present the major findings of this research on the consequences for the marital partners, then we shall examine the alleged effects of divorce on their children.

Consequences for the Marital Partners

A sensitive analyst of the effects of divorce on marital partners, Willard Waller, brought to an early classic study the same combination of brilliant insight and lack of methodological rigor that we have witnessed in his studies of dating and marital adjustment. Waller focused on the emotional aspects of adjustment to divorce and described a series of typical stages that many people go through.

First, he said, comes shock associated with the realization that one is actually being divorced. Although there may be intellectual understanding, separation and divorce frustrate deeply rooted habits quite painfully. What happens may be likened to the experience of an amputee who finds that the amputated limb still hurts. Dozens of times during the day, activities that were routine must be faced consciously and with nostalgia for the comfort and well-being that attended their performance in better days.

This disruption of habits is accompanied by ambivalence toward the partner and oneself. Self-preservation may demand that increased bitterness be felt toward the spouse and that he or she be blamed for the failure of the marriage. At the same time, the former partner may appear in some ways to be more desirable than before; even formerly disliked traits may come to be admired. An analogous ambivalence may be found in attitudes toward oneself. On the one hand, one's every action may be justified and held to demonstrate one's superiority to the former spouse. On the other hand, there may be nagging feelings of failure and a compulsive focusing of attention on what one might have done differently to avoid the breakup.

There is, of course, disruption of established sexual patterns. Some persons react by suppressing or repressing all sexual desire. This may or may not be associated with bitterness, generalized to all of the opposite sex. Many persons after the initial shock of divorce, however, go through a relatively promiscuous experimentation with sex that has overtones of revenge on the spouse and some degradation of self. Casual affairs may represent some combination of these along with attempts to reassure oneself of one's desirability and sexual adequacy.[26]

Finally, there is need to adjust to the loss of other relationships in addition to that with the former spouse, to make new friends, and to establish a new life. Alienation from the spouse is accompanied by alienation from many friends, some of whom have taken sides and all of whom serve as reminders of the relationship that is now dead. Without a spouse, one also becomes a fifth wheel at many social gatherings. Gradually, one has to develop new friendships with people who do not know of the former relationship and whose circumstances of life are consistent with one's own.

The adjustment to divorce, according to Waller, is accompanied by much frustration and unhappiness. Gradually, however, the pains ease and new habits are developed. Gradually, new friends are acquired, and one's needs for love and affection are directed toward new partners. Some persons become permanently blocked at some stage in this process, but most eventually form new relationships that replace the old.[27]

In sharp contrast, methodologically, to Waller's analysis is a study by Goode of 425 Detroit-area mothers who had been divorced from 2 to

26. Data from two national surveys showed that more than one fourth of remarried women gave birth to a child between the time of separation from their husbands and remarriage. See Ronald R. Rindfuss and Larry L. Bumpass, "Fertility During Marital Disruption," *Journal of Marriage and the Family* 39 (Aug. 1977), pp. 517–28.
27. Williard Waller, *The Old Love and the New: Divorce and Readjustment*, Carbondale: Southern Illinois University Press, 1967 (Originally published in 1930).

26 months. Goode sought to test hypotheses that (1) divorce is traumatic, (2) most divorcees are neurotic, (3) divorce often is secured for
trivial reasons, (4) adequate readjustment following divorce is rare,
(5) there are undesirable effects of the divorce on children.[28]

Goode found that divorce is preceded by a long period of conflict
and that the securing of a decree is the final result of a decision process
that lasts for an average of about two years. One third of the respondents reported waiting more than two years from the time they first
seriously considered divorce before actually filing suit.

A paradoxical situation emerged in connection with attempts to discover which of the partners first wanted the divorce and which first
suggested divorce. More often than not, the husband was the first to
desire divorce, but the wife was the first to suggest it. Goode explains it
this way. Men, by virtue of their relative dominance in the family, are
more likely to come consciously to desire a divorce. This desire and the
behaviors that lead to it tend to produce guilt feelings however. As a
consequence, the husband does not ordinarily press for divorce but unwittingly assumes behavior that eventually forces his wife to ask for
and insist on divorce. He becomes disinterested and obnoxious. The
data show that 62 percent of the wives suggested divorce; in 13 percent
of the cases, it was a mutual decision; in 25 percent of the cases, the
husband first suggested divorce.[29]

This situation may be changing rapidly. A study of Florida divorces,
for example, before and after the enactment of a no-fault divorce law,
found a complete reversal in filing patterns. Between 1962 and 1971,
when the traditional law was in effect, 62 percent of all suits for divorce
were filed by women. In 1972 and 1973, however, after the new law was
in effect, women filed only 36 percent of the suits, whereas men filed 64
percent. Whatever "chivalry" influenced divorce-filing behavior under
the old system may be giving way to the true expression of feeling and
intent under the new laws.[30]

The Goode study also yielded data on the trauma Waller found to
be associated with divorce. The respondents were divided into high- and
law-trauma groups on the basis of answers to questions concerning impact of the divorce on sleeping, health, loneliness, work efficiency, memory difficulties, smoking, and drinking. Of the respondents, 37 percent
showed little increase in symptoms and were classified as low-trauma
cases. In about two thirds of the cases, there was an increase in personal

28. Goode, op. cit., pp. 15–17. See also Gay C. Kitson and Marvin B. Sussman, "Marital
Complaints, Demographic Characteristics, and Symptoms of Mental Distress in Divorce,"
Journal of Marriage and the Family 44 (Feb. 1982), pp. 87–102.
29. Ibid., pp. 133–45.
30. B. G. Gunter, "Notes on Divorce Filing as Role Behavior," Journal of Marriage and
the Family 39 (Feb. 1977), pp. 95–98.

difficulty. Interestingly, the time of greatest difficulty was not at the time of, or following, the issuance of the divorce decree. The period of greatest trauma was the time of final separation. The divorce decree may announce the end of the marriage to the world at large, but the greatest personal crisis and the effective end to the marriage for the spouses, their kin, and their friends comes at the final separation.[31]

Apparently, most women experienced little or no discrimination against themselves as divorced persons. Only 30 percent reported any discrimination at all, and the percentage declined steadily with the age of the woman.[32] By contrast, 54 percent of the women who had been divorced for 26 months had already remarried, and 50 percent of the remainder had steady dates. Over half claimed to have kept their old friends after the divorce, and most of the others had found new friends they believed to be equal to, or better than, their old friends.

Surprisingly, even the financial adjustment failed to bear out the belief that divorce works continuing hardship. In most cases, there was little property to be divided, and the wife got most of it. Where there was a house and furniture, the wife most often got them. The husbands were generally ordered to pay child support, but because their incomes often were low, the payments tended to be low also. About half of the husbands made support payments "always" or "usually," but 40 percent made them "rarely" or "never." As contact between the former spouses dwindled, support payments tended to become less regular.

On the average, the divorced women had almost as much income, from all sources, as their husbands had earned. Moreover, the women's incomes increased with the time since the divorce, most of which was associated with remarriage. There was, of course, a large difference in income between women who had remarried and those who had not. When the women's perceptions of their economic situations were considered, however, the differences were smaller. The remarried women judged themselves as better off than during their first marriages and better off than their objective financial situations indicated. Among those who had not been remarried, the tendency was to view their financial situations as worse than objective conditions indicated, but even here the financial attractiveness of the marriage continues to fade. More women come to believe that the period while they were separated from their husbands was better than either the time of the marriage or now.

31. See Stan L. Albrecht, "Reactions and Adjustments to Divorce: Differences in the Experiences of Males and Females," *Family Relations* 29 (Jan. 1980), pp. 59–68.
32. Goode, *op. cit.*, pp. 184–88. For a good summary of the literature on one-parent families, see Jane K. Burgess, "The Single-Parent Family: A Social and Sociological Problem," *Family Coordinator* 19 (April 1970), pp. 137–44; and Benjamin Schlesinger, "The One-Parent Family in Canada: Some Recent Findings and Recommendations," *Family Coordinator* 22 (July 1973), pp. 305–9.

Thus, Goode's analysis supports Waller's at some points and contradicts it at others. He did find that the majority of couples reach the decision to divorce only reluctantly over a long period of time; that for most of them there is considerable trauma involved; that a minority experience some discrimination and may be, for a time, almost without friends; and that there is some economic deprivation.[33] On the other hand, Goode found that most divorcees kept their former friends or made other equally desirable friendships, that most quickly moved back into dating and remarriage, and that their estimates of their financial situations changed accordingly.

Bloom and Caldwell concur with Goode's finding that the separation period is fraught with trauma, but apparently it differs for husbands and wives. Women have more psychological symptoms of distress before the separation, whereas men display more such symptoms after the final separation.[34] Spanier and Hansen found that adjustment of the spouses is enhanced if their kin are indifferent to the separation—neither approving or disapproving.[35]

The factors that enhance adjustment to divorce also differ for men and women.[36] It appears easier for men to accept divorce if they have a limited commitment to marriage, if they receive approval from their friends for the divorce, and if they initiate the action themselves or make a mutual decision with their spouses. Acceptance of the divorce is lower if the decision is initiated by wives. Postmarital adjustment is easier for wives if they recall the final months of marriage as a time filled with discord and low in affective expression. Higher educational achievement among wives also serves to enhance their acceptance of divorce. Whereas divorce may be easier for some, the great majority of divorced people show some signs of attachment to their ex-spouses.[37]

If divorce is a mixed blessing, there may also be problems in remaining married. Mathews and Mihanovich, for example, studied 984 Catholic respondents and found that couples who made low marriage-adjustment scores have more problems and more serious problems than those who made higher scores. Neither did they find that problems decrease with

33. See Thomas J. Espenshade, "The Economic Consequences of Divorce," *Journal of Marriage and the Family* 41 (Aug. 1979), pp. 615–25.

34. Bernard L. Bloom and Robert A. Caldwell, "Sex Differences in Adjustment During the Process of Marital Separation," *Journal of Marriage and the Family* 43 (Aug. 1981), pp. 693–701.

35. Graham B. Spanier and Sandra Hansen, "The Role of Extended Kin in the Adjustment to Marital Separation," *Journal of Divorce* 5 (Fall–Winter 1981), pp. 33–48.

36. Linda Thompson and Graham B. Spanier, "The End of Marriage and Acceptance of Marital Termination," *Journal of Marriage and the Family* 45 (Feb. 1983), pp. 103–14.

37. Gay C. Kitson, "Attachment to the Spouses in Divorce: A Scale and Its Application," *Journal of Marriage and the Family* 44 (May 1982), pp. 379–93.

length of time married.[38] Landis found that the unhappily married, those who married young, those who are indifferent to religion, and those with more formal education are more likely to resort to divorce.[39]

Finally, Le Masters studied 36 marriages that had chronic conflict for at least 10 years. He found personal disorganization in one or both spouses in 75 percent of the cases. Symptoms included alcoholism, psychosomatic illness, neurotic or psychotic behavior, occupational problems, and extramarital affairs. He found no evidence of improvement in the marriages over time and found that husbands were more likely to suffer personality damage from their marriages than were wives.[40]

Landis has pointed out that another possible effect of divorce is to increase the likelihood of divorce in succeeding generations. He found that if neither set of grandparents is divorced, only 15 percent of their children become divorced. If one set of grandparents is divorced, 24 percent of the next generation is divorced. And, if both sets of grandparents are divorced, the probability of divorce in the next generation rises to 38 percent.[41] At first glance, these figures suggest that divorce within families is highly contagious. However, Peterson has correctly pointed out that these statistics should be regarded with caution until controls for social class are imposed. It may be that the marital failures of succeeding generations are more social linked than divorce linked.[42] This question is as yet unresolved.

38. Vincent D. Mathews and Clement S. Mihanovich, "New Orientations on Marital Maladjustment," *Marriage and Family Living* 25 (Aug. 1963), pp. 300–4.

39. Judson T. Landis, "Social Correlates of Divorce or Nondivorce Among the Unhappy Married," *Marriage and Family Living* 25 (May 1963), pp. 178–79. See also B. E. Aguirre and W. C. Parr, "Husbands' Marriage Order and the Stability of First and Second Marriages of White and Black Women," *Journal of Marriage and the Family* 44 (Aug. 1982), pp. 605–20.

40. Ersel E. Le Masters, "Holy Deadlock: A Study of Unsuccessful Marriages," *Midwest Sociologist* 21 (July 1959), pp. 86–91. See also William H. Clements, "Marital Interaction and Marital Stability: A Point of View and a Descriptive Comparison of Stable and Unstable Marriages," *Journal of Marriage and the Family* 29 (Nov. 1967), pp. 697–702.

41. Judson T. Landis, "The Pattern of Divorce in Three Generations," *Social Forces* 34 (March 1956), pp. 213–16. See also Ellen F. Greenberg and W. Robert Nay, "The Intergenerational Transmission of Marital Instability Reconsidered," *Journal of Marriage and the Family* 44 (May 1982), pp. 335–47. Charles W. Mueller, and Hallowell Pope, "Marital Instability: A Study of Its Transmission Between Generations," *Journal of Marriage and the Family* 39 (Feb. 1977), pp. 83–93.

42. James A. Peterson, "Catastrophes in Partnership: Separation, Divorce, and Widowhood," in Seymour M. Farber, Piero Mustacchi, and Roger H. L. Wilson, *eds.*, *Man and Civilization: The Family's Search for Survival*, New York: McGraw-Hill, 1965, p. 76. See also J. Richard Udry, "Marital Alternatives and Marital Disruption," *Journal of Marriage and the Family* 43 (Nov. 1981), pp. 889–97.

Consequences for Children

There has been great public concern for the presumed effects of divorce on children. Adults, knowing the trauma of divorce for themselves and their peers have assumed that children must suffer far more, that they must suffer a loss of emotional and financial security that could not help but make a deep impression on their lives. Over the years, too, the number of children caught up in parental divorces has been increasing. The proportion of divorces involving minor children today hovers around 60 percent. Today, over 7 million children see their parents divorced each year. Furstenberg and his associates, using data from the National Survey of Children, found that 2 out of 5 children experience some sort of family disruption by their middle teens.[43]

Landis confirmed that the trauma experienced by children at the time of parental divorce is widespread. He studied 295 university students of previously divorced parents, finding initially that 112 were too young at the time of divorce to remember any trauma. Surprisingly, 19 percent of the remaining respondents had considered their families to be closely united before they learned of the impending divorce, and 24 percent reported no open conflict in the family. In only 22 percent of the cases was there constant open conflict between the parents.

The reactions of children to the divorce depended on their previous evaluations of the parental marriages and their own security in their families. Over half of the children from openly unhappy homes reacted by thinking that divorce was best for all concerned. Over half of those who had believed their homes to be happy, on the other hand, reported that they were unhappy and upset. Two out of five of this group couldn't believe what was happening. After the divorce, the same split evaluation occurred between children who had thought their homes to be happy and those who knew them to be unhappy: those from apparently happy homes reported either no change in security and happiness or a change to feeling less secure and less happy; respondents from unhappy homes reported shifts toward greater happiness and security. Pett found that children's adjustment to divorce is very dependent on the social adjustment of the custodial parent.[44]

Almost half of the youngsters (44 percent) in Landis's study reported that they felt "used" by one or both parents after the divorce. The par-

43. Frank F. Furstenberg, Jr., Christine Winquist Nord, James L. Peterson, and Nicholas Zill, "The Life Course of Children of Divorce: Marital Disruption and Parental Contact," *American Sociological Review* 48 (Oct. 1983), pp. 656–68.
44. Marjorie G. Pett, "Correlates of Children's Social Adjustment Following Divorce," *Journal of Divorce* 5 (Summer 1982), pp. 25–39.

ents played on their children's sympathy, tried to get information about the other parent, told untrue things about the other parent, and sought to involve the children in continuing quarrels.

Over the long haul, one effect of the divorce was to increase the feelings of closeness of the children to their mothers and to increase the emotional distance between them and their fathers. Undoubtedly, this is associated with the mother's having custody. One cost of divorce for fathers, apparently, is loss of closeness with their children, regardless of the nature of the situation that precipitates the divorce. Only one third of the 1377 children in Furstenberg's study saw their fathers at least once a month.[45]

Finally, about one fifth of the children in Landis's study experienced shame that their parents were divorced and 1 out of 6 felt inferior to other children. Some 15 percent talked to others as though their parents were not divorced or they avoided the subject; 1 out of 10 lied about the whereabouts of the other parent.[46]

Apparently, there is foundation for the belief that children suffer trauma from their parents' divorce, just as adults do. So, also, is there reason to think that the trauma is related to the previously perceived quality of the family relationships: where the child has perceived the home to be happy, the trauma is great; where the home has been unhappy, trauma may be less conspicuous than relief that the conflict is over.

Goode's study of divorced mothers provides further data on this matter. He classified the mothers according to the trauma they experienced in connection with the divorce and then related the problems they had with their children to it. As expected, the greater the trauma, the higher the proportion of mothers who admitted that their children had been hard to handle. Of the mothers, 81 percent admitted to worrying before the divorce about the effects on the children. However, 55 percent reported no increase in problems afterwards; 18 percent said that the children were harder to handle during the separation or immediately following the divorce; 13 percent said they had been at their worst during the marriage itself; and only 14 percent thought that they were harder to handle at the time of interview.[47] Colletta found that divorced mothers with low incomes tended to experience a great deal of stress, which influenced their relations with their children. These mothers became more restrictive and demanding of their children.[48]

45. Furstenberg, et al., *op. cit.*
46. Judson T. Landis, "The Trauma of Children When Parents Divorce," *Marriage and Family Living* 22 (Feb. 1960), pp. 7–13.
47. Goode, *op. cit.*, pp. 317–21.
48. Nancy Donohue Colletta, "Stressful Lives: The Situation of Divorced Mothers and Their Children," *Journal of Divorce* 6 (Spring 1983), pp. 19–31.

Goode also sought to determine whether the mothers thought their children better off or worse off following the divorce. The evidence, he concluded, indicated that the vast majority of mothers believed them to be better off. Three fourths of the mothers who had remarried stated that their children were better off; another 15 percent said that life was about the same. Only 8 percent thought that the children were worse off in the second marriage. Among women who had not remarried, 57 percent put their children in the care of relatives while they worked. Of the mothers who used outside help, 65 percent thought that their children received "excellent" care, 24 percent said that it was "good," 8 percent said it was "average," and only 4 percent acknowledged that it was "poor."

One series of studies has tended to show that broken homes contribute to juvenile delinquency. The Gluecks used matched samples of delinquent and nondelinquent youngsters and found that 9 percent of the delinquents but only 6 percent of the nondelinquents had divorced parents. What was more surprising, however, was that homes where one parent had been widowed or where the parents were separated contributed even more significantly to the ranks of the delinquent.[49]

Although several studies confirmed the findings of the Gluecks, sociologists have been reluctant to draw firm conclusions about the relationship between divorce and delinquency for at least two reasons. First, both delinquency and divorce are heavily concentrated in lower socioeconomic strata; the apparent relationship between them may be largely spurious, with both stemming from other conditions of lower-class living. Second, there is a strong suggestion that family disorganization rather than divorce may be the crucial variable. The findings of the Gluecks regarding the effects of widowhood and separation suggest this. A study by Browning of delinquent and nondelinquent boys in Los Angeles led to the same conclusion. He states that his findings "support the hypothesis that delinquents are as likely to come from disorganized but structurally unbroken homes as they are from broken homes."[50]

These results point to the fact that the negative impact of divorce on children may be no greater than would be the effect of parents continuing to live together in an unhappy marriage. On the contrary, at least four studies have shown that unhappy, unbroken homes may have more deleterious effects on children than do broken homes.[51]

49. Sheldon Glueck and Eleanor Glueck, *Unraveling Juvenile Delinquency*, New York: Commonwealth Fund, 1951.

50. Charles J. Browning, "Differential Impact of Family Disorganization upon Male Adolescents," *Social Problems* 8 (Summer 1960), p. 43. For a careful analysis of such studies, see Karen Wilkinson, "The Broken Family and Juvenile Delinquency: Scientific Explanation or Ideology?" *Social Problems* 21 (June 1974), pp. 726–39.

51. Lee G. Burchinal, "Characteristics of Adolescents from Unbroken, Broken, and Re-

SUMMARY

All societies provide for divorce. Divorce rates vary widely among societies, and there is no apparent relationship between divorce rates and other symptoms of societal breakdown. More than half of all preliterate societies have higher divorce rates than does the United States, and some large nations have had higher rates also. Our divorce rate has been climbing steadily, however, and now is one of the highest of any modern nation.

The long-term trend in divorce in the United States has been upward. The rate of climb has been unevenly affected by wars and depressions. Wars are followed by sharp increases in divorce rates and then by a return to the level of the prewar trend. Depressions lower divorce rates temporarily and then are followed by a rapid rise.

There are, currently, over 1 million divorces in the United States each year, or about 5.1 per 1000 population. The probability that first marriages currently being contracted will end in divorce is about one in three; the probability is somewhat higher in remarriages. It is uncertain whether a recent downward trend in divorce will continue.

Divorced persons are overrepresented in urban areas. This reflects both the greater likelihood of divorce under urban living conditions and a tendency for divorced persons to migrate to cities. Divorce rates increase from east to west across the country, reflecting differences in attitudes and values and in the age, ethnic, and religious composition of the population. As blacks have come to rely less on separation, their divorce rates have been rising rapidly and now exceed those of whites. More blacks are found in the lower socioeconomic strata, and there is an inverse correlation between economic status and divorce rates.

Studies show more separations during the first year of marriage than any other. The time lag from separation to divorce results in the peak number of divorces occurring from the second to the fourth year of marriage. The mean interval to divorce is longer—around 6.5 years. The length of marriage to divorce is longer in first marriages than in remarriages and longer among blacks than among whites.

---

constituted Families," *Journal of Marriage and the Family* 26 (Feb. 1964), pp. 44–51; Judson T. Landis, "A Comparison of Children from Divorced and Nondivorced Unhappy Marriages," *Family Life Coordinator* 11 (July 1962), pp. 61–65; Paul H. Landis, *The Broken Home in Teenage Adjustment*, Bulletin No. 542 (June 1953), Pullman, Wash.: Agricultural Experiment Station; F. Ivan Nye, "Child Adjustment in Broken and in Unhappy Unbroken Homes," *Marriage and Family Living* 19 (Nov. 1957), pp. 356–61; and Helen J. Raschke and Vernon J. Raschke, "Family Conflict and Children's Self-Concepts: A Comparison of Intact and Single-Parent Families," *Journal of Marriage and the Family* 41 (May 1979), pp. 367–74.

Refined statistics indicate less of a relationship between childlessness and divorce than formerly was believed to exist. There may be from one and one-half to two times the probability that a childless marriage will end in divorce, over a marriage with children. Both the number and proportion of divorces involving children have been increasing. The proportion of divorces in which children are involved is about 60 percent. Having children is no longer a very effective deterrent to divorce.

Divorce law in the United States is state law. Legal grounds in the various states have ranged up to 40 in number, with many divorces being granted on grounds of cruelty or desertion. These have been widely used because they have little stigma associated with them, and their use tells us little about the actual causes of divorce. Until recently, most divorce law was administered through the adversary system, which again concealed the true causes of divorce and which created bitterness between the spouses.

Since 1969, most of the states have substituted no-fault divorce systems or have added no-fault grounds to their existing grounds. These seem to be reducing the trauma of the divorce process substantially, although, as yet, the new laws are very unevenly administered.

Migratory divorces apparently number from 3 to 5 percent of all divorces. Although such divorces frequently involve the open flouting of state laws, most of them are valid because they go unchallenged. Some court decisions, however, have held that obviously migratory divorces are invalid, and the whole situation is in need of clarification.

The effects of divorce on the marital partners include some trauma at the time and afterwards. There is a painful severing of former habits, ambivalence toward the partner and oneself, feelings of failure, interference with sexual patterns, and the need to form new relationships. Divorce seldom appears to be secured on frivolous grounds, and a long time generally elapses from the first serious consideration of divorce to the actual issuing of a decree. The evidence suggests that husbands more often than not desire the divorce first but that they maneuver their wives into being the ones to ask for it. That situation may be changing. Studies of divorced women show that most do not feel discriminated against, most keep their former friends, most make an adequate financial adjustment, and most remarry.

Studies of unhappy couples who do not seek divorce indicate that their problems do not lessen with time and that the partners suffer some personality damage. Statistics showing that divorce perpetuates itself in succeeding generations of the same families should be used with caution because of the possible contaminating influence of social class.

Divorce often produces trauma in children also. The effects are pronounced where the children have believed their parents' marriages to be happy. Following divorce, children tend to become closer emotionally to their mothers, who usually have custody, and to become more distant emotionally from their fathers. Where the parental home has been obviously unhappy, the children often experience relief when the divorce is final. Most mothers worry about the effects of divorce on their children, but most experience no increase in problems after the divorce. Mothers who remarry generally believe their children to be better off in the second marriage, and those who have not remarried generally are satisfied with their child-care arrangements.

Studies have shown that broken homes and juvenile delinquency are associated. However, the correlation appears to be with all forms of broken homes, including those that are emotionally broken but structurally intact, not just with divorce-broken homes. Predictions of dire effects of divorce on children appear not to be warranted.

SUGGESTED READINGS

Cauhope, Elizabeth, *Fresh Starts: Men and Women After Divorce*, New York: Basic Books, 1983. A social psychologist examines the effects of divorce on middle-aged men and women.

Hunt, Morton, and Hunt, Bernice, *The Divorce Experience*, New York: New American Library, 1977. A semipopular treatment of the problems of adjustment to divorce. For the general reader.

Luepnitz, Deborah Anna, *Child Custody: A Study of Families After Divorce*, Lexington, Mass.: Lexington Books, 1982. Examines the post-divorce experiences of 43 families in three child-custody patterns—maternal, paternal, and joint-custody families.

Weiss, Robert S., *Going It Alone: The Family and Social Situation of the Single Parent*, New York: Basic Books, 1979. Analysis of the situation of the man or woman who is responsible for the care of children following divorce.

Wheeler, Michael, *No-Fault Divorce*, Boston, Mass.: Beacon Press, 1974. An essentially journalistic account of the emergence of the no-fault divorce movement.

FILMS

Chris and Bernie (New Day Films, P.O. Box 315, Franklin Lakes, N.J. 07417), 25 minutes. Two young women, both working and divorced with young children, discuss the problems and special needs of single parents.

How About Saturday? (MTI Teleprograms, 4825 N. Scott Street, Suite 23, Schiller Park, Ill. 60176), 20 minutes. Explores emotional issues of separation and divorce from the child's point of view. Presents feelings of anger, guilt, fear of abandonment, and helplessness.

Marriage Under Stress: The Causes of Divorce (*Time-Life* Films, 43 West 16th Street, New York, N.Y. 10011), 40 minutes. Shows the pressures that force couples apart. Discusses what happens when a marriage finally is over, including the chances of, and problems, in remarriage.

Not Together Now: End of a Marriage (Polymorph Films, 331 Newberry Street, Boston, Mass. 02115), 25 minutes, color. Why a couple married and why they separated. Their lives and goals now that they are apart.

QUESTIONS AND PROJECTS

1. What is the relationship between the divorce rate in a society and the stability of the society?
2. How does the divorce rate in the United States compare to the divorce rates of preliterate societies? Of modern societies?
3. Describe the long-term trend in American divorce rates. Describe the influence of wars and depressions. What is the current divorce rate?
4. Analyze variations in divorce rates by rural-urban residence, region, race, socioeconomic status, length of time married, and parental status. Try to account for the variations.
5. What is the relationship between childlessness and divorce? Does the presence of children serve as a deterrent to divorce?
6. What is meant by the adversary system in divorce? How does it complicate divorce for the persons involved? What is the relationship between causes of divorce and legal grounds for divorce?
7. What is no-fault divorce? How widespread is it? How does it differ from traditional divorce?
8. Analyze the impact of divorce on the emotions, habits, and self-concepts of the marital partners.
9. What does research show about the way people decide to secure a divorce? What does it show about adjustment following divorce? What is the situation of unhappily married couples who avoid divorce?
10. What factors are related to the trauma children experience over their parents' divorces? What does research show about the problems of children following divorce?

11. What appear to be the relative effects of happy homes, unhappy unbroken homes, and broken homes on children?

12. Arrange a visit to a local court where divorce cases are being heard. If possible, have the judge talk with the group about how he or she views the divorce cases moving through the court. Is he or she in sympathy with present legal procedures? What changes would he or she favor?

David Strickler, Monkmeyer

19
One-Parent Families and Remarriages

Nobody really knows what makes a good stepparent. There is only one rule most stepparents say they are conscious of: Do not be cruel and justify the wicked stepparent myth. But that is hardly enough to guide anybody through the hurly-burly of family life.

An additional source of strain . . . is money. Stepmothers . . . compete with their stepchildren for the father's income and inheritance as well as his love. . . . What is more, any group of half brothers and half sisters will have grandparents who belong to some and not others. This can mean that some children in a household can expect to be richer than others—a situation not always conducive to family harmony.[1]

This excerpt was taken from an article written by a woman about her own experiences with stepparenthood. It highlights some of the problems in some remarriages, although the total article from which the quotation was taken leaves one with the feeling that the author had coped well with her problems and probably had a pretty good marriage.

So little research on the quality of remarriages has been done as yet that we cannot compare their virtues and problems fully. A news release, early in 1977, presented a fairly positive picture:

Stepfathers are as effective as natural fathers in their roles as parents, and the stepchildren are as happy as children who reside with their natural fathers, according to a study of "Stepfathers and the Mental Health of Their Children" made by a research team . . . at Western Behavioral Sciences Institute.

. . . children brought up in a home with a stepfather . . . also were

1. Brenda Maddox, "Neither Witch nor Good Fairy," *New York Times Magazine,* Aug. 8, 1976, pp. 16, 18, 19.

found to be just as successful and as "achieving." The children in the study reported getting along well with their stepfathers, and the mothers agreed.[2]

Remarriages, like first marriages, vary widely. Some are of young persons, although many are older. Some have children at the time of marriage, some do not. Their strengths and their problems vary accordingly. Most people do not remarry immediately on divorce or death of the spouse. Commonly, there is a period of living alone or of living with one's children but without a spouse.

ONE-PARENT FAMILIES

Families may be broken either through divorce or death. Widowhood will be analyzed in the next chapter, and we shall concentrate on divorce-broken families here.

Although the great majority of family households still consist of married couples, one of the most dramatic changes taking place over the last decade has been the rise in female-headed households. In 1982, 15 percent of family households consisted of women living with their children and without their husbands. Some were without their husbands because of death; the vast majority were divorced. The situation is even more dramatic for black women. In 1982, 47 percent of black households were maintained by women, up from 21 percent in 1960.[3] Although there has been a slight increase in the number of men who maintain families without their wives, they still accounted for only 3 percent of family households in 1982.

Over 13 million, or 22 percent, of children under 18 in the United States lived in single-parent households in 1982.[4] The mother was the custodial parent in 9 out of 10 cases. Once again, the situation was even more dramatic for blacks. Almost half of all black children lived in homes maintained by one parent, compared to 17 percent of white children. Only 75 percent of children lived with both parents. The remaining 3 percent or so either lived with other relatives, nonrelatives, or in institutions.

The number of one-parent families has grown enormously over the past decade and this growth is expected to continue. Although all families quite naturally experience problems, single parents are subject to

---

2. *News Feature Service*, Alcohol, Drug Abuse, and Mental Health Administration, n.d.
3. Judith Cummings, "For Black Families, the Odds are Formidable," *New York Times*, November 27, 1983.
4. U.S. Bureau of the Census, "Marital Status and Living Arrangements: March 1982," *Current Population Reports*, Series P-20, No. 380 (May 1983), p. 4. See also Barbara Bilgé and Gladis Kaufman, "Children of Divorce and One-Parent Families: Cross-cultural Perspectives," *Family Relations* 32 (Jan. 1983), pp. 59–71.

special stresses and strains. Weiss has identified three sources of strain among single parents.[5] The first is *responsibility overload*. In two-parent families, decision making is a shared responsibility. Husbands and wives have a partner with whom they can talk and plan. Single parents, on the other hand, are alone in their responsibility for making decisions and plans and caring for their families' needs and well-being. The second source of strain for single parents is *task overload*. They must take care of all those jobs that were once distributed between two people. They must work for income, maintain the home, and care for all of their children's needs. The enormity of the tasks facing single parents every day can be exhausting and relentless. Very often they have little or no time for themselves. The third source of strain identified by Weiss is *emotional overload*. Single parents must cope alone with their children's emotional needs. Because of the amount of time required to maintain their jobs, their homes, and their families, very often their own emotional needs and wants go unfulfilled.

An even more serious concern of single parents is money. Divorced women are at a financial disadvantage compared to men.[6] Many did not work while raising their families and find it difficult to enter the labor market with little or no job experience. Many are forced to take low-paying, low-status jobs to support their families. In 1982, the median income of female household heads was slightly more than half that of married couples.[7] Albrecht found that two thirds of the women in his sample reported their incomes significantly lower following divorce, compared to only 19 percent of the men.[8] Comparing female-headed households and two-parent families, McLanahan found that female heads are more likely to experience chronic stress because of low incomes and low levels of social support.[9] These factors often lead to negative self-images and pessimistic views of the future.

It is often assumed that, on divorce, court-ordered child-support payments to custodial parents allow them to maintain their families in a financially secure manner. In actuality, however, less than half of fathers who are ordered to make child-support payments do so. Some who fail to meet their obligations feel unfairly treated by the courts or are

5. Robert S. Weiss, *Going It Alone: The Family Life and Social Situation of the Single Parent*, New York: Basic Books, 1979.
6. Thomas J. Espenshade, "The Economic Consequences of Divorce," *Journal of Marriage and the Family* 41 (Aug. 1979), pp. 615–25.
7. U.S. Department of Labor, "Earnings of Workers and Their Families: Third Quarter 1982," *Bureau of Labor Statistics*, November 8, 1982.
8. Stan L. Albrecht, "Reactions and Adjustments to Divorce: Differences in the Experiences of Males and Females," *Family Relations* 29 (Jan. 1980), pp. 59–68.
9. Sara S. McLanahan, "Family Structure and Stress: A Longitudinal Comparison of Two parent and Female-Headed Families," *Journal of Marriage and the Family* 45 (May 1983), pp. 347–57.

angry at ex-wives. Others feel only negligible emotional bonds with their children or have remarried and cannot handle the financial responsibility of maintaining two households.[10]

This situation may be changing however. In 1981, the federal government gave authority to the Internal Revenue Service (IRS) to begin Operation Intercept. Operation Intercept is a program that allows the IRS to withhold tax refunds from parents who are delinquent in child-support payments. During the first eight months of operation, the IRS seized 270,714 such refunds, totaling almost 170 million dollars.[11] Although this program may aid custodial parents in the years to come, at present many one-parent families are living a hand-to-mouth existence. Over 42 percent of female-headed households live below the poverty line, accounting for almost 33 percent of the nation's poor.[12] Female heads of household are the most rapidly growing segment of the population living below the poverty line.

Two economists who have studied mother-headed families in the United States emphasize the transitional nature of this phenomenon. It is transitional in two ways. First, the larger society is in transition, in that, over the past decade, female-headed families with children have increased in numbers almost ten times as rapidly as two-parent families. Second, it is transitional in the sense that living in one-parent families is usually temporary; it is a transitional stage between divorce (or widowhood) and remarriage.[13]

REMARRIAGES

There are many different kinds of remarriages. Some remarried couples are 20 years old, some are 40, and some are 60. In some cases, there are no children. In some cases, one partner brings children from the prior marriage, in some both do. In addition, there may be children on one or both sides who live with the former spouse. The children may range from infancy to middle-aged adulthood and, eventually, there may be "your children," "my children," and "our children."

Types of Remarriages

The various types of remarriages that can be achieved through the use of previous marital status, presence or absence and age of children, age,

10. *U.S. News & World Report*, March 21, 1983, p. 70.
11. *New York Times*, December 5, 1982.
12. *New York Times*, November 27, 1983.
13. Heather L. Ross and Isabel V. Sawhill, *Time of Transition: The Growth of Families Headed by Women*, Washington, D.C.: Urban Institute, 1975. See also Benjamin Schlesinger, "One Parent Families in Great Britain," *Family Coordinator* 26 (April 1977), pp. 139–42.

and so on, are too complicated for full presentation. Either the bride or the groom may be single, previously divorced, or previously widowed, making eight possible combinations in all. Because either or both spouses may have been both divorced or widowed prior to the remarriage, the number of possible combinations is considerably larger. With so many combinations deriving from previous marital status alone, it is easy to see that dozens of variations would emerge if we were to add such elemental variables as children, age, economic status, and religion.

Two studies plotted the distribution of remarriages among the eight types for a Seattle group,[14] and a group of 2009 cases in a hypothetical community called Utopolis.[15] The highest percentages consistently involve at least one partner who was divorced previously. The largest number of cases was of the "single man-divorced woman" type. Almost equally numerous were marriages involving two previously divorced persons. "Divorced man-single woman" marriages came next, with no other type approaching these top three. At the other extreme, the lowest percentages involved persons who were previously widowed.

The Trend in Remarriages

Before 1900, the incidence of remarriage in the United States was low. About nine tenths of all marriages were first marriages, and most remarriages involved widowed persons. As the divorce rate began to climb, the remarriage rate began to rise. More of the growing percentage of remarriage occurred among previously divorced persons.

Most of the change took place after World War I. In 1917, for example, 87.4 percent of all grooms entered marriage for the first time, 8 percent were widowed, and 4.5 percent were divorced. By 1960, only 77 percent of brides and grooms were entering marriage for the first time, about 6 percent were marrying after having been widowed, and between 16 and 17 percent were remarrying following divorce.[16]

The remarriage rate continued to increase rapidly during the 1960s, paralleling the increase in the divorce rate. During the 1970s, however, the remarriage rate declined rather sharply. Because four out of five divorced persons remarry eventually, this drop may reflect two things:

14. Charles E. Bowerman, "Assortative Mating by Previous Marital Status, Seattle, 1939–1946," *American Sociological Review* 18 (April 1953), p. 171.

15. Jessie Bernard, *Remarriage: A Study of Marriage*, New York: Dryden Press, 1956.

16. Hugh Carter and Paul C. Glick, *Marriage and Divorce: A Social and Economic Study*, Cambridge, Mass.: Harvard University Press, 1970, pp. 82–83. For Canadian data, see Benjamin Schlesinger and Alex Macrea, "Remarriages in Canada: Statistical Trends," *Journal of Marriage and the Family* 32 (May 1970), pp. 300–303; and Paul Kuzel and P. Krishnan, "Changing Patterns of Remarriage in Canada, 1961–1966," *Journal of Comparative Family Studies* 4 (Autumn 1973), pp. 217–24.

less pressure on women to remarry quickly because of work opportunities and government benefits and the tendency of couples to live together for a while before remarrying.

The Incidence of Remarriage

The proportion of all marriages that are remarriages of one or both spouses has steadily been increasing. In 1980, remarriages accounted for 44 percent of the marriages in the United States compared to only 31 percent in 1970.[17] Official tabulations of remarriage figures do not take into account the number of marriages individuals have had however, so, it is impossible to know how many of these remarriages represent the second, third, fourth, or even fifth marriages of some people.

The majority of remarriages are those in which both partners have been married before. In 1980, 23 percent of marriages consisted of previously married couples. Of the marriages, 11 percent were between single women and previously married men; single men wedded previously married women in 10 percent of the cases. Only 56 percent of the marriages in 1980 consisted of couples who both were single.

People remarrying after divorce tend to be around 10 years older than those marrying for the first time. The latest available figures show the median age at remarriage for divorced men is 34.0; the median age for women now is 31.0 years. Among those remarrying after widowhood, the median age for men is 61.2 years and for women, 53.6 years.[18]

The factor of age homogamy that we find in first marriages becomes more complex when we consider remarriage. In cases in which both spouses were previously married, there is a median age difference of 3.7 years between the spouses, with husbands the elder partners. Wives were 0.9 years older than their husbands if they were divorced and marrying single men. Where the reverse was true, divorced men marrying single women, husbands were 6.5 years older than their wives.[19]

At least two factors would lead us to expect higher remarriage rates among blacks than among whites. First is the higher divorce rate among blacks; the second is the higher death rate among blacks. Both factors should increase the proportion of blacks eligible for remarriage. This expectation is not borne out however. The rate of remarriage for blacks is significantly lower than for whites.[20]

17. National Center for Health Statistics, "Advance Report of Final Marriage Statistics, 1980," 32 (Aug. 1983), p. 2. See also James A. Weed, "Divorce: Americans' Style," *American Demographics* 4 (March 1982), pp. 13–17.
18. National Center for Health Statistics, *op. cit.,* p. 8.
19. *Ibid.,* p. 3.
20. Arland Thornton and Deborah Freedman, "The Changing American Family," *Population Bulletin* 38 (Oct. 1983), p. 10.

Probabilities of Marriage and Remarriage

What may come as a surprise is that—at any age—persons who have been married before have higher probabilities of remarrying than single persons have of getting married for the first time! During the age period 20 to 24, the likelihood that divorced women will remarry is more than twice as great as the chance that single women will marry. At older ages, the differences gradually increase in favor of the previously divorced women. Sufficient cases to compare widows become available during the age period, 25 to 29. At that age and for each succeeding age, widows are more likely to remarry than single women are likely to marry originally, but widows are less likely to remarry than divorcées are. The ages at which adequate cases for divorced and widowed men become available are slightly older than among women, but the same pattern is found. Divorced men have a greater probability of remarrying than do widowed men; age by age, single men have the lowest probabilities of all of marrying.

We cannot be certain of the reason for the greater probability of remarriage than of first marriage, but the following appears plausible. A developmental task facing people in adolescence and early adulthood is the necessity to establish relationships with the opposite sex that will in time lead to the emotional and physical intimacy that precede marriage. Divorced persons, even though their first marriage fail, have at least demonstrated ability to form relationships of some intimacy. Widowed persons have done this without the imputation of failure in the first marriage. Single persons, although they may be defined as being morally superior to, and better adjusted than, divorced persons, may not have achieved a heterosexual orientation adequate to eventuate in marriage. Moreover, with each increase in age beyond the early 20s, the chances that such an orientation ever will be achieved diminishes rapidly.

Divorced men have greater probabilities of remarrying, at every age level, than divorced women do. Whereas only three fourths of divorced women remarry eventually, five sixths of divorced men do so.

The explanations for this disparity are several. During the middle years, men need wives to help care for their homes and children. Where the situation is reversed and the women have the children, however, the opposite situation prevails; men are reluctant to assume the burden of women's children. As we move into the older ages, the differential longevity of men and women begins to increase in effect. There develops a shortage of eligible men.

The traditional difference in remarriage rates for men and women appears to be lessening. If so, it may reflect two things. First, the trend toward smaller families may be lessening the deterrent effect of children on the remarriage of women. Second, the trend toward equality between the sexes may be increasing the acceptability of divorced women as marital partners.

Interval to Remarriage

The interval between the ending of the first marriage and remarriage depends on how the first marriage is terminated. The intervals for both divorced and widowed persons tend to be relatively short but are considerably shorter in the case of divorce.

Jacobson reports that one third of the women who remarry following divorce do so within one year. Almost half remarry within two years, and approximately two thirds remarry within five years. He estimates slightly longer intervals for men, but that three fifths of the men who remarry after divorce do so within five years.[21] Slightly shorter intervals are implied in Glick's findings (from survey data and from data collected by the National Office of Vital Statistics) that three fourths of all divorced persons remarry within five years.[22]

Bernard's analysis of 849 divorced women and 809 divorced men in Utopolis showed that the average intervals between first and second marriages were 4.6 years and 2.5 years, respectively. She also quotes, with approval, Landis's statement that "the large proportion of divorced persons who remarry so quickly makes one suspect that students of the family . . . have discounted too heavily the notion of the man on the street that most divorces take place so that one or both parties may be free to marry a person already selected."[23]

Acknowledging the fact that the vast majority of divorced women eventually marry again, Mott and Moore investigated factors that influence the speed with which they remarry.[24] They found that women had a higher probability of remarrying during the first year following divorce if they were not in the labor force, lived in nonurban areas, had lower education, and had no children. The obvious conclusion is that better educated, employed women have more viable options open to them.

The interval from widowhood to remarriage varies both by sex and age. Widowers remarry sooner than widows, and the disparity increases

21. Paul H. Jacobson, *American Marriage and Divorce*, New York: Rinehart, 1959, pp. 69–70.
22. Paul C. Glick, "A Demographer Looks at American Families," *Journal of Marriage and the Family* 37 (Feb. 1975), p. 17.
23. Paul H. Landis, "Sequential Marriage," *Journal of Home Economics* (Oct. 1950), p. 626, as quoted in Bernard, *op. cit.*, p. 66.
24. Frank L. Mott and Sylvia F. Moore, "The Tempo of Remarriage Among Young American Women," *Journal of Marriage and the Family* 45 (May 1983), pp. 427–36.

with age. In Bernard's 2009 remarriages, the average interval was 3.4 years for 543 widowers and 6.2 years for 445 widows.

Courtship and Wedding Behavior in Remarriages

Hollingshead studied 900 couples, 715 of whom were being married for the first time and 185 of whom had at least one partner remarrying. The courtship pattern was determined, more than by anything else, by whether the woman had been married before. Women who had been married before had courtships, before engagement, of about one-year's duration. Where the woman had not been married before, the pre-engagement courtship lasted an average of almost a year and a half, irrespective of whether the man had been married before. Similarly, women who were remarrying were less likely to have a formal engagement, were less likely to receive an engagement ring, and, if engaged, were likely to be engaged for a shorter time.

Wedding behavior also varied more according to whether the bride was remarrying than according to whether the groom was remarrying. Only about 5 percent of remarrying brides had formal weddings and only 20 to 25 percent had church weddings. Four fifths of the first weddings were church weddings, and 45 percent of those where a previously married man was marrying a single woman were church weddings. In addition, there were fewer wedding guests and the wife's family was much less likely to pay for the wedding if she were remarrying.[25]

THE SUCCESS OF REMARRIAGES

It is very difficult to estimate the success of remarriages. What criteria are we to use? Divorce rates? Duration of marriage to divorce? Marital-happiness estimates? Marital-adjustment scores? Achievement in other areas of life? There is no agreement on what good remarriages are, any more than there is agreement on what good first marriages are. In general, the data on success in remarriage are even scantier than those available for first marriages.

Divorce from Remarriage

An early study by Monahan, using data for Iowa for the years 1953–1955, reported divorce rates from second marriages to be twice as high as those from first marriages. Where one of the partners had been di-

---

25. August B. Hollingshead, "Marital Status and Wedding Behavior," *Marriage and Family Living* 14 (Nov. 1952), p. 310. See also Ersel E. Le Masters, "The Courtship of Older Persons," *Midwest Sociologist* 20 (Dec. 1957).

vorced twice before, the rate of divorce from the third marriage was
higher yet.[26] This led to the conclusion that marital adjustment involves
a rigorous selection process and that failure to make the necessary adjustment lessens the probability that they will be made in a second marriage. Failure a second time further lessens the probability of permanence
in a third marriage, and so on. Monahan also found that the duration to
divorce is shorter in second marriages than in first marriages, and it is
shorter yet in third marriages.[27]

The early Iowa data did not show the same high divorce rates for
those who remarried following widowhood. In fact, divorce rates among
the previously widowed were even lower than those from first marriages. Two possibilities were suggested. First, widowed persons often
are reasonably well-adjusted people whose prior experience with marriage was not too bad. Although there are malcontents and bitterly unhappy people among the widowed, they are fewer than in the general
population. Such persons may approach remarriage with values, attitudes, and skills that predispose them to satisfaction in their new relationships. Second, the divorce rate from remarriages of previously widowed persons must also reflect the older ages of such persons. Even
remarried couples who are unhappy are not so likely to seek divorce as
younger persons would be.

Monahan's data on high divorce rates among the previously divorced
were challenged for a few years in the late 1960s when it appeared that
the rates might be lower than expected. The experience of the 1970s,
however, again showed that divorce rates from remarriages are somewhat
higher than those from first marriages.[28] Within the first five years, as
many as 44 percent of remarriages occurring today may end in divorce.[29]

Adjustment in Remarriages

A number of studies have provided data on the quality of remarriages.
Locke, in predicting adjustment by comparing happily married with
divorced persons, secured data from 21 happily married persons who

26. Thomas P. Monahan, "The Changing Nature and Instability of Remarriages," *Eugenics Quarterly* 5 (June 1958), pp. 73–85.
27. Thomas P. Monahan, "The Duration of Marriage to Divorce: Second Marriages and
Migratory Types," *Marriage and Family Living* 21 (May 1959), pp. 134–38. Remarriages
also are more likely to be interreligious marriages. See Erich Rosenthal, "Divorce and
Religious Intermarriage: The Effect of Previous Marital Status upon Subsequent Marital
Behavior," *Journal of Marriage and the Family* 32 (Aug. 1970), pp. 435–40.
28. Carter and Glick, *op. cit.,* p. 396.
29. Marie Witkin Kargman, "Stepchild Support Obligations of Stepparents," *Family Relations* 32 (April 1983), pp. 231–38.

had remarried following widowhood and from 146 divorced persons who had remarried. He tested the hypothesis that bereaved and divorced persons are less well adjusted in their second marriages than once-married people are in their first marriages.[30] He reasoned that widowed persons in remarriages would idealize their former mates and find that their present mates suffered by comparison. The data, however, did not support this reasoning. Locke was forced to conclude that remarriages after widowhood are as happy as first marriages. He explained this finding as follows. Widowed and then-remarried persons probably are highly adaptable or they would not have entered their second marriages; if they are more adaptable, they should adjust to their second marriages in spite of idealization of the deceased spouse.

Turning to the marital adjustments of the 146 persons remarried following divorce, Locke found that approximately 45 percent rated their second marriages to be "very happy," and another 32 percent said they were "happy." Only 11 percent reported their second marriages to be "unhappy" or "very unhappy." Locke concluded that divorced persons are fairly good risks for subsequent marriages.

Locke and Klausner reported on a smaller study comparing 47 divorced and remarried persons with 64 once-married persons in Los Angeles. They found that almost equal proportions of the remarried and once-married groups fell into "good" and "fair" marital-adjustment categories.[31]

The study by Goode of 425 Detroit mothers also yielded data on the quality of remarriages in relation to the perceived quality of these same women's first marriages. Goode points out that his data on adjustment in remarriage are not definitive because none of these women had been remarried for longer than two years. He also emphasized that the most relevant comparison for previously divorced persons is not between the quality of their remarriages and the quality of all first marriages but between their own first and second marriages.

A full 87 percent of the women in Goode's sample who had remarried claimed that their second marriages were "much better" than their first ones, and an additional 8 percent said that their second marriages were "a little better."[32] The high value placed on their remarriages also was shown when they replied to the question, "Would you try to tell me how you think your life would be today, in general, if you hadn't

30. Harvey J. Locke, *Predicting Adjustment in Marriage: A Comparison of a Divorced and a Happily Married Group*, New York: Holt, 1951, pp. 298–309.

31. Harvey J. Locke and William J. Klausner, "Marital Adjustment of Divorced Persons in Subsequent Marriages," *Sociology and Social Research* 33 (Nov. 1948), pp. 97–101.

32. William J. Goode, *After Divorce*, Glencoe, Ill.: The Free Press, 1956, pp. 331–42.

got a divorce?" In reply, 82 percent said that things would have been "worse" or "the same" as during the first marriage.

Finally, Bernard analyzed remarriages thoroughly in connection with her study of the entire remarried population in Utopolis. First, she points out that divorce is a learned pattern and that persons who have overcome the societal taboo and been through the experience once may be more likely to use divorce again if their remarriages do not measure up to high standards. According to this point of view, remarried persons may demand more from their new marriages and may more quickly dissolve them if their high expectations are not fulfilled. Thus, remarriages that survive may be relatively more satisfying than most first marriages.[33]

Many analyses of divorce and remarriage have emphasized the stability of basic personality characteristics and the apparent contribution of personality problems to divorce. When we talk about the divorce-prone this is what we mean. On the other hand, even if basic personality does not change—and this assumption is being more frequently questioned—the way in which personality is expressed in behavior certainly does change over time. Bernard analyzed three factors that may contribute to greater success in remarriages.

First, an unhappy first marriage may be painful, but it contributes directly to the success of the second one. People learn, through divorce, something about what produced the failure of their marriages. Remarried persons are also likely to have increased their competence in interpersonal relationships, to have acquired more of such elusive qualities as maturity, wisdom, and tolerance. Although remarried persons may not compare favorably with the general population in these characteristics, they often are better prepared to make a success of their second marriages than they were to be successful in their first ones.

Second, failure in a first marriage often produces changes in motivation. Here we encounter a paradox. We have already stated that one divorce makes a second one easier and more acceptable. At the same time, failure in a first marriage appears to make many people determined and even desperate to succeed in the second one. Men and women who remain basically committed to family life in spite of divorce may acquire a near all-conquering will to succeed in the second one. The motivation

33. *Ibid*. Bernard *op. cit.*, pp. 270–72. See also Norval D. Glenn and Charles N. Weaver, "The Marital Happiness of Remarried Divorced Persons," *Journal of Marriage and the Family* 39 (May 1977), pp. 331–37; Anne Goetting, "The Six Stations of Remarriage: Developmental Tasks of Remarriage After Divorce," *Family Relations* 31 (April 1982), pp. 213–22; and Margaret Nelson and Gordon K. Nelson, "Problems of Equity in the Reconstituted Family: A Social Exchange Analysis," *Family Relations* 31 (April 1982), pp. 223–31.

may be mixed: the will to achieve a stable family life and the will to re-move the stigma of failure; but it may also be quite effective.

Finally, the changes associated with aging may work to the benefit of partners in remarriages. Most persons at the time of remarriage have worked through—as much as they ever will—the rebelliousness and ir-responsibility of youth. If people approaching middle age are unlikely ever to achieve the passionate commitment to one another of youth, they are more likely to accept one another as they are and not to view each flaw in one another as a catastrophe. The comfort and security that probably are more characteristic of marriage during the middle years may produce deep and lasting satisfaction.[34]

There appears to be a sex differential in regard to happiness with re-marriage. White found that remarried men are happier than men in in-tact first families. Comparing remarried women with women in intact first marriages, the opposite is true; remarried women are less happy with their lives than are once-married women. The author explains these findings by the fact that divorced women very often find it difficult to care for themselves financially and may enter marriage at least partially for financial security.[35]

Finally, Spanier and Furstenberg conducted a longitudinal study to discover if those who remarry shortly after divorce are better off than those who delay remarrying. The 180 subjects in the study were ques-tioned at the time of separation and again about three years later. There were no significant differences in well-being between those who had re-married and those who had not. Regardless of marital status, most sub-jects reported greater well-being three to four years following sepa-ration.[36]

THE EFFECTS OF REMARRIAGE ON CHILDREN

Among Bernard's 2009 remarriages, 60 percent of both men and women who remarried following divorce had children by their first marriages; among those who remarried following widowhood, from 75 to 80 per-cent had children by first marriages. The average number of children was between one and two. Comparing stepchildren with biological and adopted children, Bachrach found that stepchildren tend to be older, to

34. Bernard, *op. cit.*

35. Lynn K. White, "Sex Differentials in the Effect of Remarriage on Global Happi-ness," *Journal of Marriage and the Family* 4 (Nov. 1979), pp. 869–76.

36. Graham B. Spanier and Frank F. Furstenberg, Jr., "Remarriage After Divorce: A Longitudinal Analysis of Well-being," *Journal of Marriage and the Family* 44 (Aug. 1982), pp. 709–20.

live in large families, and to have mothers in the labor force.[37] We shall summarize what sociologists have learned about the adjustment of children in the new marriage.

American attitudes toward remarriage are complicated by a widespread negative stereotype of stepparents. The wicked stepmother is prominent in fairy tales; for many people, the word *stepmother* calls forth an image of a cold, harsh figure showing favoritism to her own children over those of her husband and in relation to whom the usual emotions are fear and hatred. The folk characterization of the stepfather is less clear, reflecting the existence of greater numbers of stepmothers than stepfathers. When he does appear, the stepfather often.is an aloof, unconcerned, intolerant person who puts up with his wife's children only because he must do so. With stereotypes such as these and the recent emergence of remarriage as a large-scale phenomenon, it is not surprising that the literature on relationships between stepparents and stepchildren is scanty.

One of the earliest studies was Nye's study of 780 boys and girls in high school in the state of Washington. He compared children in broken, unhappy unbroken, and reconstituted families and found little evidence of special problems between stepparents and stepchildren. Instead he found few differences in adjustment to broken homes, to homes with only one parent, and homes reconstituted through remarriage. In all three cases, the adjustment of children was better than in unhappy, unbroken homes. The conclusion was reached that "there are differences between the two categories of families, with the differences favoring the 'reconstructed' family including a stepparent, or the 'partial' family composed of one parent and child or children."[38]

A second study gathered data from 2145 junior or senior high school students in Washington, Ohio, and North Carolina. Using affection for parents and stepparents and feelings of discrimination and rejection as criteria, this study supported the view that reconstituted families provide a less favorable environment for children than do intact families. The adjustment of children toward stepparents was poorer than toward the real parent of the same sex. Adjustment to stepfathers usually was better than adjustment to stepmothers. Moreover, stepparents more ofen were believed to discriminate, and stepchildren were more likely to feel rejected both by the natural parent and the stepparent.[39]

Although these studies are not directly comparable, there is no doubt

37. Christine A. Bachrach, "Children in Families: Characteristics of Biological, Step-, and Adopted Children," *Journal of Marriage and the Family* 45 (Feb. 1983), pp. 171–79.
38. F. Ivan Nye, "Child Adjustment in Broken and in Unhappy Unbroken Homes," *Marriage and Family Living* 19 (Nov. 1957), pp. 356–61.
39. Charles E. Bowerman and Donald P. Irish, "Some Relationships of Stepchildren to Their Parents," *Marriage and Family Living* 24 (May 1962), pp. 113–21.

that if their findings do not conflict directly, at least they present quite different segments of reality. The hypothesis is suggested that children experience generally the best adjustment in intact homes, that there are more adjustment problems in reconstructed homes, and still more adjustment problems in unhappy but structurally intact homes.

This also is suggested by Burchinal's research in Iowa. He classified families into five types: unbroken families, broken families headed by the mother, and three types of reconstituted families—those consisting of fathers and stepmothers, those consisting of stepfathers and mothers, and those in which both parents had divorced and remarried. Measures of personality adjustment and social relationships were then compared among students in the five family types.[40] In general, the findings were of no striking differences in the adjustment of children in the five family types. There were no differences on personality measures, in participation in school or community activities, in school grade-point averages, in the number of schoolmates the respondent thought liked him or her, in attitudes toward school, or, among girls, how many of their schoolmates they liked. A few differences appeared. Students from unbroken homes were absent less often from school and those from broken homes were absent more often. It was also found that boys living with their fathers and stepmothers reported liking fewer of their schoolmates.

Goode points out that even when we establish a relationship between divorce and/or remarriage and certain personality or social characteristics of children, we still have not determined that divorce and remarriage have any effect on children. The problems, whatever they may be, may be caused by the same factors that predisposed the parents to divorce in the first place. The establishment of cause-and-effect relationships simply has not been done yet.

Goode's analysis indicated that most of the remarried mothers were satisfied with their children's adjustment. He concludes that remarriage tends to regularize the position of the children following whatever trauma was associated with the divorce and that, in most ways, reconstituted families are similar to unbroken families. Tensions between children and the new parent decrease with time.[41]

Another study of a random sample of remarried parents, their children, and stepchildren in Cleveland, Ohio, calculated total Parent-Child Relationship Scores. To the surprise of the researcher, 18 percent of the families rated "poor" on this scale, and 18 percent rated "good," whereas

40. Lee G. Burchinal, "Characteristics of Adolescents from Unbroken, Broken, and Reconstituted Families," *Journal of Marriage and the Family* 26 (Feb. 1964), pp. 44–51.
41. Goode, *op. cit.*, pp. 307, 339–41. See also Anne Goetting, "The Relative Strength of the Husband-Wife and Parent-Child Dyads in Remarriage: A Test of the Hsu Model," *Journal of Comparative Family Studies* 14 (Spring 1983), pp. 117–28.

a huge 64 percent rated "excellent." Relationships among the two sets of children in these families were not quite as good, but 24 percent still rated "excellent," 38 percent rated "good," and another 38 percent rated "poor."[42]

One recent study compared 122 children in families with stepfathers with 2747 children living with their natural parents. Comparisons were made on 68 separate social and social psychological characteristics. In the words of the researchers, no substantial differences were found. Children's experiences in reconstituted families can be predominantly positive, predominantly negative, or mixed.[43]

Lutz found that the issue most problematic to stepchildren centered, not on stepparents, but rather on the relationship between the natural parents. Stepchildren aged 12 to 18 were questioned concerning the issues they found most stressful in stepfamily living. "Divided loyalty" was the most common complaint; subjects felt a great deal of stress when they were caught in the middle of the two natural parents or when one natural parent spoke badly of the other.[44]

Bernard reports on a study in which Bernreuter Personality Inventory scores were obtained for 59 young men and women who lived in families where there had been a remarriage. Because norms on this test are available for college students, the scores of the children of remarriages could be measured against those norms. On none of the three scores— stability, self-sufficiency, or dominance—did the children of remarriages differ from the general college population. When tests were made separately for remarriages following divorce and bereavement, again no differences were found. The data did not support the view that divorce leaves children more disturbed than does bereavement.[45]

Concluding that most remarriages are not harmful to children, Bernard explains this in terms of three factors: (1) the attitudes of the children to the remarriage, (2) the new parent as a salvaging force, and (3) the inherent resiliency of human nature. The Utopolis data showed that most children, whether the first marriage was broken by divorce or death, are in favor of the remarriage of the parent with whom they are living. Even adult children generally support their parents' remarriages.

42. Lucille Duberman, "Step-Kin Relationships," *Journal of Marriage and the Family* 35 (May 1973), pp. 283–92.
43. Kenneth L. Wilson, Louis A. Zurcher, Diana Claire McAdams, and Russell L. Curtis, "Stepfathers and Stepchildren: An Exploratory Analysis from Two National Surveys," *Journal of Marriage and the Family* 37 (Aug. 1975), pp. 526–36. See also E. M. Rallings, "The Special Role of Stepfather," *Family Coordinator* 25 (Oct. 1976), pp. 445–49; Diane Reinhart Kompara, "Difficulties in the Socialization Process of Stepparenting," *Family Relations* 29 (Jan. 1980), pp. 69–73.
44. Patricia Lutz, "The Stepfamily: An Adolescent Perspective," *Family Relations* 32 (July 1983), pp. 367–75.
45. Bernard, *op. cit.*, pp. 306–11.

The only exceptions were found where custody of the children alternated between the parents and where the remarriage of a father threatened the children's interest in his property.

The stereotype of the unfeeling stepparent was contradicted in the Utopolis data by both men and women who provided wisdom, love, and understanding to help their stepchildren compensate for the trauma of divorce. Interestingly, these effects were found more often in remarriages following divorce than in those following widowhood. The stepparent replacing a decreased parent was more likely to be resented than the stepparent replacing a divorced parent.

Finally, Bernard emphasizes the inherent toughness of the human organism. She points out that most persons, whether their parents' marriages have broken or not, undergo traumatic childhood experiences. Most persons cope effectively with them and may even emerge stronger for them. Only when there is a compounding of such experiences is personality damage likely. It stands to reason that the effects of remarriage should be different in the lives of children whose lives otherwise are safe and secure, than in lower-economic groups whose problems are compounded by minority-group status and social and personal pathologies of other sorts. Perhaps the greatest increases in our understanding of the effects of remarriage on children will come when we are able successfully to control for economic status.

THE DYNAMICS OF REMARRIAGES

We have described remarriage analytically and statistically. When we are dealing with phenomena that we have been intimately exposed to over long periods of time, most of us can apply broad generalizations to the actual experiences of living men and women. When we come to remarriage, however, only a minority of college students have had direct, sustained experience. Remarriage to most 20 year olds convinced that their own marriages will be successful and lifelong, is about as academic as the family system of a preliterate society. To put some descriptive meat on the statistical bones, let us look at the dynamics of remarriage.

The Dynamics of Courtship

Courtship among persons who are remarrying—particularly women—tends to be considerably shorter than among the young. Where a triangle situation existed before divorce, this may help explain the short courtship, but this is not the major explanation. First is the shorter courtships among remarrying women than among remarrying men. Stripped of its sentimental overtones, courtship may, in some instances, be de-

scribed as convincing the woman to enter a sanctioned sexual relationship. Where the woman is sexually inexperienced, this involves cir-
cumlocution; both partners may approach warily the issue of sex. In
remarriage, however, both the man and the woman know the woman to
be sexually experienced. The man feels a freedom to approach her that
may have been difficult before a first marriage. For the woman, whatever taboos existed for sex have long since been overcome. The woman
realizes that she has as much right to sexual satisfaction as the man.

Not that courtship before remarriage becomes an orgy. Far from it.
The tonicity and the erotic content of the relationship are likely to be
lower than among the previously unmarried. The couple are older, and
their sexual needs may be less frequent and less imperious than among
younger people. The couple also have had enough experience to be better able to place sex in proportion to other aspects of marriage. Thus,
we have a paradox. Courtship before remarriage quickly becomes sexually explicit, and the percentage of couples who have intercourse is
extremely high. Yet having had intercourse is not likely to lead to guilt
or to alter seriously the probability of marriage. Sex, once a couple has
had intercourse, is likely to occupy less of the time and attention of the
couple than if they were younger.

Nor should sex be singled out as *the* area in which couples before remarriage are more intimate. They tend to anticipate most of the conditions of married life. Although young couples ordinarily go out for a
hamburger or a meal as part of their dating activities, older couples are
likely to take a good portion of their evening meals at home. Among
other things, the man is looking for someone to cook his meals. The
woman, who is used to cooking for other people may find satisfaction
in doing so. She may also assume some responsibility for his clothing and
his living quraters—doing laundry, mending, and even cleaning for him.
In turn the man often assumes some financial responsibility for the
woman. He may buy groceries, he may buy clothing for her in a way
that would be considered to be in bad taste if done by a younger man
for a young woman. He may even make a regular financial contribution
to her household.

Where there are children, they may figure prominently in the courtship. If marriage is to occur, the man and the woman must woo one another's children. Marriage may occur over the opposition of children,
but it is unlikely and, in the eyes of both partners, undesirable. Consequently, both partners are likely to move into quasi-parental roles in
relation to any young children the other may have. These roles include
efforts at the development of affection, but they also include everything
from changing diapers, to bathing, to spanking, and to having the children accompany their parents on dates.

There are many variations of course. When the couples are younger and there are no children, their courtships may be virtually indistinguishable from those of persons marrying for the first time. At the other extreme, where there are grown children (particularly of the man) who fear the loss of property interests if there is a remarriage, the courtship may be complicated by outside resistance. Among the divorced and widowed, also, are to be found people who want companionship but are loath to remarry. Among them, the courtship may reach a plateau where one or both are relatively comfortable and may remain there over a long time. Some may even decide to live together without marriage.

Remarriages, once decided on, may come about more quickly and with less fanfare than first marriages. Weddings are less likely to be church weddings, guests usually are fewer, and the ceremony is more likely to be performed by a civil official. There is less aura of initiation into a new experience, and although it may not be recognized, the role of the principals looms much larger in the remarriage ceremony. In first marriages, the emphasis is more on the ritual—on the ceremony itself—and the young man and woman are somewhat dwarfed by the pomp and mysticism. In second marriages, by contrast, the ceremony often is viewed simply as giving sanction to a relationship that already exists or would exist whether or not official provision were made for it.

The Dynamics of Marital Adjustment

Adjustment in remarriages is both like and unlike adjustment in first marriages. There is the need to establish new habits and roles. Adjustments must be worked out in each of the conventional areas—sex, in-laws, money, friends, religion, and so on. But there are differences too.

At least one of the partners is not a beginner—there is a storehouse of knowledge and experience on which to draw. The spouses are likely to be older and to have worked through the authority problems that are so prominent in young adulthood. But there are scars, too, resulting from the death or divorce that made the remarriage possible. Usually, there are more people involved; in addition to the primary families of the new spouses, there may be up to two former spouses and two sets of children. If nothing else, most remarriages are more crowded than most first marriages.

The initial adjustments probably are made more quickly in remarriages. As already described, quasi-marital and quasi-parental roles are likely to have been established before the ceremony. Too, the spouses are less threatened by the moods of their partners. Middle-aged people often know, as younger people seldom can, that the partner's being too tired to go out or to have sex or being just grouchy does not reflect on oneself. On the other hand, what emotional crises do develop early in remarriages—and all of the conventional ones do to some degree—have more potential for disrupting the marriage. Paradoxically, remarried couples both adjust quicker and divorce quicker than first-married couples.

Sexual Adjustment. Sexual adjustment probably binds the pair together more comfortably than in first marriages. With the greater likelihood of sex before marriage, remarriages may be more selective; it is difficult to imagine middle-aged people entering a marriage when they think that the sexual relationship will not be satisfactory.[46] And the sexual desires of husbands and wives are more likely to be comparable in older marriages. The man's needs typically have been declining with age,[47] whereas the woman's capacity has been increasing. Both are more likely to be comfortable with their own bodies and less concerned about "performance."

No figures are available on the frequency of marital intercourse by age and remarried status, but we might guess that, age for age, the frequency of intercourse is higher in remarriages than in first marriages. There are at least two reasons for this. First, at a given age level, the remarriages will be of shorter duration. Novelty gives stimulus to sexual participation; in remarriages there has been less time for the novelty to wear off. Second, sexual participation in remarriage is less likely to suffer the debilitating effects of differences in sexual need and of being used as a focus for conflicts originating in other areas of marriage.

Social Life. In some other areas, remarriages are more likely to suffer some disadvantage. The social life of remarried couples, for example, often has to undergo considerable reorganization. The specific patterns may vary according to whether one or both partners are being remarried and whether the new marriage follows death or divorce.

In many instances, the new couple will encounter resistance from friends. Friends of a first-married man or woman, entering marriage with someone who has been married before, may think the match inappropriate and convey their distaste to the couple. Or, the widowed person who has remarried may find that acquaintances interpret it as be-

---

46. Benjamin Schlesinger, "Remarriage as Family Reorganization for Divorced Persons—A Canadian Study," *Journal of Comparative Family Studies* 1 (Autumn 1970), pp. 101–18.

47. That the sexual needs of men decline with age should not be overemphasized. Several studies have shown that many males remain sexually active well into old age. A survey by *Sexology* magazine reported that 70 percent of the married men over 65 years of age engaged in intercourse regularly. See William H. Masters and Virginia E. Johnson, *Human Sexual Response*, Boston: Little, Brown, 1966, pp. 248–49.

trayal of the deceased spouse. Those who remarry following divorce are even more likely to encounter disapproval. Even the "innocent party" who did not want the divorce and who has been the object of sympathy may suddenly find himself or herself the object of disapproval. For the more aggressive partner in the divorce or where there has been a triangle, there is almost certain to be censure from outsiders.

Most remarried couples attempt to cope, for a time, with the cool attitudes of their social groups, and some eventually win approval for the new marriage. Strains, however, are produced in the marriage. It is not pleasant to find oneself disapproved by people whose opinions have mattered in the past. Whether the couple attempt to ignore such disapproval, or whether they acknowledge it openly, their relationship becomes a source of pain to them.

Most couples solve the problem to some degree by giving up some old friendships and making new ones among people who were not acquainted with the former marriage(s) and who accept the new relationship for what it is. It is not simple to do this however. For the months or years that the change takes, remarried couples suffer some disability that most first-married couples do not. A significant number of couples find it necessary either to change jobs, to move away, or both to escape the offended feelings of former associates.

Adjustment to Former Partners. In a real sense, the first marriage partners of the new spouses are parties to the remarriage also. Although they are not physically present, they intrude in subtle and not-so-subtle ways. Where one of the parties in the new marriage has been widowed, the spouse may find himself or herself competing with the former partner. Analyses of bereavement have indicated a tendency—particularly where the former marriage was happy, but even when it was not sasisfactory— for the surviving spouse to build up an idealized image of the deceased partner. The earlier unpleasantnesses are forgotten, whereas the good things are remembered, and the deceased spouse takes on an image larger than life. In remarriage, the new spouse, however desirable he or she may be, may be compared with this idealized image and found wanting.

In extreme cases, there may be numerous daily reminders of the former relationship. The new spouse may actually move into the home formerly shared with the deceased partner. Out of habit, he or she may occasionally be called by the former partner's name. Or there may be photographs of the former partner, unthinkingly displayed, or mementoes of the former life that are treasured to the distress of the new spouse. The competition with memories is particularly difficult because the norms of our society hold that one should not feel animosity toward a deceased person. The new spouse must woo his or her partner away from memories without appearing to be doing so.

When the remarriage has followed divorce, one must cope directly with the former spouse rather than with memories. If the former spouse was the reluctant partner in the divorce, he or she may carry a torch and may literally be a rival in the new relationship. There are instances of former spouses waging, for months and years, battles to regain their partners. Although the probability of the divorced spouse's being successful is small, considerable threat is likely to be felt by the new spouse.

Intrusion by the former spouse is likely, whether or not there remains emotional attraction, when there are children. If the new marriage has custody of the children, the former spouse usually must be permitted some entrée for visits. If the former spouse has custody, then he or she must be placated in order that continuing contacts with the children not be jeopardized. The necessity for such continuing contacts affords an aggrieved former spouse the opportunity to make demands that annoy the new partners and create strain.

Becoming a New Family. Adjustments in remarriages tend to be most complicated when there are children present from one or both of the preceding marriages. For Utopolis, Bernard found that 21.5 percent of the men and 23.4 percent of the women had children by a previous marriage, and in 5.6 percent of the cases both the new husband and wife had children. Following divorce, the typical situation was for a mother and her children to secure a new husband and father. Following widowhood, on the other hand, it was typically a father and his children who secured a new wife and mother.[48]

Marital adjustment may be viewed as a process whereby the separate value systems, attitudes, and habit patterns of the spouses yield to a new and joint way of life. That many people do not give up old patterns easily is illustrated by the greater prevalence of conflict early in most marriages. In remarriages with children, the situation is more complicated because there are more people involved. Beyond that, the presence of other people, who may be drawn into alliances wittingly or unwittingly, may strengthen one's resistance to change and prolong the time required for adjustment to occur.

A wedding ceremony, by itself, does little to weld two families into one. Instead what happens is that the two families take up common resi-

48. Bernard, *op. cit.*, pp. 211–12. See also Thomas J. Espenshade and Rachel Eisenberg Braun, "Life Course Analysis and Multistate Demography: An Application to Marriage, Divorce, and Remarriage," *Journal of Marriage and the Family* 44 (Nov. 1982), pp. 1025–36.

dence, but they attempt unknowingly to continue their old ways of life. This is almost bound to bring them into conflict. It happens in different ways.

First, when there are children, they share with their natural parent a host of experiences and memories not shared by the other partner and his or her children. In normal conversation, and without any intent of so doing, one of the partners tends to be relegated to the role of outsider. He or she has not shared the common experiences, be they joyous, sentimental, or sad. The partner who is left out, unless he or she is exceptionally patient and wise, may react defensively. He or she may try to compete for the center of attention, may retaliate by attacking the group or one of its members, or may withdraw emotionally and set the family on an alienation course.

More directly, there is a tendency for alliances to develop within the family. Family ties are particularistic, and the special consideration that has grown up between a parent and children over the years is not easily extended to the new spouse and his or her children. Each partner justifiably feels that the other shows favoritism to his own natural children. It takes wisdom for the couple to realize what is happening and to prevent it from developing into a destructively rivalrous situation.

The potential for conflicts in reconstituted families is both greater and less than in first marriages. The tolerance that comes with age and experience must be balanced against the involvement of children in whatever conflict exists; the parents may be moved to greater wisdom by having jointly to deal with the demands made by their children, and, at the same time, the children may carry the fray with a vigor that only the young possess.

Just as earlier shared family experiences work against the solidarity of the new family, so does time and new experience work for it. For months, or years, customary remembrances go back to a time when this family did not exist. But eventually the shared experiences come to outweigh the separate experiences, and the group remembers the things that "we" did together or which happened to "us." Those "other things" happened a long time ago and no longer seem real or important.

Similarly, a new set of affectional relationships develops. A stepparent may come to be as cherished as the natural parent, and the relationship may draw special strength from the fact that it was worked out without the accident of birth. The stepparent, too, may cease to distinguish between my children, your children, and our children. The terms "Mom" and "Dad," and "son" and "daughter," may apply as naturally to sociological children as to biological ones. With or without benefit of legal adoption, a common family culture comes into existence.

At what point reconstituted families become more like than unlike original families it is impossible to say. It would be absurd to state that differences do not continue to exist. The relative strengths and problems of reconstituted and original families is a topic that is just beginning to be explored.[49]

SUMMARY

Remarriages are not a homogeneous phenomenon. One or both partners may be remarrying. The remarriage may follow bereavement, or divorce, or both. There may or may not be children from one or both of the earlier marriages.

Until about the end of World War I, remarriage in the United States was uncommon, and most of it took place following widowhood. As divorce rates rose, however, so did rates of remarriage following divorce. Currently, about 44 percent of all marriages are remarriages of one or both partners.

Living in one-parent families for a while commonly occurs between marital dissolution and remarriage. Mother-headed families are much more numerous than father-headed ones, and the number of such families has been increasing rapidly.

Most divorced persons remarry. In fact, age for age, divorced persons have higher probabilities of remarrying than single persons do of marrying the first time. Again, age for age, widowed persons are more likely to wed than single persons are. Divorced persons have the highest probabilities of marrying, widows and widowers come next, and single persons have the poorest chances of all. Divorced and widowed men also have greater probabilities of remarriage than divorcees and widows do.

Intervals to remarriage tend to be relatively short and to be shorter following divorce than bereavement. Up to three fourths of divorced persons remarry within five years. Remarriages generally follow shorter courtships, more are civil ceremonies, and there is less pomp and formality than in first weddings. The fact of remarriage for the woman is more important in determining the type of courtship and wedding than is the remarriage of the man.

Early studies showed high divorce rates among couples who had remarried following earlier divorces but not among those who had been widowed. More recent studies have confirmed the fact that remarriages have slightly higher divorce rates than first marriages.

Studies of adjustment among remarried couples yield different findings. Happiness ratings and marital-adjustment scores generally do not

49. See Stan L. Albrecht, "Correlates of Marital Happiness Among the Remarried," *Journal of Marriage and the Family* 41 (Nov. 1979), pp. 857–67; and Barbara Fishman, "The Economic Behavior of Stepfamilies," *Family Relations* 32 (July 1983), pp. 359–66.

show remarriages to be less satisfactory than first marriages. The majority of remarried persons state that their second marriages are better than their first ones. Even if basic personality structure is not amenable to change, the way in which personality is expressed in behavior may change in second marriages. Three factors working to make second marriages successful are the learning that occurred during the first marriage, changes in motivation that follow an unsuccessful first marriage, and changes associated with increasing age and maturity.

Research into the effects of remarriage on children indicates that adjustment is better than in broken homes or emotionally broken homes but perhaps not so good as in happy, intact homes. Most remarried mothers report themselves to be satisfied with their children's adjustment, and personality testing of such children generally fails to show important differences between them and children from intact homes. Children find antagonism between the natural parents to be the most stressful part of stepfamily life.

The dynamics of courtship and adjustment in remarriage differ from those in first marriages. Before remarriage, couples are more likely to be intimate sexually but may devote less attention to sex than first-marrying couples do. Also, before remarriage, couples may play quasi-marital roles in different areas of life and may assume quasi-parental roles as well.

Adjustment in remarriages is similar in many ways to adjustment in first marriages. There are the same general areas in which adjustment must be made, and the new couple must establish a common way of life. Adjustment differs from that in first marriages too. Neither of the pair may be beginners and there may be more in-laws and children to be dealt with. Emotional crises may develop more quickly, and they may be resolved more quickly or may rapidly lead to divorce.

The reorganization of the couple's social life may be troubling initially. Some rejection by former friends often is encountered and, thus, some frustration experienced. Part of the solution usually involves making new friends. Sometimes, too, the problem is alleviated by moving to a new location and/or taking a new job.

Then there are former marital partners who intrude on the new relationship. Deceased former spouses intrude symbolically, and divorced partners often intrude directly. Particularly where there are children from a former marriage, contacts must be maintained with the divorced spouse.

Adjustment in remarriages is most complicated when there are children present from a former marriage. The parent and his or her children inevitably share with one another more than they do with the new spouse. This can lead to rivalry or emotional withdrawal. In extreme cases, alliances may develop within the new family that threaten its solidarity. With time, however, these divisive forces tend to yield to the accumulating shared experience in the new family and to the developing affectional relationships within it. Remarriages remain different from first marriages, but the nature of the continuing differences has not yet been analyzed adequately.

SUGGESTED READINGS

Cantor, Dorothy W., and Drake, Ellen A., *Divorced Parents and Their Children*, New York: Springer, 1983. Geared toward helping family practitioners lessen the emotional impact of divorce on children.

Duberman, Lucile, *The Reconstituted Family: A Study of Remarried Couples and Their Children*, Chicago: Nelson-Hall Publications, 1975. A report of research by a scholar who is, herself, a member of a reconstituted family.

Capaldi, Frederick, and McRae, Barbara, *Stepfamilies: A Cooperative Responsibility*, New York: New Viewpoints, 1979. A practical guide for stepparents and for single parents who are considering remarriage.

Ross, Heather L., and Sawhill, Isabel V., *Time of Transition: The Growth of Families Headed by Women*, Washington, D.C.: Urban Institute, 1975. A detailed empirical analysis of the impact of rising divorce rates and government policy on the growth of mother-headed families.

Mayleas, Davidyne, *Rewedded Bliss: Alimony, Incest, Ex-spouses, and Other Domestic Blessings*, New York: Basic Books, 1977. An unusually well-written and perceptive account of the trials, tribulations, and rewards of "synergistic" families.

FILMS

Single Parent (American Personnel and Guidance Association, 2 Skyline Place, Suite 400, 5203 Leesburg Pike, Falls Church, Va. 22041), 22 minutes. Discusses issues common to single-parent homes and the problems that can arise within different families facing these issues.

Stepparenting: New Families, Old Ties (Polymorph Films, 331 Newbury Street, Boston, Mass. 02115), 25 minutes. Members of a stepparent support group talk of the situations they encounter and how they overcome obstacles. Documentary sequences in the lives of stepfamilies.

QUESTIONS AND PROJECTS

1. Specify two different ways in which living in one-parent families is transitional.

2. The term *remarriage* refers to a number of different marriage types. Specify as many types of remarriage as you can.

3. What is the approximate incidence of remarriage in the United States? Specify the relationship between age and previous marital status to patterns of remarriage.

4. What intervals ordinarily occur between death of a spouse or divorce and remarriage? What are the probabilities that divorced and widowed persons will remarry as compared to the probability that single people will marry?

5. What differences exist in length of courtship and type of wedding between first-marrying and remarrying couples? Which has more influence—the previous marital status of the bride or that of the groom?

6. How does the divorce rate in remarriage compare with that in first marriage?

7. What bases are there for thinking that adjustment in a remarriage may be different from adjustment in the first marriage? What bases are there for thinking that it may not be different?

8. What does research show about the personality adjustment of children in remarriages compared with those living in intact families?

9. How are the dynamics of courtship before remarriage likely to differ from those that precede first marriages? Evaluate the statement: "Remarrying couples are more likely to be preoccupied with sex."

10. Why is reorganization of the couple's social life often necessary after remarriage? How is this likely to come about?

11. How do former partners intrude on the new marriage? What differences exist between remarriages following bereavement and those following divorce? What differences does the presence of children make?

12. What is the meaning of the phrase *becoming a new family* as applied to remarriages? What complications are likely to be encountered here? What factors operate in favor of the new marriage?

Irene B. Bayer, Monkmeyer

20
The Postparental Phase

Meet Jim and Mary Johnson, Americans. Both are 65 years old, married to each other and about to embark on the perilous adventure of old age. This is a crucial year for them, and their success in getting through it—especially for Jim, who has just retired—will have a lot to do with how many more years they live, and how they feel about living. The year is crucial not because they are 65—a number more or less picked out of a hat by the Social Security Administration—but because the bureaucrats who set that benchmark had no idea how important it would become psychologically. Nor had they any idea how many people would be flooding past it today along the poorly marked paths of aging.[1]

If students will refer back to the discussion of the family cycle in Chapter 8, they will see that husbands and wives average less than 50 years of age at the marriage of their youngest child. There are then about 15 years before retirement and as long as 30 years before the marriage is broken by death. The postparental phase of married life is (on the average) as long as all the earlier stages put together. Increases in longevity and prolongation of the family life cycle have drastically altered the way of life of people from their mid-40s to their 70s and 80s.

CONTINUING MARITAL ADJUSTMENT

Not much has been written about relations between husbands and wives after the children have left home, and even less has been substantiated by research. It is widely recognized that the postparental phase gives couples the opportunity to rediscover one another and to do things that

1. Alan Anderson, Jr., " 'Old' Is Not a Four-Letter Word," *Annual Editions: Marriage and the Family 82/83*, Guilford, Conn.: Dushkin Publishing Group, 1982, pp. 140–45.

they could not do earlier because of the children. At the same time, it is feared that the parallel adjustments they have made during the child-rearing years perpetuate themselves after the children have gone. Husbands frequently are portrayed as becoming more engrossed in their work and less available to their wives. Wives in turn are described as lonely and frustrated in attempts to find new meaning in life. Women's clubs and civic duties are seen as providing less than satisfactory outlets.

Unfortunately, we have no information on the proportions of couples who follow different parts of adjustment. There are data, however, on the continuing trend of adjustment after the middle years. The most comprehensive data come from Blood and Wolfe's Detroit-area study and from a study of 312 Minneapolis-area families. Hill's study covered three generations of families and, thus, affords a unique opportunity to compare intergenerational patterns. The grandparent generation were between 60 and 80 years of age, the parents were between 40 and 60, and the married children were from 20 to 30 years old.[2]

Love and Companionship

It will be recalled that studies have shown a drop in marital adjustment and satisfaction, beginning early in marriage and continuing through the middle years. The Detroit data show that the process does not end during the middle years but continues through the postparental years and on into retirement.[3] Satisfaction with love in the relationship continues to decline steadily from a high point reached during the preschool years, whereas satisfaction with companionship shows a modest increase after the children are gone. Thus, there is some basis for the idea that couples turn back toward one another when their children leave home. The most striking thing, however, is that the increase in companionship is so small. It is still lower during the postparental years than during the first 15 years of marriage.[4]

2. Reuben Hill, *et al.*, *Family Development in Three Generations*, Cambridge, Mass.: Schenkman, 1970.
3. The magnitude of this decline should not be overemphasized. Havighurst, for example, has shown that the age period from 40 to 70 constitutes a plateau during which adjustment remains relatively constant. See Robert J. Havighurst, "The Social Competence of Middle Aged People," *Genetic Psychology Monographs* 56 (Nov. 1957), pp. 297–373. Other studies have shown that the postparental but preretirement period is more crucial in the adjustment of wives than of husbands. See Irwin Deutscher, "The Quality of Postparental Life: Definitions of the Situation," *Journal of Marriage and the Family* 26 (Feb. 1964), pp. 52–59.
4. The question of whether marital adjustment improves again in the retirement years still has not been answered satisfactorily. See Stephen A. Anderson, Candyce S. Russell, and Walter R. Schumm, "Perceived Marital Quality and Family Life-Style Categories: A Further Analysis," *Journal of Marriage and the Family* 45 (Feb. 1983), pp. 127–39; Wesley R. Burr, "Satisfaction with Various Aspects of Marriage Over the Life Cycle:

Power Relationships

Other changes accompany the gradual drop in satisfaction with love and companionship. The Detroit data on changes in the power relationship of husband and wife were presented in Chapter 17 and showed that the husband's power rises during the postparental but preretirement years and then falls after he retires. The authors interpret this to mean that the gradual drop in the husband's power during the childrearing years may reflect his increasing preoccupation with his job rather than his family. After departure of the children, his power may increase again because of his wife's realization that he is likely to precede her in death. Still virile and fulfilling his primary role as breadwinner, his power may be enhanced by the wife's realization that she may lose him. Retirement changes drastically the husband's status as income-provider, and may remove much of the prestige that attached to his occupational role. The husband's power during retirement is less than at any other time in the life cycle.

Hill's Mineapolis study provides data on power in relationships of young marrieds, their parents, and their grandparents (Table 20.1). In this case, the respondents were asked to specify who makes final decisions in different areas of decision making; at the same time, interviewers independently rated who did most of the talking, who exercised the most influence, and who had the last word in the joint interview. The reports of the couples differed considerably from the interviewer evaluations.

According to the couples themselves, the vast majority in each generation had egalitarian relationships. The respondents also indicated an

A Random Middle-Class Sample," *Journal of Marriage and the Family* 32 (Feb. 1970), pp. 29-37; Spencer J. Condie and Han T. Doan, "Role Profit and Marital Satisfaction Throughout the Family Life Cycle," *Journal of Comparative Family Studies* 9 (Summer 1978), pp. 257-67; Rosalie Gilford and Vern Bengtson, "Measuring Marital Satisfaction in Three Generations: Positive and Negative Dimensions," *Journal of Marriage and the Family* 41 (May 1979), pp. 387-98; Walter W. Hudson and Gerald J. Murphy, "The Non-linear Relationship Between Marital Satisfaction and Stages of the Family Life Cycle: An Artifact of Type I Errors?" *Journal of Marriage and the Family* 42 (May 1980), pp. 263-67; Brent C. Miller, "A Multivariate Developmental Model of Marital Satisfaction," *Journal of Marriage and the Family* 38 (Nov. 1976), pp. 643-57; William H. Quinn, "Personal and Family Adjustment in Later Life," *Journal of Marriage and the Family* 45 (Feb. 1983), pp. 57-73; Boyd C. Rollins and Harold Feldman, "Marital Satisfaction Over the Life Cycle," *Journal of Marriage and the Family* 32 (Feb. 1970), pp. 20-28; Boyd C. Rollins and Kenneth L. Cannon, "Marital Satisfaction Over the Life Cycle: A Reevaluation," *Journal of Marriage and the Family* 36 (May 1974), pp. 271-82; Rosalyn Weinman Schram, "Marital Satisfaction Over the Family Life Cycle: A Critique and Proposal," *Journal of Marriage and the Family* 41 (Feb. 1979), pp. 7-12; and Graham B. Spanier, Robert A. Lewis, and Charles L. Cole, "Marriage Adjustment Over the Family Life Cycle: The Issue of Curvilinearity," *Journal of Marriage and the Family* 37 (May 1975), pp. 267-75.

Table 20.1. Family authority patterns of Minnesota families by generation

Authority pattern	Self-Reported			Observer Reported		
	Grand-parent	Parent	Married child	Grand-parent	Parent	Married child
Husband centered	22	12	15	34	24	41
Egalitarian	69	82	80	28	47	42
Wife centered	9	6	5	38	29	18
Total	100	100	100	100	100	100
N (families)	94	100	107	74	90	96

Source: Adapted from Reuben Hill, et al., Family Development in Three Generations, Cambridge, Mass.: Schenkman, 1970, p. 48.

increase in husband-centered and in wife-centered relationships in the parental and grandparental generations. Although the inference is that the power relationships change as couples move through the life cycle, it should be remembered that the data are cross-sectional—they come from three separate generations, not from the same couples through time.

The interviewers provide lower estimates of egalitarian relationships at each generational level. They also report substantial increases in wife-centered relationships at the parental and grandparental levels. Because Hill's data on the grandparental generation are not presented by retirement status, his findings cannot be compared directly with Blood's. Both studies, however, show shifts away from egalitarian norms among older couples and increasing power of the wife in later years.

Role Specialization

In one other area of marital role taking, the Michigan and Minnesota studies provide roughly comparable data. Blood and Wolfe developed a measure of role specialization to determine the degree to which husband and wife share various tasks in maintaining a home and the degree to which they perform the tasks they deem most consistent with their sex roles. The data showed more sharing of tasks during the honeymoon than at any time thereafter. A large number of wives are working outside the home during this period. As wives move out of employment and into childbearing, they begin to specialize in the traditionally wifely tasks. Husbands, freed from many domestic tasks, concentrate more on traditionally masculine tasks. This trend continues throughout child-rearing and into the postparental years. During the postparental years,

Table 20.2. Role specialization and role conventionality by generations, Minnesota families

	Grandparent percentage	Parent percentage	Married child percentage
Role specialization:			
High specialization, husband or wife always do certain household tasks	78	65	57
Medium specialization, spouses usually but not always do the same specified tasks	14	29	37
Low specialization, great shifting about, in who does tasks	8	6	6
Total	100	100	100
N (families)	99	100	107
Role conventionality:			
Both conventional in doing sex-typed tasks and combination of where wife conventional, husband crossing line	42	21	17
Husband conventional and wife crossing line and combinations where both cross line	33	62	70
Combinations of conventionality, line crossing and systemic role reversals	26	17	13
Total	100	100	100
N (families)	98	100	107

Source: Adapted from Reuben Hill, et al., Family Development in Three Generations, Cambridge, Mass.: Schenkman, 1970, p. 49.

the trend continues, and the differentiation of marital roles reaches its peak during the retirement years.[5]

Hill sought not only to determine the degree to which men stick to traditionally manly tasks of earning a living, working in the yard, doing repair jobs, and so on; he developed measures of both role specialization and role conventionality. Role conventionality refers to men doing only what is traditionally man's work and women doing only what is traditionally woman's work. Role specialization refers to the degree to which there is shifting about in the performance of various tasks or the degree to which role differentiation is rigidly adhered to.

In Table 20.2, it can be seen that role specialization increases over the

5. This often is accompanied by feelings of loneliness on the part of wives. See Leland J. Axelson, "Personal Adjustment in the Post-parental Period," Marriage and Family Living 22 (Feb. 1960), pp. 66–68. See also Dennis K. Orthner, "Leisure Activity Patterns and Marital Satisfaction Over the Marital Career," Journal of Marriage and the Family 37 (Feb. 1975), pp. 91–102.

generations. High specialization increases markedly from the married child to the parental to the grandparental generation. Correspondingly, medium role specialization is more than halved over the generations.

When we look at role conventionality, the situation is more complicated. The number of conventional couples increases steadily from 17 percent in the married-child generation to 26 percent in the grandparental generation. However, unconventionality increases, too, in the older generations. The most unconventional pattern increases from 13 percent in the married-child generation to 26 percent in the grandparental generation. A number of recent studies have found that couples tend more equally to share domestic work in the postparental and retirement years than they did when their children were living at home.[6] One study of 1193 married men aged 50 or older even found that greater participation of retired men in traditionally female tasks enhanced their feelings of well-being.[7]

Marital Dynamics

The ways in which spouses relate during the postparental years may be as varied as those of early marriage and the middle years. There is continuity as couples move from one stage in life to another.[8] However, there are differences, too, as the special problems of aging emerge.

There is reason to think that the transition to postparental status either may be smooth and uneventful or it may be traumatic. Moreover, the transition may be unequally made by the partners; one partner may take things in stride and the other be thrown into an emotional tailspin.

At one extreme, some couples literally do "stay together for the benefit of the children." The marriage or entrance into college of the last child may signal the end of a long period of distasteful obligation. Divorce may soon follow; experience attests to the fact that it may come

6. Stan L. Albrecht, Howard M. Bahr, and Bruce A. Chadwick, "Changing Family and Sex Roles: An Assessment of Age Differences," *Journal of Marriage and the Family* 41 (Feb. 1979), pp. 41–50; Elizabeth A. Hill and Lorraine T. Dorfman, "Reaction of Housewives to the Retirement of Their Husbands," *Family Relations* 31 (April 1982), pp. 195–206; and Patricia M. Keith and Timothy H. Brubaker, "Male Household Roles in Later Life: A Look at Masculinity and Marital Relationships," *Family Coordinator* 28 (Oct. 1979), pp. 497–502.

7. Pat M. Keith, Cynthia D. Dobson, Willis J. Goudy, and Edward A. Powers, "Older Men: Occupation, Employment Status, Household Involvement, and Well Being," *Journal of Family Issues* 2 (Sept. 1981), pp. 336–49.

8. Michael J. Sporakowski and George A. Hughston, "Prescriptions for Happy Marriage: Adjustments and Satisfactions of Couples Married for 50 or More Years," *Family Coordinator* 27 (Oct. 1978), pp. 321–27; Wayne C. Seelbach and Charles J. Hansen, "Satisfaction with Family Relations Among the Elderly," *Family Relations* (Jan. 1980), pp. 91–96; and Gordon F. Streib and Rubye Wilkerson Beck, "Older Families: A Decade Review," *Journal of Marriage and the Family* 42 (Nov. 1980), pp. 205–24.

as a shock to virtually unsuspecting children.[9] Or, surprisingly, couples who have longed for the day when they might be free of marital bonds, find themselves immobilized when the opportunity finally appears. In spite of their professed wishes to be free, they may be sufficiently dependent on one another that some other rationalization must be found for continuing the marriage.

At the other extreme is found an increasing proportion of couples who anticipate the day when they will be relieved of responsibility for children and, thus, free to enjoy the full fruits of whatever financial and other success life has brought. A diminishing proportion of couples define parenthood as the *prime* goal in life. Not that parenthood has been devalued, for few couples are content to do without it. But, increasingly, parenthood is viewed as occupying only one portion of the vigorous adult years—the ages from 20 to 45 or so.

And mixed with its joys are the seemingly unending frustrations of being tied down. Coping with baby-sitters, a continuous round of infectious illnesses, school schedules that discourage travel, the competing schedule demands of budding adolescents, financial demands for everything from braces to summer camps to college expenses and weddings— some couples can hardly wait for the day when they may be free to indulge their own desires. Just a measure of privacy and quiet after hectic years of crowded family living may have overwhelming appeal—the opportunity to carry on uninterrupted conversation, to watch one's own favorite TV shows, and to have the daily schedule determined by one's own instead of the children's needs. Luxuries, from new clothes, to automobiles to extended vacations may be afforded. For couples in this situation, the postparental years may represent years of fulfillment rather than years of decline.

The postparental years are not without problems, of course. The data on continuing marital adjustment indicate a tendency for many spouses to live somewhat parallel rather than truly intertwined lives.

The Preretirement Years. The postparental years often appear more unsettling for wives than for husbands because the marriage of children does not occasion drastic change in the daily routines of most husbands. They continue to spend much of their time at work. Moreover, assuming modest occupational success, these are rewarding years for men.

9. Divorce in later life may come as a shock to virtually unsuspecting spouses too. See Barbara S. Cain, "Plight of the Gray Divorcee," *New York Times Magazine,* December 19, 1982, pp. 89–93. See also Donna Hodgkins Berardo, "Divorce and Remarriage at Middle Age and Beyond," in Felix M. Berardo, *ed., Middle and Late Life Transitions, Annals of the American Academy of Political and Social Science* 464 (Nov. 1982), pp. 132–39; and Peter Uhlenberg and Mary Ann P. Myers, "Divorce and the Elderly," *Gerontologist* 21 (June 1981), pp. 276–82.

Their incomes, prestige, and power are at a maximum. Even if the pain of "losing children" is severe, men have an escape into their work.

Their wives' situation is somewhat different. Women who formerly found that there were not enough hours in the day suddenly are burdened heavily with time. For those who were not employed while their children were young, only so much time can be devoted to the diminished demands of housekeeping. If the wife seeks to fill her time with attention to her husband, often she finds him physically and emotionally unavailable; his escape into work makes her feel more alone than ever. There are alternatives available to nonworking mothers whose children have flown the nest. Some return to school to finish educations cut short by marriage and childbearing. Some seek fulfillment and escape in employment. For some, this is quite successful. On the other hand, middle-aged women who wish to work face handicaps. They *are* middle-aged and often are discriminated against in employment. Moreover, they may be untrained, or their earlier training may be out of date. As a consequence, the work available often is unskilled and poorly paid.[10]

When the families' incomes are high enough that the wives need not seek employment, a combination of community service and an expanded social life often fill the hours. Many community agencies—the United Funds, the Red Cross, hospital auxiliaries, and many more—almost entirely depend on voluntary service. Then there are women's organizations in the churches, fund drives for worthy causes, political endeavors, and special community projects to absorb time and energy. Some women thrive on this existence. Virtually everyone knows such women who are healthy, hearty, and content.

Research suggests that middle-aged women whose children have left home are happier and get more enjoyment out of life than women of similar ages who still have children at home. Data from six national surveys confirmed this to be the case.[11]

The Years Following Retirement. Most people face retirement from work at around 65 years of age. There are exceptions of course—professional people, farmers, and the self-employed, to mention a few. But increasingly in the modern world, people work in large organizations with regular retirement policies.

The adjustments that couples make to retirement may not be as variable as the adjustments in earlier years—if nothing else, physical limita-

10. Angela M. O'Rand and John C. Henretta, "Women at Middle Age: Developmental Transitions," in Felix M. Berardo, *op. cit.,* pp. 57–64.
11. Norval D. Glenn, "Psychological Well-Being in the Postparental Stage," *Journal of Marriage and the Family* 37 (Feb. 1975), pp. 105–10. See also Elizabeth Bates Harkins, "Effects of Empty Nest Transition on Self-report of Psychological and Physical Well-being," *Journal of Marriage and the Family* 40 (Aug. 1978), pp. 549–56.

tions are increasingly prominent. Then, too, the accumulating habit cage makes it less likely that there will be extreme deviation from earlier adjustment. Certainly, couples vary in preparation for retirement. Some couples plan enthusiastically for retirement, just as some couples antici-pate the marriage of their children so that they may have more time together and the opportunity to carry out long-delayed plans. Particu-larly when their income is adequate, retired couples may seek the good life. In genuine affluence, world travel is possible. On a more modest level, there still may be the winter cottage in Florida or California and the summer place at a northern lake or in the mountains.[12] Retirement may make it possible to make frequent and regular visits to children and grandchildren who now live in distant localities. It is also possible to leave again when the pleasures of the visit wane.

Other couples, of number undetermined, who have not the energy or income to live so well are content to stay in their old homes and not have to cope with the demands of other family members or with work. They may visit their children occasionally or be visited by them. Dis-engagement from much of the world is the hallmark of such couples, who socially are becoming aged whether or not they are older chrono-logically than more active couples.[13]

For still other couples, retirement is filled with threat. Either the hus-band or wife, or both, may fear that the shaky equilibrium of their mar-riage will be upset by the adjustments that must be made when they are no longer out of the home for most of the day. Although a steadily ex-panding proportion of retired couples has adequate income through social security, corporation retirement programs, and savings, retirement to some means severe economic deprivation. Problems of adjustment be-tween husband and wife may be complicated by the threat of becoming dependent on children or public agencies.

Until recently, it was believed that retirement for men was accom-panied by decreases in self-esteem and self-respect and increases in de-pression and rolelessness. This belief was tied to the primacy of the breadwinner role among men. Because so great a part of mens' identities are invested in the work role, it was believed that retirement left gaping holes in their overall self-concepts. Although this may be true for some men, research has largely dispelled this assumption.

Atchley, in a recent review of the research literature on reactions to retirement, found that retirees do not experience a drop in life satisfac-

12. Albert Chevan and Lucy Rose Fischer, "Retirement and Interstate Migration," *Social Forces* 57 (June 1979), pp. 1365–80.
13. Elaine Cumming and William E. Henry, *Growing Old: The Process of Disengage-ment*, New York: Basic Books, 1961; and Arlie Russell Hochschild, "Disengagement Theory: A Critique and Proposal," *American Sociological Review* 40 (Oct. 1975), pp. 553–69.

tion, do not have more health problems owing to retirement, and do not experience either low self-esteem or low morale in the period following retirement. Most retirees have active, satisfying lives. The factors that appear most conclusively to affect adjustment are health and family situations, not the loss of jobs.[14]

Some men of high status or expertise may continue to do some work even after retirement. Their situation is not greatly different from that of farmers, independent business people, and professionals who do not face absolute retirement at any particular age. Such people may derive a great deal of pleasure by holding onto their occupational self-concepts into very old age.

Some adopt a full-time leisure role. For those who can manage it, extravagant leisure such as foreign travel still affords high status. Occupational success makes such leisure possible, and one may conceive of oneself as a retired lawyer or banker rather than simply as a retired person. Full-time leisure affords the chance to develop interests and hobbies that had been held in abeyance during the working years. Six months after retirement, most people have settled into satisfying and long-lasting activities.[15]

A third alternative is to identify with old age itself. Some retired persons cease trying to hold onto earlier associations and confine themselves to relationships with other retired people. The men and women whose days center on the activities of Golden Age and Senior Citizens' Clubs provide the best example. Although there may be macabre overtones in this adjustment, simple observation of these groups indicates that the organizations become a consuming interest for some members.

At least one study suggests that retirement may be more difficult for women than it is for men. Szinovacz found that women retirees find it exceedingly difficult to settle fully into household work and that home chores are not a satisfactory substitute for outside employment. Because household work remains more fully their domain, they do not have the unrestricted leisure time their husbands do to pursue hobbies or interests. They then necessarily throw themselves into housework, which they find unfulfilling and unsatisfying.[16]

THE KIN NETWORK

Chapter 8 showed that married couples maintain a complex network of relationships with other kin. Within this network, relationships between

14. Robert C. Atchley, "Retirement: Leaving the World of Work," in Felix M. Berardo, *op. cit.*, pp. 120–31.
15. Atchley, *ibid.*, p. 127.
16. Maximiliane E. Szinovacz, "Female Retirement: Effects on Spousal Roles and Marital Adjustment," *Journal of Family Issues* 1 (Sept. 1980), pp. 423–40.

Table 20.3. Help given and received in various areas by generation, Minnesota sample (in percents)

	Grandparents	Parents	Married children	Totals*
Economic				
Gave	26%	41%	34%	101%
Received	34	17	49	100
Emotional gratification				
Gave	23	47	31	101
Received	42	37	21	100
Household management				
Gave	21	47	33	101
Received	52	23	25	100
Child care				
Gave	16	50	34	100
Received	0	23	78	101
Illness				
Gave	32	21	47	100
Received	61	21	18	100

* Some percentages do not add to 100 because of rounding.
Source: Adapted from Reuben Hill et al., Family Development in Three Generations, Cambridge, Mass.: Schenkman, 1970, p. 67.

parents and their married children are prominent. There is a comprehensive pattern of mutual aid in which the direction of flow is slightly more often from parents to children.[17] In Chapter 8 it was shown that mutual aid continues to 60 years of age or older, but the implications of there being three adult generations of the family were not systematically examined.

With postparental status often being achieved between 45 and 50 years of age, it follows that many families today have two living postparental generations. The younger of these generations is likely to be in full vigor and at the height of whatever financial success they will achieve; the older generation usually has passed the age of retirement. In Table 20.3, Hill presents data that specify the help given and received by all three generations in five areas—economic, emotional, household management, child care, and illness.

17. One report shows retired parents giving more help to married children than they receive from them. See Gordon F. Streib, "Intergenerational Relations: Perspectives of the Two Generations on the Older Parent," Journal of Marriage and the Family 27 (Nov. 1965), pp. 469–76. See also David J. Cheal, "Intergenerational Family Transfers," Journal of Marriage and the Family 45 (Nov. 1983), pp. 805–13; Gary R. Lee and Eugene Ellithorpe, "Intergenerational Exchange and Subjective Well-being Among the Elderly," Journal of Marriage and the Family 44 (Feb. 1982), pp. 217–24; and Ethel Shanas, "Family-Kin Networks and Aging in Cross-Cultural Perspective," Journal of Marriage and the Family 35 (Aug. 1973), pp. 505–11.

The parental generation stands at the center of the mutual-aid network. In four of the five areas, the parents give more aid than either the grandparental or married-child generations. Moreover, even in illness, the parental generation gives as much help as it receives. The married-child generation comes next, giving more help than it receives in three areas—emotional gratification, household management, and help in time of illness. As was also pointed out in Chapter 8, the married-child generation receives a great deal of financial help, and help with the care of children. The grandparents are mainly on the receiving end. Child care is not relevant for them; in all other areas, they receive substantially more assistance than they give.

Hill summarized these data by inferring ways in which each generation perceives its position and function in the family network. For the married-child generation, there is both considerable giving and receiving. The parental generation is more affluent and supportive and occupies a kind of patron status in relation to the other generations. The grandparents are meager givers and high receivers. Theirs is almost a dependency status.

Three-Generation Families

The kin network exists in spite of—or in consequence of—a trend toward the nuclear family as the basic residential unit. The traditional extended family has virtually disappeared from the American scene, and three-generation families—grandparents, parents, and children living together—typically are regarded as undesirable. Perhaps because of this, relatively little study has been devoted to either the frequency with which grandparents live with their children or what the adjustments are where doubling up does occur.

No nationwide statistics are available to indicate how many parents live with their children. The census does estimate, however, the sharing of households with relatives generally. These statistics show that from 1910 to 1947 there was an increase in related families doubling-up in the same dwelling. In 1947, almost 10 percent of all families were sharing households with other families.[18] After 1947, the sharing declined again, and by 1955, had dropped below the 1910 level. In 1955, some 3.5 percent of all married couples did not have households of their own; by 1979, the figure was 1.2 percent.[19]

18. Thomas P. Monahan, "The Number of Children in American Families and the Sharing of Households," *Marriage and Family Living* 18 (Aug. 1956), pp. 201–3.
19. U.S. Bureau of the Census, *Statistical Abstract of the United States: 1979*, Washington, D.C.

These statistics refer to the doubling-up of all family groups, not just the extent to which grandparents double up with their children and grandchildren. The census reported that there were 1,994,000 three-generation families in 1960, with only 1,245,000 of these involving a parent living with offspring and grandchildren.[20] The number of families who experience three-generation living *at some time* during the life cycle is considerably larger, and the proportion of aged persons who live with their children is substantial.

Carol Stone collected data from 5102 junior and senior high school students in Washington, finding that only 318, or 6 percent, lived in households with one or more grandparents. She found that in more than half of these cases, the grandmother alone lived with the family; in one fifth of the cases, the grandfather lived with the family; and in only about 30 percent of the cases were both grandparents present. Thus, in only about 2 percent of the sample were there three-generation families.[21]

Koller, studying three-generation families in Ohio, found such small numbers that he resorted to studying them wherever he could find them rather than drawing them systematically as a sample. In attempting to sample one community, he found that only 16 of 62 families could be classified as being concerned with three-generation living in any way. Moreover, those 16 cases were divided into three groups: those concerned with three-generation living in the past only; those living in three-generation families at the time; and those who expected to establish a three-generation household in the future. He also found that three-generation families do not last long. Most of them lasted from one to five years before the parent or parents died.[22]

As a proportion of all families, three-generation families are not numerous. When viewed from the standpoint of the grandparents, however, they are more common. Shanas estimates that a third of the old people who have children live with one child or another.[23] A U.S. Census sample survey showed that one fourth of married couples over 65 lived with their children; one third of separated, divorced, and widowed

20. Hugh Carter and Paul C. Glick, *Marriage and Divorce: A Social and Economic Study*, Cambridge, Mass.: Harvard University Press, 1970, p. 159. See also Karen Kay Petersen, "Demographic Conditions and Extended Family Households: Egyptian Data," *Social Forces* 46 (June 1968), pp. 531–37.
21. Carol L. Stone, "Three-Generation Influence on Teen-agers' Conceptions of Family Culture Patterns and Parent-Child Relationships," *Marriage and Family Living* 24 (Aug. 1962), pp. 287–88.
22. Marvin R. Koller, "Studies of Three Generation Households," *Marriage and Family Living* 16 (Aug. 1954), pp. 205–6.
23. Ethel Shanas, "Living Arrangements of Older People in the United States," *Gerontologist* 1 (March 1961), pp. 27–29.

men did so; and nearly one half of separated, divorced, and widowed women did so.[24] The loss of a mate and increasing age make living with kin more likely. Thus, we may conclude that upwards of one fourth of persons over 65 who have children live with their children. Most of these cases involve grandparents of advanced age; three-generation living typically lasts only a few years.

The weight of opinion in the United States is against three-generation living. Speaking from a theoretical framework, Parsons states: "It is impossible to say that with us it is 'natural' for any other group than husband and wife and their dependent children to maintain a common household. . . . It is, of course, common for other relatives to share a household with the conjugal family but this scarcely ever occurs without some important elements of strain. For independence is certainly the preferred pattern for an elderly couple, particularly from the point of view of the children."[25]

Among the general population, from half to over 90 percent say that it is better for children to live separately.[26] Even among aged women living alone, more than half take this position. William Smith, using data from two Pennsylvania cities, reports that only 14 percent thought that it was a good idea for older persons to live with relatives, 50 percent said that it would work sometimes, and 35 percent stated flatly that it was "no good."[27]

One of the few studies reporting on three-generation living is Koller's study of 30 families in Ohio and Virginia. He reports that his respondents recognized such living as hazardous, requiring the virtues of diplomat, statesman, and saint. Oldsters, he says, who have had authority find it difficult to give up power to their children. Their married children in turn resent this intrusion on their authority over their own lives and their children. Three-generation families were most likely to be created when the wife's mother moved into the home and conflict between the two women over management of the home was common.

Sharp issue with the American bias against three-generation living and with both the theoretical arguments and data in support of that bias has been taken by Schorr. He points out that methodologically more

24. Ernest W. Burgess, "The Older Generation and the Family," in Wilma Donahue and Clark Tibbitts, eds., *The New Frontiers of Aging*, Ann Arbor: University of Michigan Press, 1957, pp. 161–62.
25. Talcott Parsons, "Age and Sex in the Social Structure of the United States," *American Sociological Review* 7 (Oct. 1942), p. 616.
26. Alvin L. Schorr, "Current Practice of Filial Responsibility," in Robert F. Winch, Robert McGinnis, and Herbert R. Barringer, *Selected Studies in Marriage and the Family*, New York: Holt, Rinehart & Winston, 1962, p. 424.
27. William M. Smith, Jr., "Family Plans for Later Years," *Marriage and Family Living* 16 (Feb. 1954), pp. 36–40.

adequate studies in England tend to challenge this view[28] and that American data show only that three-generation living may cause problems, not that it necessarily does so.[29]

Schorr turns to the writing of Ernest Burgess rather than to Parsons for his interpretation of three-generation living. He quotes Burgess: "Where both parents and children elect to live together, the arrangement may work out more or less satisfactorily. Where the wife is working, the mother-in-law often takes on the major charge of the household responsibilities. She may be happy to function as a babysitter. . . . Although there may be some disagreements, these tend to be minor, and both generations report the relationship as satisfying."[30] Summing up, Schorr concludes that "there can be no question that there are potential strains when parents and adult children live together. But potential strains are inherent in any living situation—in work, in rearing children, in marrying. If technical and popular literature confined themselves to the strains intrinsic to each of these activities, would we conclude that we should give them up?"[31]

So the argument goes. Structurally, the American family has little place for aged parents. Apparently socialization, in this instance, works well for the vast majority of older and middle-aged persons favor grandparents' maintaining their independence and living alone. As more aging couples can maintain independence financially, more of them prefer independent living too. In 1979, two thirds of the homes owned free and clear were maintained by elderly persons.[32]

On the other hand, there comes a time when people are forced to cope with decline and death. Couples in their 50s and 60s, and some in their 70s, may still be hale and hearty; but each passing year threatens emotional and financial security. Between 55 and 64, one woman out of five is a widow. Between 65 and 74, two fifths are widows; and past 75, 70 percent are widows.[33] Old people living alone are less likely to value their independence, and feelings of filial responsibility loom larger in

28. Elizabeth Bott, *Family and Social Network*, London: Tavistock Publications, 1957, p. 218.
29. Schorr, *op. cit.*, p. 425. See also Sheila K. Johnson, "Three Generations, One Household," *New York Times Magazine*, Aug. 19, 1973, pp. 24–31.
30. Ernest W. Burgess, "Family Living in the Later Decades," *Annals of the American Academy of Political and Social Science* 279 (Jan. 1952), pp. 111–12.
31. Schorr, *op. cit.*, pp. 425–26.
32. Cynthia M. Taeuber, "America in Transition: An Aging Society," *Current Population Reports*, Series P-23, No. 128 (Sept. 1983), p. 24.
33. *Statistical Bulletin*, Metropolitan Life Insurance Company, 47 (May 1966), pp. 3–4. See also Albert Chevan and J. Henry Korson, "The Widowed Who Live Alone: An Examination of Social and Demographic Factors," *Social Forces* 51 (Sept. 1972), pp. 45–53.

their children. Even without death, illness or financial necessity frequently produce three-generation living. This produces strain. But as Schorr points out, strain is inherent in living.

Parent-Child Dynamics

An implicit theme running through our discussion of adjustment in the preretirement and retirement years and through the analysis of the continuing kin network has been that these phenomena are progressive in character. It is one thing to talk of postparental couples in their forties and fifties, another with couples who have reached retirement age, and still another with couples who are aged. Perhaps nowhere is this more evident than in the changing relationships between parents and their adult children.

The parental generation stands at the center of the mutual-aid network. They give aid on a substantial scale. They conceive of themselves as powerful, independent, and interested in promoting their adult children's welfare. This orientation, still prevailing among parents who have reached approximately 69 years of age, was shown in Streib's study of 1500 families. He reports data from 1287 men who were married and still living with their wives: 749 were retired, 538 were still working.[34] Attitudes toward occupational achievement, upward mobility, mutual aid, and continuing close interpersonal relationships were studied.

Most of the parents acknowledged that it was important for their children to do well occupationally. They approved of their children going away to college and moving to remote locations when their jobs required it. They recognized that such moves threaten family ties, and they believed that children should not ignore their responsibilities to the parents. However, they were prepared to cope with these problems rather than stand in the way of their children's advancement. Parents who had retired were a little less likely than those who were still working to emphasize achievement norms, but the majority of both the retired and working groups did so.

That the parents' assessment of their situation was realistic was indicated by the family experience of those whose children had achieved a higher level of occupational success than the parents had. Upward mobility appeared not to have adversely affected relationships between parents and children. The more successful children were more likely to keep in close touch with their parents, were more likely to offer financial aid, and were more willing to make sacrifices for their parents. Finally, when the parents were asked what they considered the chil-

34. Gordon F. Streib, "Family Patterns in Retirement," *Journal of Social Issues* 14 (Spring 1958), pp. 46–60.

dren's major responsibility to the parents to be, the vast majority emphasized the maintenance of affectional and social ties over the offering of financial help. Here, however, we begin to see more clearly the effects of retirement and lowered income. Retired parents were more likely than parents who were still working to say that financial ties are as important as affectional ties. Moreover, the percentages who emphasized financial help, although still small, were greatest at the lowest income levels. In this, perhaps, we begin to see changes in parent-married child relationships as the parents move into old age.

The Glassers, working with a sample of persons about 70 years of age who approached a family service agency for help, concluded that their problems could be conceptualized as those of role reversal. Parents, they state, who must turn to their children for material aid are dependent on their children much as the children were dependent on them earlier. The children become like parents to their own parents, and the parents become like children of their own children. For many of both generations, this leads to role conflict and personal problems.[35]

The Glassers were working with a clinical population and warned that their findings might not apply to a general population. Data from a general population have been provided by Albrecht, who took a representative sample of parents over 65 years in a midwestern community. She found that 85 percent of the aging parents maintained roles associated with independence or responsibility and that 15 percent showed dependence, distance, or neglect.[36] She further classified the parents into independent, responsible, dependent, and distant or lone groups.

The independent parents had allowed their children to become independent adults. They maintained close affectional and social relationships with them, but neither dominated them nor were dominated by them. Most of these parents maintained separate households, but occasionally lived next door. Some had remarried in their later years and concentrated on their new marital relationships rather than on their

35. Paul H. Glasser and Lois N. Glasser, "Role Reversal and Conflict Between Aged Parents and Their Children," *Marriage and Family Living* 24 (Feb. 1962), pp. 46–51.
36. Ruth Albrecht, "Relationships of Older Parents with Their Children," *Marriage and Family Living* 16 (Feb. 1954), pp. 32–35. See also Ruth Albrecht, "Relationships of Older People with Their Own Parents," *Marriage and Family Living* 15 (Nov. 1953), pp. 296–98; and Ruth Albrecht, "The Parental Responsibilities of Grandparents," *Marriage and Family Living* 16 (Aug. 1954), pp. 201–4; Patricia G. Archbold, "Impact of Parent-Caring on Women," *Family Relations* 32 (Jan. 1983), pp. 39–45; Victor G. Cicirelli, "Adult Children's Attachment and Helping Behavior to Elderly Parents: A Path Model," *Journal of Marriage and the Family* 45 (Nov. 1983), pp. 815–25; Eleanor Palo Stoller, "Parental Caregiving by Adult Children," *Journal of Marriage and the Family* 45 (Nov. 1983), pp. 851–58; and Alexis J. Walker and Linda Thompson, "Intimacy and Intergenerational Aid and Contact Among Mothers and Daughters," *Journal of Marriage and the Family* 45 (Nov. 1983), pp. 841–49.

children.[37] As a group, the independent persons were able to incorporate in-laws into the family without feeling threatened, maintained interests that gave them something in common with the younger generation, gave and accepted favors easily, and showed pride in their children.

By contrast, the responsible parents still maintained some responsibility for the second generation. In some large families, there still were adult children in the home after the parents had passed 65. Various other circumstances—the late adoption of a young child, remarriage and the acquisition of young stepchildren, prolonged education in preparation for a profession, and the return of offspring from the armed forces—combined to prolong parental responsibility in some families. Many of these were ethnic families in which traces of the old, large family system still survived. In others, there were hints of personality needs in the parents that caused them to hold on long after most parents had let go.

The dependent parents had suffered role reversals. They constituted only 6 percent of the parents and were, of course, older. Some maintained separate residences, and some lived with their children. Many had been widowed. The basis for their classification as dependent was that they required social attention, economic aid, or physical care from their children. They represented the ultimate stage in the family life cycle.

Finally, there were the lone or distant parents, widowed men and women who seldom see their children. There were more parents in this category—9 percent—than in the preceding one. Most of these people are in homes for the aged. Some feel deserted, and some, interestingly, resisted their children's efforts to care for them, apparently preferring life in the old people's home. Many of them had never had close relationships with their families, or these had been broken a long time ago. Because some of the children were stepchildren, we might entertain the hypothesis that here is a little recognized cost of remarriage.

GRANDPARENTHOOD

So far, little has been said about relationships between older couples and their grandchildren or the significance of grandparenthood for marital and personal roles. The fact that relationships between grandparents and grandchildren are mediated through parents should not blind us, however, to the importance of these relationships.[38]

The preparation for, and reaction to, grandparenthood often differ

37. Barbara J. Vinick, "Remarriage in Old Age," *Family Coordinator* 27 (Oct. 1978), pp. 359–63.
38. Geoffrey K. Leigh, "Kinship Interaction Over the Family Life Span," *Journal of Marriage and the Family* 44 (Feb. 1982), pp. 197–208; and Ann Stueve, "The Elderly as Network Members," *Marriage and Family Review* 5 (Winter 1982), pp. 59–87.

between men and women. They differ, too, according to whether grandparenthood is achieved relatively early in life or later on.

Some women, when grandchildren come early, are markedly ambivalent about them. When women marry around 22 and begin bearing children soon after, some may become grandmothers by 40, and many more by age 45. Some may think themselves too young to occupy the grandparent status. Most people know grandmothers who refuse to be called grandmother and who insist that their grandchildren refer to them by pet terms of some sort. The status of the grandchild may be ignored by the grandmother who concentrates instead on maintaining an image of herself as too young to have such a status.

Probably more often, middle-aged women find in grandchildren the opportunity to resume the maternal role directly and to gain entrée to the lives of their children. Even before the baby is born, the grandmother-to-be reassumes a role of authority as she counsels her daughter or daughter-in-law on the management of pregnancy. In addition, she is permitted to buy clothing and other items for the new arrival or to make some of them if she is so inclined.

Grandmothers frequently care for the new mother, her baby, and her family during the immediate postnatal period. After she returns to her own home, she is permitted and expected to continue a grandmotherly concern for the mother's well-being and the grandchild's care. She experiences again most of the joys of parenthood without having to cope with its exacting demands. Entering her children's homes as visitor and/ or baby-sitter, she can indulge herself and her grandchildren; when her energy or her patience wane, she has simply to leave and go to her own quiet home.[39]

The status of grandfather in middle age has less impact. Some men resist the role of grandparent just as some women do, but it is likely to be less of a problem. Aging during the middle years does not present as much threat to men; indeed aging during this period often is associated with occupational and financial success. Moreover, the man's overwhelming identification with his job until retirement forestalls the role of grandfather being of major importance. Grandchildren may be a source of pride and pleasant diversions, but they do not stand at the center of things. Retirement brings great changes. Without jobs to claim their energy, many grandfathers identify more completely with their young grandchildren. They want to visit them, to take them for walks, to buy them things, and otherwise to participate in their care.

The role of older grandfather in American culture is essentially maternal. Unless the child's father is dead or absent, the grandfather is not

39. Joan F. Robertson, "Grandmotherhood: A Study of Role Conceptions," *Journal of Marriage and the Family* 39 (Feb. 1977), pp. 165-74.

an authority figure to his grandchild or the source of financial support. Instead the grandfather baby-sits, plays with the children, and generally aids the mother in caring for them. Both grandfathers and grandchildren often derive satisfaction from this relationship, which is uncomplicated by any emphasis on discipline.[40]

WIDOWHOOD

With few exceptions, the family life cycle ends in widowhood. Although young people seldom can imagine it, one partner is destined to live out the last part of life alone—at least without the marital partner. Moreover, the period of widowhood lasts, on the average, from 8 to 16 years.

For some 25 years, widows in the United States have been increasing by more than 100,000 per year, and the total number of widows over the age of 65 is now more than 15 million.[41] The disparity between the number of widows and widowers has been widening. The ratio was about two to one 50 years ago; it is five to one today. Widowers are much more likely to change their status through remarriage, making widowhood in the United States an overwhelmingly feminine phenomenon.

That widowhood presents serious problems probably is obvious, but there are empirical data that verify this fact. Bellin and Hardt, for example, studying 1803 people over 65 in upstate New York, found that rates of mental disorder were higher among the widowed than among the still-married. These higher rates of mental illness were related not only to widowhood but also to advanced age, physical ill health, and other variables.[42] A report by Ilgenfritz based on experience in a community guidance center also emphasizes that widows suffer from fears of being alone and from loss of self-esteem as women in addition to the many practical problems related to living alone.[43]

Problems associated with widowhood are partly a function of increas-

40. For a provocative discussion of emerging roles in grandparenthood, see Bernice L. Neugarten and Karol K. Weinstein, "The Changing American Grandparent," *Journal of Marriage and the Family* 26 (May 1964), pp. 199–204. See also Arthur Kornhaber and Kenneth L. Woodward, *Grandparents/Grandchildren: The Vital Connection*, Garden City, N.Y.: Doubleday (Anchor), 1981.

41. Metropolitan Life Foundation Statistical Bulletin, July–September 1982, p. 10.

42. Seymour S. Bellin and Robert H. Hardt, "Marital Status and Mental Disorders Among the Aged," *American Sociological Review* 23 (April 1958), pp. 155–62. See also Ira W. Hutchison III, "The Significance of Marital Status for Morale and Life Satisfaction Among Lower-Income Elderly," *Journal of Marriage and the Family* 37 (May 1975), pp. 287–93; Helena Znaniecki Lopata, "Loneliness: Forms and Components," *Social Problems* 17 (Fall 1969), pp. 248–62.

43. Marjorie P. Ilgenfritz, "Mothers on Their Own: Widows and Divorcees," *Marriage and Family Living* 23 (Feb. 1961), pp. 38–41.

ing age, but not completely so. This was demonstrated in a study of almost 1000 people over 60 years of age in New York State. It found, first, that extensive association with friends is an important mechanism of adjustment to old age and widowhood. People over 70 who were still married were less likely to report high friendship participation than were younger married people. This decline did not occur among widowed men or women however. In fact, older widowed persons often had more significant friendship associations than did younger ones.[44] How can this seeming paradox be explained?

The key was found in the status of widowed persons relative to that of others in their age group. Because friends tend to be about the same age, people who are widowed early find themselves with different experiences and interests than their fellows. Without the bonds of common experiences and interests, friendships suffer. With more advanced age, widowhood becomes common and it is the still-married people who now are relatively deviant and isolated. Thus, whatever maladjustment is associated with widowhood is not a function of widowhood and advancing age alone but is also a function of the individual's position in a total social group. The individual's position in relation to other people of his or her age can make adjustment harder or easier.[45]

Widowhood for women is, in some ways, comparable to retirement among men. The death of the husband severely jolts the wife's image of herself. She is denied the opportunity to maintain her competence as companion to her husband and housekeeper for others. If she lives alone and remains active, she receives admiration from others. If she is not able to do this, her children are likely to offer her a home. This probably is the most common origin of the three-generation family.[46]

44. Zena S. Blau, "Structural Constraints on Friendship in Old Age," *American Sociological Review* 26 (June 1961), pp. 429–31. See also Greg Arling, "The Elderly Widow and Her Family, Neighbors and Friends," *Journal of Marriage and the Family* 38 (Nov. 1976), pp. 757–68; and Marc L. Petrowsky, "Marital Status, Sex, and the Social Networks of the Elderly," *Journal of Marriage and the Family* 38 (Nov. 1976), pp. 749–56.
45. See Allen J. Watson and Vira R. Kivett, "Influences on the Life Satisfaction of Older Fathers," *Family Coordinator* 25 (Oct. 1976), pp. 483–88.
46. For analyses of the roles of the widowed, see Elizabeth A. Bankoff, "Social Support and Adaptation to Widowhood," *Journal of Marriage and the Family* 45 (Nov. 1983), pp. 827–39; Felix M. Berardo, "Widowhood Status in the United States: Perspective on a Neglected Aspect of the Family Life-Cycle," *Family Coordinator* 17 (July 1968), pp. 191–203; and "Survivorship and Social Isolation: The Case of the Aged Widower," *Family Coordinator* 19 (Jan. 1970), pp. 11–25; Bernard J. Cosneck, "Family Patterns of Older Widowed Jewish People," *Family Coordinator* 19 (Oct. 1970), pp. 368–73; Jaber F. Gubrium, "Marital Desolation and the Evaluation of Everyday Life in Old Age," *Journal of Marriage and the Family* 36 (Feb. 1974), pp. 107–13; Carol D. Harvey and Howard M. Bahr, "Widowhood, Morale, and Affiliation," *Journal of Marriage and the Family* 36 (Feb. 1974), pp. 97–106; Jacqueline Johnson Jackson, "Comparative Life Styles and Family and Friend Relationships Among Older Black Women," *Family Coordinator* 21 (Oct. 1972), pp. 477–85; and Benjamin Schlesinger, "The Widowed as a One-Parent Family Unit," *Social Science* 46 (Jan. 1971), pp. 26–32.

As already pointed out, three-generation families present problems for the younger generation of adults. They also present problems for the aging widow. The younger adults have established themselves in positions of authority in the family and often admit an aging widow in a subordinate and virtually functionless capacity. Patronized by their children and others, and denied opportunity to be useful, many aging widows deteriorate rapidly both in health and outlook. Some families are wise enough to recognize that aging parents need to retain their self-respect by being admitted to the household, if at all, as full and responsible partners. Under these circumstances, it appears likely that many of the problems widely associated with old age in the United States may be avoided or at least ameliorated.

There is no escape. The life cycle of the family, as with the individual, must end in death. By this time, the family life cycle of the next generation usually is well along.

SUMMARY

Increasing numbers of couples have completed childrearing and child-launching by 45 or 50 years of age. Most such couples remain vigorous, healthy, and alert. Although they may seem ancient to their children, they have a third of their lives ahead of them. Data show that the gradual drop in marital adjustment begun earlier continues into the postparental stage. The satisfaction that wives report with the love of their husbands declines steadily into old age. Companionship-satisfaction scores show a modest increase after the children are gone, suggesting that husbands and wives do turn back toward one another slightly.

Changes in power relationships occur, too, with husbands gaining in power up to retirement but losing it thereafter. Interviewer reports, more than self-estimates, emphasize the tendency for wives to increase in power as couples move into old age. The roles played tend to become more specialized with increasing age, men coming to play the traditional masculine role and women the traditional feminine role. Role unconventionality increases, too, with age. Many couples adapt flexibly to the limitations imposed by illness and infirmity. Some couples make the transition to postparental status uneventfully, whereas for others it is traumatic. Some unsatisfactory marriages break under the strain; others continue in neurotic interdependence. Increasing numbers of couples anticipate pleasantly their release from parental burdens and embark on a life of relative leisure and companionship.

Adjustment, at this stage, often appears harder on women than on men. Women whose children have flown the nest may find themselves with too much time, with too few opportunities to use their energies, and limited employment possibilities. Retirement, once thought to be accompanied by decreases in self-esteem and self-concept, appears not to be a particularly stressful time for men. Women retirees may face more difficulties than many men.

The kin network at this stage may involve three adult generations—grandparents, parents, and married children. The parental generation stands at the center of the network, giving aid to the other two generations.

As grandparents become dependent, three-generation families appear. As a proportion of all families, three-generation families are not common; but the proportion of persons over 65 who live with their children is substantial. There is a bias against three-generation living, and data show that there often is conflict in such families. On the other hand, there is not evidence of more serious strains than in other family units at other stages of the life cycle. Most grandparents prefer to remain independent and emphasize the importance of their adult children being upwardly mobile. Both their expectations and actual experience show that upwardly mobile families are likely to be successful in maintaining close family ties and mutual aid. The older the grandparents become, the more likely they are to emphasize mutual aid.

Relationships between grandparents and parents are quite variable. Some grandparents are comfortable with their children's independence, and some seek to prolong dependence. Some grandparents become dependent in turn, and there may be a reversal of roles between the generations. In up to 10 percent of the cases, there may be estrangement and virtual loss of contact btween the generations.

Relationships between grandparents and grandchildren also are variable. Some relatively young grandparents reject their grandparent status. More often, women use grandmotherhood to regain some of the maternal role. The role of grandfather becomes more prominent following retirement, when he, too, often assumes some responsibility for child care. These relationships may be satisfying to all three generations.

The family life cycle usually ends in widowhood. In extreme old age, widowhood often is problem ridden. Evidence indicates, however, that the problems are a function of the total social situation, not of aging alone. The widowed are, mostly, women who then suffer a drastic change of status. Some widows carry on independently; some quickly become dependent. According to the wisdom and situations of the people involved, the final years in the life cycle may either be tragic or rewarding.

SUGGESTED READINGS

Brubaker, Timothy H., *ed., Family Relationships in Later Life*, Beverly
Hills, Calif.: Sage Publications, 1983. A series of articles examining a
myriad of age-related issues.

Butler, Robert N., and Lewis, Myrna I., *Aging and Mental Health*, St. Louis:
C. V. Mosby, 1977. Describes the processes of aging, analyzes treatment
and prevention programs, and catalogs organizations and programs for
the elderly.

Riley, Matilda White, *ed., Aging from Birth to Death: Interdisciplinary
Perspectives*, Boulder, Colo.: Westview Press, 1979. A symposium spon-
sored by the American Association for the Advancement of Science.
Explores the relationships between social structure and the life course.

Unruh, David R., *Invisible Lives: Social Worlds of the Aged*, Beverly Hills,
Calif.: Sage Publications, 1983. Interviews with 40 older people serve as
the basis for an examination of the social worlds of the elderly.

Ward, Russell A., *The Aging Experience: An Introduction to Social Geron-
tology*, Philadelphia: J. B. Lippincott, 1979. Written as a textbook, this
volume covers the psychological, social, familial, political, and economic aspects of aging.

FILMS

Aging (NET Film Service, Indiana University, Bloomington, Ind. 47401).
Two elderly Jewish gentlemen while playing cards reveal their attitudes toward life. A psychotherapist asserts that the greatest evil dealt
to the elderly in modern times is the idea that an old person is functionless. Having an old person as a useful participant in a domestic situation
is mutually beneficial to child, parent, and grandparent.

Four Women Over Eighty (MTI Teleprograms, 4825 N. Scott Street, Suite
23, Schiller Park, Ill. 60176), 10 minutes. Four female octogenarians
demonstrate successful responses to aging through physical activity,
continuing education, social involvement, and gainful employment.

Passing Quietly Through (Grove Press Film Division, 53 East 11th Street,
New York, N.Y. 10003), 26 minutes. Shows the death of an old man.
Intense, but never mawkish or sentimental.

The Spirit Possession of Alejandro Mamani: Aging in Another Culture
(Filmmakers Library, 290 West End Ave., New York 10023), 27 minutes. An Aymara Indian at 81 faces many of the feelings experienced
by the elderly in our own society—loneliness, rejection by sons and
daughters, and loss of stature. In addition, he believes he is possessed by
evil spirits with whom he struggles day and night.

When You Reach December (Westinghouse Learning Corp., 100 Park Avenue, New York, N.Y. 10017), color. Details the plight of the elderly
in nursing homes and those who live alone. Shows their fading health,

dwindling money, and waning courage. Reports federal and state investigations of deplorable conditions.

QUESTIONS AND PROJECTS

1. What evidence is there to indicate the trend of marital adjustment during the postparental years? What is the trend with regard to wives' satisfaction with their husbands' love? With companionship?
2. Specify the changes that occur in power relationships between husband and wife. What happens with regard to role specialization? How do you account for the changes in role conventionality?
3. Which partner usually experiences greater adjustment problems in the immediate postparental period? Why? What are these problems?
4. Which partner ordinarily experiences greater adjustment problems following retirement? Why?
5. For what reasons was retirement thought to be stressful for men? Has research borne this out?
6. Describe the mutual-aid patterns typically existing among grandparents, parents, and married children.
7. What proportion of American families are three-generation families? What proportion of people over 65 live in such families? How long do they last? Do they have more problems than other families?
8. How do parents over 65 view relationships with their adult children? What values do they emphasize? How realistic are their expectations?
9. How may grandparenthood be dysfunctional for women? How may it be functional?
10. Describe the typical grandfather role for middle-aged men. For retired men. What is meant by the statement: "The grandfather role is a maternal role"?
11. What evidence is there that widowhood brings special problems? How do friendships play a part in the adjustment to widowhood?

Name Index

Subject Index